GISSI

A Life in

GEORGE GISSING IN 1895
(reprinted from *The Album* by permission of the British Library)

GISSING
A Life in Books

❧

JOHN HALPERIN
University of Southern California

Oxford New York Toronto Melbourne
OXFORD UNIVERSITY PRESS

Oxford University Press, Walton Street, Oxford OX2 6DP
Oxford New York Toronto
Delhi Bombay Calcutta Madras Karachi
Petaling Jaya Singapore Hong Kong Tokyo
Nairobi Dar es Salaam Cape Town
Melbourne Auckland
and associated companies in
Beirut Berlin Ibadan Nicosia

Oxford is a trade mark of Oxford University Press

First published 1982
First issued as an Oxford University Press paperback 1987
Reprinted 1987

British Library Cataloguing in Publication Data
Halperin, John
Gissing: a life in books.
1. Gissing, George—Biography
2. Novelists, English—19th century—Biography
I. Title
823'.8   PR4717
ISBN 0–19–282016–8

British Library Catalouing in Publication Data
Halperin, John, 1941–
Gissing: a life in books.
Includes bibliographical references and index.
1. Gissing, George, 1857–1903—Biography.
2. Novelists, English—19th century—Biography.
I. Title
PR4717.H35 1982   823'.8 (B)   82–238962
ISBN 0–19–282016–8 (pbk)

Printed in Great Britain by
Richard Clay Ltd,
Bungay, Suffolk

To Pierre Coustillas

The writing of this book was generously supported
by a fellowship grant from the
John Simon Guggenheim Memorial Foundation

PREFACE

'THE opinions Gissing's novels contributed to the Victorian current of ideas', Jacob Korg has remarked, 'were so original that few took them seriously.' Not much has changed. Despite a modest revival of interest in recent years, Gissing remains little more than a shadowy, interesting minor figure among the Victorian novelists.

It would nevertheless be difficult to find, in the novels of his better-known nineteenth-century predecessors and contemporaries, a passage as original, striking, and prophetic as this one:

I hate and fear 'science' because of my conviction that for long to come, if not forever, it will be the remorseless enemy of mankind. I see it destroying all simplicity and gentleness of life, all the beauty of the world; I see it restoring barbarism under a mask of civilisation; I see it darkening men's minds and hardening their habits; I see it bringing a time of vast conflicts, which will pale into insignificance 'the thousand wars of old,' and . . . whelm all the laborious advances of mankind in blood-drenched chaos.

In this remarkable, prescient vision the last of the Victorian novelists penned the epitaph of the twentieth century.

The man who wrote this (I quote from *The Private Papers of Henry Ryecroft*, published 1902 to 1903) must be worth our attention. My interest in George Robert Gissing (1857–1903) lies primarily in the connections between the man's life and his art, and in the fascinating ways in which the highly charged impulses travelled between the two – in both directions. More than any other body of work with which I am familiar, Gissing's demands of the reader an awareness of biographical matters for fullest understanding. This study attempts to provide that awareness by proceeding chronologically through the life and the work together.

I have been fully alive to the dangers of this – especially in the case of a writer so many of whose books remain virtually unobtainable. On this matter I can perhaps do no better than quote from the biography of a novelist in similar circumstances. In his foreword to *The Saddest Story: A Biography of Ford Madox Ford* (1971), Arthur Mizener writes: 'Critical discussion of books a reader does not know are not very meaningful. For the reader who is familiar with Ford's work, his novels are the most important thing about him and demand careful attention; for the reader who is interested in Ford but unfamiliar with most of his books, discussions of them are a bore. I have tried to meet the needs of both these readers.'

I am pleased to acknowledge generous assistance from the John Simon Guggenheim Memorial Foundation which enabled this book to be completed several years earlier than otherwise possible. I am also indebted to the American Philosophical Society for a grant for summer research undertaken in connection with the present volume and to the Department of English at USC for defraying costs of preparing this manuscript for the press.

Parts of Chapter 1 and of the Appendix to this book have appeared in different form in two published essays. These are 'How to Read Gissing', *English Literature in Transition*, Vol. 20, No. 4 (Fall, 1977), and 'The Gissing Revival, 1961–1974', *Studies in the Novel*, Vol. 7, No. 1 (Spring, 1975). Different parts of Chapter 7 appeared separately in an Introduction I wrote to an edition of *Denzil Quarrier* published in Britain by the Harvester Press and in the United States by the Humanities Press in 1979, and in 'Gissing, Marriage, and Women's Rights: The Case of *Denzil Quarrier*', *Gissing Newsletter*, Vol. 15, No. 1 (January 1979). Part of Chapter 4 appeared in the *Gissing Newsletter*, Vol. 15, No. 3 (October 1979) as 'On *The Unclassed* as Autobiography'. I am grateful to the editors of these journals and to these presses for their kind permission to reproduce this material here.

My decision to write on Gissing, long in forming, was brought to the point by the encouragement of Pierre Coustillas, Gissing's most knowledgeable contemporary student. As the dedication of this book suggests, my debt to him is enormous. Beyond encouragement, he has provided invaluable help by placing at my disposal his encyclopaedic knowledge of the Gissing materials and answering innumerable questions I have had about them. Of special importance is that he permitted me to read in typescript an early version of his (unpublished) biography of Gissing and that he read my own typescript and made many suggestions for its improvement. This is typical of Professor Coustillas's selflessness and of his uncomplicated dedication to Gissing studies. Without his generosity, both professional and personal, the present volume might not have been written.

I am also indebted to Jacob Korg, America's most distinguished Gissing scholar. His pioneering biography (1963) made subsequent work on Gissing possible for many others. Both professionally and personally he too has been very generous. I am especially grateful to him for reading the typescript, enabling me to correct mistakes that otherwise might have passed undetected into print. Needless to say, any errors of fact or judgement are my own responsibility.

Other debts, gladly acknowledged here, are to my good friend Walter Allen, whose enthusiasm for and interest in Gissing I have found infectious, and whose comments on an early draft of the present manuscript have turned out to be invaluable; the late Alfred M. Slotnick, whose knowledge of bibliography and the Gissing materials prevented me from making several errors and who provided me with much valuable information about Gissing's earnings; the late Denise Le Mallier, a cousin of Gissing's third wife, who shared with me her knowledge of the Fleury family and unearthed many of the photographs that appear in this book; Dr Michael Safdi, who has helped me to reconstruct the probable stages of Gissing's last illness; and Peter Sutcliffe of the Oxford University Press, whose patience, wisdom, and care undoubtedly have made this a better book.

Such widespread generosity has convinced me that Gissing brings out the best in people. His present-day students seem to be inspired not only by sympathy for the ordeal that was his life but by a desire to seek ultimate justice for him as an artist. I must hope that I am not an exception to this rule.

J.H.

Santa Monica, California
May 1981

CONTENTS

LIST OF ILLUSTRATIONS

Sometimes people carry to such perfection the mask they have assumed that in due course they actually become the person they seem. But in his book or his picture the real man delivers himself defenceless . . . To the acute observer no one can produce the most casual work without disclosing the innermost secrets of his soul.

Maugham, *Ten Novels and Their Authors*

If he is a novelist he uses his experience of people and places, his apprehension of himself, his love and hate, his deepest thoughts, his passing fancies, to draw in one work after another a picture of life. It can never be more than a partial one, but if he is fortunate he will succeed in the end in doing something else; he will draw a complete picture of himself.

Maugham, *The Summing Up*

You will hear people say that poverty is the best spur to the artist. They have never felt the iron of it in their flesh.

Maugham, *Of Human Bondage*

If this had been a tale that I was inventing I would certainly have made it more probable.   Maugham, 'A Man with a Conscience'

I think Life's FAR more romantic than any books.   Rupert Brooke

Few men, I am sure, have led so bitter a life.   Gissing in 1893

※

CHAPTER I

LIFE AND ART: AN INTRODUCTION TO GISSING

> Gissing is one of those imperfect novelists through whose books one sees the life of the author faintly covered by the lives of fictitious people. With such writers we establish a personal rather than an artistic relationship. We approach them through their lives as much as through their work.
>
> Virginia Woolf, *The Common Reader* (2nd series)

> He spoke of himself, and told the truth as far as mortal can tell it.   *The Ryecroft Papers* (Preface)

> The Art of Fiction has this great ethical importance that it enables one to tell the truth about human beings in a way which is impossible in actual life.   Gissing's Commonplace Book

I

GISSING has been dead for more than three-quarters of a century now, and the world of which he wrote is even longer gone. His reputation was not one of those resurrected during the revival of interest in the Victorian novelists which began in the 1940s. Dickens, Trollope, George Eliot, and others were resuscitated; Gissing lay dormant. Indeed, 'up to . . . 1960', as one critic has put it, 'Gissing's name was apt to frighten nineteen out of twenty publishers.' And yet in the past two decades there has been a flow, steadily growing, of Gissing publications (see Appendix): new editions of his novels, most of which have long been out of print; biographies, new critical studies, reprints of older critical studies; and ultimately those final proofs of academic respectability – collections of letters, diaries, bibliographies, a Critical Heritage volume. To those who have ranked Gissing with his more celebrated peers all along, such belated recognition seems neither astonishing nor inappropriate.

George Gissing published twenty-three novels, and 111 short stories, a travel book, a monograph on Dickens ('still the best criticism of Dickens extant', the *Times Literary Supplement* said of it in 1956), and a moderate number of essays. In weight, at least, this is more than the production of any other 'major' Victorian novelist except Trollope. Gissing never achieved either the popularity of Meredith or the notoriety of Hardy, but his work was widely known and generally respected by readers and critics in the waning years of the nineteenth century. In the 1890s he was often ranked with Meredith and Hardy among the leading novelists of the time – yet he never earned much from his books. Because of his continual need for money he sold outright for ready cash the copyrights of many of his novels and rarely collected royalties under this arrangement: in his later years, when his financial needs were somewhat less pressing, some of his books were published on a royalty basis. The knowledge that if ever he were unable to work for any significant length of time he would be utterly penurious was a constant source of anxiety for Gissing (he called novel-writing 'a trade of the damned'). Between 1880, the year of his first published book, and 1903, the year of his death, twenty-one of his novels appeared, almost one a year. His best work was done in the years between 1888 and 1897. Financially his peak year was 1901. His other best earning periods were 1894 to 1895 and 1898 to 1899.

It is my opinion that no less than a dozen of Gissing's novels – *The Unclassed, Demos, The Nether World, New Grub Street, Born in Exile, The Odd Women, In the Year of Jubilee, Sleeping Fires, The Paying Guest, The Whirlpool, The Private Papers of Henry Ryecroft,* and *Will Warburton* – are first-rate. To produce a dozen good novels is no common achievement; indeed, few novelists of any nationality have written so much passable fiction. Among Gissing's novels, as among Wordsworth's poems, there is a fair share of disasters, and certainly Gissing was no Chekhov when it came to the short story. But the amount of good novels is prodigious; and *New Grub Street*, which deservedly has been his most popular novel with modern readers, is in my opinion an unqualified masterpiece. Certainly it is better than any novel by Disraeli, Collins, Reade, Kingsley, or George Moore, better than any of Mrs Gaskell's novels with the possible exception of *Wives and Daughters*, better than any of Charlotte Brontë's novels with the possible exception of *Jane Eyre*, better than any of Meredith's novels with the possible exceptions of *The Ordeal of Richard Feverel* and *The Egoist*; indeed, it may well be a greater novel than any of those I have named. This is high, but not outrageous, praise. Gissing is a major novelist; his themes are important ones, treated with sensitivity and intelligence; his perception of things is acute and detailed, his people and their problems real, 'relevant', both for his time and for ours. 'Merely on the strength of *New Grub Street, Demos* and *The Odd Women*', George Orwell said, 'I am ready to maintain that England has produced very few better novelists . . . he does not commit the faults that really matter.' Gissing published two other first-rate volumes – a critical study of Dickens, and an account of travels in southern Italy.

II

Gissing's subjects are sex, money, and class, and the three dovetail in most of his novels and stories into the single subject of marriage, the various component parts ultimately becoming indistinguishable. His treatment of this multi-dimensional theme is both recognizably 'Victorian' and totally personal, but it is in no real sense 'modern', nor do some recent attempts to establish Gissing as a twentieth-century figure make much sense. Gissing's world, the world in which his fictional characters live, seems as remote from the aeroplane and automobile, the telephone and telegraph, movies and television, as that of *Adam Bede,* which shocked and 'revolted' Gissing in 1890 because of the liaison between Hetty and Arthur. Certainly some of his books do seem pertinent to the world of today. He hated advertising, the London tubes appalled him, and he could see where the manufacture of armaments would lead. He anticipated the role science was destined to play in our lives, detested the urban sprawl and the disfigurement of the countryside by industry, and was an ecologist before anyone knew what ecology was. But his responses were always intensely personal. He foresaw, and hated, many of the 'improvements' of the new age, and he was a very nervous man; if this is what it means to be 'modern', then Gissing qualifies. But essentially he was an observer and recorder of his own time, a novelist of manners, a frustrated teacher, a realist, a classicist, a conservative. Most of his novels are the carefully plotted three-deckers of the Victorian heyday, full of guilty secrets, family disasters, lost wills, hidden identities, and clandestine marriages, with appropriate attention paid to the feelings and prejudices of Mudie's subscribers. Gissing's London 'is the fog-bound, gas-lit London of the 'eighties', Orwell has said; 'part of the charm of Gissing is that he belongs so unmistakably to his own time.' Another critic remarks that Gissing's novels give a picture of 'a London that is vanished like a bad dream'. In 1905 there was no doubt in the mind of C. F. G. Masterman as to where Gissing belonged:

> Gissing is the painter, with a cold and mordant accuracy, of certain phases of city life . . . in its cheerlessness and bleakness and futility, during the years of rejoicing at the end of the nineteenth century. If ever in the future the long promise of the Ages be fulfilled, and life becomes beautiful . . . once again, it is to his dolorous pictures that men will turn for a vision of the ancient tragedies in a City of Dreadful Night.

Gissing's good people wish vaguely to be useful, while organized philanthropy is attacked in good Dickensian fashion. The cardinal Victorian virtues of duty and hard work are unflinchingly revered by Gissing, a poor boy who worked very hard. And like many other intelligent men of his time, he was both an agnostic and a libertarian. The 'modern' note in Gissing, when it is audible, grows out of his feeling of alienation and estrangement, but when it is not simply reactionary hatred of everything that is new it takes the traditional form of the sort of paranoia about upper-middle-class snobbery one is also likely to find in Dickens, Meredith, and Hardy.

Sex, money, and class, I have said, become a single theme in Gissing's novels through his examination of marriage. Perhaps more than any of these other novelists, the subject of class obsessed him. Throughout his work there is an 'exile' theme; it always concerns men whose intellect, education, and aspirations make their most natural associates the intellectual élite of the middle classes but whose poverty dooms them forever to familiarity with the lower strata. V. S. Pritchett is certainly right to call Gissing 'the most class-conscious of our novelists'. Gissing's more sympathetic heroes tend to be men of lower- or working-class origins who hope to find a 'respectable' (in Gissing's books this means middle-class, chaste, and intelligent) woman to marry, yet are often deterred from doing so by poverty or by a past crime, real or imagined, brought on by poverty. Some of them find the right woman but back off, sensing that their lack of means or their origin will alienate the chosen lady. Some take the plunge and then discover painfully that poverty can destroy any affection, that no love can survive the corrosive effects of empty pockets, or that social inequality can eventually make enemies of husband and wife. Almost exclusively the novels and stories are about *exogamy*, marriage outside one's class. Under this single umbrella may be gathered those three obsessive concerns with money, sex, and class. For Gissing, one's financial and social position determines one's class – not necessarily one's 'natural' class (the class in which one ought to be) but rather the class in which one happens to find oneself. This in turn controls one's choice of a partner in marriage and the probable results of that choice. Marriages within a single class are more likely to succeed than exogamous ones, which are doomed by the novelist, a conservative intellectual who twice married culturally deprived women, to failure.

Gissing saw himself as unworthy of any 'respectable' woman, and this is partly because his idealized woman was the ideal of a snob. His novels tend naively to equate good manners and breeding with moral worthiness, while the poor and uneducated are usually rated at face value. Like Dickens, Gissing could sympathize with the plight of the poor without wishing to live among them; unlike Dickens, however, he did not fill his novels with people to whom is attributed moral superiority because of the fact of their poverty. There is a fear of the mob in Gissing, as there is in Dickens. The exile motif expresses Gissing's feeling that he himself was a natural aristocrat – in a spiritual, intellectual sense, of course – and that the circumstances of his life forced him always to live outside and below his natural class, in 'exile'. This is the heart of Gissing's conservatism. He sympathized but did not identify. He felt that reform could usually be little more than an unwonted disruption of the status quo. And he felt that wealth, because it often fostered and promoted culture, was more a virtue than a vice.

By 'culture', however, he did not mean education. To be an educated man in an imperfect world is torture; better to be less educated, less fastidious, and thus less dissatisfied. As we shall see, Gissing's education prepared him to live in one social class and the facts of his life compelled him to live in another. In the novels what is always memorable is the collision between the man of intellect, educated sufficiently to be disappointed by the limitations fate has imposed on him, and the grinding necessity of his earning, by whatever means available, an income large enough to satisfy his own yearnings or his family's wants – both of which are always more than minimal. Here the civilizing effects of education are seen to be in fact most pernicious, tantalizing without being able to assuage. No other novelist has written so movingly of the pulverizing effects of poverty and the money-race on the sentient spirit and of the ways in which human feelings can be degraded by economic pressures. It is the focus on the individual confronted by circumstances, social and financial, beyond his control that gives such power to Gissing's best novels – the confrontation of men and economic systems, the brute force of money, the negation of the individual in a money-grubbing system. Scrunch or be scrunched, as Mr Boffin might say. But where Dickens retreats into metaphor, Thackeray into amused tolerance, Mrs Gaskell into hope and prophecy, Gissing stands unflinchingly literal, brutally honest. Perhaps no other novelist except Trollope evokes so fully the texture, the atmosphere, the feel of daily life in the nineteenth century; certainly no other English novelist – not even Dickens – deals so specifically with the consequences of economic systems and failures in the lives of ordinary people. Gissing's usual subject is what Biffen in *New Grub Street* in a memorable phrase calls 'the ignobly decent' – that is, the frustration of the normal and reasonable expectations of average people. Gissing never waxed romantic about love in a hut (the famous passage from 'Lamia' is quoted in the twenty–fourth chapter of *New Grub Street*); healthy relationships, to remain healthy, must be fed with good food and comfortable surroundings. Gissing's idealistic characters who are also impractical always come to bad ends.

So the reasons for Gissing's long obscurity are not difficult to identify. His novels are not pleasant; many verge on the depressive. As in Hardy's work there is little or no poetic justice, and people with good intentions often come to pathetic ends. Such themes are demoralizing, and certainly some of Gissing's fiction is almost unendurably gloomy. And yet we almost always tend to believe in the reality of his people and their milieux, which accounts in large measure for the affective power of his novels.

One may ask: Whence cometh all this gloom? The answer to this question lies in the facts of Gissing's life and personality; no English novelist put more of himself into his novels than George Gissing. To read his books without a detailed knowledge of his biography is to read blindfolded. The critic who attempts to deal with Gissing's fiction phenomenologically or from a narrow structuralist approach acutely diminishes the chances of understanding his subject.

The things Gissing wrote about both obsessed him and happened to him. Written directly from life, his novels are almost without exception parts of a spiritual autobiography, extracts from the story of his own existence. But this is not all. Sometimes Gissing took a cue from the characters he created and imitated them himself – not surprising, since his characters are so often projections of himself. Oscar Wilde's argument that life imitates art is convincingly dramatized in the life of his contemporary Gissing, who was prone

in 'real' life to act out roles and situations he had dreamed up as a
novelist years before.

It is the story of Gissing the novelist, the great neurotic whose
books are so extraordinarily full of his own problems and prejudices, fears and fixations, that I wish to tell. A fatalist who in his
twenties looked in his handkerchief when he coughed and at thirty
was sure he was about to die, Gissing believed that peace and
happiness eluded most men, and certainly had eluded him. A
compulsive reader, a student of languages, an accomplished classicist, a mostly self-taught intellectual, the fastidious, introspective,
hypersensitive Gissing craved order and solitude yet frequently
complained of loneliness. Simultaneously a recluse and a claus-
trophobe, he rarely introduced his friends and relations to each
other and thought the custom of people living together in close
physical proximity was monstrous. A terrific hypochondriac, he
had all kinds of dietary fetishes (he experimented with vegetarianism, then switched to an all-meat diet, then back to vegetarianism,
and so on throughout his life; he thought his third wife's mother
was systematically trying to kill him with her cooking), worried
constantly about the weather (the single most important concern of
his letters), and never really rested. He tried riding a bicycle for
exercise but found it made him too nervous. When a friend H. G.
Wells wrote that 'the *genre* of Gissing's novels is nervous exhaustion', he could just as well have been referring to the atmosphere in
which the novels were written as to the books themselves. James,
who met Gissing in 1901, said later that he was a man 'quite
particularly marked out for what is called in his and my profession
an unhappy ending'. Gissing was a self-destructive and impractical
man, with little common sense.

But this is only part of the story. He was also a notorious *poseur*,
a self-dramatizer, a man who revelled in personal disasters, only
some of which were genuine. Several of his contemporaries report
that Gissing loved jokes and was capable of great hilarity, that he
could be a joy-loving, cheerful man, that he was attractive to
women, liked to talk, liked to be invited out, hated to be ignored.
In all probability he was what modern psychology would term a
manic-depressive; he allowed the depressive mood to take over
when he put pen to paper. A restless man, he was easily dissatisfied;
almost every novel he wrote was begun, cast aside, then again
begun, abandoned once again, and finally finished in a great burst of

concentrated energy. It is entirely possible that he threw out half of his literary productions (think of Trollope, who never altered a word).

Gissing's protagonists, as might be expected from the foregoing, are remarkable among other things for their savage moodiness, their bad cases of nerves, their neurasthenic misanthropy. This is largely the result of Gissing's pessimism, his vision of himself and of the world he lived in – a vision shaped partly by his reading of Schopenhauer, which provided him with a philosophical justification for his condition and the conclusions to which it drove him. But partly, too – primarily, in fact – his view of things was a result less of his reading than of 'temperament'. 'He always liked to speak of the gloomy side of things', Morley Roberts said. 'I possess many letters of his which end with references to the workhouse, or to some impending black disaster.'

'Gissing loves unhappiness', Pritchett has written. 'To understand him one must look first and last at his personal life, for he was, excessively, a personal writer.' At what point Gissing's fiction becomes 'excessively' personal is open to question, but Pritchett's conclusion is surely right. Why is it, for example, that Gissing wrote some of his best books during his unhappiest years and that in his relatively more relaxed last years there is a falling off in his work? This cannot be explained by the ageing process, for Gissing died in his prime, at the age of forty-six. As the *TLS* put it in 1905, 'Gissing's work, though always good, was only great when it was gloomy.' As a writer he needed misery as an oyster needs sand to produce pearls. 'Art, nowadays, must be the mouthpiece of misery, for misery is the key-note of modern life', announces the protagonist of *The Unclassed,* his second published novel. It is probably true, as C. P. Snow has written, that 'In your deepest relations, there is only one test of what you profoundly want: it consists of what happens to you.' What Gissing consciously wanted and what happened to him were not always the same things, though this judgement does not take into account the possibly self-destructive urges of the subconscious man; but to see this, or anything else of importance about him, we must certainly look to the novels – in many ways his 'deepest relations'. They reveal Gissing even more clearly than do his letters, in which there is always some measure of self-dramatization. Fiction, after all, is likely to be more revealing than conscious autobiography, in which there is often some holding back. 'An autobiography can distort; facts can be realigned. But fiction never lies; it reveals the writer totally', V. S. Naipaul has said. One of Gissing's great contemporaries knew this well enough. 'A writer of imaginative prose . . . stands confessed in his work', Conrad wrote in 1912. 'He stands there, the only reality in an invented world, among imaginary things, happenings and people. Writing about them, he is only writing about himself . . . Indeed, everyone who puts pen to paper . . . can speak of nothing else.'

IV

Sounding like a combination of Matthew Arnold and the elder Heyst in Conrad's *Victory,* Gissing wrote to his brother Algernon in 1885: 'Keep apart, keep apart, and preserve one's soul alive – that is the teaching for the day. It is ill to have been born in these times, but one can make a world within a world.' The 'world within a world' is the world of fiction – here less an escape from the 'outer' world than a reflection or extension of it. *The Private Papers of Henry Ryecroft,* in some ways Gissing's most autobiographical book, ends on this remarkable note: 'May I look back on life as a long task duly completed – a piece of biography; faulty enough, but good as I could make it – and, with no thought but one of contentment, welcome the repose to follow when I have breathed "Finis".' Gissing saw his own life as 'a piece of biography', and his novels duly constitute an extended piece of autobiography. The idea of the novelist as biographer or historian is of course a common one in the nineteenth century, reaching a kind of apotheosis in the work of James. In the fiction of Jane Austen, George Eliot, Trollope, Hardy, and many of their contemporaries, the novelist-biographer relates the 'true history' of a fictional personage – plausible, but not really real. Gissing's 'histories' often are in fact case-histories of his own thoughts and actions – and thus really real.

In my search for the man – the man who wrote novels – I cannot hope to produce a more eloquent or informed assessment than that given by Gissing's sister Ellen after his death:

in this strange misshapen life there was a central cord which held all the parts together; there was a principle deeply imbedded in his nature which caused him to prefer that he himself should suffer rather than bring suffering upon others; and in this lay the secret of the life which to outsiders appeared only steeped in gloom, but out of which, for those who knew him, there shone a gleam of imperishable gold.

This touches upon another facet of Gissing which probably explains more fully than the easy term 'masochist' much of his suffering: his innate kindliness, his concern for others, his constant desire to help, to teach, to be of use. One senses his 'passion of sympathy for the suffering poor' without his writing it down in his Commonplace Book and despite his intellectual antipathy to the lower classes. Unfortunately, like Richard Feverel, he tried to 'save' too many women. He had a problem with women, as we shall see – and all of his novels begin and end with that problem.

It is appropriate, then, that we too begin with that problem. To speak of it is to commence the story itself. 'The story of Gissing', one critic has said, 'is better than any of his novels.' To say this is to slight the novels; but certainly Gissing is one of those writers – unlike his contemporaries Meredith and Hardy, for example, who were selfish to the point of cruelty to others – one would especially like to have spent an evening with.

✥

CHAPTER 2

YOUTH AND EXILE, 1857–1876

Oh this learning! what a thing it is !
The Taming of the Shrew

Within the walls of a college, I should have lived so happily, so
harmlessly, my imagination ever busy with the old world.
The Ryecroft Papers

Walk with me, reader, into Whitecross Street.
Workers in the Dawn (Gissing's first novel; opening sentence)

I

WALK with me, reader, into Manchester, if you please. It is 31 May
1876, dusk. The students of Owens College (later to be the
University of Manchester) have been worried of late by the
disappearance from their cloakroom of money, clothing, books. A
police trap has been laid for the thief: some marked money (five
shillings and two pence, to be exact) has been left in an obvious
place and a detective hidden in a contiguous room. A handsome,
tall, well-built, freckled but pale youth of eighteen, with thick
brown hair and blue-grey eyes, walks among the lockers. He is one
of the College's outstanding scholars, a boy who four years earlier
received the highest mark in the Manchester district when he sat for
the Oxford Local Examination, a scholarship student who in his
career at Owens has carried off the prizes for German, Greek,
Latin, English, and poetry, and who the previous year – at the age
of seventeen – had passed the matriculation examination for the
University of London. He looks nervously around the room; sees
the money; takes it. Immediately he is arrested; he is taken to
prison. The Principal of the College is especially upset by the news;
the thief was to have been his guest at dinner that evening. Later, at
a special meeting of the College Senate, all the boy's awards are
revoked and he is summarily dismissed.

I begin with this incident because it is significant of much that
happened to the youth and explains a good deal of what was to
come; in fact an understanding of the motive for the theft and of the

importance of this moment in his life is central to any examination of his life and art. For of course the thief was George Gissing.

II

It is typical of Gissing's life that he came from a town 'ingeniously designed for the torment of any man who cares for beauty and tradition'. This is Wakefield in the West Riding district of Yorkshire. Here on 22 November 1857, in a room above his father's chemist's shop, George Gissing was born. The old three-storeyed brick building in the market centre, like the rest of Wakefield, is still there. What was once the shop of Thomas Gissing, pharmacist, and then for many years part of the Boots chain of pharmacies, is now an Oxfam shop.

Gissing's father, an amateur botanist, would-be poet, and some-time Liberal politician (in local elections only), was an avowed agnostic with an interest in education – a hard-working and intelligent man and himself the author of several volumes devoted (separately) to plants and poetry. He was 'taciturn' but 'pleasant', according to Henry Hick, a childhood friend of George Gissing, and a great reader and an advocate of culture. Early he won the undiluted and lasting admiration of his intellectually precocious eldest son (years later George remarked that he owed everything to his father and that he regularly saw him in his dreams but some obstacle arose to prevent them coming together).

Thomas Gissing was fond of airing his hatred of snobbery and hypocrisy, but he prohibited his children from associating with the children of other tradesmen, and he chose his own friends from among the professional classes. This ambivalence is important. He was not, strictly speaking, a member of the prosperous middle class, nor yet was he of the more humble working class. Today we undoubtedly would classify him as lower-middle-class and be done with it, but in the middle of the nineteenth century his position was ambiguous: he had the education and the intellectual pretensions of the comfortable bourgeois and the income (never very much) of an ordinary worker. George Gissing grew up in a household in which such distinctions were often spoken of, and very early in life he seems to have picked up from his father the exaggerated interest in class that was to be a lifelong characteristic. To which class, exactly, did he belong? His fear and abhorrence of – even paranoia about – the working classes began with his father's social pretensions. Certainly Gissing was *not* born into the lower classes, as some (perhaps those who have read only the early slum-life novels) have assumed, but rather into that twilight zone between 'middle' and 'working' – a guarantee in itself that one's life will be devoted at least in part to sorting the problem out. It is in this way that the 'exile' motif, the man 'exiled' from his natural or appropriate social class, came into Gissing's life at an early age. The novelist always remembered his father, as Pierre Coustillas has aptly put it, 'with that admiring pity one feels for worthy men and women handicapped by their origin and overtaken by fate'. Gissing also inherited from his father an interest in physical nature and a passion for literature.

Gissing's mother has been called 'The Unknown Mrs. Gissing' – and rightly so, despite the fact that she outlived her eldest son by ten years. Margaret Bedford married Thomas Gissing in February 1857. The wedding took place in the parish church of Grasmere, in the yard of which may be found the simple grave of Wordsworth. The odds are that Mrs Gissing was utterly immune to this influence and contiguity; her interests were more domestic. She was both less educated and more religious than her husband, and to the end of her days remained uninterested in ideas. Gissing's mother was the disciplinarian of the family, and he was never close to her; in fact he never liked her very much. Years later he described her as 'a stranger' to him and said that he could not remember ever having received a caress from her. It must have contributed to the feeling he had all his life – articulated in *Born in Exile* – that he was 'unlovable' to women. In any case, it is in this sense that Gissing's mother remains largely 'unknown' to us. The only other account of her we have from among Gissing's early friends is a brief one by Hick, who calls her 'most kindly and charming' but remembers that she once locked his cousin's sister up 'in a dark cupboard' for being 'naughty' and left her there for a long time.

Gissing had two brothers and two sisters, all younger than he. William, born in 1859, would die young. Algernon, the other brother, was unsuccessful both as a solicitor and a novelist, but he seems always to have 'got by'. He was three years younger than George. Margaret and Ellen were, respectively, six and ten years younger than their eldest brother. Neither of the girls escaped the narrow Anglican puritanism of their conventional mother, though Gissing seems always to have felt the younger sister, Ellen, more in sympathy with him than the elder (and more religious) Margaret. But the novelist was never very close to any members of his family, though he was to correspond prodigiously with Algernon. 'I never in my life exchanged a serious confidence with any relative, – I mean, concerning the inner things of one's heart and mind', Gissing noted in his Commonplace Book in 1889. The children grew up wanting for little, though of course there were no luxuries.

Gissing as a boy is described by all who knew him as thirsting for knowledge, tireless in his studies, and fascinated by almost every aspect of physical nature – a passion which, as I have said, he inherited from his botanist father and which contributed to his lifelong penchant for sketching whatever interested him (his interest and skill in sketching led him to sprinkle a sizeable number of artists among his literary characters – and to contribute his own illustrations to *By the Ionian Sea*). He read everything he could get his hands on. As a schoolboy he is remembered chiefly for the ferocity of his devotion to his studies, his hunger for learning, and his high marks. Compulsiveness, signs of great natural intelligence, and tremendous intellectual curiosity are the hallmarks of Gissing's boyhood. He worked hard 'because he could not help it', Hick says. He describes Gissing as 'a rather shy, ingenuous boy, a general favourite with his school fellows'. He recalls discussing literature and languages with Gissing and notes that the future novelist's 'love of the sound of words was well marked even then'.

In December 1870 Thomas Gissing died of congestion of the lungs – the same ailment that was to kill the novelist thirty-three years later to the day. The elder Gissing's illness may have been precipitated by some sudden financial calamity: it is not clear, but if this is so it certainly helps to account for the large number of precipitate economic reversals (in both directions) to be found in Gissing's novels. The loss of this guide, philosopher, and best friend was traumatic. At the age of thirteen he was left with a parent with whom he had nothing in common and with brothers and sisters who were too immature to be intellectual companions. From this time onward the shadow of loneliness and incipient unhappiness begins to loom over Gissing's life.

Gissing's mother was left with five children to bring up and very little money with which to do it. The house and chemist's shop were immediately sold and the family moved to more modest lodgings in Wakefield. A fund in the town was raised by public subscription for the schooling of the Gissing boys, and all three were sent as boarders (further reducing Mrs Gissing's domestic expenses) to the Lindow Grove School at Alderley Edge in Cheshire, a decent place run by non-sectarian Quakers in which the teaching standards apparently were high. All three brothers did well there. George, who avoided games and devoted himself exclusively to academic pursuits, soon became head boy, amazing the teachers with his scholarly zeal. He worked as he ate, and read as he walked. He saw himself as the head of a large family; he felt he must get on quickly. Being poor, he knew he would need scholarships to continue his studies, and he drove himself accordingly.

At fifteen, if we take Harvey Rolfe in *The Whirlpool* as a portrait of the novelist at that age, Gissing was loutish, ungainly, scholarly, conceited, bashful – and tormented by his bashfulness. At any rate this is how he saw himself. His sister Ellen describes him at sixteen as 'a tall boy with dark auburn hair, high white brow and eyes slightly short-sighted so that the lids had to be drawn together when looking at any distant object'. She said 'he shewed a marked gentleness of manner' and was 'over-sensitive . . . to what others were feeling or thinking'; this was, she says, 'all through [his] life, a very strong characteristic'. She also remembers him at home on vacations using 'scathing words to denounce the boyish pursuits and love of adventurous literature' of his younger brothers. The uneasy relationship between the overbearing Godwin Peak and his unintellectual younger brother in *Born in Exile* is obviously drawn from Gissing's memories of his own youth.

Gissing did equally well in all subjects during his two years at Lindow Grove, carrying off a good many of the school's prizes. In May 1872 he passed the Oxford Local Examination, having almost worked himself into exhaustion in the process ('overwork was Gissing's most settled habit', as Korg has said). On the basis of this performance Gissing was offered a three-year tuition-free scholarship to Owens College, which was exactly what he was hoping for. He matriculated there in January 1873.

Founded in the early 1850s, Owens offered something between a secondary and a university education; many of the young men who went there did so to prepare for Oxford, Cambridge, or London University, as Gissing did. During his first two years at Owens he continued to board at Alderley Edge, but in his third year he moved into Manchester – a change that was to have far-reaching consequences. Sounding suspiciously like Dickens on the blacking-factory episode – Gissing carefully read Forster's *Life of Dickens* in 1874 – he declared later to Morley Roberts: 'It was a cruel . . . thing that I, at the age of sixteen, should have been turned loose in a big city, compelled to live alone in lodgings, with nobody interested in me.' Turned loose he certainly was, but Gissing did most of the unfastening himself. For a boy of studious habits, with no experience of less intellectual temptations and an extremely sentimental cast of mind, the results of such sudden freedom were to be disastrous.

Roberts remembers Gissing at this time as a young man of exceptional promise who hated science and was fascinated by Hogarth's paintings, a great talker when in the mood but often reserved, and capable of great hilarity on occasions. He describes the future novelist as 'curiously bright, with a mobile face. He had abundant masses of brown hair combed backwards over his head, grey-blue eyes, a very sympathetic mouth, an extraordinarily well-shaped chin – although perhaps both mouth and chin were a little weak – and a great capacity for talking and laughing.' I had perhaps better add here that Roberts, one of the earliest and closest of Gissing's few lifelong friends, is not always to be trusted. In _The Private Life of Henry Maitland_ (1912), the first attempt at a biography of Gissing which turned out to be largely fiction, Roberts made up a great deal – not all of it to Gissing's credit. There is sympathy here, but there is also (as in Wells's even more disloyal reminiscences of Gissing) a tendency to patronize, to condescend, and to denigrate. One must pick and choose carefully among the 'facts' served up by Roberts, who was himself a novelist.

Gissing's academic career prospered. He won prizes for English poetry, Greek, Latin, and German. He rested little, and avoided social engagements so that he might work. He regularly rose at 4 a.m. and worked until 10 p.m. In June and October of 1874 he sat for the matriculation examinations of London University and to the surprise of no one performed brilliantly – winning national prizes for English, Latin, and history, and carrying off more of Owens's prizes too (this time those for Greek, Latin, history, mathematics, and classics). It was clear that he had a distinguished university career ahead of him. During the autumn of 1875, his last at Owens, he began preparing himself to enter the University of London in the autumn of the following year. His teachers and schoolmates predicted that he would become a professor of classics at one of the universities. He was a fine literary scholar and an exceptionally brilliant linguist.

During the first months of 1876 Gissing, now just turned eighteen, was living by himself in a furnished room near the College. He had, of course, complete freedom of action, his mother and brothers and sisters being far away and his few friends at the College kept, most of the time, at arm's length. One day, Roberts tells us, Gissing showed him a photograph. It was that of a young girl, about seventeen, who wore 'her hair down her back. She was not beautiful, but she had a certain prettiness . . . and she was undoubtedly not a lady.' Her name was Marianne Helen ('Nell') Harrison, and it turned out that she was a prostitute whom Gissing had met and picked up in a public house. During the early stages of their affair the naîve, romantic, sex-starved Gissing had been an easy prey for Nell and her landlady-pimp, but as he got more passionately involved, the relationship began to change. He became Nell's lover instead of merely her client. Roberts advised him to give her up, and was horrified by the petulant retort that he had better watch what he said about Gissing's future wife.

John George Black, another friend, also slept with Nell; a venereal disease was his reward. Gissing himself had a bout of gonorrhoea in February 1876, but not even this could cool his passion. 'He haunted the streets which she haunted, and sometimes saw her with other men', Roberts reports. Gissing seems to have viewed her as a victim of society and to have set out to redeem her. Attempting to give Nell the means of a respectable livelihood off the streets, Gissing bought her a sewing-machine and suggested that she became a sempstress. Nell wasn't interested in sewing; her indoor occupations were more strenuous. Still, Gissing continued to see her as saveable. He gave her, eventually, all his money, even selling his father's treasured watch for additional funds. For Nell Harrison, however, there was no such thing as enough money. She was a hopeless alcoholic and had become a prostitute to feed her habit – a habit which she never succeeded in overcoming. Gissing completely misread her from the start, attributing to her special qualities she never had or could have had – such as the desire to improve herself, to learn, to become respectable, and so on. At eighteen he understood neither his own sexual needs nor those of the women he met. He projected on to Nell his own idealistic social values. Of course she was immune to all of them.

The more money Gissing gave Nell the more she spent. The sewing-machine remained unused. But he persisted in his mad desire to marry her, assuming that married life would provide a moral framework which would enable her to readjust. His friends – Roberts, Black, Hick, and others – pleaded with him to give her up, but he refused to listen. For the first time – but by no means the last – he insisted on acting self-destructively. He would, he said, save her, save her at all costs (*The Ordeal of Richard Feverel*, not surprisingly, was always one of his favourite novels). During the spring of 1876 Gissing took Nell on several short trips. Completely infatuated, for the first time in his life he began to neglect his studies. His scheme to save her cost more and more. His scholarship funds were exhausted and he began to take things from the locker-room of the College. The thievery was repeated over and over again, ultimately leading to the College's hiring of a detective and the laying of the trap I have already described. On 31 May 1876 the trap was sprung and the culprit caught; and Gissing's world came crashing down upon him.

All those years of academic preparation and overwork, of fondly laid plans to overcome the financial circumstances of his background and to justify his father's faith in education and in himself, went down the drain. Caught, jailed, and dismissed from the College, his admission to the University of London was cancelled. Like any ordinary criminal, he had committed a crime and been arrested. Overnight he was transformed from a respectable college student to a common felon, a prostitute's fancy-man. The effects of this mighty and sudden transformation were, as we shall see, to last throughout Gissing's lifetime and to determine many of his most characteristic social attitudes. They also were to give shape to his art. The affair with Nell and the stealing episode were of course always connected in Gissing's mind and were, I think, largely responsible for that confluence I have spoken of in his work of sex, money, and class. In driving these events of 1876 farther and farther away from the surface of his life as time went on, Gissing also turned them, inevitably, into vastly influential subconscious forces – obsessions, in fact. He was to make out of them a single monolithic 'guilty secret', as Gillian Tindall has called it, of which the guilt went so deep and the secret of his past became so important to maintain that Gissing found himself trying to exorcize them in everything he did, and in story after story.

The 'guilty secret' appears in different guises. Sometimes it takes the form of a secret marriage, sometimes of a secret identity or birth, sometimes a past indiscretion real or imagined. In Gissing's case the guilt was many-sided – a liaison with an unworthy woman, a venereal disease, a crime and a prison-term. Such things did not happen to respectable people, and Gissing above all as a young man without money and prospects yearned for respectability. How, now, could he ever become respectable? How could he ever live among gentlemen, much less call himself one? Until the last few years of his life he was absolutely convinced, despite his other achievements, that he was unworthy of the love of any respectable woman. He saw himself as an exile, deserving as a result of his accomplishments to live among his intellectual peers but fated by circumstances to live below and away from them. Again and again his fiction portrays the martyrdom of the outsider. In the years subsequent to 1876 his guilt took many forms, but surely Tindall is right to detect in the stealing episode and its results an indiscretion that seemed to Gissing more *social* than sexual or financial:

what Gissing had so calamitously done was to commit a *working-class crime*. He had disgraced his family and himself by doing something not just against the law but utterly out of keeping with the class with which the whole Gissing household fervently wished to be associated. In his temporary abandonment of honesty, he had blundered back through those very social barriers which, by dint of work and scholarships, he had himself so laboriously climbed.

This disaster – which led to others in Gissing's life, though none quite like this – deprived the world of a brilliant classical linguist, but it just as surely guaranteed, by forcing him to begin earning a living almost immediately, that a significant contribution to English fiction would be made instead. Literature has prospered rather than suffered from this arrangement.

We will be returning to these themes again and again as we review Gissing's books and stories, but for the moment let us go back to the month of June 1876. This is a period of Gissing's life about which, understandably, he was absolutely silent later. Not a single letter written by him during the summer of 1876 is known to exist. The Principal of Owens put up bail for Gissing, and he was released from prison on the day after he was arrested. The incident caused general astonishment, especially as Gissing was so well respected in the College community and because a promising career had been so irretrievably ruined. Here was a contemporary tragedy in plain dress. Gissing's mother, apparently, was quick to blame but slow to understand her eldest son. On 6 June Gissing was sentenced to one month's hard labour, a sentence which he served in Manchester. Sentences were not suspended in those days. Immediately the Owens College Senate voted to dismiss Gissing and to rescind his prizes. The Senate committee investigating the matter found the circumstances of the case aggravating rather than extenuating: there was no sympathy for a man whose mistress was a prostitute and on behalf of whom he had stolen from his classmates. It was discovered that Gissing's friends Roberts and Black had known of the affair with Nell; they received reprimands.

Upon Gissing's release from prison in July 1876 he returned to

Wakefield, but his story was of course known and no possibility existed of his getting work there – or of his resuming his studies elsewhere, for that matter. No second subscription would be taken up in the town for the convicted thief. Gissing may have held, briefly, a clerkship of some sort in Liverpool in August, but this is uncertain. In September he once again became the beneficiary of a subscription relief fund – this one raised largely at Owens College, at the instigation of the administration. There was some sense that perhaps the College had behaved with gratuitous harshness to this inexperienced, impecunious, fatherless boy.

Amongst the Gissing family and its friends it was decided, ultimately, that the black sheep should go to America, where there would be no prejudice against him, where he could become a new man. He would take several letters of recommendation with him; perhaps he would make his fortune there. He would also, of course, cease to be dependent upon his resourceless family (they had been counting on him to help them); and many thousands of miles would be put between him and Nell. Gissing seems to have concurred in these plans without much enthusiasm. He was told that the family's friends would do whatever could be done to rehabilitate Nell. Using the money raised for him by Owens College, Gissing sailed for Boston in September 1876 – having told none of his Manchester acquaintances except Roberts what he was doing. At eighteen he had cut himself off from virtually all who knew him. It was the first of many exiles.

CHAPTER 3

⚵

WORKER IN THE DAWN, 1876–1882

'Paint a faithful picture of this crowd we have watched, be a
successor of Hogarth, and give us the true image of *our* social
dress, as he did of those of his own day. Paint them as you see
them.'   *Workers in the Dawn*

'The one object I have in life is to paint a bit of the world just as
I see it. I exhaust myself in vain toil; I shall never succeed; but I
am right to persevere, I am right to go on pleasing myself.'
                                                      The Emancipated

'A perfectly decent fellow may be driven by circumstances to
commit a crime and if he's found out he's punished; but he may
very well remain a perfectly decent fellow.'
                                     Maugham, 'Footprints in the Jungle'

I

GISSING began by liking America very much. He moved into a
small boarding-house in Boston and almost immediately discovered
the local public library, where he went, every day at first, to read
George Sand's novels, and Boswell – whom, like the protagonist of
A Life's Morning, he admired greatly. His letters to his family
during this period make a series of comparisons between England
and America unfavourable, in his new-found euphoria, to his
homeland. Like all of his letters, they are full of details about the
food and the climate – two of his most consistent concerns wherever
he went. He was amazed, he told his family, by a new invention
called the telephone. Letters he brought with him had procured
personal introductions to William Lloyd Garrison and William
Dean Howells – but, as yet, no work.

It is clear from Gissing's letters that he was hoping in America to
begin a literary career of some sort – as a journalist, a critic, or a
free-lance writer. At Alderley Edge, and again at Owens, he had
written a good deal of poetry, and at Owens some of his critical
exercises found their way into school publications, but as yet he had
produced no fiction, and nothing he had written had been published
outside the world of school magazines. Now, however, his first

published piece appeared – a critical essay in the *Boston Common-wealth* (28 October 1876) on two paintings on show in Boston. But this was all. He was fascinated by the spectacular presidential election campaign of 1876, by the famous centennial exhibition in Philadelphia, by the optimism and energy of the Americans – but he could find no work. His funds running low, he moved in December to suburban Waltham, Massachusetts, where he took a temporary teaching post at the local high school. He taught languages – German, French, and English. One of his students in later years described him as being at this time (he was now nineteen) 'a tall, broad-shouldered figure with a shock of light brown hair worn rather long, dull light blue eyes, and a full sandy beard'.

Gissing enjoyed teaching – he was a natural teacher – and the Waltham people clearly liked him. So that when, on 1 March 1877, he failed without explanation to meet his classes, there was general astonishment in the little town. He was not sick, he was not simply away for the day; he had packed up and vanished. The reasons for Gissing's sudden departure remain vague, but Coustillas has unearthed one possible explanation. While receiving letters from Nell urging him to return to England, he had also made the acquaintance of one of his pupils, an attractive girl only a year younger than himself by the name of Martha Barnes. He began to feel attracted to Martha, and what probably happened next is reconstructed shrewdly by Coustillas: 'Haunted as he was by the sense of his responsibilities, he must have been smitten with remorse after allowing his passion for his pupil to develop. His past, he already thought, made him forever unacceptable to a young girl of good family, and he found in flight from Waltham the only means of remaining faithful to Nell.' We hear of him next in Chicago.

II

Whelpdale's narrative in *New Grub Street* of his experiences in Chicago – once stripped of its blasé humour – is a fairly accurate account of Gissing's stay there, though in later years the novelist's memories of this period were recounted to friends with more painful emotion than appears in Whelpdale's version. He arrived with five dollars, immediately paid out $4.50 for a week's room and board, and then set about looking for work. After much hesitation he went to see the editor of the *Chicago Tribune* and offered to write stories of 'English life' for the paper's weekend supplement. The editor suggested that he submit some stories; he would see if he liked them. Gissing wrote his initial piece of fiction during the first week of March 1877 – literally to keep from starving. The circumstances under which this introduction to authorship took place are vividly described by Whelpdale:

Impossible to write in my bedroom, the temperature was below zero; there was no choice but to sit down in the common room, a place like the smoke-room of a poor commercial hotel in England. A dozen men were gathered about the fire, smoking, talking, quarrelling. Favourable conditions, you see, for literary effort. But the story had to be written, and write it I did, sitting there at the end of a deal table . . . I stand amazed at my power of concentration as often as I think of it!

The story was called 'The Sins of the Fathers'. It was written in two days, and the editor of the *Tribune*, to Gissing's astonishment, gave him $18.00 for it – enough to pay his room and board at the boarding-house for an entire month. Thus fortified, Gissing immediately wrote another tale, called 'R.I.P.', which was also accepted by the *Tribune*. His career as a writer of fiction had begun.

'The Sins of the Fathers' is virtually pure autobiography, an accurate portent of what was to be Gissing's usual genre. It is about a well-educated, middle-class man who falls in love with and engages himself to a destitute lower-class woman. The hero attempts to help her by getting her sewing to do. (Gissing, we should remember, was corresponding with Nell throughout his stay in America.) He quarrels with his father, who opposes the marriage, and goes off to America, where he gets a job teaching in a New England secondary school. Later he hears that the girl is dead; but since he knows that she would not have made an adequate intellectual companion, he is by no means devastated by the news. Soon thereafter he marries a respectable, well-heeled woman. The original fiancée reappears, the reports of her death having been greatly exaggerated. There is a terrible scene, a struggle, and finally the deposed girl drags the man to their deaths in freezing water: the story ends with this double drowning. 'R.I.P.' is also about an exogamous relationship which ends in disaster. This time a French nobleman marries a peasant girl; his family drives her out; she kills herself. Finis.

For several months Gissing earned his living by selling tales to various Chicago papers. Between March and July of 1877 at least seventeen stories of his were published (there are others which may be his but of which the authorship is still disputed; many of Gissing's earliest stories were unsigned). I shall mention some of them briefly

here. 'Too Dearly Bought' is a Dickensian tale about an old man
and his granddaughter who, living in the midst of urban squalor,
dream of going to the country. Ultimately the grandfather steals
some money to get them there (Gissing was to use part of this plot
later in *A Life's Morning*). The story is interesting both for its
idealization of the country at the expense of the awful city (a
conspicuous theme in the fiction) and for its description of the
thief's state of mind at the very moment of the theft: 'His brain was
in a whirl. All his hopes, his longings, his vain schemings, flashed
. . . through his mind . . . a cold shudder passed over his body . . .
and his tongue felt parched against his palate. He could not reason;
he stood a prey to quick succeeding passions and emotions.'

In the next story, 'The Warden's Daughter', a man wrongly
convicted of theft escapes from prison with the help of the warden's
crippled daughter, who has always had great 'compassion for the
unfortunate'; later they marry. In 'Gretchen' we learn that to
become an artist a man must be both a great genius and near to
starvation. In this story the artist-hero, the first of many in
Gissing's fiction, falls in love with a lady he sees in a picture – an
idea the novelist was to use again much later in *Will Warburton*.
'Twenty Pounds', which tells us that 'to be dishonest is worse than
going mad', is also about a man who steals money; here the
protagonist gets into trouble by having to change a large bill (this
anticipates the plot of *A Life's Morning*). 'Joseph Yates' is another
story about a theft of money, and also of interest because it contains
the first of several idealized wives in Gissing's fiction – the sort of
wife he was always to dream about but never to have. This one,
Bessie Yates, tells her hard-pressed husband that she can endure 'all
things . . . poverty, trial, sacrifice' – but not disgrace. Not, of
course, that she enjoys being poor. But the point of the story is that
there are worse things: it is, for example, better to be poor than
dishonoured. Poor Gissing! 'Brownie' is a grisly Hardyesque tale of
an uncle who murders his niece in order to keep his farm.

Most of these stories, it will be seen, revolve around crimes of
various kinds, very often theft: obviously Gissing continued to be
haunted by the events of the previous year. None of the stories is
first-rate; most, as a matter of fact, are inept. But they were
produced when the writer was only nineteen.

III

In July 1877 Gissing left Chicago. He had had only one story accepted during June and July, he was short of money again, and out of ideas. Homesick for England, he headed east – this time for New York City. But there was no work for him there. A newspaper in Troy, in upstate New York, had pirated 'The Sins of the Fathers', he discovered. Taking a chance, he chose Troy as his next destination. At Troy he was to find himself in a situation that was to make him, as Jacob Korg says, 'a celebrated case among starving authors'. For several days, having no other recourse, he lived on peanuts bought from a street-vendor (this too forms part of Whelpdale's narrative in Chapter 28 of *New Grub Street*). Starvation, remarks Morley Roberts, was for Gissing 'one of the initiation ceremonies into the mysteries of literature, and he was always accustomed to say, "How can such an one write? He never starved".'

Eventually Gissing decided to go home. He wrote to England for money, and apparently borrowed some more in Boston, to which he returned to buy his passage back to Liverpool. For a short time he avoided starvation by working as an assistant to a travelling photographer. At some point he saw Niagara Falls, which was to provide the setting for the final scene of his first published novel. But generally he did not use much American material in his fiction. In a novelist who so often wrote autobiography, this suggests that much of his time in America was too unpleasant even for fiction.

Gissing embarked for England some time in September – a year after leaving his homeland – and landed in Liverpool on 3 October 1877. He returned to Wakefield six weeks short of his twentieth birthday, hungry and in debt: a failure by any standards. He had not been expected back, and was not made especially welcome. Algernon was articled as an apprentice solicitor and still dependent on his family for support. William was working in a bank but earning barely enough for himself. The two girls were at home with their mother. Gissing obviously could not become a burden to his family. Again he packed his bags, this time determined, like many before him, to make his fortune in the city. His mother was not sorry to see him go. 'George's speedy departure for London', Coustillas remarks, 'relieved the Gissing household of a troublesome son whose name in the town was pronounced only in a whisper or with knowing looks'. In London he hoped to earn his living as a writer. He knew that he could expect no help or even encouragement from his family, though he remained on relatively good terms with his brothers. Gissing at this time must have been acutely cognizant of the mortgage his past held on his future.

IV

He took a furnished room near Gray's Inn Road and began looking about for the means of earning a living. Not much is known about these early months in London – Gissing never said much about them – except that at some point Nell came to live with him. He published a story ('The Artist's Child') in *Tinsley's Magazine* for January 1878, signing his full name for the first time, and did some private tutoring to make ends meet. Towards the end of 1877 he made one of many moves to another boarding-house, this one off Tottenham Court Road; it is likely that the move coincided with Nell's reappearance upon the scene, about which he remained extremely secretive with his friends and relatives. His brother Algernon met her in January 1878 and his brother William met her the following spring, but Roberts, for example, was never allowed to lay eyes on her, and there is no mention of her at all in Gissing's letters to his mother and sisters.

The letters written early in 1878 do reveal, however, that he had begun to write a novel. He worked a good deal at the British Museum both for the sake of the light and the warmth there and also in order to do the sort of literary hack-work which Alfred Yule, in *New Grub Street*, always hoped might turn into a permanent meal-ticket. But Gissing apparently failed to sell any critical pieces during this period.

Certainly he was very poor. He complained to Algernon that he could not afford to buy any shoes or even a new pair of trousers. He was sure that no employment would be offered to him because of his shabby appearance, and he was largely right. In February 1878, however, he found some new pupils to tutor, and this made things a little better; but he remained in perpetually difficult circumstances. Even so, 'My early years in London were a time of extraordinary mental growth, of great spiritual activity', Gissing was to say later. 'There it was that I acquired my intense perception of the characteristics of poor life in London.' *The Ryecroft Papers* gives an account, largely autobiographical (though it leaves Nell out altogether), of what life was like for Gissing in those days – the changing of lodgings to save a few pennies (and because Nell's old habits were not to the liking of landladies), the going without a meal to buy a desired book (or drink for Nell), the gazing through shop windows at food he could not buy, the walking of immense distances to save fares. His clothing was probably very ragged. He ate in cheap places when he could afford to eat at all. He became, partly through personal embarrassment, a sort of recluse, subject to what Ryecroft calls 'the profound solace of misery nursed in silent brooding . . . I wanted only a little walled space in which I could seclude myself, free from external annoyance. Certain comforts of civilised life I ceased even to regret . . . I just locked my door, and . . . went to bed.' Yet he managed to do an enormous amount of reading during this period, and he kept up his Greek and Latin. Wherever he lived his precious store of books and the Owens College prizes he had been able to keep went with him and were proudly displayed. Roberts, who was one of the few friends of his past life to be admitted to his new one, describes these years in harrowing terms, and sums up:

This was the kind of life that [Gissing], perhaps a great man of letters, lived for years. Comfortable people talk of his pessimism, and his greyness of outlook, and never understand. The man really was a hedonist, he loved things beautiful – beautiful and orderly. He rejoiced in every form of Art, in books and in music, and in all the finer inheritance of the past. But this was the life he lived, and the life he seemed to be doomed to live from the very first.

Gissing continued during the first part of 1878 to work on his still untitled novel. Despite his passion for freedom from 'annoyance', the domestic conditions that generally obtained during this period of his life – as during much of the rest of it – could not have been conducive to work. Roberts reports that Nell's habits perpetually compelled Gissing to move from one place to another, 'for even the poorest places . . . could hardly stand a woman of her character in the house'. She continued to drink; and at intervals she deserted Gissing and went back, for the sake of more drink and the money he was unable to give her, to her old trade on the streets. Again and again she returned in tears and he took her in: 'no man on earth could have made more desperate efforts to help her than he made', says Roberts. Still, wherever the pair went Nell managed to associate herself with the worst elements of the neighbourhood and to quarrel with everyone. In September 1878, several moves later, they were living in Gower Place.

The autumn of this year was an important period in Gissing's life. On 22 November he was to come of age and would be eligible to receive his share of what little money his father had left (eventually, in April 1879, he got about £300). Also during this autumn he finished his novel and began circulating it to publishers. No one wanted it. Gissing pretended not to be surprised, but he must have been bitterly discouraged. The book was never to be published, and it has not survived in manuscript; apparently the novelist destroyed his first offspring. This would not be the last time that an entire book-length manuscript was thrown out.

Briefly at the end of 1878 Gissing worked as a clerk in a charity hospital, an experience he was to make use of in *New Grub Street*. Early in 1879 he met Eduard Bertz, who was destined to be one of the closest friends he ever had – and, eventually, the recipient of his most revealing letters.

Four years older than Gissing, the radical Bertz was an exile from Bismarck's Germany. Like Gissing, he was studious, intellectual, hard-working, poor, interested in literature, and generally incompetent in practical matters. Like Gissing, he had lost his father as a boy; made a living primarily by tutoring; was extremely sensitive to grossness and vulgarity; required an ordered household life in order to work. He too moved from one house to another seeking peace and quiet and was never satisfied, no matter where he was. He was also a confirmed hypochondriac. Needless to say, the two men got on very well indeed, and Gissing unreservedly poured out to Bertz the endless story of his domestic troubles. They met, oddly enough, through a newspaper advertisement Bertz had placed, seeking intellectual companionship, very much as Waymark and Casti meet one another in *The Unclassed*, Gissing's second published novel (in which Bertz appears not as Casti but as Eggers, the unhappy teacher). The two soon became fond of talking the night away in each other's company – almost always in Bertz's rooms rather than Gissing's, since Nell, like Mrs Casti in *The Unclassed*, waxed unpleasant when she was not included in the conversation. As in the relationship between Mrs Casti and Waymark in Gissing's novel, Nell grew jealous of Bertz and became fond of slandering him to Gissing to assuage her feelings.

In *The Unclassed* Gissing uses Casti's first meeting with Waymark as an opportunity to give us, in the picture of the man Casti sees, an interesting and detailed self-portrait:

He was rather above the average stature, and showed well-hung limbs, with a habit of holding himself which suggested considerable toughness of sinews; he moved gracefully, and with head well held up. His attire spoke sedentary habits; would have been decidedly shabby, but for its evident adaptation to easy-chair and fireside. The pure linen and general tone of cleanliness were reassuring; the hand, too, which he extended, was soft, delicate, and finely formed. The head was striking, strongly individual, set solidly on a rather long and shapely neck; a fine forehead, irregular nose, rather prominent jaw-bones, lips just a little sensual, but speaking good-humour and intellectual character. A heavy moustache; no beard. Eyes dark, keen, very capable of tenderness, but perhaps more often shrewdly discerning or cynically speculative. One felt that the present expression of genial friendliness was unfamiliar to the face, though it by no means failed in pleasantness. The lips had the look of being frequently gnawed in intense thought or strong feeling. In the cheeks no healthy colour, but an extreme sallowness on all the features. Smiling, he showed imperfect teeth. Altogether, a young man . . . whose intimacy but few men would exert themselves to seek; who in all likelihood was chary of exhibiting his true self save when secure of being understood.

Such is Gissing's picture of himself as he thought he appeared to Bertz at the time of their first meeting (17 January 1879). It is an instance by no means anomalous of the way in which Gissing unreservedly wrote himself – physically as well as emotionally – into his books.

In March 1879 Gissing was working on two lectures entitled 'Faith and Reason' and 'The State Church from a Rationalist's Point of View', scheduled to be given at a local working men's club. This was the first fruit of his marathon discussions with Bertz, who felt – as Gissing did at this time – that the educated poor had an obligation to help the uneducated poor to improve themselves. For a short while Gissing had a mission; a series of lectures was planned. In January 1879 he wrote to Algernon: 'Scarcely one man in ten thousand is capable of original thought . . . No material advance will ever be effected if we do not take for our earliest watchword – popular education.'

Gissing was soon disillusioned with this plan of improvement as he became better acquainted with the sort of man he thought he wanted to educate. This bitter experience was to find its way into several of the novels – most notably *Thyrza* – and Gissing's disillusionment was to be translated as time went on into undiluted hatred of the lower classes and of all schemes for educating them. 'Faith and Reason' was delivered as planned in March 1879, but this was the full extent of Gissing's career on the public platform; no other lectures were given, though more were written.

The payment of Gissing's share of his father's legacy enabled him to move with Nell from Huntley Street, Bloomsbury, to Edward

Street, near Regent's Park, in the spring of 1879. He had been living largely on tutorial fees (and eating almost nothing but lentils in one of his vegetarian periods attributable more to poverty than to preference), rising usually at 5 a.m. for the two-hour walk to his chief pupil's Chelsea home – to be told, as often as not, that the man didn't want a lesson that day. The new lodging seemed to be to his taste. He got on quickly with the writing of his lectures for the working men's club, and he began another novel despite the utter failure of his first attempt. The new book was to be *Workers in the Dawn*, written between May and November 1879 (after finishing the novel he and Nell moved again – this time to Hanover Street, Islington). The original title of the book was 'Far, Far Away' – which, as Gissing wrote to Algernon, 'conveys the *idea* of the book, which is very greatly directed to social problems, principally the condition and prospects of the poorer classes'. While waiting for a decision from the publishers, he set to work on a number of new stories.

v

We come now to two most important events in Gissing's life – his first marriage, and the publication of his first novel. These may well be considered together, since *Workers in the Dawn* is in part about Gissing's life with Nell. The book was not published until May 1880, but Gissing worked on it during a good part of 1879, as we have seen, and finished writing it within a few days of his marriage.

Why did he do it – why did he marry Nell? Gissing complained bitterly of her to Bertz and wrote of her mercilessly in his first novel, as we shall see. And yet on 27 October 1879, in the parish church of St. James, Hampstead Road, he legalized his relationship with her. None of Gissing's friends or relatives was invited to the ceremony; few were even told of it. His decision to marry – especially considering the difficulties of divorce for a poor man in those days – defies understanding. He took exactly the foolish step which, in *Workers in the Dawn*, he had made his hero take (that is, to try to save a prostitute by marrying and educating her), and shown to be disastrous. The novel – which I must repeat was finished within a few days of the marriage ceremony – demonstrates clearly that Gissing no longer had any idea of trying to save Nell; his few remaining illusions about her had been shattered. The writer, as Tindall says, knew more than the man, and the man was unable to make proper use of what the writer knew and had actually written. This is one astonishing example of the odd relationship between Gissing's work and his life. His fictional protagonists yearn for respectable women while they marry beneath themselves; as a novelist Gissing *knew* what torture this could be for a sensitive man, yet as a man susceptible to women he seems to have forgotten what in fact he knew. Not only was Nell alcoholic, not only did she continue to sell herself in the streets to feed her habit, not only was she ignorant, foolish, wilful, and defiant, but she was also both vulgar and slovenly, two traits which, as Gissing's writings show again and again, he especially abhorred. There is no rational explanation for what he did (though a few clues exist in *Workers in the Dawn,* as we shall see). There are some irrational explanations: that the marriage was a masochistic joke he played on himself; that Nell claimed to be pregnant and that he was taken in by her (Casti in *The Unclassed* has this trick played on him by his future wife – who bears, as we have seen, some other resemblances to Nell); that he simply resigned himself to formalizing the existing situation, having come to feel that no respectable woman would ever have him. The fact that Gissing and Nell were married according to the rites and ceremonies of the Established Church in no way illuminates the question, especially when one considers the novelist's repeated assertions to his friends that he entertained no religious beliefs whatever. Nor does Morley Roberts's characterization of Gissing as a man who 'did not like to be disturbed in any way whatsoever'. He could not have found a more effective way of disturbing himself.

In a letter to Algernon, Gissing describes *Workers in the Dawn* as '*not* a book for women and children, but for thinking and struggling *men*'. Unfortunately too much struggling was required, and it sold very poorly; since Gissing ended by using some of his father's money to pay for publication of the book himself, the affair was a total fiasco from start to finish. No one, however, can be at a loss to see why the book failed so miserably. Even as a first novel by a twenty-two-year-old writer it is an awful performance. The 1,234 pages of its first edition would have made it difficult to finish in any case. Gissing had not as yet learned what should be left out of a novel – he was still too much his own subject. Nor do the characters in the book speak to one another. They deliver speeches, often sermons: practically the whole novel is exposition. The children are absurdly precocious and often orate like hardened philosophers. Gissing was to develop an excellent ear for dialogue later.

The novel's hero, Arthur Golding, is the first of the long series of fictional self-portraits. The chief preoccupations of his life are work and love. Should he dedicate himself to helping others, as Gissing had recently thought of doing, or to art? Should he devote himself to the drunken prostitute he has made the mistake of marrying, or to the ideal woman who both understands and encourages his artistic calling? These questions are asked for over 1,200 pages until Arthur puts an end to them for ever by jumping into the Niagara Falls in the middle of winter. He was heading in the direction of art and the ideal when the end came. It is possible that Gissing, who must often have wanted to get away from Nell and felt guilty in consequence, thought of suicide as a solution to his dilemma. The several deaths by drowning in the early fiction suggest that this was the means that occurred to him when such thoughts held sway. 'There's a point in the life of every man who has brains, when it becomes a possibility that he may kill himself', says Basil Morton in *The Whirlpool*. 'Most of us have it early.' Gissing probably did.

Arthur's father dies when Arthur is still a boy – being unable to recover from the ill effects of having 'yielded to a terrible temptation' and robbed his employers, at a single blow having 'hopelessly shattered' all his prospects in life. Like Gissing, Arthur has the good fortune to grow up with well-developed sensibilities and a great deal of intellectual curiosity, but like the usual Gissing hero, he is condemned by his poverty to a level of existence much below that which he desires and feels himself fit for. Arthur suffers a great shock, at the age of eight, on finding himself out of his proper class: he runs away from the Norman family largely because he cannot endure being patronized by the well-off. It is the daughter of this family, Helen, who becomes his ideal woman (Helen was Nell's real name, and this may be an exercise in wish-fulfilment; but Nell herself is to appear in this novel very much in her own person, as we shall see).

Arthur spends most of his adolescent years as the informally adopted son of a stationer named Tollady, who seems to be Gissing's idea of what his father might have been like in old age had he lived. Tollady's library, significantly, is large on the literary side, sparse on the scientific side except for botany, and bereft of theology. An ardent botanist, Tollady has at one period of his life, like Thomas Gissing, kept a herbarium, the contents of which he collected himself.

Arthur is urged by Tollady to 'be a successor of Hogarth, and give us the true image of *our* social dress'. We know that Gissing always admired Hogarth, and undoubtedly this first novel is consciously Hogarthian in its examination of the poorer classes. But like his fastidious creator, Arthur instinctively shrinks from the ugly, preferring to contemplate the beautiful instead. We can *see* Gissing in this novel trying to resolve this problem which was to plague him for the rest of his life. The problem was the writer's desire to live amid what is soft and gentle, and the necessity of living elsewhere – having constantly in front of him as subject-matter for his books only what he loathed. Arthur at seventeen 'felt within himself the stirrings of a double life, the one, due to his natural gifts, comprehending all the instincts, the hopes, the ambitions of the artist; the other, originating in the outward circumstances of his childhood . . . showing him . . . the ever-multiplying miseries of the poor amongst whom he lived'. The 'double life' surely is Gissing's own. And, on Hogarth:

The art to which he was devoted was not the same in which Hogarth had excelled. He felt that it would be impossible for him to take up his pencil for the delineation of such varieties of hideousness. Beauty was the goddess that he worshipped at the inmost shrine of his being, and to the bodying forth of visible shapes of beauty his life must be devoted, or he must cast aside the pencil for ever . . . how should he go for his models to the slums and the hovels amidst which his wretched childhood had been passed?

Roberts said years later that Gissing's 'very repugnance to his early subjects led him to choose them. He showed what he wished the world to be by declaring and proving that it possessed every conceivable opposite to his desires.'

Workers in the Dawn attacks the existence of public houses and examines the evils of drink. Despite its impatient and often unkind account of the poor, it manages to show us many of the worst horrors of poverty. It depicts the lower classes as beyond, in their bestiality, either education or the well-meaning attempts of philanthropists. And it describes London as a nineteenth-century Waste Land, a horrible place in which, for the sake of peace and an end of suffering, it is better to be dead than alive. Here is a little Hogarth from *Workers in the Dawn* – Whitecross Street on Christmas Eve: 'Out of the very depths of human depravity bubbled up the foulest miasmata which the rottenness of the human heart can breed . . . stifling a whole city with their infernal reek. The very curs that had followed their masters into the gin-palaces shrank out into the street again, affrighted by the brutal din.'

'Its object', said Gissing of *Workers in the Dawn*, 'is to depict real life', and certainly the more naturalistic chapters of the novel are powerfully written. But Gissing had not as yet learned to tell a story or to populate it with more than a few credible creations. Helen Norman, like Miriam Baske in *The Emancipated*, becomes with equal facility first a religious fanatic and then an aggressive agnostic. Instead of using his characters to achieve mimetic adequacy, Gissing employs them to attack most forms of speculative philosophy, whose great fault, he was coming to feel, was inability to promote sympathy for the *individual*.

Much of the second volume of *Workers in the Dawn* is taken up with Arthur's flirtation with a working men's club, described as a nice idea but on the whole irrelevant to the life of a serious artist (which is how Gissing had come to see it just a few months previously). Arthur retraces many of Gissing's steps. From viewing education of the average working man as the only answer – and wanting, in consequence, to help open a working men's library (here is part of the plot of *Thyrza* in miniature) – he comes to see the whole thing as a useless exercise. This part of *Workers in the Dawn* includes much discussion of Schopenhauer, Comte, and Shelley, all of whom Helen reads carefully while in Germany. This leaves her roughly where Gissing's reading in speculative metaphysics had left him in 1879: 'the mystery of life and death begins and ends with a vast doubt . . . boundless conjecture.' Gissing got his account of student life at Tübingen directly from Bertz, who provided him with an outline for the chapter in which it is described (Volume I, Chapter XIV). This is typical of the book's chief problem: characters are made to personify ideas rather than real people, and as a result we never have much interest in them.

In its focus on the horrors of slum life *Workers in the Dawn* may seem to take a Radical point of view, but in fact, like Gissing's later novels, it adopts a very conservative tone about the poor: it is best to leave them alone because nothing really can be done; give them money and it will only be spent on drink; sanity can only be preserved by doing whatever it is one is destined to do in life; education only makes the ignorant more dissatisfied and unhappy.

The strain in the novel between helping others as the only acceptable morality and personal egotism as the only possible defence against the world's madness is reflected in the story of Arthur's love for two women – Carrie Mitchell, actually Nell, and Helen Norman, between whom and himself 'there is always that horrible difference of caste.' Indeed, the novel clearly portrays Gissing's sexual schizophrenia – his need for sensual love from, and desire to play providence to, an unsophisticated girl; and his need of the moral approval of a 'respectable' woman. This is part of the 'double life' that Arthur talks about in the novel. Was Gissing right to abandon at so tender an age any hope of marrying a respectable woman? Was his decision to try to save Nell an intelligent one? Or was she beyond help, and he simply destroying in the attempt what was left of his own life? *Workers in the Dawn* argues that the Helens of this world are always beyond the reach of the Arthurs, and that the Carries will always be the ruination of the Arthurs. It also argues that art is a more sacred calling than philanthropy: this is the only aspect of Arthur's 'double life' that is ever clearly resolved. Urging him to give up his foolish notions about helping the unfortunate and to concentrate instead upon his painting, Helen makes an impassioned speech late in the novel:

I bid you give yourself henceforth solely to art, for you are born to be an artist. The feelings of infinite compassion for the poor which work so strongly in your mind . . . you must not allow . . . to lead you astray . . . nothing in this world is more useful than the *beautiful*, nothing works so powerfully for the ultimate benefit of mankind . . . in becoming a pure artist you would do far more to advance the ends [of civilization] than by wearing away your life in petty efforts to do immediate good. Genius has always had, and always will have, laws to itself.

This is pure Gissing; he had already decided to take this advice, and was only lecturing himself.

The Arthur–Carrie relationship is the most autobiographical thing in the novel. Gissing's Pygmalion theme begins here, in Arthur's attempt to make Carrie a spiritual as well as a physical companion. His pitiful efforts to teach his wife to read, write, and speak correctly – all of which she meets with stubborn sullenness – provide the most moving scenes in the novel. However, a man who sulks on the second night of his marriage because his wife won't read Coleridge with him is probably not an ideal husband; Gissing must have been difficult to have around the house.

Arthur's predicament is clearly stated: 'What he intensely loved, he could not but wish intensely to respect. The pity which had originated his love was in itself a species of respect; he had convinced himself by force of emotion that Carrie could not deserve the suffering she endured, and he had almost reverenced her as an instance of unmerited misfortune . . . He could not believe that such outward perfection could exist with a common-place and sterile nature.' Arthur dreams of finding a girl as beautiful as Carrie who has no trouble with her *h*'s. By persistent correction of his wife's pronunciation he finally manages to enrage her.

Arthur has to marry Carrie to see what she is really like. Gissing, already knowing what Nell was really like, married her anyway: the account of Carrie, written before Gissing's marriage, makes this clear. Carrie has no hesitation about going to bed with Arthur, and so he ends up with her. Something like this must have been one of Gissing's reasons for choosing lower-class partners. They were sexually accessible; he could feel superior to them; he need not worry about being rejected by them. Women like Helen Norman were more difficult to approach, more selective, less promiscuous. They might also inquire into one's past, as Helen inquires into Arthur's.

Gissing portrays Arthur as hating his life with Carrie. He can have no friends in when she is at home; he thinks of his previous existence without her as a time of 'vanished joys'. At one point he lectures her: 'What peace can I have if I know that . . . you are taking the surest means, day by day, to degrade yourself and render yourself altogether unworthy of my affection?' This is especially interesting. Is Arthur more worried about 'saving' his wife or finding a way to justify, rationalize, his desire to sleep with her? In any case, whatever hopes he has for her are short-lived. Soon after his marriage, having become thoroughly acquainted with her cunning ways of obtaining drink, he sums up her character in these terms:

She seemed to have no innate respect for truth, and had acquired a facility in deception which made it all but impossible to arrive at the truth by questioning her. The knowledge of this terrible flaw in her character gave Arthur many sleepless nights. How could he tell what ruinous schemes were ripening in the brain of the girl who slept so peacefully by his side? . . . his suspicions never ceased to be fed with only too substantial evidence. *Distrust* haunted him like a passion.

Carrie finally dies of her life on the streets, as Nell was to do. Arthur goes to America to escape his past mistakes, but ends by drowning his sorrows in the Niagara Falls. Gissing's epitaph for Arthur is another bit of sorrowing self-portraiture: 'The secret of his life lay in the fact that his was an ill-balanced nature, lacking . . . a firm and independent will . . . he was one of those men whose lives seem to have little result for the world save as useful illustrations of the force of circumstances.' Here is one possible clue to why Gissing married Nell. If you see your life as an allegory of unluckiness then what you do may have the effect of a self-fulfilling prophecy. Another clue might reside in Arthur's 'precious sense' of his role in the marriage as that of performing 'a lofty task which seemed necessary to his existence'. Less complicated clues may be found in Carrie's threat to Arthur – 'I could force you to support me' – and in Arthur's comment about their life together that 'Though we may scorn the world's opinion, we must still fear its tongue.'

When Carrie finally leaves Arthur to get more money for drink, he is intensely relieved – as Gissing was when he later walked out on Nell. Arthur thinks of the departed Carrie as a 'weight to which he had immutably bound himself' and which 'was dragging him down, down into the foul atmosphere of a brutal existence'. Arthur perceives his marriage as Gissing perceived his even before he married: a great error capable of turning 'a moment's folly' into a hellish existence.

Workers in the Dawn, then, chronicles the death of Gissing's love for Nell at the moment when he had decided to marry her. 'Excess of compassion had by degrees developed in him to a feeling which he had mistaken for love', Gissing says of Arthur. 'My wife? My wife?' Arthur moans to Helen. 'This degraded, horrible, brutalised creature to call herself my wife!' Gissing was about to give Nell the right to do so as he wrote this. Certainly he had given up his plans for reforming her. 'All my efforts are vain!' Arthur says. 'I cannot raise her to my level; but I feel only too well that she has the power to drag me down to hers. It is my fate to suffer.' The book emphasizes what Gissing calls 'the immutable power of destiny'. Mr Tollady's fatalism obviously is congenial to the novelist. 'History pursues its path, using us as its agents for the working out of prescribed ends', Tollady tells Arthur. 'To think that we men can modify those ends is the delusion of ignorance or madness.'

Another theme in *Workers in the Dawn* that was to become typical of – or at least recognizable in – the later fiction is the violent excoriation of landladies and the boarding-houses they keep, a subject on which Gissing was becoming a reluctant expert. Landladies he always saw as gouging and rapacious, boarding-houses as noisy and unpleasant. Gissing's horror of domestic discord is everywhere present in the novel, perhaps most comically in the character of Mr Venning, who spends his Sundays sitting at home merely to enjoy the silence there.

VI

As *Workers in the Dawn* was making its rounds among the publishers in December 1879 and January 1880 and being turned down by one after another, Gissing was undauntedly working on some stories. 'If ever literature was a man's vocation it is certainly mine', he wrote to Algernon. 'I feel that no amount of discouragement will make me cease writing; indeed I cannot conceive of my life otherwise than as being spent in scribbling.' In late February he gave up on the publishers and agreed to pay Remington and Company £125 to bring out *Workers in the Dawn*. The advertising expenses, estimated at £20, were to be paid out of sales; the author was to receive two-thirds of any profits (in this same year Disraeli received a record advance of £10,000 from Longmans for *Endymion*).

During the first two months of 1880 Gissing wrote six stories, none of which appeared during his lifetime. 'The Last Half-Crown' is about an unsuccessful writer who gives his last bit of money to some starving neighbours and then drowns himself in the river. 'Cain and Abel' is a gruesome tale of murder and revenge emphasizing the role of predestination in human affairs. 'All for Love' is a *novella* with all the trade marks of the early Gissing: exogamy, two climactic drownings in icy water, blackmail, revenge, and murder. More than anything else Gissing had so far written, this story turns on 'the dreadful', 'the fatal', the horribly *guilty* secret – in this case a woman has married for the second time thinking that her first husband is dead, only to discover that he is very much alive (Gissing was to use a similar plot-device in *Denzil Quarrier*). 'All for Love' is focused on the question of how to get rid of an inconveniently extant spouse – a subject by which Gissing, for obvious reasons, was obsessed during this period of his life. 'My First Rehearsal' is a jolly tale of a man who wants to become an actor and is swindled out of everything he has by another man pretending to be a theatre-manager. 'My Clerical Rival' and 'An Heiress on Condition' stand alone in this group by virtue of their happy endings. The former tells the story of a man who pursues his ideal woman and, after a brief comedy of errors, wins her. The latter has another idealized heroine, an artist-hero yearning after her, and a melodramatic climax based on the revelation of a concealed identity.

VII

About the time he concluded the publishing agreement with Remington, Gissing began a new novel. Called first 'A Child of the Age' and later 'Will-o'-the-Wisps' or 'Wills-o'-the-Wisp', the new story was destined to be destroyed by the novelist in manuscript. 'The subject of the novel', he wrote to Algernon, 'is the dissipation of illusions, the destruction of ideals, in short the failure of a number of people to gain ends they have set up for their lives, or, if they *do* gain them, their failure to find the enjoyment they expected.'

Obviously the novelist was in a lugubrious frame of mind. 'I must sternly face the fact that only a short time may remain to me in which to develop what intellect I have', he wrote to William in March 1880. '"The night cometh when no man *can* work" is a good sentence to have before one's eyes.' Gissing was only twenty-two and in generally good health. But Nell had been spitting blood, William himself was briefly ill, and clearly the novelist was having mortal thoughts. When William died suddenly on 16 April of a ruptured blood vessel in the lung, aged twenty, Gissing's fatalism seemed amply justified. Besides his feeling of loss, his letters during this time show him even more firmly resolved to make a name for himself quickly in case he too was destined to die young. Nell's continuing poor health reinforced his feeling of mortality. He even began to suffer from pains in the chest, and imagined that he had inherited William's ailment. Throughout the spring of this year he spent an average of two evenings a week with Bertz at the latter's Bloomsbury flat – the two men, as always, talking the night away.

In May 1880 *Workers in the Dawn* was published. In July the sale of the book was so poor that Gissing's two-thirds' share of the proceeds came to only sixteen shillings. He complained bitterly to Remington about inadequate advertising. During the summer and autumn a few reviews of the novel appeared. The *Athenaeum* was lukewarm, complaining of the radical division between good and bad people, prejudice against the well-to-do, and a certain stiffness in the writing, while praising warmly the portrait of Helen Norman. In the *Academy*, Saintsbury also criticized the unsubtle characterization, but lauded Gissing's 'sincerity' and 'imagination'. The *Manchester Examiner and Times* gave the novel more praise than it deserved. The *Spectator* review was mixed, but it did acknowledge a certain raw power in the book. These were the only major reviews of *Workers in the Dawn*, which was generally ignored by the London literary world.

The novelist complained about reviewers' alleged inaccuracies, about their unanimous feeling that he knew nothing of upper-middle-class life (quite true), of the charge that the book was more a tract than a work of art (also quite true) – and was especially irked by their taking him to be 'a working-man'. A careful reading of his book would, he believed, show such a description to be grossly absurd. To Algernon, Gissing wrote a brief explanation of the novel's pessimism, declaring it the result of 'my temperament, and the special mood in which it was written. If you knew much of my daily life you would wonder that I write at all, to say nothing of writing cheerfully. But . . . I have . . . *written off* a whole period of my existence.' In another letter to Algernon he says of his work that he wishes, in it, 'to bring home to people the ghastly condition . . . of our poorer classes, to show the hideous injustice of our whole system of society . . . I shall never write a book which does not keep . . . these ends in view.' He could not know it, of course, but the perspective from which he would view the 'condition' of the poor and the 'injustice' of society was to alter considerably as the years went by – and much sooner than he dreamed.

Perhaps the most important result for Gissing of the publication of *Workers in the Dawn* was the friendship it initiated between himself and Frederic Harrison, to whom he sent a copy of the book. Harrison, forty-nine in 1880, was a distinguished Positivist philosopher and social critic and a frequent contributor to the most important journals of the day. He was well known as a writer and lecturer on social subjects, and he had many connections in literary and journalistic circles. Harrison disliked the novel's scenes of low-life brutality but was impressed by its power of sympathy for the suffering poor, the 'religion of humanity' which the book, in the tradition of Comte and George Eliot, clearly propounds: and he helped Gissing by introducing him to John Morley, the Radical editor of both the *Pall Mall Gazette* and the *Fortnightly Review*, and by telling a number of his friends – among them Matthew Arnold – to read *Workers in the Dawn*. Morley immediately asked Gissing to contribute some articles to the *Pall Mall Gazette*; Gissing sent in some pieces on contemporary socialism and German politics, with which he was helped by Bertz and for which he was paid the relatively handsome sum of eight guineas. As he had been selling his clothes piecemeal in the autumn of 1880, this new source of income was especially welcome. In November 1880 (about the time of Gissing's twenty-third birthday) Harrison asked him to tutor his two sons: the novelist was to teach them for the next four years, and soon afterwards he got more tutoring work through some of Harrison's connections.

During the latter part of 1880 and the early part of 1881 Gissing was leading a curious sort of double life – appearing in fashionable homes as tutor and guest and returning at night to cramped misery and a drunken wife. The novelist reported to Algernon that at one social gathering a lady asked him how he managed his butler; he replied that he preferred a maid. These new activities represented financial salvation for Gissing. But he was not getting on with his new novel, and ultimately, having other projects in mind, he put it aside altogether. The poor sale of *Workers in the Dawn* must have been a factor in his decision not to try the public's patience with another similar production. By Christmas 1880 only forty-nine copies of the novel had been sold; indeed, it is a measure of the book's permanent obscurity that in later years *The Unclassed* was generally thought to be Gissing's first novel. Still, though he had not as yet made his way as a writer of novels, he was slowly becoming known in London literary circles, largely through the benign influence of Harrison and John Morley. He knew his métier was that of a writer of fiction; and though he produced only three short stories during the next three years, he had made up his mind to persevere – and persevere he did.

VIII

In February 1881 Gissing and Nell moved again – this time to Wornington Road, Westbourne Park, in the West End. This address was more convenient for the novelist's tutoring. By March 1882 he had ten pupils, all children of wealthy families, and was earning 45 shillings a week from this work alone. It was also more convenient for his new career in journalism, which included now a quarterly article on English affairs for *Le Messager de l'Europe*, a Russian journal which paid him £32 a year for the several years of his contributions. The only part of each piece recognizable to Gissing upon its appearance was the signature 'G.R.G.' at the end, the rest having been translated into Russian in the editorial offices in St. Petersburg. Around this time Gissing also became intimate once again with his old Owens classmate Morley Roberts, and was soon dividing many of his evenings between Roberts and Bertz (who had taken lodgings close to Westbourne Park). Roberts tells us that he had been seeing a good deal of Gissing for over six months before he was told about the novelist's marriage and invited to his home – upon which occasion he was unable to stay because Nell, invisible in the next room but certainly audible, was so sick with drink as to need all his host's attention. (When Gissing's sisters visited London in the spring of 1881 he met them away from his lodgings; they left without knowing he was married.) Nell's poor health continued: her medical bills compelled Gissing to borrow money from his mother (that must have been a bitter moment). What with one thing and another he found himself during much of this year hardly able to do any serious writing. Occasional optimism alternated with bouts of despair. 'I am slowly obtaining a footing among people worth knowing', he told Algernon; his new Russian adventure, for example, initiated a brief correspondence with Turgenev, whom Gissing admired greatly. But at the same time he was depressed both by his inability to get on with his fiction and the spiritless life he saw going on around him. 'Our age . . . is thoroughly empty, mean, wind-baggish, and the mass of people care so little to find employment in intellectual matters that they are driven to all manner of wild physical excesses for the sake of excitement', Gissing wrote to Algernon. About his own work at this time he commented: 'for composition I absolutely require a period of mental and bodily peace to *precede* the actual writing': of course he could not find it. 'Yet I know very well that this alone is my true work, and it shall not be sacrificed to whatever exigencies.' The 'exigencies' are not otherwise identified, but Gissing adds: 'How I wish I could give you a real insight into my daily existence for the past years! But to do so would be to write a miserable letter . . . people who live from hand to mouth have to be content to do without . . . comforts.'

The new novel he was not getting on with was given various titles during the first half of 1881 – 'Heirs of Poverty', 'Heirs of Toil', 'Children of Toil', 'The Disinherited' were a few of these – but ultimately, like its predecessor, it remained unfinished and unpublished. The titles suggest, however, that he was finding his way towards the material of his next published novel, *The Unclassed*. Later in the year he began to write another book, called 'Mrs. Grundy's Enemies'.

Austin Harrison, Frederic's eldest son, has left on record his impressions of the man who taught him the classics in the early eighties. Gissing was always carefully dressed, Austin reports, his moustache meticulously waxed. He walked like an athlete, seemed always to have a wistful or dejected expression on his face, yet could startle his pupils by breaking into uproarious laughter. He was sensitive, calm, and kindly to the Harrison boys but would not tolerate inattention or misconduct. He was an excellent teacher. He was treated by the Harrison family as a friend and often invited to stay for meals, during which – invariably, Austin says – his father and his tutor would debate the issues of the day. Austin was especially impressed by Gissing's 'humanity': 'I felt . . . attracted towards a man with so much learning who yet seemed so woebegone and deplorably miserable. And yet he loathed misery and degradation.' Gissing was often invited to Mrs Harrison's receptions. Like Peak in *Born in Exile,* he generally felt out of place at such gatherings and was especially irritated by the easy bearing of his fellow guests. Unlike them, of course, he had to return home to an alcoholic wife whose drunken fits demanded almost constant (and expensive) medical attention. 'For people who are not anxious about tomorrow's dinner, life in London is very fine', he wrote to his sister Ellen in November 1881; 'otherwise it is a cruel sort of business.'

Sometime during the latter half of 1881 the novelist decided that he must separate from his wife. 'My writing has suffered most grievous interruptions', he told Algernon. 'I suppose a perfectly peaceful and intellectually-active life is one of those blessings I shall always only be looking forward to till there is no time left for it.' His letters to his brother show that he was deeply depressed: 'I am doomed to do everything under the most harassing difficulties, in nothing is my path ever lightened, but rather forever more and more encumbered . . . the months and years go, go, with never a better, but always a dark, outlook, and perhaps the best years of all are already gone.' Gissing was twenty-three.

In July 1881 he rented a room for Nell in Hastings. He himself moved in August into new lodgings in Gower Place, Euston Square. Nell did not stay long in exile; rebelling, she returned to her husband less than a month after her departure, and work again became virtually impossible. To Algernon he wrote: 'I struggle with absolute anguish for a couple of hours of freedom every day . . . To say that I am like a man toiling up a hill with a frightful burden upon his back is absolutely no figure of speech to me; often . . . I am on the point of stumbling and going no further.'

However during the autumn of this year he did manage to finish a story, 'The Quarry on the Heath'. Here he tried out several ideas he was to expand later. The encroachment of the factory on the countryside became a central theme in *Demos*; the story's setting, a town very much like Wakefield, was to be used again in more detail in *A Life's Morning* and *Denzil Quarrier*; the central character, Lashmore, was to give his name, slightly changed, to the protagonist of *Our Friend the Charlatan* (Lashmar). 'The Quarry on the Heath' (also unpublished during the novelist's lifetime) is another formula Gissing tale of this period, a tragic love story replete with guilty secrets, unfulfilled amorous desires, and yet another suicide by drowning.

The autumn of 1881 was an especially bad time for Gissing; he said very little to anyone about it. 'I am getting most frightfully nervous, indeed so completely nervous that I dread the slightest variation from my humdrum life', he told Algernon. 'The door-bell ringing, even, or the postman's sudden knock puts me into palpitation and head-swimming.' He continued to struggle on with the old life until, in January 1882, a new crisis brought his relationship with Nell to another impasse. Not for the first time, she was overcome in a public place by one of her alcoholic fits. Gissing took her to University Hospital; they were unable to help her. He had by now run out of all patience with Nell; her methods of getting drink often included plotting with the lodging-house servants against her husband, lying to him, even cheating him of money. Gissing knew that she was hopelessly addicted to alcohol and that drink was slowly driving her insane. He also knew that his only hope of getting work done lay in separation from her. His attempt the previous year to effect a separation had failed; he was determined to see this one through. After a series of terrific scenes, he put Nell into an invalids' boarding-house run by two old ladies in Battersea. This cost him fifteen shillings a week – a large proportion of his small income – but he felt he must be rid of her at any cost.

As soon as Nell was out of the house he got back to work. In February 1882 he moved to rooms in Dorchester Place, near Blandford Square. Here he made rapid progress on 'Mrs. Grundy's Enemies' during the winter and spring: and the absence from home of his wife enabled him to take on some additional pupils – one of them the Duke of Sutherland's nephew, another the grandson of Sir Stafford Northcote. Bertz was in America at this time, but Gissing saw a good deal of Roberts. Occasionally of an evening they would make and eat together a stew of miscellaneous ingredients cooked over the fire, and talk about books. Gissing shared his solitude with a tomcat named Grimmy Shaw, who was fond of going to sleep on

his writing-table. He also spent a number of evenings with Algernon, who was now living in London; the two talked much of places
they wished eventually to see, Italy being Gissing's first priority. At
this time he was reading Gibbon, having purchased in May a huge
six-volume set of the *Decline and Fall* for six shillings and sixpence
and carried the whole thing home in stages to Dorchester Place
from the Euston Road. These various details – the stew cooked over
the fire, the cat named Grimmy, the endless evening talks about
literature and travel, the purchase and transportation of Gibbon –
will be familiar to any reader of *The Unclassed*, which was to make
free use of them (the Gibbon story is also told in *The Ryecroft
Papers*).

With Algernon close at hand, much of Gissing's letter-writing
during the first half of 1882 was directed to his sisters. Like Milvain
in *New Grub Street*, Dymchurch in *Our Friend the Charlatan*, and
Warburton in *Will Warburton*, Gissing had female relatives living in
the country to whom he regularly wrote letters full of advice – often
about what to read, almost always touching in some way upon the
theme of self-improvement. As Milvain exhorts his sisters to
educate themselves and make use of their education, so Gissing,
throughout the early eighties, exhorted Margaret and Ellen. 'If you
only could know how much of the wretchedness of humanity is
occasioned by the folly, pigheadedness, ignorance and incapacity of
women you would rejoice to think of all these new opportunities
for mental and moral training', he wrote to Ellen in February 1882.
This is the closest he came to revealing to his sisters anything of the
life he had been leading in London.

IX

Though he maintained his separation from Nell, Gissing continued
to be plagued by her. During the summer of 1882 she escaped from
the invalids' home and lived in a variety of places, along the way
causing her husband to be sent a continuous stream of abusive
letters complaining of his cruelty and neglect. Gissing increased her
allowance to £4 per month, but stayed away from her.

'Mrs. Grundy's Enemies' was finished in September, and Gissing
sent it on its rounds of publishers. After several rejections, the novel
was accepted by Bentley. Buoyed by this, undismayed by the
publisher's offer of only £50 for the book, and ignorant of Bentley's
reputation as a scoundrel, Gissing immediately began a new novel,
'The Burden of Life' – later retitled *The Unclassed*. Also in this

month he moved again – to Oakley Crescent, Chelsea, where he was to live for the unprecedentedly long period of eighteen months. Bertz was still abroad, but Roberts visited Gissing every Sunday; the two were fond of reading Greek and discussing literature together, often on empty stomachs, very much in the manner of Reardon and Biffen in *New Grub Street*. In October Nell, having had an eye operation and being virtually helpless, threw herself on her husband's mercy, and in a weak moment Gissing took her in. After less than a month, however, he had to put her out again; she went off to live with some people at Brixton.

In the autumn of 1882 Gissing was also working on two more pieces (neither of which, again, was to be published during his lifetime). 'The Lady of the Dedication', among other things, is about the absolute and arbitrary power publishers and editors have over aspiring authors. Adler, the writer in this tale, often must go 'to bed with a most unpleasantly hearty appetite . . . Unless he parted with some of his books, there was absolutely nothing convertible into supper.' This is certainly the Gissing of the recent past. The Gissing of the more immediate present is evoked in the description of Adler as a man who, despite his poverty and obscurity, 'was doubtless the subject of conversation in not a few genial circles, where appreciation of literature was heightened by the soothing effects of recent dining'. The narrator goes on to describe Adler as 'a young man of education and talents' reduced to 'living . . . from hand to mouth' owing to 'a restless heart and impetuous qualities little consistent with prudence'. The question is: will he starve before gaining a measure of success in letters? Unfortunately, he lacks assurance; and it is difficult for him to ask others for help, since he considers this a form of begging.

Gissing is of course describing himself. Ultimately, because an editor's wife (for which read Frederic Harrison) likes Adler, he is given some measure of literary exposure and thus a means of living; and he is reunited with his long-lost love, an idealized working-class girl in the tradition of Bessie Yates named, this time, Ellen (instead of Helen), who conspicuously displays confidence in everything her lover does, patience with his literary and pecuniary troubles, understanding of all his various problems, and so on. 'The Lady of the Dedication' is a slight advance upon Gissing's previous stories. It shows him beginning to move away from melodrama in his shorter tales and dealing with more ordinary, realistic, subjects.

The other piece he worked on during this time was 'The Hope of Pessimism', a longish essay showing the influence of Schopenhauer on his thought and his disillusionment with Comte and Positivism, with which *Workers in the Dawn* had dealt in the main sympatheti- cally. 'The harsh experiences of these years were teaching him to modify his faith that society could be transformed by rational means', Korg says. Gissing was also growing more and more conservative, and this plainly shows in 'The Hope of Pessimism'. In it he mounts a full-scale attack on nineteenth-century Radicalism as being too idealistic, too unrealistic, to be of use to anybody. Largely because he thought the essay might offend Harrison and his other Positivist and Radical friends, Gissing ultimately decided not to publish it. Still, it gives an interesting insight into his thinking at this time. The Positivists typically substituted the 'religion of humanity' and sociological ethics for metaphysics and orthodox religion; inherently optimistic, Positivism was seen by Gissing now as mere mindless, groundless hoping-for-the-best. 'The Hope of Pessimism', by contrast, is a remarkable expression of what we would think of today as twentieth-century pessimism. Helen Norman's philosophy in *Workers in the Dawn* makes it clear that what first attracted Gissing to Schopenhauer was his sympathy with the sufferings of mankind. In *The Unclassed* – which Gissing had already begun as he was writing 'The Hope of Pessimism' – Waymark speaks almost pure Schopenhauer dogma: he believes in mortifying the will to live and in putting faith instead in the doctrine of philosophical necessity, the idea of fate. 'We shall not escape from the eternal truth that the world is synonymous with evil', Gissing says in this essay. He goes on to refer to 'the weariness of being' and 'the burden of breath':

We enter the gates of life with wailing, and anguish to the womb which brings us forth; we pass again into the outer darkness through the valley of ghastly terrors, and leave cold misery upon the lips of those that mourn us. The interval is but a feverish combat . . . Those brief intervals of rest which nature grants we embitter for each other by the inexhaustible envy of our hearts. Our passions rack us with the unspeakable torment of desire, and fruition is but another name for disillusion. Every epoch of existence feeds on the vision of some unattainable joy . . . we lament for that which we have not, and our nightly dreams mock us with a visioned happiness . . . Our bodily frame is a . . . seat of lusts which obscure the soul . . . We lay our selfish plans as though for an eternity of life, and fate mocks the bitterness of our disappointment.

Still only twenty-four, Gissing had already developed that streak of fatalism which was to form an important part of his character for the rest of his life. Certainly he had his reasons.

As he had done three years earlier when writing *Workers in the Dawn*, Gissing in this essay suggests that one may be forced to choose between helping others and single-minded devotion to one's own interests – as in Arthur Golding's case, the interests of art. 'There is', he says in 'The Hope of Pessimism', 'only one kind of worldly optimism which justifies itself in the light of reason, and that is the optimism of the artist.' In art alone 'good does prevail over evil' and the natural egotism of man is sublimated 'into pictures of absolute significance' and 'images of pure beauty'. Not for the last time, Gissing was taking a road already travelled by one of his own characters. The essay ends, however, with this view of the future: 'The grave will become a symbol of joy; those who have departed will be spoken of as the happy ones.'

It was in this frame of mind that *The Unclassed* was written.

1. Thomas Waller Gissing (the novelist's father) in 1869

2. Margaret Bedford Gissing (the novelist's mother) in 1879

3. George Gissing in 1888

4. George Gissing (profile)
in 1888

CHAPTER 4

⚜

ART AND MISERY, 1882–1885

When I think of all the sorrow . . . that has been wrought in my
life by want of a few . . . pounds . . . I stand aghast at money's
significance . . . Hateful as is the struggle for life in every form,
this rough-and-tumble of the literary arena seems to me sordid
and degrading beyond all others.   *The Ryecroft Papers*

Some men are born not to make money.
                              Gissing to Clodd in 1903

'Art, nowadays, must be the mouthpiece of misery, for misery
is the key-note of modern life.'   *The Unclassed*

I

His November 1882 article for *Le Messager de l'Europe* was
Gissing's last. Some of the income thus lost to him was made up by
taking on additional pupils, but because of the allowance he gave
Nell he was still hard pressed for money. His landlady of the
moment found a way to reduce the expense of his lodgings, thus
making her husband suspiciously jealous and causing Gissing,
eventually, to move again. There is an incident a little like this in
Will Warburton.

I must now outline the brief history of 'Mrs. Grundy's Enemies'.
Gissing read proofs in January and February 1883. About this time
Bentley took fright at some things in the book. We shall never
know precisely what they were, but reading between the lines of
Gissing's correspondence tells us that the novel attacked, probably
with little subtlety, prudery in all its forms, as well as Radical
idealism and democratic socialism. Undoubtedly it was brutally
realistic, in Gissing's best Hogarthian style. Bentley asked the
novelist to take the offending passages out. After some hesitation
Gissing agreed. In March he thought he had done what Bentley
wanted; still the publisher balked, demanding more excisions.
Gissing made a few more; and in April Bentley sent him a cheque
for the promised advance of £50. In October 1883 the book was
advertised and Gissing awaited its appearance. Early in 1884 his
letters show him still expecting the novel to appear at any moment.

During the summer and autumn of 1884 he made, at Bentley's request, more revisions. But the novel was never published. Neither the manuscript nor the proof has survived.

Furious but undaunted through all this, Gissing continued to work on *The Unclassed* during 1883. His letters to Algernon, now a solicitor living in Wakefield, are full of technical questions about legal matters connected with the plot. Gissing's concentration on this project left him little time for other writing, but he did publish a couple of stories, some descriptive sketches, and even a poem or two in the course of this year. Most of these appeared in *Temple Bar*, published by Bentley, whose bad conscience over the non-appearance of 'Mrs. Grundy's Enemies' apparently assuaged itself in accepting everything else Gissing sent to him. The novelist also got a piece into the *Pall Mall Gazette* – an unsolicited descriptive essay called 'On Battersea Bridge', published the day after he sent it in (this incident is recounted in *The Ryecroft Papers*). It is a measure of Gissing's advance in the literary world that he could now get into print much of what he wrote. Still, he had produced little fiction since *Workers in the Dawn* appeared in 1880.

Bertz came back penniless from America during the summer of 1883, and Gissing helped him to place some journalism before he was again off on his travels. In September 1883 Nell was arrested along with three men for involvement in a public disturbance. She claimed she had been assaulted, but her testimony was impeached. Harrison took this opportunity to advise Gissing to get a divorce, and offered to help. To gather evidence of Nell's usual mode of life Gissing hired a detective to watch her for several weeks, but nothing came of this. By the late autumn he had given up the idea of a divorce. He continued to send her a pound a week, but ceased for all practical (and probably moral) purposes to regard her as his wife – as Arthur ceased to regard Carrie as his wife in *Workers in the Dawn*. Gissing did not see Nell again until she was dead.

His letters during this time make interesting reading. In May 1883, with 'The Hope of Pessimism' sitting in his drawer, he told his sister Margaret that 'the only thing known to us of absolute value is artistic perfection. The ravings of fanaticism . . . pass away; but the works of the artist . . . remain, sources of health to the world.' In July, writing to Algernon, he sounds a good deal like the protagonist of *The Unclassed*. 'My attitude henceforth is that of the artist pure and simple', he says. 'The world is for me a collection of phenomena . . . to be studied and reproduced artistically.' Everything he observes, he says, is for him a 'situation'; 'the afflictions of others' are little more than 'materials for observation'. He wrote this while in the midst of *The Unclassed,* which makes unsparing use of incidents from his own life as well as of the new 'detached' philosophy he had evolved from his reading of Schopenhauer and his growing conservatism.

Late in the year his letters to Algernon were full of advice about writing, for not having prospered as a lawyer Algernon had decided to try his hand at fiction. Gissing tells his brother to cultivate detachment and avoid didacticism; to eschew faultless characters and to keep his plots simple; to read George Eliot but not Scott, who is too discursive; and to make sure that every chapter of a novel contains some incident of interest. Algernon was never successful either as a solicitor or as a novelist, though he did become a prolific writer of fiction; his books continued to appear long after his brother's death, but he never achieved any reputation as a novelist, or any popular success.

But by far the most important event of this period for Gissing was the completion of *The Unclassed* in December 1883 and its acceptance in February 1884 by Chapman and Hall. Chapman had been hesitant to take a novel in which a young prostitute was a central character, but ultimately he decided to publish the book if some deletions were made to the satisfaction of his reader, who was George Meredith. Meredith helped Gissing with the revisions; they went quickly, and in March the contract was signed. Chapman gave an advance of £30 (very little, but his was an old and highly respected firm publishing a possibly controversial book by a virtually unknown novelist) and a royalty of five shillings on every copy sold over 400. Any book brought out by Chapman and Hall was likely to be sufficiently advertised, and Gissing, though he complained privately about the paltry advance, seems on the whole to have been satisfied. He began another novel immediately; at the rate he was being paid for his work he could not afford to stop writing for a minute. But the new story, called 'A Graven Image', was never completed.

In May 1884 Gissing moved again, this time to Milton Street, near Regent's Park. In June *The Unclassed,* dedicated to Morley Roberts, was published. This was really the beginning of Gissing's writing career. During the years between 1877, when he began to write fiction, and 1884, when *The Unclassed* appeared, he had published only one novel – a total failure – and a handful of stories. Between 1885 and 1895 he published fourteen novels, including some of his finest ones. The publication of *Demos* in 1886 would bring him his first popular success, and moderate fame. But *The Unclassed* is the turning-point in Gissing's career as a novelist; one of his better novels, it represents an impressive artistic advance. The years between 1880 and 1883, though full of suffering and virtually empty of tangible achievement, had seen his coming to maturity as a writer.

II

Two days after the publication of *The Unclassed* we find Gissing writing to Algernon: 'When I am able to summon any enthusiasm at all, it is only for ART . . . Human life has little interest to me, on the whole – save as material for artistic presentation. I can get savage over social iniquities, but even then my rage at once takes the direction of planning revenge in artistic work.' This is interesting for two reasons. First, it shows how prone Gissing was to use fiction as a response to events in his own life. Second, it sounds very much like a paraphrase of Waymark's views in *The Unclassed*. Algernon expressed dismay that Waymark's cynicism should be shared by his brother. Gissing's reply, considering his newly discovered 'detachment' as an artist, is a bit ingenuous. 'You evidently take Waymark's declaration of faith as my own. Now this is by no means the case', he tells his brother. 'Waymark . . . alone is responsible for his sentiments . . . I cannot be responsible for what [my characters] say.' He goes on to assert that he has not 'for a moment advocated any *theory* in the book . . . I make . . . the clearest distinction between *The Unclassed* and George Gissing.' I say this is ingenuous because the most casual reading of *The Unclassed* shows how much of him there is in Waymark. As in *Workers in the Dawn*, Gissing wrote into this tale his own spiritual history, the autobiography of George Gissing during the years 1880 to 1883. Algernon's question – that of the resemblance of the protagonist of *The Unclassed* to the novelist himself – is indeed of central importance.

'Only as artistic material has human life any significance', declares Waymark. 'The artist is the only sane man.' And he adds that for him life is chiefly interesting 'as the source of splendid pictures, inexhaustible materials for effects'. A novelist himself, he used to write, he says, 'with a declared social object. That is all gone by. I have no longer a spark of social enthusiasm. Art is all I now care for.' This is Gissing the pessimist looking back at Gissing the Positivist – the same Gissing who tells Algernon that life is interesting only as the raw material of art. The author of *The Unclassed* reviews the author of *Workers in the Dawn* in these terms: 'I was not a conscious hypocrite in those days of violent radicalism, working-men's-club lecturing, and the like; the fault was that I understood myself as yet so imperfectly. That zeal on behalf of the suffering masses was nothing more nor less than disguised zeal on behalf of my own starved passions . . . I identified with the poor and ignorant; I did not make their cause my own, but my own cause theirs.' In Waymark's words, 'ranting radicalism' is worthless, though there had been a time when 'Radicalism of every kind broke out in me, like an ailment.'

Near the end of his life, in *The Ryecroft Papers*, Gissing was to write: 'And to think that at one time I called myself a socialist.' Gissing's statement to Algernon that the protagonist of *The Unclassed* was not himself was of course nonsense.

Like Gissing, Waymark admires Hogarth, whose 'pictures harmonised with his mood'. Waymark's first book was written in that 'mood' but was scarcely noticed by the reviewers. Those who did notice it remarked that there was some 'powerful' writing in it, but generally condemned it as morbidly naturalistic; 'it was destined to bring the author neither fame nor fortune.' Like Gissing, Waymark is a cynic who has considered suicide. A student of Schopenhauer (Chapter XXVII, called 'The Will to Live', is largely a discussion of Schopenhauer's philosophy), Waymark believes in 'the doctrine of philosophical necessity, the idea of Fate'. Like Gissing he is a great walker; is fascinated by the life of the streets; loves the theatre; hates science, 'progress', everything new; is poor but well educated; lives in lodgings; tutors pupils to make extra money; longs for the companionship of women; and believes that life is governed by 'personality'. He speaks of himself as 'a student of ancient and modern literatures, a free-thinker in religion, a lover of art in all its forms, a hater of conventionalism'. And he is described as a man for whom 'poverty was [a] familiar companion, and had been so for years'. Waymark even complains in striking Gissingesque phrasing of the 'hand-to-mouth existence' his impecuniousness forces him to lead. It is precisely this anomalous existence that renders him 'unclassed', in 'exile' from his natural social sphere, 'in a limbo external to society'.

Waymark's relations with women may also remind us of Gissing's. Waymark's sexual fantasy is the same as Golding's in *Workers in the Dawn*: to be married to a respectable woman (Maud Enderby, the successor of Helen Norman) while sleeping with a decidedly less respectable one (Ida Starr, an ex-prostitute, a Carrie Mitchell with self-respect). Maud excites Waymark's social instincts, Ida his sexual ones; there is the intellectual preference for the gentlewoman and the physical preference for the lower-class girl (plus the subterranean feeling that he is not worthy to sleep with the respectable woman).

'A refined and virtuous woman had hitherto existed for him merely in the sanctuary of his imagination; he had known not one such. If he passed one in the street, the effect of the momentary proximity was only to embitter his thoughts, by reminding him of the hopeless gulf fixed between his world and that in which such creatures had their being.' It is a characteristic passage; to see a 'hopeless gulf' between oneself and a virtuous woman (remote enough to be perceived as a 'creature' rather than an ordinary being) is typically Gissing. As respectable women seem to be beyond his reach, so are humble women idealized by Waymark into fantasy wives completely unlike poor Nell. Ida is clean, well organized, desirous of self-improvement and of being of use to others – a literary reproach to the Carrie-Nell character of his nightmares and an excellent example of how Gissing tended to respond in fiction to real-life problems. Ida, who becomes a respectable sempstress despite a sordid past (she went to prison for theft), is the Nell of Gissing's youth transfigured by wish-fulfilment. Why didn't his wife improve herself for *him*, as Ida does for Waymark?

There is also a good deal of Nell in Harriet Casti, a vulgar, scheming, dishonest woman who traps her husband into a marriage he does not really want and in a short time makes him 'dread . . . seeing his wife's face and hearing her voice'. Her usual companions, like Nell's, are 'gross and depraved people, who constantly drag her lower and lower'; during Casti's absences from home, he complains (as Gissing himself often had cause to) that 'women have called to see her who certainly ought not to enter any decent house', eliciting objections from the landlady. Casti's account of how his wife has destroyed his peace of mind and thus his inclination to work (he is a poet) is, again, a statement of Gissing's plight. He *cannot* do anything as long as he is married to this woman, Casti says; and he adds:

My nerves are getting weaker every day; I am beginning to have fits of trembling and horrible palpitation; my dreams are hideous with vague apprehensions, only to be realised when I wake . . . my work is at an end for ever. It is all forsaking me, the delight of imagining great things, what power I had of putting my fancies into words, the music that used to go with me through the day's work . . . Quietness, peace, a calm life of thought, these things are what I *must* have; [but] . . . I find they are irretrievably lost.

It is typical of Gissing not to limit self-dramatization to a single character, but to write something of himself into several. And autobiographical themes run throughout the novel. The attack on religious asceticism (here principally in the character of Miss Bygrave, Gissing's Mrs Clennam) is one of these. Another is the preoccupation with money.

What can claim precedence, in all this world, over hard cash? It is the fruitful soil wherein is nourished the root of the tree of life; it is the vivifying principle of human activity. Upon it luxuriate art, letters, science; rob them of its sustenance, and they droop like withering leaves. Money means virtue; the lack of it is vice. The devil loves no lurking-place like an empty purse. Give me a thousand pounds to-morrow, and I become the most virtuous man in England. I satisfy all my instincts freely, openly . . . What cannot be purchased with coin of the realm?

In many ways Waymark is the archetypal Gissing protagonist: there can be no doubt at all about his real identity. In fact in 1886, when Gissing was faced with the possibly simultaneous publication of two of his novels, he suggested that *A Life's Morning* appear under the pseudonym of Osmond Waymark.

III

Although Chapman advertised *The Unclassed* prodigiously (the notice in the *Pall Mall Gazette*, of all places, mis-spelled Gissing's name) the novel received little public acknowledgement, and what it did receive was mostly unfavourable. 'Confound the prudery of the British Public and the creeping parasites of critics', Gissing exclaimed. He also had to deal with the objections of Harrison, who called Waymark's anti-Positivist philosophy 'moral dynamite'. In a letter to Harrison, Gissing said that he had always had a quarrel with society and that *The Unclassed* represented nothing new in his thought: 'ever since I can remember I have known this passionate tendency of revolt.' Harrison also guessed something of Gissing's past history from the book and apparently learned the rest of the 'guilty secret' in the course of several painful discussions with the novelist.

The *Evening News* lauded the novel's 'terrible realism' and compared Gissing favourably with the French naturalists. The *Academy* pointed to similarities between Gissing and Zola but gave

The Unclassed fainter praise. The *Graphic* called the book unpleasant; the *Athenaeum* pronounced it inept. Gissing had expected to
be condemned for writing about low life again, and especially for
giving a prostitute such a prominent place in his book; he was
surprised to find his technique (which the reviewers generally
thought heavy-handed) more roundly criticized than his subject-
matter. When, some months later, he wrote a mild letter of
remonstrance about the reviews to the *Pall Mall Gazette* – the gist
of which was that he, like Thackeray, felt debarred by public taste
from writing of things as frankly as he would have liked – he was
rewarded by an immoderate and nearly illiterate attack on his letter
(not his novel) in *Punch* – for so many years the organ of Thackeray
himself. 'I am getting used to abuse in place of criticism', the
martyred novelist wrote to his brother. The fact is that Gissing was
treated fairly by the critics as often as not and that other novelists
have had much worse critical treatment to complain of (Hardy, for
example). The literary advice Gissing gave Algernon during this
time demonstrates the impact upon him of the sort of criticism his
books had received. He advocates a cautious honesty. 'I have found
by several pieces of unpleasant experience that moral indignation is
simply not marketable.' But one cannot give up the truth for the
sake of one's readers: on the contrary, the artist should try to lead
rather than follow. 'Let novelists be true to their artistic conscience,
and the public taste will come round.'

Discouraged by reviews of *The Unclassed*, Gissing went off to
Wakefield for a short rest. Here he began to think about a new
novel which would, he said, 'depict the religious, political and
social movements now at work among the masses' – ultimately
Demos, which fortunately did not attempt quite all of this and
which in any case he did not begin to write for another year. While
in Wakefield he worked on a short story called 'Mutimer's Choice'
(published posthumously) which reflects his savage mood during
the summer of 1884 (summers, during which his wealthy friends
were out of town, always seem to have troubled him). It is an
unpleasant little tale of sexual jealousy and monomania, with such
recognizable Gissingesque elements as suicide and exogamous
marriage.

In August 1884 Gissing was invited to stay with the Harrisons at
their summer home in Bonscale, near Ullswater, in the Lake
District. The invitation was joyously accepted, and the novelist
spent a happy fortnight in the country. Letters written upon his
return to London show him resenting more than ever the noise and

dirt of city life. During the latter months of this year he continued
to revise the ill-fated 'Mrs. Grundy's Enemies' for Bentley, and
worked on a couple of stories – taking a break in September to visit
a family named Gaussen, friends of the Harrisons, in Oxfordshire.
Mrs Gaussen, an intellectual, a philanthropist, a world-traveller,
and a great beauty, captured his fancy immediately: she combined
all the qualities he most admired in women. Gissing was asked there
in order to examine the Gaussen children; ultimately he was to tutor
one of the boys. Mrs Gaussen and her fine sixteenth-century
country home would be the inspiration for the heroine and the
setting of *Isabel Clarendon*, the plan of which he began to work out
that autumn.

Gissing was invited out a good deal during 1884. The more
invitations he accepted the more he realized, as Korg has said, that
'he was at heart not a rebel at all but the most conventional of
Victorians, who loved good manners, pleasant surroundings, and
cultivated conversation.' Yet he remained uneasy among his well-
to-do friends because of the 'guilty secret' of his past and the inner
conflict his worries about class inspired. He was still too poor to
feel on equal terms with the urbane people he met in society; to
acquaintances who asked for his address he generally replied that
he had none. He saw himself still in that 'limbo external to
society'.

When he left Oxfordshire Mrs Gaussen had told Gissing that she
would call on him in town. The prospect terrified him. At heart a
snob, he could not bear to think of receiving her in shabby
lodgings. In September 1884 he moved from Milton Street to
Rutland Street, near Hampstead Road, and later in the same year to
a leased flat in Cornwall Residences near the Marylebone Road.
Here he was to live for the astoundingly long period of six years,
having escaped for the time being from hated boarding-houses. 'I
shall be free from the thralldom of landladies', he wrote exultantly
to Algernon, and he hired a woman to come in and clean for him.
He liked the upper-middle-class ambience of the neighbourhood
(he was living behind Madame Tussaud's). Roberts, however,
found the new flat 'a horrible place of extraordinary gloom' and
reports that 'its back windows overlooked the roaring steam engines
of the Metropolitan Railway.' Furthermore, he says, 'there was not
a spark or speck of colour in the place.' Gissing's own feelings
about the location tended to fluctuate according to his mood the
longer he lived there. Directly across the street from his flat was the
Marylebone workhouse – which, according to Roberts, Gissing

considered 'his only possible refuge', should he fail as a writer. He regarded it, Roberts says, 'with a proprietary eye'.

During the winter of 1884 to 1885 Gissing saw a good deal of the Gaussens, who had a house in town and supplied him with many social evenings, and worked on several projects, cutting down the number of pupils he took in order to devote more time to his writing. *Isabel Clarendon* was finished in March 1885. He submitted it to Chapman and Hall and was asked to cut it by one-third – a request with which, after some grumbling, he decided to comply. Meredith helped him once again, and the revision was completed during the summer and autumn of this year. Gissing was pleased with the final product, the revising of which had helped to alert him to some artistic problems. 'The ending is as unromantic as could be, and several threads are left to hang loose; for even so it is in real life; you cannot gather up and round off each person's story', he wrote, in his new-found Jamesian vein, to Algernon. (As a matter of fact, the *Pall Mall Gazette*'s review of *Isabel Clarendon* would compare its ending to that of a James novel.) After stating his grounds of objection to the old Victorian method of revealing everything through an omniscient narrator, Gissing went on: 'Far more artistic . . . is the . . . method of merely suggesting . . . it is better to tell a story precisely as one does in real life, hinting, surmising, telling in detail what *can* be told and no more . . . it approximates . . . the dramatic mode.' Perhaps he was taking to heart the charges of heavy-handedness levelled at *Workers in the Dawn* and *The Unclassed*; perhaps he had read carefully *The Portrait of A Lady*, which the ending of *Isabel Clarendon en l'air* and the name Gissing chose for his heroine suggest (James's novel had appeared in *Macmillan's Magazine* in 1880 to 1881).

During the autumn of 1885 Gissing completed both *Isabel Clarendon* and *A Life's Morning*, and began *Demos*. The work was done at immense personal expense, as letters he wrote to Wakefield during the year show. In June, in the midst of his revisions of *Isabel Clarendon*, he moans to Ellen: 'This kind of life is too hard. I can't endure it. I grow more and more low spirited and incapable of continued work. Suddenly in the middle of writing I am attacked by a fearful fit of melancholy and the pen drops, and I get nothing done. For hours I walk round and round the room and sicken with need of some variety in life.' During the summer, as he neared the end of his work on *Isabel Clarendon* and began to contemplate the plots of *A Life's Morning* and *Demos*, he found himself reacting savagely to trivial annoyances. 'I have to go out to buy sugar, and dread it; the grocers here object to sell sugar by itself . . . yet I cannot always order other things, and I cannot carry the sugar home myself. These little things burden my life to utter misery.' He was discovering that not having a landlady meant doing one's own shopping. He began to take long walks to escape from his flat, which no longer seemed much more comfortable than ordinary lodgings. Amidst exhortations to Ellen to continue her reading – all of Keats, he says, and *Diana of the Crossways,* just out – he told Margaret in August that it had been 'more than three weeks since I opened my lips to speak to anyone but the servant . . . I . . . live in utter solitude.' The recluse wrote to his brother about the same time that 'there was much to be said for civilization, if one is in a position to enjoy it'. Not being in that position, Gissing lived 'a very hermit's life'. The London season was over, but much as he loved the country, he could not afford to go anywhere, and he could not afford to stop writing. The alternative was the workhouse across the street.

Gissing's mood clearly betrays his professional anxiety. His work was unappreciated by the public. Though he had been writing for some years now he had never earned more than a bare subsistence; without his tutoring he would have gone under long ago. He was twenty-seven, and a failure. At times he could not write a word. Seeing 'no one and [going] nowhere', he lived in fear of drying up altogether. He did not wish to devote his life to teaching. It was at this time, in September 1885, that he uttered to Algernon the doctrine of separation and preservation I have discussed earlier: 'Keep apart, keep apart, and preserve one's soul alive – that is the teaching for the day. It is ill to have been born in these times, but one can make a world within the world.' The 'world within' was the world of fiction; despite his despair and his loneliness, Gissing continued to work, populating that inner world with the creatures and the visions of his moods. He would not give up, at least not yet. 'Surely I shall get a footing now before very long', he wrote to Algernon, in a rare burst of optimism, later that autumn. 'Confound it, I only want a couple of hundred a year. I am certain of it if I can live another two years or so; just now is the climax of the struggle, I believe. Thank goodness my powers obviously grow.' His next few books would make or break him, he told his brother. He attributed his new-found energy ('Two complete novels between June and November, not bad?') to vegetarianism, to which he had resorted once again. Just for the moment, anyway, he was buoyant.

IV

Having completed his revision of *Isabel Clarendon* in August 1885, Gissing made short visits to the Harrisons and the Gaussens before going back to work. He finished *A Life's Morning* (at first called 'Emily') in October. But already the idea for *Demos* had taken hold; and Gissing's interest in his subject was suddenly accelerated when, in September 1885, a number of prominent socialists – among them William Morris – were arrested for assaulting a policeman during a demonstration. Gissing nonchalantly remarked that Morris 'will inevitably coarsen himself in the company of ruffians', but the incident helped to stoke the fire of his imagination, and he now gave serious thought to his projected 'socialist' novel.

His approach to *Demos* was made from a perspective significantly different from that of *Workers in the Dawn* – and even that of *The Unclassed*. For Gissing was moving farther and farther to the right as the years went by; as his comment on Morris suggests, his new book about the working classes ('my special line of work', as he termed it) would be much less sympathetic than anything else he had done on the subject. 'I shall call it *Demos* and it will be rather a savage satire on working-class aims and capacities', he told Algernon. In November he was attending socialist meetings – including one at Morris's home – to gather material: he was to use Morris as his model for Westlake, and Miss Morris for Stella. The meetings he planned to depict were to be drawn directly from life.

The roots of Gissing's growing conservatism are not hard to identify. As he got older and saw more of comfortable middle-class life, he began to feel that a social code, though not always observed, did exist at least in theory for these people – while among the poor, anarchy, cruelty, and insensitivity were rife. 'He was repelled by their food, their table manners, their common eating houses, their low humour and mockery', Korg has said. 'The furnishings of their homes . . . were dreary, vulgar, and tasteless' to him. The life of the poor was organized along lines that favoured the survival of the toughest, the most violent and unscrupulous; the lives they led offered no opportunity for the experience of art or beauty. Unlike Dickens, Gissing was unable to see any connection between poverty and goodness; the good working-class person is rare in his books, though certainly there are many who aspire to better things. But he was always ready to see common people as base, sordid, mean, and vulgar; like Dickens, he had an instinctive fear of the mob, a tendency to regard mass phenomena of any sort with loathing. No doubt these feelings were due in part to that fear of his I have mentioned of sliding backward and being re-absorbed by his origins. He demonstrated, as Tindall says, a 'squeamish dislike of working-class coarseness and [a] general tendency to become intolerant . . . of *any* alien mode of life'. If you are worried about your own orthodoxy of course one way to prop it up is to attack the unorthodoxy of others. Gissing's diffidence led him to avoid the company of those he did not know well, in particular those of inferior station or education. Most of the friends he made after his return to England from America were comfortably off. While he sympathized with the plight of the poor he saw the social fabric as something permanent; institutionalized charity was to him merely a half-witted disruption of the inevitable status quo. 'I believe in the distinction of classes', his character Denzil Quarrier says. 'So long as nature doles out the gift of brains in different proportions, there must exist social subordination.' *The Private Papers of Henry Ryecroft* argues similarly. On this question the novelist never changed his mind. He regarded all lower-class movements as 'threatening culture in its best sense', Roberts says of his friend. 'The very word "progress" had no meaning for him – but disturbance.' No wonder the *Spectator*'s review of *Demos* called it 'the book of a pessimist with no belief in the power of . . . progressive ideas'. Nor was Gissing's conservative élitism unconnected with his theories of education, or his lifelong passion for the classics. Samuel Vogt Gapp many years ago perceived the relationship between Gissing's characteristic turn of mind and his love of Greek and Roman literature. His conservatism, Gapp said, was in part a result of his classical training.

It is a familiar fact that the classic literature was an aristocratic one. It took little account of slaves, of poor artisans, of the hordes of freedmen who filled the Circus Maximus . . . It was a literature written by men who reclined at ease in their villas. It was often . . . the product of an imperial court . . . Proletarian literature was simply inconceivable in ancient times. In the education of modern times the classic literatures have found a similar . . . destiny. They are not taught to artisans; a classic education is synonymous with a professional training; it is the privilege of the professional classes, of lawyers, doctors, divines, of the wealthy classes, or of statesmen.

Methodical study of the classics, Gapp concludes, often produces a conservative attitude of mind. Gissing, he says, 'shared to the full [classical] ideals and never . . . deserted them'.

Of course familiarity with the classics is itself a mark of caste. 'Few indeed there are who know the classics so well as he did, who read them for ever with so much delight', says Roberts. To be uneducated, in Gissing's eyes, was not to know Greek. No wonder the novelist ferociously kept up his studies. No wonder he wrote about socialism and the working classes 'from a very conservative point of view'. Paul Elmer More rightly says that Gissing's distrust of science and of the masses grew out of his love of the classics, from which 'came his notion of the one only salvation through the aristocratic idea, the essential idea of Greek literature'. Nor can we ignore the role played by the novelist's hatred of the contemporary, or his chronic pessimism. 'As some sort of disappointment always awaited him in the present', Coustillas remarks, 'he perpetually sought a refuge in the past.' 'To Gissing', Korg explains, 'the most striking defect of modern industrial civilization was its inability to share the heritage of antiquity. His social criticism is unintelligible when it is divorced from his love of classical culture.' Ultimately, after all, Gissing was in spirit and impulse – if not always in income – a member of the conservative middle class. In 1905, reviewing *Will Warburton*, Edward Garnett declared that the novelist 'was marvellously representative of the English middle-class with all its thin-blooded idealism, its nervous susceptibility to class distinctions, its self-consciousness, reserve, [and] conscientiousness of purpose'.

In November 1885 Chapman finally accepted *Isabel Clarendon* (though the contract was not signed for several months), offering terms of an equal share of profits after deducting production and advertising costs plus ten per cent; in all likelihood he paid Gissing no advance at all. It was at this point that Gissing, determined not to bring out simultaneously two novels under his own name (for he thought that *Isabel Clarendon* and *A Life's Morning* would be published at about the same time; in fact *A Life's Morning* did not come out until 1888), submitted 'Emily' (*A Life's Morning*) to Smith, Elder under the pseudonym of Osmond Waymark (the author's identity was of course known to the publisher). It was accepted almost immediately. With a sigh of relief Gissing turned to his story of socialism, which current events were destined to make immediately interesting to the reading public. Socialist agitation in 1885 – the year of the founding of the Fabian Society, and the year after the founding of Morris's Socialist League – arose primarily out of unemployment problems resulting from the end of agricultural prosperity and the attendant economic recession. The government was blamed, and demonstrations went on throughout the year, climaxed by the scuffle between the police and the socialist sympathizers and the arrest of Morris in September. Gissing saw this as an opportunity to write something of popular interest, and for the next few months he worked on *Demos* with single-minded intensity.

v

Neither *Isabel Clarendon* nor *A Life's Morning* is among Gissing's better achievements, though both are of interest for the light they shed on the manifold connections between his life and his work.

Gissing's extreme moodiness during 1884, when he was writing *Isabel Clarendon,* and again during the summer of 1885 when he was revising it, is reflected in the character of his protagonist, Bernard Kingcote. Kingcote is subject to what Gissing calls 'an illness of nerves' to a greater degree than any other Gissing hero. It was his destiny to suffer and he was 'born with the nerves of suffering developed as they are in few men'. Kingcote says: 'I do not know what it is to have the same mind for two days together . . . My moods are tyrannous; my moods make my whole life. Others have intellect; I have only temperament.' For Kingcote, Gissing tells us, things 'which most men accept as the everyday rubs of the world were . . . among the worst evils of existence' (such as shopping for sugar?). 'Few men surpassed Bernard Kingcote in ingenious refinement of self-torture.'

Kingcote's personality represents Gissing's as perceived by himself. In *Isabel Clarendon* he follows the prescription for the artist laid down by Waymark in *The Unclassed* and observes his own misery objectively in the cause of art. There can be no doubt of this. Kingcote's 'fits of depression, his pacing to and fro for hours in misery, his impracticality, his sudden decisions followed by regrets, his frequent mournfulness in the company of "polite triflers" in drawing-rooms, are part of the author's recorded experiences', as Coustillas points out. Kingcote's 'nerves' are Gissing's. Both live on a small income, are poor but highly educated, and see themselves as members of a class with 'no social standing'; Kingcote is another of the novelist's social 'exiles'. Gissing's description of Kingcote's feelings about his anomalous position is pure autobiography: 'Aristocracy of race cannot compare in . . . intensity with aristocracy which comes only of the influence of the intellect and temperament. Kingcote would have chosen death rather than an existence elbow to elbow with [lower-class] people.' The novelist thought of himself as the kind of 'aristocrat' he describes here – an aristocrat of 'the intellect and temperament' living amidst cultural peasants. This is his 'exile'. By the end of the novel he has become (like Will Warburton in Gissing's last novel) totally *déclassé*: 'He began with thoughts of glory; he would finish his career as a shopkeeper . . . it would cost him a twinge . . . to put up his name over the shop, and invite the attention of all who remembered it.' This is the same fate that befalls Warburton, and obviously such a consummation haunted Gissing for years.

Kingcote too has a 'guilty secret' of sorts: his humble origins and the dependence upon him of his unrefined sister and her children. Such connections would obviously be a disadvantage if known among the upper-middle-class set upon whose fringes he is able to live during the first half of the novel. His unwanted relations symbolize for Kingcote his past life of suffering. This past, and various youthful excesses he now regrets, are evoked by Kingcote in terms which must remind us of Gissing himself. 'There is nothing I hold more in horror than the ghost of my former self', Kingcote tells Isabel. 'How can one be responsible for the thoughts and acts of the being who bore his name years ago? The past is no part of our existing self; we are free of it, it is buried.' If only it were so! 'I am no common thief, a person who steals from his friends and goes to prison for it', Gissing is saying here. 'I am more than the husband of an alcoholic prostitute who once infected me with a venereal disease. I am not the same person who made those awful blunders.'

Kingcote's black cynicism is an accurate picture of Gissing's mood during 1884 to 1885. Glimpses of the 'perfect content' and 'ideal domesticity' of other people stir Kingcote to 'bitterness' and 'misery'; he senses he will never have such happiness. He sees himself as a man who, at twenty-nine, has 'wasted my time, lost my best years'. One of the chief causes of Kingcote's pessimism is the inability 'to win a woman's love. To me that has always been the one, the only thing in the end worth living for.'

Kingcote's pessimism makes him almost inert. His passivity, while a fascinating example of the pathology of authorship, ruins *Isabel Clarendon*: for who, besides a biographer, a critic, or a psychoanalyst, can be interested in a neurasthenic hero who throws up his hands and sinks into a chair at the slightest annoyance? Roberts says that 'there is no more intensely depressing book in the entire English language': he was not the only one to think so. Still, for the critic and biographer *Isabel Clarendon* is of great autobiographical interest from the very first page. Introducing Kingcote, Gissing wrote that 'he had not the face of a man at ease with his own heart, or with the circumstances amid which his life had fallen. A glance of pleasure . . . was often succeeded by the shadow of brooding, and this by a gleam of passion, brief but significant.' The novel begins with this portrait of an extraordinary man condemned to live in ordinary surroundings, and tells the story of how he escapes them – only to return to them in the end, a victim of the circumstances of his birth, and of his past.

Isabel Clarendon reflects Gissing's fear that one day, after their mother died, he might have to live with his sisters and support them. The lack of intimacy between Kingcote and his sister reflects the difficulties Gissing always felt in intercourse with his female relatives. Indeed, the description of Kingcote's mother explicitly suggests Mrs Gissing: 'Mrs. Kingcote, though behaving to [him] with all motherly care, did not win [his] love, neither appeared to miss it. She was a woman to whom the external facts of life sufficed; details of housekeeping occupied her all but exclusively.' Isabel Clarendon is an idealized version of Mrs Gaussen, fitted out with all the usual paraphernalia of Gissingesque wish-fulfilment applied to sexually unattainable women. The novelist was fond of tormenting himself with the proximity of superior women beyond his sexual reach, and for several years in the mid-eighties Mrs Gaussen was the chief of these. Debarred by his poverty, his family commitments, and his sense of social inferiority from marrying Isabel, Kingcote makes himself miserable over her instead.

In *Isabel Clarendon* the typical wife is pictured as greeting her husband when he comes home at the end of the day 'with questions, with complaints, with frettings'. The novel's most quoted passage refers explicitly to the difficulty the unusual man has in finding a suitable wife: 'The woman who may with safety be taken in marriage by a poor man given to intellectual pursuits', says the narrator of *Isabel Clarendon*, 'is . . . extremely difficult of discovery.' Gissing was writing from the heart. Did he speak of Nell to Mrs Gaussen? Or did he, like Kingcote with Isabel, conceal his guilty secrets?

Kingcote's feelings about money are those of his creator. Having lost his wallet during a country ramble, Kingcote in the opening chapter refuses to throw himself on the mercy of an innkeeper for a meal and a bed because 'he was too proud to subject himself to possible suspicion, especially that of his social inferiors.' There are both class snobbery here and the paranoia of a man who fears that others may not think him honest. Another passage in the novel expresses the same point of view we encountered in *The Unclassed* about the ease with which one may be happy and good when there is enough money around: 'Could not I . . . be gently gracious to all . . . if I had wherewith to keep my soul from the bitterness of hunger?' Kingcote muses. 'How easy to cultivate a charm of manner when every need is so waited upon with fruition!'

Gissing's exemplar in this novel of how *not* to educate women is Rhoda Meres, who 'could render . . . an ode of Horace, could solve a quadratic equation, could explain to you the air-pump and the laws of chemical combination, could read a page of Ælfric's "Homilies" as if it were modern English. And all the while . . . she knew nothing at all.' This sort of educational 'progress' does not allow either the intelligence or the spirit to develop: it touches the mechanical springs of learning only. 'Let the mind take care of itself', Kingcote says. A girl or boy who has a bent for knowledge will manage to acquire it without force-feeding. 'Make him a sound creature, that's the first thing. Occupy him with vigorous bodily pursuits; keep his mind from turning inwards; save him from reflection. If every boy in England could be so brought up, they would be a blissful generation.' Thus speaks the novelist who, as a boy, hated games and was perhaps more ravenous for learning than any of his contemporaries. What had changed? 'Knowledge of the world' had intervened.

Some people are better off without an education. For the sensitive lower-class person who has no chance of escaping his milieu, for example, education will only create dissatisfaction where before there was acceptance – or blissful ignorance. What is the point of giving people glimpses of an existence that can never be attained?

If only the schoolmaster could be kept away; if only progress would . . . leave these worthy clodhoppers in . . . peace! They are happy; they look neither before nor after, for them the world has no history, the morrow no futile aspirations . . . Oh, leave them alone, leave them alone! . . . Do not heed the folly of those who say that culture is always a blessing; the truth is that, save under circumstances favourable to its enjoyment and extension, it is an unmitigated curse . . .

Thus Kingcote to his sister on the education of her children.

We may be surprised to find Gissing arguing here that 'culture' can be 'an unmitigated curse' and vocational training all that is necessary for some. In fact these sentiments reflect a characteristic aspect of his thinking. What is good for him and sets him apart may only do harm to those without his gifts. He values his own education, but he also sees how it can render a person unfit to live in the social and financial circumstances in which he finds himself. Might not one be happier as a lotus-eater, unconscious of how the other half lives?

Kingcote's inability to 'be affectionate with children' is something we will see more of in later Gissing characters. Also typical is his need, despite his reserve, to 'find a confidant, and pour forth in sympathetic ears the stream of his miseries'. Gissing was constantly doing this with Bertz, with Roberts, with Algernon, with almost anyone who would listen. As Asquith says in *Isabel Clarendon*, 'The great preservative of sanity is free intercourse with one's fellow men – to see the world from all points, and to refrain from final conclusions.' The last phrase also reflects the novelist's opinion that speculative philosophy is useless time-wasting; 'reflection' leads nowhere.

Kingcote's interlude in an isolated country cabin represents a long-standing fantasy of Gissing's, one that he was to indulge at some length in *The Ryecroft Papers*. Gissing loved the country, hated London's clamour, but was unable to be happy in any one place for long. His neurasthenia plainly inspired the description of Kingcote's arrival in the city after an absence of many months: the 'roaring crowd' makes him 'wish for deafness . . . Every sensitive chord of his frame was smitten into agony . . . [and] stirred him to a passion of loathing. His very senses rebelled; he felt sick, faint.' Gissing's aversion to dishonest landladies and irresponsible lodging-house servants is personified here in the portrait of Mrs Bolt and her establishment, upon which Gissing vents the frustrations of his early lodging-house years.

Also significant is the advice Thomas Meres gives Ada Warren on the writing of fiction. Ada's stories, Meres tells her, show a great deal of promise; their fault is excessive subjectivity – they are too obviously derived from 'personal experience, which the writer is not far enough away from to describe with regard to artistic proportion'. Such criticism was sometimes levelled at Gissing's early books by publishers' readers and critics; and Meredith must have said something like this during their discussions of *The Unclassed* and *Isabel Clarendon*. The frequently epigrammatic style of the latter novel may be in homage to Meredith; such an exclamation as 'How the imps of the air exploded as soon as he was gone!' has a Meredithian ring.

In *A Life's Morning*, the other novel written in 1885, the Gissing *persona* is split. The hero, Wilfrid Athel, shares with his creator a passion for Greek literature, Boswell, self-cultivation, hard work, vegetarianism, and intellectual women; he also suffers from insomnia and loathes the masses. Another man faced with a choice between an intelligent upper-middle-class woman for whom he has great respect (Beatrice Redwing) and a lower-class girl (Emily Hood) whom he wishes to sleep with, Athel's selection of the latter is not, for once, a source of tragedy; for Emily, a governess, is highly educated and will make him a satisfactory wife despite the exogamous relationship.

There is a temperamental affinity between Gissing and his hero, who early in the novel declares himself to be 'distracted by the numberless desires that seize upon me, depressed by the hopelessness of satisfying them. I cannot even enjoy music from the mere feeling that I do not enjoy it enough . . .'. Here is a touch of moodiness worthy of Kingcote. And for the first time in his fiction Gissing also puts a good deal of himself into a heroine. Emily is refined but poor, respectable yet shy of 'society', educated enough to be dissatisfied with her working-class background and associates. 'Circumstances willed that she should suffer by the nobleness of her instincts.' Again we have a character whose refined temperament clashes with a sordid milieu, and the suggestion that those with finely honed sensibilities suffer more than others. Emily's neurasthenia, like Gissing's, is the result of the over-exposure of a sensitive nature to undistinguished surroundings and of a passion for peace and quiet. 'Emily loved silence, the nurse of the soul', Gissing declares. She shrinks from the London streets, preferring the quiet of the country. 'Others might find their strength in human fellowship; she would fain live apart.'

Throughout much of the novel Emily is also the keeper of a guilty secret of the first order (she cannot tell Wilfrid that her refusal to marry him stems from her father's theft of some money and his employer's threat to expose him unless she herself consents to be the employer's wife). Emily comes from a town ('Dunfield') very much like Wakefield; and 'The Shadow of Home' (a chapter-title) hangs over her throughout the book. The house she grows up in is drawn from the Wakefield house – the likeness 'is accurate in detail', according to Hick. 'The misery of her parents' home haunted her, and by no effort could she expel the superstition that she had only escaped from that for a time, that its claws would surely overtake her and fix themselves again in her flesh.' Emily sees her family as capable of making, some time in the future, precisely those demands upon her which Gissing and Kingcote feared. 'Not only is it your right but your very duty, to spare every penny you can', Emily imagines her parents saying to her. 'If anything happened to prevent your earning money, you would become a burden upon us.' Emily is constantly aware of the tenuousness of her independence from 'home' and of how quickly, should she ever be unable to work for any length of time, her independence would evaporate – 'only too well aware of the fate which might come upon her in consequence of the most trifling mishap'. This was a source of anxiety to Gissing throughout his career; indeed, at the end of his life his anxieties were the same. He never had any margin for relaxation. The agnostic Emily is closer to her father than to her religious, house-bound mother, with whom her relations are cool (Mrs Hood is certainly drawn from Mrs Gissing). She is also subject to fits of melancholia and fatalism. Ultimately, like many another Gissing heroine, she rejects the moral temptations of asceticism. Hers is unique among the marriages in the early novels in having the blessing of the novelist. Exogamous marriage *can* work, apparently – when the partner from the lower sphere is willing to devote herself equally to cultural self-improvement and household management.

Still, as the astute Mrs Rossal remarks, marriages of socially unequal partners 'very seldom prove anything but miserable, and *always* bring a great many troubles'. The exogamy theme, resolved happily in the story of Wilfrid, remains an issue in that part of the novel concerning Richard Dagworthy, a self-made industrialist, wealthy but unrefined, whose great ambition in life is to become socially respectable. How should he use his wealth to become cultured? His answer: by marrying above himself and letting his wife instruct him in the ways of society. He marries an upper-middle-class woman between whom and himself there can be no real sympathy; she dies young. Doomed by his origins to fail at his pet project of self-improvement, Dagworthy ultimately becomes little more than an appetite personified. Clearly he is a forerunner of Mutimer in *Demos*, written just after *A Life's Morning*. Indeed, some of the passages describing Dagworthy's disastrous marriage could as easily describe Mutimer's marriage to Adela:

After the first few months of their marriage, the two lived, as far as possible, separate lives; Mrs. Dagworthy spent the days with her mother and sister, Richard at the mill, and the evenings were got through with as little friction as might be between two people neither of whom could speak half a dozen words without irritating or disgusting the other . . . Gradually he came to understand that he had been deceived by artificialities which mocked the image of something for which he really longed, and that something was refinement, within and without, a life directed by other motives and desires than those he had known, a spirit aiming at things he did not understand.

Mutimer's longings – and the results of them – are almost exactly the same.

The encroachment of Dagworthy's factory upon the surrounding countryside also anticipates an important theme of *Demos* and one that Gissing was to come back to in several later novels. He hated industry's rape of the land, having seen a good deal of it in Yorkshire. In his environmentalism he is peculiarly modern, and unique among the Victorian novelists. We get a first taste of it here in *A Life's Morning*. The country around Dunfield 'was blighted by the curse of . . . industrialism.' The grass has 'absorbed too much mill-smoke to exhibit wholesome verdure'; 'Take in your fingers a spray from one of the trees . . . and its touch left a soil'; the river is 'foul . . . with the refuse of manufactures'. Smoke from the local coal-pits has a habit of blowing in the open windows of train-carriages, 'giving a special flavour to . . . bread and meat', making sandwiches 'smoky'. A local colliery town is described as 'vomiting blackness . . . a region of blight and squalor . . . [and] smoke-fouled streets'. The theme combines Gissing's love of the country with his hatred of 'progress', notes sounded even more loudly in *Demos*.

Emily, herself the product of a loveless match, arrives at a point of view typically Gissingesque long before Hardy made it famous in *Jude the Obscure*: 'the public ceremony of marriage . . . she deemed a barbarism. As a sacrament, the holiest of all, its celebration should, she felt, be in the strictest privacy; as for its aspect of a legal contract, let that concession to human misery be made with the smallest, not the greatest, violation of religious feeling.' Failed marriages, says Mrs Rossall – sounding a good deal like the rueful husband of Helen Harrison – are usually the result of hastily taken decisions; and she adds, 'I often think a man's majority ought to come ten years later than it does. Most of you are mere boys till thirty at least, and you go and do things that you repent all the rest of your lives.'

Again bad housekeeping comes in for its share of blame for failed marriages. Mrs Baxendale tells the story of a husband so maddened 'by his wife's perpetual absence from home . . . that he at length fairly turned the key on her in her bedroom, and through the keyhole bade her stay there till she had remembered her domestic duties' (a similar story about a racalcitrant wife is told in *Denzil Quarrier* with the same lip-smacking approval).

'After Emily, two children were successively born; Fate was kind to them and neither survived infancy.' This sort of pronouncement appears frequently in some later novels (especially *The Nether World*) in connection with the struggles of the impecunious. Mrs Baxendale, an apostle of charity, sounds a note also to be heard with more insistence in the later novels (e.g. *New Grub Street*) – help for the poor, when it comes at all, almost always arrives too late to be of use: 'only let your misery drive you out of the world, and people will find out all at once how very easily they might have saved you.' Sometimes as little as one pound a week (Gissing's allowance to Nell) may be the source of such salvation; 'I have vast faith in the extra pound a week', says Mrs Baxendale.

Though in general less fatalistic than some of Gissing's other novels, *A Life's Morning* refers again and again to 'the farce of life' and the 'inevitable gloom' arising from *circumstances* – a synonym for Fate in its most immutable, inscrutable, Schopenhauerian guise. 'Possibilities rendered futile by circumstances', 'the power of circumstances' – such phrases are invoked to 'explain' why things happen, and also to justify what Mrs Baxendale calls the 'heathen doubt' of many intelligent people. One of the novel's chief weaknesses lies in Gissing's tendency to soliloquize unsubtly on these and other causes of human misery; when doing so his prose becomes nearly impenetrable. 'It is the miserable contradiction in our lot that the efficiency of the instincts of beauty-worship waits upon a force of individuality attainable only by the sacrifice of sensibility', Gissing could write. Or: 'Frustration of desire joined with irritated instincts of ascendancy to agitate him almost beyond endurance.' Can anyone wonder why his early novels were not best-sellers? In *Isabel Clarendon* Gissing was particularly sensitive to the advantages of the 'dramatic' method and the protracted revisions of that novel undoubtedly were a factor in this. *A Life's Morning*, scribbled furiously in less than three months, is one of his most carelessly written novels and remains, with justice, one of the least known to modern readers.

Several other items will complete the catalogue of standard Gissing themes. Again the amount of money a man has is seen as the single most important determining factor of the quality of his life. The novel insists upon the utterly different worlds inhabited by rich and poor – two nations governed by a different set of laws, as *Sybil* puts it. Gissing refers to 'the inestimable advantage of those born

into the material refinement . . . wealth can command', which
enables a man to keep his mind 'disengaged from anxiety' about
seemingly trivial concerns – as, say, the soiling of his clothes (for a
poor man a cleaning bill may mean going without a meal). Such
anxiety can easily make a mockery of all other interests and
aspirations, not least of all a desire for learning. Adversity can
undermine self-respect – what the novelist calls 'the conscious
dignity of manhood'. Hood, for example, having been subject to
this kind of anxiety all his life, knows 'that poverty is the mother of
degradation'; he feels like a criminal long before he does anything
wrong, realizing as he does how low his resistance would be to
'some luckless chance' that could tempt him, with the lure of
money, into crime. Such proves to be the case; and in this way we
are shown, some years before *New Grub Street,* how inevitably
'poverty degrades'. 'It is the deepest curse of such a life as his',
Gissing says of Hood, 'that it directs the imagination in channels of
meanness, and preoccupies the thought with sordid fears.' 'A mere
struggle to support existence' leaves no time for anything else: it
even chokes off 'the impulses of affection'. As so often, on this
subject Gissing is especially eloquent:

that love and joy, the delights of eager sense and of hallowed aspiration,
should be smothered in the foul dust of a brute combat for bread, that the
stinted energies of early years should change themselves to the blasted
hopes of failing manhood in a world made ill by human perverseness, this is
not easily . . . borne with patience. Put money in thy purse; and again, put
money in thy purse; for, as the world is ordered, to lack current coin is to
lack the privileges of humanity, and indigence is the death of the soul.

Despite these horrors, Gissing has not changed his mind about
the brainlessness of attempts from above to improve the lot of the
poor. Again indiscriminate education is rejected as a panacea.
Wilfrid declares that 'an appetite for knowledge' is 'the unhappiest
gift a man can be endowed with; it leads to nothing but frustration.'
Ignorance can be bliss. Colliers must be 'really happy', Emily
muses, 'for they know nothing of their own degradation'. Wilfrid
sees Beatrice's plan to stage concerts in the poor districts of London
as doomed from the start: to attempt to 'humanise ruffians' by
placing before them 'an artistic ideal' is 'paltry, imbecile, charlatan'.
Wilfrid, who had thought of a political career as a means to help the
disadvantaged, ultimately takes up politics in a wholly different
mood: 'Respect for the masses he had none; interest in their affairs
he had none.' In the end politics lures him only because it is 'a

recognized profession for gentlemen, and offered brilliant prizes'. Later novels go more deeply into the nature of political charlatanism, reminding us again and again that politicians, no matter what they say, can do nothing about the way the world is ordered – about 'circumstances'.

A Life's Morning evokes for us once more the 'vulgarity' of lodging-houses; the novelist's pathological fear of having to do menial work; and the precarious existence of the scrupulous artist. 'Art, you know, is only contemptible when it supports the artist', Wilfrid snarls at his father.

VI

Though he didn't know it yet, Gissing's darkest years of struggle and penury – 'the awful decade' (1876 to 1885), as he was to call it – were over. Still, these early years continued to give a colouring to everything he wrote, long after his first attempt at a pot-boiler, *Demos*, had rescued him from obscurity.

CHAPTER 5

৵

THE PASTURES OF POVERTY, 1886–1888

As covetousness is the root of all evil, so poverty is the worst of all snares. *Moll Flanders* (1722)

'I believe people make a great deal of money out of novels, don't they, Mrs. Ormonde?'
'I have heard of one or two who tried to, but didn't.'
Thyrza

People say that suffering ennobles one; it's a lie, it only makes one brutal. Maugham, *Mrs. Craddock*

I

As socialist agitation continued through the early weeks of the new year (1886), Gissing worked away on the novel he had begun the previous autumn. The first two volumes of *Demos* had been completed when contemporary events conspired to make his subject even more relevant. On 8 February a group of Free Traders, socialists, and radicals of various shades held a huge rally in Trafalgar Square to protest against the effects of the economic depression and demand action on behalf of unemployed workers. On their way to Hyde Park, the demonstrators vented their dissatisfaction upon some of the Pall Mall clubs; the window-smashing so beloved of London mobs went on for hours. The Trafalgar Square riots, as they came to be called, were widely reported. The day after the riots Gissing rushed to the offices of Smith, Elder, and told them about his novel, leaving with them the two volumes he had completed. Pronouncing the writing superior to anything of George Eliot's, Smith, Elder quickly reported to Gissing the decision to publish – if the last volume could be written at once. Working furiously, Gissing found himself reading proofs of the first volume as he was working on the third. Though he was sceptical about the comparison with George Eliot, he did feel the book might be superior in its genre to anything written since her heyday; and in an unusual burst of optimism he predicted for *Demos* 'a great success'. Rashly he accepted terms of £100 outright for the novel; the success he was so sure of would have made a royalty arrangement more profitable, but he was unable to refuse ready cash, especially an amount so significantly larger than any he had received before. And the publishers knew their man. Anonymous publication was decided on – both to attract the curiosity of potential readers (most of whom would not have heard of Gissing) and to emphasize the novel's controversiality. Smith, Elder meant to suggest, of course, that the author was a personage of some importance who was reticent about putting his name to so topical a book. Large advertisements of the book began to appear almost immediately, and *Demos: A Story of English Socialism* (a timely subtitle) was published in March 1886 – three months ahead of *Isabel Clarendon* and, as it turned out, two years before *A Life's Morning*. It thus became the third of Gissing's novels to be published though in fact it was the seventh written (after the unnamed first novel, *Workers in the Dawn*, 'Mrs. Grundy's Enemies', *The Unclassed*, *Isabel Clarendon*, and *A Life's Morning*).

The book's topicality induced Smith, Elder to send out an unusually large number of review copies and much attention was paid to it in the press. Reactions varied, sometimes determined by the political persuasion of the journal or the reviewer: generally the Liberal press was hostile, the Conservative press friendly. As it turned out, *Demos* received a good deal of additional publicity because of the passions it aroused. For the most part it was treated with respect, even by unfriendly reviewers; the notices were more often good than bad. *The Times*, calling the book 'remarkable', compared it favourably with *Alton Locke*. The *Athenaeum* also compared the author of *Demos* with Kingsley – and Mrs Gaskell and Charlotte Brontë as well – but discovered less to like in the book than *The Times*, complaining that the socialists were drawn unsympathetically. The *Spectator* shrewdly noted the 'aristocratic' bias of the author but suggested that he knew less about middle-class life than about working-class life. Mutimer was praised as 'a real and living figure'. '*Demos* is the book of a pessimist with no belief in the power of what are called progressive ideas', the *Spectator* announced (Gissing especially liked this review). 'He is certainly not a socialist, nor even an ardent democrat', remarked the *Westminster Review*. The *Guardian* joined the chorus of praise for Mutimer. The conservative *Scottish Review* called *Demos* 'one of the most valuable publications we have seen for a long time'. Harrison liked the book, though he complained once again of Gissing's 'aristocratic temperament'. Morley Roberts, who read it in America and immediately guessed the secret of its authorship, called it 'masterly' and a work of genius. Almost all of the book's contemporary readers were struck by the powerful description of the East End graveyard.

Overall the impression the novel made was indelible; and after the identity of the author was revealed, Gissing's name was often associated with hostility to the working classes and anti-democratic sentiments. Certainly it marks a further turn to the right for Gissing. The book has always been unpopular in Russia and in Marxist circles generally (the representatives of Marxism in *Demos* are the villainous Keene and the opportunist Roodhouse). Modern criticism has often attempted – perversely, I think – to assess the accuracy of its account of English socialism in the eighties instead of dealing with it as fiction. *Demos* is not a historical novel; it is a discussion of social behaviour and class. Gissing made no real attempt to write contemporary history, though certainly he wanted to cash in on current social and political unease. As always, his object was to create a work of art. And in this he succeeded, for *Demos* is his first great novel. Contemporary critics for the most part treated it as a novel and not as a tract, realizing that the author was making a personal statement; in this they were more incisive than some of their recent descendants.

II

There are some methods of expression, even in printed words, which seem to carry with them the very accents of the writer. It is then we read and almost forget that we read because we seem to hear the spoken word. It is possible for the student of Gissing to learn those peculiarities of his thought and diction which made him original and . . . remarkable . . . He has, with other greater and lesser masters of the English tongue, this power of subjectively audible speech.

Roberts, not always so perceptive a student of Gissing, hits upon an aspect of *Demos* which is very much to the point – the quality of 'subjectively audible speech' that makes it immediately identifiable as a Gissing novel. Though there are fewer direct autobiographical connections than in the earlier books, the ideas and themes that run through it faithfully reflect the author's true convictions.

Demos is a novel about class, and together with *Born in Exile* and *Will Warburton* it is one of Gissing's most comprehensive treatments of the subject. It is virulently anti-working-class and the novel even condemns the ordinary charitable instincts of humanity when the beneficiaries are the disadvantaged. A product of Gissing's horrible struggles of the early eighties, it is one of the most reactionary novels he ever wrote, and one of the most powerful.

The focus is upon the disastrous marriage of Richard Mutimer, a working-class man enriched by the accident of a rich cousin's demise intestate, and Adela Waltham, a poor but refined middle-class lady. To marry Adela, Mutimer gives up a working-class girl (Emma Vine) who would have suited him perfectly. For Mutimer the marriage to Adela 'would represent the union of classes – of the wage-earning with the *bourgeois*'. Again the working-class man chooses between a sexual partner of his own class and a social superior; the exogamous choice, as always, is fatal. Adela, who succumbs to the Mutimer marriage at the insistence of her impecunious family, quickly learns that 'the monstrous gulf between men of that kind and cultured human beings', the 'gulf which lies between the educated and the uneducated', may not be bridged. When, late in the novel, the discovery of a lost will deprives Mutimer, now a socialist leader, of his legacy, he becomes a working man once again – much more easily than he had become a capitalist (one is reminded of the quick change of both uniform and class performed by Ralph Rackstraw and Captain Corcoran at the end of *H.M.S. Pinafore* which had its *première* eight years before *Demos*).

These peregrinations through the class structure give Gissing the opportunity to articulate some of his favourite ideas. The novel's most quoted passage treats specifically of class differences. During a train-journey Adela looks upon the face of her dozing husband and muses.

It was the face of a man by birth and breeding altogether beneath her. Never had she understood that as now; never had she conceived so forcibly the reason which made him and her husband and wife only in name. Suppose that . . . sleep of his to be the sleep of death; he would pass from her consciousness like a shadow from the field, leaving no trace behind. Their life of union was a mockery; their married intimacy was an unnatural horror. He was not of her class, not of her world; only by violent wrenching of the laws of nature had they come together. She had . . . [tried] to convince herself that there were no such distinctions, that only an unworthy prejudice parted class from class. One moment of true insight was worth more than all her theorising on abstract principles. To be her equal this man must be born again, of other parents, in other conditions of life.

Besides commenting directly on Gissing's own marriage, passages such as this are of course violently anti-working-class.

Mutimer, the socialist leader, is the embodiment of *demos* – in Greek, 'the mob'. He is a common working man who has tried to step beyond the bounds fixed by fate for a man of his class and he affords Gissing an opportunity to attack the pretensions of the class as a whole. Here is one of his most unadorned comments: 'The fatal defect in working people is absence of imagination . . . Half the brutal cruelties perpetrated by uneducated men and women are directly traceable to lack of the imaginative spirit, which comes to mean lack of kindly sympathy.'

Demos goes on taking aim at the working classes. 'Probably no costume devisable could surpass in ignoble ugliness the attire of an English working-class widow when she appears in the street.' In the presence of 'those fellows', says Eldon of working men, 'I feel that I am facing enemies . . . I have nothing in common with them but the animal functions . . . They are . . . the enemies of every man who speaks the pure English tongue and does not earn a living with his hands.' Elocution was always of great importance to Gissing. Poor Mutimer assumes the Carrie Mitchell role in this novel – that is to say, the burden of Nell: 'Aspirates troubled him . . . and the syntax of his periods was often anacoluthic.' Mutimer is always ill at ease among the cultured and refined. Indeed, his veneer of respectability is paper-thin; haranguing a crowd, 'his accent deteriorated as he flung out his . . . words; he spoke like any London mechanic, with defect and excess of aspirates, with neglect of g's at the end of words, and so on.' There is more than a touch of monomania here. Surely this reflects Gissing's own insecurities – his dread of being taken for a common working man, his worries about sartorial adequacy, about his address, about the presentability of his wife, and so on.

The attack on the working classes in this novel is inseparable from the political theme which so interested Gissing's contemporaries: the condemnation of socialism and all its professed values. The average socialist working man, *Demos* declares, neither speaks nor thinks of 'the social question' between meetings, which he attends for the sake of diversion, like a prizefight, and for company afterwards in the local pub – a nasty charge, given nineteenth-century English socialism's support of the temperance movement. The novelist's description of the socialist crowd at one of these gatherings reveals his class snobbery: 'One moment their eyes would be fixed upon [the speaker], filmy, unintelligent, then they would look at one another with a leer of cunning . . . Socialism, forsooth! They were as ready for translation to supernal spheres.'

Gissing's prime example of the dilettante socialist working man is Daniel Dabbs, a publican characterized as follows:

he had got into the habit of listening to inflammatory discourses every Sunday night, and on the whole found it a pleasant way of passing the evening . . . it affected him with an agreeable sensation, much like that which follows upon a good meal, to hear himself pitied as a hard-working, ill-used fellow, and the frequent allusion to his noble qualities sweetly flattered him. When he went home to the public-house after a lively debate, and described the proceedings . . . he always ended by declaring that it was 'as good as a play' . . . The expositions of doctrine he passed over; anything in the nature of reasoning muddled him . . . Had he been called upon to suffer in any way for the 'cause of the people,' it would speedily have been demonstrated of what metal his enthusiasm was made.

The novelist's account of a socialist mob on the rampage betrays both personal fear and political hostility: 'Demos was roused, was tired of listening to mere articulate speech; it was time for a good wild-beast roar, for a taste of bloodshed. Scarcely a face in all the mob but distorted itself to express as much savagery as can be got out of the human countenance . . . Demos was having his way; civilisation was blotted out, and club law proclaimed.' The blood shed is Mutimer's, assassinated by an anonymous member of this rock-throwing pack of animals. Rampaging *demos* anticipates with pleasure not so much changes in the social fabric as 'an uproar which would give them unwonted opportunities of violence and pillage . . . A crowd of Englishmen working itself into a moral rage is as glorious a spectacle as the world can show', writes Gissing.

This is harsh. Elsewhere in the novel there is a more rational and leisurely discussion among intelligent men of the merits of socialism, but the conclusions are no different. Wyvern – the clergyman who, as Roberts observes, 'is very often but Gissing in disguise' – dissects the socialists dispassionately: 'they preach the childish theory of the equality of man, and seek to make discontented a whole class . . . These men . . . are not sincere.' Less dispassionate is Eldon, who also speaks with Gissing's voice often in this novel. He pronounces socialism's epitaph in plain terms: 'English Socialism! It is infused with the spirit of shop-keeping; it appeals to the vulgarest minds; it keeps one eye on personal safety, the other on the capitalist's strongbox; it is stamped commonplace, like everything originating with the English lower classes.'

One might expect (of another writer) that educating the masses and raising their standard of living would be offered as a panacea for the disgraceful degradation the novel describes. Of course *Demos* offers no such thing. In a pivotal passage Eldon tells Adela that she 'must distinguish between humanity and humanitarianism. I hope I am not lacking in the former; the latter seems to me to threaten everything that is most precious in the world' – that is, the distinctions between the classes so important to the class-conscious novelist. 'The sight of distress touches me deeply', Eldon says. 'To the individual poor man or woman I would give my last penny. It is where they rise against me as a class that I become pitiless.' This Swiftian sentiment lies at the heart of Gissing's social theology. Paranoid on the subject of class, he was prone to see himself threatened less by individuals than by movements – the obverse, surely, of most people's feelings. In the same spirit Adela, a kindly and feeling woman, comes to see by the end of the novel what sort of 'humanitarianism' is useful and what sort is not:

there is a work in the cause of humanity other than that which goes on so clamorously in lecture-halls and at street corners, other than that which is silently performed by faithful hearts and hands in dens of misery and amid the horrors of the lazar-house; the work of those whose soul is taken captive of loveliness, who pursue the spiritual ideal apart from the world's tumult, and, ever ready to minister in gentle offices, know that they serve best when nearest home.

In *The Unclassed, Isabel Clarendon,* and *A Life's Morning,* Gissing argues the case against educating the unrefined but never so uncompromisingly as he does through Wyvern in *Demos*:

I have a profound dislike and distrust of . . . universal education. . . I used to have a very bleeding of the heart for the half-clothed and quarter-fed hangers-on to civilisation; I think far less of them now than of another class in appearance much better off. It is a class created by the mania of education, and it consists of those unhappy men or women whom unspeakable cruelty endows with intellectual needs whilst refusing them the sustenance they are taught to crave. Another generation, and this class will be terribly extended, its existence blighting the whole social state. Every one of these poor creatures has a right to curse the work of those who clamour progress, and pose as benefactors of their race.

It is better to be utterly ignorant than to learn that one is deprived of the very things that learning has taught one to value.

'Arry Mutimer (Gissing obstinately spells it without the aspirate throughout the book), the protagonist's younger brother, is one casualty of the mania for education. He belongs, says the novelist, to 'a distinct class', identified as 'the sons of mechanics' who are 'ruined morally by being taught to consider themselves above

5. Margaret Gissing (the novelist's sister)

6. Ellen Gissing (the novelist's sister)

7. William Gissing (the novelist's brother) in 187[

8. Algernon Gissing in old age

manual labour'. To make such a person immune 'from the only kind of work for which he was fitted', Gissing argues, is madness: it gives 'fatal momentum to all his worst tendencies'. In *Demos*, as Roberts says, Gissing 'shook off the idiotic Victorian belief that education beyond that of a man's class would always make him a better and more noble citizen'.

Only once does *Demos* betray the sort of reflexive sympathy for the suffering poor to be found in *Workers in the Dawn*. This occurs during the account of Emma's visit to a cemetery in the East End, justly noted by critics as an example of Gissing at his lyrical best:

Here lie those who were born for toil; who, when toil has worn them to the uttermost, have but to yield their useless breath and pass into oblivion. For them is no day, only the brief twilight of a winter sky between the former and the latter night. For them no aspiration; for them no hope of memory in the dust; their very children are wearied into forgetfulness. Indistinguishable units in the vast throng that labours but to support life, the name of each, father, mother, child, is as a dumb cry for the warmth and love of which Fate so stinted them.

Demos picks up some old threads and weaves a few new ones.

'To one who lacks money the world is but a great debtors' prison', it is said. The enormous differences between the two nations, rich and poor, are insisted upon in *Demos*, as in *A Life's Morning*. But to this theme Gissing now adds a twist: the idea that society is organized so as to keep its poorest members just barely alive, giving them only enough to sustain physical existence while ensuring that their emotional life is a continuous torture. 'Just keeping afloat' is said to be 'the whole principle of the capitalist system of employment'. The system determines how much you need in order to keep working and then gives you that much and no more. 'It's calculated exactly how long a man can be made to work in a day without making him incapable of beginning work on the day following – just as it's calculated exactly how little a man can live upon, in the regulation of wages.'

Gissing was no friend of the industrial plutocracy. While it betrays contempt for the workers, *Demos* does not defend their masters. On the contrary, the new class of industrialists and the political Establishment are attacked with special bitterness. 'Men with large aims cannot afford to be scrupulous in small details', snarls the narrator. The environmentalist theme touched on in *A Life's Morning* is taken much further into a remarkably sustained and prophetic condemnation of the rape of the countryside by heavy industry. The novel's very first paragraph describes the town of Belwick, 'with its hundred and fifty fire-vomiting blast-fur-naces', as a hell in the middle of 'greenery'. Hoxton, its neighbour, is delineated in language reserved for Gissing's most emotional out-bursts: 'a region of malodorous market streets, of factories, timber yards, grimy warehouses, of alleys swarming with small trades and crafts, of filthy courts and passages leading into pestilential gloom; everywhere toil in its most degrading forms . . . working folk of the coarsest type, the corners and lurking-holes showing destitution at its ugliest.'

While in charge of the Wanley works Eldon tried to preserve the surrounding areas, to keep the countryside unsullied by industry. Mutimer, the new working-class boss without taste, wants to construct an 'ideal' community of workers in the middle of this green valley. As a result there is much tearing up of the countryside in the interests of 'progress' – and a good deal of commentary in the novel on how spurious these interests are. 'It used to be all fields and gardens over there', says Mutimer proudly to his sister as they stand on the churned-up site of his New Wanley. 'See what money and energy can do!' Gissing was unimpressed by the examples of Robert Owen, Charles Fourier, Thomas Hughes, and others who had attempted to establish communities of workers along socialist lines. His account of Mutimer's rape of the land is acidulous.

Building of various kinds was in progress in the heart of the vale; a great massive chimney was rising to completion, and about it stood a number of sheds. Beyond was to be seen the commencement of a street of small houses, promising infinite ugliness in a little space; the soil over a considerable area was torn up and trodden into mud . . . the benighted valley was waking up and donning the true nineteenth-century livery.

At the end of *Demos,* when Mutimer is disinherited and Eldon comes back to power, New Wanley is joyously destroyed. Mutim-er's awful project, it is said, 'has ruined one of the loveliest valleys in England'. Eldon vows to 'sweep away every trace of the mines and the works and the houses, and . . . restore the valley to its former state'. The reactionary wants to go back to an earlier time. 'It may be inevitable that the green and beautiful spots of the world shall give place to furnaces and mechanics' dwellings', Eldon tells Adela, but he will have no part in such 'desolation and defilement'.

'Then you think grass and trees of more importance than human lives?' Adela asks him.

'I had rather say that I see no value in human lives in a world from which grass and trees have vanished', Eldon replies.

Significantly it is the working-class man who cares nothing for natural beauty, the middle-class man who wants to preserve it.

The novel's most remarkable passage articulates a vision of the future which is strikingly prophetic. Eldon predicts that some day grass and corn will be produced by 'chemical processes' for 'a hungry Demos' uninterested in 'the beautiful'. 'There will not be one inch left to nature; the very oceans will somehow be tamed, the snow-mountains will be levelled. And with nature will perish art . . . Do you imagine the twentieth century will leave one green spot upon the earth's surface?' No other Victorian novelist looked to the future with such foreboding. 'Progress will have its way, and its path will be a path of bitterness', says Wyvern. 'Everywhere the tendency is towards the rule of mean interests, ignoble ideals', says Eldon. The narrator of *Demos* describes the contemporary era as one in which 'falsehood is the foundation of the social structure, and internecine warfare is presupposed in every compact between man and man.' Gissing's description of a railway station seethes with a neurasthenia brought on by the vision of 'progress' in the modern mechanical age he so much hated: 'In the station was a constant roaring and hissing, bell-ringing and the shriek of whistles, the heavy trundling of barrows, the slamming of carriage-doors; everywhere a smell of smoke. It [was as if] . . . all the world had become homeless, and had nothing to do but journey hither and thither in vain search of a resting-place.' As the eighties became the nineties and the roar of progress grew louder, Gissing would react ever more violently.

In this novel, as in *A Life's Morning*, there is a happy ending after much tragedy: Eldon and Adela walk hand in hand through a garden from which all trace of the hated New Wanley works has been expunged. To reach this victory over *demos* was no easy matter; for some there is no victory at all. 'We are interesting in proportion to our capacity for suffering, and dignity comes of misery nobly borne', Gissing concludes. He adds: 'Only the gentle and helpless have to suffer; that is the plan of the world's ruling [force].' Old habits of thinking die hard. He never forgot his Schopenhauer; and he never became reconciled to the modern age.

Like other Gissing heroines before and after her, Adela comes to reject the puritanism of her upbringing and to rejoice in the happiness of marriage, after Mutimer's death, to a cultural equal (Eldon). 'The Puritanism of [Adela's] training led her to distrust profoundly [the] impulses of . . . nature'; 'pleasure in the ordinary sense she did not admit into her schemes of existence.' By the end of *Demos* Adela's love for Eldon has revealed to her the emptiness of the anti-pleasure philosophy: 'Her soul was bare to her and all its needs. There was no refuge in ascetic resolve, in the self-deceit of spiritual enthusiasm.' An undeviating agnostic, Gissing puts into the unlikely mouth of his clergyman in *Demos* an unadorned rejection of the vale-of-tears view of life. We must live for the present and not for the future, Wyvern says: 'Those who are enthusiastic for the spirit of the age proceed on the principle of countenancing evil that good may some day come of it. Such a position astonishes me. Is the happiness of a man now alive of less account than that of the man who shall live two hundred years hence? Altruism is doubtless good, but only so when it gives pure enjoyment.' This is a condemnation of asceticism as a moral philosophy rather than an invitation to hedonism. Gissing was no believer in gratuitous self-denial. In this he was consistent through-out his life. Years later he wrote to Gabrielle Fleury: 'I abhor . . . asceticism. It means every sort of intellectual vice, it involves needless suffering . . . it is through joy, not sorrow, that men become morally better.'

Direct autobiographical equivalents are scarcer here than in preceding novels, though it must be plain by now how characteristic a Gissing performance *Demos* is philosophically. Still, the novelist has not kept himself altogether out of the book. There is something of him in his 'unclassed' protagonist Mutimer and in his cultural aristocrat Eldon, as well as in the clergyman Wyvern. Mutimer's pursuit of Adela is fraught with all the neuroses attendant upon exogamous relationships in Gissing's novels.

The pale anguish of her face was his joy; it fascinated him, fired his senses, made him a demon of vicious cruelty. Yet he durst not as much as touch her hand when she sat before him. Her purity, which was her safeguard, stirred his venom; he worshipped it, and would have smothered it in foulness . . . He would have had her resist him, that he might know the pleasure of crushing her will.

Gissing's fantasies about 'respectable' women clearly embodied a measure of sado-masochism.

Eldon, who yearns passionately for a woman his social equal, is another fastidious man with a guilty secret – a liaison with a lower-class woman during his early years. Gissing describes Eldon's immature fixation as 'a glorious madness' and a 'reckless passion', and comments: 'However unworthy the object of his frenzy . . . the pursuit had borne him through an atmosphere of fire tempering him for life, marking him for ever from plodders of the dusty highway.' By the mid-eighties Gissing undoubtedly saw himself in this way – that is, as a man who had already lived several lives and was wiser for the experience, however unhappy. Eldon also shares Gissing's naturally conservative temperament: 'Hubert's . . . character [was] so compact of subtleties and refinements, of high prejudice and jealous sensibility, of spiritual egoism and all-pervading fastidiousness, that it was impossible for him not to regard with repugnance a man [Mutimer] who represented the . . . uncultured classes.'

Finally, a word about the plot of *Demos*. It hangs largely upon wills. Old Mr Mutimer dies while in the process of altering his will, thus intestate. The Wanley works are inherited, accidentally, by his working-class cousin Richard. The finding of a new will late in the novel disinherits Mutimer and puts him back where he came from. He suffers a further disappointment when an anonymous benefactor who has promised to leave him a legacy dies while altering his will. This is the first of several Gissing plots which hang upon wills. His use or over-use of wills reflects both their popularity among Victorian novelists (especially Dickens) as a plot-device and Gissing's own interest in money – as well as a fantasy he surely entertained throughout much of his life of inheriting money from some appreciative patron. It is interesting to note in Gissing's novels some of the most traditional motifs of nineteenth-century fiction side by side with the most prophetic 'modern' themes.

Emma Vine has a theory of story-telling which Gissing recounts for us. Over the years she has become a skilful teller of tales to children, but she is always careful not to make her stories too saccharine, and thus misleading.

Emma had two classes of story: the one concerned itself with rich children, the other with poor; the one highly fanciful, the other full of a touching actuality, the very essence of a life such as that led by the listeners themselves. Unlike the novel which commends itself to the world's grown children, these narratives had by no means necessarily a happy ending; for one thing Emma saw too deeply into the facts of life, and was herself too sad, to cease her music on a merry chord; and, moreover, it was half a matter of principle with her to make the little ones thoughtful and sympathetic; she believed that they would grow up kinder and more self-reliant if they were in the habit of thinking that we are ever dependent on each other for solace and strengthening under the burden of life.

III

Gissing corrected the proofs of *Isabel Clarendon* in March 1886; in April the novel was announced by Chapman and Hall. Gissing, who thought it 'vastly better from a literary point of view' than *Demos*, predicted lugubriously that it would be 'a flat failure'. *Isabel Clarendon* was published in June to an almost total critical silence. The few reviews which did appear were mixed; the *Saturday Review* and the *Guardian* were especially hostile. Kingcote and Isabel were praised. The similarities to Meredith's work were noticed.

Sales of *Demos*, meanwhile, were relatively brisk. Over 500 copies were sold in the first month after publication – a good performance in view of the high price of the cloth edition. As the book's authorship was unveiled, Gissing became a lion of the literary season. The sale of Continental rights for *Demos* to Tauchnitz gave him a new constituency of readers (French, German, Russian, and even Polish translations of *Demos* appeared in the nineties). A six-shilling edition of 1,000 copies, with Gissing's name on the title-page, was brought out by Smith, Elder in November 1886; cheaper reprints appeared in 1888, 1890, and 1892. More than three years after its original publication the novel was serialized by the *Manchester Weekly Times*. The popularity of *Demos* diverted Gissing from the disappointment he would otherwise have felt at the failure of *Isabel Clarendon*. *Demos*, however, did not enrich him personally, since he had sold the copyright to the publisher; but he hoped its success would enable him to get a higher price for his next book.

Having disposed of *Demos*, *Isabel Clarendon*, and *A Life's Morning* – and having for once both a clean desk and some money in his pocket – Gissing, detecting signs of his 'emancipation' and enjoying the new attention he was receiving in London drawing-rooms, decided it was time at last to do what all of his middle-class friends periodically did – take a vacation. The attention he was attracting and the prospect of travel exhilarated him. 'Thank heaven I can go without the torture of feeling myself *nobody*', he wrote to Ellen. 'I can't endure to be *nobody*. I knew that would have to come to an end.' Referring to the 'huge success' of *Demos*, Gissing declared that his turn had come at last.

He spent the latter part of March and the first half of April 1886 in Paris. Always an observant and at times a passionate traveller, Gissing considered this first trip to Europe, brief as it was, 'the beginning of a new life'. Characteristically, one of the first places he visited was the Paris morgue. At this time he came to love French architecture, French food, French theatre, though later his Francophilism was to wane. During these weeks he had more peace of mind than he had known for years. Still, there was some teaching to be done, and a new novel to write, and by mid-April he was back in London, where his new success could not lighten all his recurring glooms. He wrote to Ellen: 'How impossible for me ever to live the ordinary kind of domestic life! Solitude has long since been an essential to me' – in order to work, he meant. He turned down a number of invitations, walked twenty miles a day, and went back to work.

IV

In June 1886 Gissing sent copies of *The Unclassed* and *Isabel Clarendon* to Hardy (who had already read *Demos*), commenting in an accompanying letter that *The Unclassed* was 'saturated with by-gone miseries' and that he did not dare to read it again himself. He also mentioned the 'refreshment' and 'help' he found in Hardy's work. The new novel, *Thyrza*, was begun at this time. Knowing he had an audience now and wishing not to disappoint it, Gissing wrote slowly and methodically. After several false starts and much destruction of manuscript, he made real progress on it during the latter months of the year and finished it in a great burst of writing in January 1887. Smith, Elder had had a big success with *Demos*. But they knew Gissing, his insecurities, and his impecuniousness (in the same month in which he finished writing *Thyrza*, the author of *Demos* had to borrow money from his brother). The publishers offered £100 for the copyright of *Thyrza* or £50 plus a ten per cent royalty. Gissing was devastated by the meagreness of his reward. He considered going to other publishers, but the prospect of more uncertainty of this sort was too nerve-racking. After some agonizing he chose the advance-plus-royalty arrangement, which was only to make him worry more about sales once the book was published. 'The present terms', Gissing told Algernon in January, 'mean that I shall live in deadly fear of poverty through the rest of the year, – that I cannot help the Wakefield people with a penny . . . that I cannot buy new clothing, – that in brief I shall be harassed through all the next book and do poor work.' And he added, moodily but prophetically: '"Thyrza" cannot be a popular book, nothing like so much as "Demos."' Smith, Elder, it should be pointed out, treated most of its authors – among them Charlotte Brontë – in the same shabby way; the firm is infamous in literary history for its savage handling, largely at the instigation of the urbane George Smith, of Victorian writers.

Gissing's letters late in 1886 reflect his deep immersion in the new book, which he described to Ellen as 'grim' and 'tragical'. 'No one else can write' this story, Gissing told his sister. It 'will contain the very spirit of London working-class life'. He wept (in good Dickensian fashion) over some of the final chapters as he was writing them, according to another of his notes to Ellen. 'It is good, better in many respects than *Demos*', he said. And he added: 'I value the book more than anything I nave yet done . . . Thyrza herself is one of the most beautiful dreams I ever had or shall have.' *Thyrza* was always one of his own favourites among his novels: the idealized prostitute, the aborted lecture-hall scheme, the 'unclassed' status of several of the leading characters and some other factors involved him very personally in this tale. 'The pathetic parts of my own stories affect me deeply when I open the book to revive my memory of them', he noted later in his Commonplace Book. 'The tears always come when I read parts of "Thyrza".'

Gissing spent a good deal of time while writing *Thyrza* researching his working-class subject on the spot in Lambeth in the manner of Zola. The influence of non-English writers upon the book was explained to Bertz on the grounds that so much of his own culture derives from foreign literature that he could not be his 'real self when unable to refer to the foreign authors' he values. To Margaret he wrote: 'The writers who help me most are French and Russian; I have not much sympathy with English points of view. And indeed that is why I scarcely think that my own writing can ever be popular.'

In 1879 in the flush of his social idealism he had written to Algernon advocating 'a complete system of education, supplemented by a thorough network of free libraries' for the working-class poor. On these matters he had undergone a complete change of heart in the intervening seven years, but the new novel expresses his continuing interest in the subject, if now from a different perspective. The year 1886 was among the most economically depressed in England's recent history; ways of relieving the sufferings of the indigent were being urgently sought. Socialist agitation, as we have seen, was at its height. Yet *Thyrza* again shows Gissing's hatred of idealisms which seek to alleviate suffering through social 'systems'. It is in fact an attack on all measures of reform, launched with much sermonizing and little subtlety. Whatever Gissing may have learned about the dramatic method from his revisions of *Isabel*

Clarendon is mostly forgotten in *Thyrza,* one of his less inspired performances. Again, however, we can have no difficulty in recognizing a familiar voice.

Thyrza: A Tale was published by Smith, Elder in April 1887. Gladstone, who read it upon publication, said later he was impressed by its chief lesson: that unpractical visionaries may do less to benefit the world than unidealistic men with a solid political base, practical abilities, and uncomplicated personal ambition. One of the book's major movements pits the idealistic, soft-hearted, but unpractical Walter Egremont against the unprincipled, self-seeking politician James Dalmaine. Both wish to improve the lot of the workers of Lambeth – but for different reasons. Egremont's idealism is ultimately destroyed, as Gissing's was, by a disillusioning collison with *demos*; Dalmaine's indestructible private ambitions, made of stuff sterner than sentimentality, actually bring some measure of relief to the hapless ghetto.

Among the passages in the novel which must have impressed Gladstone is a discussion between an admirer of Egremont, Paula Tyrrell (who later marries Dalmaine), and her indolent but more clear-sighted brother John. Men like Egremont, John Tyrrell says, 'get it into their heads that they're called upon to reform the world' because they haven't got anything else to keep them busy. He goes on:

Social reform, pooh! Why, who are the real social reformers? The men who don't care a scrap for the people, but take up ideals because they can make capital out of them. It isn't idealists who do the work of the world, but the hard-headed, practical, selfish men. A big employer of labour 'll do more good in a day, just because he sees profit 'll come of it, than all the mooning philanthropists in a hundred years. Nothing solid has ever been gained in this world that wasn't pursued out of self-interest.

'In all which,' says the narrator, 'it is not impossible that Mr. John Tyrrell hit the nail on the head.' Dalmaine, 'a man with a future', understands well enough that the present is 'the age of the practical. Let him who would be an idealist, the practical man in the end got all that was worth having.' It matters little that 'the single working man for whom he veritably cared one jot was Mr. James Dalmaine' himself; selfish ambition at least achieves results. 'No man will succeed with us in politics who has not got a reputation of solid earnestness. Therefore, the more stupid a man, the better chance he has', Dalmaine says.

The long aside late in the novel on the career of Cornelius

Vanderbilt – a boor personally odious in many ways, yet a great benefactor of mankind as a result of personal vanity – preaches the same lesson. Even Egremont finally learns that 'to sneer at . . . the practical philanthropists . . . is . . . to speak contemptuously of the rain-shower which aids the growth of the corn.' His friend New-thorpe had tried to convince him of this: 'With the mud at the bottom of society we can practically do nothing; only the vast changes to be wrought by time will cleanse that foulness.' Egremont's plan, which includes lecturing on social and cultural subjects to working men and opening a free local library, fails to take into account the appalling material the would-be reformer has to work with to achieve his ends. 'The working man does not read, in the strict sense of the word', the narrator of *Thyrza* declares. 'Fiction has little interest for him, and of poetry he has no comprehension whatever.' If the common man reads anything it is the newspaper – 'the very voice of all that is worst in our civilisation'. The free library of Lambeth is doomed from the start. 'The working class', as Dalmaine says, 'will never value anything they [sic] don't pay for.' Reform, *Thyrza* tells us, can never come out of the quixoticism of meddling idealists.

Egremont, who has kind feelings and genuinely wishes to benefit others, brings only disaster to his working-class acquaintances. The attempt to cross class lines, as so often in Gissing's stories, leads to disaster. Mingling with those he wishes to help he falls in love with a girl, Thyrza Trent, who is the promised bride of an intelligent working man, Gilbert Grail. Thyrza returns Egremont's passion, thus ruining the hopes of poor Grail. Later Egremont tires of Thyrza, who dies of a broken heart. Everyone is disappointed in one way or another as a result of Egremont's actions – and Lambeth loses its free library.

Like its predecessors, *Thyrza* tells us that it is not a good thing to educate people beyond their means, their class, or their reasonable expectations. The only truly 'happy people of the world', the novel says, 'are the dull, unimaginative beings from whom the gods, in their kindness, have veiled all vision of the rising and the setting sun, of sea-limits, and of the stars of the night, whose ears are thickened against the voice of music, whose thought finds nowhere mystery'. 'The untaught vulgar are very defective in the senses; they hear, feel, see, taste, smell, very imperfectly', Gissing's Common-place Book declares.

So by the end of *Thyrza* the wiser Egremont thinks little of his former plans. Like Kurtz, he has changed his mind: 'Let the people rust and rot in ignorance!' At the centre of *Thyrza* is Egremont himself. While not as closely modelled on the novelist as Waymark or Kingcote or Arthur Golding, there is plenty of Gissing in him. Unlike Gissing, he has private means (his father was a successful tradesman), but his instinctive sympathy for the deprived and his working-class background make him, too, 'unclassed'. Of Egremont, Gissing says: 'there seemed to be a gap between him and the people born to refinement who were his associates, his friends'. Like the novelist, Egremont wonders 'if his life were to be a struggle between inherited sympathies and the affinities of his intellect'. Egremont goes off to America to get over his various disappointments, retracing the novelist's path. His lecturing scheme also reminds us of Gissing's, as well as the desire to teach workers to read. The idealism disintegrates and is replaced by a general scepticism and finally antipathy to the poor.

Egremont also becomes tangled in the 'two-women' theme. The choice is between Annabel Newthorpe, intelligent, respectable, middle-class, sensually unexciting, and Thyrza Trent, unintellectual, working-class, and – for a time at least – sexually attractive to Egremont. There is a suggestion here, typical of Gissing, that perhaps 'respectable' people do not make love as passionately as their more humble counterparts. Egremont's attachment to Thyrza is called 'perishable' and 'prudential' and 'poor, worldly, ignoble, in comparison with [the] sacred . . . ardour' she has for him. Egremont is one of the few protagonists to draw back from the perils of exogamy – even though *his* working-class girl vows to 'work very hard, so that he shouldn't be ashamed of me'.

The narrator introduces Egremont to the reader thus:

Mr. Egremont had not the look of a man who finds his joy in the life of Society. His clean-shaven face was rather bony, and its lines expressed independence of character; his forehead was broad, his eyes glanced quickly and searchingly, or widened themselves into an absent gazing which revealed the imaginative temperament. His habitual cast of countenance was meditative, with a tendency to sadness. In talk he readily became vivacious; his short sentences, delivered with a very clear and conciliating enunciation, seemed to indicate energy. It was a peculiarity that he very rarely smiled, or perhaps I should say that he had the faculty of smiling only with his eyes. At such moments his look was very winning, very frank in its appeal to sympathy, and compelled one to like him. Yet, at another time, his aspect could be shrewdly critical.

Mrs Ormonde's assessment of Egremont is equally revealing. She says to him:

you have much that is feminine in your character. You have little real
energy; you are passive in great trials; it is easier for you to suffer than to
act. Your idealism is often noble, but never heroic. You have talked to me
of your natural nearness to people of the working class, and I firmly believe
that you are further from them . . . than many a man who counts
kindred among the peerage. You have a great deal of spiritual pride, and it
will increase as your mind matures.

This is not to say that Gissing wears only one hat in *Thyrza* – as
usual there is something of him in several other characters. Chief
among these is Gilbert Grail, who seems always to be on the
'threshold of the promised land, hopeless of admission'. His
exclusion from the bourgeois paradise does not breed in him,
however, any 'revolutionary spirit. His personality was essentially
that of a student; conservative instincts were stronger in him than
the misery [poverty] which accursed his fortune.' As a young man
'extreme shyness held [Grail] from intercourse with all women save
his mother and sister', but as he matures he puts 'supreme faith' in
the ability of the fair sex to make him happy and so searches for 'a
pure and noble creature' to suit him. The choice, of course, is
circumscribed by his means and his class. Reserved, silent, lonely,
unhappy, intensely subjective, self-absorbed yet secretly craving
companionship, a great reader, and a lover of books, Grail obviously has much of Gissing in him.

The reclusive scholar Newthorpe, who sounds and lives like the
protagonist of *The Ryecroft Papers,* is a 'genial pessimist', who finds
pleasure 'in urbanely mocking at his own futility', at his incapacity
for anything except quiet study. 'There's tragedy in me, if you have
the eyes to see it', he remarks complacently. And there is Bunce, the
working man embittered by poverty and an unfortunate marriage,
who contemplates suicide by drowning.

The attack on asceticism is carried forward in the character of
Thyrza, for whom suffering and deprivation do little. It is
emphasized in the character of Mary Bower, a low-church fanatic
whose 'chapel-going', it is said, makes her more 'unkind' than
otherwise; and in the account of the rest of the Bower family, which
cultivates the image of piety to mask the most hideous grasping
materialism.

If self-denial is not a prescription for happiness, neither is
marriage, which is portrayed in *Thyrza* as another destroyer of
idealisms. For Bunce, unhappily married, 'the memory of bondage
to a hateful woman clings like a long disease which impoverishes the
blood' and poisons the thoughts. Totty Nancarrow, contemplating

marriage, understands that 'couples who wedded and went to live in one furnished room seldom get along well together. It was well if the wife did not shortly go about with ugly-looking bruises on her face, or with her arm in a sling.'

And there is the familiar neurasthenia, and hatred of the metropolis. On his way to work, Grail is almost overcome by the physical environment:

he went to work through a fog so dense that it was with difficulty he followed the familiar way. Lamps were mere lurid blotches in the foul air, perceptible only when close at hand; the footfall of invisible men and women hurrying to factories made a muffled, ghastly sound; harsh bells summoned through the darkness, the voice of pitiless taskmasters . . . Gilbert was racked with headache . . . he longed for nothing more than to lie down and lose consciousness of the burden of life.

This is what it is like to *have* to go to work, whether you feel up to it or not. The physical properties of London – described here in terms reminiscent of *Bleak House* – are largely responsible for Gilbert's headache, his desire for unconsciousness. Like its predecessors, *Thyrza* has a great deal to say about the quality of urban life. 'Windows glimmered at noon with the sickly ray of gas or lamp; the roads were trodden into viscid foulness; all night the droppings of a pestilent rain were doleful . . . and only the change from a black to a yellow sky told that the sun was risen.' Gissing's description of the Caledonian Road is of a waste land:

It is doubtful whether London can show any thoroughfare . . . more offensive to eye and ear and nostril. You stand at the entrance to it, and gaze into a region of supreme ugliness; every house front is marked with meanness and inveterate grime; every shop seems breaking forth with mould or dry-rot; the people who walk here appear . . . to be employed in labour that soils body and spirit. Journey on the top of a tram-car from King's Cross to Holloway, and civilisation has taught you its ultimate achievement in ignoble hideousness. You look off into narrow sidechannels where unconscious degradation has made its inexpugnable home, and sits veiled with refuse. You pass above lines of railway, which cleave the region with black-breathing fissure. You see the pavements half occupied with the . . . most sordid wares . . . the public-houses look and reek more intolerably than in other places.

The description of Lambeth as 'redolent with oleaginous matter; the clothing of the men was penetrated with the same nauseous odour' is clearly derived from the sections of *Bleak House* which conjure up Krook's oily neighbourhood, and Totty Nancarrow's 'Little

Shop with the Large Heart' in the midst of a slum is equally
Dickensian. Consider, however, such a passage as this:

The life of men who toil without hope yet with the hunger of an unshaped
desire; of women in whom the sweetness of their sex is perishing under
labour and misery; the . . . song of the girl who strives to enjoy her year or
two of youthful vigour, knowing the darkness of the years to come; the
careless defiance of the youth who feels his blood and revolts against the lot
which would tame it ; all that is purely human in these darkened multitudes
speaks to you as you listen. It is the half-conscious striving of a nature
which knows not what it would attain, which deforms a true thought by
gross expression, which clutches at the beautiful and soils it with foul
hands.

The lyricism of the opening, reminiscent of the graveyard scene in
Demos, is Dickensian in spirit and tone; but the final sentence,
undercutting a good deal of the sympathy in what precedes it, is
very un-Dickensian indeed. Poverty, however, is not always an
evil. One of Gissing's favourite arguments was that an artist must
face starvation in order to do anything, as Roberts recalled.
Egremont is handicapped by his money: he has never gone without
his dinner. The 'true artist', Gissing says in *Thyrza,* 'will oftener find
his inspiration in a London garret than amid the banality of the
plutocrat's drawing-room.' He found his inspiration where
Hogarth found his. The worthlessness of Virginia Woolf's idea that
you have to have a room of your own and five-hundred a year to be
a writer is proved by the early material circumstances of most of her
nineteenth-century predecessors, not least Gissing. And her
offhand remark that working-class writers such as Gissing are
boringly obsessed by the subject of money and their own sufferings
is one of many examples in her work of her insensibility to the
problems of those not born, as she happened to be, into the social
and intellectual purple. One wonders how she would have done in
the cramped quarters occupied by her favourite novelist Jane
Austen – like Gissing a neurasthenic and a loner who wrote books
in noisy and crowded circumstances.

Gissing's argument that artists must find motivation in poverty
does not contradict another familiar argument – that for the
ordinary man or woman just a little money can mean the difference
between happiness and misery. 'What spaces between those two
worlds!' Egremont muses. For the person without the over-
developed sensibilities of the artist – that is, for most of the world's
population – life is 'a simple thing . . . with limitless cash, a perfect

digestion, and good-humour in place of brains!' For those without limitless cash a trivial occurrence can mean the difference between living and dying. As the necessity of having one's clothes cleaned may force the poor man to go without a meal, so the slightest physical indisposition in the susceptible poor can become a serious ailment when means to combat it are lacking. 'The difficulty these poor things have in getting rid of a cold', remarks Mrs Ormonde of her charges; 'with many of them . . . such a condition is chronic . . . it goes on . . . until they die of it.'

Undoubtedly *Thyrza* is more pessimistic than *Demos*. The book ends with most of the major characters either dead, unreconciled to one another, or utterly disillusioned. 'Few things in life turn out as we desire', Grail says, sounding like a refugee from a Hardy novel; 'to have done one's best with a good intention is much to look back upon – very few have more.' 'The great fact of all', says Egremont, 'is the contemptibleness of average humanity'. Few people, muses Thyrza, are 'exempt from the sorrow that goes about in the world, blighting lives and breaking hearts.' Ultimately she dies of unhappiness, having decided that 'to sleep is better than to wake' – for 'how should we who live bear the day's burdens but for the promise of death.' Even Schopenhauer's Will to Live is extinguished in her, betrayed by her love for an unworthy man and the accident of her humble birth.

v

Reviews of *Thyrza* were sparse but for the most part favourable. The *Athenaeum* and the *Saturday Review* were lukewarm and *The Times* critical (mostly of the novel's sentimentality), but the *Guardian*, the *Whitehall Review*, and the newly established *Murray's Magazine*, among others, gave the book high praise. The novel's realism was appreciated, its pessimism accepted. Ellen Gissing liked the tale; but Bertz found in it no dramatic interest. Generally the reviewers preferred Thyrza to Egremont; Gissing's understanding of the female character was cited by several of them (indeed, the *Whitehall Review* speculated that 'George Gissing' might be the *nom de plume* of a lady novelist).

More importantly, the appearance of another Gissing volume called forth in the popular press the first two detailed studies of him as a novelist. W. T. Stead, the well-known controversialist who had written a series of exposés in the *Pall Mall Gazette* several years earlier on prostitution in London, had his attention caught by *The Unclassed*, one of the few English novels of the nineteenth century with a prostitute (Ida Starr) as a major character. It led him to the other books, and in June 1887 he published in the *Pall Mall Gazette* a highly laudatory piece called 'George Gissing as a Novelist'. He praises Gissing chiefly for his 'courageous presentation of truth' and 'profound . . . knowledge of the lives of the London poor'. His novels, Stead writes, 'are dramatic expositions of modern life . . . in all its hideousness'; he compares them to Balzac's *Comédie Humaine*. Stead notes both Gissing's increasing pessimism since *Workers in the Dawn* and his inability, in Stead's opinion, to portray the middle classes (this charge always displeased Gissing; he would have been enraged by Morley Roberts's pronouncement that 'beyond the lower middle class his knowledge was not very deep. He was mentally an alien'). Stead concludes: 'There is no English novelist of the present day better qualified to speak . . . of the English working classes'; he hopes that in future works 'Mr Gissing will confine himself to those phases of life with which he is familiar'.

The second essay on Gissing, much longer, appeared in April 1888 in *Murray's Magazine*. Its author, Edith Sichel, an amateur literary critic who later became a friend of Gissing's, managed to please the novelist more than the eminent Stead had – though Gissing had reservations about this piece too. Called 'Two Philanthropic Novelists: Mr Walter Besant and Mr George Gissing', the essay prescribes more middling paths for social novelists than those mapped out by Gissing's pessimism and Besant's sentimentality. Gissing is preferred because of his greater ability to face truths, no matter how unpleasant; Besant, in comparison, is called 'an intelligent child'.

As might be expected, Gissing was rarely happy with anything written about him. He told Miss Sichel later that his books were 'in no sense philanthropic but works of art'. But the appearance of these two essays, both generally sympathetic, was an indication of his arrival, before his thirtieth birthday, on the literary scene. From now on almost everyone who read books would know who he was. In this same year, 1886, his earnings reached £100 for the first time.

VI

After finishing *Thyrza* in January 1887 Gissing went off to Sussex for a brief holiday. The terms given for the novel were so poor that he could not afford to stop working for long, and by early February he was back in London. He wrote to Smith, Elder that he wished to see no reviews of the new book ('They irritate me and interrupt my work'). About this time he also turned down an offer from the *London Figaro* to publish his portrait; at this stage of his career he thought 'publicity' vulgar. Despite his embargo on reviews, he could not help knowing that notices of *Thyrza* were good, or that the first edition sold only 412 copies despite healthy advertising. Though he had, as we have seen, immense personal affection for *Thyrza*, Gissing was astonished to see that some of the reviewers preferred it to *Demos* . 'I assure you there is nothing like the same power in the book', he wrote to Ellen. 'It will be a long time before I do anything better than *Demos* artistically.'

Despite great industry, everything Gissing wrote for the next year or so remained either unfinished or unpublished. The period from the spring of 1887 to the spring of 1888 must have been one of the novelist's most frustrating. We can be more specific about Gissing's activities now, for it was during this time that he started to keep a diary. During 1887 he wrote all or part of three books never published: 'Clement Dorricott: A Life's Prelude', finished in May; a satire on the literary scene called 'Sandray the Sophist' (never finished); and 'Dust and Dew', later called 'The Insurgents' – almost completed in December 1887, begun anew several times thereafter, and ultimately abandoned altogether in 1888. 'Clement Dorricott' was the only one of these manuscripts sent to a publisher – in this case Bentley, which suggests that Gissing did not think much of it. He hoped Bentley would serialize the new story in *Temple Bar*, but terms for the book were never negotiated. Bentley offered to publish it in volume form, but Gissing seems to have considered it an unworthy successor to *Demos* and *Thyrza* and demurred, despite his terrible poverty and the offer of an advance. Bentley eventually returned the manuscript, and Gissing destroyed it (and apparently that of 'The Insurgents' too). Letters suggest that 'Clement Dorricott' was about the theatrical world; and some of the characters' names were to be used again in subsequent works – Elgar in *The Emancipated*, Glazzard in *Denzil Quarrier*. Gissing's attempt to write two stories about the contemporary artistic scene shows that he was inching his way towards the subject of his masterpiece, *New Grub Street*.

In April Gissing had to borrow money again – this time from Smith, Elder. He also had to fall back upon bread and dripping for his meals, and all thoughts of another European jaunt were of course dashed. It was especially frustrating because he had thought himself on the brink of emancipation from penury after *Demos* (in

1887, the year after *Demos,* he earned only £60). He gave up most of his visiting and locked himself up to write. In May he declared that his loneliness made him unfit for any company. 'It is my rule henceforth to dine with no one', he wrote to Ellen. 'I cannot get the kind of people who suit me, so I must be content to be alone.' 'My life is that of a hermit', he wrote to Margaret. 'I do not even take a newspaper.' He retained one pupil but gave up the others. The allowance to Nell continued to be paid.

During this awful spring there were some pleasant interludes. He attended the opera several times (the extent to which singing delighted him may be judged by the unusual number of singers in his novels). He was also reading and re-reading Charlotte Brontë, a lifelong favourite. After re-reading *Villette* he wrote to Margaret: 'Charlotte Brontë I find more and more valuable. She is the greatest English woman after Mrs. Browning. George Eliot is poor in comparison with her. No page of her is without genius, and she wrote a style such as you find in no other writer. She strengthens me enormously.' To Bertz, who had gone back to Germany (thus occasioning a long series of intimate letters from Gissing for which posterity can be grateful), the novelist wrote during the same month (April 1887) that he could not read Trollope: 'the man is such a terrible Philistine. Indeed, of English novelists I see more and more clearly that there is *only one* entirely to my taste, and that is Charlotte Brontë. A great and glorious woman! George Eliot is miserable in comparison!' At the same time he noted in his Commonplace Book: 'In no modern writer have I such intense *personal* interest as in Charlotte Brontë.'

This interest, which has never been adequately addressed by his critics, is probably due to several factors. First, her publisher was also Smith, Elder, and George Smith had known her well; indeed, he introduced her to Thackeray, whom she idolized (and who was one of Gissing's heroes as well). While dining with Smith during the summer of 1887 Gissing heard him give an account of the famous episode early in his career when Charlotte Brontë turned up in his office to reveal the identity of 'Currer Bell', the author of *Jane Eyre.* Smith was fond of regaling Gissing with stories of the Brontës and Thackeray and other literary giants of preceding decades, and Gissing, as might be expected, was fascinated by it all – and of course delighted to remember that the publisher of the Brontës and Thackeray was also publishing him. Next, Charlotte Brontë was not only a woman, but a brilliant woman – and not only a brilliant woman but a *passionate* brilliant woman – a combination of characteristics that must have intrigued Gissing. His comments on George Eliot, though surprising (few today would rate her below Charlotte Brontë as a novelist), are comprehensible when considered in this light. Despite her notorious private life – or perhaps because of it – George Eliot wrote of love in her novels much more chastely, much less directly, than Charlotte Brontë did. Perhaps George Eliot – that 'great horse-faced blue-stocking', as Henry James called her – symbolized for Gissing the sensual coldness of the superior woman, while Charlotte Brontë, so much more unconventional in so many ways, represented almost everything he thought of as being ideal in a woman (no doubt Smith's recollections would not have hindered this view of her). But of greatest importance by far, I think, is that Gissing saw Charlotte Brontë as an *outsider* (as indeed she was) – regarded by others as 'an insignificant stranger', as he put it in one of his letters, who got her 'revenge of time' through her art. He thought of her as victorious 'over oblivion' and of her work as 'a rebellious triumph over the world's brute forces'. Gissing thought of himself as facing the same challenges, especially during those disillusioning months of 1887. What she did he could do. He was fond, according to Roberts, of quoting her contemptuous exclamation, 'cultivate happiness! Happiness is not a potato.' His admiration for her work never waned.

During the summer months Gissing averaged, by his own account, seven hours of work a day, and yet continued to make almost no money at all. Again he borrowed from Algernon. Being in a misanthropic mood, he refused invitations from Smith, the Harrisons, and others. In June 1887 during one of his rare evenings out the novelist met Edward Clodd, a successful banker and a passionate lover of literature. Seventeen years older than Gissing and on familiar terms with many of the literary giants of the age (he was, for example, an old friend of Thomas Hardy), Clodd was destined to become one of the most intimate confidants of the novelist's last years and the recipient of some of his most interesting letters. Much later Clodd recalled his impressions of Gissing in 1887. 'He was shy,' Clodd said, and 'had a hunted-hare look; he struck me as morbidly self-conscious.' When Clodd asked him for his address, Gissing (with typical diffidence) replied: 'I haven't one, but let me write to you.'

During the summer Gissing visited working men's meetings, switching his *venue* from Lambeth to Clerkenwell, a very poor region of slums and tenements specializing in the manufacture of light metals. He continued to be unimpressed by the quality of the speeches he heard at these meetings. 'A more disheartening scene is difficult to imagine', he wrote to Margaret of one such get-together. He characterized the participants as 'vulgar blatant scoundrels!' Many details of Clerkenwell, unforgettable to any reader of the book, were to be used in *The Nether World*, his next novel.

In June 1887 the Queen's Golden Jubilee celebrations convulsed the capital, and Gissing declared himself disgusted both by the glorification of royalty and the behaviour of the festive masses. In a letter to Ellen he called the celebration 'the most gigantic organized exhibition of fatuity, vulgarity, and blatant blackguardism on record . . . The inscriptions hung about the street turn one's stomach.' He added: 'it certainly degrades humanity to yell in this way about a rather ill-tempered, very narrow-minded and exceedingly ugly farmer's daughter.' The novelist in Gissing, despite his disgust, was taking careful note of the goings-on. 'The "Jubilee" was amazing', he wrote to Algernon. 'At night the great streets were packed from side to side with a . . . current of people, all vehicles being forbidden. You walked at the rate of a funeral horse from top of Bond Street to the Bank, by way of Pall Mall, Strand, etc. Such a concourse of people I never saw.' Gissing was to reconstruct skilfully the atmosphere of the Jubilee celebrations some years later in *In the Year of Jubilee*; several scenes in *The Nether World* also reflect his careful observation of the London crowds in June 1887.

Gratified by the critical success of *Thyrza*, Gissing was disappointed by its failure to sell. Mudie had ordered only 85 copies of the novel as against 200 of Rider Haggard's *She*; but Gissing declared to Ellen that his own novel would be read 'when Haggard's was waste paper', and he added: 'I cannot and will not be reckoned among the petty scribblers of the day . . . Two things I aim at in my work: the love of everything that is beautiful, and the contempt of vulgar conventionality.'

In July Gissing took a short holiday in Surrey and paid a flying visit to Wakefield. He was working unproductively and chafing at the fact. Still in his misanthropic mood, he refused in September to attend Algernon's wedding, and wondered if Mrs Frederic Harrison's praise of *Thyrza* was sincere. His misanthropy reached the stage, Roberts reports, at which he 'would seldom associate with anybody whom he did not know already'. It was at this time that Gissing gave Roberts, whom he considered impractical, lessons in how to keep a fire going on the least amount of coal. Later, in the autumn, the novelist was feeling more optimistic. 'The gloomiest days are over', he wrote to Ellen in October. 'I begin to be content with my lot and find it enough to work all through the day.' Characteristically, however, he couldn't resist adding one of his favourite expressions: 'Soon enough the night cometh.' Roberts, who saw a good deal of Gissing during this time, says that 'Damn the nature of things!' was another of the novelist's favourite exclamations. In any case, the rare optimistic mood did not last long. Soon he was giving sustained thought to the gloomy underpinnings of his fiction – and concluding, as he told Ellen, that 'All my work is profoundly pessimistic as far as mood goes.' There were, he admitted, a few hopeful signs: if he lived another ten years, 'there shall not be many contemporary novelists ahead of me, for I am only beginning my work.' He was just thirty.

VII

In November 1887 Smith, Elder finally got around to 'Emily'. In need of a serial for the *Cornhill*, they proposed to Gissing that it appear there throughout 1888. It would be published in cloth near the end of the run; the novelist would be paid £50. Gissing agreed, but reluctantly; the money, and exposure in the *Cornhill*, were welcome (the same journal had launched the careers of Trollope and Hardy), but he feared that the story itself, written in 1885, was not worthy of the reputation he had made since then. Smith, Elder wanted a title other than 'Emily'. Gissing suggested 'Her Will and Her Way', then settled on *A Life's Morning*. As the first proofs reached him his fears about the novel's reception were intensified, but it was too late to do any serious rewriting. He told Ellen she would be disappointed in the tale: 'the whole is feeble'. He was particularly dissatisfied with the 'happy' ending (Emily's marriage to Wilfrid) he had provided at the behest of James Payn, Smith, Elder's reader. The story, he wrote to Ellen later, in the midst of its serial run, 'is disgusting me, and I feel it gets poorer and poorer; I can only hope that it will very soon be forgotten.'

The *Cornhill* was still, in the late eighties, one of the most respected and widely read of British periodicals, and the serialization of *A Life's Morning* brought Gissing a good deal of publicity. Magazine publication, however, was to cut deeply into sales of the heavily spaced-out, three-volume cloth edition which appeared in November 1888; only 383 copies of the first edition were sold. With typical parsimoniousness, Smith, Elder reduced its payment to Gissing by one-half, citing poor sales as the reason. They did not bother to tell him that the American rights had been sold to

Lippincott for £60 – not a penny of which, needless to say, reached the novelist's pocket. Indeed, the £25 Gissing received for the first edition of *A Life's Morning* would seem to be all he ever got for the book. Again he had to borrow money, this time from his mother.

The months of January and February 1888 were again bad ones for Gissing. He could not get on with 'The Insurgents', and soon abandoned it altogether. He was suffering from fatigue, headache, and a fresh bout of depression. Early in February he laid aside his other projects and began a new novel called 'Marian Dane', which was discontinued one day later. His state of mind was suicidal; he saw no one for days. On one day he recorded in his diary: 'Suffered anguish worse than any I remember in the effort to compose.' On another: 'Two days of blank misery . . . feeling almost ready for suicide.' He was getting nowhere but was afraid to let this get about among his friends: 'I dare not tell anyone the truth.' No book, he decided, could be written in his present state of mind, and for the first time in over ten years he ceased to write altogether.

Desperately needing a change of scene, Gissing decided to spend the last two weeks of February 1888 in Eastbourne, and Roberts accompanied him. Eastbourne was a bizarre choice, cold, windy, and damp in February, and the visit did not go well. Gissing's moodiness finally got the better of his companion, and Roberts went back to London. Gissing stayed on.

On the last day of February, returning to his lodgings in Eastbourne after a trip to Lewes, Gissing found a telegram awaiting him. It said: 'Mrs Gissing is dead. Come at once.' Roberts claims to have been with Gissing when he opened the telegram, and in *The Private Life of Henry Maitland* he treats us to a touching account of the novelist's facial expressions as he read the news. As we have seen, however, Roberts was in London by then and Gissing had to telegraph the news to him. The novelist reached town the next day, was met by Roberts, and the two set off together for the house in Lambeth in which Nell was said to have died. Gissing half suspected some ploy on his wife's part to get money, and sent Roberts into the house first to interview Nell's landlady. But dead poor Nell certainly was. It had happened in a tiny, miserable room barely furnished. On a bed bereft of blankets, despite the cold weather, lay the emaciated body of Helen Harrison Gissing, covered with a flimsy gown. With stark objectivity the novelist recorded in his diary what he saw:

On a door hung a poor miserable dress and a worn out ulster . . . Linen she had none; the very covering of the bed had gone save one sheet and one blanket. I found a number of pawn tickets, showing that she had pledged these things during last summer, – when it was warm, poor creature! All the money she received went in drink . . . I drew out the drawers. In one I found a little bit of butter and a crust of bread, – most pitiful sight my eyes ever looked upon. There was no other food anywhere. The drawers contained a disorderly lot of papers: there I found all my letters, away back to the American time.

Gissing was moved to see that she had kept mementos of her life with him – his photograph and one or two books in addition to the letters. Scattered around were pledges she had signed to abstain from drink. Nell had died of drink and syphilis, cold and hunger; but the doctor who was called in euphemistically wrote 'chronic laryngitis' on the death certificate. Gissing settled with a local undertaker the details of the plain burial (cost: six guineas). Then he 'looked long, long, at her face . . . but could not recognize it', he confided to the diary. 'She had changed horribly.' Pathetically, he added: 'In nothing am I to blame; I did my utmost . . . Fate was too strong. But as I stood beside that bed, I felt that my life . . . had a firmer purpose. Henceforth I shall never cease to bear testimony against the accursed social order that brings about things of this kind. I feel that she will help me more in her death than she balked me during her life. Poor, poor thing!' When he left the room the novelist took with him a small parcel of Nell's belongings, having decided not to attend the funeral. But on the next day he returned to Lambeth to see her again, this time in her coffin. 'Cut a little hair from her head, – I scarcely know why', he wrote in the diary. On this second visit her features seemed to him more recognizable; acting on impulse, he redeemed her pawned wedding-ring.

On 1 March he wrote to Algernon to inform him of Nell's death – adding at the bottom of the letter: 'now it behoves me to get to work . . . This memory of wretchedness will be an impulse such as few men possess.'

This 'impulse' was to be at the heart of *The Nether World*, a passionate book he began to write in a white heat on 19 March 1888 – less than three weeks after Nell's horrible death – and which he finished in July. Unlike most of Gissing's novels, this one, as we shall see, deals almost exclusively with the poor and virtually ignores the more prosperous classes. It was to be one of Gissing's most moving accounts of the effects of poverty on the human spirit. In a sense this was the dead Nell's first real bit of 'help' to her husband: by dying just when she did, at his most fallow period as a writer, she both stimulated his creative imagination and gave it a subject to work upon.

On 5 March Nell was buried at Tooting, the only mourners being her landlady and her landlady's husband to whom, in accordance with a popular practice in nineteenth-century England, Gissing had paid £3 to replace him at the ceremony.

CHAPTER 6

ꗘ

APPRENTICE TO LIFE, 1888–1889

The one need of my intellectual life is to deal a savage blow at
the influences which ruined all my early years.

The Emancipated

I have had no time; I have only been preparing myself – a mere
apprentice to life.

Gissing in 1900

I

AFTER Nell's death Gissing's psyche was a battlefield of sentiments. One part of him felt nothing but 'blank misery', as he
confessed to Ellen. At first he could write nothing. Nell's grisly end
preyed upon him; he must have felt some guilt for not having
known she was in want. According to Roberts, Gissing 'grieved for
her, grieved for what she might have been, and for what she was'.
He remembered now the heartbreaking messages she would send
asking for forgiveness. 'My dear chap', Gissing said to Roberts,
nearly in tears, 'she had kept my photograph . . . all these years of
horrible degradation.' In mid-March he told Ellen he thought he
might not live through another winter. He would not go out. 'All
day long I do absolutely *nothing*, I do not even read. Goodness
knows how I get through the hours . . . I cannot interest myself in
anything; I do not live, but merely support existence . . . I am a
hermit wherever I go. I merely carry a desert with me.'

And yet there was much to give him relief, and perhaps the guilt
he felt was due in part to a sense of thanksgiving. With Nell's death
an important segment of his old 'guilty secret' had disappeared – in
the flesh, anyway. The income he had been paying her could now
be devoted to his own needs. He was free of a terrible incubus.
Roberts's feelings on the matter were unequivocal:

There was nothing on earth more desirable for him than that she should die,
the poor wretch truly being like a destructive wind, for she had torn his
heart, scorched his very soul, and destroyed him in the beginning of his life.
All irreparable disasters came from her, and through her. Had it not been
for her he might then have held, or have begun to hope for, a great position
at one of the universities.

Of course the most interesting result of Nell's death was that it left the novelist free to marry again, or at least to think about marriage. No longer would such thoughts have to be part of a fantasy life. Surely the most important fact of Gissing's existence in the eighties was his chronic loneliness, which accounts for much of his savage moodiness and misanthropy. One should not suppose, however – as many Gissing scholars have done – that the novelist was always alone during these years or that he remained celibate. His libertinism, his strong sexual drive, his attractiveness to women and their attractiveness to him, his interest in the life of the streets and his taste for working-class girls all suggest that he availed himself of whatever opportunities came his way. Clearly he was not averse to picking women up – he met his first two wives in that way. Consider this passage in *The Crown of Life* about young Piers Otway, 'racked . . . with amorous frenzy' and footloose in London. 'He feared the streets at night-time; in his loneliness and misery, a gleam upon some wanton face would perchance have lured him, as had happened ere now. Not so much at the bidding of his youthful blood, as out of mere longing for companionship, the common cause of disorder in men condemned to solitude in great cities.' 'Never did silly mortal reap such harvest of experience', says Henry Ryecroft of his early years in London: 'never had any one so many bruises to show for it.' In *Eve's Ransom* the young Maurice Hilliard, alone in London, is 'all but frenzied with the violence of his sensual impulses'. Gissing's private writings are more reticent on such matters, naturally, but this tends rather to support my surmise than otherwise – especially when we remember that the novelist expected his diary to be read by others after his death. Still, there are some glimmerings in the letters. 'A . . . young man thinks chastity ridiculous', Gissing told Gabrielle Fleury some years later. He added: 'I am not made to live in solitude', and referred to a 'wandering of the desires' when younger. Waymark too has 'wandering desires'. In 'The Hope of Pessimism' Gissing had written: 'Our passions rack us with the unspeakable torment of desire . . . Our bodily frame is a house of torment, and the seat of lusts which obscure the soul.' Although the novelist was lonely for companionship, he probably was not sexually deprived; only rarely during these years does he complain of *sexual* frustration. One advantage of not moving much in 'respectable' circles was that he could meet women on a casual basis without causing scandal. Despite his passionate sentimentality about women and his lifelong desire for domestic stability, he was always more interested in living with women than in marrying them – a habit of mind he never really left behind him. 'I doubt if any of his ideas concerning women were at all romantic', Roberts said. He added: 'He was a man not without a certain sensuality' – and he went on to suggest that it was largely this side of Gissing's nature that 'kept him alive in spite of all his misery'. Coustillas refers to the novelist's 'chronic amorousness' and to 'his strong sexual instinct', apparent most often when he was living alone.

In any case he felt now, in the spring of 1888, the need for change. He thought of going abroad, hoping this time to see Italy, but felt he could not do so with a clear conscience until he had another novel ready and thus the prospect of some income while he travelled. He began to feel his loneliness more and more during the summer. 'It seems so miserable that a man at my age should be so utterly companionless', he wrote to Ellen. 'What I want is domestic society.' As he was writing *The Nether World* – March to July 1888 – he had brief moments of rebellion, though the work was going well. In May he noted in his diary his 'agony of loneliness. This becomes intolerable; in absolute truth, I am now and then on the verge of madness . . . This life I *cannot* live much longer; it is hideous.' There was a brief flurry of interest in a Miss Curtis, whose acquaintance Gissing had made, apparently, at Eastbourne, but after rushing off to see her one day in April he recorded the end of any hopes he might have entertained in that direction. This disappointment was mitigated by a more pleasant incident. Going one day to the Grosvenor Library to take out a subscription, Gissing was delighted when, upon identifying himself, he was saluted by the librarian: 'Ah, a very familiar name to us.'

As *The Nether World* progressed Gissing became aware of how sad a book it was. He tried to warn the people at Wakefield, who often seemed to take personal offence at his literary productions. 'I have no ambitions to dance jigs before the public', he wrote to Margaret in mid-April. 'You would wish for a more sanguine tone of writing, but . . . I am not sanguine with regard to any of the affairs of men.' The sombre hues of the new book were the result of many things in Gissing's life – solitude, overwork, poverty, his awful diet, fear of failure, the resolve he had made at Nell's bedside 'to bear testimony against the accursed social order', and – a new note – the suspicion that he would die soon. 'Strange how sternly I am possessed by the idea that I shall not live much longer', Gissing wrote in his diary in June 1888. 'Not a personal thought but is coloured with this conviction. I never look forward more than a year at the utmost; it is the habit of my mind, in utter sincerity to expect no longer tenure of life than that.' Gissing was thirty. 'Death, if it came now, would rob me of not one hope, for hopes I simply . . . have not', he wrote in his diary. Having decided he had but a short time to live, the novelist went on to give the probable cause of his death: 'I am haunted with the idea that I am consumptive. I never cough without putting a finger to my tongue to see if there is a sign of blood.' It was to take another decade, but finally he did manage to will bad lungs upon himself.

Of his complete solitude while he was writing *The Nether World* he remarked to Ellen: 'no one troubles me with invitations this season . . . I have secured this freedom by my constant refusals.' And yet he noted in his diary: 'I have lived in London ten years, and now . . . when I am very lonely and depressed, there is not one single house in which I should be welcome if I presented myself, not one family – nay, not one person – who would certainly receive me with good will.' This was not true; there were people who would gladly have received him had he made the effort to visit them.

In June and July Gissing reported he was reading Ibsen, whose work must have appealed to his current state of mind ('I never enjoy anything now – *never anything*', he wrote in his diary); survived another 'suicidal mood'; and, on 22 July, announced the completion of *The Nether World*.

As soon as the novel was finished, Gissing took it to Smith, Elder and then rushed off to Wakefield. Surprised to find himself in the grip of 'cheerfulness . . . I cannot think whence it comes', he went with the family in August to Seascale, Cumberland, for a holiday. This was not a success. The regular attendance of his mother and sisters at church twice on Sundays irritated him. His mother's monomaniacal domestic interests enraged him, as they always did: 'It is a sad, sad thing, that anyone would be rendered incapable of spiritual activity by ceaseless regard for kitchenware and the back steps.' Obviously she was uninterested in his work. He stayed with the family in Yorkshire for a while before going, in September, to visit Algernon and his wife in Broadway, Worcestershire. He had heard nothing from Payn, Smith, Elder's reader, about *The Nether World*; he was hoping they would give him enough for the book to enable him to go abroad immediately. Gissing's *Cornhill* serial had made him better known, and the brisk sale of the new cheap edition of *Demos* also should have heartened the publishers – so Gissing reasoned. But Payn ultimately told him he must wait longer to hear their decision on *The Nether World*; the cloth edition of *A Life's Morning* would be published in November, and no new book by Gissing could be brought out until the spring of 1889 without interfering with the sale of the earlier novel.

Gissing decided on a European tour anyway. Equipped with a frying pan, a spirit lamp, a kettle, a saucepan, and a German acquaintance named Plitt (of whom practically nothing is known; his chief virtue, it would seem, was his willingness to share the expenses of the trip), the novelist set off for the Continent on 26 September 1888. He planned to revisit France, and to fulfil the old yearning by seeing Italy at last.

II

The Nether World, set in penurious Clerkenwell, which Gissing had been studying carefully, is his most exhaustive treatment of poverty. Its great theme – poverty degrades – anticipates the argument of the more famous novels of the early nineties, *New Grub Street, Born in Exile,* and *The Odd Women.* But in *The Nether World* Gissing looks at poverty longer and harder than anywhere else, regarding the poor with his characteristic contempt, but also with the new passionate conviction that something has gone wrong in the social organism – the new understanding that settled upon him in the aftermath of Nell's death. There is at least some sympathy for the hapless and helpless and indignation at a state of things that could allow people to live and die like animals, unnoticed, and unattended.

'The effect of a struggle with mean necessity is seldom anything but degradation'; 'poverty makes a crime of every indulgence'; 'the anxieties which degrade' – *The Nether World* is about what poverty does to people, spiritually as well as physically. Chiefly, Gissing argues, it degrades them morally; they become spiritually diminished by 'the anxieties which degrade'. Gissing writes of this process with as much passion as he ever summoned on any subject: 'Oh that bitter curse of poverty, which puts corrupting poison into the wounds inflicted by nature, which outrages the spirit's tenderness, which profanes with unutterable defilement the secret places of the mourning heart!' The book both begins and ends with passionate perorations designed to call attention to the suffering of the indigent and to the 'brute forces of society' they face. This is not to suggest that Gissing suddenly became the champion of the poor. On the contrary. 'The London poor', he writes, are the 'least original and least articulate beings within the confines of civilisation.' The well-known account of the working-class mob on holiday at the Crystal Palace leaves an indelible impression. On 2 April (Easter) 1888 Gissing noted in his diary: 'Spent day at Crystal Palace and brought back a lot of good notes.' In *The Nether World*, during what is called 'a great review of the People', the novelist describes what he saw:

how respectable they are, how sober, how deadly dull! . . . Not one in a thousand shows the elements of taste in dress; vulgarity and worse glares in all but every costume. Observe the middle-aged women; it would be small surprise that their good looks had vanished, but whence comes it they are animal, repulsive, absolutely vicious in ugliness? Mark the men in their turn: four in every six have visages so deformed by ill-health that they excite disgust; their hair is cut down to within half an inch of the scalp; their legs are twisted out of shape by evil conditions of life from birth upwards . . . Since man came into being did the world ever exhibit a sadder spectacle?

The Gissing-*persona* of *The Nether World*, Sidney Kirkwood, is another poor man of working-class background with a passion for education and the instincts of an artist (he is a talented metal-worker and designer of jewellery). Ultimately he is defeated by lack of means and opportunity for self-advancement. At one time given to lecturing on social topics to his fellow workers, as the years go by Sidney becomes more and more sympathetic to their plight and indignant at the state of things that permits conditions so inimical to exist: 'As a younger man, he had believed that he knew what was meant by the struggle for existence in the nether world; it seemed to him now as if such knowledge had been only theoretical . . . He understood how men have gone mad under pressure of household cares.' As time goes by a 'profound' and 'ever-deepening' sympathy animates Sidney. Living amidst the poor, he comes to see their lives as inevitable products of unjust social conditions. While his compassion may deepen, Sidney learns to give up idealisms, to shun all *hopefulness* as 'the fatal error'. He is a Schopenhauerian. He is no ascetic. And he desperately wants the love of a woman.

There is something of Gissing too in Scawthorne, a self-made intellectual who, as 'a grave, gentle, somewhat effeminate boy, with a great love of books and a wonderful power of application to study', had suffered so much from want and worked so hard to get ahead that success, when it finally comes, arrives with the 'loss of all his pure ideals . . . Probably no one who is half-starved and overworked during those critical years comes out of the trial with his moral nature uninjured.' By the weight of sheer, uninterrupted, single-minded effort, Scawthorne ultimately makes the great leap forward into middle-class clerkdom, only to find that, 'notwithstanding his mental endowments, his keen social sense, his native tact, in all London not one refined home was open to him, not one domestic circle of educated people could he approach and find a welcome . . . Never had it been his lot to exchange a word with an educated woman' – a highly self-indulgent picture of the novelist's own position before the publication of *Demos*. Scawthorne's story illustrates a favourite Gissing maxim: whatever class you are born into remains your class forever, no matter how many artificial barriers you may pass in your social progress.

Sidney's conviction that the less hope one has for the future the less disappointed one is likely to be contributes to the novel's pessimism, but more importantly it is part of Gissing's continuing attack in *The Nether World* on idealistic schemes of philanthropy. 'Of all forms of insolence there is none more flagrant than that of the degraded poor receiving charity which they have come to regard as a right', declares the novelist. *The Nether World* propounds a sort of *laissez-faire*, social Darwinist view of the problem of poor relief. It is wrong to tamper with a social fabric which by its nature is unalterable and in any social system there will be rich and poor.

Michael Snowdon is the useless philanthropist. The 'struggle between the idealist tendency . . . and stubborn everyday sense, supported by his knowledge of the world', drives Michael to the fringes of madness; his blind fanaticism is Gissing's metaphor for the futility of all attempts to help the poor. Michael's 'playing with people's lives, as fanatics always do', brings nothing but misery to a number of people. In the end he becomes a monstrous angel of charity – monomaniacally self-indulgent, no less selfish than any ordinary egotist. In Dickens's novels it is often the charitable plutocrat, the Cheeryble brothers or the chastened Scrooge, who is singled out for unstinting praise; in *The Nether World* the would-be dispenser of charity, substituting philanthropy for religion and having become the victim of selfish delusions, goes crazy and dies.

These themes contribute to the monolithic pessimism of *The Nether World*: it is Gissing's darkest novel. The pessimism is rarely subtle, and it is everywhere – especially evident in passages about 'Fate', which is seen by the characters as a powerful negative force in their lives; indeed, they consider themselves its hostages. And with good reason: Fate in *The Nether World* is up to no good. The 'vice inherent in the nature of things', as Sidney puts it, makes it inevitable that everything will turn out for the worst in the worst of all possible worlds. As in Hardy's later novels there is the sense of a world out of control. The phrase 'things were wrong somehow' runs through *The Nether World* like a refrain; so do references to 'the tyranny of circumstances'. Mankind's 'faith that a good deed will not fail of reward' is said to be 'pathetic'; there is no poetic or any other kind of justice. 'How can . . . any of us help what we're driven to in a world like this?' Sidney asks.

The novel abounds in fortuitous deaths – deaths seen as an end of suffering for the world's 'superfluous' population. Most striking of all in this connection are the novelist's comments on children. The 'only piece of good fortune' to happen to the Hewett family in the course of two years is the death of the youngest child. 'Thank goodness for that', the father exclaims. The children one sees in the streets of the nether world are not the innocent, dewy-eyed, lovable, playful progeny of Dickens's poor: 'On all the doorsteps sat little girls, themselves just out of infancy, nursing or neglecting bald, red-eyed, doughy-limbed abortions in every stage of baby-hood, hapless spawn of diseased humanity, born to embitter and brutalise yet further the lot of those who unwillingly gave them life.' Here Gissing uses images of city life for what Korg has aptly called an 'iconography of degradation.'

The waste-land motif that was so vital a part of *Demos* comes back with a vengeance in *The Nether World*. Descriptions of an inner city in the clutch of alien forces are unprecedentedly vivid. The London streets are full of 'thin clouds of unsavoury dust', the air has a 'stifling smell and a bitter taste'. As in *Bleak House* and *Thyrza*, the physical environment takes its touch and texture from the moral life in its midst. When it rains, along with the water descends 'the smut and grime' that characterize the neighbourhood; 'the pavement was speedily over-smeared with sticky mud . . . Odours of oil and shoddy . . . grew more pungent.' In Shooter's Gardens, rock-bottom Clerkenwell, 'the walls stood in a perpetual black sweat; a mouldy reek came from the open door-ways; the beings that passed in and out seemed soaked with grimy moisture, puffed into distortions, hung about with rotting garments.' Gissing's debt to Dickens is plain here. When, after weeks of fog, darkness, and rain the sun momentarily appears, Clerkenwell, like a shy tramp peering into the beam of a flashlight, cringes in all its ugliness from the unfamiliar illumination. Gissing puts some characters on a train travelling from the city to the country to underline the contrast between the slums and what lies beyond them:

Over the pest-stricken regions of East London, sweltering in sunshine which served only to reveal the intimacies of abomination; across miles of a city of the damned, such as thought never conceived before this age of ours; above streets swarming with a nameless populace, cruelly exposed by the unwonted light of heaven; stopping at stations which it crushes the heart to think should be the destination of any mortal; the train made its way . . . beyond the outmost limits of dread, and entered upon a land of level meadows, of hedges and trees, of crops and cattle.

In a Commonplace Book entry for 1889 Gissing addresses himself specifically to the differences between himself and Dickens in so far as their literary treatment of the poor is concerned: 'I am constantly astonished to think of the small use Dickens made of his vast opportunities; in the matter of observation among the lower classes. The explanation . . . is, that he did not conceive of a work of fiction as anything but a *romance*. The details which would to me be most precious, he left aside as unsuitable because unattractive to the multitude of novel-readers.' Gissing was no romancer; the 'details' most precious to him were those which most vividly illuminated the ordinary daily existence of the poor.

Still, in terms both of subject-matter and of plot, *The Nether World* owes a good deal to Dickens and the more 'romantic' (that is to say, early Victorian) school of nineteenth-century realism. The subject is the urban poor, the plot hinges on murder, revenge, lost identities, secret relationships, unexecuted wills, and so on. The Byass family and Pennyloaf Candy are pure Dickens. The idea for the Peckover/Snowdon marriage (each thinks the other has money) probably came from the story of the Lammles in *Our Mutual Friend*. There is much here, in sum, that is both like and unlike Dickens. Ten years later Gissing was to attempt a resolution of his ambivalent feelings about his great predecessor by writing a critical study of Dickens. But by then he had long since given up writing low-life novels.

III

'For me Rome is the centre of the Universe. I must go thither . . . if I beg my way. I dare not read a book about Rome, it gives me a sort of *angina pectoris*, a physical pain, so extreme is my desire to go there.' So Gissing had written to Ellen three years earlier. In Paris in October 1888, noting in his diary Smith, Elder's offer of £150 for

The Nether World and his acceptance, he saw the money in very
specific terms: 'This will enable me to go to Italy.' He added: 'The
knowledge that I am safe from penury for a year has helped me
wonderfully.' It was the highest price he had ever received for a
book – though it was not especially generous, considering his new
fame. The publishers said, predictably, that they could not offer
more because the sale of his other books remained slow.

Gissing went to work learning Italian. His lifelong passion for
Italy stemmed from his study of the classics; he looked forward to
the journey south with enormous excitement. 'Italy, Italy! think
that I am really going thither at last, a thing I never dared to hope',
he wrote to Bertz. 'My real life is beginning.' The death of Nell, the
temporary abatement of financial anxiety, the opportunity to travel
– Gissing saw the possibility of a new life opening up before him.

He spent several weeks in Paris going to the theatre, visiting
museums and art-galleries, attending public lectures – and scouting
out the graves of Gautier, Murger, Heine, Balzac, Rachel,
Michelet, and Chopin (the tombs of some of these are described in
his diary; it is typical of Gissing that he spent so much time in
cemeteries – on his first visit to France, he had rushed directly off to
the city morgue).

Several days before he left Paris, Gissing wrote in the diary of his
growing interest in European culture and his waning interest in the
problems of the poor – problems he felt relieved to leave behind in
England. 'I experience at present a profound dislike for everything
that concerns the life of the people', he observed. He now
considered himself 'a poet, pure and simple . . . an idealist student
of art'. It was in this cathartic spirit, now that *The Nether World*
was behind him, that the rest of his European tour was undertaken.
As Korg has noted, it was the beginning of a permanent change in
Gissing, for when he returned to England and to novel-writing he
ignored many of the low-life themes that had dominated his first
decade of writing.

Along with Plitt, Gissing departed by train for Marseilles late in
October. He could not take his eyes from the passing countryside –
it was his first glimpse of southern Europe. At Marseilles they took
ship for Naples. As Italy came into sight at last, Gissing wrote to
Ellen: 'It makes me choke in the throat and tears come to my
eyes.' The Mediterranean shore led him to dream of the ancient
civilizations he loved so much.

It was almost inevitable that a classical scholar from the North
would fall in love with Italy, and Gissing quickly proceeded to do

so. 'Impossible, impossible to imagine it!' he wrote to Bertz. And to Ellen: 'No words can give the faintest idea of it [Naples]; no painted picture is of any use. You must come here or be content to know nothing about it . . . No, no; one can't speak of it! . . . I live in a sort of half craziness, and it will be long before I can write coherently.' Five days after his arrival Gissing was making invidious comparisons with French culture. 'In every way I prefer the life and customs to those of France', he wrote in his diary – not least because his anti-democratic temperament welcomed life 'under a monarchy once more!' (France was a republic).

As he had done in Paris, so here in Naples – and again in Rome, Florence, and Venice, for that matter – Gissing made straight for the cemeteries and wandered happily among the tombs of the dead, noting inscriptions and memorial tablets.

Always frugal, he had no trouble paring his living expenses to the bone in Italy. But he did not deprive himself. Typically, he wanted to see everything; *The Emancipated* – and, much later, *By the Ionian Sea* – give eloquent testimony to all that he did see, and to all that he so carefully remembered, on this and future visits to Italy. He was especially struck by the rich street life of the South – the hawking of merchandise up and down every avenue, the tremendous traffic at all hours, the crowds of people and their animals everywhere, the ubiquitous clergy, and the constant sound of the street-organs, which he came especially to love (and even to miss in other Italian cities). He liked the food, particularly the profusion of fresh fruit, and he acquired readily enough the custom of taking a moderate amount of wine with his meals. He was delighted by the Italian temperament and seemed for a while fully to forget the problems of the poor, even though there were a great many more poor in Italy than in England. Almost every day he took long walks through the towns surrounding Naples, noting places of literary and historical interest. He went off for several days to Pompeii, Amalfi, Salerno, and Paestum.

On 15 November 1888 *A Life's Morning* was at last published. The novelist confided to his diary: 'I rejoice unspeakably that I am out of the way.' Telling Bertz a copy would be sent to him, Gissing added: 'I implore you not to speak to me about it. It is trash. Wait for "The Nether World", and, I beg, do not think I am falling into dotage.' Besides Bertz, Algernon was the only other person to receive a copy of *A Life's Morning* from the publishers, upon Gissing's instructions (even Harrison was excluded).

Despite Gissing's well-founded fears, the critical reception of *A*

Life's Morning was astonishingly good. Among two-dozen or so reviews of the novel there was only one really savage notice (in *Vanity Fair*). The *Spectator* condemned the book but was not too severe. Several reviewers assumed that *A Life's Morning* was written after *Demos* and *Thyrza* (a reasonable assumption) and rated it an advance over its supposed predecessors (certainly unreasonable; but one should never underestimate the appetite of Victorian readers for happy endings). The *Whitehall Review* called it Gissing's masterpiece. The *Saturday Review* said the novel had 'a wider sense of beauty and a broader feeling of human possibilities' than any of Gissing's previously published books. It noted the influence of Meredith upon his work. The *Athenaeum* pronounced *A Life's Morning* 'excellent' (though the reviewer did object to the book's moralizing and the orotundity of its style). The *Guardian* gave Gissing generous praise but condemned what it called the 'moral' of his book – 'that life is a hopeless and degrading toil for all who have not the means of culture; and that the means of culture are wealth, power, and worldly position.' If the reviewers preferred any character in the novel it was Beatrice Redwing; neither Wilfrid nor Emily was a general favourite. Still, not for the first time Gissing fared better with the reviewers than he deserved. Some echoes of the warm reception received by *A Life's Morning* reached the surprised novelist in Italy, but Gissing, to his credit, never liked the book much, always refused to take it seriously, and often referred to it contemptuously in later years – 'miserable rubbish' he called it in 1898, by which time the novel had already gone through several of the ten English editions which made it, ironically, one of Gissing's most popular tales with contemporary readers.

IV

On his thirty-first birthday – 22 November 1888 – Gissing climbed Vesuvius on horseback with a guide, lunched on bread, cheese, and wine, and in the evening met a British expatriate acquaintance, John Wood Shortridge, at a nearby inn for dinner. They were surrounded by German travellers and spent a pleasant evening; the incident is faithfully recreated in the sixth chapter of *The Emancipated*. The novelist stopped at Capri on his way back from Naples; and on 29 November he set off for Rome, ridding himself of Plitt (though they were to meet again).

As might be expected, Gissing took to Rome immediately, visiting the Forum and the Colosseum on his first day there, the graves of Keats and Shelley in the Protestant Cemetery on the second, and rarely slowing the pace thereafter. He found Roman street life quieter and less interesting than Neapolitan. He spent the month of December systematically studying Roman culture and art, especially painting and sculpture (as the heroine of his next novel, Miriam Baske, was to do). Generally he was interested in secular and pagan Rome, and in Christianity primarily as history. Religious painting he found '*deadly uninteresting* . . . The art of Christianity makes no appeal to me, because I do not feel – have *never* felt – the least vital interest in Christianity itself', he wrote to Bertz. In a later letter to Bertz he says: 'I have been taught in these days how intensely classical are my sympathies; if indeed I needed the lesson.' His next holiday, he vowed, would be devoted to Sicily (he never went there) and Greece. 'It only remains for me to go to Greece, then I shall have all the ground work of education. The education itself must be the work of my life', he wrote to Ellen. To Margaret he grumbled about the prudery and asceticism which resulted in the draping of some of Michelangelo's figures in the Sistine Chapel (where he spent many hours) and the placing of fig-leaves on statues. Nevertheless: 'in the museums of the Vatican I walk about in a state of exultation, waving my arms and *shouting* in a suppressed voice', he told his sister. 'I thought I had formed an idea of ancient Rome but I had done nothing of the kind. I had not a notion of such magnificence. What paltry houses our modern towns consist of in comparison!'

Obviously this was a time of contentment for Gissing. He noted in his diary 'wonderful happiness of mind' and attributed it to 'the consideration of beautiful things, wholly undisturbed by base necessities and considerations'. As he had done in Naples, in Rome he took one excursion after another, visiting a number of towns around the city.

At the end of December he left for Florence. On New Year's Eve he walked around the city, dining amidst tumultuous Florentines. The 'exuberant spirits' around him suddenly made him feel 'wretched', he wrote in his diary. 'At midnight they all began to shout and stamp and ring bells, etc. – a terrific uproar. I rushed out into the street.'

Thus ended 1888.

v

Gissing found Florence less exciting than Naples or Rome – more Christian, less pagan, and uncomfortably colder. 'Amidst the most splendid artistic work of the Renaissance, I felt a heart-ache for the Forum Romanum', he wrote to Bertz in January. In the same letter he let loose a blast against English tourists in Italy: 'Many of them are absolute shop-boys and work-girls. How in heaven's name do they get enough money to come here? And where are the good cultured people?' He wished, obviously, to think of himself, in his European travels, as keeping exclusive company. He concludes rather intemperately: 'Every day I saw people whom I should like to have assaulted. What business have these gross animals in such places?'

After more than three months away from England, Gissing was beginning to get restless. He received news in January that the first proofs of *The Nether World* were ready – a reminder that he must soon get back to work. He was also getting lonely; but when Bertz invited him to visit Germany on his way back to England, Gissing declined on the ground that he had not enough money to avoid cutting a poor figure among new acquaintances. 'I am not respectable enough in appearance', he wrote to Bertz. 'I should . . . have embarrassed [your friends], and discredited you.' This sounds like the old Gissing. But he remained jubilant about his Italian experiences. What he had seen and learned on this trip he would never forget; 'all these things are realities to me, and, as long as I keep my memory, no one can rob me of them', he told Ellen. Still, he quickly tired of Florence. Late in January he departed for Venice, which he liked better. No Italian city, however, had for him the excitement of Naples; he missed in the others the Neapolitan street life, especially the distinctive street organs: 'my whole life is brightened by a little music, however poor' (Henry Ryecroft says the same thing about himself). While in Venice he corrected the proofs of the first half-volume of *The Nether World* – telling Bertz, 'This time I . . . honestly . . . believe the work to be good.' He prophesied that in the twentieth century, because of the modern passion for 'improvement' and rebuilding, 'the Italy of antiquity and of the Renaissance will . . . be only a tradition, supported by the evidence of a few museums and much-restored buildings.' Deciding to set his next story partly in Italy, he began to work out while in Venice the plan of *The Emancipated*.

Having by the latter part of February 1889 finished correcting the proofs of *The Nether World* up to the end of the second volume, Gissing decided to return home in time for the novel's publication, scheduled for early April. Before his departure he sent off to Smith, Elder an epigraph for the title-page (printed in the first edition only) – a quotation from a speech of Renan's he had just read, of which the English translation reads: 'A painting of a dung-heap might be justified if a beautiful flower grew out of it; otherwise the dung-heap is merely repulsive.' Late in February he left Venice, returning to England via Brussels – where he wandered about thinking of Charlotte Brontë, her stay there, and her use of the city as a setting in *Villette*. He arrived back in London, after an absence of nearly six months, on 1 March. Exactly one year had passed since the death of Nell.

VI

'So it is all over – alas! alas! But the memory remains, and you shall see what I make of it.' So Gissing wrote, thinking of his new novel, to Bertz on the day he arrived back in England. After a brief trip to Wakefield, during which he finished correcting the last proofs of *The Nether World*, he returned to London on a day of 'sludge unutterable' and tried to re-apply himself to the gruelling routine of earning a living by his pen.

Walking around the West End one evening he was struck anew by the comparative wealth of the people he observed there entertaining themselves: 'With not one penny to spend on pleasures, I am entirely shut out from the new theatres and palaces that I should like to see', he confided to his diary. 'For years I have not had a single pleasure that was unalloyed – that was not consciously interfered with by miserable thoughts', he wrote to Ellen. The latter part of March he devoted to working in earnest on *The Emancipated* (at first called 'The Puritan'). He spent some time at the British Museum gathering information on Naples in 1880, the scene of the book's opening chapters. He found it hard to keep momentum going – not only because he was 'rusty', but also because, as Korg reminds us, this was in effect 'the beginning of a new phase of his career', his first sustained examination of the less sensational material of middle-class life that had grown so interesting to him during his six months away from English squalor. From the middle of March to the end of May 1889 he waged a mighty battle with his new book, writing at least three different versions of the first half-dozen chapters. Finally he laid aside the theme of poverty – but not without a struggle.

Gissing had some society at this time, including that of Roberts, the Gaussens, and the Harrisons. 'Found idiots there', he remarked of one visit to the Gaussens. 'The deuce take these interruptions of regular work.' Towards the end of March, Roberts introduced him to W. H. Hudson, then an obscure naturalist surviving (barely) on the income of a boarding-house run by his wife. Hudson, his friend the painter Alfred Hartley, Roberts, and Gissing were to meet fairly regularly for a while to rail against the philistines and discuss art and literature.

On 3 April 1889 *The Nether World* was published, and Gissing sent copies off to Roberts, Bertz, and the family at Wakefield. Roberts loved it. The novel shocked and sickened the family, as Gissing's more depressing slum-life studies always did, but he refused to let himself be disturbed by their reaction. Bertz took his time with the book, finally writing to praise it highly. Among other things he called it the most 'classical' of Gissing's novels to date; but he warned that the public was likely to be less enthusiastic. The novelist replied that he would 'never again deal directly with that subject', and added: 'Heavens! the labour that book cost me!' Each novel, he said, was harder to write than the last. 'I exhaust myself in toil – and the public pays no heed.'

In April, Algernon consulted his brother about his own career. He had not made much money either as a lawyer or a novelist; might he do something with short stories? 'I myself cannot write them', came back the reply. 'This . . . matter of short stories is an exceedingly difficult one.' He went on to give Algernon some general literary advice: he should 'have nothing whatever of a *disagreeable* kind' in his fiction; he should 'keep clear of sexual complications'; 'avoid . . . what is called sentiment'; and be, whenever possible, optimistic – 'a great aid . . . in writing for the public'. Gissing concludes poignantly: 'The accursed complication of literary endeavour with the struggle for subsistence is . . . one of the most harassing things humanity has ever known. The utter impossibility of giving help in the struggle makes it seem all the harder, to those who are aware of it.' Plitt turned up briefly to tell Gissing of a mistress he had kept in Rome. The envious novelist recorded in his diary that he 'made me so wretched in my loneliness that work was impossible'.

The notices of *The Nether World* were mixed. The *Academy*, the *Saturday Review*, and the *Spectator* ignored the book altogether. The *Daily Chronicle* and the *Illustrated London News* were lukewarm, the *Athenaeum* hostile. *Vanity Fair*, the *Whitehall*

Review, and the *World* praised the novel. The book's 'brutal accuracy' was lauded by the *Guardian*. Frederick W. Farrar, the well-known Archdeacon of Westminster (and the author of the best-selling *Eric, or Little by Little*), contributed to the *Contemporary Review* a long essay on *The Nether World* which managed to avoid mentioning the novelist's name anywhere (only an English cleric would be capable of that, Gissing noted to Bertz). Farrar praises Gissing for a realism that has 'in it none of that leprous naturalism . . . of Zola and his school'. He added that 'not one touch of wretchedness' was exaggerated in the book.

Its publication also provided the occasion for a long article on Gissing by Bertz, which appeared in the *Deutsche Presse* later in the year. Much of this essay may be dismissed as special pleading, but parts of it are of interest if only because the opinions expressed are those of Gissing's most intimate friend. According to Bertz, 'Gissing . . . cannot turn aside from human misery; it fascinates him to capture in words what has shaken him to the very core' – a fair reflection of the autobiographical impulse behind so much of Gissing's work. 'There is a pronounced aristocratic trait in his character', Bertz observes, 'which stems from his spiritual thirst for beauty – every contact with the common inspires him with feelings of aversion.' Bertz goes on to comment on Gissing's 'deeply pessimistic view of the world', due largely to the gap observed everywhere by the novelist between the actual and the ideal and to the 'resignation' of the novelist when faced by this insoluble problem.

As usual, Smith, Elder made a tidy profit from *The Nether World*, none of which (after the £150 he was paid for the copyright) found its way into Gissing's hands. As early as September 1889 a six-shilling edition was announced. The book continued to do fairly well for years.

VII

In late May 1889 Gissing paid another visit to Wakefield ('this home of Puritanism', as he called it), where he finally began to make some progress on the new novel. But he was still unhappy. 'I am deeply discontented with the outer circumstances of my life, wherever it be led', he wrote to Bertz. 'I wonder whether I shall ever have a home of my own? Most probably not.' In this he was right. Gissing's stay in Wakefield was extended to mid-August, both because his flat in London was being painted and because he found, to his astonishment, that he could work in Yorkshire. He paid his mother for his room and board. Close and extended exposure to her and his sisters soon irritated him in the usual ways, however, and he complains in his diary about 'the paltry kind of talk that always goes on at meals . . . never does an abstract subject come up; only local facts, and those the meanest.' Still, the new novel was getting itself written, despite periodic bouts of depression, and on 15 August it was finished. He wondered whether it might not be too 'emancipated' for any publisher. A few days later he and his sister Margaret went up to London, where the novelist delivered the manuscript to Bentley, who, he thought, might offer more for it than Smith, and then travelled on with her to Guernsey for several weeks' holiday. At the end of August they moved over to Sark for another fortnight's stay. The brother and sister seemed to get along well enough, though Gissing notes in his diary 'The usual Sabbath difficulties' (presumably Margaret wanted him to go to church with her). Soon he was 'desperate for lack of conversation'; by mid-September they were back in London.

Bentley liked *The Emancipated* and asked Gissing to suggest terms. The novelist offered to sell the copyright for £250; Bentley said he would think it over. Late in September Gissing noted that he had only £5 left in the bank – a desperate situation. Fortunately Bentley offered a fairly generous price for the new novel – £150 outright, £50 more when 850 copies were sold, and an additional £50 when 1,000 were sold. Gissing accepted immediately.

VIII

The Emancipated is the first of a series of novels about the middle class which Gissing wrote during this period of his life. The old denunciatory tone is replaced here by a more urbane irony, as Korg notes; it is as if Gissing had finally placed behind him the dark periods of his life (indeed, he told Bertz at this time that he would never again read his early novels – they would remind him too acutely, he said, of his past sufferings). Of course the early period was always part of his memory, part of what he was and thus of his work; but for the next few years the novelist's focus is on the genteel, with whom he now felt more at home, rather than on the downtrodden.

The novel's opening chapters, set in Naples, reflect Gissing's love of the place in their tender, passionate description of the city and the surrounding countryside. Gissing knew the area around the Bay of Naples well and uses it unstintingly here. Cecily Doran even sketches it, as the novelist himself did; and Mallard's visits to such places as Amalfi and Paestum are also drawn directly from Gissing's experiences. There is cogent description of the uproar of the Neapolitan streets – of the hawkers, the organ-grinders, the church bells, the priests, soldiers, thieves, and costermongers who contribute to the startling and continuous cacophony.

But as a fresh beginning *The Emancipated* is a disappointment. It is mostly about religion and art: more specifically, it elucidates the moral and educational process that must take place in the puritan psyche before it can be reconciled to the respectability of art. Religion here appears in the person of Miriam Baske, who undergoes the sort of secular conversion Gissing undoubtedly wished on his sister Margaret ('My poor sister is a Puritan' and busies herself with 'some dirty little pietistic work', Gissing noted while in Sark with her). Art is embodied in Ross Mallard, a more restrained and middle-class version of the old Gissing-*persona*: Bernard Kingcote in a frock coat. The 'emancipation' at issue is that from narrow prejudice, mostly female, in social and religious matters. Gissing was later to explain the novel's title to Bertz thus: ' "The Emancipated" simply means the English people who have delivered themselves from the bondage of dogma and from the narrow views of morality that go therewith.' The book does not argue for the emancipation of women – except from ignorance; indeed, it suggests that some women think too much, are too much emancipated from traditional roles. On the subject of the emancipation of women from ordinary domesticity the novel is sometimes incoherent – declaring, as Gissing himself believed, that ignorant women make poor wives, but that truly emancipated women make worse ones.

The commentary on religion is not subtle. Gissing attacks English puritanism with special vigour. Miriam, in early sections of *The Emancipated*, is his exemplar of the perils of puritanism. Repressed, cold, joyless, she refuses to open herself to literature, art, music, or other 'frivolous' amusements. This is the result of the training she received during her youth in Yorkshire; she has been an apt pupil. Gissing writes as a man with a special grudge against Yorkshire and puritanism. Later, when Miriam's eyes have been opened by the growth of new feelings, new emotions, new tastes, she comes to see that 'The religion of my childhood was one of bitterness and violence and arbitrary judgment and hatred.' Going back to her Yorkshire town after some months in Europe and 'approaching with new eyes that narrow provincial life, she could scarcely believe it had once been her own' – something Gissing himself was surely used to feeling whenever he went home.

Throughout he refuses to admit that puritanism's adherents might be sincere. 'The vast majority of English people are constantly guilty of hypocritical practices', he says, which 'is mere testimony to the rootedness of their orthodox faith'. Puritanism is the national hypocrisy, Clifford Marsh says, and Elgar, in response, ties puritanism to *demos*:

The representative English bourgeois is a hypocrite in essence, but is perfectly serious in his judgment of the man next door . . . Puritanism has aided the material progress of England; but its effect on art! . . . Depend upon it, the democracy will continue to be Puritan. Every picture, every book, will be tried by the same imbecile test. Enforcement of Puritan morality will be one of the ways in which the mob, come to power, will revenge itself on those who still remain its superiors.

The close connection Gissing saw between 'the mob' and bourgeois morality helps explain both his lifelong anti-democratic bias and his hatred of asceticism and English puritanism – feelings perceptible everywhere in his work. 'The multitude will *never* be humanised', Marsh declares in *The Emancipated*. 'Civilization is attainable only by the few; nature so ordains it.' Art must suffer wherever *demos* reigns: 'Democracy is the fatal enemy of art.' Neither Greece nor Italy has ever had a genuine democracy, Marsh argues, and yet these two countries have produced the world's greatest art. Here is Gissing the classicist speaking. 'Democracy is simply the triumph of ignorance and brutality', Marsh continues. 'Socialism, communism, collectivism, parliamentarism, – all these have one and the same end: to put men on an equality; and in proportion as that end is approached, so will art in every shape languish. Art . . . is nourished upon inequalities and injustices!'

The novelist's assumption that puritanical Christianity is antipathetic to art is another reason why he prefers pagan art to that of the Renaissance. We have seen how thoroughly bored he was in Rome and Florence by the religious subjects of the Renaissance painters, technically brilliant though they might be. 'His real interest in religion', says Morley Roberts, 'seemed to lie in his notion that it was a curious form of delusion almost ineradicable from the human mind.' An entry in the Commonplace Book for 1887 sums up Gissing's feelings about religious doctrines and the controversies they spawn: 'The one thing which must excite me to irresistible laughter . . . is the existence of religious prejudice. To think that people will loathe you, because you cannot enter into their way of thought with regard to the Universe! It is far more comical than "You be eternally damned for your theory of Irregular Verbs!"'

Several familiar themes run through *The Emancipated*. One of these, in counterpoint to Miriam's early prejudices, argues the superiority of artists to other men and of art to other things. 'An artist is privileged', Cecily declares. 'The common terms of society have no application to him.' 'An artist', Mallard says, 'should have nothing to do with domesticities' – an artistic 'privilege' very close to Gissing's heart. Elgar tells his wife that soon they would 'hate the sight of each other' should he fail as a writer: he would have to take a clerkship, and move his family into a garret. 'I think that would kill my love in time', Cecily admits. 'Of course it would', Elgar says. Here is the plot of *New Grub Street*.

The Emancipated has a good deal to say about marriage, and some of Gissing's characteristic neuroses on this subject are displayed. 'How absurd it was for two people, just because they were married, to live perpetually within sight of each other! Wasn't it Godwin who, on marrying, made an arrangement that he and his wife should inhabit separate abodes, and be together only when they wished?' Thus muses Elgar. In Gissing's view the mere fact of any couple living together for long 'makes love impossible . . . How many wives and husbands love each other? Not one pair in five thousand.'

Even so, Elgar cannot read the marriage-column in a newspaper without feeling 'a distinct jealousy of all the male creatures there mentioned' (Kingcote in *Isabel Clarendon,* on the other hand, laughs uproariously at the accounts he reads in newspapers of other people's happiness).

Elgar's creative impulses resemble Gissing's. 'The one need of my intellectual life is to deal a savage blow at the influences which ruined all my early years', he says. No one can know, he adds, 'the fierce hatred with which I am moved when I look back'. He can write, he declares, only 'on some subject which deeply concerns me – me myself, as an individual'. Hating the ruinous 'influences' of his early years, he is moved most profoundly as a writer by himself as subject. Elgar also lacks the social graces:

He . . . was not the kind of man who shines in company. He had never been trained to social usages, and he could not feel at ease in any drawing-room but his own. The Bohemianism of his early life had even given him a positive distaste for social obligations and formalities. Among men of his own way of thinking, he could talk vigorously, and as a rule keep the lead in conversation; but where restraint in phrase was needful, he easily became flaccid, and the feeling that he did not show to advantage filled him with disgust.

This is a fairly exact description of Gissing in his early thirties. He still could not forget the 'Bohemianism' – a euphemism – of his early years. At ease with his friends, he was never completely comfortable in other people's drawing-rooms.

But the Gissing of 1888 to 1889 is personified mostly in Mallard. The fact that Mallard is middle-class rather than working-class signals the change of focus I have mentioned. Gone are the Arthur Goldings, Osmond Waymarks, Bernard Kingcotes, and Sidney Kirkwoods. Like Edwin Reardon, Godwin Peak, Denzil Quarrier, and Everard Barfoot – protagonists of the next novels Gissing was to write – Mallard moves among middle-class acquaintances in a way that would have been impossible for the heroes of the earlier novels, as it would have been for the younger Gissing himself.

Mallard burns 'with inner fires'. His face is so designed, says the novelist, to express 'bitter ironies or stern resentments'. Like Gissing, he has 'a heavy moustache, but no beard'. In his clothing too he resembles the novelist: 'To matters of costume he . . . gave little thought, for his clothes, though of the kind a gentleman would wear . . . had seen their best days, and the waistcoat even lacked one of its buttons' – a sign of careless bachelorhood. 'The necessity of donning society's uniform always drew many growls from him; he never felt at ease in [evening clothes], and had a suspicion that he looked ridiculous.' So he shuns polite society. At the end of the novel Mallard's wedded bliss is described in terms obviously appealing to the novelist. The little house Mallard and Miriam occupy is 'inwardly rich with whatever the heart or brain can desire. Hither came no payers of formal calls, no leavers of cards, no pests from the humdrum world to open their mouths and utter foolishness. It was a dwelling sacred to love and art.'

Like Golding, Waymark, Kingcote, Egremont, Gilbert Grail, and a good many heroes in later Gissing novels, Mallard has in England a mother and sisters. With them are associated in his mind thoughts 'grim, cold and sunless . . . These relatives still lived where his boyhood had been passed, a life . . . alien to his sympathies, but their house was still all he could call home. Was it to be always the same?' Gissing would admit to Ellen later that he drew on the Wakefield milieu for his attack in *The Emancipated* on 'cold' convention and life 'alien to his sympathies'. As we know, the question of whether or not he would ever have a real home of his own was one he was asking himself in the late eighties. 'Since I was a boy, I have known nothing of domestic regularity', Mallard declares. Like Gissing, he is 'a lonely man . . . but not content with loneliness'. He is also said to represent 'a curious instance of the Puritan conscience surviving in a man whose intellect is liberated'. Without 'this conscientiousness . . . [he] would have had worldly success long ago' as an artist. 'The one object I have in life', he says, 'is to paint a bit of the world just as I see it. I exhaust myself in vain toil; I shall never succeed; but I am right to persevere, I am right to go on pleasing myself.' This is an eloquent evocation of Gissing's attitude towards his work and of the mixture of idealism and fatalism with which he approached it.

Mallard's moodiness also resembles the novelist's. 'Do you *never* relax?' Elgar asks Mallard. It was something Gissing's friends often wondered about him. Until the end of the novel Mallard, in the tradition of the earlier protagonists, is a grim man. 'What joy in the world that does not represent a counterbalance of sorrow? What blessedness poured upon one head but some other must therefore lie down under malediction?' Mallard even composes his own epitaph (a favourite pastime of Gissing's): 'Here lie I, Ross Mallard; who can say no good of myself, yet have as little right to say ill; who had no faith whereby to direct my steps, yet often felt that some such was needful; who spent all my strength on a task which I knew to be vain; who suffered much and joyed rarely; whose happiest day was his last.'

The Emancipated is less pessimistic than its predecessors, having been written – though with much difficulty – in the aftermath of the novelist's exciting travels abroad. But while the subjects and the milieux of the books may change, the Gissing touch is always recognizable.

IX

In September 1889 Gissing told Bertz that he was working on the outline of a new novel to be called 'The Head Mistress', which would deal with the 'female education' question. The scene was to be a girls' school in the provinces. The novelist noted with some satisfaction that his name was tolerably well known now wherever he went: '*I cannot stand obscurity.*' Writing to Algernon in October,

Gissing predicted that *The Emancipated* 'will give a good deal of offence, for the satire is rather savage in places, especially that directed against religious formalism. At [Wakefield] the book will not be liked, but I cannot help that.' From now on, he said, he intended to please himself about what he wrote. 'The better I become known . . . the freer hand I shall have, and it is by no means my intention to neglect this advantage.' Several weeks after he wrote to Ellen: 'Have I not gone through enough misery? Who has experienced more – other things being equal?' Already he was thinking of another journey abroad, he told Ellen. 'That is my way of making life endurable. Other people have domestic interests . . . if my life is to be a lonely one, I must travel much.'

Much of October 1889 was devoted to correcting the first proofs of *The Emancipated*. He also worked on his plan for the new novel, reading up on 'Women Literature', as he called it, at the British Museum in his spare time. 'The Head Mistress' was destined to be abandoned before completion, but Gissing would make use of his reading in several subsequent novels, most notably in *The Odd Women*.

In November he concluded a letter to Bertz with several poignant comments. 'I suffer more and more from my solitude', he said. As a result of this, and because of his poverty, he admits that he writes far too much, but he cannot help it; 'perhaps some day I shall earn enough to enable me to take more time.' Meanwhile he had already begun to think about the novel to come after 'The Head Mistress'. It will be 'a tremendously savage book, the scene once more in London', he told Ellen. 'Not, however, among work people but among the poor and wretched educated.' It would probably be called 'Revolt'.

Making good his pledge to render his life more 'endurable' through travel, Gissing now decided to use some of the money he had earned from *The Emancipated* to realize another long-cherished goal. 'If I do not take the opportunity . . . now, who knows whether I shall ever be able', he wrote to Margaret. On 11 November he left for Greece.

🙞

CHAPTER 7

THE WRONG WORLD, 1889–1891

'We all have a secret desire to believe love imperishable.'
'An amiable sentiment; but it is better to accept the truth.'
The Emancipated

The truth is that I have never learned to regard myself as a
member of 'society.' For me there have always been two
entities – myself and the world, and the normal relation
between these two has been hostile. *The Ryecroft Papers*

I am in the wrong world. Gissing to Bertz in 1890

I

'THREE years ago, it seemed to me a wildly extravagant hope that I
should ever see Greece, but here I am!' Gissing wrote triumphantly
to his mother on 18 November 1889. He had sailed from Marseilles
to Piraeus, with a stop in Genoa. First, of course, he had to see the
Acropolis, and the elevated, wind-blown scene is recorded gran-
diloquently in his diary:

The declining sun, from the front of the Nike Apteros; its rays streaming
wildly from behind clouds, and falling athwart the Saronic Gulf, between
Aegina and Salamis, against the hills of Argolis . . . From the west streamed
brilliant sunlight, whilst all the north and east was covered with huge
purple-black clouds . . . The Erechtheion gleamed against that cloud-
background, its yellow marble wonderfully illumined, every stone distinct
. . . Beneath the dark clouds was Pentelicon; its summit hidden, itself
darker than the sky, a bluish-black. Later, as the sun set, the eastern clouds
became fiery underneath, and Pentelicon, its clefts and flanks, glowed
unimaginably; such colour as one sees on imaginary mountains in the fire
. . . As the sun grew low, the shadow of the Mouseion gradually rose on
the Acropolis, which lost its glory. And when the sun had disappeared
altogether, sinking splendidly behind the hills of Argolis, the cloud on
Pentelicon suddenly faded to a delicate blue-grey, all its mouldings, its
reliefs and depressions, exquisitely marked in degrees of tenderness; the
mountain below, a deeper grey . . . A few minutes, and the afterglow had
begun. The western sky became brilliant amber; the zenith and the east
became a dark deep azure, awing the eye, whilst the great cloud again

flushed softly. And this lasted . . . until Pentelicon had blackened into night.

Soon he was visiting local cemeteries and lugubriously noting burial customs. On 22 November he was still sufficiently preoccupied to mistake, in a diary entry, his age. 'This is my birthday. Thirty-three, n'est-ce-pas?' He was thirty-two.

Like almost all visitors to modern Athens, however, Gissing was soon disappointed. Epithets like 'mean' and 'dirty' began to appear in his diary. 'I don't like the Greek people', he wrote. 'Utterly alien from my sympathies'. Athens 'does not possess a single painting of any kind', he noted. And there was 'No vivification of the old life'. After only a week in Greece the novelist had made up his mind to go back to his beloved Naples; soon he was looking up train and boat time-tables.

Gissing spent his time in Athens taking long walks about the city and its environs, searching out the places with historical and literary associations, working on his command of ancient Greek (he now re-read Sophocles, Aristophanes, and Plato), and making notes for possible future use (the opening scenes of *Sleeping Fires* would be set in modern Athens; in *New Grub Street* Reardon's description of the Acropolis is taken from Gissing's diary). 'This is the last letter from Athens', Gissing wrote to Bertz on 14 December. 'My education slowly progresses; in a few years I hope to be a decently cultivated man.'

A last sunset on the Acropolis moved him to another burst of lyricism:

The sun emerged below clouds into the open rift of sky, and shot glory in every direction; its shafts of light smote upwards athwart the sullen clouds and made them a wild, strange yellow. To the left of the sun, the gulf was a glory of golden mist . . . the shape of Aegina floated in it vaguely. To the right . . . over dark Salamis, there lay delicate strips of pale blue . . . The Acropolis glowed – ablaze . . . for a moment all was nearly crimson. Then suddenly the sun passed again into the lower stratum of cloud, and the glory died.

On 17 December Gissing left Athens. Travelling by way of Patras, Corfu, and Brindisi, he reached Naples two days later.

II

The familiar noises of Naples made Gissing feel at home, though he lamented the absence of the organ-grinders – silenced by a new law.

Still, there was plenty to hear. On Christmas day he noted 'a ceaseless clamour; perpetual ringing of church-bells, explosions of fireworks and yelling'. As the year drew to an end he went over his accounts. He had earned £150 from literature in 1889 – more than in any other year, but certainly very little for a writer of his expanding reputation (and the following year his income was to be the same).

A diary entry for January 1890 records that he was thinking of a 'new novel, which probably will not be "The Head Mistress"'. Later in the month he fell ill briefly with congestion of the lungs, a first touch of the malady that was eventually to kill him. He spent the rest of his time in Naples visiting previously unseen sites south of the city and working hard on his Italian and his German, and on 20 February he sailed for England. On board ship he noted 'an old affliction, the circumfluence of English people', as he wrote to Bertz.

In another note to Bertz Gissing reported that the ship's parson, hearing a clergyman 'in the first class' mention his, Gissing's, name and recognizing it immediately, said to him: 'I hear you are a celebrated author.' The novelist, who needless to say was not travelling first class, saw in this event, he told Bertz, 'a symbolical significance. It is my fate in life to be known by the first-class people and to associate with the second class – or even the third and fourth. It will always be so.' Gissing was sufficiently impressed by this incident to write of it in similar terms in his diary: 'This is symbolical of my life. It is first-class people who know me, whilst I myself am always compelled to associate with the second-class.' Certain barriers could never be overcome by the druggist's son from Yorkshire, even with literary success. The theme of the artistic outsider, the exiled aesthete, took on more rather than less significance in Gissing's novels as time went on. It was to be a dominant concern in the next two – *New Grub Street* and *Born in Exile*.

On 28 February 1890 Gissing was back in London after an absence of a little more than three months. It was the second anniversary of Nell's death.

III

Gissing had £77 left in the bank – enough, he calculated, to support himself for the next six months. 'Ten years hence I shall perhaps be able to have a home like other wealthy people', he wrote sardonically to Ellen upon his return to the Baker Street flat, 'but I don't think it will be in England.' Having heard nothing for months about *The Emancipated*, he wrote to Bentley to inquire about it. On 13 March he began a 'new story', deciding that materials already gathered for 'The Head Mistress' could 'lie over' for a while. As it turned out the story, of which only thirty-one pages were written, was abandoned. Little is known about it except that the title was 'Hawkridge' and the setting the Channel Islands.

A few days after Gissing noted in his diary that he did 'not really have enough to eat', six author's copies of *The Emancipated* unexpectedly arrived from Bentley. Gissing distributed them among Algernon, Bertz, Roberts (who said it was 'the best thing I have done yet', the diary records), his painter friend Hartley, and the family at Wakefield. The first announcements of the new book appeared. Late in March the novelist was heartened to see a new cheap edition of *The Nether World* advertised.

The Emancipated infuriated Gissing's family as never before. Ellen wrote to him immediately to say she disliked it from beginning to end. 'Naturally. Wrote a reply of very quiet self-defence. But no use', he recorded in the diary. Ellen saw something of herself and her sister Margaret in Miriam Baske before her emancipation from religious fanaticism – and of Wakefield's values in the conventions condemned by the novel. She complained bitterly of her brother's attack, as she saw it, on everything the Wakefield family valued. The novelist's reply, to his credit, was uncompromising:

My part is with the men and women who are clearing the ground of systems that have had their day, and have crumbled into obstructive ruin. To those who live in quiet corners of the earth, where those systems still seem solid edifices, and who know nothing of the true state of things in the greater part of the world, we seem mere reckless destroyers. This is an inevitable misconception. Short of ceasing altogether to write, I have no choice but to present myself before your imagination in this distorted fashion.

On 7 April 1890 Gissing abandoned 'Hawkridge' and the next day began a new story, tentatively entitled 'A Man of Letters'. There can be no question that this was the start of what was to become that autumn, after many more new beginnings, *New Grub Street*.

During the last weeks of April reviews of *The Emancipated* began to appear. As might be expected, the press, while by no means entirely unenthusiastic, was generally cool to this attack on conventional values. The *Illustrated London News* and the *Academy* were lukewarm but not unfriendly. The *Saturday Review*, noting that

Gissing had made a name for himself 'by his vivid portraiture of low London life', congratulated him 'on having made his escape' from the nether world. The *Westminster Review* complained of the novel's 'morbid' pessimism and its unendearing protagonists. The *Guardian* spoke for many readers when it summed the novel up thus: 'Considered as a treatise on the particular subject dealt with, the book deserves to be read; but as a work of fiction, it is by no means equally satisfactory, for there is a prevailing lack of lightness . . . that make some think an emancipated world would be a dreary place to live in.' In his comment on *The Emancipated*, Bertz with some justice lectured Gissing 'on the necessity of "condensation"'.

IV

In early May Gissing visited Wakefield; again he found that he was able to work efficiently there. By the end of the month he was writing the sixth chapter of 'A Man of Letters'. The work going well, he stayed on, refusing the few invitations forwarded from London; convinced he never would again dine 'at a civilized table', he sold his one dress suit. In mid-June he noted in his diary: 'thus happily *finished vol. 1.*' From this point, however, the diary records increasing problems, climaxed by a familiar announcement: 'Absolutely determined to abandon my story, and commence a new one.' He was not, he wrote in his diary, afraid of work. And 'No one could deny my courage. I had half finished the other novel.' But he began a new story, 'Storm-Birds', quickly completing three chapters in nine days. But by mid-July he was stuck again: 'feeling terribly wretched. The struggle to get my story clear driving me almost to madness.' And so it went throughout the summer. 'Getting on well, now', the diary says on 28 July. 'Broke down with wretchedness', it records the next day. At the beginning of August there were periods of 'blank misery' and 'Utter wretchedness'. His peace of mind was not improved by a note from Smith, Elder announcing that only 412 copies of *Thyrza* had been sold since its publication in 1887 and offering a meagre £10 for the copyright (this was the only novel of Gissing's whose copyright he had not sold outright).

During his stay in Yorkshire, Gissing wrote one of his most revealing letters to Bertz. In it he told his friend that he would 'never be able to make [himself] at home again in England', that his life there was 'indefinitely wearisome'. Exiled from London by his own choice, Gissing complained, characteristically: 'It is absurd that I should be mouldering here in a Yorkshire village; it is a scandalous waste of life, when already I have wasted so many years . . . I am in the wrong world.'

I cannot make friends, not even acquaintances, in England; and the small success of my books embitters me against the country . . . I shall move about on the Continent, and hope someday to find a wife there, which will never happen in England . . . I am so much more myself, when abroad. In the society of people here I am stiff and awkward and contemptuous. Abroad, I do not expect people to recognize me as an author, and consequently I am able to be simply a man . . . My *London* life is in the past; I cannot *live* in London now, and I think never shall again. But it was invaluable to me. I have not yet made half the use of it that I shall be able to. I want to drink wine, to talk and laugh, to feel that I am living, and not only a machine for producing volumes. I want to hear music, above all things. If only I live a few months more! . . . Don't lose patience with me. I shall do something some day.

Gissing forgot when he wrote this letter how restless he could grow abroad. We know he easily became dissatisfied with his life wherever he happened to be.

What Gissing said to Bertz about finding a wife reflects his intensifying loneliness. In August he met a Wakefield girl named Connie Ash and, in his solitary state, imagined for a few days that he had fallen in love with her ('wretchedness confused with hope' was his description of his state of mind); but she gave him no encouragement. He was even more desperately lonely. 'If another five years such as this last is before me, I shall either end in the Asylum or the Thames', he told Ellen. He wrote to Bertz: 'This solitude is killing me. I can't endure it any longer. In London I must resume my old search for some decent work-girl who will come and live with me. I am too poor to marry an equal, and cannot live alone.' The most interesting aspect of this much-quoted but often-misunderstood statement is that Gissing does not propose here to marry a 'decent work-girl'; on the contrary, he proposes to 'live with' one, the idea being that a lady would never consent to such an arrangement and that he is too poor to marry one. These sentiments should be remembered in the light of what happened later.

Throughout the month of August 1890 Gissing struggled furiously with his various embryo novels, sometimes discouraged, sometimes elated. During the third week of August he returned to London (it would be several years before he saw Wakefield again) and towards the end of the month commenced yet another story. But he saw almost immediately that it was no good. He began a

novel called 'Hilda Wolff'. It went well for several weeks, and
Gissing's mood was almost sunny. He noted happily that Smith,
Elder was advertising *Demos, A Life's Morning,* and *The Nether
World* in a cheap uniform edition. But in mid-September the diary
records 'Complete breakdown again. Am at the end of Vol. 1 [of
'Hilda Wolff'], but feel it won't do.' Undecided as to the direction
his next story should take, he bought a new cheap edition of *The
Return of the Native* and re-read it avidly. The evenings he spent
wandering around looking for company. His plaintive diary entries
continue. 'Feel like a madman at times. I know that I shall never do
any more good work till I am married.' He began a new tale
tentatively called 'Victor Yule' (obviously another strand of *New
Grub Street*). 'Curious that I feel in good spirits about this new
story', he wrote in his diary. 'I seem to have hit the possible vein
again once more.' On 22 September he dropped 'Victor Yule' and
picked up 'Hilda Wolff' again. The next day he went back to 'Victor
Yule'. 'A bad, bad time with me: the wasting of my life in
bitterness', Gissing recorded in his diary.

'We are both unhappy creatures', the novelist wrote to Bertz,
'and it will be miraculous if either of us ever attains to much peace
on this side of the eternal silence . . . I live alone, as usual, and dare
not, as yet, make any effort to change this state of things; my
financial position is too shaky.' He told Bertz that for the past
several weeks he had conversed with no one except his servant; and
he went on to discuss once again, at some length, the marriage
question.

Marriage . . . is impossible owing to my insufficient income: educated
English girls *will* not face poverty in marriage, and to them anything under
£400 a year is serious poverty. They remain unmarried . . . rather than
accept poor men. I know that my danger, if I become connected with a
tolerable girl of low position is very great: I am weak in these matters. But
then . . . there is no *real* hope of my ever marrying any one of a better kind,
no *real* hope whatever! I say it with the gravest conviction.

On 24 September 1890, at the Oxford Music Hall, he met Edith
Underwood.

Gissing was desperate. He had threatened to take home with him
the first 'decent work-girl' he could find; his solitude was killing
him. His state of mind may be glimpsed in that of Cecil Morphew
in *The Whirlpool*, who is described as 'mad' with sexual desire: 'I
simply couldn't live alone any longer – I couldn't', he says,
explaining how he happened to pick up a young woman in the park.

'Starved emotions made me a madman', Gissing admitted to Gabrielle Fleury a decade later. 'He was very hard up and hopeless and he was fearfully oppressed by sex necessity', said H. G. Wells of the Gissing of this period. 'I believe he was too poor for prostitutes.' Gissing's experience with Nell had made him understand how 'weak in these matters' he was – how susceptible to sexual temptation, how easily he could become enmeshed in the 'dangers' posed by any attractive girl of 'low position' who would sleep with him and to whom he would not be expected to offer marriage. He continued to feel tainted by his relationship with Nell and the disease she had given him.

At least one, and possibly two, of the stories he was struggling with at the time concerned a poor man of intellect who married an impatient, unsympathetic woman, and the misery of such a union. With his usual gift for self-fulfilling prophecy, Gissing had already begun to consider in his writing many of the problems that were about to beset his personal life.

Ironically, his desperation and misery during the summer of 1890 helped produce both one of the greatest novels in the English language and one of the unhappiest marriages in English history. It is typical of Gissing's life that these events should be so closely linked; it was the old story, as Osmond Waymark might have said, of misery goading art to life. For exactly one week after he met Edith, Gissing recommenced writing a book he now called *New Grub Street*. Within ten weeks of their first meeting he had finished it. Out of the false starts, the cancelled beginnings, the abandoned fragments, and out of this new friendship destined to be so fatally destructive, emerged a masterpiece.

Edith Underwood was 23, a respectable girl of humble origin who lived with her family in Camden Town. Her father was a 'working-sculptor' – a sort of carpenter's assistant. Contemporaries who have described her are agreed that she was no beauty.

According to Roberts, Gissing sought her out at first as a result of desperate physical need. Roberts's imaginative version of their initial meeting, often quoted since, is that when the novelist found his solitude unendurable one day he rushed out into Baker Street and spoke to the first woman he saw. This was Edith. Roberts continues: Gissing's 'solitude, this enforced and appalling loneliness, which seemed to him necessary for work if he was to live', had eaten into him so deeply as to destroy 'his nerve and what judgment he ever had' with regard to women. And he adds: 'In all his relations with women it seems as if his own personal loneliness was the dominating factor . . . the misery of the man who lives alone and yet cannot live alone.' Roberts concludes that the novelist recognized how uncongenial an intellectual companion for him Edith was but that 'his body meant to have its way . . . He admitted that he did not love her in any sense of the word love. He admitted that she had no great powers of attraction, that she seemed to possess no particularly obvious intellect.' But Gissing's passions were 'fatally roused', Roberts says, because Edith, unlike Nell, was 'respectable', and he had feared he was debarred forever from having a relationship with any woman even remotely so. 'He was in love with the sex but not with the woman', Roberts says. Gissing's friend is not always a reliable witness, but in this his assessment of the situation strikes me as acute. It is backed up by that of Wells – no more than Roberts inclined to be accurate about anything touching Gissing, but on the subject of the novelist's second marriage certainly incisive: 'he felt that to make love to any woman he could regard as a social equal would be too elaborate, restrained and tedious for his urgencies, he could not answer questions he supposed would be asked . . . and so, for the second time, he flung himself at a social inferior whom he expected to be easy and grateful.' Wells adds: 'Never did a man need mothering more and never was there a less sacrificial lover.' Wells did not meet Gissing for another six years, but the novelist was prone in his last period to confide in Wells, and the foregoing may be taken as the comment of an informed and intimate acquaintance.

Edith was not shy about going to Gissing's flat several times a week unchaperoned; from late September through December 1890 they saw each other alone regularly. The few people to whom Gissing mentioned Edith were told that their relationship was Platonic, and some of Gissing's modern students have taken this description of it at face value. It could not, however, have been anything other than a physical relationship. That is what Gissing craved, he could hardly have expected intellectual companionship. Considering how jealously he guarded his working hours from interruption and how badly in need of funds he was, it is clear that he would not have spent so much time with Edith during this autumn unless they were sleeping together. In the diary her visits to the flat were usually couched in such euphemistic phrases as 'spent the evening', or 'stayed an hour'. No one should be beguiled by such language. Certainly Roberts never was as his own language makes clear.

Edith's father (rightly, in the circumstances) disapproved of

Gissing, but took little interest in the affair. As in *The Odd Women*, the young man suggested to the young lady a free union, and was turned down; the torments and the expenses inflicted upon Gissing by his first wife remained fresh in his mind. He hesitated. In a letter to Bertz written in October, Gissing mentioned casually that he had 'made the acquaintance of a work-girl who will perhaps come to live with me when I leave this place, at Christmas' (his lease was up then). He told Bertz he had got to finish his novel, for he was practically penniless – and added: 'I must consider nothing but mere physical needs. I . . . can only recover something of my old self by the change of life I have referred to [that is, taking a mistress]. Otherwise, there is nothing before me but lapse into mental and bodily ruin.' Any doubt about the nature of his relationship with Edith should be removed by this statement. Inducing Edith to be his mistress indefinitely was not so easy as he supposed, however. Soon he was writing in a quite different vein to Algernon: 'I can't stand my solitary life any longer and it must not surprise you if you suddenly hear that I am going to be married again.'

It seems that Gissing underestimated Edith Underwood, who was not so immune to considerations of dignity and the future as he imagined. In a letter to Ellen written around this time he said he sought for nothing in a woman 'but good temper and sincerity . . . I have ample experience of what it means to live with an uneducated wife'; it is intimated that he won't make again the mistake he made once before. 'If there is only no brutality, I shall be quiet and contented', he adds. A beautiful and intelligent companion would never be his anyway: so why not, after all, marry Edith, who seemed tractable and pleasant? He was working steadily and well now; clearly Edith's visits were a good stimulus as well as a release.

During this autumn Gissing had to sell some of his books to avoid borrowing money (those bare shelves haunted him, as *The Ryecroft Papers* testify) while he worked over his new manuscript. Edith's visits continued. Bentley's report that only 491 copies of *The Emancipated* had been sold out of 1,000 printed did not slow him down – rather it induced him to fresh efforts. After so many false starts *New Grub Street* was now being written with comparative ease. In between stints of writing the diary records poetry-reading sessions with Edith. The old dream of educating a working-class girl, a dream sublimated into various plots in novel after novel, persisted in real life.

'My wretched birthday . . . Am 33 years old', he noted on 22 November 1890, getting his age right this time. Two weeks later (on

6 December) he finished *New Grub Street,* writing Reardon's death scene last. The manuscript was submitted to Smith, Elder. Gissing's plans were uncertain, largely because he had no money and no idea how much he could get for the new book. When his lease expired at the end of the month he would either take new lodgings in London or rent a place in the country. Either way he was apparently reconciled now to the idea of marrying again. At Christmas dinner at Edith's home he announced that he had decided to settle in Exeter for a year or two, which would give him simultaneously the advantages of a city and of the surrounding Devon countryside. He had already made plans to have his furniture removed from his London flat when Smith, Elder's terms for *New Grub Street* came through: £150 for all rights (the same figure had been offered for *The Nether World* and *The Emancipated*; the publisher's reader liked the new novel a bit better but was afraid of its gloominess). Unfortunately Gissing could not afford to refuse this offer – 'unfortunately' because once again he would have done better financially with a royalty arrangement. He was never to reap any real monetary rewards from this great book – never to earn a penny from cheap reprints or translation rights. Nor was Smith, Elder the sort of house to take pity upon an author who had made a bad deal.

On New Year's Eve Gissing recorded in his diary 'anything but cheerful thoughts. The future full of doubt.'

v

In January 1891 Gissing went off to Exeter to look for suitable lodgings. He had by this time told Roberts of his plan to marry Edith. As he had done before Gissing's first marriage, Roberts begged his friend to reconsider; but 'he was peculiarly obstinate, and nothing that I could urge had the least effect upon him.' Roberts surmised that Gissing's past life made him especially determined to do nothing now 'which might seem in any way dishonourable'. Describing Edith as the woman who was 'to bear his children, to torture him for years, to drive him almost mad, and once more to make a financial slave of him', Roberts says there was never a possibility of her becoming 'in any remote degree what he might justifiably have asked for in a wife . . . She possessed neither face nor figure, nor a sweet voice, nor any charm – she was just a female.'

Once again we must ask – why did he do it? Why did he marry her? *New Grub Street,* after all, shows us in several of its plots the pulverizing effects of marriage on an intelligent man who allies himself to an uncongenial woman. Gissing said that in *Workers in the Dawn* he had 'written off' a whole period of his existence. In *New Grub Street* he once again worked out in a piece of fiction the probable consequences of his own future actions – and then went ahead and performed those actions anyway. One cannot escape the conclusion that he was still punishing himself for his past crimes – performing an act of aggressive, irrational 'respectability' to make up for previous irregularities. In spite of his apparent fore-knowledge of the consequences, he married again, perhaps because, in Korg's words, 'a part of him wanted to suffer those conse-quences' as a sort of penance.

On 14 January 1891 Gissing left London, the scene of his struggles of the past thirteen years, and moved himself and all his belongings to rented rooms (part of a house) in Exeter. The marriage date was fixed for 10 February. Abruptly, however, Edith postponed it – apparently because her family, not unreasonably, had misgivings about the ill-assorted match. It was reset for 25 Feb-ruary at Gissing's insistence: it would be then or never, he stormed. Unfortunately for all concerned, Edith gave in.

The novelist devoted much of February to getting the rooms in Exeter ready for Edith and taking long walks in the Devon countryside, which was to be described so eloquently in *The Ryecroft Papers*. Also during this month he read Lyell's *Elements of Geology*, Hugh Miller's *Testimony of the Rocks*, and other works on science and theology – which make it clear that he had already hit upon a major theme of his next novel, *Born in Exile*.

Proofs of *New Grub Street* began to arrive. He worked on them, and wrote to most of his friends and relatives of his coming marriage. In the letter to Bertz he said: 'the family is a respectable one . . . The girl is peculiarly gentle and pliable, with a certain natural refinement which seems to promise that she might be trained to my kind of life.' He told Ellen that Edith was 'not unintelligent . . . though she has had no education in the proper sense of the word, her letters are all but perfect in orthography . . . When I have accustomed her to speak without the vile London accent, she will have a reasonably refined mode of speech.' Shades of Carrie Mitchell and Nell Harrison! Had he forgotten already where such Pygmalion-like experiments might lead, what training someone 'to my kind of life' might involve? He was obviously ready to let history repeat itself – or, rather, to repeat it himself.

On 24 February Gissing went to London, and on the 25th he was married to Edith Underwood at the Registrar's Office, St. Pancras (nearly two decades later Clive Bell and Vanessa Stephen would be married in the same place – and several years after that, again in the St. Pancras Registrar's Office, Vanessa's sister Virginia would marry Leonard Woolf). Edith's father and sister were witnesses; no one from the Gissing family was invited. Immediately after the ceremony, Gissing's diary reports, the newly married pair 'drove in fog to Paddington, and caught the 11:45 for Exeter'.

A few weeks later the novelist wrote to Mrs Frederic Harrison refusing an invitation and explaining that he had been compelled to marry a woman of 'the artisan class' in order to carry on his work and that he intended henceforth to sever all relations with educated people. 'Of course I shall have no society here', he wrote to Ellen of his life in Exeter. He saw himself as being in a sort of exile: 'My ambition now is to make my name known, whilst personally I remain unseen and unheard of . . . We shall have to see whether I can keep my mind active without the help of congenial minds. I have the feeling of being deserted by all who ought to be my companions: but then these miseries are useful in giving a peculiar originality to my work.'

Like Waymark, Gissing considered misery a necessary ingredient of his art. If it was misery he was after, he was to find more than he bargained for in his second marriage. It is not wholly accidental, then, that many of his best novels were written in the nineties, during some of the most domestically 'miserable' years of his life. Coustillas is surely right to refer to Gissing's 'regular genius for masochism'.

VI

New Grub Street is perhaps the greatest novel ever written about the collision of the creative impulse with material circumstances. Into this book Gissing put everything he knew about the barriers thrown up to artistic genius by mean necessity. It is a spiritual autobiography, a personal history. There is something of the novelist or of situations in which he found himself in almost every major personage and happening in the novel. This will not be surprising when we remember how many times Gissing began, cast aside, and then again began this story, and the number of characters and themes that must have passed through his head during this procreative ordeal. I have said that Gissing's fiction is most effective when it was most autobiographical. The brilliance of *New Grub Street* derives largely from the novelist's unstinting use of his own experiences and feelings to tell the story – or rather, the stories. For each of the leading literary men in the novel – Reardon, Biffen, Whelpdale, Milvain, Yule – represent some aspect of Gissing as artist. It has been fashionable among readers of *New Grub Street* to see Reardon as the Gissing-*persona* and the others as objects of various kinds of satire, and this view is not wholly unjust; but it should also be clear to any reader of the novel who is also a student of Gissing's life that all of these men have their origin in the novelist's self-dramatizing impulse.

Certainly Reardon is the fullest expression here of that impulse. A classicist, a scholar, a novelist who struggles fiercely with every book yet has no other means of keeping himself and his family alive, Reardon shares with Gissing the trait of impracticality – a trait by which the novelist, with some justice, was always characterized by his friends. Reardon also dresses carelessly, works often without hope, and usually expects, in good Schopenhauerian fashion, the worst. A highlight of his life has been a trip to Greece and Italy, about which he constantly talks. He has married a respectable woman, a lady – an event which in his most impecunious days he feared could never come to pass. His relationship with his wife is ultimately destroyed by his failure as a writer and thus as provider: he turns out to be not 'good enough' for her after all. Reardon's greatest friend meets him evening after evening to talk of the classics (especially Greek metrics, on the subject of which Gissing published a letter in *The Times* in February 1891), the writing of fiction, and women.

Reardon is acutely aware of the tenuous division between subsistence and starvation and of what fate awaits the artist who ceases to produce saleable artifacts. 'Suppose I could never get more than this poor hundred pounds for one of the long books which cost me so much labour?' Reardon worries. What then? 'He knew what poverty means. The chilling of brain and heart, the unnerving of the hands, the slow gathering about one of fear and shame and impotent wrath, the dread feeling of helplessness, of the world's base indifference. Poverty! Poverty!' In a well-known passage Reardon recites to his wife one of Gissing's constant themes:

Can I think of a single subject in all the sphere of my experience without the consciousness that I see it through the medium of poverty? I have no enjoyment which isn't tainted by that thought, and I can suffer no pain which it doesn't increase. The curse of poverty is to the modern world just what that of slavery was to the ancient. Rich and destitute stand to each other as free man and bond. You remember the line of Homer I have often quoted about the demoralising effects of enslavement; poverty degrades in the same way.

'Poverty makes a crime of every indulgence', *The Nether World* taught us; in *New Grub Street* it is the phrase 'poverty degrades' that echoes through the pages. In the artist's case it 'degrades' by forcing him to work against the grain – to work whether he feels like it or not; it makes him desperate to produce at any cost. Reardon knows he is temperamentally unsuited to the competitive level of the Grub Street market-place. 'If I had had the means, I should have devoted myself to the life of the scholar', he tells Milvain. 'That, I quite believe, is my natural life; it's only the influence of recent circumstances that has made me a writer of novels.' He believes that his books are produced not by his true self but rather by 'his accursed poverty', which forces him to write for a living. These sentiments are of course Gissing's own, spoken directly to the reader in his own voice. In this aspect of Reardon's character the pretence of fiction is dropped altogether.

The self-destructive, impractical side of Reardon is insisted upon with a vehemence approaching self-mockery. 'Practicality was not his strong point', it is said early in the novel. 'My nature is feeble and luxurious. I never in my life encountered and overcame a practical difficulty', Reardon says of himself. The more deeply embittered Biffen tells Reardon that 'we have both of us too little practicality. The art of living is the art of compromise. We have no right to foster sensibilities, and conduct ourselves as if the world allowed of ideal relations . . . What right have we to make ourselves and others miserable for the sake of an obstinate idealism? It is our duty to make the best of circumstances.' Reardon refuses to take this advice (Biffen does not take it himself), clinging instead to his 'obstinate idealism'. Shortly thereafter he dies of congestion of the lungs, in a chapter savagely entitled 'Reardon Becomes Practical'. Then Biffen poisons himself. Milvain's verdict is that both men were 'hopelessly unpractical' and thus 'bound to go to the dogs . . . in such an admirable social order as ours'. Reardon's impracticality is portrayed as an analogue of his aesthetic sensitivity. Surely the fatalistic Gissing saw himself in the same mould.

Few passages in Gissing's fiction can be as unblushingly auto-biographical as that in which Reardon talks to Biffen about his travels through Italy and Greece.

The best moments of life are those when we contemplate beauty in the purely artistic spirit – objectively. I have had such moments in Greece and

Italy; times when I was a free spirit, utterly remote from the temptations and harassings of sexual emotion. What we call love is mere turmoil. Who wouldn't release himself from it for ever, if the possibility offered? . . . Haven't I told you . . . of that marvellous sunset at Athens? . . . On Parnes there were white strips of ragged mist, hanging very low; the same on Hymettus, and even the peak of Lycabettus was just hidden. Of a sudden, the sun's rays broke out. They showed themselves first in a strangely beautiful way, striking from behind the seaward hills through the pass that leads to Eleusis, and so gleaming in the nearer slopes of Aigaleos, making the clefts black and the rounded parts of the mountain wonderfully brilliant with golden colour . . . This lasted only a minute or two, then the sun itself sank into the open patch of sky and shot glory in every direction; broadening beams smote upwards over the dark clouds, and made them a lurid yellow. To the left of the sun, the gulf of Ægina was all golden mist . . . To the right, over Black Salamis, lay delicate strips of pale blue – indescribably pale and delicate . . . What does a man care for any woman on earth when he is absorbed in contemplation of that kind? . . . it is infinitely preferable to sexual emotion. It leaves . . . no bitterness of any kind. Poverty can't rob me of those memories.

The reader of this book will see how much of the description of the Athenian sunset is taken directly from the novelist's diary; and the last line of the quotation was one Gissing frequently used in letters to friends and relatives when describing his travels. As for the rest of what Reardon says – among other things it must be one of the most eloquent hymns to senility ever penned. Such language may suggest to us the depth of suffering Gissing underwent throughout much of his life as a result of nagging sexual need and loneliness on the one hand and the desire on the other to rise above merely physical considerations. The novelist may have wished for the sort of calm Reardon identifies here as an ideal, but rarely if ever did he achieve it.

Biffen, to whom the speech is made, has spent much of his own life yearning to see Greece and Italy, as the younger Gissing did. He is a would-be novelist of the school of Zola. Gissing satirizes the literary ambitions of his own youth by portraying Biffen as wishing to take down verbatim the conversation of grocers – those he calls, in a memorable phrase, the 'ignobly decent'. The result of such transcription, Biffen admits, 'will be something unutterably tedious. Precisely. That is the stamp of the ignobly decent life. If it were anything *but* tedious it would be untrue.' Reardon's comment on this appalling literary system is in effect Gissing's on his younger self, the Gissing of *Workers in the Dawn*. 'I couldn't do it', says Reardon; neither, any more, could Gissing. 'Since Dickens's time there has arisen a school of fiction which, with incredible labour, strives to set before us the reality of things, to impress by a scrupulous fidelity of presentment', Gissing wrote, some years later, in a preface to *The Old Curiosity Shop*. 'The method has been in . . . few instances successful.' He told Gabrielle Fleury that 'Extreme naturalism in fiction has always been repugnant to my feeling, and to my critical sense'; he told Eduard Bertz that he had 'grown to abhor Zola's grossness'. And he was to attack the school of naturalism head-on in an essay written in 1895 called 'The Place of Realism in Fiction'. In his pursuit of what he calls 'absolute realism', Biffen seeks out 'the essentially unheroic', wishing to write of 'that vast majority of people who are at the mercy of paltry circumstance'. Dickens could have done it, says Biffen, but his tendency to melodrama and comedy got in the way. Needless to say, a book so 'unutterably tedious' as Biffen's (entitled 'Mr. Bailey, Grocer') is turned down by every publisher. Ultimately he joins the list of Gissing *alter egos* who commit suicide.

In other respects too Biffen reminds one of Gissing: the yearning after the companionship of a respectable woman, the loneliness, the tutoring of students in Greek and Latin (and the hatred of doing it), the long evening discussions with Reardon about women and classical literature, and so on.

The great apostle of 'practicality' in *New Grub Street* is of course Jasper Milvain, that 'man of his day' both satirized and admired by Gissing. The satire is part of the novel's main thrust: an attack on the modern tendency to turn literature into trade, a commodity to be bought and sold like any other. But 'Jasper of the facile pen' also represents a side of Gissing himself – within an area that might be called wish-fulfilment, or fantasy. Milvain may be a hack, he may throw standards out the window, he may be utterly cynical – but he knows how to make 'literature' profitable, and this is a practical talent that Gissing, who would soon employ a literary agent, wished he possessed himself.

Again Milvain has a mother and two sisters in the country, and he goes to London to make his way in the world of letters. He too starts with nothing and struggles mightily to progress a few inches at a time. Ultimately he discovers that pleasing himself is preferable to trying to please others, and he sets about making money in Grub Street as a sort of literary stockbroker. He reneges on his offer of marriage to Marian Yule chiefly because he sees that the alliance would reduce his social, and thus professional, opportunities. 'I have only one superstition that I know of', he says, 'and that forbids me to take a step backward.' Unprincipled though he is, he is hard to dislike; he is never under any illusion about his moral nature, and he has more charm than most of his fellow rogues. 'It is men of my kind who succeed', he says. 'The conscientious, and those who really have a high ideal, either perish or struggle on in neglect.' Gissing knew this well enough – and, on some issues, feels as Jasper does. They are entirely at one on the subject of poverty: it is the worst crime of all. So Milvain often speaks with Gissing's voice – as here : 'Want of money makes me the inferior of the people I talk with, though I might be superior to them in most things.' Milvain's intelligence and sensitivity, combined with his lack of means, 'declass' him, as Gissing felt himself declassed. The difference is that Jasper acts practically and aggressively and sometimes dishonestly to put poverty behind him for ever – something his creator could never quite do. And so Milvain is rewarded at the end of the novel with Amy Reardon, a consistent (if hateful) representative in the story of solid, unfeeling respectability (she would have made a marvellous Forsyte). The point is that he does *not* make the mistake of marrying beneath him – as the impractical Gissing was about to do for the second time.

Whelpdale and Yule also represent aspects of Gissing's experience. As I noted in Chapter 3, Whelpdale's adventures in America, narrated in Chapter 28 of *New Grub Street,* are taken directly from Gissing's American odyssey of 1877. Whelpdale's 'hapless wooing' of women, and his fear of being unable to find a respectable one who would accept him, is another familiar theme; so is the would-be novelist side of Whelpdale – 'a clever fellow', as Milvain says, 'but he can't hit a practical line.'

Yule, whose story probably provided the germ of the novel, is partly self-dramatization too. The young Gissing had thought of making his way in the profession of letters as a journeyman scholar and critic, free-lancing articles on learned subjects for the popular press. Yule thought this a promising beginning when a young man; but the editorship he wanted never came along, and after 'many long years of unremitting toil' he finds at the end of his life only 'failure and destitution'. One of the reasons for Yule's position is his marriage; his uneducated wife is unpresentable in polite company, which means he lacks the social credentials (pursued so single-mindedly by Milvain) to get ahead in his profession. Yule married because he could not live alone efficiently; later, when he sees how much his wife has cost him professionally, he is correspondingly bitter. The blameless Mrs Yule was an ordinary work-

ing-class girl when Yule married her; and Gissing, who was about
to walk in Yule's footsteps, comments in *New Grub Street*: 'The
London work-girl is rarely capable of raising herself, or being
raised, to a place in life above that to which she was born; she
cannot learn how to stand and sit and move like a woman bred to
refinement, any more than she can fashion her tongue to graceful
speech.' Gissing had already met the 'London work-girl' who was
to be his next wife when he wrote this: the situation perfectly
recapitulates the Carrie Mitchell sections of *Workers in the Dawn*.

Yule treats his hapless wife cruelly; he patronizes her, ignores
her, enslaves her in domesticity, and rarely permits her to be seen
by others. He never takes her out. Aspects of this behaviour were to
be replicated by Gissing with Edith; as time went by and he got to
know her better he grew ashamed to introduce her to his friends and
took her virtually nowhere. Mrs Yule is a passive woman (as
Gissing, in the autumn of 1890, thought Edith was), an apt subject
of tyranny; Edith turned out to be less docile.

One of Yule's constant complaints becomes a chief theme of the
novel, which calls our attention to some of the commercial aspects
of 'literature' so despised by Gissing. 'The evil of the time', says
Yule, 'is the multiplication of ephemerides. Hence a demand for
essays, descriptive articles, fragments of criticism, out of all proportion to the supply of even tolerable work.' Milvain describes the
contemporary epidemic of literary hack-work in these succinct
terms:

Literature nowadays is a trade. Putting aside men of genius, who may
succeed by mere cosmic force, your successful man of letters is your skilful
tradesman. He thinks first and foremost of the markets; when one kind of
goods begins to go off slackly, he is ready with something new and
appetising. He knows perfectly all the possible sources of income.

Milvain describes Reardon as a man who doesn't know how to
market his wares: 'he sells a manuscript as if he lived in Sam
Johnson's Grub Street.' Of course this is a description of Gissing
himself.

The successful writer, Milvain argues, is a good businessman who
can sell his product several times over when he puts it on the
market; only the 'impractical' are left behind. An energetic writer
ought to be able to write his two novels a year easily enough, if he
cares to work. But for Reardon, literature cannot be reduced to
matters of marketing and gross output. The circulating library
system was still demanding from publishers the ponderous three-

decker (and would continue to do so for another four years – until 1894), and Reardon finds the necessity of filling up the required space a terrible ordeal. 'To make a trade of art', he says, 'is [an] unpardonable sin . . . [and] a brutal folly.' 'How silly it is to talk like this', says Amy, who has been listening to Jasper on the subject. 'Art must be practised as a trade, at all events in our time . . . What *does* the subject matter? Get this book finished and sold.' No wonder becoming 'practical' is characterized in *New Grub Street* as a disease leading to death. 'The world has no pity on a man who can't do or produce something it thinks worth money. You may be a divine poet, and if some good fellow doesn't take pity on you you will starve by the roadside. Society is as blind and brutal as fate', the novel tells us.

The clash between art and materialism – between the creative man wanting to do something worthwhile and the circumstances of his life which force him to be mediocre or die – is at the centre of *New Grub Street*. Nowhere else in Gissing's work is the malignity of matter so emphasized or the life of the artist characterized so despairingly. The idea that a novelist who cannot turn out several saleable books a year is only being finicky or temperamental is a comment on how deeply the rampant commercialism of the later nineteenth century had penetrated all strata of professional life and attitudes. This is Gissing's *The Way We Live Now*.

The fact that five writers in *New Grub Street* have problems stemming from too little money, difficulties with women, and considerations of class, stamp the book as an especially recognizable Gissing performance. Marriage to a lady plunges Reardon into the sort of 'financial slavery' Roberts mentions as one of Gissing's chief worries after his second marriage. Biffen's depression and suicide are largely due to his inability to earn enough money from his books to marry a respectable woman. Milvain's rejection of the unglamorous Marian is of a piece with his literary opportunism: he understands that social success is a prerequisite of literary success in the world of literary 'business'. A result of Whelpdale's failure to achieve commercial prosperity as a writer is his inability to find a suitable wife; while a result of his ultimate success in literary hackdom is his acceptance by a respectable woman (Milvain's sister). Yule's financial and professional failure is traced directly to his marriage to an unsuitable woman, by which he declassed himself at an early stage of his career. Money, class, and women are bound inextricably together.

New Grub Street shows Gissing deciding that marriage without financial security is suicidal. The fact that he proposed to Edith while he was writing it should by now seem not so much inexplicable as inevitable. 'You're such a sentimental fellow', says Milvain to Whelpdale. 'I believe you seriously think that love ought to endure throughout married life.' What the novel shows us is that it only 'endures' when there is money sufficient to sustain it comfortably. Reardon finds out quickly enough how tender feelings 'can be embittered by misfortune. Some great and noble sorrow may have the effect of drawing hearts together, but to struggle against destitution, to be crushed by care about shillings and sixpences – that must always degrade.' As in *The Nether World*, poverty not only disillusions and diminishes: it also *degrades*. The famous passage from 'Lamia' –

> Love in a hut, with water and a crust,
> Is – Love forgive us! – cinders, ashes, dust.

– is quoted by Milvain to explain the collapse of the Reardon marriage and to postpone his own.

Reardon perceives readily enough how 'the dread and shame of penury . . . made [Amy's] heart cold to him . . . He had won the world's greatest prize – a woman's love – but could not retain it because his pockets were empty . . . A little money, and he could have rested secure in her love . . . Upon him, too, penury had its debasing effect.' Amy is degraded by poverty from a sympathetic wife to an inimical accountant and Reardon from a struggling artist to a desperate failure. When she threatens to leave him unless he finds a way to earn more money from his books and agrees to give up his plan to moonlight as a hospital clerk, a memorable bit of dialogue takes place. 'Amy, are you my wife, or not?' 'I am certainly not the wife of a clerk who is paid so much a week', is the chilling reply. She will not be 'declassed' along with her husband; like Rosamond in *Middlemarch*, she married for better, not for worse.

'Man has a right to nothing in this world that he cannot pay for ', the narrator muses cheerily after Amy walks out on her husband. 'Did you imagine that love was an exception? Foolish idealist! Love is one of the first things to be frightened away by poverty.'

'Poverty', says Milvain, sounding like Shaw's Andrew Undershaft, 'is the root of all social evils; its existence accounts even for the ills that arise from wealth. The poor man is a man labouring in fetters.' Money, Amy agrees, 'is the most powerful thing in the world. If I had to choose between a glorious reputation with poverty and a contemptible popularity with wealth, I should choose the latter.' Amy, we are told, 'knew how subtly one's self-respect can be undermined by sordid conditions'. So too Marian Yule understands how much 'better' and 'kinder' a man her father would have been had he had more money. 'It is poverty that has made him much worse than he naturally is; it has that effect on almost everybody.' Even Mrs Yule, a character who seems at times transplanted from *The Nether World*, sees readily enough that 'Poverty will make the best people bad, if it gets hard enough.'

This was a central theme of *The Nether World*; the speech Reardon makes to Amy on the ineffable distance between the two nations of rich and poor also recalls that novel. The rich, says Reardon,

pass so close to us; they see us, and we see them; but the distance between is infinity. They don't belong in the same world as we poor wretches. They see everything in a different light; they have powers which would seem supernatural if we were suddenly endowed with them . . . The power of money is so hard to realise; one who has never had it marvels at the completeness with which it transforms every detail of life. Compare what we call our home with that of rich people; it moves one to scornful laughter. I have no sympathy with the stoical point of view; between wealth and poverty is just the difference between the whole man and the maimed.

The Milvain sisters, in receiving 'an intellectual training wholly incompatible with the material conditions of their life', are said to be especially unfortunate. 'To the relatively poor (who are so much worse off than the poor absolutely) education is in most cases a mocking cruelty.' It is a nice question whether or not Gissing is right in this; the 'absolutely' poor would no doubt prefer 'relative' poverty to the little they have. The fact is that Reardon, despite his eloquence, is living in conditions vastly more comfortable than those in which hundreds of thousands of Londoners lived in the latter decades of the nineteenth century. So was Gissing. What both yearn for is release from *anxiety* about money and the freedom to spend theirs from time to time on entertainments and amusements; money as the means of subsistence is not the first concern. I think this is an important distinction – not always acknowledged by Gissing, whose streak of self-pity was broad. In some ways *New Grub Street* represents a partial return to the earlier fictional mode, especially in its concern with poverty and its effects on the educated and the 'quarter-educated' (as the novel puts it). The protagonists of this story, however, are not denizens of the nether world struggling for survival, but rather the 'ignobly decent' and the 'decently ignoble' – those who most feel and miss the things they are deprived of.

Tindall suggests that 'one of the private uses of *New Grub Street*' for its creator was as 'a make-believe exploration and rejection of the idea that a really desirable girl might be for him, and thus a rationalization of the marriage he was actually making'. Considering the re-acquaintance Gissing made with himself in this book and the conditions of his life at the time, it is astonishing nevertheless that what self-knowledge he did manage to achieve and articulate was not sufficient to deter him from the step of 'criminal reckless-ness' (as he later described it) that he took at the St. Pancras Registry Office on 25 February 1891.

'As a rule', Milvain tells Whelpdale, 'marriage is the result of a mild preference, encouraged by circumstances, and deliberately heightened into strong sexual feeling . . . the same kind of feeling could be produced for almost any woman who wasn't repulsive.' Gissing wrote this warning into *New Grub Street* but did not heed it himself. Perhaps nothing in the novel is more remarkable than the following exchange between Reardon and Biffen near the end of it. It was a mistake 'for me to marry such a girl as Amy', Reardon says.

'I ought to have looked about for some simple, kind-hearted work-girl; that was the kind of wife indicated for me by circumstances. If I had earned a hundred a year she would have thought we were well-to-do. I should have been an authority to her on everything . . . No ambition would have unsettled her. We should have lived in a couple of poor rooms somewhere, and – we should have loved each other.'

'What a shameless idealist you are!' said Biffen . . . 'Let me sketch the true issue of such a marriage. To begin with, the girl would have married you in firm persuasion that you were a "gentleman" in temporary difficul-ties, and that before long you would have plenty of money to dispose of. Disappointed in this hope, she would have grown sharp-tempered, querul-ous, selfish. All your endeavours to make her understand you would only have resulted in widening the impassable gulf. She would have miscon-strued your every sentence, found food for suspicion in every harmless joke, tormented you with the vulgarest forms of jealousy. The effect upon your nature would have been degrading. In the end, you must have abandoned every effort to raise her to your own level, and either have sunk to hers or made a rupture. Who doesn't know the story of such attempts?'

Who, indeed? Biffen here charts with astonishing accuracy the course Gissing's second marriage would take – even down to the sharp temper and querulousness of the wife and the torment and ultimate escape of the husband. *New Grub Street* shows throughout what a mistake the marriage was and what its consequences were likely to be. Gissing was reading proofs on the day the ceremony took place.

VII

Gissing at thirty-three 'was especially interesting-looking, and most obviously lovable and sympathetic when any of his feelings were roused', according to Morley Roberts. 'His grey eyes were very bright and intelligent, his features finely cut, and at times he was almost beautiful; although his skin was not always in such good condition as it should have been, and he was always very badly freckled.' The novelist brushed his hair straight back from the forehead without any parting, as photographs taken at this period show. Roberts describes Gissing's hair as 'very fine [and] of a brown colour, perhaps of a rather mousy tint, and it was never cut except at the ends of the nape of the neck'. When he washed his face he would fasten his hair back with an elastic band always carried in a pocket, Roberts reports. 'His forehead was high, his head exceedingly well shaped but not remarkably large.' He wore a moustache. He was physically robust and capable of walking great distances without tiring. 'Seen nude, he had the figure of a possible athlete', Roberts says. He almost always had a pipe in his mouth. He remained obstinate – 'extremely difficult to influence, even for his own good' – and conservative, regarding 'all kinds of reform not merely without hope, but with an actual terror', as Roberts put it. 'He lived in the past, and was conscious every day that something in the past that he loved was dying and must vanish.' Yet he hated British Imperialism, and militarism generally, and vowed that his children, if he had any, would never serve in the armed forces.

Gissing at first was relieved to get out of London and into Devonshire. He had begun to find the city oppressive to the spirit because it represented the '*triumph* of the vulgar man', as he wrote in his Commonplace Book. He looked back with distaste on his days of urban drudgery, especially the cheap dinners he was forced to eat.

In Gower Place, it was bread and milk: that starved me. In Wornington Road, it was German sausage (for weeks): that made me ill. For two or three months at 7K [the Baker Street flat] it was Desiccated Soup: that again pinched my stomach. Potatoes mashed with dripping, – bread soaked in hot water with dripping or butter, – and other such expedients have often served me.

Now he looked forward to living for once in a well-ordered house and eating regular meals.

Meanwhile he continued to work on proofs of *New Grub Street*. 'I am astonished to find out how well it reads. There are savage truths in it', he reported to Algernon. 'It is certainly a much better book than I thought', he told Bertz. In the same letter there is this aside: 'It is my belief that the multitude was never more remote than now from true culture . . . We have to recognize that the progress of our time is purely material.' *New Grub Street*, in showing 'the triumph of the vulgar man', argued precisely this – that spiritual growth had not kept pace with material progress, which was now everybody's first consideration.

Two days before he wrote this letter to Bertz, Gissing began a new book, tentatively entitled 'Raymond Peak'. By late March 1891 he had completed its first chapters. He wrote the tale slowly, but for once without the usual false starts. This is undoubtedly because his domestic life for once (but not for long) was relatively peaceful. Gissing's only real disappointment with Edith during these early days of their marriage came about when she confessed she could not get through *The Nether World*, the first of his books he had given her to read; the language was too difficult, she said. However, she liked *New Grub Street* – remaining, obviously, oblivious to its true message. Ten days after the marriage Gissing told Ellen that there was 'much docility and some capacity for household work' in Edith, and he remained pleased with her. He worried, though, about her lack of education. 'It is commonly supposed that one could not find a mature English person who had never heard of "Pilgrim's Progress",' he noted in his Commonplace Book, 'yet I find that this is [Edith's] case, and doubtless that of many other people in her class.'

Smith, Elder advertised *New Grub Street* widely, and Gissing received the first of several requests for an interview. He turned it down, informing the *Pall Mall Gazette* that he 'had nothing to tell the public'. On 7 April the book was published, and Gissing sent copies to the usual small group of friends and relatives. In the accompanying note to Bertz he announced he had written half a volume of a new novel, now called 'Godwin Peak' – 'a study of a savagely aristocratic temperament'.

Reviews of *New Grub Street* began to appear in mid-April; and while the novel was to receive some mixed notices and to spark controversy in the press, it was immediately clear that this time Gissing was going to get some sustained critical acclaim. Even where there were reservations about the book (as in the *Athenaeum*, *Murray's Magazine*, the *Pall Mall Gazette*, the *Guardian*, and the *National Observer*), this was generally due to its pessimism rather than to its subject, characters, or style; indeed, the few negative reviews were mild. Generally *New Grub Street* was greeted with a chorus of praise. The *Whitehall Review* said the novel conveyed 'a sense of perfect reality'. The *Court Journal* lauded the 'unexaggerated truth of . . . its sad pictures'. The *World* announced that it was the 'best of all' Gissing's books. 'There is power in every line', said the *Illustrated London News*. The *Saturday Review* declared that the theme of art's degradation by commercialism is 'cruelly precise in every detail'. The reviewer ranked Gissing as a storyteller along with Stevenson, Kipling, and Meredith. The *Spectator* pronounced *New Grub Street* the work of a 'master'. Writing in the *Author*, Walter Besant commented that 'the fidelity of Mr. Gissing's portraits makes me shudder.' *New Grub Street* was mentioned in a *Daily News* leader – an unusual distinction for a novel.

Demos made Gissing known, but it took *New Grub Street*, his ninth published book, to make him popular. Its appearance turned out to be a watershed in his career. *New Grub Street* was chiefly responsible for getting him mentioned along with Hardy and Meredith in the nineties as one of the leading novelists of the age: and it also became his first genuinely popular success , going into a second edition in three volumes just seven weeks after it first appeared (nothing like this had happened to any of Gissing's previous novels – not even *Demos*). Within two years it went through five cheap editions in England, and also appeared in Germany, France, Australia, and Russia (the Russian title, translated into English, meant 'Martyrs of the Pen'). As we know, Gissing received no direct financial benefit from the novel's success. Indirectly, however, it helped him enormously, for it was to create a greater demand for his fiction, and to stimulate editors to ask him for stories. Throughout the mid-nineties he would earn a comfortable income writing short pieces of fiction for journals and magazines. His average yearly income for the eight years 1892 to 1899 was about £345, as compared to an average income of about £120 during the six years 1886 to 1891.

Among Gissing's circle, Bertz rated *New Grub Street* the novelist's 'maturest and most interesting' publication; Roberts loved it;

and even Gissing's mother and Ellen praised it, though with the usual reservations about his gloominess. To Bertz, Gissing replied that he had written *New Grub Street* 'in utter prostration of spirit; no book of mine was regarded so hopelessly in the production'. He added: 'When I read to you the MS. of "Workers in the Dawn", we did not foresee this endless series of 3-vol. novels . . . Alas! there will be many more.' In his letter to Wakefield, Gissing said he was too old to change his view of things. 'I have reached the stage at which one is content to be ignorant. The world is to me mere phenomenon . . . and I study it as I do a work of art – but without reflecting on its origin' (Osmond Waymark speaks again!). His health has not been so good for years, he says; his only complaint is the dullness and vulgarity of his Exeter neighbours.

Gissing's diary entries for May 1891 alternate between exultation over the success of the novel and complaints about the weather, lack of money, and the neighbours. Late in May he noted: 'Look at my position, with a novel succeeding as "New Grub Street" has done. I cannot buy books, I cannot subscribe to a library; I can only just afford the necessary food from day to day: and have to toil in fear of finishing my money before another book is ready. This is monstrously unjust. Who of the public would believe that I am still in such poverty?' A few days later he bought Hardy's *Two on A Tower* and purchased a subscription to the circulating library in Exeter.

He continued to make steady progress on 'Godwin Peak', as it was still called; in mid-June he finished the second volume. He went for long walks, 'botanizing' and studying the geology of Devonshire – as the protagonist of *The Ryecroft Papers* would do. On 17 July he finished 'Godwin Peak' and on the 20th sent it off to Smith, Elder along with a letter asking for £250 for all rights. 'I don't suppose I shall get it', he wrote to Algernon. He added that he was beginning to find Exeter dull.

While awaiting Smith, Elder's verdict, he and Edith left Exeter for several weeks' holiday, going first to Clevedon and then to Burnham, on the Bristol Channel. Edith was pregnant now, and often peevish – Gissing's patience with her was having its first serious trial. He told Bertz he dreamed of being a fellow of Oxford or Cambridge, far away from material anxieties and with only scholarly work to do. Despite his own financial anxieties he lent Algernon £10. He was mulling over two possibilities: writing a one-volume novel in the manner of some of the more popular novelists of the day who had bypassed the requirements of the terrible triple-decker; and turning his professional affairs over to A. P. Watt, a well-known literary agent. Watt would take a ten percent commission, but the agent would do better in negotiations with publishers, Gissing thought, than he had ever been able to do himself. In the meantime there were other decisions to be made. With a child expected in December he would have to think about ways of augmenting his income. He resolved to try some short stories. He had not written any for seven years.

VIII

Upon his return to Exeter in August 1891, Gissing heard from James Payn of Smith, Elder, who said that he had not as yet read 'Godwin Peak' but that in any case the firm could not possibly pay £250 for it in the light of the 'financial failure' of *New Grub Street*. As I have suggested, Smith, Elder's dishonesty was bottomless. Gissing replied mildly, 'saying that if they will give £150 at once, I will take it, but that if even that sum is contingent upon [Payn's] opinion when he has finished MS, I must withdraw and go elsewhere.' Payn returned 'Godwin Peak' unread, saying he could not get to it for a month or so and that he would not in any case advise Smith, Elder to give more than £150 for anything by Gissing; he was too pessimistic ever to succeed with the public. This was the novelist's reward from this firm of cut-throats for the profits it made on *New Grub Street*. Gissing immediately put the manuscript into the hands of the agent Watt, asking him to get at least £200 for it. Watt sent it first to Chatto and Windus; they offered £120. Watt sent it to Longmans. 'I know that my books have still no market value, and that I must continue to work for small sums', Gissing wrote to Bertz. And he added, sounding yet again like the hero of *The Unclassed*: 'The artist makes all such miseries subserve his higher ends.'

Gissing began work on a short story, gave it up in a few days, and in early September decided that, for inspiration, he needed 'a large canvas'. He spent much of the month racking his brains for a subject. Around this time he was heartened by a letter from the new publishing firm of Lawrence and Bullen offering to bring out any one-volume novel he might produce – and suggesting relatively generous terms of £100 on account and a royalty of one-sixth of sales. Gissing responded immediately. He would write the tale they wanted, he said; it would be a political novel, and it would probably be called 'The Radical Candidate'. He had got that far, at least, in his thinking about the new book; but he confessed in his diary that he could not concentrate on any work until the fate of 'Godwin Peak' was settled. Watt wrote to say that Longmans had made no offer for the novel and he was sending it on to Bentley. Gissing replied that he needed money badly (he had £27 left in the bank) and that the book must be sold before the end of the year.

Early in October 1891 Gissing began to write the political novel he had promised Lawrence and Bullen. He worked quickly – perhaps because he was not particularly interested in it. His worries over the fate of 'Godwin Peak' and his financial anxieties generally were distracting, and they help to account for the mediocrity of this book (eventually *Denzil Quarrier*), which was written at desperate speed and oddly sandwiched between several of his finest productions. Throughout October he laboured over 'The Radical Candidate'. On 12 November, after a furious burst of work, he finished the book, and two days later he sent it off to Lawrence and Bullen. It was, he wrote to Bertz, 'the length of the ordinary 2-vol. novel . . . I think the book won't be bad, but it *may* give some offence to the extreme philistine wing.' Of his own affairs at this time he added: 'I seem to stand in a more dangerous position, financially, than for several years.' But he was writing more easily now than he had for some time, and this undoubtedly was due in part to his continuing comfort and the regularity of his domestic arrangements.

He now began to work on several short stories, one of which – 'A Victim of Circumstances' – remains among his best known. Later in November came a note from Lawrence and Bullen asking Gissing for a new title: 'booksellers have assured him', wrote A. H. Bullen, the editor of Middleton, 'that women will be frightened' away from a book called 'The Radical Candidate' (then as now women were the chief consumers). 'Confounded nuisance', was Gissing's reaction. The result was one of the less euphonious of Gissing's titles: *Denzil Quarrier*. The publishers immediately sent him a cheque for £105 – remarking, however, that 'the story doesn't seem . . . very strong.' 'You will excuse me for thinking that hereafter you will do stronger work than *Denzil Quarrier*,' Bullen wrote candidly. He promised none the less that they would push the new novel as much as they could, and said he thought it would do well. Lawrence and Bullen immediately sold the American, Continental, and colonial rights: the proceeds of these sales were not large, but Gissing did share in them and was pleased with his new publisher's energy and efficiency. This was the beginning of what was to be a lengthy, pleasant, and relatively lucrative publishing connection for Gissing. Unlike Smith, Elder, the new firm was both honest and encouraging: and it proposed a number of cheap reprints of his earlier books and royalty arrangements on his future ones, enabling him for the first time in his career to begin sharing in the revenues generated by his novels. He had finally broken the harpy clutch of George Smith.

Gissing's thirty-fourth birthday on 22 November passed by without comment. Already by the latter part of the month and the first days of December he was thinking about a new novel on the 'woman question' – something he had been mulling over since his abortive attempt several years earlier to write a book about a girls' school. Throughout December 1891 Gissing was reading proofs of *Denzil Quarrier*. As the time of Edith's confinement drew closer, he found more and more domestic duties devolving upon himself, and the word 'misery' occurs with regularity in the diary – the crescendo of epithets subsiding temporarily on 10 December with the birth of his first child. Gissing's account of this event is laconic, to say the least: 'The blackguard business draws to an end. Went to the study door, and heard the cry of the child. Nurse, speedily coming down, tells me it is a boy. Wind howling savagely. So, the poor girl's misery is over, and she has what she earnestly desired . . . The baby has a very ugly dark patch over right eye. Don't know the meaning of it.' Thus the novelist's first unrapturous moments of fatherhood. Gissing's son began life, as Korg says, 'by disrupting his sensitive father's routine'. The child's continuous crying both depressed and annoyed him. The boy was called Walter Leonard because Gissing thought the names 'inoffensive '.

'Godwin Peak' was rejected by Bentley, and Gissing wrote in despair to Bertz that the story was not really a bad one: 'I believe it rather strong. Possibly the reluctance of publishers is due to the subject: a man pretends to study for the Church solely to gain personal ends.' Later in December Watt succeeded in selling 'Godwin Peak' to the firm of Adam and Charles Black of Edinburgh. The terms were £150, half down and half on publication, which was expected to be in October 1892 (the book was published in May, three months after *Denzil Quarrier*). Once the agent's commission had been deducted, Gissing collected only £135 for a book considered by many critics one of his masterpieces. In fact *New Grub Street* and *Born in Exile* together brought him a total of only £285.

A few days before Christmas Gissing finished correcting proofs of *Denzil Quarrier* and returned them to Lawrence and Bullen. He was in a black mood. 'Hard frost – overflowing of a cistern – troublesome baby – general misery', the diary reports. He was still trying to work out the details of his new story on the 'woman question', but the domestic upheaval of his establishment interfered with any sustained concentration. Christmas Day 1891 was characterized by the novelist as 'the most uncomfortable I have ever known. [Edith] . . . not able to walk. Much quarrelling with nurse.' The year ended with Gissing's dawning consciousness of the nature of Edith's disposition under conditions less than ideal. 'She in brutal temper, reviling everyone and everything. A day of misery . . . and bitter repentance. Did nothing.' His domestic tranquillity threatened to come to an abrupt end along with the year 1891 – during which, despite the publication of *New Grub Street* and the writing of *Born in Exile* and *Denzil Quarrier*, he had earned only £156.

IX

The two novels written during this year vary significantly in quality and interest. *Born in Exile* (as 'Godwin Peak' would be called) is one of Gissing's most sustained pieces of fictional autobiography and among his most fascinating performances. *Denzil Quarrier*, focusing on a subject in which the novelist in fact had little interest, is pitched at several removes from his own life and remains one of his least inspired productions. The juxtaposition of these two books may lend further support to my contention that Gissing as novelist is most successful when he is most autobiographical.

Roberts declared that *Born in Exile* was Gissing's 'greatest book among the novels'. Gissing told Bertz plainly that 'Peak is myself – one phase of myself.' And he added: '"Born in Exile" was a book I *had* to write. It is off my mind, and now I go on with a sense of relief.' For Gissing, writing the novel obviously was a cathartic experience. Why?

The answer is that *Born in Exile* was Gissing's fullest expression to date (among the later novels equalled only by *Will Warburton*, perhaps) of his 'exile' psychology. Let us recall the letter he wrote to Ellen in January 1891 about his new life in Exeter. 'I remain unseen and unheard of', he says. 'I have the feeling of being deserted by all who ought to be my companions.' This was written about six weeks before he began *Born in Exile*. Obviously the subject of his *déclassé* status was on his mind, especially as he was about to admit to one and all, by marrying Edith Underwood, that an alliance with a woman of his own class was out of the question.

This was one reason why, after all, he decided to leave London. He could not take Edith to meet Mrs Harrison or Mrs Gaussen. Indeed, he was not deserted by all those who should have been his companions; he deserted them. He knew that Edith would not be invited to Wakefield after the wedding, nor would Ellen or Margaret hasten to Exeter to meet her. *Born in Exile* is not really about the clash between science and Christianity, though that is one of its ostensible subjects, nor is it about any repressed longing of Gissing's to be a clergyman, as several inattentive readers of the novel have thought. But it is very much about his yearning for a measure of middle-class respectability – very much about class. The themes of exogamy, cultural and social 'exile', of a sensitivity verging on paranoia about class, are central concerns of *Born in Exile,* woven together around the single character of Godwin Peak.

With the help of relatives and family friends in his home town of Twybridge, the fatherless, penniless Peak, son of a pharmacist's assistant, is sent on a scholarship to a preparatory school, Whitelaw College. He has a brilliant record there, carrying off a number of school prizes. He intends to go to the University of London and is about to begin his studies for the Local Examination when an incident occurs which makes him decide to leave the school: his uncle opens a restaurant in the town. This humiliation, as Peak sees it, has the effect of declassing him in the eyes of others. He feels he cannot stay at Whitelaw, and a university education is now out of the question. He disappears for several years and later surfaces in London as a free-lance journalist. His first years in the city are lonely and difficult. He has a disappointment in love. Ultimately he acquires some money, but dies abroad – in his thirties, alone, 'in exile'.

These, in broad outline, are the facts of Peak's life, and we need not analyse them in detail to see how autobiographical the story is. Substitute the uncle's restaurant for the stealing episode at Owens – both of which are humiliating for their working-class ambience – and the mysterious disappearance for the trip to America, and the stories of Peak and Gissing are virtually identical. The novelist, of course, could not know that he would also die young and in Europe – 'in exile' – but so he did; it is a measure of this book's autobiographical impulse that the future as well as the past is described, not for the first time, with such accuracy.

The novel tells chiefly of one endeavour of Peak's – to make a 'good' marriage, a marriage of the sort Gissing always dreamed of making: with a woman beautiful, well-off, highly educated, and socially sophisticated. A man who will do *anything* – assume any disguise, adopt any hypocrisy – to make such a marriage, Peak is a shamefaced caricature of Gissing himself and his own amorous aspirations (Peak, by the way, is extremely passionate). Peak's ideal of womanhood (embodied in this novel by Sidwell Warricombe) is Gissing's; and the hypocrisy of Peak's religious conversion is simply part of his attempt to seduce and become assimilated by the respectable middle class to which Sidwell belongs. Placing the Warricombe home just outside Exeter also gives Gissing a chance to write of the Devonshire area he had come to know well. And the many discussions of religion and science that take place in this novel reflect the novelist's reading of 1890 to 1891 – especially Lyell's *Geology* and Hugh Miller's *Testimony of the Rocks*.

Early in the novel the adolescent Peak is described thus: 'No common lad. A youth whose brain glowed like a furnace, whose heart throbbed with tumult of high ambitions, of inchoate desires; endowed with knowledge altogether exceptional for his years . . . but as likely as not [apt] to rush headlong on traverse roads if no judicious mind assumed control of him.' The figure Peak cuts at Whitelaw College undoubtedly also has its origin in Gissing's memory of himself at Owens:

He was not generally liked, for his mood appeared unsocial, and a repelling arrogance was sometimes felt in his talk. No doubt – said the more fortunate young men – he came from a very poor home, and suffered from the narrowness of his means . . . A deadly bashfulness forbade him to be natural either in attitude or speech. He felt his dependence in a way he had not foreseen; the very clothes he wore . . . seemed to be the gift of charity.

Of course Gissing at Owens, living on a Wakefield scholarship, would think that the boys spoke behind his back of his poverty. Peak, at least, is allowed to escape one trap Gissing fell into in Manchester – amorousness. Left to his own resources, Peak as a schoolboy is not tempted by 'casual allurements . . . to wreck amid trials exceptional', as Gissing puts it. Still, Peak has many of his creator's characteristics at nineteen: one of these is a penchant for 'moody solitude', another 'an excess of nervous sensibility'. Like Bernard Kingcote, he is highly susceptible to the modern affliction of 'nerves'. 'Life is a terrific struggle for all who begin it with no endowments save their brains', the novel tells us. Peak is unable to 'abandon himself in natural repose'. He leaves Whitelaw College determined to make it 'remember the student who seemed to have vanished amid the world's obscure tumult.'

As Peak matures, his creator's idiosyncrasies become more recognizable. Peak's first months in the metropolis, like Gissing's, are months of 'gnawing discontent . . . furious revolt . . . black despair'. A great walker, Peak often takes rambles through the wealthier districts of the West End: 'Why was no one of these doors open to him? There were the men of culture and capacity, the women of exquisite person and exalted mind. Was he the inferior of such people? By heavens, no!' We recall Gissing's bitter diary entry on the walk he took through the West End, making similar observations.

Always Peak remains morbidly sensitive about his early years. He is especially touchy on the subject of 'the unspeakable cause' of his abrupt departure from Whitelaw College. When he dines out he wonders if his friends have been able 'to obliterate from their minds . . . disagreeable thoughts' of his past life, his guilty secret. Peak thinks, for example, that Mr and Mrs Warricombe know his 'story' and 'shudder'. There can be no doubt, as Korg has said, that this aspect of *Born in Exile* dramatizes Gissing's moral conflicts resulting from the Owens College stealing episode. He wondered for years, whenever he went to the homes of his middle-class friends, whether they had heard the story of his humiliation. The several warning speeches Buckland Warricombe makes to his sister about Peak show us that for Gissing such worries were real and persistent. 'Peak . . . lacks the sense of honour generally inherited by men of our world. A powerful intellect by no means implies a corresponding development of the moral sense', Buckland says. Gissing could not forget that he was once a thief; he had been to gaol. Peak muses: 'How many years before the past could be forgotten, and his claim to the style of honourable be deemed secure?' Could anyone feel such guilt merely because, years before, his uncle had opened a restaurant in a college town?

Born in Exile is a sort of textbook compendium of the novelist's views, as they had evolved by 1891, on class questions. Peak's pride is largely the product of a 'savagely aristocratic temperament', to borrow the phrase Gissing himself used in the letter he wrote to Bertz about the book. Peak sees himself as 'one of the few highly favoured beings who, in despite of circumstances, are pinnacled above mankind' – a bit of sardonic self-characterization by Gissing. 'There's nothing I hate like vulgarity', Peak says, and throughout the book the conservative social theme is prominent. The hero cannot stand the thought of his sister marrying a shopkeeper: 'one could not dissociate him from the counter.' When his unlettered uncle decides to open the restaurant, Peak reacts strongly: 'the public proximity of an uneducated shopkeeping relative must be unwelcome to a lad who was distinguishing himself.' Later in the novel Gissing has Peak articulate a number of other social prejudices in a set-piece of exposition:

you can't call a man a democrat who recognises in his heart and soul a true distinction of social classes . . . The division I instinctively support is by no means intellectual. The well-born fool is very often more sure of my respect than the working man who struggles to a fair measure of education . . . my prejudice . . . is ineradicable . . . Birth in a sphere of refinement is desirable and respectable; it saves one . . . from many forms of coarseness. The masses are not only fools, but very near the brutes . . . I don't deny the possibility of social advance; I only say that at present the lower classes are always disagreeable, often repulsive, sometimes hateful . . . The mere sound of their voices nauseates me; their vilely grotesque accent and pronunciation – bah! I could write a paper to show that they are essentially the basest of English mortals. Unhappily, I know so much about them.

No 'democrat' himself, Gissing believed most of this. 'Whatever the mob enjoys is at once spoiled for me', Peak says.

The 'quarter-educated', as they are called in *New Grub Street,* are excoriated again, and it is the sweating working classes who are attacked, not the system that presses them down. 'I hate the word *majority* ; it is the few, the very few, that have always kept alive whatever effectual good we see in the human race', Peak declares. The novel's reactionary social philosophy is never vague or unsubtle. Peak, it is said, 'exulted in the prerogatives of birth and opulence, felt proud of hereditary pride, gloried that his mind was capable of appreciating to the full those distinctions which, by the vulgar, are not so much as suspected'. Dickens's sympathy was always with those who were locked out; Gissing's main concern is to get inside, and to stay there. Why, Peak asks himself, should he submit 'to an unending struggle with adverse conditions? . . . Nothing easier than to condemn the mode of life represented by [the] wealthy middle class; but compare it with other existences conceivable by a thinking man, and it was emphatically good.' All of these 'aristocratic instincts', as Gissing calls them, are his own. At times he seems to forget he is writing a novel, so directly does he speak to us of himself and of his own disappointments.

Like Gissing, Peak is sensitive to accent, enunciation, the spoken word. Peak's long reverie on the subject of his own speech must surely have in it something of the insecurity of the Yorkshire druggist's son: 'Peak after each of his . . . remarks, made comparison of his tone and phraseology with those of the other speakers. Had he still any marks of the ignoble world from which he sprang? Any defect of pronunciation, any native awkwardness of utterance? . . . Preciseness must be avoided, for in a young man it seemed to argue conscious effort.' Peak sees his birth into the working classes as having placed him 'in a social sphere where he must ever be an alien'. 'I was born in exile – born in exile', Peak says over and over again. The word 'exile' recurs as a refrain. 'My life has been one of slavery and exile . . . from the day of my birth', Peak tells Sidwell. 'Whether I remained with my kith and kin, or turned my back upon them in the hope of finding my equals, I was condemned to a life of miserable incompleteness . . . I was born in exile. It took a long time before I had taught myself how to move and speak like one of the class to which I belonged by right of intellect.' Peak sees as an emblem of his social alienation his status as a lodger living in somebody else's rooms: 'as on the day of his arrival, he was an alien – a lodger. What else had he ever been, since boyhood? A lodger in Kingsmill [Manchester], a lodger in London, a lodger in Exeter. Nay, even as a boy he could scarcely have been said to "live at home", for from the dawn of conscious intelligence he felt himself out of place among familiar things and people.' And:

For six years he had shifted from quarter to quarter, from house to house, driven away each time by the hateful contact of vulgarity in every form, – by foulness and dishonesty, by lying, slandering, quarrelling, by drunkenness, by brutal vice, – by all abominations that distinguish the lodging-house of the metropolis. Obliged to practise extreme economy, he could not take refuge among self-respecting people.

We can see why so many stories Gissing wrote in the nineties are set in a lodging-house; the place was a symbol for him of social anomalousness. Real people live in real homes amidst families, not in somebody else's rooms. His fate, Peak reflects, is 'Solitude, now and for ever, or perchance some base alliance of the flesh, which would involve his later days in sordid misery' (Gissing was writing in the first months of his second marriage – a 'base alliance of the flesh' if ever there was one). 'I belong to no class, town, family, club', Peak says. 'The result of all these years' savage striving to knit myself into the social fabric' has been failure.

Gissing could never forget a scene he witnessed in a restaurant during his destitute days in London. 'The fact of social difference is always illustrated to me', he wrote in his Commonplace Book in the year *Born in Exile* was published, 'by that young fellow – proletarian of some kind, who had evidently a little unfamiliar money in his pocket – who came into the restaurant where I was dining, and awkwardly ordered a beefsteak. He could not eat it, and after a few vain trials began to wrap it up in his handkerchief. A waiter brought him a newspaper, into which the poor fellow cast his meat, and hurried away.' The man in alien circumstances is the vintage Gissing theme – the man out of place, embarrassed, humiliated, anomalous.

Other familiar themes abound in *Born in Exile*. The chief of these is marriage. Peak's attitudes toward women are amply expounded in the course of this long novel. He tells Earwaker: 'I hate emancipated women! . . . Women ought neither to be enlightened nor dogmatic. They ought to be sexual.' Later Earwaker declares to Peak: 'Women are born for one thing only, the Church of England marriage service.' The truly educated women, Peak muses, 'are to be found in every age, but how many of them shine with the distinctive ray of womanhood? These are so rare . . . The truly emancipated woman . . . is almost asexual.' The lot of many men, then – 'until the new efforts in female education shall have overcome the vice of wedlock as hitherto sanctioned' – is to marry ignorant women (women, for example, who had never heard of *Pilgrim's Progress*). 'Nature provides the hallucination which flings a lover at his mistress's feet. For the chill which follows upon attainment she cares nothing', *Born in Exile* announces. Obviously Gissing was beginning to feel 'the chill'.

He was to explore the 'woman question' more fully in his next two books. Here he expresses a side of himself he apparently recognized – his need, born of myriad insecurities, to be or feel superior to the women he became involved with, and the quickness with which he tired of them once the original 'hallucination' (i.e. sexual desire) had subsided.

Like Peak, Gissing spent a good deal of his life looking for an intellectual woman who would live with him ; unlike Peak, the novelist was scared to death he might find one. What then? That part of Gissing theoretically seeking a woman his intellectual equal is articulated in Peak's pursuit of Sidwell Warricombe. 'My one supreme desire is to marry a perfectly refined woman,' Peak declares. The perfect woman, for him, will have 'always lived among people of breeding and high education, and never had her thoughts soiled with the vile contact of poverty'. During a scene in the Warricombes' drawing-room Peak mentally compares his ideal woman, Sidwell, both with 'an average emancipated girl' and 'a daughter of the people. How unsatisfying was the former; the

latter, how repulsive! Here [in Sidwell] one had the exquisite mean.'
Gissing had just married 'a daughter of the people'; that he would
soon grow dissatisfied with her was inevitable (his next liaison
would be with an 'emancipated girl'). Long had Peak searched for
'the prize which most men claim as a mere matter of course, a wife
of social instincts correspondent with his own', Gissing writes. Like
Trollope, miserable early years made Gissing especially responsive
to the imagined joys of ordinary life. It was the tragedy of Gissing's
life that, unlike Trollope, he attained these things only in his
imagination. Says Earwaker of Peak: 'His mate must be somewhere
. . . but he will never find her.'

This is certainly Gissing's view of his own situation. But why
should he be singled out for such misery? *Born in Exile* gives us a
large part of the answer: Peak is too much in love with a class to fall
in love with a woman. 'The woman throned in his imagination was
no individual but the type of an order', the novel declares.

[Peak] could not . . . inflame himself with the ardour of soul reaching to
soul; he was preoccupied with the contemplation of qualities which
characterise a class. The sense of social distinctions was so burnt into him,
that he could not be affected by any pictured charm of mind or person in a
woman who had not the stamp of gentle birth and breeding.

Gissing's self-destructiveness set him at variance with his own
ideals; and we need look no further to see why his first two
marriages were such utter failures (though there were other reasons,
of course).

When Marcella Moxey tells Peak, in reference to his matrimonial
goals, that 'there was never a man who united such capacity for
great things with so mean an ideal', it suggests at least that Gissing
perceived the shallowness of his sexual values. But he persisted in
them, and I think the clue to why he did so may be found in *Born in
Exile*. It is embodied in a remarkable speech about himself that Peak
makes to Sidwell. 'To myself . . . I seem anything but lovable,' he
tells her. 'I don't underrate my powers – rather the opposite . . .
but what I always seem to lack is the gift of pleasing – moral grace
. . . I criticise myself ceaselessly; expose without mercy all those
characteristics which another man would keep out of sight. Yes,
and for this very reason, just because I think myself unlovable – the
gift of love means far more to me than to other men.' Such feelings
usually are the result of a sense of inadequacy; Peak's surely are
identical with Gissing's. Gissing thought more about love than
other men because, more than other men, he thought himself

unlovable. At the same time his notions about love were hopelessly idealistic (some of the letters he wrote to Gabrielle Fleury express feelings that have no relation to life; we shall come to them in due course). Thus it is not remarkable that Peak constantly thinks about women; that his mental life is dominated by what the novel calls 'erotic reverie'. Surely the speech Peak makes on his own unlovableness goes far toward explaining Gissing's extremely passionate nature, his worship of superior women, and his liaisons with inferior ones.

The novelist's domestic claustrophobia, of which we have seen prior evidence, is articulated in *Born in Exile* in a short sermon on the married uses of wealth. One of the advantages of money, the book says, 'is that it allows husband and wife to keep a great deal apart without any show of mutual unkindness, a condition essential to happiness in marriage' (it is no accident that Godwin Peak is named after the man who advocated separate dwellings for husbands and wives). Also typical of Gissing is Peak's desire to mould the woman he marries: 'Little by little she would learn to think as he did . . . Godwin had absolute faith in his power of dominating the woman he should inspire with tenderness.' No wonder Gissing's wives had a tendency to grow violent. There is also in *Born in Exile* the familiar digression on women's speech – intonation, accent, diction, and so on. Peak is described as a man with 'fastidious ears'. To be grammatical is not enough for him; women must emit 'conversational music. Of course there existed a world where only such speech was interchanged, and how inestimably happy those men to whom the sphere was native!' Some of this undoubtedly is self-parody. Still, one has the feeling that Nell and Edith must have had a good deal to put up with; and it is perhaps no accident that Gissing's third wife, according to Morley Roberts, had 'a voice that was absolute music'.

Another familiar theme is the attack on the new commercialism and its awful product, urban blight. The country outside Exeter is said to be spoiled by commercial growth. Also characteristic is the attack in the novel on orthodox Christianity and the 'new sophistry' of its most zealous practitioners, who are eager, at any cost, to accommodate the Church and its dwindling membership to the new sciences, especially geology. Christianity is denounced as 'at best a helpful delusion . . . as it has been understood through the ages, [Christianity] can no longer be accepted . . . that was the truth, the truth, the *truth!*' Gissing's sister Margaret disliked this book more intensely than any other her brother wrote (knowing in advance how Wakefield would react, Gissing did not send a copy of *Born in Exile* home). 'It is a pity you should write on a subject you so little understand as Christianity', Margaret said to him, on behalf of the family.

It would be as responsible for me to deny the existence of all the beautiful things you have seen and told me of in foreign countries, simply because *I* have not seen them, as it is for you to deny spiritual things you have never seen or felt, when there are thousands of people who have seen them, and are therefore as certain of them as of their own existence. How anyone can disbelieve the Bible merely because it is not written in the latest scientific language seems remarkable.

'How impossible to reply to such stuff as this!' the novelist noted in his Commonplace Book.

Born in Exile is in many ways the archetypal Gissing novel – even more so than the better-known and more widely discussed *New Grub Street. Born in Exile* is too discursive, too self-indulgent, too much a 'fluid pudding' to be one of Gissing's greatest works, but it is certainly one of his most interesting. It brings together in closest proximity the themes of class, money, and women so central to all his work; and the exile motif is nowhere else so ubiquitous. Considerations of the results of exogamous marriage fill every chapter. It should be clear now why this was a novel Gissing told Bertz he *had* to write – and why he felt such a sense of relief once he had written it. The guilty secrets of the early years were at least partially exorcized by being exposed to the reading public, even heavily disguised. Rarely in the novels does Gissing speak to us so directly for so long: rarely is the narrative voice so unmuffled by invention, factitiousness, obfuscation.

Few scenes in Gissing's novels are more powerfully written than that in which Peak declaims to Christian Moxey his Schopenhauerian view of existence: 'If ever I crush a little green fly that crawls upon me in the fields at once I am filled with envy of its fate . . . To have passed so suddenly from being into nothingness – how blessed an extinction!' To feel this way, Peak concludes, is 'to be a true pessimist'.

Denzil Quarrier, written hurriedly in two months and devoted partly to a subject in which Gissing had little interest – politics – is one of his less successful works. It is also one of his least autobiographical novels. Quarrier's manic nature, his scholarly side, and his small store of common sense may remind us of

Gissing, but generally the few resemblances between them have more to do with opinions on political and social matters than details of private life and behaviour. As I have argued, the farther Gissing gets away from himself the less interesting his books turn out to be.

There are some characteristic themes here. 'Oh, these English provincial towns! What an atmosphere of deadly dullness hung over them all!' muses Glazzard, reflecting Gissing's growing boredom with Exeter. The preservation of the countryside is also a concern. But the novel's chief topics are politics, marriage, and women's rights, and from the start it is clear that the treatment of them is going to be unconventional. Indeed, convention itself is under attack here. Thus: 'conventional wrong-doing, when it injures no one, is not wrong-doing at all, unless discovered'; indeed, conventional ideas of 'wrong doing' are largely the result of 'imbecile prejudice'. 'We have to do with monstrous social tyrannies', Quarrier says. 'Social law is stupid and unjust, imposing its obligations without regard to person and circumstance. It presumes that no one can be *trusted.*'

Of course Gissing had many reasons for attacking conventional values and beliefs. No one is more bitter about privilege than the man who is denied it. In *Denzil Quarrier* the protagonist's grudge against society has to do with a woman. Quarrier married Lilian not realizing she was committing bigamy. When he finds out, Quarrier's love for her remains unchanged; they decide to go on living together as husband and wife. What matters to Quarrier is how he feels, not what the law says. Society, he believes, by its very nature forces people to tell lies. 'She *is* my wife, in every sense of the word that merits the consideration of a rational creature!' Years later Gissing would be saying this, or something like it, to his friends about Gabrielle Fleury. Again, uncannily, his future is prefigured in his fiction, for in May 1899 he would 'marry' another woman while his present wife was still very much alive – and he would 'marry' her in precisely the same way that Denzil 'marries' Lilian, walking through a farcical ceremony in France for the benefit of some friends and relations. In the autumn of 1891 Gissing wrote a novel in which his characters face situations, and resolve them, exactly as he was to do nearly eight years later.

Gissing's hatred of conventional values in this novel smacks of protesting too much; the issue on which his hero chooses to contest society's law is not a good one. Presumably the novelist was not advocating bigamy. On the other hand he was married to someone he was beginning to discover he did not love and undoubtedly there is some special pleading going on. It is no accident that Lilian is the most sympathetic character in the book, though technically she is its chief 'criminal', the bigamist. *Denzil Quarrier* suggests that convention is especially despicable when it deprives deserving people of what they want. To put it another way, it shows Gissing sneering at something he now knew he could never have while married to Edith: ordinary middle-class respectability. If you cannot have something you want, one way to respond is to say that you do not want it anyway, that it is not worth having. Among other things this is what Gissing does in *Denzil Quarrier*.

The exogamous 'marriage' between Quarrier and Lilian forces them to keep a 'guilty secret'. She comes from a respectable but working-class background, and is largely uneducated; his origins are the educated middle classes. It is almost a replay of Gissing's two marriages, though Lilian is superior to both Nell and Edith. But she is nervous with Quarrier's friends, afraid she will betray ignorance.

Her ultimate resolution of her problems is a familiar one to the reader of Gissing – suicide by drowning. In two early stories, 'The Sins of the Fathers' and 'All for Love', Gissing had tried out a similar idea: in each someone marries supposing a former lover or spouse to be dead, in each the absent one turns up inconveniently, and in each there are several deaths by drowning. But in these stories – written, respectively, in 1877 and 1880 – the young Gissing's mode is melodrama rather than analysis, and questions of class and conventional conduct are hardly touched upon. Lilian marries Quarrier knowing that Northway, her husband, is still alive; but she is unable to resist the blandishments of respectability, promotion into a higher social sphere, and a man she can love. She is a sort of female Arthur Golding, tied to a lower-class spouse while courting a middle-class lover. Arthur, of course, is saved from immorality by Helen Norman's rectitude – but his end is the same as Lilian's. Now, a dozen years after *Workers in the Dawn* was written, such virtue as Helen's seems less relevant to Gissing than domestic happiness, achieved at whatever cost. But what happens when this happiness is found to be in defiance of society's rules? *Born in Exile* raised a similar question. In both novels those who sneer at conventional values come to an unhappy end, while the solid middle-class people are around at the finish. If Gissing expresses contempt for convention in these books, he also acknowledges its terrible power. In the end the message of *Denzil Quarrier*, like that of *Born in Exile,* is a conservative one: the social fabric is too powerful to be rent by puny protest; for your own safety, observe the conventions (or be seen to observe them) – even if you find them absurd.

Lilian's situation leads Gissing to one of his favourite topics – the education of women. 'The ordinary girl [is] sent forth into life with a mind scarcely more developed than that of a child. Hence those monstrous errors she constantly [commits] when called upon to accept a husband', Quarrier says. 'Not one marriage in fifty thousand [is] an alliance on terms fair to the woman. In the vast majority of cases, she [weds] a sort of man in the moon. Of him and all his world she [knows] nothing.' Because of the ignorance of women (in part sexual, clearly), most men who marry come to regret it, according to Quarrier; and he suggests that women without families of their own should help to train young girls so as to emancipate them from such deplorable ignorance (here, perhaps, is the germ of Gissing's next novel, *The Odd Women*).

The marriage theme and the question of female education also incline Gissing to say a good deal in *Denzil Quarrier* about feminism and women's rights – a subject with which he had been tinkering on and off for years, going back to 'The Head Mistress'. The novel is certainly unsympathetic to feminism. Its chief proponent, Mrs Wade, complacently watches Lilian drown when she alone could save her – because she wants Quarrier for herself. She believes in 'freedom' but not, so she says, in marriage; yet she spends much of the novel chasing Quarrier around. She thinks that women are silly, worthless, and a 'great reactionary force': in political and social matters, she says, they always demonstrate 'a native baseness . . . They worship the vulgar, the pretentious, the false.' Such a woman as Mrs Wade is by any standards a bizarre representative of the women's-rights movement – unless, of course, the novelist is making a point. Nor is Quarrier, although a strong advocate of women's education, any more sympathetic to organized feminism. Women's rights, he says, are 'humbug' and 'twaddle'. Women, he declares, haven't 'the faintest understanding of political principles'.

Queen's College had been founded in 1848, Bedford College in 1849. The influential Society for Promoting the Employment of Women opened its doors in the fifties; the Married Women's Property Act, though not passed into law until 1882, was first introduced in Parliament in 1856. Mill's *The Subjection of Women* was published in 1869; Girton College was founded in 1872. The seventies saw the agitation for women's rights reach a sort of crescendo, and Gissing, whose novel is set in the years 1879 to 1880, was very much interested in the subject. But his attitude was ambivalent. He knew that well-educated women were hard to find. He wanted women to receive the sort of education that would make them fit wives for educated men – he felt, as Quarrier says, that they should not be sent ignorant into the world. On the other hand, he knew how slatternly housekeeping could interfere with a man's work and peace of mind, and he thought that increased liberty made some women unmanageable, encouraging them to neglect their homes and their children and abuse their husbands. It is no accident that in his critical study of Dickens, Gissing chooses Ruth Pinch as his favourite Dickensian character. The prospect of an England in which women had forsaken the linen closets for the hustings scared Gissing to death.

Mrs Wade's questionable credentials as a feminist form part of the leisurely commentary in *Denzil Quarrier* on politics, which makes it plain that in Gissing's eyes anyone with an announced political creed is likely to be untrustworthy. People get involved in politics, the novel tells us, not to help others but because of 'the wish for power' and the 'delight in ruling' that comes with power. Quarrier thinks the most efficient form of government is autocracy. 'I have no objection to an autocrat; I think most countries need one' (one recalls Gissing's preference for Italy's monarchy over France's republic). 'There are no such things as natural rights', Quarrier says. 'Nature gives no rights; she will produce an infinite number of creatures only to torture and eventually destroy them . . . civilization is at war with nature.' He expresses a stoical point of view about human suffering – to which, he believes, there can be no political solution. 'One is bound, in common sense, to close eyes and ears against all but a trifling fraction of human misery', he declares. 'Men are perishing by every conceivable form of cruelty and natural anguish.' People 'are being burnt, boiled, hacked, squashed, rent, exploded to death in every town . . . of the globe'. To dwell on these things 'would lead to madness . . . We have to say: It doesn't concern us! And no more it does. We haven't the ordering of the world; we can't alter the vile cause of things.' There is no *political* answer to anything. Quarrier predicts a world torn in the future between the 'Teutons' (by which he means the Americans and the English) and the Slavs. Very prescient, indeed.

Nor is *Denzil Quarrier* a party novel: Gissing seems to hate all political factions equally. Political aspiration is equated here with various kinds of moral charlatanism. In the local election the

Liberal–Radical candidate, Quarrier himself, is living a lie. The Tory, Welwyn-Baker, is incompetent and lazy (too lazy, as a matter of fact, to appear in the novel). Among the book's other would-be politicians, Mumbray is an embodiment of cant and humbug; Northway, who believes that political parties are 'worthless', is an extortionist of professional calibre; and Eustace Glazzard sublimates his political ambitions in treachery and sadism. Quarrier says he could have been a Conservative as easily as a Radical – it makes no difference: 'There's foolery and dishonesty' on all sides; 'What sensible man swears by a party?'

Yet at the heart of *Denzil Quarrier* is not politics but rather the unequal marriage and the guilty secret it hides – vintage Gissing and the best thing in the book. The domestic scenes rather than the public ones give this so-called political novel its chief interest and its intermittent power. Here, as so often, Gissing's primary subject is the relation of the sexes and the social backgrounds against which their sad comedy is played.

❧

CHAPTER 8

THE MAN OF LETTERS, 1892–1894

Sweet are the uses of adversity.   *As You Like It*

A man, when he marries a woman like that, thinks he's going to
lift her up to his own station. The fool! It's she who drags him
down to hers.   Maugham, *The Merry-Go-Round*

Art, you know, is only contemptible when it supports the
artist.   *A Life's Morning*

I

THE year 1892 did not begin auspiciously for Gissing. Edith
remained in poor health; she spent much of January in bed with
neuralgic headaches. He was forced, as he put it, 'to nurse the
yelling baby'. 'Each night finds me wearied out with anxieties and
sheer physical fatigue . . . Driven all but to desperation.' By mid-
January his agonies with the baby were so acute that he decided to
send it out to nurse. Throughout the rest of the month he worked
on his revision of 'Godwin Peak', ultimately hitting upon the title
Born in Exile. He noted particular problems in revising 'the love
chapters [between Peak and Sidwell] – always very difficult for me'.
On 5 February he finished the revision; on the same day *Denzil
Quarrier* was published by Lawrence and Bullen. Gissing sent
copies to the usual small group. With Bertz's volume he enclosed a
note: 'If you don't care much for it, just make a cross at the head of
your next letter, and never mind further comment' (as it turned out,
Bertz liked the book). In another letter to Bertz he noted that
Kipling, Hall Caine, and J. M. Barrie had all made 'enormous
reputations' in the past year: 'I wish my receipts from literature
were one quarter of what each of them earns.' 'Lord, lord! what a
life it is, this of literature!' he wrote to Algernon. He was amazed
to hear that Mrs Humphry Ward had earned £18,000 from *David
Grieve*: 'Incredible! Five hundred a year for life! And in ten years
no one will care to read the book.'

On 19 February Gissing began a new novel. As yet he had no
working title; but the description he gave to Bertz of the subject

leaves no doubt that the new tale (after many false starts and new beginnings, with nothing completed until October) was *The Odd Women*:

It will present those people who, congenitally incapable of true education, have yet been taught to consider themselves too good for manual, or any humble, work. As yet I have chiefly dealt with types expressing the struggle of natures endowed *above* their stations; now I turn to those who are *below* it. The story will be a study of vulgarism – the all but triumphant force of our time. Women will be the chief characters.

Here was a class of 'exiles' of another sort.

Denzil Quarrier, meanwhile, was being treated with unexpected generosity by the press. The *Daily Chronicle* was ecstatic. *The Saturday Review* said *Denzil Quarrier* showed 'a mind well abreast of the time. A bolder theme may possibly suit this author better.' Gissing delightedly sent this to Ellen – who, along with Margaret and their mother, had objected to the bigamy theme as being too audacious. *The Times* compared the novel, not unfavourably, with works of Dickens and Meredith. The *Guardian* and the *Illustrated London News* found the book unpleasant, but the *Athenaeum* gave special praise to the handling of political matters, and the *Whitehall Review* singled out the novel's plot for special compliment. The *Academy* and the *Graphic* were unenthusiastic. The *New Review* published a nasty notice by H. D. Traill – redressed two months later when, in the same journal, Edmund Gosse recommended *Denzil Quarrier* as one of the year's best novels. Initial sales of the book were brisk.

II

Gissing received word from A. & C. Black that *Born in Exile* would be published in the spring rather than the autumn, and late in February the first proofs began to arrive. In March he was interested to hear that a lecture had been given in London before the Ethical Society entitled 'The Novels of George Gissing'. The lecturer's name was Clara Collet, MA. The paper's main thrust, he discovered, was to contradict the general impression that Gissing was a fatalist; the lecturer defended his books as a becoming mixture of idealism and realism. Gissing was intrigued, but did not get in touch with Miss Collet (she took the initiative the following year). Also this spring a highly laudatory article on his books was published by Morley Roberts in the *Novel Review*. Roberts gets a good deal wrong, but in several particulars – for example, his assertions that Gissing is 'one of the few authors read by other literary men' and that he creates feminine characters 'whom women themselves actually regard as feminine' – he strikes the right note. The lecture and the article, along with the favourable reviews and respectable sales of *Denzil Quarrier,* put Gissing in a rare optimistic mood. 'I begin to have hope of escaping the workhouse', he wrote to Ellen.

But the latter part of that spring of 1892 was not so pleasant. He found the new novel difficult to get on with, abandoned it, took it up again. In mid-April Walter was brought home, and the domestic disorder Gissing dreaded recommenced. He found once again that he could not work; and suddenly he and Edith began to quarrel. She was proving incapable of any sustained management of the household. She could not get along with, supervise, or even control the series of nurses and servants who came and went with maddening regularity; the novelist ended by taking care of the child himself throughout much of the day. An entry in his Commonplace Book is revealing: 'I am never so impressed with a sense of social distinctions as in seeing a houseful of servants ruled by a dignified and gracious mistress . . . most women are hopelessly incapable of anything of the kind, and the exceptional instances give one a high idea of all that is implied in rank and education. The last thing to be looked for in a woman of low social standing is the power of ruling subordinates.' Well, he had married 'a woman of low social standing', and the result was predictable. His disenchantment with Edith set in in earnest. Roberts, who visited them in Exeter during this spring, said later 'they were then living on the verge of a daily quarrel . . . a dispute was for ever imminent . . . [Edith] frequently broke out into actual violence and the smashing of crockery.' (He also observed that 'her locutions were vulgar, and she had no natural refinement.') Eventually, Roberts says, it was 'nearly impossible for any one to enter [the] house for fear of an exhibition of [her] rage'. Gissing must have been haunted by memories of his ordeal with Nell; the whole thing seemed to be happening all over again. Edith, he told Roberts, had 'developed the temper of a devil, and began to make his life not less wretched . . . than the poor creature had done who was now in her grave'. He began to wonder if his wife was mad.

But what depressed him most was his inability to work. The new book grew by inches – largely because he could not trust Walter to the care of his mother. No servant would stay long in the house with Edith throwing dishes at her; and her violence made the novelist fear for the child's physical safety. Servant after servant, nurse after nurse, came, saw, and left. As a consequence, according to Roberts, Gissing himself 'often did the household work when he should have been writing. He was dragged away from his ordinary tasks by an uproar in the kitchen', or some argument between Edith and a servant over who was to do what in the house that day. In all likelihood one of Edith's problems was that she was forced by her position to give orders to women of her own class who could see what she was and resented her ascendancy – undoubtedly exercised without tact.

The diary now begins a familiar melancholy refrain – 'wasted day', 'couldn't work', 'did nothing', 'domestic uproar', and so on. 'Cannot even read nowadays', Gissing wrote on 30 April. And, a few days later: '[Edith] constantly groaning with neuralgia, and discontent at our loneliness'. 'Loneliness' is a euphemism for his refusal to take her anywhere or to introduce her to anybody; he had married Mrs Yule, and he knew it. In mid-May: 'Uproar in the house, owing to breakage of plates and dishes. Misery.'

In the midst of all this turmoil – appropriately, perhaps – *Born in Exile* was published. It offended nearly everyone. The major exception was the *Daily Chronicle*, which pronounced the new book Gissing's 'best'. But this was the minority point of view. The *Speaker* commented that the novel's only distinction was to equal the pessimism of *New Grub Street*, which had seemed impossible: 'One does not appreciate gloom best by having three large . . . volumes of it . . . the book is like a large dinner composed entirely of very cold mutton.' The *Morning Post* called *Born in Exile* 'arid'. The *Saturday Review* was genuinely abusive. It characterized Peak as 'the most unlovable creation that ever appealed to the misdirected sympathies of a reader . . . Part prig, part snob, all egotist, Godwin Peak inspires us with feelings where disgust and boredom strive for mastery.' *The Times* found the novel interesting, but heavy going; like many other reviewers of the book, *The Times* writer wondered why Peak shouldn't simply have 'persevered in his own work' rather than 'masqueraded as a clergyman' (a question too complicated for anyone who did not know the novelist to answer). The *Guardian* found *Born in Exile* interesting but too painful. The *Academy* summed up the response many readers, both past and present, have had to this most difficult of all Gissing's novels:

The story is almost necessarily a melancholy one, but it is singularly able; and those readers who do not at an early stage give it up as dull will gratefully admit that it is brilliant. The cleverness of the book is attested by the fact that Godwin Peak neither forfeits the reader's sympathy nor wins his admiration. We take him for what he is; and though the whole result is unsatisfactory, it includes much that is worth having.

The book sold fairly well despite the reviews, with three cheap editions published in England between 1893 and 1896, and a second colonial edition brought out in 1895.

Bertz worried about its melancholy tone. 'You will not find that Peak's tone is to be henceforth mine – do not fear it', Gissing replied. 'I hope to be more and more objective in my work from now on', he added. He went on to tell his friend that in future books he planned to deal with what he called 'the flood of blackguardism' he saw 'pouring forth over . . . society' wherever he looked – with the 'extending and deepening Vulgarity' of the time. And he goes on in this letter to speculate whether he himself would

ever be the subject of a serious study in one of the leading periodicals – as Meredith and Hardy and Marion Crawford – and all the rest of them – have been again and again? It is doubtful: probably not before my death . . . It is true that there are occasional little signs of spreading recognition, but this affects only a . . . very small section of the public.

He concludes, however, on a more hopeful note: 'The subjects ideally adapted to one's mind and mood are of course very few; they occur only in moments of happy inspiration. One has often to struggle vehemently with what seems uncongenial matter – and indeed there comes a reward from such struggle. One's powers grow in the process.' In mid-May Gissing's diary records another beginning made on the novel about women. The fragment was abandoned again three weeks later. This sort of thing was to go on throughout the rest of the spring and early summer. Meanwhile, Gissing's sister Margaret, at his invitation (largely as a result of Edith's complaints about their solitude), came to visit them for two weeks. This was Edith's first contact with her husband's family, and the experiment soon proved unsuccessful. Edith found in Margaret another Gissing to vent her rage upon; Margaret was delighted to go home.

A series of letters from Gissing to Bertz gives a revealing picture of his state of mind during the summer of 1892. Two extracts:

It is hard indeed that one's work must always be performed under conditions more or less unfavourable. We are always being told that a struggle against adverse circumstances is for the good of our art, and that with prosperity comes relaxation of effort. It is so, undoubtedly, with some men, but chiefly with those who have nothing very particular to say.

The summer has, for me, been all but wasted. I have begun several stories, but in each case only to destroy what I wrote . . . I must get a book done so as to have some money before the end of the year . . . I am getting a very solid bad-reputation for gloominess and misanthropy.

III

After more false starts (on 1 July he noted in his diary that he had begun the new novel seven different times; on 10 July he recorded an eighth beginning; on 30 July: '*Decided to throw aside all I have written!*') he hit upon the vein he was to mine in the final version of *The Odd Women*. He worked away at it throughout the rest of the summer despite his little son's ups and downs in health and another series of angry nurses. 'It deals with the women who, from the marriage point of view, are *superfluous*', he told Bertz. For the next months the writing went smoothly. *The Odd Women* was finished on 4 October 1892 and dispatched to Lawrence and Bullen the next day. Of this book Gissing wrote in his diary: 'the writing has been as severe a struggle as ever I knew. Not a day without wrangling and uproar down in the kitchen; not an hour when I was really at peace in mind. A bitter struggle.'

After finishing it he took Edith and Walter to Weymouth for a short holiday, after which he went on to visit Algernon in Worcestershire while Edith and the child went to stay with her married sister in London. Within a few days her relatives had had enough of her, and Edith was ordered out. Gissing took lodgings for the three of them in Birmingham for three weeks; he wanted to gather material for use in his next novel, which he tentatively planned to set in the industrial Midlands.

Bullen was pleased with *The Odd Women*, though he asked for some minor revisions, especially in early chapters. He offered Gissing 100 guineas plus a royalty that amounted to about 10½ per cent on the three-volume edition and one-sixth on a subsequent cheaper edition. He also volunteered to reprint *The Emancipated* in a cheap edition the following year if Bentley could be brought to terms (he could). Gissing was delighted, and agreed to these proposals.

By mid-November he was working on the first proofs of *The Odd Women*. His thirty-fifth birthday, on 22 November, passed apparently unnoticed. In early December proofs arrived of his story 'A Victim of Circumstances', which would appear in the January

1893 number of *Blackwood's Magazine* and for which Gissing, to his astonishment, now received a cheque for £20. The editor invited him to send more short fiction. In the midst of this relatively productive period another domestic row broke out, and Gissing noted in his diary: 'Had to go down into the kitchen and map out on paper a daily scheme of house-work. Bah!' He wrote to Roberts, who had proposed another visit, that 'our domestic confusion makes it impossible to receive visitors.'

Bringing Bertz up to date on his various writing projects, Gissing told him about a book he intended to write on middle-class life which would insist 'on the degree to which people have become *machines,* in harmony with the machinery amid which they spend their lives.' The title would be 'The Iron Gods' and the setting Birmingham. Gissing's weariness – *The Odd Women* would be his twelfth published novel in thirteen years – is apparent in this aside to his closest friend:

There is nothing more wearying and distressing than a failure of one's confidence, time after time, in a scheme of literary work. I know it myself only too well. Again and again and yet again I have begun a novel; only to write a few chapters and throw them aside as useless. Many, many months have I thus wasted. If I had confessed to you all such failures, you would have feared for me very often. But I have to keep most of my miseries to myself.

Gissing hired a study to work in away from the house in Exeter and settled down to write 'The Iron Gods.' It went well at first. Late in December he wrote to Ellen: 'You will, I am sure, enjoy your holidays. Ah, how I envy this going about among people. Never to speak with a soul outside one's own household is very trying.' On 31 December he recorded the following in his diary: 'The year 1892, on the whole profitless. Marked by domestic misery and discomfort. The one piece of work. "The Odd Women", scribbled . . . as the autumn drew to an end, and I have no high opinion of it. Have read next to nothing; classical studies utterly neglected. With my new plan of [working] away from the wretched home, I may hope to achieve more in year to come.' Still, 1892 had not been so terribly bad for him as a writer. He had earned about £275 from his work during this year, a new high.

IV

Bullen sold Continental and American rights to *The Odd Women*; Gissing shared in these sales. The novelist told Bertz, in reply to another query about the new book, that it was about women 'who are *odd* in the sense that they do not make a match; as we say "an odd glove".' He began to think of possible subjects for short stories; the large payment he received from *Blackwood's* had been earned with comparative ease. 'I wish I could do something more than write 3-vol. novels', he told Bertz now, early in 1893. There would be a great outpouring of short fiction from Gissing during the years 1893 to 1896. 'Before long, I shall go back to London for good', he went on to inform his friend. 'I want the streets again.' Similar sentiments were expressed to Algernon: 'I fear that I have wasted two years here in Devon. It is obviously in London that my material lies.' The novelist's restlessness, along with his impatience at self-imposed exile in the country, were soon to spur another move.

Meanwhile his domestic difficulties continued. There is a pathetic diary entry for 24 January 1893:

an anguish of suffering in the thought that I can never hope to have an intellectual companion at home. Condemned for ever to associate with inferiors – and so crossly unintelligent. Never a word exchanged on anything but the paltry everyday life of the household. Never a word to me, from anyone, of understanding sympathy – or of encouragement. Few men, I am sure, have led so bitter a life.

Bertz was in Germany, and Roberts denied the house by Edith's bad temper. Gissing's few London friends were out of reach. His family liked nothing he did, and his wife, 'so crossly unintelligent', was not interested. Truly, he was leading the life of an exile.

During the last week of January he worked on a new short story and finished correcting proofs of *The Odd Women*. Walter, now more than a year old, was beginning to dislike his mother, Gissing thought. In February Bullen suggested doing cheap reprints of *The Unclassed* and *Isabel Clarendon,* and added: 'We count it a privilege to publish your books. If we lose money in issuing popular editions of your earlier novels it won't trouble us. The pleasure of seeing your books collected would atone for any loss; but we fancy they might ultimately be profitable.' George Smith could never have written such a letter. Gissing's grateful comment: 'Was ever struggling author thus addressed?' He worked away on 'The Iron Gods'. Late in the month he was delighted to see a new cheap edition of *Born in Exile* announced – and rather less delighted to lend poor Algernon another £10. In March and April he was making painful decisions about 'The Iron Gods'. Ultimately he decided to abandon it altogether. It thus joins the list of nearly completed Gissing novels we shall never know very much about. He had planned an uncharacteristically happy ending, and perhaps that was one reason he had trouble in finishing it. What little of it remains extant may be found in the Birmingham setting of *Eve's Ransom*.

Gissing now turned his attention to shorter fiction. He sold one story to the *English Illustrated Magazine* this spring for eleven guineas, and planned to write more. At the end of March he spent a week in London alone, savouring the city, and being finally sick of Exeter looking for a new place to live – chiefly in the suburb of Brixton. He found some unfurnished rooms there to his liking, and the move was planned for June. At the same time he hired another room to work in away from home, in Kennington.

The Odd Women was published in April. At the end of the month Gissing braced himself to receive his mother on a visit to Exeter. The preparations for her arrival occasioned more domestic upheaval: 'perpetual rows', says the diary, and 'misery'. When his mother arrived in mid-May, Gissing decided after a day or two that the house in Exeter was too small to hold them all and went off to Burnham for a week. By the end of this month, May 1893, reviews of *The Odd Women* had begun to appear.

v

The 'odd' women are, depending on one's point of view, either 'useless, lost, futile' human beings leading wasted lives, or 'a great reserve', a potential element of the work-force neglected and abused. They are unmarried and likely to remain so, being without money, without 'social position, and unable to win an individual one'. They are female 'exiles' from a society which stresses respectable social status as the ultimate goal of every woman's existence, and marriage as the chief means to that end. Monica Madden marries Widdowson for the same reasons Jane Austen's women often marry, and Gissing articulates the reason with utter clarity: 'As things went in the marriage war, she might esteem herself a most fortunate young woman . . . She felt no love . . . but between the prospect of a marriage of esteem and that of no marriage at all there was little room for hesitation. The chances were that she might never again receive an offer from a man whose social standing she could respect.'

In a remarkable passage the book's heroine, Rhoda Nunn, attacks the conventional view of love as popularized by the romantic novel:

If every novelist could be strangled and thrown into the sea we should have some chance of reforming women . . . Love – love – love; a sickening sameness of vulgarity. What is more vulgar than the ideal of novelists? They won't represent the actual world; it would be too dull for their readers. In real life, how many men and women *fall in love*? Not one in every ten thousand, I am convinced. Not one married pair in ten thousand have felt for each other as two or three couples do in every novel. There is the sexual instinct, of course, but that is quite a different thing; the novelists daren't talk about that. The paltry creatures daren't tell the one truth that would be profitable. The result is that women imagine themselves noble and glorious when they are most near the animals.

In the real world, Gissing believed, that 'hallucination' which pulls men and women together – 'the sexual instinct' – ultimately fades away; little remains after marriage but the habit of living together, the 'chill'.

What, then, are women to do: marry and be disappointed, or stay unmarried and 'odd'? The novel shows us how the lot of the unmarried woman is as unhappy in late Victorian England as it was in Jane Austen's time. *The Odd Women* tells the story of Rhoda Nunn and Mary Barfoot, who attempt to give the 'odd' women enough practical education to enable them to survive economically without marrying. In typical Gissing fashion, however, both those who do marry and those who do not have unhappy fates awaiting them. Ultimately the novel offers no solution at all to the dilemma of the 'odd' women.

In book after book Gissing had discussed the working-class woman's need for an education of more than a perfunctory kind – 'education . . . in self-respect and self-restraint' – and in *The Odd Women* this argument is presented perhaps more cogently than in any of the other novels. His treatment of the subject is the expression of a lifelong interest. Shortly after the novel was published, in response to a query from Bertz as to whether he believed in female emancipation, Gissing replied:

I am convinced there will be no social peace until women are intellectually trained very much as men are. More than half the misery of life is due to the ignorance and the childishness of women. The average woman pretty closely resembles, in all intellectual considerations, the average male *idiot* – I speak medically. That state of things is traceable to the lack of education, in all senses of the word . . . I am driven frantic by the crass imbecility of the typical woman. That type must disappear, or at all events become altogether subordinate. And I believe that the only way of effecting this is to go through a period of what many people will call sexual anarchy.

Certainly 'more than half the misery' of Gissing's own life had been 'due to the ignorance and the childishness of women'. He told William Blackwood: 'Everything that concerns the education of women – the *one* interest of our time, the one thing needful – strongly appeals to me.'

The Odd Women is not vague about the sort of education Gissing thinks women should have. 'The odious fault of working-class girls . . . is that they are absorbed in preoccupation with their animal natures', he says, echoing the words of his heroine. Such girls need to be trained to be useful: they must not remain simply sexual or ornamental. 'When the whole course of female education is altered; when girls are trained as a matter of course to some definite pursuit; then those who . . . are obliged to remain at home will do their duty there in quite a different spirit. Home work will be their serious business.' This is said by Rhoda, one of the novel's more aggressive feminists; we can see what female 'emancipation' meant to Gissing. He wanted women trained to run a house, not a business – to be wives and mothers, not executives or politicians.

The Odd Women, then, makes no plea for women's rights. *Born in Exile* taught that truly emancipated women are always 'asexual' and that woman's one role is to be a wife. *Denzil Quarrier* taught that women should not be sent forth into marriage in total ignorance. 'The vast majority of men make a marriage that is doomed to be a dismal failure', *The Odd Women* argues, simply because women have been taught so little. What is important to Rhoda Nunn and to Mary Barfoot is not that women be trained as lawyers or doctors, 'but that women in general shall become *rational and responsible beings*', as Miss Barfoot puts it (her italics). In order to join the professions? No: to become a productive 'worker out in the world, a new ruler *of the home*' (my italics). Women make poor wives because of their ignorance; if they were trained to work and to think, they would make better managers.

The novel says much about women in general and the nature of marriage in particular. Mary Barfoot, off the platform, remarks to Rhoda: 'surely between ourselves we can admit that the vast majority of women would lead a wasted life if they did not marry.' And, in another mood: 'Rhoda, when one thinks how often a woman is a clog upon a man's ambition, no wonder they regard us as they do.' 'Most women, whether they marry or not, will suffer and commit endless follies', says Mary Barfoot. Like Mrs Wade in *Denzil Quarrier*, she is a feminist who thinks little of women.

Widdowson's views on marriage are not dissimilar (at times he sounds like a character out of *Jude the Obscure*, published the following year): 'How many marriages were anything more than mutual forbearance? Perhaps there ought not to be such a thing as enforced permanence of marriage . . . perhaps, some day, marriage would be dissoluble at the will of either party to it.' Like Hardy writing *Jude*, Gissing was wondering how to get rid of his wife. The theme of the husband walking out would be more fully developed in *In the Year of Jubilee* – and then tried out by Gissing in real life several years later. Elsewhere in *The Odd Women* marriage is characterized as 'a long . . . bitter struggle for predominance'. 'Some marry for a good reason, some for a bad, and mostly it all comes to the same in the end.'

Gissing's own life is most intimately reflected in two relationships: that between Everard Barfoot and Rhoda, and that between Monica Madden and Widdowson. Of Everard, his cousin Mary says: 'I have heard him speak bitterly, and very indiscreetly, of early marriages; his wife was dead then, but every one knew what he meant'. A widower who wants the companionship of women without having to marry them, to Everard 'the brutality of enforced marriage doesn't seem . . . an alternative worth considering'. He will only marry again, he declares, when he finds an attractive woman who is his intellectual equal. 'Let beauty perish if it cannot ally itself with mind; be a woman what else she may, let her have brains and the power of using them! . . . for the life of wedlock, the durable companionship of man and woman, intellect was his first requirement.' Poor Gissing. It was precisely this 'durable companionship' that he missed in his marriages: he had no one to talk to. Because this combination of feminine virtues is so difficult to come by, Everard, Gissing writes, is often vulnerable to 'the indulgence of casual impulse' where women are concerned. Having had enough of marriage the first time round, he proposes to Rhoda what Gissing proposed to Edith and would propose to Gabrielle Fleury – that they live together as man and wife without being married. But Rhoda senses in Everard what was certainly true of Gissing – the need for 'submission', for 'subduing [women] to his will' – and she backs off. When he discovers that her will is equal to his own and that he cannot rule her, he backs off too, and the affair is ended. There is a great deal of discussion in the novel about free unions: it was a condition in which the amorous but twice unhappily married Gissing was interested (and in which he was to end his days in France).

There is a good deal of Gissing too in the Monica –Widdowson story. The novelist sympathizes, for example, with Monica's passionate craving for privacy in a marriage with an uncongenial mate. Every night she is wretched 'because she must needs go to the same chamber in which her husband would sleep. She wished to be alone . . . to lie awake, to think without a disturbing presence, to shed tears if need be.' We know about Gissing's domestic claustrophobia – how he felt about marriage's enforced intimacy. Monica, tied irrevocably to a man she does not love, finally tries (unsuccessfully) to evade her fate. Her attempt to escape with the timid Bevis to France comes to nothing – though it foreshadows Gissing's own flight to France with a lover some years later, also to escape an unhappy marriage (in fact Bevis has a mother and sisters in England who, it is said, would feel disgraced if it were known that he ran off with another man's wife).

It is a measure of the depth of Gissing's autobiographical impulse when writing fiction that he portrays and caricatures a good many of his own less congenial qualities in the person of Widdowson. Of course there is much in Widdowson that is nothing like Gissing; but in Widdowson we see Gissing looking at himself as husband from a wife's point of view – and understanding, perhaps, why his relationships with the women he married were so explosive.

Autobiographical resonances in the Monica–Widdowson story may be found in the early scenes set in Clevedon and along the Bristol Channel, where Gissing and Edith had been on holiday; and in the honeymoon Widdowson and Monica embark upon in the Channel Islands, where the novelist had taken his sister Margaret. As for his relationship with Monica – 'Never had it occurred to Widdowson that a wife remains an individual, with rights and obligations independent of her wifely condition. Everything he said presupposed his own supremacy; he took for granted that it was his to direct, hers to be guided.' Seduced by a garbled understanding of Ruskin, Widdowson tells his wife that 'an educated woman had better become a domestic servant than try to imitate the life of a man . . . This, to his mind, was the perfect relation of wife to husband. She must look up to him as her benefactor, her providence.' This is ironic self-parody; but surely Gissing speaks partly in his own voice here – the voice of a man whose insecurities must be fed by relationships with *inferior* women. Certainly it is the novelist's own voice which Widdowson uses to lecture Monica on her domestic duties: 'A woman ought never to be so happy as when she is looking after her home.' If it were good enough for Ruth

Pinch, then why not for Monica Widdowson – or Edith Gissing? Widdowson's opinion of women's intellectual capabilities strikes me as about half self-parody and half true conviction: 'He regarded [women] as born to perpetual pupilage . . . they were simply incapable of attaining maturity, remained throughout their life imperfect beings, at the mercy of craft, ever liable to be misled by childish misconceptions.' For Widdowson, 'Women were very like children; it was rather a task to amuse them and to keep them out of mischief. Therefore the blessedness of household toil, in especial the blessedness of child-bearing and all that followed.' This part of Ruskin's teachings Gissing surely accepted. Being imperceptive, women – even a married woman – ought to adopt men's opinions on most if not all matters, Widdowson believes. 'Look to me for guidance', he tells Monica. 'I am no tyrant, but I shall rule you for your own good.' Gissing adds: 'To regard her simply as a human being was beyond the reach of his intelligence.'

What contributes a little spice to this story is that Monica ultimately rebels – and, as in the Everard–Rhoda part of the novel, there is a contest of wills. Widdowson's reverie towards the end of the book about the mistakes he has made as a husband contains, for the Gissing reader, a number of familiar echoes. Perhaps, muses Widdowson, he married a woman too close to his own social status to be ruled by him as a woman should be ruled by her husband.

Would [I] not have been a much happier man if [I] had married a girl distinctly [my] inferior in mind and station? . . . We are unsuited to each other. We do not understand each other. Our marriage is physical and nothing more . . . I do not love her mind, her intellectual part . . . I don't know what her thoughts really are, what her intellectual life signifies.

Widdowson's disillusionment in his marriage reflects Gissing's in his during the summer and autumn of 1892, and there is perhaps a touch of authorial wish-fulfilment at the end of the book in Monica's death in childbirth. This would have been a convenient end to Gissing's domestic troubles. Death had saved him once; perhaps, subconsciously, he was counting on it to do so again. Not long after *The Odd Women* was published Edith became pregnant again.

'Are we to believe', writes Gillian Tindall, 'that Gissing managed to marry two women, both of whom went mad while living with him, and that this was a total coincidence?' A key to answering this question undoubtedly lies in the relationship between Widdowson and Monica in *The Odd Women*. Living with Gissing, if it were even remotely like living with Widdowson, could easily drive a woman – even two women – mad. 'Anyone may marry one highly neurotic woman by accident', Tindall reminds us, 'but to . . . [marry two] argues a particular emotional taste.' Perhaps only a neurotic woman would have married him; or perhaps this is what he believed. 'It seems to me', Tindall continues, 'that the reason Widdowson is so thoroughly convincing is that he is a caricature of certain aspects of Gissing himself . . . [When he says] "I can't take things the simple way that comes natural to other men" – [that is] a Gissing admission if there ever was one.'

The Odd Women, like *Born in Exile*, manages to be one of Gissing's most interesting novels without being one of his greatest. From a biographical point of view it is of course much less rich than the earlier book; but it does help to clarify some of the novelist's views on women.

During the years 1893 to 1896 Gissing was to write five more novels – four of which (*In the Year of Jubilee, Sleeping Fires, The Paying Guest*, and *The Whirlpool*) are among his finest achievements (I except *Eve's Ransom*). Between 1890 and 1893 he had written three of his better works – *New Grub Street, Born in Exile*, and *The Odd Women* (also *Denzil Quarrier*). These years were among the unhappiest of his life, proving once again that in some men creativity thrives on misery.

VI

Before moving back to London, Gissing began to plan his next novel, which would be set in the metropolis. About it he wrote to Bertz: 'I have done with *questions*. I am going to write a novel, pure and simple . . . It will be a reversion to my old style without any spirit but that of art.' Books which advocate systems of behaviour or moralities rarely have any effect on anybody, Gissing says. Toward the end of this long letter to his friend he reports that *The Odd Women* is being reviewed sympathetically. 'Most writers insist upon its "absorbing" interest. This is a pleasant surprise to me.' The book was selling fairly well (332 copies of the three-volume edition up to July 1893), and Bullen had voluntarily raised the author's royalty from 10½ per cent to just under 13 per cent. Gissing noted around this time that he had a balance at his bankers of a little over £116 but that he still had to furnish his London flat. Late in June the family moved to Brixton.

The reviewers of *The Odd Women* were indeed enthusiastic. The *Glasgow Herald* used words like 'ingenious' and 'remarkable' and declared that Gissing had become one of the leading novelists of the day. The *Saturday Review*, which had lambasted *Born in Exile*, was more tolerant of *The Odd Women*. The reviewer complained that Gissing's beliefs about marriage were unfathomable (a likely possibility), praised Widdowson, but noted that 'Mr. Gissing's women are far truer to nature than his men.' The *Athenaeum* declared that Gissing had 'not written anything stronger or more striking'. The *Pall Mall Gazette* pronounced *The Odd Women* 'the most interesting novel of the year', and continued: 'His people live. You might brush against any of them in the Strand from morning till morning again . . . *The Odd Women* is a great vindication of realism from the charge of dullness.' The *Women's Herald* (as might be expected) praised the book lavishly. The *Illustrated London News* called *The Odd Women* Gissing's best book to date. The *Spectator* and the *Morning Post* also gave it high praise. There were the usual charges of gratuitous gloom and sordidness, this time from the *Review of Reviews*, the *Academy*, and the *Guardian*. Gissing's new novel also brought forth an essay on his work in the *Echo* in which he was called, now, a 'writer of the first rank'; his 'vivid powers of description' were compared with those of 'a Turner or a Whistler', and 'the middle and working classes' were described as the area of his special expertise. The writer of the essay noted that though his views on the artisan classes were reactionary, they deserved attention because they were based on an intimate acquaintance with the subject.

Among those who read *The Odd Women* with interest and determined to meet the author was Clara Collet; now that Gissing was within reach she was not to be denied. When they finally met in July 1893 she was thirty three. The first woman to earn a degree in political economy at London University, she was an indefatigable humanitarian, involved in some of the most advanced political and social organizations of the time. She was the 'new' woman *par excellence*, and Gissing was much taken with her. He had held back at first because of embarrassment about his marriage; but he ended by confiding to her most of his domestic difficulties. She did what she could for him by making a friend of Edith and taking her out now and then to give the novelist a quiet day at home. Ultimately she offered to undertake the entire expense of Walter's education. Gissing was deeply moved, as well as mightily relieved – for this was one source of constant financial anxiety. Miss Collet remained a good and loyal friend for the rest of his life, as we shall see.

The chorus of critical praise for *The Odd Women* made Gissing, once again, a literary lion of the hour; this, coupled with the family's move to London, secured the novelist a number of invitations. A member of the Athenaeum asked him to spend a weekend at his country house; Gissing refused. Miss Collet invited the family for a weekend visit; Gissing refused. The Lord Mayor invited him to a literary dinner at the Mansion House; Gissing refused. His clothes were not right, his wife was not right, and he was still shy of Society. Nor would he permit himself, just yet, a more sanguine view of the future. 'The struggle of life gets harder as one goes on, instead of being lightened', he wrote to Algernon, who certainly knew what his brother was talking about. 'It would be a strange sensation to look forward with easy confidence for a year or two.' Yet soon he would have something approaching this, if only temporarily.

The Brixton flat adequately furnished and the family comfortably ensconced there, Gissing settled down to work in his Kennington study. His first item of business was to revise *The Emancipated* for the cheap edition Lawrence and Bullen was bringing out. Then he wished to get on with the new novel (tentatively entitled 'Miss Lord of Camberwell', ultimately *In the Year of Jubilee*). But of greatest importance now was the series of short stories he began to produce rapidly during the summer of 1893, a series commissioned by Clement Shorter – editor of no less than three literary journals (the *English Illustrated Magazine*, the *Illustrated London News*, and the *Sketch*). Shorter asked for tales principally of lower-class life and offered to pay eleven or twelve guineas each for them. Gissing supplied him with several stories in July, but quickly hit upon the idea of using the well-known literary agent William Morris Colles to get higher prices than those Shorter was offering (Watt, the novelist felt, was not aggressive enough). Colles, an admirer of Gissing's work, was delighted. He approached the *National Review* and *To-Day*, journals which offered to pay an average of fifteen to eighteen pounds per story of 6,000 words. This encouraged Gissing; in August 1893 alone he wrote seven tales, spending no more than a few days on any one of them. It was more lucrative and less exhausting than writing novels; and it enabled him to take his time with the novels he did write – one reason why he produced some of his best longer fiction during this period of his life. 'I am entered upon the commercial path . . . But I shall try not to write rubbish', Gissing told Bertz. The fact that his work commanded a price in the literary market-place did a good deal to restore his professional self-confidence in the mid-nineties. Yet Gissing never really mastered the short story: only a few of the hundred or so he wrote are first-rate. He liked the larger canvas; the stories were written quickly to make money, with the inevitable result.

We might look briefly at some of the stories he produced in August 1893. By far the most interesting is 'A Lodger in Maze Pond'. Shergold, the protagonist, spends most of his time thinking about women; he falls prey to them one after another. A man with little money who never completed his university education, he has a chequered past. As a university student he got involved with the eighteen-year-old daughter of a tailor, a girl he picked up in a tobacconist's shop. He married her against the advice of his friends. 'Any sane person' could have predicted the result: 'a hideous disaster'. Shergold attempts suicide, leaves his wife, and then foolishly agrees to live with her again. His wife dies soon afterwards: he is 'free but terribly shattered'. Here is a thinly veiled recapitulation of the circumstances of Gissing's first marriage. Shergold goes abroad, and upon his return to England gets involved with another lower-class woman – his landlady's almost illiterate daughter, whom in an insane moment he promises to marry. Why has he repeated his mistake? Because he is 'a fool about women', as he says himself; a sentimentalist, he has an 'incessant hunger for a woman's sympathy and affection'. Anyway, he argues, most 'men marry without passion' because there is no choice; one just picks the most convenient female available. One reason why Shergold keeps getting entangled with lower-class women is that it is easier to get them into bed with him than middle-class women, of whom he is afraid. 'I find it an impossible thing to imagine myself offering marriage – making love – to a girl such as those I meet in the big houses', Shergold declares. Here Gissing articulates once again his great insecurity – his feeling that he was not worthy of a woman of refinement. As a result of mere 'idiot desire', Shergold ends by marrying the landlady's awful daughter – with the plan of educating her afterwards. 'A Lodger in Maze Pond' is twenty pages or so of pure autobiography.

If 'A Lodger in Maze Pond' is about women and class, 'A Capitalist' is about money and class. Ireton is a writer who marries unhappily, gets divorced, goes abroad, and spends much of his life upon his return to England working hard to make others rate him a 'gentleman'. Temperamental and moody, Ireton as a young man laboured as a clerk in a drug warehouse; now, walking into a chemist's shop and smelling the drugs there make him feel sick. In his early years he barely got by; he was bothered less by bad food and bad lodgings than by 'the feeling that [he] was everybody's inferior'. He develops 'a furious hunger for money' and makes a lot of it buying and selling paintings. A character who wishes above all things to appear to be respectable; who is temperamental, and aristocratic in outlook; who has fought with every weapon available to put his past, and especially his poverty, behind him; who suffers from unpleasant private memories of that past; who feels sick in chemist's shops – such a character could only be a creature of George Gissing.

'The Day of Silence' is a Freudian's delight. It is about three people – father, mother, and seven-year-old son – who live in a one-room Southwark garret. The place is noisy, close, and unventilated. The mother worries constantly that the boy will be run over in the street (one of Gissing's great enemies was the London omnibus). On a rare holiday the father and son go boating, and drown; on the same day the mother, who works as a charwoman, dies of exhaustion. 'In the little home there was silence' at last. This is one way to quiet a house, certainly. Of course Gissing's own household was a source of worry to him – especially the safety of little Walter, so often at the mercy of his mother's temper. In his Commonplace Book the novelist recorded his sympathy for children who suffer from 'idiot mothers; perpetual slapping, scolding, weeping.'

'Our Mr. Jupp' is about a selfish man who lives with his mother and sister but refuses to help them financially and never takes them anywhere. This little tale may reflect Gissing's guilt about his treatment of Edith – or perhaps his neglect of his uncongenial female relatives.

VII

Throughout the autumn of 1893, Gissing worked on 'Miss Lord of Camberwell' – giving it up and going back to it innumerable times, in his usual way. Visiting his old Baker Street flat in September, he learned that his successor in the place had committed suicide. 'The atmosphere I left behind me . . . overcame the poor man', Gissing mused. In September the novelist gave Colles a bundle of stories to dispose of at higher rates than those offered by that 'scoundrel' Shorter, who was often slow to pay. Early in October Lawrence and Bullen, to Gissing's delight, announced a new cheap edition of *The Emancipated*. In the middle of the month he 'once more re-began "Miss Lord"' – for perhaps the half-dozenth time, he calculated. 'Did ever man work on such a method as this?' His bank balance, he noted, was slowly dwindling (his total earnings for 1893 would be only £194 – more than £80 below his earnings for 1892). He gave up the outside study as a needless expense and worked at home. In late October and early November he took a short holiday with Algernon and his family.

Colles, meanwhile, was selling Gissing's stories at a fairly steady and profitable rate – nearly £14 for the very brief 'Day of Silence', for example. Sending a bunch of his printed stories to Bertz, Gissing commented: 'pray do not take much trouble in criticizing these short productions. You know they are really pot-boilers.' On 21 November he recommenced 'Miss Lord' for perhaps the dozenth time; the next day he noted, simply, 'My birthday; age, 36.' Early in December he agreed to do six more stories for Shorter at twelve guineas each. He was also pleased to hear that the cheap edition of *The Emancipated* was selling briskly: 250 copies in the first ten weeks.

Among the stories written for Shorter's *English Illustrated Magazine* in December 1893 is 'Comrades in Arms', which extols the virtues of having as few attachments and dependants as possible, especially when young. The protagonist is another writer, this one contemptuous of public taste and fearful of accidentally writing a best-seller. He lives in lodgings and relishes his isolation. When you are poor it is better to be lonely and free than attached to someone and thus responsible for his welfare, the story tells us. Here is Gissing unmarrying himself again in imagination. Another story, 'In Honour Bound', is the most autobiographical of this group. Filmer is a 'literary recluse', a poor but brilliant scholar whose only possessions in his miserable garret are books. He goes often to the British Museum, seems indifferent alike to his clothing and his diet, and values chiefly his independence, his leisure to do what he likes (he is writing a book on philology). He is 'proud amid [his] poverty' and shrinks from society and most companionship. As a result of a typical Gissingesque reversal of fortune, he suddenly loses the small competence he has been living on. Finding he can think of his charlady 'without repugnance' and discovering that she has a little money of her own, he works himself up to propose marriage to her – only to find that she has just married someone else. (In *Will Warburton* circumstances of a similar kind occur, with a denouement somewhat reversed.) Filmer's willingness to 'declass' himself comes to nothing but embarrassment.

Gissing told Bertz he was writing more stories. 'Some of them are not bad, I think.' He complained bitterly of the trouble he was having with the new novel. The 'toil of rewriting . . . is the curse which always lies upon my . . . work; sometimes I rewrite chapters six or seven times, until I hate the very thought of them . . . The least defect of health, and the least domestic trouble, puts an end to . . . regularity.' And he added: 'I cannot say that life gives me much more satisfaction than of old. Society I shall never have; to that I am practically reconciled.' In mid-December he was astonished to hear that Roberts had gone off to Italy with a married lady and that they were living together there. Late in the month Gissing received a letter from *Pearson's Weekly* asking, for publication, some questions about his work and literary tastes. Usually he paid no attention to such queries, but this time he determined to help himself to some free publicity if he could. What he wrote appeared in the journal the following June. Among other things, he said that he liked *New Grub Street* best among his own books, and that his favourite novels were *Villette, The Ordeal of Richard Feverel*, and *The Return of the Native.*

On the first day of 1894 'Miss Lord of Camberwell' was recommenced yet again, and this time the work went well. During January, Gissing was asked by a member of the Philomatic Society of Paisley for some biographical facts which could be used as part of a lecture on *Demos*. He replied, saying:

the beginnings of my literary career were hard enough to have discouraged most men. In those days . . . I met only with abuse because I tried to depict the world as I saw it. I am told that there still exists a prejudice against me among ordinary readers; though the intelligent people . . . only charge me with undue timidity in handling the facts of life.

He joined the Society of Authors, largely to please Colles. This was to bring him in subsequent years the acquaintance and friendship of some other leading literary men of the day. Also during this month he agreed to write a 60,000-word story to run serially for thirteen weeks in Shorter's *Illustrated London News*. The manuscript would have to be submitted within six months; he would be paid £150. Gissing was delighted to earn so much for such a short work: and he was also happy to have something other than the detested 'Miss Lord' to work on. Of this novel he confessed to Bertz he was altogether 'tired . . . it has been on hand too long.' As for the shorter pieces: 'these minor efforts are doing me good with the public; they make my name better known, and enable me to ask higher prices.' By the end of January he had already planned a good deal of Shorter's serial, deciding to set it partly in and around

Birmingham and thus make some use of the discarded 'Iron Gods' (the serial would turn out to be *Eve's Ransom*). Soon, despite 'idiotic domestic troubles', he was working steadily and well, completing the first volume of 'Miss Lord' ('heaven be thanked') and embarking on the second.

The seven stories Gissing wrote for Shorter in December, which represented three weeks' work, earned him about £88, and two stories Colles placed in the *National Review* brought the novelist another £25. *The Odd Women* and *Denzil Quarrier* had not as yet made a profit for Lawrence and Bullen; still, Bullen sent Gissing a cheque for 25 guineas, saying he expected to recoup on these books eventually. He also told Gissing he would like to bring out a cheap edition of *Born in Exile*. The future, at the end of January 1894, looked to Gissing less grim than usual; and as a matter of fact the year 1894 would witness his highest earnings to date: just under £440.

In late January Walter developed bronchitis, and Gissing was advised to give the child a change of air. The family took lodgings by the sea in Hastings for three months, and here the novelist settled in to write the second volume of 'Miss Lord of Camberwell'. This he finished late in February. In March Walter seemed no better; but Gissing was heartened by a cheque from Colles for nearly £26, payment for two more stories sold from among the group he had written the previous December. The novelist was also pleased to see the cheap edition of *Born in Exile* announced. Meanwhile he was staggering toward the final pages of 'Miss Lord'. 'Thank God the end of the book is in view. Think it won't be bad, on the whole, and it has been written under fearsome circumstances', he recorded in his diary. The daily battles with Edith were becoming fiercer.

The family went off to Eastbourne for two weeks. Here Gissing had received the news of Nell's death while on holiday in 1888; six years later he was finishing one of his greatest novels there. Early in April they all returned to Brixton. Gissing complained that he had little time to read. 'Thomas Hardy once said to me "Novel-writing makes one so illiterate." When not actually writing, I am laboriously thinking about writing.'

On 12 to 13 April the momentous battle with 'Miss Lord' came to an end. The diary records the event: 'To-day I sat down to the final chapter of "Miss Lord", and wrote . . . with indescribable struggle. I am utterly tired of the thing, and within a page of the end cannot realize that it will ever be finished . . . In the evening *finished my interminable novel.*' Almost immediately he began to work out plans for the serial he had promised Shorter: 'Thinking of my story for the *Illustrated London News,* and got some ideas.' Gissing spent the next few days looking (principally in Streatham) for another house to lease; he also saw Bullen, who told him that 400 copies of the new edition of *The Odd Women* had been sold. When he sent 'Miss Lord' to Bullen, he enclosed with it a note. 'I am of opinion that "Miss Lord" is not without value as a study of a well-defined social class', he wrote. 'I have much more hope for this new novel than I had for any of its predecessors. Hope to be disappointed, perhaps; but do . . . see it as an honest picture of something that exists.' On 18 April he began to write *Eve's Ransom,* then called only 'my old Birmingham story'. As always, he was plagued at the outset by a series of false starts, and throughout May 1894 he worked steadily at the new serial, only to discard what he had done. He started again in June. Late in May he visited Halesworth, Suffolk where his father had been born (in 1829), looking up the record of his baptism in the church register. At the railway station Gissing bought a copy of the current *English Illustrated News* and found one of his stories in it. 'How proud he would have been, the dear, kind Father! How little could he dream, when a lad running about lanes and fields, that, more than half a century hence, his son's literary work would be sold, to that son himself, at Halesworth!'

Gissing decided to take the family to Clevedon for the summer. Just before his departure he received a cheque from Bullen for 50 guineas as partial payment for 'Nancy Lord', as the new book was now called. Bullen offered an advance of 100 guineas, a four-shilling royalty on the three-volume edition, and a one-shilling royalty on the cheap one-volume edition to follow. The profits from foreign sales would be shared equally between the author and publisher. Gissing accepted immediately. Colles was appalled; he thought he could have secured much better terms, especially by selling the new book for serial publication first. But Gissing was determined to remain loyal to Lawrence and Bullen, which had befriended him during dark days and treated him fairly, he thought, ever since. As it turned out, Lawrence and Bullen's six-shilling, one-volume edition of *Eve's Ransom,* issued the following spring at the conclusion of the story's serial publication, went into a second printing before it had been out a month, and Gissing's faith in his publishers seemed justified (though *In the Year of Jubilee,* more than three times longer, did not do nearly so well, as Colles had predicted).

Shortly after arriving at Clevedon, Gissing received a letter from W. T. Stead (years earlier a lonely defender of *The Unclassed*), now editor of the *Review of Reviews*. Stead asked Gissing, 'as one of the foremost novelists of Great Britain', for his signature to a memorial in the cause of international peace. The novelist, a hater of Imperialism and war, willingly gave it. Once established at Clevedon, Gissing went to work again on *Eve's Ransom*. Begun with 'a horrible struggle – sinking misery', the story progressed quickly ('Feeling better about my work. It may not be utter trash, after all') and was completed in twenty-five days of concentrated writing. 'Heaven be thanked, finished the thing, and decided to call it "Eve's Ransom"'. 'A poor title, but my head whirls', Gissing wrote in his diary on 29 June 1894. Publication was originally scheduled for the autumn, but the illustrator's alcoholism and the necessity of finding another one delayed the story's appearance until early the following year. In the event Gissing's next two novels were published in the order in which he wrote them — *In the Year of Jubilee* in December 1894 and *Eve's Ransom* from January to March 1895 (in cloth in April 1895).

At the end of June Gissing wrote a longish letter to Bertz. 'It is surprising how very little genuine interest I have in the movements of our time', said the author of *Workers in the Dawn*. 'To be sure, I study them to a certain extent but my real pleasure is in things ancient.' He commiserates with his friend's loneliness. 'Serious literary toil compels solitude. I know, as regards myself, that I shall *never* have society; my methods of work do not allow of it.' Anyway, he added, 'I am afraid of crowds.' Gissing concludes his letter with a striking *non sequitur*: 'Women are tenacious of life, and a great deal of nonsense is talked about their sufferings.'

During the summer of 1894 the three-volume system of novel-publishing once and for all went the way of most of the circulating libraries – into the wilderness. People had got into the habit of buying cheap one-volume novels, and Gissing could look forward from now on to writing shorter tales, along the lines of *Eve's Ransom* – meant to be purchased rather than borrowed. In fact, *In the Year of Jubilee* would be the last novel he wrote under the old three-decker system, though some of his later novels would be as long.

In July 1894 he went carefully over the manuscript of 'Nancy Lord', finishing his revision and in the process hitting upon the title *In the Year of Jubilee*. He explained to Clara Collet that it was satirical, and in keeping with the tone of the book: 1887, the year of

Queen Victoria's Golden Jubilee, 'signified so much that is contemptible – snobbery, blatant ochlocracy [mob rule], shams gigantic and innumerable – all thrown together into an exhibition of human folly not often surpassed for effectiveness'. During this month and the next he corrected proofs both of *Eve's Ransom* and *In the Year of Jubilee*, and took long walks through the countryside around Clevedon (described in *The Ryecroft Papers*). He was also house-hunting, determined to give up the rooms in Brixton, which he thought bad for Walter's health, by the end of the summer. Late in August the family returned to London, and Gissing once more undertook the arduous search for satisfactory lodgings. He rented rooms in Dorking for two weeks and continued the hunt, finally finding a house he liked in Epsom which he took for a year. They moved in mid-September, the proofs of *In the Year of Jubilee* and *Eve's Ransom* following the novelist from place to place and being dispatched by him piecemeal back to, respectively, Bullen and Shorter. Several years later, in *The Whirlpool*, Harvey Rolfe would search for lodgings in the London suburbs very much as Gissing did during this nomadic summer of 1894.

VIII

Of the two books completed during the spring and summer of 1894, *In the Year of Jubilee*, written and rewritten over many months with enormous difficulty and suffering, is vastly superior to *Eve's Ransom*, a serial pot-boiler stitched together in three weeks. Both are interesting but the earlier novel is one of Gissing's greatest achievements while the other is little more than an intriguing mediocrity. Despite all the complaints about the pain *In the Year of Jubilee* had given him, Gissing sensed it was one of his finest novels, as his note to Bullen makes clear ('I have much more hope for this new novel than I had for any of its predecessors'). None of his best novels was written easily.

In the Year of Jubilee is in a sense another *New Grub Street* – many of the major characters embody aspects of Gissing himself, their stories taken directly from his life. Both Tarrant and Peachey, the two chief male characters, make exogamous marriages, leave their wives, and hide from them; Gissing had already done so once and would soon do so again (Peachey, as a matter of fact, walks out on his wife twice). Tarrant's ideal of marriage is one in which husband and wife live, in perfectly friendly fashion, apart. Two other characters, Samuel Barmby and Horace Lord, pursue women according to principles reminiscent of Gissing's. Barmby declares that 'even the long pursuit of a lofty ideal does not render a man proof against the elementary forces of human nature.' Lord falls in love with a sort of superior prostitute: he 'had all her faults by heart, and no longer tried to think that he respected her, or that, if he married such a girl, his life could possibly be a happy one; but still she played on his passions, and at her beck he followed like a dog.'

'Petty domestic detail . . . is the whole of life', Gissing wrote in his Commonplace Book. 'To occupy furnished lodgings is to live in a house owned and ruled by servants; the least tolerable status known to civilisation', *In the Year of Jubilee* tells us. These two principles intersect in the story of Arthur and Ada Peachey, illustrating how a domestically disorganized household can destroy a marriage. Note the manifold connections with Gissing's life. The Peacheys live in Brixton. They have one child, a son, whom the domestically inept mother and wife mistreats, and a servant problem of magnificent proportions due largely to her inability to get along with the help. The novel declares: 'Now-a-days, every woman who can afford it must have another woman to wait upon her, no matter how silly, or vulgar, or depraved she may be; the result, of course, is a spirit of rebellion in the kitchen. Who could have expected anything else?' Says Tarrant: 'The servants have learnt that splendid doctrine that every one is as good as everybody else . . . And this kind of thing is going on in numberless houses . . . an utterly incompetent mistress and a democratic maid in spirited revolt.' The utterly incompetent mistress, Ada Peachey, is of course Edith Gissing – an almost exact portrait (even in their given names) down to their temper-tantrums. In one scene Ada is found 'smashing every breakable object in her bedroom – mirrors, toilet-ware, pictures, chimney-piece ornaments.' She is a 'product of sham-education and mock refinement grafted upon a stock of robust vulgarity'. That she uses a finer accent than her servants signifies only that she has grown up 'amid falsities', so that with the help of money she can 'dwell above-stairs, instead of with [her] spiritual kindred below.' The very fine line of demarcation between Edith and her succession of serving-girls is denoted here. Like Edith, Ada has 'frequent ailments, more or less genuine, such as afflict the indolent and brainless type of woman', and which keep her in bed when she should be doing or supervising housework. 'Bottomless ignorance and imbecile vanity had been the girl's ruin.' Her husband, though sorely tried, does not often lose self-control.

But Peachey is driven to a wrathful frenzy whenever his wife's heedlessness or ill-temper affects the well-being of his child.

For motherhood she had no single qualification but the physical. Before her child's coming into the world, she snarled at the restraints it imposed on her; at its birth she clamoured against nature for the pains she had to undergo, and hated her husband because he was the intermediate cause of them. The helpless infant gave her no pleasure, touched no emotion in her heart . . . She rejected it at night because it broke her sleep; in the day, because she could not handle it without making it cry. When Peachey remonstrated with her, she stared in insolent surprise, and wished that *he* had had to suffer all her hardships of the past year.

This would appear to be undiluted autobiography and Arthur Peachey is the novelist himself, barely disguised. In Part 4 there is a long and detailed description of the married pair's relationship. In his apprehension for his little son and his dislike of his wife, Peachey's situation reflects the novelist's:

Peachey could not be said to have any leisure. On returning from business he was involved forthwith in domestic trouble and broils . . . Peachey lived only for his child . . . whose newly prattling tongue made the sole welcome he expected or cared for on his return from a hard day's work . . . he never left home without dread of perils that might befall [the child] in his absence. On the mother he counted not at all; a good-tempered cow might with more confidence have been set to watch over the little one's safety . . . On approaching the house he suffered, as always, from quickened pulse and heart constricted with fear. Until he knew that all was well, he looked like a man who anticipated dread calamity.

This, according to Roberts, is an exact description of Gissing's usual state of mind while living with Edith in the mid-nineties. Roberts says: 'He always left his own house with anxiety and returned to it with fear and trembling. This woman of his home was given to violence, even with her own young children. It was possible, as he knew, for he often said so to me, that he might return and find the baby badly injured.'

Peachey sustains sanity by dreaming of another life away from his wife: 'Ah, if he were but unmarried, what a life he might make for himself now that the day's labour brought its ample reward.' His business is just beginning to prosper, and he finds it doubly disillusioning that his marriage should begin to disintegrate just as he is achieving some measure of professional success. Ada's 'indolence, incapacity, and vicious ill-humour' open her husband's eyes to the true nature of married life.

Before his marriage he had thought of women as domestic beings. A wife was the genius of the home. He knew men who thanked their wives for all the prosperity and content that they enjoyed . . . Nowadays he saw the matter in a light of fuller experience. In his rank of life married happiness was a rare thing, and the fault could generally be traced to wives who had no sense of responsibility, no understanding of household duties, no love of simple pleasures.

Peachey's 'natural delicacy' keeps him loyal to his household for a while, but finally he has had enough. 'From morning to night the house rang with brawls between mistress and servants; in her paroxysms . . . Ada behaved like a candidate for Bedlam.' Peachey decides 'that he would rather die than continue living with his wife'. Like Sidney Kirkwood in *The Nether World*, he understands 'how men have gone mad under pressure of household cares'. He has a sister in Kent, and to her he determines to take his little boy. He waits until Ada is out of the house; then he packs up his belongings, takes the child to his sister, and moves into a flat in London, keeping his new address secret from all but a few carefully chosen confidants.

In his new lodgings

Peachey awoke each morning with a vague sense of joy, which became delight as soon as he had collected his senses. He was a free man. No snarl greeted him as he turned his head upon the pillow; he could lie and meditate . . . could go downstairs to a leisurely meal, cheered perhaps by a letter reporting that all was well with his dear little son. Simple, elementary pleasures, but how he savoured them after his years of sordid bondage! It was the blessedness of divorce, without squalid publicity. It was the vast relief of widowerhood, without dreary memories of death and burial. In releasing himself from such companionship, the man felt as though he had washed and become clean.

In all this we can see Gissing beginning to work himself up to another leave-taking. Of course as soon as he was alone again he would want another woman; but, living with one like Edith, it is easy to see why he wanted so badly to be free. He had forced Nell to take lodgings away from him. The role he was destined to play opposite Edith *three years later* is almost exactly as it is described in *In the Year of Jubilee*, down to the taking of the boy to his sister's and the secret new address. Gissing seems to know, before the event, not only how he will feel when he has taken this step, but also how his wife will react – her terrible rage, her compulsive attempts to find both husband and child, the 'deuce of a kick-up' she will make at her sister-in-law's house. All of this was to happen

– once again turning fiction into 'real life', and 'real life' into art. Uncanny prescience? The re-enacting in actuality of events already worked out in the fiction? Most novelists use some of their experiences as the material of fiction; Gissing used his fiction as a sort of testing-laboratory for actuality. The immense power of *In the Year of Jubilee*, like that of *New Grub Street*, lies in its autobiographical content.

Lionel Tarrant also makes an exogamous marriage and then leaves his wife (the novel is a dream-fantasy, with inconvenient wives imperiously abandoned by impatient, would-be bachelor husbands). Tarrant, however – as we shall see – emerges from his experiment in marriage with the sort of sexual truce Gissing always sought and, like Peachey, was unable to find. The novelist's description of Tarrant as an aspiring writer, poor but educated, signals another self-portrait. Tarrant has 'never had a home'. A cynic, he is 'critical of To-day, apprehensive of To-morrow'. His politics are conservative. Travelling to the United States (and living for a while in a cheap boarding-house), he comes to loathe democracy as 'the most hateful form of society yet developed'.

On the subjects of love and marriage Tarrant speaks in Gissing's clearest tones. The ideal woman, he tells Nancy, devotes 'perfect love' to her children. To her husband she must make 'rational acquiescence'. The good wife finds ways to help her husband in his work; she is his 'friend' as well as his lover. Tarrant enjoys Nancy's company, 'which is more than one man in ten thousand can say of his wife. The ordinary man, when he wants to dissipate, asks – well, not his wife . . . A man's wife is more often than not his enemy.' Reference is made to 'a poor devil of an author who daren't be out after ten at night because of the fool-fury waiting for him at home'. Such a marriage is 'mutual degradation'. For Tarrant, 'the most wonderful phenomenon in nature' is an uneducated woman who is neither vulgar nor foolish.

A number of Tarrant's other expressed feelings about marriage are instantly familiar to the Gissing reader. The unhappy marriage is one of Tarrant's favourite subjects. 'There is not one wife in fifty thousand who retains her husband's love after the first year of marriage', he says. By marrying outside your class, 'You are not hiding away from Society because you are unfit for it, only because you can't live as your social equals do'. Tarrant has probably ruined his life by acting honourably and marrying the pregnant Nancy. 'If henceforth he loved her, it must be with husband's love – a phrase which signified to him something as distinct as possible from the ardour he had known; a moral attachment instead of a passionate desire.' The result of all such calculation and miscalculation is usually a relationship which is 'a defilement and a curse'. The world, remarks Gissing, 'is perhaps more brutalised by marriage than by anything else'. The novelist's desire for Edith, such as it was, had utterly disappeared within a year of his marriage. The 'moral attachment' a married man feels for his wife seems to be light years away from the 'ardour' of the unmarried man for the unmarried woman. Again, the 'hallucination' of sexual desire is followed by the 'chill' of perpetual contact.

Two alternatives are offered to Tarrant, and he takes them both. At first, craving 'liberty', he simply leaves his wife. 'A man who finds himself married to a fool, is a fool himself if he doesn't take his own course regardless of his wife', he says. Later, however, he finds a compromise. Since he comes to like Nancy but dislikes living with her, why not stay married but live apart? The 'enduring tenderness of a reasonable love' that succeeds passion may best be sustained at a reasonable distance: 'forced together, he and his wife would soon be mutually detestable'. Tarrant declares: 'Husband and wife should interfere with each other not a jot more than two friends of the same sex living together.' The good wife is an obliging friend who drops in only when she is asked. Tarrant delivers a long speech on this subject to Nancy:

man and wife . . . see a great deal too much of each other – thence most of the ills of married life: squabblings, discontents, small or great disgusts . . . People get to think themselves victims of incompatibility, when they are merely suffering from a foolish custom – the habit of being perpetually together. In fact, it's an immoral custom . . . The common practise of man and wife occupying the same room is monstrous, gross . . . The only married people who can live together with impunity, are those who are rich enough, and sensible enough, to have two distinct establishments under the same roof. The ordinary eight or ten-roomed house, inhabited by decent middle-class folk, is a gruesome sight.

Gissing would probably not have been happy for long cooped up with *any* woman, and for Tarrant/Gissing the ideal relationship seems to be the wife as mistress and the husband as bachelor.

If Tarrant is another educated man without means, Nancy is another of those social anomalies so beloved of the novelist. 'Haunted by an uneasy sense of doubtfulness as to her social position': 'What *is* my position?' she impatiently asks. Nancy is the daughter of a well-to-do musical-instrument salesman, himself basically uneducated. Uncertain as to the rank of life in which Nancy should be raised, he gives her an education of sorts; the result is that peculiar brand of social 'exile' Gissing depicts so well. 'I have made her neither one thing nor the other', Mr Lord concludes sadly. Her liaison with Tarrant is also vintage Gissing, for Tarrant is another 'exile' – the educated poor man, the struggling artist with the instincts of an aristocrat. The result of their marriage is an oddity among the novels: two 'Gissings' wedded to one another.

The class theme is extended in the stories of Jessica Morgan and Samuel Barmby, both of whom are 'declassed' by a misplaced passion for education. These people yearn for culture but are beyond its reaches.

Jessica chases success through the route of the BA examination, for which she memorizes facts so ferociously as to strain her health to breaking point (in fact she is nearly killed by books, like Leonard Bast in *Howards End*). She keeps failing. Education is not for everybody. Gissing writes of her efforts with less sympathy than contempt:

Her brain was becoming a mere receptacle for dates and definitions, vocabularies and rules syntactic, for thrice-boiled essence of history, ragged scraps of science, quotations at fifth hand, and all the heterogeneous rubbish of a 'crammer's' shop. When away from her books, she carried scraps of paper, with jottings to be committed to memory. Beside her plate at meals lay formulae and tabulations. She went to bed with a manual and got up with a compendium.

Barmby has one of the novelist's favourite debilitating cultural diseases – disregard for aspirates. Gissing mischievously makes him read Milton aloud – 'Ail, orrors, ail! and thou profoundest Ell,/Receive thy new possessor!' – and describes him as a man who seeks culture but hates books. That Barmby is one of the kindest-hearted men in *In the Year of Jubilee* does nothing to mitigate the savage contempt with which the novelist treats his intellectual pretensions. Mary Woodruff, the Lords' wise housekeeper, speaks directly for Gissing when she says: 'Education makes life very much harder to live. That's why I don't hold with educating the poor . . . beyond reading and writing. Without education, life is very plain, though it may be a struggle. But from what I have seen of highly-taught people, I'm very sure they suffer worse in their minds than the poor ever do in their bodies.'

The treatment of Ada Peachey is anti-feminist, the point being that she has no business doing anything besides keeping house. Mr Lord makes a speech on the subject: 'the most worthless creature living is one of those trashy, flashy girls . . . calling themselves "ladies", – thinking themselves too good for any honest, womanly work . . . They're educated; oh yes, they're educated! What sort of wives do they make, with their education? What sort of mothers are they? Before long, there'll be no such thing as a home. They don't know what the word means.' A married woman undertakes by contract certain responsibilities. 'Let women be as independent as they like as long as they're not married', says Luckworth Crewe in this novel. 'But a wife must play second fiddle, and think her husband a small god almighty.' Even Nancy ultimately comes around to this view.

'Is it not a woman's place under the sheltering roof? What right had a mother to be searching abroad for tasks and duties? Task enough, duty obvious, in the tending of her child.' And: 'Nature doesn't intend a married woman to be anything *but* a married woman . . . who can doubt it is Nature's law? . . . One might as well revolt against being born a woman instead of a man.' Tarrant puts to rest her last doubts at the end of the book by reminding her that 'Not one woman in a thousand can bear a sound-bodied child; and not one in fifty thousand can bring up rightly the child she has borne.' This is her 'part in the life of the world'. *The Whirlpool*, written as Gissing's tolerance of Edith's domestic deficiencies was coming to an end, insists on these things even more urgently.

The anti-feminist theme is also carried forward in a number of gratuitous attacks on the female sex, inspired by Gissing's growing hatred of his wife. 'Out of every five hundred women, you can reckon on four hundred and ninety-nine being fools', Crewe declares. The women's dress shop he opens with Beatrice French is run according to this simple principle, and prospers accordingly. And only an angry husband could have written such a sentence as this: 'It is a notable instance of evolutionary process that the female mind, in wrath, flies to just those logical ineptitudes which most surely exasperate the male intelligence.' Gissing's truest feelings, as always, went into his fiction. In letter-writing, in the composition of a diary, in any form of *conscious* self-revelation, there is always some holding back, some reservation; but fiction never lies, especially Gissing's. *In the Year of Jubilee* shows more incisively than any of the novelist's private papers the true state of his marriage in 1894.

The ecology theme of *Demos* is carried forward here in the

description of the spreading suburbs and in the greedy passion of Crewe for 'developing' the countryside. Suburban Camberwell and Brixton are described as both remote from London and yet firmly within its grubby grasp. The following passage about land speculation could well have inspired several chapters of *Howards End*:

London, devourer of rural limits, of a sudden made hideous encroachments upon the old estate, now held by a speculative builder; of many streets to be constructed, three or four had already come into being, and others were mapped out, in mud and inchoate masonry, athwart the ravaged field. Great elms, the pride of generations, passed away, fell before the speculative axe, or were left standing in mournful isolation to please a speculative architect; bits of wayside hedge still shivered in fog and wind, amid hoardings variegated with placards and scaffolding black against the sky. The very earth had lost its wholesome odour; trampled into mire, fouled with builders' refuse and the noisome drift from adjacent streets, it sent forth, under the sooty rain, a smell of corruption, of all the town's uncleanliness.

Crewe is also the chief advocate in this novel of 'advertising', a new phenomenon of the nineties hated by the novelist with one of his most singular passions and violently attacked by him in all subsequent novels as the most visible sign of modern triviality and decay. Posters for 'somebody's "Blue"; somebody's "Soap"; somebody's "High-class Jams"' fill the city of London; advertisements for soap and pills ring the piers along the Thames. All that is hateful about the present, all that is destructive of beauty and taste, is symbolized for Gissing in advertising. The bathing-machines at Crewe's resort are plastered with advertisements. 'Nay, the very pleasure-boats on the sunny waves declared the glory of somebody's soap, of somebody's purgatives'. Crewe plans to put his advertisements even on the walls of caves. To Nancy he expounds – with tongue only slightly in cheek – the credo so detested by Gissing:

How could we have become what we are without the modern science of advertising? Till advertising sprang up, the world was barbarous. Do you suppose people kept themselves clean before they were reminded at every corner of the benefits of soap? Do you suppose they were healthy before every wall and hoarding told them what medicine to take for their ailments?

Here again the last of the Victorian novelists sees clearly into the future: today's paradise of advertising would not surprise him, as it undoubtedly would Thackeray or Trollope or George Eliot. Perhaps no passage in *In the Year of Jubilee* so uncannily strikes the modern note as this description of King's Cross underground station:

> They descended and stood together upon the platform, among hungry crowds, in black fumes that poisoned the palate with sulphur. This way and that sped the demon engines, whirling lighted waggons full of people. Shrill whistles, the hiss and roar of steam, the bang, clap, bang of carriage-doors, the clatter of feet on wood and stone – all echoed and reverberated from a huge cloudy vault above them. High and low, on every available yard of wall, advertisements clamoured to the eye; theatres, journals, soaps, medicines, concerts, furniture, wines, prayer-meetings – all the produce and refuse of civilisation announced in staring letters, in daubed effigies, base, paltry, grotesque. A battle-ground of advertisements, fitly chosen amid subterranean din and reek; a symbol to the gaze of that relentless warfare which ceases not, night and day, in the world above.

It is this aspect of Gissing's vision, the nervous reaction to the noise, dirt, and triviality of contemporary life, that I have called peculiarly 'modern' – fuelled, of course, by hatred of the present, a temperamental preference for everything that is dead, dying, and gone. As he wished always to be somewhere other than where he was, so he recoiled from his own time with a passion consistent and unflinching. His phobia is reflected in much of his work through the mid-nineties – even the private jottings. 'In a big advt. on the walls', he notes in his Commonplace Book, 'it is stated that 60,000 bullocks are slaughtered yearly to make somebody's beef-tea. Another announced that, every minute, 7 of Beecham's pills "reach their destination".'

Eve's Ransom, set in Birmingham, Paris, and London, is an indifferent trifle among the works of Gissing's fruitful middle period: certainly it is several levels below the achievement of *In the Year of Jubilee*. Written quickly as a serial and composed partly of discarded sections of unfinished books, *Eve's Ransom* is a pastiche of interesting ingredients which add up to little. It is one of the most 'scenic', and Jamesian, of the tales written since *Isabel Clarendon*, but it is not fleshed out enough to take seriously.

   Maurice Hilliard, the unappealing protagonist, is another Gissing *persona*, harking back to the heroes of the early London years – of the Waymark/Kingcote rather than the Reardon/Tarrant school of autobiography. A young man living in lodgings, lonely, pessimistic, passionate, dreaming of making money and travelling, shrinking from Society (yet sometimes talking the night away with a cherished friend), Hilliard embodies many of the characteristics of Gissing's early self-portraits. It was 'difficult to ascertain his social standing', the novelist writes of the young Hilliard; he had 'an education just sufficiently prolonged to unfit him for the tasks of an underling, yet not thorough enough to qualify him for professional life'. He is a graduate of Mason College, Birmingham, described by the novelist as a place 'where young men are taught a variety of things, including discontent with a small income'. He dreams of meeting a woman who will be a companion as well as a lover. When Eve Madeley offers to be his friend, Hilliard – echoing Shergold in 'A Lodger in Maze Pond' – replies: 'It's no use to me. I must have more, or nothing.' His sentimentality combined with his sensual passion make it difficult for any intelligent woman to put up with him. His other attitudes toward women are familiar (for example, they are machines for the spending of money and the ruining of their husbands' lives).

The title of the novel refers to Eve's 'ransom' from poverty by Hilliard, who acquires a little money, and ultimately her 'ransom' from Hilliard by Narramore, who has more. Along the way a great deal is said about the imagined pleasures of the rich. Eve wonders: 'How do people feel who are quite sure they can never want as long as they live?' The novel does contain some fine writing, especially when Gissing compares the industrial town with the countryside beyond it. 'That's the end the human race will come to', Hilliard observes of Birmingham. 'It'll be driven mad and killed off by machinery.'

At the end of *Eve's Ransom* Hilliard, who in the usual Pygmalion-like pattern of sexual relationships in Gissing's novels has fallen in love with an inferior woman he has hoped to educate, loses her to a richer man. This, however, turns out to be no cause for regret. On the contrary, Gissing's misogynic mood of 1894 resulted in a 'happy' ending being tacked on to the novel. The idea is broached here that a man is better off without such an encumbrance as a wife. It is an ending only Gissing could have written: 'Maurice Hilliard, a free man in his own conceit, sang to himself a song of the joy of life.' The 'joy' is that of solitude, which now seemed to Gissing so alluring a state. Arthur Peachey's paradise is Hilliard's ultimate reward; the novel is really about his own 'ransom'. All of this makes for indifferent fiction but fascinating autobiography.

᯼

CHAPTER 9

ACHIEVEMENT AND DISASTER, 1894–1897

> For nothing makes man's loss grievous to him
> But knowledge of the worth of what he loses:
> For what he never had, he never misses.
>   . . . From a man that's blind
> To take a burning taper, 'tis no wrong,
> He never misses it; but to take light
> From one that sees, that's injury and spite.
>   Middleton, *Women Beware Women*

> Why will these literary men make these unfortunate marriages?
> It's all very sad, very sad.   Maugham, *Cakes and Ale*

> What a simple matter life would be, but for women!
>   *The Whirlpool*

I

THE first days at Epsom, in September 1894, were relatively peaceful. Gissing had found 'quietude', he told Bertz, while managing to remain near London. He added that the next book of his Bertz would receive (*In the Year of Jubilee*) was a 'picture of certain detestable phases of modern life'. And he wondered out loud if he should permit Lawrence and Bullen to reprint *The Unclassed*, as they were now proposing to do (the new edition appeared in November 1895).

During this September Gissing was heartened to hear that Bell and Company had purchased 1,200 copies of *Denzil Quarrier* and 750 of *The Emancipated* for its Colonial Library, and that the firm had requested 1,500 copies of *In the Year of Jubilee* (these orders were all for the one-volume 'cheap' – six shillings – edition, of course; most new novels by major novelists eventually reached this format now that the three-decker was in its death-throes). The novelist suddenly found himself engaged, simultaneously, upon proofs of *In the Year of Jubilee*, *Eve's Ransom*, and 'A Lodger in Maze Pond' (for the *National Review*). Shorter asked him for more stories. In mid-September Gissing received the £150 promised for *Eve's Ransom* (first mistakenly announced as 'Eve's Pardon'), though it would not begin to appear until the following January.

Gissing was finding it a pleasant novelty to be able to decide which journals to publish in and which to ignore. On 4 October he both 'began and finished', according to the diary, a short tale called 'Their Pretty Ways' (published the following year in *Lloyds Weekly Newspaper*). This little piece about domestic discord tells the story of two couples, the Rushes and the Wagers, who decide to share a house. Soon enough a 'note of dissonance . . . sounded . . . from below-stairs', and the men, who come home in the evening in expectation of a quiet dinner, encounter disorder instead: 'each was taken apart by his tender spouse, and, in spite of hunger, compelled to hear a catalogue of complaints against cook and housemaid.' Mrs Rush, obviously drawn from Edith, 'had but the vaguest ideas of domestic economy; when her husband insisted on speaking gravely of sordid matters, she pouted, rambled into all manner of irrelevant subjects, and at length, accusing him of never having loved her, burst into tears.' The husbands decide they must split the households up because their wives cannot get along with their servants or one another.

On 10 October Gissing recorded in his diary: 'But for my little boy, I would not, and could not, live with [Edith] for another day. I have no words for the misery I daily endure from her selfish and coarse nature.' He began to take Walter, now nearly three years old, with him on some of his long walks through the Surrey lanes; as his interest in the child grew he no longer begrudged the time spent with him.

During the latter part of October Gissing completed five more tales, and 'loaned' Algernon another £10. And he bought a dress suit, noting that he was beginning to be deluged with invitations to dine out – some of which he now wished to accept. He attended several dinners hosted by the Society of Authors, which only confirmed him in his belief that the most commercially successful writers of the day (such as Anthony Hope, author of *The Prisoner of Zenda* and guest of honour at one of the dinners) were businessmen rather than artists: 'respectable shopkeepers' and 'very commonplace tradesmen' was Gissing's verdict. Writers of the stature of Hardy, Meredith, James, and Kipling (whose early work Gissing admired) were usually not to be seen at these gatherings, and Gissing found them dull. He did make some new friends, however – including Eliza Orme, a prosperous conveyancer who was to become a loyal friend of his later years. He also met several editors who were to ask him for stories.

Early in November Gissing wrote another short piece. Called

'An Inspiration', it concerns a man and woman who were lovers when young; separated for many years, they manage to find each other again. This little tale is obviously a warm-up for *Sleeping Fires,* written shortly afterwards.

These latter months of 1894 saw an end of Gissing's public obscurity. Thanks to his new agent and his growing reputation, there was a constant demand for his work; paragraphs about him and essays on his novels appeared more frequently in the press; the sales of his books were on the increase; people knew his name, if not always his work. Now, when asked for a story, he could sometimes afford to refuse – or to name the subject and terms of payment himself. His income was dramatically rising. In 1893 his total earnings had been just under £200. During 1894 he made nearly £440 (about £157 from stories). His best year before 1894 had been 1892, when he had earned about £275. In 1895 he would make nearly £520. During 1894 his expenses barely exceeded one half of his income and he began to acquire some peace of mind on money matters. Indeed, he could not work quickly enough to supply all the people who asked him for stories and novels, as he told Bertz at the end of November 1894. He added: 'I am beginning to have a literary past; in meeting the young writers of to-day, I feel a veteran. And how strange a thing it is when, in walking about the streets of London, I pass the streets where I lived in those days of misery! Of course *that man* and *I* are not identical. He is a relative of mine, who died long ago; that's all.' He was thirty-seven.

For the time being the news was all good. The rights for a French translation of *The Odd Women* were sold for 20 guineas. Bell's bought another 500 copies of *The Emancipated.* Orders for *In the Year of Jubilee* were holding steady, though the book was not yet published. Lawrence and Bullen decided to do the cheap edition of *The Unclassed.* A cheque for £38 arrived from Shorter for three stories he had bought. If Gissing was unhappy, it was because the situation at home had not improved; he had no new novel under way to follow *Eve's Ransom* (between October 1894 and March 1895 no less than six publishers – one of them Smith, Elder! – asked him for a one-volume novel, all on generous terms); and the writing careers of Roberts and Algernon were apparently being snuffed out by the demise of the three-decker. Both had financial recourse to Gissing, who was proving himself more adaptable in the new literary market-place.

II

On 1 December 1894 *In the Year of Jubilee* was published in three volumes, and Gissing sent copies to Clara Collet, Bertz, Roberts, and Hudson (Algernon would have to wait for the one-volume edition, and Wakefield would have to wait indefinitely). The first notices began to appear during this month. The book was widely reviewed, and aroused controversy: its savage attack on suburban middle-class pretentiousness, along with the revolutionary views on marriage it offered, managed to offend a number of readers. The *Daily News, Saturday Review, National Observer, World, Bookman,* and *Pall Mall Gazette,* among others, were disapproving. Praise came from the *Morning Post,* the *Review of Reviews* ('Some day the reading public will wake up to find they have an English Zola in Mr. Gissing'), the *Athenaeum,* the *Academy,* and *To-Day* (which published the novelist's portrait). The *Daily Telegraph* felt that Gissing's characters were commonplace, but depicted with great skill. The *Sketch,* which also published a photograph of the novelist, was enthusiastic. In the *Illustrated London News* James Payn, Gissing's old enemy at Smith, Elder, concluded that *In the Year of Jubilee* was quite as good as anything he had written.

The most interesting notice (because of its consequences) was an unsigned attack in the *Spectator.* The reviewer said that Gissing was *the* contemporary chronicler of lower-middle-class manners, but that the 'general effect' he produced in his books was 'false, misleading, even libellous . . . it is in essence caricature.' Gissing is accused of exaggeration, prejudice; of seeing the idiosyncrasies in people but not their humanity. 'The brutish stupefaction of his men and women' is too 'inevitable' to be real, the writer declares. Gissing is not 'realistic', because he is too selective in what he will show and say; rather he is 'an idealist of the new school' (Zola's), a renderer of selected 'detail' rather than of truth. Gissing's vision, the reviewer concludes, is 'distorted': he sees only 'the vulgarity, sordidness, and ugliness of life'.

A few days after this notice appeared Roberts told Gissing he intended to write a critical article on him for the *Fortnightly Review.* Stung by the *Spectator*'s assault, Gissing in a long letter outlined what he thought his friend's line of defence should be. His chief argument was that the *Spectator* critic knew little of the class depicted in the novel. Reviewers, he said, never sufficiently studied his books: if they did they would not find his vision 'distorted'. As to the charge (made in this instance by Payn, and by other reviewers from time to time) that his characters are 'commonplace and sordid' – this, says Gissing, is untrue, and the impression ought to be corrected.

The most characteristic, the most important part of my work is that which deals with a class of young men distinctive of our time – well-educated, fairly bred, but *without money*. It is [the] fact . . . of the *poverty* of my people which tells against their recognition as civilised beings. 'Oh', said someone to Bullen, 'do ask Mr Gissing to make his people a little better off!' There you have it. Now think of some of the young men, Reardon, Biffen, Milvain, Peak, Earwaker, Elgar, Mallard. Do . . . books containing such . . . men deal, first and foremost, with the commonplace and sordid? Why these fellows are the very reverse of the commonplace: most of them are martyred by the fact of possessing uncommon endowments . . . This side of my work, to me the most important, I have never yet seen recognised.

What enraged Gissing was that his most autobiographical characters were the ones often singled out for censure as 'commonplace and sordid': it was doubly insulting.

  In the Year of Jubilee was not one of the novelist's best-sellers. Two months after publication only 365 copies of the three-volume edition had been sold. But the controversies it spawned stimulated further interest in Gissing and his work (and thus helped to boost the circulation of *Eve's Ransom*). Goaded by Colles, Methuen now offered to publish *Eve's Ransom* in one volume when it should have concluded its serial run, but Gissing decided to stick to Lawrence and Bullen, which had promised to continue the arrangement of a one-shilling royalty on each six-shilling volume sold, along with an advance of 50 guineas upon publication and half-profits of all subsequent editions.

  Despite these favourable omens, the last weeks of 1894 turned out to be gloomy ones for Gissing. The weather was bad, all three members of the family had colds, he was getting little work done, he had to send more money to Algernon, and the arguments in the press over *In the Year of Jubilee* were bothering him. 'I yield at once under . . . almost any kind of trouble', Gissing wrote to Bertz. In mid-December he read Moore's new novel *Esther Waters* and pronounced it 'miserable writing'. He was pleased by Jerome K. Jerome's request for half a dozen tales, 1,000 words and £3 each, for *To-Day* (the series tentatively to be entitled 'Nobodies at Home') – but he had few writing ideas at this time. The final diary entry for 1894 is heartening: 'Find that I earned by literature in 1894 no less a sum than £453–12–5 [actually, it was rather less]. Bravo! I see that my total expenses were £239–6–9.'

A week later he was advising Algernon to turn his hand to 'shorter things' such as 'Vignettes of country life and scenes . . . A piece you might write in one morning is vastly more likely to sell than the results of six weeks' toil.' He told his brother not to start over again as a novelist: 'it means the utter waste of life; it means destruction in the prime of manhood.' Gissing was delighted by Lawrence and Bullen's huge advertisements for *In the Year of Jubilee* and some of his other works, and by the first number of *Eve's Ransom* in the *Illustrated London News* (5 January 1895). Shorter wrote asking him to have his portrait done by a man who was photographing the 'sixteen leading novelists' of the day.

Gissing was also beginning to plan his next novel. When Smith, Elder asked him for a one-volume tale he replied evasively, but he was more encouraging to Fisher Unwin; the firm had offered £150 for a 30,000-word story (a large sum for such a short work) to be submitted by 31 March and published as part of its 'Autonym' series. On 15 January he began the new book, called from the start *Sleeping Fires*. Gissing had decided to set its opening scenes in Athens, and now re-read the diary record of his journey to Greece. The next day a paragraph appeared in the *Literary World* on the Gissing 'boom', informing the journal's readers that Mr Gissing, though presently in England, spent most of his time in Italy. 'Didn't know of the "boom"', Gissing wrote in his diary. He also recorded the 'loan' of yet another £10 to Algernon. On 19 January he signed the agreement with Fisher Unwin for the new book, and two days later began it all over again. During the latter part of January and the early weeks of February he cast aside and then recommenced the novel several times, in his usual fashion. Around this time he reluctantly sent £5 to Roberts, noting in his diary that he could 'ill afford' to be the banker of others. In mid-February he learned that 'A Lodger in Maze Pond' was being published in translation in France. The 'boom' was beginning to make itself felt.

Late in February Gissing received a letter from Martha Barnes, the girl with whom (probably) he had been briefly involved while teaching in Waltham, Massachusetts, at the age of 19. She had been following his career, she said: 'read some of my books; writes very nicely, and like an educated woman. Replied to her. Strange, strange!' On 1 March he finished *Sleeping Fires,* one of his better pieces of work. He then immediately began several short stories he had already promised. Feeling exhausted, he took the family off to

Eastbourne for a short holiday at the end of March. 'I . . . am very often reminded that the years of best energy are gone and will return no more', the thirty-seven-year-old novelist wrote to Bertz. Beyond 'the fatigue of inventing and writing', he explained to Roberts, 'I [also] keep house and bring up the boy, and the strain . . . is rather severe.' Edith, it seems, had ceased to exert herself altogether. Upon their return from Eastbourne, Gissing found a cheque for £150 from Unwin for *Sleeping Fires*.

Late in March he agreed to write a 25,000-word story for Cassell's Pocket Library: it would be due in the autumn, the remuneration £50 (this would be *The Paying Guest*). Colles continued to urge upon Gissing the writing of short pieces to satisfy the current public appetite, but the novelist had not altogether forgotten his real vocation. 'I work slowly', he replied, and 'shall never be able to turn out very much. What I *am* bent on doing, is to write books which will be read, not only to-day, but some years hence . . . I dare not lose the respect of the highest class of readers for the sake of immediate profit.' Having his eye on posterity, Gissing had always refused to be 'popular', to write down to his audience; the new vogue for his fiction made him a little suspicious, made him wonder if perhaps quality was being sacrificed. As for his inability 'to turn out very much', he wrote more novels than any other major nineteenth-century novelist except Scott and Trollope and lived fewer years than any of them except Jane Austen and the Brontës.

During the first week of April 1895 Gissing visited Wakefield, alone. On the way back he stopped off at his brother William's grave near Manchester and visited the school at Alderley Edge they had attended as children. No doubt the tragedies of his early Manchester days were much on his mind. Upon his return to London he found a request from Shorter for six more stories and a cheque for 50 guineas from Lawrence and Bullen. *Eve's Ransom* had been published in one volume on 2 April: 800 copies were sold on publication day, and another 700 during the next three months; there was a second edition in May 1895 and a third in 1901, and Gissing eventually earned nearly £250 from this least ambitious of the novels written in the mid-nineties.

Although *Eve's Ransom* sold better than any of Gissing's earlier novels except the equally mediocre *A Life's Morning*, it got from contemporary reviewers the rough treatment it deserved. Few wholly favourable notices appeared. Several journals issued warnings that must have hit Gissing in a vulnerable place – for, as we have seen, he worried now about frittering away his time and talent on trifles. 'The temptation to beat one's work out thin is one of the most dangerous that can beset an author of rising popularity', the *Pall Mall Gazette* said. 'Wherefore let Mr. Gissing look to himself.' 'It is hoped that he is not going the way of so many writers, and producing too rapidly for his own reputation', the *Bookman* declared. The *Critic* said more or less the same thing; the substance of *In the Year of Jubilee*, controversial as some of it might be, was wholly missing in this new work. Eve was considered uninteresting as a character; Hilliard (deservedly) was more of a success with the reviewers. The *Manchester Guardian* and the *Daily Chronicle* were more positive, though the latter's critic found the 'happy ending . . . profoundly depressing'. In the *Saturday Review* H. G. Wells devoted part of a longish essay on what he called 'The Depressed School' of fiction to *Eve's Ransom*, declaring that 'we do not believe that any social stratum is so dull as [the] melancholy world' depicted in the novel. He shrewdly added: Gissing 'cannot imagine a happy marriage under a thousand a year . . . That horror of being hard up, the fixed idea of the dismalness of middle-class life, is not only the keynote of this book, but of all his work; it reduces it from the level of a faithful presentation of life to *genre*. It is the *genre* of nervous exhaustion.' Wells went on to express his admiration for Gissing's other novels, and the rest of the piece formed an appropriate prelude to the friendship the two men were soon to establish. 'We must needs admire' Gissing's work, Wells says, 'because it is so remarkably well done, and we must needs read it to its bitter end for the grim interest of it that never fails.'

III

Sleeping Fires, completed in March 1895, became Gissing's fifteenth published novel since *Workers in the Dawn* appeared in 1880. It is the first of three consecutive masterpieces written during the last very explosive years of Gissing's second marriage; together with its successors, *The Paying Guest* and *The Whirlpool*, it represents a final burst of the creative energy that began in 1888 after the death of Nell and was to end, to all intents and purposes, in 1897 with the publication of *The Whirlpool* and Gissing's separation from Edith. For his last novels, with only a few exceptions, are less interesting than their predecessors. The only great novel of the last period is *Will Warburton*, published posthumously. *By the Ionian Sea*, a brilliantly sustained piece of narrative, and *Charles Dickens*, a first-rate piece of criticism, are works of non-fiction. *The Private Papers of Henry Ryecroft,* a long-time favourite of many readers (the first of Gissing's books to appear in a modern paperback edition), is a brief memoir-essay, fascinating for its autobiographical content but only marginally a novel. His last years of life, remarkably chaotic though they were and punctuated by failing health, were probably Gissing's happiest – or least unhappy – and one may legitimately suppose that in his case, as in Osmond Waymark's, the 'art and misery' equation always applied: art, for Gissing, throve on adversity and shrivelled up in the sunshine.

Edmund Langley, the protagonist of *Sleeping Fires,* possesses many familiar characteristics of the Gissing hero. The resemblances to the novelist are discernible through the disguise of a private income and a strain of dilettantism: Langley is in the Egremont/ Mallard/Quarrier/Hilliard line rather than the Golding/Waymark/ Kingcote/Peak line of protagonists. He has deep feeling for the ancient civilizations; and since part of the novel is set in Greece, Gissing is able to give free play to his enthusiasm – not for modern Athens, needless to say, but for ancient Greek culture, which in *Sleeping Fires* represents a past worshipped in preference to a hated present. The Temple of Theseus is described as 'A sanctuary . . . so old, so wondrous in its isolation, that all the life of to-day around it seemed a futility and an impertinence.'

There is also the almost obligatory description of the Acropolis: 'rocks and ruins all fawny gold, the work of art inseparable from that of nature . . . neither seeming to have bodily existence; the gorgeous purples of Hymettus; that cloud on Pentelikon, with its melting splendours which seemed to veil the abode of gods' – and so on, the diary entries quarried again. The novel describes many of the places Gissing visited during his brief trip to Greece some years earlier. Indeed, Langley's precipitate return from Athens follows exactly Gissing's path: by sea to Naples via Brindisi, with a stop in Corfu.

Langley describes himself as an 'old-fashioned Tory': he is emphatically anti-Radical. Louis Reed, in fact, virtually dies *of* Radicalism: if he had not been sent abroad by his guardian to escape the influence of the Radical Lady Tresilian, a woman of fashion who devotes her life to helping the poor, he would probably have remained healthy. Langley's discovery that Louis is his illegitimate son stimulates him to muse along lines Gissing's thoughts must often have followed whenever his life with Edith became unbearable: 'A son of that age [18], a handsome, intelligent lad, overflowing with the zeal and the zest of life; with such a one at his side how lightly and joyously would he walk among these ruins of the old world! What flow of talk! What happiness of silent sympathy!' Gissing, who knew little of 'silent sympathy', transferred his domestic interest to his young son as the boy grew up; here is a projection of what it might be like to be Walter's father some years hence (the comparative 'joys' of being a father and a husband is also a theme of *The Whirlpool*). From *In the Year of Jubilee* onwards, fatherhood is almost always a theme in Gissing's books.

In *In the Year of Jubilee* Tarrant does the decent thing and marries the pregnant Nancy. This is precisely what Langley, faced with a similar situation, does not do: he does not marry Louis's mother (he is twenty-three at the time), and *Sleeping Fires* argues that he is right not to do so. For once the male evades the trap laid by the female. It is another way-station marking Gissing's progressive hatred of the institution of marriage. 'The . . . ceremony of marriage is of no account', Langley declares. He adds that 'a parent is bound by every kind of law in the interests of his child', and is willing to support the son but not the mother. Langley's marriage to Louis's mother would have been exogamous. By the mid-nineties Gissing's characters no longer need to find out the consequences of such relationships: they are known, and often avoided. Louis's mother was 'on the brink of hopeless degradation' – presumably prostitution – when Langley met her. As Nell had been for Gissing, she was for Langley 'the moment's fancy of sensual youth', without charm, depth, or beauty. 'A lad can be fooled by the most worthless woman', Langley declares, speaking from the novelist's heart. But this lad is not fooled. To have married her would have been 'to lay the foundation of life-long misery', he says of the woman he has impregnated. It would have been to bow one's head to 'the silliest cant. What sort of marriage would that have been? Have we not known of such?' We have indeed. 'My selfishness . . . saved me from worse than folly', Langley says. He adds: 'What real love can you feel for a woman whom you can't respect?' 'But what has marriage to do with love?', asks Lady Revill, to whom Langley tells the story of his past.

Agnes Revill was the love of Langley's youth. They had had to part as a result of Langley's indiscretion with Louis's mother, which he had confessed to Agnes's father. This indiscretion was his 'guilty secret' – a 'hidden . . . sorrow of which he spoke to no one'. He was very young when he had had this fling; like Hubert Eldon in *Demos*, his past costs him much sorrow before he finally (after sixteen years) gets the very respectable lady he has always wanted.

The quick pleasure of a passing infatuation melts on the tongue; the power of wanting that which has value lingers, grows stronger – especially when one is deprived of the prize. In his misery, Gissing was still hoping for a turn of luck.

Langley feels that his early mistakes should not prevent him forever from gaining the love of a respectable woman. That Gissing was beginning to acquire a new self-confidence is clearly demonstrated by *Sleeping Fires*. He was now a fashionable novelist with a comfortable income: why shouldn't a respectable woman have him at last? It perhaps was not too late to attain happiness – even if, like Arthur Peachèy, he had to leave home to find it. Langley's passion to get Lady Revill back, her own secret passion to have him back, and their coming together at last may thus be seen as a result of Gissing's own 'sleeping fires' in the mid-nineties: 'For the fire that so long had slept within [Langley], hidden beneath the accumulating habits of purposelessness, self-indulgent life . . . thought of as a . . . flash amid the ardours of youth – the fire of a life's passion, no longer to be disguised or resisted, burst into consuming flame . . . No hapless lad, tortured by his twentieth year, suffered keener pains than Langley.' Gissing had had enough; before long he would burst the inimical bonds that held him, in an attempt to assuage his 'life's passion'.

Had Edith read or understood *Sleeping Fires* it would have warned her as clearly as *In the Year of Jubilee* of what lay ahead. For the later novel argues with great eloquence that life is not over at forty, it is not too late to love in early middle age. 'If the best of life is over, so is the worst, thank God!' says Lady Revill; she is the same age as Gissing, thirty-seven. Langley, a few years older, speaks about the advantages of mature over youthful love: 'we know what may be asked, and what may not. No castles in the air; no idealisms of boy and girl; but two lives that have a want, and see but . . . one hope of satisfying it': being together. *Sleeping Fires* is Gissing's *Antony and Cleopatra*.

As one might expect, the attack on self-denial and asceticism is carried forward from the earlier books. 'The old prejudices', as they are called here, are attacked with as much gusto as in *Denzil Quarrier*. 'Oh, how the proprieties imprison you! How the petty hypocrisies of life constrain the nobler part of you!' So Langley complains to the icy Lady Revill, before she melts. 'Turn ascetic – torment yourself – find merit in misery', he taunts her. 'This is the greatest sin and folly of all!' He goes on: 'Health and joy are the true repentance. All sins against the conscience – what are they but sins against the laws of healthy life? . . . Health and joy . . . is what life demands of us.'

Sleeping Fires is an exuberant, eloquent little tale that has always been too quickly passed over by Gissing's critics. It is a brilliant story, highly dramatic, and wonderfully passionate. I believe it is one of the greatest short novels ever written, though no one has ever heard of it. But this neglected masterpiece deserves to be read – not only for what it tells us of Gissing's state of mind early in 1895 (though at first glance it seems remote from his own experience) but also on its merits as a superb piece of English fiction.

IV

'These short stories are becoming a great trial', Gissing wrote in his diary in mid-April 1895. But as he was getting about £15 apiece for them he persevered, and in fact he was to write more stories during this year than any other. Edward Clodd wrote to invite him to visit Aldeburgh for a week. He told Clodd he would come for a few days – and volunteered the information that urban women of the lower classes were still prey to 'gross superstition' and other 'exasperating barbarisms'. 'It is easy to imagine the case of a fairly sensible workman driven mad by his wife's imbecility', Gissing informed Clodd, who had not met Mrs Gissing. Evidently his patience was growing thinner. During his visit to Clodd he met the novelist Grant Allen, the author of *The Woman Who Did* (a popular tale of a free union), some of whose conversation he was later to use in *The Ryecroft Papers* (Autumn, 12). Also present was Shorter, who extracted a promise from Gissing to write six more stories for the *English Illustrated Magazine* at 12 guineas each and twenty short pieces for *The Sketch,* of the sort he had done for Jerome's *To-Day,* at three guineas each (an order totalling about £145). Gissing was delighted to get away from Epsom at Derby time ('blackguardism [at] its height', he noted in his diary) and he enjoyed Clodd's gathering. 'He looked like the very last man to have cultivated an intimacy with the slums', said W. Robertson Nicoll, who met Gissing about this time. 'He was well dressed, bland, debonair and communicative.' The novelist's old Wakefield friend, now Dr Henry Hick, visited Gissing at Epsom at the end of April. 'George was practically the same as when I had known him twenty years earlier', Hick wrote.

The novelist now began to work out the plot of the tale he had promised Cassell's Pocket Library for October. Meanwhile proofs of *Sleeping Fires* arrived. An advertisement for *Eve's Ransom* promised a 'Second Edition ready shortly'. At the end of April Gissing noted that his bank balance stood at £436 – and that more than 1,000 copies of the six-shilling edition of *Eve's Ransom* had been sold. Except for his inability to get going on another 'big' book – and of course the situation at home – things were looking up. He began to write a novel called 'The Spendthrift' on 1 May; the diary records the usual stops and starts until the story was abandoned two weeks later. Another tale called 'The Enchantress' also was begun and then discarded. 'I destroy far more than I publish', Gissing admitted to Colles.

A cheque from Bertz for £27 arrived. 'Astonished', Gissing recorded in his diary: 'a debt due to me for more than ten years'. He responded with a long letter to his old friend. He did not really need the cash, he said. 'The money I earn is small compared with the literary reputation I have somehow managed to achieve; but still it is sufficient for my present needs.' He went on to say that in the 'old days' (the early and mid-eighties) '*my* debt to you was a great one, inexpressible in cash. But for your companionship I might have sunk to miserable depths.' To Bertz's strictures on *Eve's Ransom*, he conceded: 'To be sure, Eve was not worth it all; therein lies the sting of the story . . . It certainly is not one of my best.' He concluded: 'I am rather overburdened by the demand for short stories. This work is not altogether congenial to me, but it is the only kind that brings in much money. My books don't sell; though perhaps they may some day. The second edition of "Eve" is only a second thousand.'

In mid-May he wrote a short essay, at the request of the editor of *The Humanitarian*, on 'The Place of Realism in Fiction'. An interesting little piece, it attacks literary naturalism – which chooses 'vulgar, base, or disgusting subjects' – and argues that such terms as 'realism' and 'realist' be discarded and works of literature judged as either 'sincere' and 'craftsmanlike', or not. Sincerity, or 'the spirit of truthfulness', is of chief importance: 'no novel can possess the slightest value which has not been conceived, fashioned, elaborated, with a view to depicting some portion of human life as candidly and vividly as is in the author's power', Gissing says. But 'Reality' is impossible to define since 'every novelist beholds a world of his own, and the supreme endeavour of his art must be to body forth that world as it exists for him. The novelist works, and must work, subjectively.' Thus there can be 'no science of fiction'; literature is 'dead material' until life is breathed into it by the writer's 'shaping spirit of imagination'. The critic's only job can be to decide whether or not a work of art is truthful – 'that is to say, to judge the spirit in which it was conceived, and the technical merit of its execution'. If it is anything, realism therefore is no more than 'artistic sincerity in the portrayal of contemporary life'. Art is what the artist selects as subject-matter. 'The Place of Realism in Fiction' expresses a point of view identical with that of Hardy in such essays as 'The Profitable Reading of Fiction' (1888) and 'The Science of Fiction' (1891), both of which Gissing undoubtedly read.

During June he began to collect notes for a historical novel with a Roman setting, a project he had long thought about. Throughout the next eight and a half years he was to work on *Veranilda* sporadically, leaving it unfinished at his death. Of the short stories he wrote at this time, 'The Justice and the Vagabond' is an unpleasant little tale extolling the virtues of travel and attacking the tyranny of family life. 'Travel is conquest', the story says; to stay at home and care for one's wife and children is merely to 'play at life'. At the centre of 'The Firebrand' is one of Gissing's political charlatans, this one a radical demagogue lampooned as a hypocrite and a coward.

At the end of June, Gissing wrote another of his confessional letters to Bertz. 'It is strange how many letters I get from women', he told him, 'asking for sympathy and advice. I really can't understand what it is in my work that attracts the female mind.' Gissing's fiction was always popular with women, as he himself was. In most of his books there are at least two, and usually more, women in leading roles, treated with understanding if not always with sympathy. Undoubtedly women perceived his interest and responded in kind. Gissing was a man with whom a number of women wished to become involved in one way or another.

On 13 July he attended, at Shorter's invitation, a dinner meeting of the famous Omar Khayyám Club. The meeting was held near Box Hill so that the crippled Meredith, who was being honoured that evening, could be present. Hardy was there; so were Edmund Gosse and Theodore Watts, among others. Clodd was in the chair. After the meal several of the diners, Hardy included, were called upon to say something about Meredith, and when his turn came Gissing told the story of his interview with Meredith years earlier on the occasion of Meredith's acceptance of *The Unclassed* for Chapman and Hall. Afterwards both Meredith and Hardy asked Gissing to come and visit them. Accounts of the dinner were given in several newspapers. The *Daily Chronicle* referred to Meredith,

Hardy, and Gissing as the three foremost novelists of the age, and Gissing proudly sent copies of the article to Wakefield and to Bertz.

Certainly his reading public had been growing. After *Demos* all his novels – including, in this July of 1895, *In the Year of Jubilee* – were reprinted in cheap one-volume form; many of them had appeared as well in foreign and colonial editions. In the mid-nineties it was undoubtedly true that Gissing's name was as highly respected as Hardy's (Meredith had achieved a degree of fame and respect beyond them both), though his books never generated the substantial profits his two famous contemporaries could count on. In this he was following a path a younger writer of his generation would soon tread: Conrad's name, like Gissing's, commanded great respect during the latter years of his life, but his books generally had disappointing sales.

v

After a false start at the end of June 1895, Gissing wrote *The Paying Guest* quickly in the first two weeks of July. It is another miniature masterpiece. Its obsession with matters of class place it with *Demos*, *Born in Exile*, and *Will Warburton*, though its format does not allow the same leisurely development of theme. Still, Gissing's success here, as in *Sleeping Fires*, demonstrates his talent for the *novella*, with which he was always more comfortable than the short story.

The Paying Guest is set in suburbia, where worrying what the neighbours think seems to be all there is to do. The Mumfords are afraid of losing caste by 'taking lodgers' – thus the euphemism they adopt which Gissing appropriates for his title. To them, as a 'paying guest', comes a girl from a family rich but vulgar and unrefined. Louise is ashamed of her family, and Mrs Mumford is ashamed to have Louise's friends and relatives with their uncultured pronunciation in the house. Louise brings disharmony – and, ultimately, fire – to the Mumford establishment; she is noisy, violent, and bad-tempered. This does not prevent Mr Mumford from becoming infatuated with her. By the end of *The Paying Guest* everyone has concluded that the mixing of the classes, their physical proximity, is a mistake.

During the year 1895 Gissing wrote approximately three dozen short stories, roughly a third of the total number he produced during his writing life from 1877 to 1903. Most of these tales appeared either in 1895 or 1896, and many of them were reprinted in the collection called *Human Odds and Ends*, published in 1897. I have already mentioned several of the stories written during 1895; I shall examine a representative number of others to convey some notion of their general flavour.

'The Medicine Man' is about a physician who ruins himself, both morally and vocationally, by marrying 'a woman of no character and inclined to drink'. He justifies his gouging and fraudulent treatment of the poor by saying it does not matter what he tells them since they cannot follow medical directions. This, says Gissing, who had not lost his hatred of 'reform', is 'a truth which should be laid to heart by all excessively anxious about the ignorant poor'. 'Raw Material', which focuses on a woman who tries to pass herself off as an experienced servant and fails miserably, and ultimately becomes a prostitute, anticipates an incident in *Will Warburton*. The central character of 'An Old Maid's Triumph' is a governess who is sacked after thirty years of service but is able to survive on her meagre savings because, throughout her life, she has never spent an unavoidable shilling, 'out of sheer dread of some day finding herself destitute, helpless at the mercy of a world which never spares its brutality to those who perforce require its compassion'.

'The Tout of Yarmouth Bridge' is another attack, harking back to an earlier vein of Gissing's, on lodging-houses and the women who run them. He never forgot, and he never forgave. Here the landlady steals her lodgers' belongings, cooks their food badly on purpose – and even lets, without so much as cleaning it, a flat just vacated by a family in which there has been scarlet fever, to another couple with children. 'A Song of Sixpence' is an interesting tale about a woman fairly well educated and with a musical career before her, who makes the mistake of marrying a drinking husband. In an alcoholic rage he throws her down a flight of stairs, as a result of which she loses a leg and her career.

The tenor of 'A Profitable Weakness' may be judged from its opening: 'Only to the few and the very fortunate of men is it granted to earn a livelihood by the exertion of their best powers. Men in general owe their sustenance to the meaner of their faculties, often enough to the basest possibility that is in them.' The central character of this tale is a teacher who hates teaching, detests the noise children make, and has no power of discipline over them – undoubtedly a version of Bertz in the early 1880s. Unlike Bertz, this teacher develops a practical strain and manages to get himself adopted by a rich benefactor.

'The Beggar's Nurse' is about a woman whose years of toil in a local poor-house on behalf of the degraded have in turn degraded her into a beast who tortures her charges. 'A Parent's Feelings' is a charming slum-life tale about a mother who regularly beats her children for the fun of it (she has beaten one to death). The youngest girl of the family, who has had her nose broken in a fight with her mother, puts nails in her shoes for the next encounter. The protagonist of 'The Little Woman from Lancashire' is a poor woman with pretensions to refinement who marries a low-bred working-class man, inherits some money, and goes in for 'society' with some success – though her speech always betrays her origins. When she refuses her husband's request to forgo her fashionable career he beats her and locks her up. The quarter-educated protagonist of 'At High Pressure' lives in a constant state of nervous tension. She reads all the new periodicals, writes dozens of letters, but takes no hand in the running of her family's lower-middle-class household, in which domestic discord reigns. 'A Free Woman', in Gissing's most unsubtle vein, also attacks women who eschew domestic duties. Charlotte Grubb hates cooking, mending clothes, tending children, and so on, and swears not to give up her freedom by marrying. She is proud never to have prepared a meal, washed a plate, or sewn a stitch. She is encouraged, by 'women of the higher classes [who] were making speeches, and calling for a great many more or less unintelligible things', to neglect her young brothers and sisters.

'A Son of the Soil', a reworking of an incident in *Workers in the Dawn* (the story of Mr Tolladay's mother), is about a man who abandons his widowed mother, dependent upon him for support, and goes to London seeking adventure and advancement. A child of his age, he is discontented, dishonest, and ignorant; his only interests are fleshly, and it is not long before he contracts a disease – presumably venereal, though unspecified. Failing to find work and beginning to starve, he writes at last to his mother: the letter comes back marked 'Dead'.

'Out of the Fashion' is one of the few tales in this group that features a likeable woman: it gives us another idealized picture of the perfect housewife. Despite the fact that her husband loses one job after another, Mary never complains. She is cheerful and supportive; she has no great expectations. Not highly educated, she has much native intelligence and common sense. Her chief interests are books, music, and her husband's welfare. She does the house-keeping efficiently, shedding 'the light of home' about her wherever she goes and guarding her little family 'from the degrading effects of manifest poverty'. She keeps her strength up without having to take holidays; and she knows better than to 'brutalise the bread-winner' by ruining his mental equilibrium with impossible demands. When the piano has to be sold, she sings to her husband instead. Mary, Gissing concludes, represents a 'type of vanishing virtue. Wife, housewife, mother – shaken by the harsh years, but strong and peaceful in her perfect womanhood. An old-fashioned figure, out of harmony with the day that rules.' Indeed, Mary is the most anomalous, the 'oddest' of all the 'human odds and ends' among this group of characters.

'The Prize Lodger' is set in several lodging-houses in Islington, where Gissing lived from November 1879 to July 1880. Again lodging-house landladies are pilloried – chiefly Mrs Elderfield, who tyrannizes over her chief tenant. 'Transplanted' is another vintage Gissing piece which attacks the charitable impulses of the well-to-do. A wealthy lady takes pity on a London tramp and sends him to work as an under-gardener in her country house. He almost dies of overeating – but survives to acquire congestion of the lungs. Ultimately he develops a violent hatred of the lady who tried to help him and slices up some of her favourite plants.

As I have said, Gissing never really mastered this form. He preferred the larger canvas, and did better with it. But it is interesting to note the continuity of themes.

VI

In mid-July 1895 Gissing took the family for a holiday at Gorleston: 'E. sulking all day in bedroom, with no meals'. The novelist had once again managed to choose lodgings poorly run by a gouging woman, and when they decided to move to others in Yarmouth Edith and the landlady got into a fight which brought a police inspector on the scene.

Upon their return to Epsom the diary begins to take on a familiar tone. 'A time of great domestic misery. No servant heard of . . . and of course no work possible.' He began, however, to churn out the tales for Shorter – doing sometimes two a day from late August to late September. In a letter to Hardy he described these pieces as 'blotched impressions of miserable, squalid lives. They are not worth much, but such work must needs be done'. He persevered, the money being necessary: another child was expected in January. He wanted to do 'a good solid novel', but as yet could not find the time. To Bertz he sketched his position in the contemporary literary scene:

The *distant* attitude . . . has become one of my characteristics in the eyes of the reading-public. I am looked upon as . . . a recluse, and it is well known that I never sought the favour of influential people; and these things certainly serve me. Happily, I can now meet men in a very independent way. It is known to very few how poor I am; most people think my books have a *large* sale, and . . . treat me with great respect. I suppose the sale of the books is really increasing a little.

He concluded: 'The extent to which novelists are becoming *mere* men of business is terrible.'

Early in September he visited Meredith, now sixty-seven, at Box Hill. Meredith greeted him cordially, spent much of the afternoon with him, and invited him to dine later in the month. 'His talk of simple matters; strong interest in women often appearing. Pleaded for imagination in the novel – must be fruit for the reader to take away', Gissing noted. 'Said he had a miserably hard time in his youth.' After dining with Meredith at Box Hill, he noted 'Dinner poor'. Meredith was extremely parsimonious.

An invitation from Hardy to visit Dorset for several days arrived and was promptly accepted.

On 14 September Gissing went to Dorchester, where Hardy met him at the station. 'Signs of easy circumstances, but cooking of course bad. Mrs. Hardy a foolish, unrestful person, and disagreeable in face' (this was of course the first Mrs Hardy, Emma Lavinia Gifford). The next day Gissing walked with his host through Egdon Heath, Hardy pointing out to him places of interest along the way – getting the names of wayside flowers wrong, according to Gissing – and talking to his guest of his new novel, *Jude the Obscure*. 'He spoke of the difficulty he had in describing in decent language an odd scene – that in which, at a pig-killing, a girl throws a pig's *pizzle* at a man and hits him.' Gissing liked Hardy less than the cultivated, suave Meredith. He is Meredith's 'intellectual inferior', he noted in his diary. 'I perceive that he has a good deal of coarseness in his nature – the coarseness explained by humble origin.' Hardy's father was a mason; Meredith, cleverer at obfuscating his origins, was the son of a bankrupt tailor. Gissing reported that Hardy 'did an odd thing at breakfast – jumped up and killed a wasp with the flat of a table-knife! He seems to me to be a trifle spoilt by success; he runs far too much after titled people, and, in general, the kind of society in which he is least qualified to shine . . . Cannot let himself go in conversation; is uneasy and pre-occupied', Gissing complained of the older man. Hardy was not as skilful as the urbane Meredith at putting the nervous Gissing at his

ease. On the last day of the visit Hardy told Gissing what a trivial
man Tennyson had been (Gissing was none the less to name his
second son after the late Laureate), while Mrs Hardy 'talked
fretfully of being obliged to see more society than she liked . . . and
even said that it was hard to live with people of humble origin –
meaning Thomas, of course'. Gissing sums up his impressions: 'On
the whole very little pleasure from this visit. It is disagreeable to see
a man like Hardy so unsettled in his life . . . all this is the outcome
of misery in his marriage . . . the atmosphere of success does not
suit him. Vastly better if he had married an honest homely woman
who would have been impossible in fashionable society.' And yet
Gissing was too ashamed of his own wife to take her anywhere, let
alone to Max Gate. Did he, perhaps, fear a middle age like Hardy's
(Hardy was fifty-five in 1895): the trappings of success yet the
continuing misery of being chained to an inimical woman?

Gissing sent an account to Bertz of his visits to Meredith and
Hardy. He called Meredith 'a scholar' and said 'there is a fine
dignity about him . . . I feel proud to sit in his room.' Hardy, he
declared, 'is a man of far less intellectual vigour and distinction . . .
Born a peasant, he yet retains much of the peasant's views of life.'
His description of Hardy continues: 'He evidently does not read
very much, and I grieve to find that he is drawn into merely
fashionable society, talks of lords and ladies more than ordinary
people' (Meredith was a more notorious toady and tuft-hunter but
better at concealing his snobbery). 'Most unfortunately', Gissing
went on, Hardy 'has a very foolish wife – a woman of higher birth
than his own [Emma's father was a lawyer] who looks down upon
him, and is utterly discontented . . . I admire Hardy's best work
very highly', Gissing declared, 'but in the man himself I feel
disappointed. To my great surprise, I found that he did not know
the names of flowers in his own fields.' He concluded: 'A strange
unsettlement appears in him; probably the result of his long
association with such a paltry woman.' Preoccupied as he was with
the surface lives of these two famous contemporary novelists,
Gissing is not seen in a flattering light here – though perhaps it
should be said on his behalf that he was describing two of the most
selfish and unfeeling characters of his or any other age. In any case,
the increased intimacy with such eminent men shows how solid his
position had become in the literary world. Hardly a month went
by now without something by or about him appearing in the press,
often next to his photograph.

During the latter half of September Gissing resumed work on the rest of the stories promised to Shorter and read proofs of the new edition of *The Unclassed*. Examining his accounts, he realized that he would earn more than £500 in 1895. During the last week of the month he made out his will, appointing Algernon and Miss Collet joint executors; the latter accepted on condition that Edith should be named the legal guardian of the children 'with coordinate powers'. In the first week of October he finished Shorter's sketches, wrote a new preface to *The Unclassed* for Lawrence and Bullen, and paid a flying visit to Hick in New Romney, near Dover. He was cheered to hear that more of his stories were being translated into French.

A word must be said about the new edition of *The Unclassed* (for which the novelist was paid an advance of 50 guineas). The book was much sought after when Gissing became well known in the nineties but obscure and hard to find before then. In the course of revising, Gissing cut it by about one-third. It was hard work; he had to immerse himself once again in his unhappy life of the early eighties. Coustillas has summed up eloquently this retrospective ordeal: 'It was with unspeakable self-torture that he re-shaped the story; in the process, he relived the past, with its misery and its dogged idealism, the martyrdom of his life with Nell transposed in the rash marriage of Julian Casti, the undying hope of Ida Starr's redemption.' The new preface was largely an appeal for indulgence of this autobiographical early book. It was, the author said, the work of a very young man, 'who dealt in a romantic spirit with the gloomier facts of life' (it is difficult to see where or how the novel is 'romantic'). The English press welcomed the volume enthusiastically, much more enthusiastically than it had in 1884. The novel went into colonial and American editions, and interestingly enough became a best-seller of 1896 in the United States. It was one of Gissing's better novels; only now, eleven years after original publication, was it getting the recognition it had always deserved.

Gissing continued to turn down most requests for stories and *novellas*. As a matter of courtesy he acceded to Shorter's orders for the *English Illustrated Magazine*, but during the last quarter of 1895 he let his output of tales slacken off, feeling he needed to get back to the large canvas and more serious work. He was now formally elected a member of the Omar Khayyám Club: at its December dinner he met, among others, the dramatist Pinero. *Eve's Ransom* was being translated into French, *In the Year of Jubilee* into German. He began to receive letters from people asking for his autograph. Around this time he wrote a tale, 'The Foolish Virgin', for the *Yellow Book*; this is about a friendless and impoverished woman who makes a reasonable life for herself as a domestic helper: the story anticipates that of Minnie Wager in *The Whirlpool*, Gissing's next novel. He also renewed his acquaintance with his old Owens College friend Black, now a clerk in the Record Office and the father of six children, and with Frederic Harrison, whom he had not met since his 'exile' to Exeter. In November he read proofs of *The Paying Guest* and saw his new edition of *The Unclassed* published. The £75 he received from Cassell for the former (an advance of £50, plus £25 for the American rights) and the fifty guineas he received from Bullen for the latter – not to mention the money Shorter was paying him – left him very flush indeed during the last weeks of 1895, his most prosperous year. His thirty-eighth birthday was allowed to pass on 22 November without comment.

During the next two months Gissing wrote three long letters to Bertz. Sending the new edition of *The Unclassed* to his friend, he admitted that the book was painful to him for several reasons but he felt that the revision had made it 'less crude and absurd'. Responding to his friend's complaints of loneliness, Gissing told him that solitariness 'is really preferable, for the wise man, to all but a very few forms of companionship. Intellect and character in any case tend to solitude; associated with poverty, they are all but universally *condemned* to it.' Somewhat ingenuously for once, he complained to Bertz of lack of funds. He continued, he said, 'to make new acquaintances. If I were to accept all the invitations I receive, I should dine in town about once a week, but I am afraid of excessive distraction.' On the various Imperialist imbroglios then in progress in Africa and elsewhere, he commented: 'The so-called civilized world is . . . full of rampant barbarians – most of them reckless of everything in the furious chase after wealth and power. More likely than not, they will bring about terrible things in the immediate future.'

Despite its passionate plea for liberalized divorce laws, Gissing found little to like, when it appeared, in *Jude the Obscure*. 'A sad book!' he wrote to Hick. 'Poor Thomas is utterly on the wrong tack, and I fear he will never get back into the right one.' Hardy was to write no more novels though he lived until 1928.

VII

Sleeping Fires was published in cloth in December 1895 and *The Paying Guest* in January 1896. Cassell's incredible advertisement, which appeared in the *Sketch*, the *Academy*, and the *Pall Mall Gazette*, read in part: 'Mr George Gissing's story "The Paying Guest" is . . . his first comedy . . . To read the book one would think that Mr Gissing had been converted suddenly to a cheery optimism. There is no moment of gloom from cover to cover. The vein is the lightest, and the volume will be a welcome surprise to many who have regarded this most able writer as the apostle of melancholy.' By any odds this is an eccentric valuation of the tale – which, as Cassell himself admitted, satirizes 'the grotesque ambitions of suburban life'. 'They are puffing it in a shameless way and making the author ridiculous', Gissing commented bitterly; he vowed he would have nothing more to do with Cassell. In a letter to Hick, Gissing referred to *The Paying Guest* as 'a paltry story' and 'literary trash'; the tales he was writing for Shorter he called 'brief rubbish'. He agreed with Roberts rather than Bertz in preferring *Sleeping Fires* to *The Paying Guest*, in which he was undoubtedly right; the reviewers liked them both, though *The Paying Guest* was more unreservedly praised. The reading public bought both books at a brisk pace.

As so often, press responses to Gissing's new productions were generally fair. Certainly the reviewers were right to see these books as an advance over the mediocre *Eve's Ransom*. In the *Saturday Review* Wells was patronizing and vague about *Sleeping Fires*, but the *Athenaeum* called it 'a brave venture in a new style'. The *Academy*, the *Sketch*, the *Speaker*, the *Pall Mall Gazette*, and *The Times* all gave *Sleeping Fires* high marks.

The *Daily News* review of *The Paying Guest* called Gissing 'the English Balzac of middle-class suburban life'. Said the *Academy*: 'Even Mr Gissing will find it hard to equal *The Paying Guest*.' In the *Saturday Review* Wells declared the new book 'delightful' and observed that it showed 'Gissing at his best, dealing with the middle-class material he knows so intimately'. Praise also came from the *Weekly Sun*, the *Globe*, and the *New York Times*, among others.

Publication of the novels called forth two long essays on Gissing in American newspapers. In the *New York Times* Harold Frederic, its London correspondent (and the future author of *The Damnation of Theron Ware*), noted that one began to hear Gissing's name 'mentioned in literary conversations at dinner tables of non-bookish people. Very often it happens that, when the names of Meredith and Hardy are quoted, that of Gissing is bracketed with them.' The two older novelists, Frederic declared, had had their day; now Gissing was having his. Until recently, he said, it was habitual to dismiss Gissing 'with the remark that he was too "pessimistic"'; people now are reading Gissing with relish, according to Frederic. He pronounced *In the Year of Jubilee* Gissing's most 'important' work, and *The Odd Women* 'as painful a book as I have ever read'. *The Unclassed* was singled out as Gissing's most 'interesting' novel: 'It is hard to understand now what London critics were about eleven years ago in letting this piece of solid and honest work pass unnoticed.' In the *Boston Evening Transcript* Kate Woodbridge Michaelis called Gissing 'one of the strongest and most thoughtful of presentday novelists'. Making a series of guesses about Gissing's personal circumstances based on his books, Mrs Michaelis reached the astonishingly incisive conclusion that the novelist must be 'unhappily married to an unappreciative wife . . . It would also seem that he had been shut out from the companionship of any truly happy man or woman' and that he was 'blessed with a large number of unpleasant women friends and relatives'. Mrs Michaelis discusses admiringly most of the sixteen novels. *The Unclassed* is called the 'saddest and grimmest' of the books, *The Emancipated* the most 'repulsive' (for its attack on the female intellect). Her three favourites are *The Odd Women* ('the most successful thing ever written with which to make one's self entirely miserable'), *New Grub Street* ('A more powerful and heart-breaking book . . . it would be hard to find . . . No student of letters can afford to neglect it'), and *In the Year of Jubilee* (a 'vivid' and 'masterful' treatment of 'the tragedy of marriage'). She hears, says Mrs Michaelis, that Gissing is now at work on what he thinks will be his 'greatest book'.

VIII

The new book, eventually *The Whirlpool*, certainly one of his best, he had indeed begun to think about early in 1896. Its first title was 'The Common Lot', and it suffered even more than the usual number of interruptions before being brought to completion. Despite his new prosperity (£560 in the bank as of 4 January), the first month of the new year was an especially difficult time for him. Edith grew increasingly irritable while awaiting her confinement, and Gissing had to take in hand once again much of the domestic management ('Got up early, lit fires, got breakfast, peeled potatoes . . . Of course, can do nothing at all, not even read'). They had almost no visitors except Miss Collet. The diary records 'gloom' for several days running. But he did dine with Shorter and some of his friends at the Savile Club, where he listened with fascination to Shorter telling how the previous summer he had bought all the surviving remnant manuscripts of Charlotte Brontë from her husband Nicholls for about £500.

On 20 January the novelist's second son, called Alfred Charles, was born. Gissing notified his mother, Algernon, and Clara Collet. The letter to Algernon is less than ecstatic: 'Unfortunately, another boy. Edith wished a girl. The youngster . . . will give infinite trouble.' The following week he wrote to Hick in an equally laconic fashion: 'A few days ago, another boy was born into this dolorous household. Happily he doesn't make much noise.' He predicted to all his correspondents that he would be unable to get any work done for months, and he was right. For the first few weeks after Alfred's birth he and Walter, now four years old, slept together on a sofa-bed; the novelist spent much of his time looking after his elder son while Edith attempted to suckle the infant. During the rest of January and throughout February 1896 he made no progress on 'The Common Lot'. Edith, he noted in his diary, was 'in her familiar mood of surly revolt and anger against everyone'. There was another succession of servants and nurses.

Early in February Gissing received from Bullen a request to do a reprint of *Isabel Clarendon* as a sequel to the successful new edition of *The Unclassed*. Not having a copy in the house, Gissing went to Mudie's, where a clerk remarked conversationally that Gissing was very popular these days and 'thought by many one of our cleverest writers'. The novelist took the book home, began to read and revise it, but found there was too much to do and gave up in despair. 'It was written after the failure of "The Unclassed",' he told Bullen, 'and in sheer need of a few pounds. I am quite decided that we must not reprint it.' It was not reprinted, and thus became very scarce for years.

The diary entries for February 1896 make depressing reading. One day there is 'Endless misery in the house'; on another, 'E. . . . constantly in sullen rage, at nothing at all'; on another, 'Gloom. Within, misery and uproar.' Towards the end of the month he wrote a letter to Bertz full of gloomy political prognostications and exuding hatred of jingoistic Imperialism, which he continued to see as principally a product of 'capitalist greed'. The new novel, he declared, was coming into focus 'very slowly . . . I am afraid it will take me a long time.' As he thought, he could not work on it in the midst of the uproar in the house occasioned by the birth of his second child. Like Walter's appearance upon the scene in 1891,

Alfred's meant to the harried father, initially at least, little more than an irritating interruption of his routine and exacerbation of his already difficult relations with his wife. Careless gasfitters caused an explosion in the house at Epsom, and the family had to move temporarily into lodgings. Gissing saw this addition to his 'private misfortunes and miseries' as another barrier to work. 'If this kind of life goes on', he wrote to Algernon, 'I see not the faintest hope of earning a living . . . Impossible to dream of work, and will be for a long, long time.' He none the less finally finished the series of sketches for Shorter. But he decided that the only way to restore some peace in the household was to get the nervous Walter away from his hysterical, nagging mother, thus reducing her household duties and his own concerns for the child's health. Without consulting Edith, he now took Walter to Wakefield where, for £10 a term, he would enrol his son in the new preparatory school his sisters had recently started. On the way back to London he did some sightseeing in Wales, carefully exploring Caernarvon – the setting of Part the Second, Chapter 11 of *The Whirlpool*. He wrote to Bertz from there that he had come away from Epsom 'in search of thorough mental quietude'.

It had become clear to him that some further change must be made in his domestic circumstances. His home had become 'utterly impossible', he wrote to Algernon in explanation of Walter's move to Yorkshire. 'I will not allow him to hear perpetual vilification of his father and all his father's relatives and friends.' In a letter to Miss Collet he said that Edith had begun to open his personal letters so 'that she may find new forms of vulgar abuse . . . she brings revolting charges against me, and prays fervently . . . for misery to befall me and mine. No one could bear it.' He was convinced that he had married another lunatic – nor was this conviction dispelled upon his return home without Walter, when there was (as the diary puts it) 'a terrible scene with E.; won't bear speaking of'. As their mutual hatred grew he began to see that it might become as impossible for him to live with Edith as it had been for him to live with Nell. It should be stressed, however, that the fault for the degenerating situation could not be entirely Edith's. Gissing had completely misjudged her, for which she was not to blame. At the last moment she had decided they were mismatched and tried to evade him. Since their marriage he had refused to be seen with her virtually anywhere in public (except during their summer holidays, always taken far away from his acquaintances): this enraged her and led her to demean his pretensions to respectability, his friends and relations. There was also his own well-developed sense of self-pity, which must have been a terrible irritant. 'It is fairly clear that Gissing . . . had a quite peculiar capacity for driving others frantic with indignation while continuing to regard himself as the only sufferer', Tindall says. 'No doubt Edith wanted to hit her husband as often as he wanted to hit her.'

IX

Gissing found he missed Walter terribly; the little boy had been his only real companion at home for several years. *The Whirlpool*, as we shall see, is partly a product of Gissing's newly aroused protective feelings for his son. By the end of April 1896 things had quietened down a little, and he was able to make some progress on the novel. During the next month there were the usual false starts and much destruction of manuscript: the book was now called 'Benedict's Household'. 'The theme is the decay of domestic life among certain classes of people, and much stress is laid upon the question of *children*', he told Bertz. He asked his friend for 'information about the terms and conditions of study at the *School of Music* at München' (Alma in *The Whirlpool* attends a music school in Munich). He concluded: 'My book is a laborious one, but I am not ill-pleased with it so far . . . A strange, strange life, this of literature – isn't it?' As usual when working on a novel he went through sunny spells and dark ones. 'The old fervours do not return to me, and I have got into the very foolish habit of perpetually writing against time and to order. The end of this is destruction', he told Roberts. 'Have got over a knotty point, the story of Benedict's [Benedict's name was later changed to Rolfe] early life. Very difficult to tell this briefly.' Indeed it was, since he was writing largely about himself. Lawrence and Bullen professed themselves delighted at the early prospect of a novel from him; they had had nothing new from him for two years. Unknown to Gissing, his publishers were in deep financial trouble.

In mid-May he visited Meredith again and found the elder novelist 'revising his works for the Library edition . . . says he is "slashing" at them – probably a great mistake.' At the end of the month, worried about money again, Gissing agreed to do a story for *Cosmopolis*: 6,000 words for £20. He wrote it in early June. The tale, called 'A Yorkshire Lass', is about a widower who marries his housemaid and the effects of this exogamous relationship on his snobbish daughter, who grows hysterical and is driven to the edge of madness by the loss she perceives in her social status. It is a very neurotic performance, even for Gissing. 'I am grievously ashamed to have put it so prominently before the public'. he wrote to Bertz of 'A Yorkshire Lass'. He considered the story 'poor and empty'.

Gissing told Hick in mid-June that he was 'overwhelmed with work . . . Ceaseless scribbling day and night . . . I am labouring at a long book, very slowly.' Yet he was resigned to it. 'In literature there is hardly such a thing as holiday; no sooner is one bit of writing finished than the mind has to renew its toil in preparation for the next', he wrote to Algernon. He added a sad postscript: 'We get, I fear, a very small margin of satisfaction out of life. One keeps hoping that years will bring improvement, but cares and responsibilities increase as one gets older.'

At an Omar Khayyám dinner on 20 June Gissing met, among others, J. M. Barrie. A few days later, at another gathering, he met Justin MacCarthy, Israel Zangwill, Andrew Lang – and saw Frederic Harrison once again. Zangwill later remembered Gissing in 1896 as a man 'in the flower of his age: a tall, handsome, strapping Anglo-Saxon, scarcely suggesting the literary recluse . . . the pessimist and misogynist'.

From mid-July until mid-August the Gissings, Walter included, took a holiday at Mablethorpe in Lincolnshire. Once again the novelist and his elder son slept together. Walter's wilfulness, excitability, and bad temper worried him, but he understood the boy's nature well enough. 'What a terrible lesson is the existence of this child, born of a loveless and utterly unsuitable marriage', he wrote in his diary. He was getting no work done at all and was deeply depressed. 'Nothing gives me much pleasure now-a-days', he wrote to Bertz. 'I have lost heart and hope – at all events for the present.'

Upon his return to Epsom late in August Gissing went immediately back to work on 'Benedict's Household', having decided to revise the entire manuscript (he did not, as some scholars have surmised, throw it out and start again). He laboured ferociously, refusing all invitations and even turning down a request for a story from the high-paying *Blackwood's Magazine*. In September, however, he did allow Hick to pay a visit to Epsom. Hick's account is revealing. Gissing got him a room at a nearby inn, saying 'that the house was not fit for a visitor . . . it was evident that he was having trouble with his wife . . . Things looked bad.'

By the end of the month Gissing had finished, he calculated, more than a third of the novel. 'I don't think it will be altogether bad, and there is a most grave purpose in it', he told Bertz. 'I write slowly, and have to re-write, and re-re-write, alas!' When he was about half-way through he hit upon a better title for the book. It would be called *The Whirlpool,* he told Bertz: 'It deals with the morbid activity of money-getters and pleasure-seekers.' He spent the rest of the month working hard on it; making rapid progress now, he doggedly continued to refuse most invitations. Luckily Alfred, the baby, was less nervous and easier to manage than Walter had been.

On 20 November 1896, at another Omar Khayyám dinner, Gissing met Arthur Conan Doyle and H. G. Wells. Wells was destined to be the closest friend of Gissing's last years, but consistently and perversely disloyal to his memory. While Gissing lived he did what he could for him. Their acquaintance began in a curious way. Wells rushed across the room and breathlessly announced to Gissing that *New Grub Street* was a perfect picture of his own existence at one time: he had once been a struggling author who lived in a flat in Mornington Road near Regent's Park and had a wife named Amy (since divorced). Nine years younger than Gissing, Wells had had a huge success with his novel *The Time Machine* (1895). In 1896, when Gissing's earnings fell off to £290, Wells earned over £1,050. He was an optimist, a scientist, a socialist, highly ambitious, largely self-educated, happily married now after the early divorce. In these things they were very different men indeed. But both had 'starved', neither was religious, and each had come from lower-middle-class backgrounds (Wells's father was a shopkeeper in Bromley). As we have seen, Wells had written favourable reviews of *Eve's Ransom* and *The Paying Guest,* and Gissing was well enough disposed to him to accept an invitation to visit him and his wife at their new home in Worcester Park in December – the first of many times that Wells helped break down the solitary habits of his new friend. On 26 November Wells initiated a correspondence with Gissing which was to last, with few interruptions, until Gissing's death.

Gissing immediately 'liked Wells's wild face and naïve manner . . . He seems the right kind.' Wells recorded his impressions of Gissing at the time. He was 'extremely good looking' and 'well-built', though 'slightly on the lean side'; and 'blond, with a good profile and a splendid leonine head'. He spoke 'in a rotund, Johnsonian manner, but what he had to say was reasonable and friendly'. 'He assumed that modern science and all that were merely degenerate', Wells wrote later, and 'regarded Christianity as a deplorable disaster'. According to Wells, Gissing told him that he could not reciprocate his invitation by asking him 'to my home . . . Impossible – quite impossible . . . I have no home . . . One must have a habitation, and here, somehow or other, I live; but I have never yet asked mortal to come and see me here [not true] – and probably never shall. For which let my friends be grateful.' Gissing informed Wells that he accepted few invitations. 'I am so much afraid of wasting other men's time that it is a very rare thing indeed for me to call upon anyone.' He was 'a damaged, joy-loving human being', Wells said, whom the uncertainties of life had rendered too nervous to ride a bicycle.

Gissing's thirty-ninth birthday passed without comment. He was hard at work on *The Whirlpool*. In early December he gave Bertz an updated account of the new book. 'I have put into this novel a great deal that I really wanted to say', he told his friend. 'I often marvel at my own stubborn patience' – in writing it in the midst of so many difficulties, he meant. Of one thing he was quite proud: 'Except Kipling [who lived in America], I have now met every English writer of any standing, and with several of them I am on very good terms.'

In mid-December he visited Wells and his wife and liked them both. 'He tells me he began life by two years' apprenticeship to drapering' – later described in Wells's only first-rate novel, *Kipps*. 'Astonishing, his self-education. Great talent. His wife, a nice woman, formerly his pupil in biology, when, after taking the London B.Sc., he coached science.' Ironically, Gissing always admired Wells's literary abilities more than Wells admired Gissing's.

On 18 December, back at Epsom, he finally finished *The Whirlpool*, which he described as 'The hardest bit of work I have done yet'. Certainly no book of his since *In the Year of Jubilee* had cost him so much time and effort; perhaps no book of his since *The Unclassed*, thirteen years earlier, had been written in circumstances so inimical to creative energy. Bullen offered an advance of 150 guineas (instead of the usual 100) and paid down half the advance on the spot. In addition, the novelist would have the usual one-shilling royalty per copy sold and half-profits on all foreign sales. Gissing told Bullen he believed deeply in the new novel, thought it one of his best, and asked him to advertise it generously. After all, as he wrote to Algernon, 'the contrast between my reputation and cash results grows something more than ludicrous.'

x

So often during Gissing's career adversity and struggle produced a great novel. *The Whirlpool* is not only one of his finest tales; it is probably the best-written of them all, virtually free from the awkward constructions that occasionally interrupt the flow of some of the others, even *New Grub Street*. Gissing was perhaps more moved himself by *The Whirlpool* than by anything else he had written since *Born in Exile*; the lyrical prose, the richly allusive style of this novel is the result. Often one hears echoes of Dickens, Trollope, James – and, if there can be echoes of the future, of Conrad, Virginia Woolf, and Edith Wharton: surely Mrs Wharton got her ending for *The House of Mirth* (1905) from *The Whirlpool*, and a number of other parallels might well be drawn between Alma Rolfe and the more famous heroine of the later novel, Lily Bart. *The Whirlpool* also shows us once again how close the connections are between Gissing's fiction and his life.

The twin themes of the novel are epitomized in two of its epigrammatic pronouncements: 'Art and housekeeping won't go together'; and 'What a simple matter life would be, but for women!' *The Whirlpool* articulates the nature and the lessons of Gissing's second marriage, though Alma is not much like Edith. Over it all lies the shadow of Harvey Rolfe, Gissing's brooding *alter ego*.

The two passages I have quoted reflect the problems Alma creates for Rolfe. He married her thinking her docile and domestic. Edith's bad temper is sublimated in the novel in Alma's desire for a career, which inevitably leads to chaos in the household, intractable servants, lack of supervision of the Rolfes' child, unpredictable meals, and all the rest. When his wife decides to become a violinist Rolfe finds he cannot sympathize with her goals and resents her abandonment of the household. Like *Denzil Quarrier*, *The Odd Women*, and *In the Year of Jubilee*, *The Whirlpool* attacks women who neglect their households to pursue careers, affairs, or whatever: they should stay at home and take care of their families.

The novel opens with the robbing of a fashionable house by a band of dishonest servants, and problems of 'housekeeping' and domestic stability continue to make themselves felt throughout the book. The ideal domestic establishment is defined as one without a servant problem: 'A small house – just large enough for order and quietness, and to keep a room for the friend that comes' (this is where Mallard and Miriam happily end up in *The Emancipated*). Women, *The Whirlpool* argues, should not 'be ashamed of housework; there are all sorts of things . . . that every woman is better for doing.' The book is filled with domestically incompetent women – such as Mrs Leach – unable to rule over their servants, and all bearing some resemblance to Edith Gissing.

The obverse of them all is Mrs Morton:

she conceived her duty as wife and mother after the old fashion . . . it seemed to her no merit that in [her] little ones she saw the end and reason of her being. Into her pure and healthy mind had never entered a thought at conflict with motherhood . . . From her they learnt to speak . . . the names of trees and flowers . . . Later she was their instructress in a more formal sense . . . By method and good will she found time for everything, ruling her house and ordering her life.

Here are many of Gissing's fantasies drawn together into one ideal woman. Another sympathetic character is Minnie Wager, who makes a useful citizen of herself by learning to cook (her father had distinguished himself by abandoning his children and sending cheques from time to time for their support – an action startlingly similar to proceedings Gissing himself was soon to take).

Just as women generally make a mess of household affairs, so they are also perceived in this most misogynic of Gissing's novels as incapable of friendship; 'brainless'; generally incomprehensible; responsible for most of the frivolities of 'society'; and absurdly suspicious and jealous ('Jealousy without love, a passion scarcely intelligible to the ordinary man, is in woman common enough').

Alma Rolfe is one of Gissing's most interesting characters, and perhaps his greatest heroine. She is educated, cultured, refined, and domestically inclined and companionable until her passion for a career sets in. She is also an able musician. (In this she uncannily anticipates Gabrielle Fleury, an accomplished pianist, whom Gissing was to meet in the year after *The Whirlpool* was published.) But Alma grows restless. 'The domestic side of things', as it turns out, 'simply was not her forte'; Rolfe misjudged her in this. Their relationship, degraded into a contest of incompatible wills, begins to resemble Gissing's second marriage.

Alma's husband is another undisguised self-portrait – a character we would recognize whether or not he was married to an incompetent housekeeper. He is like the novelist in desiring a well-ordered household, in his hatred of 'parties', his antipathy to the noise and dirt of cities and his partiality to the country. *The Whirlpool* is Gissing's *Mansfield Park* : it is one of his most negative and carping novels, revealing at almost every turn the author's impatience with

9. Eduard Bertz in 1891 (on the back of this photo, in Bertz's hand, is written: 'For my Dear old Friend George Gissing. August, 1891.' The photo was found in Gissing's wallet after his death)

10. Morley Roberts in 1911 (National Portrait Gallery, London)

11. H. G. Wells in the 1890s
(National Portrait Gallery, London)

modern life and values. In other ways Harvey Rolfe is a warm-up for Henry Ryecroft – they have more than their initials in common: he is at home in the country, likes to lead an outwardly simple life with much time for quiet contemplation, and so on.

Other aspects of Rolfe's personality and experience in *The Whirlpool* resemble Gissing's. As a young man from the Midlands, Rolfe 'had known the pastures of poverty, and the table as it is set by London landladies' when he came to the metropolis. As he grows older he notes with relief the decline in him 'of baser appetites, so long his torment and his hindrance'. There was a time 'when the senses raged in him, and only by miracle failed to hurl him down many a steep place'. Ultimately his bad habits are overcome when 'there developed in him a new social pride which made him desire the acquaintance of well-bred people.'

The description of Rolfe at the time the novel opens is another of Gissing's self-portraits:

Something of cynicism appeared in his talk of public matters; politics amused him, and his social views lacked consistency, tending, however, to an indolent conservatism. Despite his convivial qualities, he had traits of the reserved, even of the unsociable, man: a slight awkwardness in bearing, a mute shyness with strangers, a hesitancy in ordinary talk, and occasional bluntness . . . suggesting a contempt . . . he did not intend . . . Rolfe had a shaven chin, a weathered complexion, thick brown hair . . . middle-age had touched his countenance, softening here and there a line which told of temperament in excess.

Rolfe both looks and sounds like Gissing. He thinks that 'the educated man who marries on less than a thousand [a year] is either mad or criminal.' As a young bachelor he believes that a child who dies is fortunate to have escaped life's miseries. After his marriage he cannot, like Gissing, bear to be bothered by household questions: 'All domestic matters were a trial to his nerves.' Again like Gissing, Rolfe loves music. At parties 'the merest chatter, meaningless repetition of commonplaces' and 'sheer vulgarism' make him furious – though 'he enjoyed human fellowship, timely merrymaking'. But for the most part Rolfe is reclusive and introspective – a 'bookish', 'methodical' man, especially 'persistent . . . in his historical readings'. He believes neither in science nor religion, but rather in books – in learning generally, and in old-fashioned social values. Like Reardon, he knows that 'misery' degrades people. He loves to travel (like Gissing in Italy the *following* autumn, he once 'nearly died at some miserable roadside inn').

When their son is born and Alma ignores the boy, there is a sudden reversal of feeling about children. Fatherhood transforms Rolfe. 'That first wail of feeblest humanity, faint-sounding through the silent night, made a revolution in his thoughts, taught him on the moment more than he had learnt from all his reading and cogitation.' Rolfe's relationship with his son Hughie recapitulates Gissing's experience with Walter. 'All pleasures, aims, hopes that concerned himself alone, shrank to the idlest trifling when he realised the immense debt due from him to his son; no possible sacrifice could discharge it.' Morley Roberts describes Rolfe as the 'later' Gissing and says the novelist told him that Rolfe 'would probably never have developed at all after a certain stage but for the curious changes wrought in his views and sentiments by the fact of his becoming a father'. Roberts adds that Gissing himself 'would never have remained so long with his second wife . . . if it had not been that she was . . . a mother'. Rolfe's lecture to Mrs Abbott on the upbringing of children reflects the novelist's conversion: 'You know, it isn't a matter of course for people to see that they are under an enormous obligation to the children they bring into the world; except in a parent here and there, that comes only with very favourable circumstances.' The more Alma neglects her son, the more Rolfe devotes himself to the boy.

Alma pursues her career and chaos reigns in the house. Rolfe's 'days of quietude were over . . . No more dreaming among his books; no more waking to the ordinary duties and cares of a reasonable life'. Formerly a calm, quiet man, Rolfe grows agitated; like many a Gissing hero before him, he becomes subject to attacks of 'nerves' and 'smothered petulance'. Secretly he wishes Alma 'to become a mere domestic creature' – he admits it to himself; and how much better for her family if she would become one, the novel argues.

Rolfe grows more and more depressed by his failing marriage. Finally even 'that History which he loved to read' becomes for him merely 'the lurid record of woes unutterable'. In his new pessimism he begins to resemble the morbid protagonists of Gissing's early novels: 'How could he find pleasure in keeping his eyes fixed on century after century of ever-repeated torment – war, pestilence, tyranny; the stake, the dungeon; tortures of infinite device, cruelties inconceivable?' His vision of the contemporary scene also begins to recall that of the earlier protagonists:

Somebody said to me once: 'Well, but look at the results; they're not so bad.' Great heavens! not so bad – when the supreme concern of mankind is to perfect their instruments of slaughter! Not so bad – when the gaol and the gallows are taken as a matter of course! Not so bad – when huge filthy cities are packed with multitudes who have no escape from toil and hunger but in a wretched death! Not so bad – when all but every man's life is one long blunder, the result of ignorance and unruled passions!

This is the language of Waymark, Kingcote, and Kirkwood. As Rolfe's pessimism deepens, he begins to have terrible nightmares:

No sooner had he lain down in darkness than every form of mortal anguish beset his thoughts, passing before him as though some hand unfolded a pictured scroll of life's terrors. He seemed never before to have realised the infinitude of human suffering. Hour after hour . . . he travelled from land to land, from age to age; at one moment picturing some dread incident of a thousand years ago; the next, beholding with intolerable vividness some scene of agony reported in the day's newspaper.

Rolfe's morbidity leads him to worry about his child. Hughie, he concludes, 'lived in the golden age' at three years old. 'A year or two more, and the best of life would be over with him; for boyhood is but a leaden time compared with the borderland between it and infancy; and manhood – the curse of sex developed' – Rolfe's thoughts trail off here. This remarkable passage may be paired with Reardon's memorable paean to senility in *New Grub Street*. At age four or five 'the best of life' is over, Rolfe believes, for after that one is subject to 'the curse of sex'. Should the child die, he muses, 'it would be no reason for sorrow; how much better to fall asleep in playtime, and wake no more, than to outlive the happiness and innocence which pass for ever with childhood . . . Intelligence that has learnt the meaning of a doubt compares but sadly with the charm of untouched ingenuousness.' Here is an old Gissing theme. Rolfe finds 'solace in remembering that after no great lapse of time he and those he loved would have vanished from the earth, would be as though they had not been at all; every pang and woe awaiting them suffered and forgotten . . . the brief flicker of troubled light quenched in eternal oblivion'. This is Rolfe's Schopenhauerian 'substitute for the faith and hope of the old world'.

Late in the novel Rolfe is led by his unhappiness and his growing pessimism into a long reverie about his childhood; not surprisingly that childhood resembles Gissing's in several ways. Rolfe's father – 'a man whom he could admire and love' – died when Harvey was a boy; and 'he held it the supreme misfortune of his life that, in those early years which count so much towards the future, he had [not] been . . . under his father's influence.' At fifteen 'bashfulness cost him horrid torments . . . exasperating his conceit.' He disliked girls; his choice of male friends was poor. 'Games and sports had no attraction for him; he shut himself up in rooms, and read a great deal, yet even this, it seemed, not without an eye to winning admiration.' Here is Gissing's portrait of himself as an adolescent – the adolescent who declined an invitation to a play in Manchester because he had some reading to do. At twenty, Rolfe recalls, he was 'a lank, ungainly youth, with a disagreeable complexion and a struggling moustache . . . Self-centred, but painfully self-distrustful, he struggled to overcome his natural defects of manner.' He began to work for a living and to know what it was not to have enough to eat. 'It came back to him, his first experience of hunger – so very different a thing from appetite. He saw the miserable bedroom where he sat on a rainy day. He smelt the pawnshop. His heart sank again under the weight of awful solitude.' So Rolfe, still miserable at forty, married, and a father, muses on what he thought were his most miserable days – much as Gissing must have mused throughout that awful year of 1896.

Ultimately Rolfe can no longer pretend to himself that he loves Alma. In wooing her he had obeyed 'no dictate of the nobler passion . . . as at every crisis of his life, he had acted on motives which would not bear analysis, so large was the alloy of mere temperament, of weak concession to circumstance.' He sees that he should have been firmer with Alma all along: 'With a little obtuseness to the "finer" feelings, a little native coarseness in his habits toward women, he would have succeeded vastly better amid the complications of his married life.' At the end of his long reverie Rolfe consoles himself by reflecting that he has been able to avoid some dangers. Though Alma is a poor wife and mother, at least she is a refined and intelligent woman. Thankfully, he has not committed 'the most woeful of all blunders': he has not married 'a woman worse than himself'. Nor, after all, has he been 'guilty of that crime of crimes, the begetting of children by a worthless mother'. As we know from Gissing's diary entries about Walter, it was precisely this crime of which he accused himself (9 August 1896: 'What a terrible lesson is the existence of this child, born of a loveless and utterly unsuitable marriage').

One of Rolfe's ambitions is to become an expert on a particular period of history and to write a book about it, as Gissing hoped to do in *Veranilda*, set in sixth-century (AD) Rome. On the subject of education, Rolfe speaks in the tone Gissing adopted in *Isabel Clarendon* and would adopt again in *The Ryecroft Papers*:

If I followed my instincts, I should make [my] boy unfit for anything but the quietest, obscurest life. I should make him hate a street, and love the fields. I should teach him to despise every form of ambition; to shrink from every kind of pleasure, but the simplest and purest; to think of life as a long day's ramble, and death as the quiet sleep that comes at the end of it. I should like him not to marry – never to feel the need of it; or if marry he must, to have no children . . . The best kind of education would be that which hardened his skin and blunted his sympathies. What right have I to make him sensitive? The thing is, to get through life with as little suffering as possible. What monstrous folly to teach him to wince and cry out at the sufferings of other people! Won't he have enough of his own before he has done? Yet that's what we shall aim at – to cultivate his sympathetic emotions, so that the death of a bird shall make him sad, and the sight of human distress wring his heart.

Here is a pure expression of Gissing's pessimism and his resultant conservatism. 'The thing is, to get through life with as little suffering as possible.' His life with Edith had robbed him of the peace of mind which enabled him to write with comparative optimism just a few years before. In *The Whirlpool* he sounds more like the author of *Workers in the Dawn*, *The Unclassed*, and *Demos* than the author of *Eve's Ransom* and *Sleeping Fires*.

Rolfe and Alma manage to reach an uneasy understanding of sorts at the end, but their temperamental incompatibility is still emphasized: 'Only death could part them; but how much better for him and for her if they had never met! Their thoughts and purposes so unlike; he, with his heart and mind set on grave, quiet, restful things, hating the world's tumult, ever hoping to retire beyond its echo; she, her senses crying for the delight of an existence that loses itself in whirl and glare.' Gissing's old feelings of hopelessness were returning: he was beginning to view his life with Edith as fatalistically as he had once viewed his life with Nell. Unlike either Nell or Edith, Alma takes the quick way out through an apparent suicide. Surely some part of Gissing wished that Edith would disappear as conveniently as Alma does (and as Monica did in *The Odd Women*).

As in so many other books, Gissing pleads in *The Whirlpool* for the preservation of rural life and values and attacks London as the venue of noise and tension. The peace and quiet of the scenes in Basil Morton's rural home articulate the novelist's longing for peace and quiet in his own. *The Whirlpool*, like *In the Year of Jubilee*, is particularly unfriendly to commuter trains, which make much of the novel's noise: they are depicted as a source 'of roar and crash and shriek' inimical to sanity. London is the whirlpool, the vortex of urban chaos. Hugh Carnaby talks of 'this damned London': 'Great God! when there is so much of the world clean and sweet, here we pack and swelter together, a million to the square mile! What eternal fools we are!' Gissing even takes the extraordinary step of having one of his characters killed off by bad drains: outside the novels of Charles Kingsley, who developed a sort of theology of drains, poor Henrietta Winter must be the only character in Victorian literature to suffer such a fate. By contrast, at the Mortons' country place 'No tramp of sooty smother hung above the house-tops and smirched the garden leafage; no tramp of crowds, clatter of hot-wheel traffic sounded from the streets hard by.'

In *The Whirlpool*, as in *Demos, In the Year of Jubilee*, and some of the other books, there is a prophetic sense of what 'improvements' and developers are doing to the countryside. Rolfe predicts sadly that it is 'the destiny of every beautiful spot in Britain' to be 'developed'. And the attack on modern values is also carried on in Gissing's broadside against war in general and British Imperialism in particular – a theme running through several of the novels and taken up more fully in *The Crown of Life*. Two passages on the subject in *The Whirlpool* are especially interesting – and, again, astonishingly prophetic. In the first of these, Rolfe tells Carnaby: 'Who believes for a moment that England will remain satisfied with bits here and there? We have to swallow the whole, of course. We shall go on fighting and annexing . . . until the decline and fall of the British Empire . . . We shall fight like blazes in the twentieth century. It's the only thing that keeps Englishmen sound; commercialism is their curse.' Gissing put his finger here on a major cause of the two twentieth-century wars that were indeed to cost England her status as a world power. As he says: 'We shall fight like blazes in the twentieth century.' The other passage, sadly, has a more personal application. Speaking to Morton about the savagery of war, Rolfe alludes to the increasing violence of sports, especially English football; worries that women are abandoning golf and tennis for cricket and cycling; and concludes bitterly: 'We may reasonably hope . . . to see our boys blown into small bits by the explosive that hasn't got its name yet.' On 1 July 1916 Walter Gissing was to die at Gommecourt during the second battle of the Somme.

The copious (and by no means disinterested) advice Redgrave gives Alma about being an artist expresses Gissing's point of view on the subject – a point of view, as I have noted before, not unlike that of Henry James (or George Eliot, for that matter): 'To be a great artist, one must have more than technical qualifications. It's the soul that must be developed . . . Experience means emotion . . .You may practise . . . day and night, and it won't profit you – until you have *lived* . . . From a cold and conventional existence can come nothing but cold and conventional art . . . The springs of art are in the old world. Among the vines and the olives one hears a voice.'

Another character endowed with elements of the Gissing *persona* is Cecil Morphew, whose poverty, insecurity, social anomalousness, and 'guilty secret' (an unwholesome sexual liaison) make him 'unworthy of any good woman's love'. This, the narrator ingenuously remarks, 'pointed to something [in the past] which had had its share in the . . . smirching of his character; something common enough, no doubt'. Morphew, like Will Warburton after him, comes from a middle-class family but is eventually forced by circumstances to become a shopkeeper, the fate Gissing so often reserves for his declassed characters. As Morphew immerses himself in his new shopkeeping life he sloughs off many of his cultural habits: 'the intellectual disease of the time' took hold of him: he lost the power of mental concentration. He becomes 'indolent' and 'desultory' in his reading. It is he who is enamoured of the young lady done in by drains. After her death he recalls the loneliness of his youth, referring at one point to 'the awful misery' he suffered living by himself: 'I was often enough nearly mad with – what is one to call it?' The answer, of course, is sexual desire. 'Why isn't there a decent name for the agony men go through at that age?' he asks. The lady of the drains having made him wait too long, he picks up a young woman in the park, and becomes unhappily involved with her. He 'suffers all the more' from this situation because he has 'delicate instincts'.

And Hugh Carnaby's neurasthenic temperament resembles Gissing's. When a man running for a train inadvertently bumps against Hugh on the platform, 'he clenched his fist, and . . . might have lost himself in blind rage . . . he inwardly cursed railway stations, cursed England, cursed civilisation.'

From beginning to end *The Whirlpool* chronicles the effects on a sensitive nature (Rolfe's) of a crumbling marriage and miserable domestic circumstances. It is the spiritual autobiography of one awful year of Gissing's life: 1896. As so often in his most autobiographical performances, there are a passion and pulsation here that could spring only from his deepest feelings. It is impossible to convey at second-hand a sense of the gritty reality of this marvellous but neglected book.

The Whirlpool is a fitting climax to Gissing's astonishing burst of creativity in the mid-nineties, astonishing when one considers the circumstances in which the great novels of these years – *In the Year of Jubilee, Sleeping Fires, The Paying Guest*, and *The Whirlpool* – were written. Their appearance attests to a principle of Gissing's life on which I have insisted before: the tendency to be most productive when his personal life would seem to be least conducive to creative energy. As an artist he did indeed thrive on misery. A change in his domestic life was not far off, as *The Whirlpool* was completed in December 1896, and with that change came an end to the long period of hard work and brilliant writing that had commenced in 1888 with the death of Nell and produced, before the great books of the mid-nineties, such remarkable earlier tales as *The Nether World, New Grub Street, Born in Exile*, and *The Odd Women*.

XI

Near the end of 1896 the novelist was asked by an old acquaintance from Owens College days who now worked for the publishers Blackie and Son (Glasgow) if he was interested in writing a book on Dickens as part of a series of monographs. Gissing sent a tentative affirmative, confiding to his diary that he welcomed a change from 'fiction-grinding'.

Having suffered from a nagging cough for over a month, the novelist consulted a physician later in December. Dr Beaumont told Gissing that there was 'a weak point' in his right lung. 'This may be a grave matter, and may not.' Iodine and syrup of hypophosphites were prescribed. Gissing confessed to Miss Collet that the cough worried him: 'it is very like that from which my father suffered just at my age, and which killed him at 42.' The novelist resolved to follow a more healthy diet.

On New Year's Eve 1896 came proofs of *The Whirlpool*, which would be Gissing's seventeenth published novel since 1880: he worked on them throughout January. The book was scheduled to appear in April 1897.

Shorter asked for a 'bright little love story' for the *Illustrated London News*, and for once was refused. 'I couldn't do it', Gissing confided to his diary. 'Days too miserable to chronicle; ceaseless quarrel and wretchedness.' But he did manage to do some reading, saw several acquaintances whom he had put off meeting until *The Whirlpool* was finished, and he contemplated a possible new serial tale. His life at Epsom, however, was now intolerable due to Edith's temper, and he found it impossible to live or work there. 'Misery in house', he noted on 5 February. Four days later the diary breaks off for the unprecedentedly long period of four months – not to resume again until 2 June 1897. On 10 February Gissing was, as he said himself, 'driven from home'. For the second time in two decades he left a wife who had made his life unbearable.

๛

CHAPTER 10

INTERREGNUM, 1897–1898

The springs of art are in the old world. Among the vines and the olives one hears a voice.   *The Whirlpool*

At forty, or near it, a man . . . gets used to his slippers and his pipe – especially if comfort . . . [has] come after half a lifetime of homelessness.   *The Whirlpool*

What you want is what happens to you.
                     C. P. Snow, *In Their Wisdom*

I

MORLEY Roberts has described Gissing's appearance on his Fulham doorstep on the afternoon of 10 February 1897: 'I found him in the most extraordinary state of nervous and physical agitation . . . he was almost crimson, and his eyes sparkled with furious indignation. He was hot, just as if he had come out of an actual physical struggle.' According to Roberts, Gissing broke out: 'I can't stand it any more. I have left her for ever.' Roberts says he told Gissing he had done the right thing and that he should not change his mind. Gissing declared that Edith had 'behaved like a maniac; she shrieked, she struck him. She abused him in the vilest terms, such as he could not or would not repeat to me.' After the novelist had calmed down a bit, Roberts says, 'the prospect of his freedom . . . inspired him with pathetic and peculiar exhilaration.' Gissing, Roberts observes here, was 'perhaps the most sensitive man alive', and yet had had to endure at Epsom the humiliation of seeing his neighbours 'coming out upon the doorstep, eager to inquire what disaster was occurring in the next house. There were indeed legends in the Epsom Road that the mild looking writer beat and brutalised his wife, though most knew, by means of servants' chatter, what the actual facts were.'

The 'most sensitive man alive' slept in London on the 10th. The next day he went to Dover to visit his friend Hick. He told Hick he could not put up with his wife's behaviour any longer, and that he had left her. He said that when he had informed Edith of Dr

Beaumont's diagnosis of a tuberculous patch in one lung, she cursed him for marrying her. 'He was determined not to return to his wife, though he was much grieved for the children', Hick reports. He then examined Gissing, rejected Beaumont's diagnosis, and told the novelist that he had a patch of emphysema at the base of the left lung. Gissing stayed with Hick and his wife for several days. On Hick's recommendation they went up to London together to consult Dr Pye-Smith, a well-known specialist. Pye-Smith confirmed Hick's diagnosis. He suggested that Gissing live out of London for a while, preferably in Devon or Cornwall, and take more exercise in the open air. He told the novelist to gain some weight if he could (he weighed 157 pounds at the time).

The next day Gissing left for Budleigh Salterton in Devon, a little seaside town he had become familiar with while living in Exeter. It was here he had decided to settle for the time being to nurse himself back to health. He took rooms in a small hotel. Edith was prevailed upon to send some clothes to her husband and to forward his mail. Roberts is certainly wrong to claim that three days after he left Epsom Gissing returned home with his tail between his legs, the victim of a 'miserable peace' patched together by Miss Collet and another friend. As it turned out, the novelist stayed in Budleigh Salterton for nearly four months, slowly recovering his health while peace terms were negotiated with Edith.

From his rural retreat Gissing sent accounts of himself (he had left his diary in Epsom so we have no entries for the spring of 1897). To Bertz he wrote that he had settled in Devon for reasons of health. With Algernon he was more candid: 'I have simply been driven from home – chased away with furious insult . . . My one consolation is that the greater part of life is struggled through – past and over. It is nothing less than a miracle that we . . . have escaped sheer beggary. I wonder . . . whether this family curse will show itself in the next generation. I shall do my best to raise up my boys in a spirit of savage egotism.' To Hick, both doctor and friend, he wrote more copiously. Late in February he told Hick that huge meals and long walks had made his cough virtually disappear. 'Things at a standstill at Epsom', he reported. In mid-March he wrote again. 'I have done no work whatever. It is impossible, whilst my affairs are thus unsettled.' He was walking and reading a good deal – and worrying about the money he was spending, since he had virtually no income now. He would receive 75 guineas from Lawrence and Bullen when *The Whirlpool* was published, but apart from the vague offer from Blackie for the Dickens monograph and a few ideas he had for some fiction, his future prospects were meagre. By the end of March, however, the reports he was receiving from Epsom, largely from Miss Collet, were more encouraging. Edith was beginning to show signs of remorse. It is to Gissing's credit that he did not blame her for everything. 'It was grossly selfish' and 'utterly unintelligent' of him to take her out of her natural sphere, he admitted to Miss Collet. 'She . . . would have made an ordinary mate for the lower kind of London artisan.' He continued his regimen of walking and reading, re-reading all Dickens and every book he could lay his hands on about ancient Rome in preparation for *Veranilda*. Margaret and Walter spent some time with him at Budleigh Salterton, and so did the Wellses. Wells later recalled that visit to Devon. Gissing, he said, was 'a damaged and ailing man, full of ill-advised precautions against the imaginary illnesses that were his interpretation of a general malaise'. Wells, of course, was wrong about the 'imaginary' nature of Gissing's illness. Gissing spoke of Italy 'as one speaks of a lost paradise'; he was determined to go back there, and urged the Wellses to accompany him. He seemed to think, however, that sooner or later he would return to his wife and child.

The Whirlpool was published on 5 April 1897. It was a fortunate time. No other English novel was commanding any attention, and virtually every important journal and newspaper reviewed at length the famous writer's new book. On the whole the reviews were favourable. The *Guardian,* the *Academy,* and the *Pall Mall Gazette* found the novel utterly convincing. The review in the *Bookman* contains a passage which may help us to comprehend what it is in Gissing's work that was always so interesting to women: 'No novelist has taken more pains to understand the condition of the average woman's life to-day, to study her ambitions, to mete out to her an austere kind of justice.' The *Saturday Review* thought *The Whirlpool* Gissing's best novel with the possible exception of *In the Year of Jubilee*. Warm praise for the book also came directly to Gissing from Meredith and Barrie, among others.

In the *Contemporary Review* Wells published a long essay on Gissing, focused on *The Whirlpool*. He called it 'the most vigorously designed' of Gissing's novels. In his best patronizing vein, Wells declared that 'in the case of no other writer does one perceive quite so clearly the steady elimination of immaturities . . . his first novels must have been published when he was ridiculously young.' He noted that Egremont, Quarrier, Mallard, Tarrant, and Rolfe 'are all . . . successive Waymarks'. All the novels, he said, are 'depressing'. He concluded with some forced faint praise: 'Mr Gissing has written a series of extremely significant novels, perhaps the only series of novels in the last decade whose interest has been strictly contemporary.' In a letter to Wells, who was appropriately nervous about his friend's reaction to the essay, Gissing generously admitted that much of the energy of his past life had been 'frittered away in mean squabbling and sordid cares', which probably accounted for his slow development as a writer. As for the 'depressing' aspect of his work: Gissing said he tried in his fiction to adopt a stance of impersonal detachment, his only assurance of sanity. 'I have a conviction that all I love and believe in is going to the devil; at the same time, I try to watch with interest this process of destruction.' Gissing was still Waymark.

In America the new novel brought forth a critical essay on Gissing, entitled 'A Novelist of the Hour', in the *Sewanee Review*. The author, Greenough White, commented that 'in Mr Gissing's work our generation may see itself photographed. The book is startlingly modern, and its reader may realize and repeat his father's sensations when reading a novel of George Eliot's fresh from the press.' In Gissing, White said, 'the realistic movement in English fiction' had reached its height. In a longish essay in *Harper's* on Gissing's work, James declared that Gissing 'has the strongest deepest sense of common humanity, of the general struggle and the general grey grim comedy'. James went on: 'For this author . . . I profess, and have professed ever since reading *New Grub Street*, a persistent taste – a taste that triumphs even over the fact that he almost as persistently disappoints me . . . The whole business of distribution and composition he strikes me as having cast to the winds.' James thought *The Whirlpool* inferior to *In the Year of Jubilee*.

There was some carping. The *Sketch*, the *World*, and the *Review of Reviews* found *The Whirlpool* too negative. The *Athenaeum* and the *Illustrated London News* criticized Gissing's powers of construction. But the fact that a new novel by Gissing provoked such widespread attention and interest made it plain that no longer could he be considered a 'neglected' novelist. Indeed, he was now very much in the forefront of English letters.

One result of all this critical attention was a tremendous sale for *The Whirlpool*: it sold better in England than any of Gissing's previous novels. It went through three English editions in 1897 alone. In America the book went through five editions. There was also a large Colonial sale. In view of these encouraging sales figures

Gissing determined to raise his own prices. In the month after *The Whirlpool* was published he turned down, as being not enough, an offer of 16 guineas for a story of only 3,500 words.

II

Throughout the rest of April and May 1897 Gissing remained at Budleigh Salterton, reading Roman history, awaiting the all-clear from Epsom, and beginning to formulate plans for the serial novel Colles had been asking for. 'A story *must* be written in the summer, or I go to the workhouse', he told Hick. Bertz, meanwhile, had sent him a letter full of praise for *The Whirlpool*. At the end of it Bertz wrote: 'It is remarkable how greatly you are now inclined to pessimism in your delineation of women and marriage; that makes a great difference from your earlier books; your realism is much more consistent or at least more pronounced than formerly.' Gissing's reply may give some idea of his mood: 'I wonder how many more changes of the year I am destined to see. I *hope* for a good many, as I have still a lot of work to do; but I fear the best of life is over.'

By mid-May the novelist had decided that he must go back to Epsom. Though Edith 'refused to come to *any* terms – save the old', as he wrote to Hick – he could not stay away much longer. He was afraid of her effect on young Alfred; and in any case his distance hardly contributed to his peace of mind. As he told Hick, 'I am tortured out of all possibility of work by letters.' Furthermore, he could not afford to maintain three establishments: Walter in Yorkshire, Edith and Alfred at Epsom, himself in Devon.

On the last day of May Gissing returned to Epsom. There is no recorded account of his first meeting with Edith after nearly four months, but apparently she made an effort to be pleasant. The next day he was examined in London by Pye-Smith, who said his health was much better but that he 'must now choose a suitable place of abode – high and dry'. Pye-Smith ordered him not to live in or near London; he told the novelist he had emphysema, which could be reversed if he took proper care of himself. The lease on the house in Epsom was up at the end of the year, and Gissing put off any thought of moving until then.

The best medicine he got during this spring was the report of sales figures for *The Whirlpool*, about which he was triumphant. Still, at one shilling per copy its huge success only helped him a little financially ('Each 2,000 only means £100!' he told Hick). Early in

June he had his portrait done by William Rothenstein, who recalled later how much he had liked Gissing – 'a wistful, sensitive nature, a little saddened . . . and perhaps . . . lacking in vitality, but with a tender sense of beauty'. He thought that Gissing, even more than Hardy, who had also sat for him, was 'obsessed by the melancholy of life'. During the sitting 'that remarkable youth' Max Beerbohm came in, and the three men lunched together.

Throughout June Gissing carried on with his reading of Roman history. 'I mean to take the conflict between Christian ideals and the old Roman spirit', he told Bertz. His subject was sixth-century Rome, about which practically nothing was, or is, known. 'This is the outcome of a desire I have nursed for ten years', he told his friend. He noted with distaste the approach of another Jubilee, this one the sixtieth anniversary, on 22 June 1897, of the Queen's ascent to the throne.

Meanwhile he had a living to earn. On 9 June he began another novel, called at first 'Polly Brill'. This was the book Colles had been badgering him for, and Gissing worked away at it rapidly. Writing in the midst of an extended domestic peace and avoiding the usual false starts and fresh beginnings (largely because the story failed to engage his interest), he finished the tale just five weeks later, on 14 July, and sent it off to Colles immediately. The final title was *The Town Traveller*. He told Colles that his expenses were high and his income low in 1897, which was to be his worst year – 'the year of terror', he called it – since 1888. Earning only £102, he had to draw on his savings. He asked Colles to get the best terms possible for the new book. Colles was free to take him out of the hands of Lawrence and Bullen if he liked.

Little need be said of *The Town Traveller*, concocted solely to make money as a serial. It is an uncharacteristically lighthearted tale, identifiable as by Gissing only by the obsessive interest in money, the knowledgeable account of lodging-house life, and the unmercifully satirical treatment of Cockney speech (the problem of aspirates resurfaces, but this time in more jocular surroundings). Gissing's re-reading of Dickens shows through in the comic treatment of lower-middle-class life. But the tone throughout is that of false heartiness, as if Gissing could not help but know how badly he was writing. *The Town Traveller* must be his worst novel, if that distinction does not belong to the unreadable *Veranilda*. The tale is in any case a bizarre successor to *The Whirlpool*. I have suggested that Gissing's fiction is at its lowest ebb when he strays farthest from autobiography. *The Town Traveller* is a singularly disembodied performance ('When Mr Gissing is cheerless, he is convincing, but when he is cheerful, he is denied credence', a perspicacious American reviewer would remark of it). Few of Gissing's other books were produced so effortlessly. Indeed, his reading of Roman history never slackened while he was writing the novel, as the diary plainly shows. During this period he also re-read Forster's *Life of Dickens*, and looked through Georg Brandes's *Impressions of Russia* (1890), which contained information he was to use later in *The Crown of Life*.

In mid-July he wrote to Blackie in Glasgow agreeing to do the book on Dickens, for which he had begun to collect notes. He looked forward to the job as a pleasant change. He also suggested to Lawrence and Bullen that they bring out a volume of his recent stories and sketches made up largely of the tales that had appeared in Shorter's journals between 1893 and 1896. Bullen pronounced this an excellent idea, planned the collection for autumn publication, and said he would call it *Human Odds and Ends*. Gissing would receive an advance of 75 guineas for the volume and the usual royalty of a shilling per copy sold. Things seemed to be looking up. Edith was being relatively co-operative.

Late in July 1897 Gissing took Edith, Alfred, and Walter on holiday to Castle Bolton, Wensleydale, a secluded little place whose scenery the novelist was to make use of in *The Crown of Life* and *The Ryecroft Papers* (Winter, 23). He described the area in a letter to Hick, adding that he was now 'gasping for breath on the least provocation'. During the first week of August he had trouble with Edith again. She began to nag both boys unmercifully, and Gissing became restless. The diary records a number of sleepless nights. Worse was to come. In mid-August Edith grew violent again. 'Much misery today; grumbling, snarling, rage and universal idiocy. What a life!' He thought poor Walter's 'position in this family of discord . . . most unfortunate. He and his mother always quarrelling. How *can* he respect her?' Again: 'Infamous uproar all day; E.'s behaviour worse than ever.' And again: 'E.'s frenzy of ill temper' was spoiling everything. By 24 August Gissing had decided to spend the winter in Italy – alone: 'To this plan I shall fiercely adhere.'

As his health worsened the desire to work grew stronger in him, but he felt he could not accomplish much as long as he was living with Edith. Roberts dates Gissing's physical decline from this period but blames it primarily upon the novelist's self-destructive working habits:

No man of letters can possibly sit for ever at the desk during eight hours, as was frequently 'his brave custom' . . . If he had worked in a more reasonable manner, and had been satisfied with doing perhaps a thousand words a day . . . his health might never have broken down in the way it did. He had been moved . . . towards these hours, partly by actual desperation; partly by the great loneliness which had been thrust upon him; very largely by the want of money which prevented him from amusing himself in the manner of the average man, but chiefly by his sense of devotion to what he was doing.

Roberts goes on to describe one of Gissing's average work-days:

After breakfast, at nine o'clock, he sat down and worked till one. Then he had his midday meal, and took a little walk . . . about half-past three, he sat down again and wrote till six o'clock or a little after. Then he worked again from half-past seven to ten. I . . . doubt whether there is any modern writer who has ever tried to keep up work at this rate who did not end in a hospital or a lunatic asylum, or die young.

In Wensleydale, meanwhile, things were coming to a head. One day late in August Edith, in Walter's presence, called her husband a liar and threatened to hit him with a plate. 'Still raging, she then addressed herself to Walter, and commiserated with him on having such a father, a father unlike all others, – who never bought him a toy . . . and who was never in a decent humour.' For Gissing, this was the last straw. 'There it is. Decisive, I should think, for ever.' On the same day that he wrote this sad scene into his diary Gissing received the first proof sheets of *Human Odds and Ends*. Two days later Walter was sent back to Wakefield and the others returned to Epsom. Gissing was determined now to break with Edith permanently. He told Hick that Edith and Alfred would be put in lodgings (for £50 per quarter) under the watchful eye of Eliza Orme, that the furniture would be stored, and he would spend the autumn and winter in Italy, working on his Dickens monograph and some other projects he had in mind. He had promised the Dickens volume for the end of November 1897; he decided to settle in Siena to write it. After that he planned to tour Calabria. 'There – it is a great decision, and has cost me much. The details have been laboriously elaborated, and I would not unsettle them for much fine gold.' He looked forward to 'solid work – for the first time in six years'. He told Hick that he would be leaving 'with much anxiety on my mind – anxiety about the little children, the chance of life and death, etc., etc. It is not like my Italian travel 8 years ago, when – save for cash – I was independent.' Now, he said, he had to earn 'a good £200 a year apart from my own living and casual expense' to support his various establishments. 'If I live, I think I can do it – but there is no occasion for merriment.' He was very grateful to Miss Orme: 'What toil and misery she is taking off my hands!' His departure was set for the third week of September. He hoped to see enough of southern Italy this time to produce 'a book of travel-sketches'. 'I have come to the moment in my life when I must make a new start', he wrote to Bertz. 'I *feel* that I am doing the right thing.'

When he finally informed Edith of his plans, 'Fury and insult' were the result, and 'great misery' reigned in the house for days afterwards. On 17 September he and Edith finally parted, by no means amicably. 'Misery to the very end – rage and ill feeling', the diary reports. Gissing and his second wife were not to live together again: the spark of eroticism that kept bringing him back to Nell was never an important factor in his relationship with Edith after the first few months of their marriage.

Gissing paid flying visits to Algernon and to Wakefield, and on his last night in London wrote to Wells and dined with Bullen, to whom he proposed doing a collected edition of his works (Bullen, financially hard-pressed, turned him down). To Wells he wrote: 'One more chapter of life closed – one more step towards the happy Finis.' On 22 September 1897 he left England for his third visit to Italy. He would be away this time for nearly seven months. Behind him lay the wreckage of his second marriage, among the debris two fatherless children. In his haste to begin yet another new life, Gissing had left his younger son to the tender mercies of the boy's erratic mother.

III

The novelist reached Siena on 25 September. Charmed by its undisturbed medieval flavour, he settled into inexpensive lodgings and began to write his study of Dickens. He was reasonably satisfied, but bothered by two things: he missed his children; and his health now started seriously to deteriorate. He began to cough blood, and he had trouble maintaining his weight. In a fatalistic mood he wrote to England to amend his will, appointing Algernon, Miss Collet, and Edith joint guardians of his children. By mid-October, feeling better, he was progressing rapidly on the monograph, producing an average of 2,000 words over seven hours each day. He was impressed by his own capacity for work now that he was back on his own. 'How improbable, this, a few years ago! It is strange how much more control I am getting over myself.' Late in the month he informed Bertz that he was nearing the end of the monograph. 'It seems that the only way to achieve popular success is to keep on publishing incessantly, year after year, till you have forced people to know you', he wrote to his friend.

In a long eloquent letter to Jane Wells, Gissing expressed ambivalent feelings:

Does one *like* Italy? The fact is, I always feel it is a terrible country; its unspeakable beauty is inseparable from the darkest thoughts; go where you may, you see the traces of blood and tears . . . here one *remembers* so much more than in other countries. Age after age of strife and tyranny, of vast calamities, of unimaginable suffering in the palace and the hut. You feel something pitiless in the blue sky that has looked so tranquilly on all this. And the people – you see centuries of oppression on their faces, hear it in their voices. Yes, yes, one likes Italy; but in a very special sense of the word.

Here is a foretaste of the brilliant writing that was to be sustained so remarkably in *By the Ionian Sea*.

In October a long appraisal of Gissing's work was published in the *National Review*. It was oddly out of date, referring to *Eve's Ransom* as Gissing's latest novel (the piece was written in 1895 and never brought up to date). The author, Frederick Dolman, speaks of the novelist as 'a writer of great, if not supreme, power' and argues that Gissing's pessimism has been responsible for the slow growth of his literary reputation. The essay's failure to mention his last three books left Gissing, as so often with critical assessments of his work, unimpressed.

On 5 November the novelist finished his book on Dickens, sent it off to Colles, and several days later left for Rome. He stayed only two days, departing quickly for his beloved Naples, which he had not seen for seven years. He still found it, he wrote to Wells a few days later, 'the most interesting town . . . in the world'. He was preparing for the Calabrian journey. On the evening before his departure for the South he felt feverish. He noted peevishly in his diary that he was tired of the 'atmosphere of illness and death' that seemed always to surround him.

In England, meanwhile, *Human Odds and Ends* had been published to generally scathing reviews – and deservedly so, for Gissing's stories, as I have said, are uniformly mediocre, and a collection of them made this only too plain. The *Academy* called most of the tales 'mere scraps and suggestions' rather than stories, which is just. The *Bookman* was more temperate, but *The Times* noted with distaste the apparent relish with which Gissing depressed his reader in piece after piece. The *Graphic*, the *Sketch*, and the *Guardian* were less courteous in their appraisals of the book. Gissing earned only seven shillings beyond the advance of 75 guineas he was paid for *Human Odds and Ends*, the publication of which did his reputation no good.

IV

Charles Dickens: A Critical Study is one of the best books ever written on Dickens. Like most of Gissing's other works, it tells us a great deal about himself – as books by one writer about another so often do. It also demonstrates Gissing's skill and insight as a critic and scholar, a side of him that had been waiting to go to work for many years. What is perhaps most remarkable is that it was one of the first to pinpoint the sources alike of Dickens's genius and his limitations.

Dickens's most important asset as a novelist, Gissing argues, is his humour: when his characters come alive, this is often the reason. Dickens's humour had, of course, its didactic purposes: 'Only because they laughed with him so heartily, did multitudes of people turn to discussing the question his page suggested.' Also, says Gissing, Dickens was 'truly and profoundly national' in his point of view – and this 'intense nationality' enabled him 'to utter the thoughts of voiceless England'. His observation of apparently ordinary things was 'wonderfully minute . . . It is the property of his genius to perceive romance in the commonplace and the squalid.'

On the other side of the ledger are Dickens's woeful defects – for example 'characterization spoilt by the demand for . . . intrigue', resulting largely from his inability to construct plots, to develop 'character through circumstance . . . the art of adapting simple probabilities to the ends of narrative he never mastered.' Quite rightly, I think, Gissing attributes Dickens's 'astonishing lack of skill when it came to inventing plausible circumstances' to his 'love of the stage' and his usual failure 'to see mentally as whole the work on which he was engaged' as he wrote it. Another weakness is a lack of 'historical knowledge . . . no true understanding of what is meant by history'; this helps explain why, 'when he exhibits victims of social wrong', he 'takes no due account of the effect of conditions upon character'. Indeed, 'Few really great men can have had so narrow an intellectual scope' – which also helps explain why 'No distinctly intellectual person figures in his books.'

I find it difficult to quarrel with any of Gissing's conclusions about Dickens. Surely he is right to see as a result of these mixed elements in so talented a man a series of uneven literary achievements: unequalled greatness when he is good, second-rate melodrama when he is bad. 'Permit Dickens to show us the life he knew in its simple everyday course and he is unsurpassed by any master of fiction; demand from him a contrived story, and he yields at once to the very rank and file of novelists.' Gissing's verdicts on individual novels seem to me equally just – for example, his declaration that, without qualification, *Little Dorrit* is 'the best book of all'. Gissing was writing at a time (just twenty-seven years after his death) when Dickens's later novels were considered a falling-off – when, that is, the achievement-and-decline view of Dickens's work was at its height. Dickens was considered fit for children and Christmas and little else. It is to Gissing's credit that he paid no attention to this absurdity. 'It is the privilege of a great writer to put into his work the finest qualities of his heart and brain, to make permanent the best part of himself', Gissing says here. 'Be he a true artist, he gives us pictures which represent his own favourite way of looking at life; each is . . . the world as *he* prefers it.'

Wherein lay Gissing's interest in Dickens, an interest sufficiently developed to move him to spend several months of his life in 1897, and more time later, writing about the great man? Dickens's fascination for Gissing had a number of sources. He was awed by Dickens's power, alien to him, 'of pursuing his imaginative tasks amid distractions which most men would find fatal . . . [His] fiction-writing went on as usual, with never a hint of difficulty owing to circumstances.' On the other hand, he himself had done something which, he was certain, Dickens could never have done: 'Dickens could never have struggled for long years against the lack of appreciation. In coldness towards his work he would have seen its literary condemnation, and have turned to a new endeavour.' But it is in their similarities that Gissing is most interested. Both men loved to travel but hated 'the supercilious Englishman abroad', as Gissing puts it; both loved the English countryside, and yearned for it most when penned up in the metropolis; both venerated the past and detested many aspects of modern life. Dickens's age and his own – not very far apart, after all – appeared to Gissing to be periods 'in which the English character seemed bent on exhibiting all its grossest and meanest and most stupid characteristics. Sheer ugliness of every day life reached a limit not easily surpassed.' All in all, Gissing sums up, 'A time of . . . ugly religion, ugly law, ugly relations between rich and poor, ugly clothes, ugly furniture.' When Dickens died at fifty-eight, Gissing was already in his thirteenth year; their hatred of the 'modern' age is a hatred of the same age. The London of the two novelists is the same London, though observed forty-five years apart. Indeed, many scenes in *The Nether World* could easily be transplanted to *Bleak House*. But it is typical of Gissing's hatred of the present to idealize the recent as well as the more distant past, finding his own time, if more respectable, also 'decidedly duller'. Gissing's feeling that Dickens's 'age' was better than his also leads him to see it as a period when 'there was more of the picturesque, more of the beautiful, than we see to-day', and to speak of his own time as one in which there is 'destruction of so much one would fain preserve. Think, for instance, of Yarmouth as seen in *David Copperfield* and the Yarmouth of this year's railway advertisements . . . Our people . . . have advanced in the understanding of business, a word which will justify most atrocities, and excuse all but every form of shamelessness.'

Hatred of the modern and veneration of the past is in each novelist the product of a temperamental conservatism. In seeing the so-called great Radical of his time as a genuine conservative at heart, Gissing is not indulging, as it might seem, in psychological projection: he is being profoundly incisive, taking a point of view, completely correct, which was to escape Dickens's critics for another half-century.

Dickens's conservatism lies, I think, in his unquestioning belief in God, money (characters worthy of redemption are often rewarded with it), and class (his bourgeois characters speak a pure English, no matter what their actual origins). Gissing picks up some of this and adds a few things of his own. As he points out, Dickens was sceptical about the virtues and effects of 'popular education' – for example, Charley Hexam in *Our Mutual Friend* – and uneasy about 'the spread of a genuinely democratic spirit' (the fear of the mob is everywhere in Dickens, most notably in *Barnaby Rudge* and *A Tale of Two Cities*). In these matters the two novelists were at one. Dickens, himself 'a considerable capitalist', as Gissing points out, 'Never desired . . . a political revolution', and he reminds us how much he hated American republicanism. He goes on: 'He was never a democrat; in his heart he always held that *to be governed* was the people's good; only let the governors be rightly chosen . . .

Dickens knew – no man better – how unfit are the vast majority of mankind to form sound views as to what is best for them.' This is an accurate summary of Gissing's views on these matters as well as Dickens's; it is a good example of the temperamental affinity between the two.

Political action was not the answer. What, then, was one to do about the poor? Gissing's response was – nothing; the poor you will always have with you, no scheme of relief can change that. Dickens's answer was almost identical, but with one addition: 'He distrusted legislation; he had little faith in charitable associations . . . His saviour of society was a man of heavy purse and large heart, who did the utmost possible good in his own particular sphere.' Dickens put his faith in 'private benevolence' rather than public aid. Gissing's summing-up of Dickens's views on this question is a perfect synopsis of his own: 'Dickens, for all his sympathy, could not look with entire approval on the poor grown articulate about their wrongs . . . He . . . thought that humble folk must know "their station." He was a member of the middle class, and as far from preaching "equality" in its social sense as any man that ever wrote.' This is only a slight distortion of Dickens's views on such matters. Both men, beginning with little and achieving much, became in the course of their lives middle-class snobs. There was always somewhere in the background a fear of backsliding. Well into middle age Dickens had nightmares about his deprived childhood; each house he lived in was more gargantuan than the last. Of course both sympathized with the poor: how could they not? But in both the sympathy was more intellectual than practical. Dickens fought some abuses, but generally he tended more to sentimentalize the poor than to help them.

Closely related to these questions in Gissing's mind as he wrote his study of Dickens were certain considerations about nineteenth-century puritanism – and what he calls 'social tyranny'. Gissing cites Dickens's distrust of institutionalized religion and religious fanaticism of all shades, his irritation and disgust with the English clergy, and goes on to discuss standards of social 'respectability' created and maintained by English puritanism. 'Since the Puritan revolution', Gissing says, 'it has unhappily seemed necessary to our countrymen . . . to profess in a peculiar way certain peculiar forms of godliness, and this habit, gradually associated with social prejudices arising from high prosperity, results in the respectable man.' Echoing a theme of *Denzil Quarrier*, Gissing adds: 'Though the Englishman may dispense with a gig, and remain respectable, he must not be suspected of immorality . . . We must hold it as an article of faith that respectability not only does not err, but knows not temptation.' This sort of 'social superiority', Gissing argues, which is 'merely obstructive', earned Dickens's 'boundless contempt'.

Dickens was 'by birth superior to the rank of proletary, inferior to that of capitalist', Gissing writes. His grudge throughout his life against his own unhappy childhood 'was in essence a *class* feeling', he argues. 'To the end his personal triumph gratified him . . . as the vindication of a social claim', and 'what he had undergone turned to his ultimate advantage.' How well Gissing knew these feelings himself! His literary success no less than Dickens's was 'a social claim'; he too made literary use of 'what he had undergone'. Dickens 'wore himself to a premature end in striving to found his title of gentleman on something more substantial than glory,' says Gissing, who was himself engaged in an identical kind of 'striving' with similar physical results. 'He treats . . . of the lower middle class, where he will be always at his best . . . To the lower middle class, a social status so peculiarly English, so rich in virtues yet so provocative of satire, he by origin belonged.' Here again Gissing could be describing himself.

Gissing's discussion of Dickens's fictional women is revealing. Both alternately idealized and despised women. It is not to Gissing's credit that he was enthralled by Dickens's most nauseatingly saccharine, lily-white heroines. 'One discerns absolutely nothing of "exaggeration"' in Dickens's women, Gissing says. 'Not a word, not a gesture, goes beyond the truth.' Everyone knows how completely Dickens failed with most of his women; Gissing, like the rest of the Victorian audience, needed an angel of the hearth to worship. He found one in Dickens. Ruth Pinch, he says, 'is no imbecile – your thoroughly kind-hearted and home-loving woman never will be.' Such a woman never makes 'a sound of complaining or of strife, never a wry face, acidly discontented with a husband's doings or sayings. Upon my word – is it a bad deal?' Gissing concludes his discussion of Ruth with this declaration: in Dickens's novels women can see the 'ancient deformity of their sex, and will recognize how justly he pointed out the way of safe reform; no startling innovation, no extravagant idealism, but . . . a kindly glorifying of one humble little woman, who saw her duty, and did it singing the while.' With his peculiar and complicated feelings about women, Gissing was the perfect Dickens reader.

Both novelists were also good haters, and when it came to the things they detested in women they were again on common ground. Consider this remarkable passage in which Gissing is discussing Dickens's gallery of 'foolish, ridiculous, or offensive' lower-middle-class women:

nothing is asked of them but a quiet and amiable discharge of household duties; they are treated by their kindred with great . . . consideration. Yet their characteristic is acidity of temper and boundless license of querulous or insulting talk. The real business of their lives is to make all about them as uncomfortable as they can . . . they are unintelligent and untaught; very often they are flagrantly imbecile . . . their voices shrill upon the terrified ear. It is difficult to believe that death can stifle them; one imagines them upon the threshold of some other world, sounding confusion among unhappy spirits who hoped to have found peace . . . Many a woman . . . has brought the arts of ill-temper to high perfection.

And, Gissing adds, Dickens might also have dealt with the 'shrew who proceeds on the slightest provocation from fury of language to violence of act', neglects her children, and soothes her nerves 'by flinging at the remonstrant husband any domestic object' handy. Gissing has taken the Dickens shrew and recast her as the wife he has just left.

Dickens's shrews do not resemble Edith so perfectly in Dickens's pages as they do in Gissing's. Such women, Gissing goes on, bring their households 'to the verge of despair by . . . persistent sourness and sulkiness':

No reason whatever can be assigned for it; when she takes offence, it pleases her to do so. She has in perfection all the illogicality of thought, all the maddening tricks of senseless language, which, doubtless for many thousands of years, have served her like for weapons. It is an odd thing that evolution has allowed the persistence of this art, for we may be quite sure that many a primitive woman paid for it with a broken skull.

So much for Edith, whom he may well have wished to pay back for all her abuse of him with 'a broken skull'. Similarly Mrs Joe Gargery: 'Mrs. Gargery shall be brought to quietness; but how? By a half-murderous blow on the back of her head, from which she will never recover. Dickens understood . . . that there is no other efficacious way with these ornaments of their sex. A felling and stunning and all but killing blow, followed by paralysis and slow death. A sharp remedy, but no whit sharper than the evil it cures.' It is probably a good thing that Gissing left home when he did.

'It was (and is) precisely because so many men admire the foolish in girlhood that at least an equal number deplore the intolerable in wives', Gissing concludes. Perhaps no other passage in *Charles Dickens: A Critical Study* so plainly shows the extent to which he was writing about himself and his own feelings even in this work of literary criticism.

Roberts is surely wrong to say that Gissing produced the Dickens book solely for money. Gissing also wrote prefaces to the novels published in the incomplete Rochester Edition of Dickens's works (the prefaces were later collected in a volume called *The Immortal Dickens*), published articles on Dickens in various journals, and did an abridgement of Forster's *Life of Dickens* for Chapman and Hall. Obviously there was more here than a momentary interest. Roberts comes closer to the truth when he contradicts himself and acknowledges that, after all, the two men had much in common, most importantly their interest in 'the lower middle class and the class immediately beneath it.' Gissing's attacks on the Establishment, like those of Dickens, had their origin not in 'any native liberalism . . . or even . . . sympathy for the suffering of others, but came directly out of his own personal miseries and trials'. Both men, Roberts concludes, were 'essentially . . . conservative, and . . . lived in an alien time'.

v

On 16 November 1897 Gissing left Naples for the month-long tour of southern Italy so vividly described in *By the Ionian Sea*. The diary entries for November and December teem with detailed accounts of what he saw, which he was to draw on liberally when writing the travel book several years later. It was at times a difficult journey: the novelist was the first foreigner seen in some of these places for more than a century.

Gissing was forty on 22 November. The diary entry for that day notes simply, 'My birthday'. During the last week of November he had a serious attack of pulmonary congestion, brought on by 'that old enemy, the right lung', while at Cotrone; a local doctor helped nurse him back to health. Colles wrote to say he had sold the American rights to *Charles Dickens* for £50, and that the English edition was scheduled to appear on 15 February 1898. He had only disappointing news to report about *The Town Traveller*: it did not seem to interest the serial press. 'I shall give no more thought to [serialization] in writing fiction', Gissing declared in disgust. 'It is very clear that my work is not of a kind that is found acceptable in that market.'

In mid-December Gissing returned to Rome via Naples, spending a night at the Abbey of Cassino, a monastery he planned to use as a setting for some scenes in *Veranilda*. He took rooms in Rome and continued his explorations of the city and his study of archival material. He was to stay four months.

VI

Letters from Miss Orme about his wife upset the novelist just after Christmas: 'Infinite worry from that vicious idiot . . . Wrote severely to E., telling her that she must behave better, or I will take the little child away.' On New Year's Eve he was working on the proofs of *Charles Dickens: A Critical Study*.

In January 1898 Wells told Gissing that he and his wife would visit Rome in March: it would be their first trip to Italy. Gissing was delighted by this prospect, but could not help pouring out to Wells all his problems. His wife, he said, was ruining his peace of mind. 'With people of the educated class she cannot live – their proximity simply maddens her . . . the child . . . might just as well be in the care of a drunkard or a lunatic, as of this furious and hateful woman.' There was little he could do; his living with her would only make her more violent, and drive him mad. 'I see there is going to be a long, hard fight through the years that remain to me', Gissing told Wells. 'How would you relish literary labour under such conditions?' He said he was getting little work done. 'Probably I shall spend next Christmas in the workhouse.'

Despite a nagging cold Gissing managed to send off the corrected proofs of the Dickens book early in January. He continued his ramblings around Rome, trying to preserve his precarious health and infuriated by the reports of Edith he was receiving from England. In reply to a letter from Bertz generously praising *Human Odds and Ends,* Gissing replied that he had 'a poor opinion' of his short stories. 'I don't know what the papers are saying about them, and indeed don't care.' If this was true it was just as well. 'I could do with a little more money', he told his friend. 'It surprises me that my books do not sell better . . . the books are extensively read. But the publishers' account is *nil* – after the first half-year. This means that I have to keep writing, writing, when I should like to rest. I have nothing to fall back upon.' He was deeply depressed. 'Italy is a splendid country for the young and strong', he wrote to Ellen. 'For invalids it offers little comfort and many dangers; to send Keats to Rome was the height of folly . . . [it] might have been a deliberate plan for shortening his life.' The cold and damp were making him miserable, but he remained in Rome to continue gathering material for *Veranilda*. 'I have gravely injured my health', he admitted to Wells. 'It must come to an end, this kind of life I am leading.' He was somewhat cheered by the arrival of a cheque from Colles for £40 – partial payment for the Dickens book.

During the first part of February he devoted a good deal of time to finding lodgings for the Wellses: the letters he wrote to his friend are obsessively concerned with food, the climate, clothes, heating, plumbing, and related matters. Finally he found what he wanted at a hotel and liked it so much he moved into the same establishment himself. Meanwhile he commiserated with Wells on the rough handling in the *Athenaeum* of *The War of the Worlds*, just published. Who, he asks, writes their reviews? 'Are they women, soured by celibacy and by ineffectual attempts to succeed as authors? Even as they treat you this time, they have consistently treated me, – one continuous snarl and sneer. They are beastly creatures.' He told Bertz he would visit him in Potsdam on the way back to England in April. He asked his friend not to plan too much during the visit. 'I dread the sight of strangers', he wrote, sounding like Henry Ryecroft, adding that his health was now 'utterly ruined'.

On 12 February some genuinely good news arrived. Methuen had offered Colles an advance of £250 for *The Town Traveller* and an American publisher another £100 for American rights. This was by far the largest advance Gissing had ever received: he wrote to Colles immediately accepting the terms. The novel was not to be serialized and Methuen would publish it in April.

Miss Orme now recommended a legal separation from his wife and offered the services of her solicitor. Gissing consented. He also asked her to look for rooms for himself somewhere in the London suburbs. A cheque for £24 arrived from Lawrence and Bullen for miscellaneous royalties. Blackie sent the first author's copies of *Charles Dickens: A Critical Study* and a cheque for £30. Suddenly money was no longer a worry.

The year 1898 looked like being a prosperous one for him (it was to be his best earning year to date: £525 altogether, up 500 per cent from the miserable total of the previous year). Still, he found that his poor health made it difficult to work. He was grateful to Bertz for telling him about a new remedy for tuberculosis called creosotal. Gissing made inquiries about it, obtained some, and found that it gave him relief.

Towards the end of February Gissing dispatched a large number of author's copies of the Dickens book to his friends and family. He read in the Italian press an account of the Dreyfus affair and Zola's indictment. 'France seems sunk in infamy', he noted in his diary. He tried to write some fiction but managed to do little: the news from home was disconcerting. Miss Orme wrote to say that 'E.'s behaviour is more outrageous than ever'.

Blackie now asked the novelist to do a volume on Thackeray as a companion to the Dickens book: 'At present the thing seems impossible', Gissing noted. But he was delighted by the apparent success of *Charles Dickens*. 'I shall be glad if people in general recognize the fact that I am not confined to novel-writing', he told Bertz. 'I am told that it is selling very well, and that there have been many laudatory reviews', he remarked, somewhat complacently, of the monograph.

In fact this was true. As *The Whirlpool* had the previous year, *Charles Dickens: A Critical Study* received a great deal of attention in the press, provoking a number of long articles and a great many reviews. Gissing's reputation was at its height; Dickens's was at its lowest ebb. The combination interested people. Here was a leading novelist of the present-day commenting on a great favourite of the previous generation. The two men wrote about many of the same kinds of people. The public was curious to know what the living novelist would say of the dead one. The publishers, detecting the interest, sent out a huge number of review copies.

In the *Daily Chronicle* William Archer, the famous dramatic critic, published a piece called 'Mr. Gissing on Dickens'. 'Without swerving from his allegiance to an artistic ideal more serious and strenuous than Dickens ever conceived', Archer wrote, Gissing 'shows that the keenest sense of a great man's limitations is not inconsistent with the most ardent appreciation of his unique and beneficent genius.' He observed that Gissing 'traces many of Dickens's limitations to the very source of his greatness – the fact that he was a typical incarnation of middle-class English character.' In the *Outlook* W. E. Henley called Gissing 'as ardent a seeker after Truth . . . as devout and as expert a student of character . . . as accomplished an artist in fiction . . . as we have'. He declared: 'I have read nothing about Dickens which has pleased me half so well.' And he commented that Gissing had all the qualities of a great critic – 'sanity, clarity of thought and style, a point of view, the capacity for appreciation', 'excellent sense', and 'intellectual cour-age'. The unsigned review in *Literature* called Gissing's book 'the best study of Dickens we have ever read'. Other raves appeared in the *Guardian* and the *Inquirer*. In *Longman's Magazine* Andrew

Lang urged Gissing to tackle Thackeray, Fielding, or Scott next. Several journals (for example, the *Academy*, the *Sketch*, the *Daily Graphic*) raised their eyebrows over the violent discussion of women. In America the *New York Tribune* commented that Gissing was 'equipped as perhaps no other writer of to-day is equipped for a thorough and sympathetic examination of . . . Dickens'. The *Mercure de France* called the volume 'One of the best ever written on Dickens'. Dickens's readership had of course been tremendous, and by reaching out to what remained of it Gissing undoubtedly brought to himself some new readers and a great deal more critical attention.

VII

Gissing took the Wellses, who arrived on 8 March 1898 for a long stay in Italy, all over Rome. They were occasionally joined by the novelist E. W. Hornung (the creator of Raffles) and his brother-in-law Arthur Conan Doyle. The four novelists were a harmonious quartet.

Wells later recalled this period of Gissing's life:

he was in flight from his second wife. The dreadful intimacy of that isolated life at [Epsom], without a thought in common, an intimacy of perpetual recrimination, had become intolerable . . . the poor wife, perplexed and indignant beyond measure by this strange man who had possessed himself of her life, was progressing through scenes and screams towards a complete mental breakdown . . . letters would arrive . . . that left Gissing white and shaking between anger and dismay for the better part of a day.

'Perhaps', Wells said, 'Gissing was made to be haunted by Fate. He never turned and fought. He always hid or fled.' Hornung's reminiscence of Gissing is more generous. The novelist, he said, was 'lovable', had 'abundant humour', and 'a glorious laugh . . . an appreciative sympathy, a cordial humanity'. Brian Dunne, an American who made Gissing's acquaintance at this time, later recalled him as 'one of the most cheerful, luxury-loving people I have ever met'.

In mid-March Miss Orme's solicitor sent the novelist the Agreement of Separation. A pound a week was suggested for household expenses; Gissing raised this to 25 shillings, or £5 a month. He also had some of the stored furniture delivered for her use; he worried about the state of his books and papers, but Edith seems to have preserved them in good order. After a few days of peace she settled into her usual routine and set about making enemies of all her new

London neighbours. She also threatened to go before a magistrate and declare that her husband had deserted his family. Needless to say, Gissing found plenty to brood about. He was doing little real work but managed to turn out a story or two while in Rome. He noted with satisfaction that *Eve's Ransom* was appearing serially in translation in the *Revue de Paris.*

On 12 April the Roman party broke up. The Wellses left for Naples and Gissing went off to Berlin on his way to visit Bertz in Potsdam. He had not seen his old friend since 1884. 'Find him looking very old; silvery hair', he noted in his diary. Germany struck him as dull: 'The sheer *commonness* of it all, after Italy.' He had warned Bertz in advance that he wanted no society. 'Let us say nothing to anybody, but creep about in secret, like two old fogies.' Accordingly they did little. Gissing, who disliked the new militarism he saw everywhere (and went out of his way to attack in *The Ryecroft Papers* – Spring, 19), was glad to leave Germany behind him four days later. He spent two nights with Hick in Dover. Hick examined him and pronounced him relatively fit. The novelist went on to London, where he was astonished to find that he still had more than £200 in the bank. He embarked on a round of visits to his friends, and also made a quick trip to Wakefield. Through it all he burned to get back to work.

Gissing took a room in a hotel while deciding on a place to live. This was a matter of great importance, and he put off anything else until it was settled. It was also a matter of great delicacy. He did not want Edith, in her bitter mood, to know his address. He wished to avoid both her visits and her letters. When, early in May, he found a suitable house in Dorking, Surrey, his chief concern remained keeping his whereabouts a secret from his wife. 'Will you on every opportunity industriously circulate the news that I am going to live henceforth in Warwickshire?' he wrote to Roberts. 'I earnestly beg you not to breathe a word . . . to anyone', he wrote to Hick. Wells and Miss Orme knew his address, he said, but few others. 'My one fear is that some idiot may discover my address, and make a newspaper paragraph out of it', he told Bertz. 'Of course I must hide myself, in constant fear of attack by that savage.'

His first job after moving to Dorking was to correct the typescript of *The Town Traveller* for Methuen. 'Poor rubbish', was his verdict on it. Algernon picked this moment to ask for £25. 'Alas! Just the money I wanted for my new furniture', the novelist confided to his diary. Gissing dined with Meredith, pottered about the house in Dorking trying to fix it up properly, and began to think about fiction-writing again. The housekeeper he hired, sour but efficient, satisfied him; he settled in. His first guest was Wells, who came to dine.

Half a dozen or so stories date from this spring of 1898, and they bolstered Gissing's income as he awaited payment for *The Town Traveller*, now scheduled for publication in August. One of the tales, 'Fate and the Apothecary', may serve to show what the novelist was thinking during these days. The hero of this story is a pharmacist whom class pride renders rude to his customers. Unmarried at thirty-eight, 'natural shyness had always held him aloof from reputable women . . . Nicely dressed and well-spoken and good-looking women above the class of domestic servants he worshipped from afar, and only in vivacious moments pictured himself as the wooer of such a superior being.' Gissing's sexual insecurities and fantasies were the same at forty as at twenty. The pharmacist's professional tactlessness finally puts him out of business with 'just enough money to bury him'.

Early in June Gissing learned from Miss Orme that Edith was now actively trying to find him. About this time she disappeared briefly from view, and Gissing was terrified that she would turn up on his doorstep. Having fought with her landlady, Edith had been given notice and gone in search of her husband by seeking out his brother in Worcestershire. Gissing suggested to Miss Orme's solicitor that the separation agreement be redrafted so as to force Edith to give up Alfred. 'She threatens to give all possible trouble', he lamented in his diary. Edith had apparently told Algernon she would go to Wakefield next. 'If I am discovered, I suppose I must flee abroad', Gissing wrote to Hick. He added: 'Ah, but life is bad and hard. I often wish I were out of the way. Then someone or other would look after the two boys, and that madwoman would be supported by her relatives.'

Methuen now inquired if Gissing would write introductions to a new edition of Dickens's novels they were planning; F. G. Kitton, a well-known Dickens scholar, would provide the notes. It would be called the Rochester Edition. The novelist referred Methuen to Colles for terms. Colles asked for 10 guineas on publication per introduction, 3,000 words each. Methuen planned to bring out eleven volumes at the rate of two a year; Gissing's earnings, after Colles's commission was deducted, would be about £100. This was good pay for relatively little exertion, and the novelist accepted the terms immediately.

On 23 June he received a letter from a Frenchwoman, Gabrielle

12 (*left*) Auguste Fleury
(Gabrielle's father) in 1886

13. (*right*) Anna Fleury
(Gabrielle's mother) in 1886;
this is the French mother-
in-law whom Gissing
found so uncongenial

14. Gabrielle Fleury in 1886

15. Gabrielle Fleury-Gissing in 1904 or 1905
(in mourning; Gissing was fond of the dog, named 'Bijorese')

Fleury, inquiring if she could have French translation rights to *New Grub Street* and proposing to come to England to discuss the matter with him. Gissing replied non-committally – the first exchange in an interesting correspondence. A few days after this he wrote to Wells of the results of a physical examination he had had: 'decided phthisis [of the right lung] . . . strong gouty tendency – uncertainty of heart – bad emphysema – liver at any moment to give serious trouble – disposition to eczema' on the arms. His state of mind may be gathered by the proposition he made to Wells: 'I have a fine, lurid idea. Could it be given out that I am *dead*? Then, with comfort and half a dozen intimates, I might work steadily for a year or two, preparing posthumous books.' Writing to Bertz he was no more sanguine: 'I am overwhelmed with anxiety about money, and see only difficulties in the future.' He observed sadly that he hardly knew his sons. 'My children will have strange thoughts of their father, when they grow up!'

Something need be said now of Clara Collet, who in all likelihood brought her friendly relationship with Gissing to a crisis of sorts once he became separated from Edith. Miss Collet destroyed most of his letters to her written from early 1898 to mid-1899. One of them has survived, and the following extract from it is illuminating:

One who suffers incessantly – even though as the result of his own folly – should not be sternly treated . . . A woman must always more or less despise the man who, in his relations with women, has shown himself lacking in sense, lacking in self–respect, lacking in delicacy, lacking in ambition . . . It would be folly to hope that you could ever forget all this; I do not even wish that you should. Your place as a human being is vastly removed from mine; you stand far, far above me.

It sounds as if Gissing were tactfully turning down a proposal from his correspondent for a closer intimacy. But the letter also shows us that Gissing, forty and still emotionally starved, was ready to form another attachment should the occasion arise. There is some evidence that he carried on an affair with a Mrs Williams, a widow eight years his junior whom he met in Rome and continued seeing in England during the summer of 1898. At one point he may have asked her to come and live with him. Mrs Williams, who had children, wanted a more conventional relationship. 'Some woman ought to sacrifice herself for Gissing', Wells is supposed to have told the unyielding Mrs Williams, who however shortly remarried. Gissing had to wait for the right person to come along. On 6 July 1898, she did.

Four days earlier Gissing had gone over to Wells's place at Worcester Park for a visit. It was here that Wells taught him to ride a bicycle. Despite Wells's disclaimer, Gissing apparently made progress as a cyclist, and took to this form of exercise for a time. At Wells's, on 6 July, Mlle Fleury tracked Gissing down. She wanted to discuss her proposed translation of *New Grub Street*. She was invited to lunch, and afterwards the novelist and the would-be translator strolled in the garden at Worcester Park 'confabulating', as Wells puts it. Here is his description of her (one must remember that he always disliked her):

She was a woman of the intellectual bourgeoisie, with neat black hair and a trim black dress, her voice was carefully musical, she was well read, slightly voluble and over-explicit by our English standards, and consciously refined and intelligent. To Gissing she came as the first breath of Continental recognition, and she seemed to embody all those possibilities of fine intercourse and one-sided understanding for which he was craving.

Roberts, who liked Gabrielle, would describe her as 'a very beautiful woman, tall and slender, of a pale but clear complexion, [with] very melancholy lovely eyes'. Gissing remarked to Wells after this first meeting that Gabrielle was 'the very best kind of Frenchwoman, uniting fine intellectuality with the domestic sense'. Here at last, it seemed, was that ideal woman he had been looking for.

Gabrielle Fleury was twenty-nine in 1898. Her origins were solidly middle-class: her father was the trusted officer of a shipping company, her mother the daughter of a lawyer. She was studious, well read, and fluent in several languages. The poet and philosopher Sully-Prudhomme had once fallen in love with her, but he was her senior by thirty years and the match had not come off. Her friends thought of Gabrielle as being not only bright and open-minded but also somewhat dashing. She moved with ease (and without a chaperon) through the Parisian *salons* of the time, seeking the company of writers, artists, and musicians. She had become an intimate friend of the family of Alfred de Musset. From the first meeting Gissing was impressed by her knowledge of literary matters and her conversational powers: she seemed to him, as Coustillas puts it, 'the ideal mate for a man of letters'. The novelist immediately gave her the permission she sought to translate *New Grub Street* and arranged to meet her again three weeks later in Dorking to discuss excisions.

VIII

Four days after he met Gabrielle, Gissing wrote in his diary: 'Thinking about "The Crown of Life".' The 'crown of life' is love. Gissing had always wanted to write under this sort of inspiration, and now he thought he had it.

He began to draft *The Crown of Life* on 15 to 16 July, eagerly looking forward to Mlle Fleury's next visit ten days hence. He wrote to Wells: 'I have suddenly fallen upon a mood of work – such as comes rarely in these latter days. I labour all day long, and thank Heaven for the chance of doing so.'

Edith continued to cause trouble, and was now told she must leave her London lodgings. Gissing had her informed that if she agreed to give up Alfred she could live wherever she liked. Meanwhile, on 26 July, duly came Mlle Fleury armed with Smith, Elder's permission to translate *New Grub Street*. 'A sweet and intelligent creature', Gissing wrote of her in the diary. He gave her several of his books. They had a long talk, and apparently both spoke frankly of their personal situations. The letter Gissing wrote to her the next day was a love letter. They obviously covered a lot of ground during this second meeting. 'How often shall I see your beautiful hazel eyes . . . looking at me with kindness, with indulgence for my morbid weakness and all my wearisome peculiarities!' A few days later he wrote, 'Do you not know how sensitive I am to kindness from *anyone*? And what can be the effect upon me of words . . . from a woman whose face has thrilled me, and in whom I divine something very like my ideal of womanhood? . . . I think of you ceaselessly, and to think of you is to long for your presence.' He describes for her the dreariness of his average day: breakfast at 8:30, work from 9:00 to 1:00, dinner followed by a walk or cycling until 4:30, work again from 5:00 to 8:00, a light meal and early bedtime. 'It is the life of a hermit; not a happy life; haunted with desires of the impossible, oppressed by a great loneliness.' He adds: 'If I could some day tell you the story of my life, you would see in it a dreary sort of tragedy, but it would explain *me*.' Gabrielle's letters do not survive – she probably destroyed them after Gissing's death – but clearly she reciprocated his passion: he could not have written to her in this way otherwise. But he was not prevented by these developments from going to see Mrs Williams now and then at the cottage she had conveniently taken in Dorking.

Early in August Edith assaulted her landlady and the woman's husband with a stick and had to be restrained by a policeman. She went immediately into other lodgings. Gissing renewed his plea to Miss Orme's solicitor to get Alfred away from her if he could. Edith informed the solicitor that her terms for agreeing to a legal separation included a house of her own and custody of both boys: this effectively stalemated all negotiations. She would not consider a divorce. A few days later she vandalized her ex-landlady's garden and wrote the first of some poison-pen letters to Miss Orme. Gissing wrote plaintively to Roberts: 'All work impossible owing to ceaseless reports of mad behaviour in London . . . my literary career is at an end.' The novelist's only solace, besides his correspondence with Gabrielle, was his visits to Mrs Williams. He told Wells she was saving him from 'melancholy madness'. Wells continued to urge her charms in preference to those of Gabrielle – who, he told Roberts, was 'a tiresome weak sentimental middle-class Frenchwoman who wrote her letters on thin paper'.

Gabrielle continued to write 'letters on thin paper', and Gissing continued to write passionate responses. During the first ten days of August 1898 he dispatched to her a series of letters amongst the most revealing he ever sent to anyone:

Eight years ago, I was poor and solitary and tormented by my emotions. It seemed to me that I should never succeed in literature – which meant that I could never hope to win the love of a woman who was my intellectual equal. In recklessness . . . I offered marriage to the first girl I happened to meet – and the result was what might have been expected. Few men have paid more bitterly for such foolish weakness . . . I have no words to utter the sense of worship with which I think of your pure and noble nature . . . Dearest, you are very far above me, and it is strange, strange, that you should care to be loved by me . . . I love you beyond all that I ever imagined of love. You are the incredible woman – the ideal of a passionate heart.

It is interesting to note Gissing's overt equation of success in literature with the winning of an intellectual woman. A few days later he wrote to Gabrielle in a similar vein. 'In you I have met the woman who corresponds most wonderfully to my ideal', he says. He goes on to sketch for her this ideal. It is a woman 'nobler' than he. She is intelligent. She loves music and art. She is both passionate and tender. 'And with all that she has domestic instinct, so seldom found with the other qualities.' He had thought he should never meet such a woman; now he has met her, and fallen in love with her. He told Gabrielle she had 'terrible power' over him and besought her to 'use it kindly'. He concludes:

I cannot live as now much longer. Before meeting you, I was thinking very often of suicide. My two little children would then be taken care of by somebody, and many people who are troubled by my troubles would come to quietness of mind. But now, now, I am hungry for life – the true life, which I have never known. My nature is a strange compound of the bohemian and the bourgeois; I am passionate but at the same time very domestic. To the woman who loved me I should be absolutely faithful . . . I have never felt proud of anything I have done. If *you* loved me, I should know for the first time what pride means – I shall know what it is to live with dignity.

All of Gissing's books together were not enough to create in him self-esteem. He was not respectable until a respectable woman thought so.

Gabrielle had appeared at just the right time. 'One great danger was before me', he wrote. 'I am not made to live in solitude, and it was only too likely I should have sought the companionship of some woman, who, sooner or later, would have involved me in new unhappiness.' Mrs Williams, perhaps? He urged Gabrielle not to judge his opinion of women from his 'wretched *books*': 'I recognize no restraint whatever upon a woman's intellect.' Summing up his beliefs for her, he declared that he had no religious faith and could not conceive of a 'personal deity. My religion is the mysterious beauty of the universe, and the infinite power of loving that is in the human heart.' A few days later he wrote: 'The love of a true woman is always precious. That of a woman who is one's intellectual equal (or superior) is a blessing beyond any other known to this life of ours.'

Gissing had spent a lifetime looking for a woman like Gabrielle, one who would reciprocate both his love and his respect. And so if a lifetime's passion is poured into these letters, we must not be surprised. He saw her as his last chance of happiness – his last chance to enter that charmed circle, so easily entered by other men, from which he thought he was always to be excluded.

Roberts says that Gissing ended by telling Gabrielle almost everything about his past life, only leaving out 'the early disaster which had maimed and distorted his natural career and development'. Unlike Wells, Roberts watched with pleasure as they grew intimate. Gissing had finally met a woman whom Roberts describes as 'beautiful and accomplished' and, among other things, 'a capable and feeling musician'. She played the piano. For what it is worth, Wells called Roberts's account of Gabrielle 'ridiculous'.

In August 1898 Gissing put *The Crown of Life* aside to begin the prefaces to Dickens he had agreed to write. During the rest of the month he worked on introductions to *The Pickwick Papers, David Copperfield,* and *Dombey and Son.* Late in August he informed Wells that his mother had arrived for a month's visit and wondered how he would get through the time. He now received his author's copies of *The Town Traveller* and a cheque from Colles for £215 – the novelist's advance from Methuen less the agent's commission and expenses. The copy sent to Wells was accompanied by a note apologizing for this 'thin book'.

A brief flare-up of temper on Wells's part now occurred. In a letter either lost or destroyed Gissing apparently waxed sentimental about the charms of Mlle Fleury, and Wells replied savagely that his first duty ought to be to his wife and children. As usual, Gissing responded with more generosity than Wells deserved: 'this is candour with a vengeance. But you are too severe. My error has been in bearing so long with a woman who has used me so unmercifully. Of course I did it for the children's sake . . . To them is my first responsibility, and I shall always recognize it.' From this time Gissing confided little to Wells about his hopes with regard to Gabrielle, and indeed there is a notable absence of intimate matter in his letters to his friend for the next six months.

But his correspondence with Gabrielle continued to blaze. 'Already you have taught me to use the future tense instead of the conditional', he told her. The reading public and many of his friends, he says, have sometimes accused him of being a 'woman-hater'. 'The reason is plain enough. I had always such a high ideal of the woman I could love, and of late years it has seemed to me fantastic, unattainable . . . Imagine what it means to me, to be writing to the *ideal woman herself.*' He goes on: 'My thought on every subject has undergone a . . . wonderful change. No more wandering of the desires – no more restless discontent with life – no more brooding on dark philosophies!' He reminds her that his life up to now 'has been a story of vain hope. From twenty to thirty-three, I worked hard for success in literature – always regarding it as the mere stepping-stone to that much greater thing, the love of the ideal woman.' He warns her not to take the gloom of his books as an index to his personality. With her to inspire him, he says, his life could be renewed: 'Fate owes me a second lifetime.' He warns her that a 'spiritual' love is not enough for him. He needs 'another form of contentment . . . it is *in my nature* to desire the love of a wife . . . my heart aches with longing for intimate affection.' He acknowledges the terrible obstacles barring them from living together. Still, he says, 'it can only be the spirit of hope that has kept me alive through such evil years', and he will go on hoping.

IX

The Town Traveller, published late in August 1898, was an immediate commercial success. Less than two weeks after its appearance the novel had sold nearly 2,500 copies, and a second edition of 1,000 copies was depleted by the end of September. Its popularity may be measured by the fact that Methuen in 1902 printed 20,000 copies in a sixpenny edition. The novel was reprinted twice again, the last time as recently as 1956 . French translation rights were also sold. The book did so well that Methuen was to offer Gissing a new career-high advance of £400 for *The Crown of Life*. The novelist, to his credit, never took the success of *The Town Traveller* seriously, telling his friends it was vulgar and ignoble, as indeed it is, and asking them not to read it.

Once again the press was extraordinarily generous. Here, said the reviewers, was a marvellous phenomenon: Gissing converted to comedy. They proceeded to fall over themselves praising the book. The *Pall Mall Gazette* and the *Critic* (London) lauded its brightness and wit, and also its realism: 'Mr Gissing has never got much more inside London than here', said the *Gazette*. The *Saturday Review* thought it an ingenious story. The *Morning Post* said that Gissing, who 'has made for himself a distinct position among English writers by the production of some of the most depressing novels ever penned', had now reached a new phase – no doubt as a result of his study of Dickens. The *Guardian* also compared Gissing's 'new' manner to Dickens's. The *Daily Chronicle* sparked a controversy by raising, in a leader, the question of the authenticity of Christopher Parish, the Cockney clerk in the novel whose speech is so unmercifully parodied, and by printing some correspondence from readers on the question. Is this portrait of an East London junior clerk authentic, asked the *Chronicle*, or an unfair exaggeration? For several weeks the arguments raged back and forth in the correspondence columns of the *Chronicle*, to the delight of Gissing and Methuen. Not all the reviews were favourable. Gissing's old adversary the *Athenaeum* was lukewarm, and adverse notices appeared in the *Bookseller*, the *Scotsman*, and *Outlook* (US). Generally, however, Gissing was more fortunate with the critics than he deserved.

Despite all this, the novelist wrote to Clodd to say that he was still 'preoccupied by the accursed struggle for money'. He could not take time to write a book on Thackeray – 'who, be it said between us, appeals to me much more strongly than Dickens' – because of 'the very trifling payment' involved. In the same week he wrote to Bertz about *The Town Traveller*, saying he was 'disgusted' with it, and about *The Crown of Life*, giving his friend a preview of it: 'the question of Peace will be involved. It is a love story, but with large issues – philosophic . . . and cosmopolitan.' He told Bertz about Edith's latest antics, but nothing of Gabrielle. As for Alfred: 'I fear his life is sacrificed – my own fault. The marriage was *criminal*.'

On 7 September 1898 the event Gissing had been dreading for so long came to pass. Edith, with Alfred in hand, appeared on his doorstep. She had got his address from the furniture-storage company. Fortunately 'there was no scene', the diary reports. 'I gave her to understand that our parting was final, but that I should not take Alfred away from her as long as she keeps well.' The child, not yet three years old, did not recognize his father; Gissing only remembered after they had gone that he did not address a single word to his younger son. He and Edith spoke quietly; she promised, upon leaving, never to return. He was not to see either of them again.

Throughout September he wrote copiously to Gabrielle, who had gone back to France. He felt he should make it clear to her that he saw no prospect of obtaining a divorce; nor could he (as yet) bring himself to suggest to her a free union. There was little he could do but pour out his feelings. It was she who was shaping *The Crown of Life*, he told her. 'Of course the heroine is not *you* . . . but your influence has greatly affected my imagination.' And a few days later: 'You know that my life has been lonely in an extraordinary degree. I have *never* known the pleasure of confiding absolutely in man or woman . . . Cannot you imagine how often I have longed for real companionship? Of course I have suffered horribly from need of a woman's love, but perhaps more from aching desire of intellectual intimacy.' He had believed, he said, that he had nothing to look forward to but more solitude. 'I thought I should never exchange words of true sympathy; that I should die, at last, lonely and silent – a whole world of thought and emotion for ever suppressed. It will not be so now! I shut my eyes to all obstacles in our way.' His moods varied. 'The world is a place of tragedies, my Gabrielle! . . . In the end, human life must be a tragedy; to the end, I suppose, it will be made endurable by love.'

Gissing continued to work on the Dickens prefaces and *The*

Crown of Life. It was decided that Gabrielle should come over for a visit so that they could discuss their plans. Gissing determined now to ask her to live with him. The few letters he wrote during the autumn of 1898 are addressed almost exclusively to her; he did not wish to confide in Wells, Roberts, Bertz, Hick, Clodd, or anyone else until his future happiness was decided. In one letter he asks Gabrielle again not to take to heart the nasty remarks he has made in his books about women and marriage: 'I so often wrote in a bitter mood.' He goes on to anticipate the subject of their talk when she comes to visit: 'I am convinced that a profound love between two intelligent persons *demands* a life in common, and will be satisfied with nothing less.'

When Gabrielle came to England a week later she knew that the novelist could not obtain a divorce. Indeed, he had told her that Edith's *'one* consolation [is] the thought that I cannot marry again.' Gabrielle arrived in Dorking ready to reach some sort of accommodation with him nevertheless. A week later she left. The diary makes a terse announcement: 'We have decided that our life together shall begin next spring.'

Gabrielle was determined to persevere. Her mother, who knew only a little of Gissing's domestic circumstances, supported her staunchly. The couple would live in Paris, at Gabrielle's parents' flat. Gabrielle had a small income; the flat was large; living with her parents would pare their household expenses to a minimum.

As soon as Gabrielle departed Gissing went back to work on *The Crown of Life*. At the end of October he was pleased to hear that *Eve's Ransom* had been published in cloth in France and that Gabrielle had sold translations of two of his stories to Paris journals. Newspaper reports of a possible war with France, sparked by the Fashoda incident, bothered him. He paid another visit to Mrs Williams. He reported to Gabrielle: 'My breathing gives me no trouble at all; I can walk rapidly with ease; my mind is clear and cheerful . . . I am become an extravagant optimist.' Early in November he informed her that he had completed about half of *The Crown of Life*, which he thought might well be the best thing he had ever done. 'I marvel at my own happiness', he told her.

Roberts was the first of his English friends to whom he confided his future plans. 'Absolute silence – it goes without saying', Gissing wrote to him. 'You will be the only man in London who knows this story . . . If ever by a slip of the tongue you let a remark fall that my wife was dead, *tant mieux*.' He begged Roberts to find out as much as he could 'about the marriage and divorce laws of all the separate

States of North America,' just in case he could find a way out of his marriage. This was the beginning of a long, and fruitless, investigation by Gissing of the marriage and divorce laws of different countries of the world. It was clear that he intended to keep his relationship with Gabrielle a secret. Roberts – and Wells, when he heard of the situation some time later – advised Gissing against secrecy and deception. But the novelist had never lost his fear of society's strictures, of being thought unconventional or not respectable. He had come too close to being thoroughly unrespectable. And so, seven years after he wrote of such a couple in *Denzil Quarrier*, he and Gabrielle decided to live a lie, to tell her friends they were married and to tell his nothing at all. Certainly the novelist was more reticent, less intrepid, than the characters of *The Odd Women*, his most explicit examination of the concept of free union. Written six years earlier, it described a situation he had now to face himself. Then he had deplored duplicity and deception under such circumstances. 'I believe if a few men and women in prominent positions would contract marriage of a free kind, without priest or lawyer, open and defiantly, they would do more benefit to their kind than in any other possible way', says Mrs Cosgrove in that novel. In 1892 Everard Barfoot had not feared society's verdict. If Rhoda 'declared herself willing . . . to defy the world's opinion by becoming his wife without forms of mutual bondage – she was the woman he had imagined, and by her side he would go cheerfully on his way as a married man.' Gissing in 1898 had the same problem but less self-assurance: he was not prepared to be quite so brazen. One cannot help but be struck yet again by the resemblance of events in the novelist's life to those he put into his novels years earlier.

Finally he confided in Bertz, telling his friend that 'For the first time in my life I am happy!' In a long correspondence stretching back more than twelve years, this is the first genuinely good-humoured letter Gissing wrote to him.

Three months earlier the novelist had written to Gabrielle of his past life: 'Ten years ago, I desired literary reputation, but it seemed very, very far away. I suppose I may say that I have won it. In my wretched London lodgings, I longed for a little house in some beautiful part of the country, and thought it beyond possibility; yet here I am, in that very house . . . Shall I not, then, dare to hope for the supreme blessing – the crown of life?' Two months earlier, again going back a decade in memory, he had written: 'if you had known me ten years ago, you would never have cared for me. I had terrible faults, resulting partly from natural disposition, partly from an abnormal experience. I was mentally very immature; I was *gauche* and often *farouche*; in a word I was uncivilized.' He mentions vaguely 'that experience which was to serve me so well in literature, though at the time it seemed a mere disaster'. He talks about his years of 'terrible struggle' in London. Now, he says, he has mellowed, he has become civilized. He is ready for a civilized woman.

Wells had wanted some woman to 'sacrifice' herself for Gissing. Gabrielle now committed herself to making this sacrifice. 'Little by little, my existence has come out of darkness', Gissing wrote to her; 'step by step, from poverty to comfort, from obscurity to reputation; and now I have before me the supreme attainment – the crown of life!'

❧

CHAPTER 11

THE CROWN OF LIFE, 1898–1900

All at once, he thought amid his triumph of those unhappy ones whom the glory of love would never bless; those . . . born to a vain longing such as he had known, doomed to the dread solitude from which he by miracle had been saved.

The Crown of Life

The consensus of opinion among his friends and family was that he had started out with . . . 'a sound constitution' and had persistently undermined it by emotional strain, by eating the wrong sort of food, by continuing to work even when exhausted or actually ill on the grounds that other people had done it and so could he, and by never, ever, taking any real rest.

Tindall, *The Born Exile*

Passion and neurasthenia mean instability.

Huxley, *Brave New World*

I

GISSING was forty-one on 22 November 1898. His birthday found him working hard on *The Crown of Life,* which he expected to finish in January. He now changed literary agents, asking James B. Pinker to handle his work instead of Colles. He had increased his allowance to Edith to £2 a week, and as he would soon be supporting three establishments again he felt the need of a more aggressive agent. Pinker had that sort of reputation. He worked for some of the most distinguished writers of the day, including James, and later Conrad.

Virtually the only letters Gissing wrote now were to Gabrielle. He says in one of them that she represents to him a lifetime of striving: 'I loved you many and many a year before we met.' At the end of November he commented to her on *The Crown of Life* in these terms: 'In part it will aim at showing the worst side of English "Imperialism" – of that hateful spirit which, by its greed and arrogance, threatens such disturbance to the peace of the world, – the spirit represented in literature by Rudyard Kipling (a man who is doing, I fear, great harm).' In December he began to look forward to their spring reunion. But in the middle of the month, as he contemplated his future happiness, he was suddenly beset by guilty feelings about his past life. He wrote to Gabrielle: 'one troublesome thought mingles with my delight. I look back on my by-gone life, and I contrast it with the purity of yours . . . will you forgive me everything? Can you forget? . . . Indeed, *I* have all but forgotten; it is only now and then that the dark thought comes back. Say that you forgive me . . . Say that you will never look at that dark, hateful time.'

He also told her that Pye-Smith found his emphysema arrested. Although there was still a weakness of the throat and chest, it was possible, the doctor felt, that the spot in his lung might disappear altogether. At the same time Gissing declared himself pleased with *The Crown of Life*. 'The book excites me. I feel that I am saying something that ought to be said, and which will interest all the best readers . . . its aim is the encouragement of Peace.' He added a comment that could serve as an epigraph for almost any one of his novels: 'Of course the chief interest of the book . . . is the love-story, and as I draw towards the end I feel very strongly the emotions with which I am dealing artistically.' He concluded: 'A few days and it will be 1899 – the year to which all my life has unconsciously pointed . . . Ah, how I hoped, long ago, that I should win the love of a beautiful and noble woman!' Gabrielle was working on her translation of *New Grub Street*, and her letters were full of inquiries about English word-meanings. It is clear from the correspondence that Gissing was more truly bilingual than she was.

On New Year's Day 1899 Gissing addressed to her another passionate letter, once again full of self-reproach. His pride in himself, he says, 'has not saved me, as it should have done, from base things' in the past. It is also his pride

that has accounted for my solitude. Being poor and miserable, I have kept [my] sorrows to myself, have lived out of sight of people who could not understand me. Above all, my pride has held me from seeking the acquaintance of such women as would have been likely to excite my deeper emotions; I could not bear the thought of becoming enslaved to anyone who would probably regard me . . . with compassion.

Here is an accurate distillation of the emotion that prevented him for years from seeking the love of a truly congenial woman. He goes on to thank Gabrielle for the 'sacrifice' she will be making for him.

On 13 January Gissing received news of Gabrielle's father's death. Three days later he finished *The Crown of Life*, telling her that he could continue to work while she grieved only because of the seriousness of his subject: 'it is not a trivial novel that I am now completing . . . Under the guise of fiction, this book deals with the most solemn questions of life . . . it has never been my habit to write flippantly, idly; I have never written to gain money, to please the foolish. And my reward is that – however poor what I have done – I do not feel it ignoble.' Certainly he never wrote 'to please the foolish', but he had often enough written for money. Several days later he was able to report that Pinker liked *The Crown of Life*.

During the last week in January the novelist visited Wakefield and saw Walter, now seven years old. Walter was 'very tall for his age, and very intelligent', he told Gabrielle. 'It is noticeable that he excels in English composition . . . To me he is very affectionate.' He informed his mother and sisters that he would be moving to the Continent in the spring but did not say why. He gave Algernon, who was in poor health, £50 – an enormous slice of his resources given the expenses he would soon be incurring. On the way home he stopped off to see Miss Collet, to whom he confided his great secret. Her reaction was, 'Why not declare the truth, like George Eliot?' Gissing told Roberts that this would be difficult to do: Gabrielle and her mother 'would suffer terribly from the results . . . She has all sorts of semi-aristocratic relatives; it would be a terrific scandal.' For the sake of Gabrielle's relatives, Gissing wrote to Roberts, they would have to pretend to be formally married. Undoubtedly he did not like the idea of being involved in scandal himself. Miss Collet, as usual, proved to be a staunch friend, telling him that, whatever happened, 'Gabrielle shall never be without a friend and a home in England whilst I live.'

Pinker reported an offer from the *Pall Mall Gazette* of £25 for a 5,000-word story, and Gissing set to work on it late in January. Meanwhile Methuen offered £300 for *The Crown of Life*, plus a twenty percent royalty on the first 2,500 copies sold and 25 per cent thereafter. For the American edition Gissing would get £100 plus a fifteen percent royalty. The book would appear in the autumn. The £400 Gissing received for this novel was a career record. In February, despite a long bout of influenza followed by lung-congestion and pleurisy ('I am beginning to pay the penalty of many years of insufficient food and every kind of unhealthiness', he told Wells), he finished the story for the *Pall Mall Gazette* – called 'A Poor Gentleman' – and wrote another preface for the Rochester Edition of Dickens. His poor health continued into March. He felt so ill that he abandoned his diary altogether for two months – from late February to late April 1899. In March he went back to work briefly on *Veranilda* (tentatively called 'The Vanquished Roman').

The stream of letters to Gabrielle continued. 'I should not have lived through 1899 . . . but for you', he wrote. 'I was sinking, losing courage. Not even duty to the little boys would have kept me alive.' But still he had his dark moods. 'I cannot help feeling bitter against these men who are able to offer you legal marriage.' He writes angrily of English divorce laws:

What a vile, what an insensate law, is the law of divorce in England. A man is [insulted], outraged, ill-used, day after day, month after month, year after year, by his so-called wife; he behaves with perfect honour, with incredible patience, yet the insults have become ever more ferocious; he knows not an hour of peace under his own roof . . . finally he is *driven from home*, with every brutality that can be uttered – and the law refuses to break such a marriage! It drives me mad to think of this hideous folly and injustice.

But he cannot believe, he says, that their relationship will not be a fruitful one. It is an interesting statement.

I say to myself: 'Consider the story of your life. You began with nothing whatever but a good education. You were self-willed, passionate, foolish, and for years it seemed as if there could be no future for you. Nevertheless, by dint of hard work, you slowly, slowly, made your way in literature. Just when hope was beginning to shine, you ruined everything by an insane marriage. Yet still you worked on, insensibly hoping. At length there came to you the incredible thing – the love of a perfect woman. Is the story to end here? Is that love to be frustrate? I *cannot* believe it!'

If, as he goes on to speculate, 'emphysema can be produced by mental suffering', then it can be reversed by happiness. Gissing says: 'One reason why I think of my past life so bitterly, is because I *know* that my health was destroyed by the moral torments I underwent . . . my suffering . . . would have *killed* a weaker man . . . There is in me a *great* capacity for happiness . . . in my whole life I have not known one entirely happy day.' His doctor, he reports, recommends that he live in the mountains rather than in a city.

Gissing's awe at what was happening to him did not dissolve. But neither did the darker mood ever leave him: 'my English public will never *like* my books. I have not the true English note – the foolish optimism which is indispensable to popularity.' He goes on in this vein: '*My motives are too subtle*. You know that I constantly use *irony*; and this is never understood; it is all taken in the most stupid literal sense.' He is proud of his growing European reputation and hopes it won't be undermined by a French translation of *The Town Traveller* – which book, Gissing declares, 'I do not care much for' (the novel was never published in France). About this time Gabrielle read *Demos* and liked it. He told her it was 'one of my best, and . . . has more movement than most of my books'.

11

We must now review Gissing's writings of these months: the prefaces to Dickens (six of the eleven he wrote were completed by March 1899, the others were written between August 1899 and February 1900); 'A Poor Gentleman', one of Gissing's more interesting tales; and of course *The Crown of Life*.

There are no surprises in the prefaces to Dickens. Thackeray, Gissing declares, is the greater 'realist' (realism is defined as 'a severe chronicle of actual lives') but Dickens cannot be judged strictly by these standards. The realist, Gissing says in the preface to *Dombey and Son*, shows how things *would* turn out; Dickens showed how things may turn out for the best. 'His view of art involved compliance with ideals of ordinary folk . . . An instinctive sympathy with the moral . . . prejudices of the everyday man guided Dickens throughout his career . . . [He was] *a representative Englishman of the middle class.*'

Dickens's great *métier*, according to Gissing, is the depiction of London, its 'roads of mountainous ugliness, streets and byways remarkable only for degrees of discomfort and dirt and sordid struggle'. The portrait of London in *Oliver Twist* is brilliant in its 'squalid mystery and terror', its aspects of 'the grimly grotesque', its 'labyrinthine obscurity and lurid fascination'. People still see London with Dickens's eyes, Gissing says, and adds: 'The novelist's first duty is to make us see what he has seen himself, whether with the actual eye or with that of the imagination.' The artist's business 'is not to report life *in extenso*, but to convey to another mind some impression which it had made upon his own . . . To depict London was one of the ends for which Dickens was born.' Rob the Grinder may be 'the most truthful picture of London boyhood' ever painted. And the evocation of the city in *Bleak House*, more than anywhere else in Dickens the city Gissing saw, receives special attention: 'murky, swarming, rotting London, a marvellous rendering of the impression received by any imaginative person who in low spirits has had occasion to wander about London's streets'.

The Old Curiosity Shop is pronounced the work of 'an utterly conservative mind, ever looking backwards, lamenting every change, and dreading the new time that advanced'. He reminds us that Dickens's art is primarily concerned with the uncultured. 'The uncouth and the underbred play so vast a part in human life that to neglect them is to falsify; but only the rarest genius can turn them to worthy use.' While Dickens sympathizes with these people 'he never demands that they shall be raised above the status of poverty', Gissing says approvingly. '*Morally, he would change the world; socially, he is a thorough conservative.*'

The preface to *Bleak House*, while praising the novel, attacks Dickens for the excessive attention paid to low-life and the exaggerated delicacy of virtuous sentiment portrayed among the lower orders: 'Though virtue may exist in the ignorant and the poor and the debased, most assuredly the delicacies of virtue will not be found in them.' If anything is true of the English lower classes, Gissing declares, it is that, even 'supposing them to say or do a good thing, they will say or do it in the worst possible way . . . we can only mark with regret how the philanthropist often overcame the artist.' (See Appendix, p. 367.)

'A Poor Gentleman' is about an impoverished gentleman-bachelor living in lodgings in Islington. He has lost his money by making bad investments. Shy, irresolute, nervous, he is a vegetarian and a teetotaller, and he wears a moustache. He is lustreless in dress without being shabby. He walks everywhere, disdaining public transport. An apprentice bookbinder, he lives almost entirely in solitude. 'Poverty', the story says, 'is the great secluder . . . a sensitive man who no longer finds himself on equal terms with his natural associates, shrinks into loneliness, and learns . . . how very willing people are to forget his existence.' Furthermore: 'strange knowledge' comes to such men. They become familiar with 'wondrous economies, and . . . feel a sort of pride in [the] ultimate discovery of how little money is needed to support life'. The protagonist of this tale hides in horror from friends who knew him in palmier days: he tells the few acquaintances he has left that he lives among the poor to 'study' them. The utterly poor, the story concludes, have no idea of any other sort of life and so do not really suffer from want; it is only the declassed, who have known a breath of purer air, who suffer in this way.

The Crown of Life, Gissing's nineteenth published novel and
twenty-first published book, contains many familiar ingredients,
plus a few new elements. Gissing told Bertz that 'it is first and
foremost a love-story, but, blended with this, it contains a . . .
vigorous attack on militarism.' While the novel declares that love is
'the only thing in life *worth* thinking about', it also tries to
distinguish between different kinds of love – emphasizing, ultimately, the healing power of reciprocated feeling. 'How vast is the
distinction between love and sensuality, I hope to make clear',
Gissing had written to Gabrielle the previous autumn. The result is
a story largely about sexual desire. The effect of such desire on the
Gissing-*persona* of this novel – Piers Otway, who 'raves and
agonizes' night after night 'lying upon his bed' – is the central focus.
But other related concerns are woven through the novel, making
it one of Gissing's richest books as well as one of his most
shapeless.

We first see Piers Otway living in a house 'just too large to be
called a cottage; not quite old enough to be picturesque' – a suitably
anomalous home for a Gissing hero. This hero also happens to be
illegitimate, and illegitimacy is used as another symbol of social
anomalousness. Typically, his father dies intestate, and Piers
inherits nothing. But it is characteristic of Gissing's sympathy for
the anomalous man that he makes Piers become more successful
than his legitimate brothers, who ultimately lean on him for
support (just as Algernon leaned on Gissing).

As a poor young man, Piers falls in love with Irene Derwent,
wealthy and respectable. Being declassed by circumstances, he must
make money in order to reach 'the only end he felt worth living for
– an ideal marriage . . . there was for him but one prize worth
winning, the love of the ideal woman.' *The Crown of Life* is written
with the singular passion of a man who knows what it is to be
continually frustrated and to find the 'ideal woman' after years of
disappointed searching.

Like Gissing, Piers is promiscuous when young. Had he 'sought
patiently for his perfect wife', the novelist comments, 'somewhere
in the world he would have found her, could he but have subdued
himself to the high seriousness of the quest'. A few months earlier
Gissing might not have been so confident of this. He goes on: 'In a
youthful poem, [Piers] had sung of Love as "the crown of life" . . .
That crown he had missed, even as did the multitude of mankind.'
Irene seems impossibly above him, being the daughter of a rich
physician.

He stared forward into the coming years, and saw nothing that his soul desired. A life of solitude, of bitter frustration . . . the woman he longed for would never become his. He had not the power of inspiring love. The mere flesh would constrain him to marriage, a sordid union, a desecration of his ideal . . . What is life without love? . . . to him love meant communion with the noblest. Nature had kindled in him this fiery ambition only for his woe . . . Images of maddening beauty glowed upon him out of the darkness . . . He smothered cries of agony . . . For the men capable of passionate love (and they are few) to miss love is to miss everything.

In Gissing's letters to Gabrielle – as throughout his life – the same issues are raised, the same fears are present, the same goals are coveted, the same frustration is evident. Indeed, except for some of the political and moral issues it raises, *The Crown of Life* might well be a love-letter from first to last, an explanation to Gabrielle of everything that preceded her meeting with the novelist. Piers's general state of mind may remind us of Gissing's at the time he met Gabrielle: 'A terror fell upon him lest he should be fated never to know the supreme delight of which he was capable, and for which alone he lived . . . He trembled at the risks of every day; what was his assurance against the common ill-hap which might afflict him with disease, blight his life with accident, so that no woman's eye would ever be tempted to rest upon him?'

Throughout much of the story Irene seems to Piers an impossible ideal. Out of respect for her he gives up some of his more unsavoury habits. Seeing a man pick up a prostitute on a London street, 'a feeling of nausea' comes over him. His love cleanses him, makes him more fastidious. He becomes imbued with the idealist's fervour. In the lyrical passion of the next passage we may see the effect upon the novelist of his meeting and correspondence with the 'ideal woman':

what was marriage without ideal love? . . . The ordinary man . . . marries because he must, not because he has met with the true companion of his life; he mates to be quiet, to be comfortable, to get on with his work . . . Love in the high sense between man and woman is of all things the most rare . . . is not a great mutual passion the culminating height of that blind reproductive impulse from which life begins? Supreme desire; perfection of union. The purpose of Nature translated into human consciousness, become the glory of the highest soul, uttered in the lyric rapture of noblest speech.

Alter a phrase here and there and we could be reading almost any one of the letters Gissing wrote to Gabrielle during the winter of 1898–9. 'Men woefully deceive themselves', the novelist says, 'yearning for women whose image in their minds is a mere illusion, women who scarce for a day could bring them happiness, and whose companionship through life would become a curse'.

In Piers Otway's case, the temper which defies discouragement existed together with the intellect which ever tends to discourage, with the mind which probes appearances, makes war upon illusions. Hence his oft-varying moods, as the one or other part of him became ascendant. Hence his fervours of idealism, and the habit of destructive criticism which seemed inconsistent with them . . . Intensely self-conscious, he suffered much from a habit of comparing . . . himself with other men . . . who achieved things . . . He could not read a newspaper without reflecting, sometimes bitterly, on the careers and position of men whose names were prominent . . . Nothing so goaded his imagination as a report of the marriage of some leader in the world's game. He dwelt on these paragraphs, filled up the details, grew faint with realisation of the man's triumphant happiness . . . Portraits of brides in an illustrated paper sometimes wrought him to intolerable agitation – the mood of his early manhood.

Piers's love for Irene resembles Gissing's for Gabrielle in its intensity and texture – in detail, not merely in outline. It begins as an infatuation, growing by stages to a sort of idolatry. For Piers, the novel tells us, 'was one of those men who cannot live without a woman's image to worship . . . He mused upon her features till they became the ideal beauty; he clad her, body and soul, in all the riches of love's treasure-house; she was at length his crowned lady, his perfect vision of delight.' There is not even a pretence of fiction here: Gissing speaks directly of Gabrielle.

When Irene finally consents to be his, Piers's response recalls Gissing's after his conference with Gabrielle at Dorking in October 1898: 'You gave me the ideal of my life . . . something to live towards . . . I have loved you without hope; loved you because I had found the only one I could love . . . on and on to the end . . . You have given me a new life, a new soul!' The final sections of *The Crown of Life* reflect the novelist's happy frame of mind in January 1899: he was finishing the book in the certain knowledge that he and Gabrielle would be living together several months hence. She drew the novel out of him as surely as she drew out of him the love-letters of 1898 to 1899.

The 'modern' in all its aspects is attacked in the novel with special vehemence. Never, perhaps, did Gissing so savagely assault the values of his age. The 'modern tendencies which vulgarise' are insisted upon, as they were in *In the Year of Jubilee* and *The Whirlpool*. 'Our man of business is a creation of our century, and as bad a thing as it has produced', Piers declares. 'Commerce must be humanised . . . We invented machinery, and it has enslaved us – a rule of iron, the servile belief that money-making is an end in itself . . . Think how much sheer barbarism there is around us, from the brutal savage of the gutter to the cunning savage of the Stock Exchange!' The most memorable passage Gissing ever wrote on the vulgarity of commerce and its effects on contemporary urban life is to be found in this novel:

Piers Otway saw it all in a lurid light. These towering edifices with inscriptions numberless, announcing every imaginable form of trade . . . arrogant suggestions of triumph . . . titles of world-wide significance . . . vulgar names with more weight than those of princes . . . no nightmare was ever so crushing to one of Otway's mood. The brute force of money; the negation of the individual – these, the evils of our time, found their supreme expression in the City of London. Here was opulence at home and superb; here must poverty lurk and shrink, feeling itself alive only on sufferance; the din of highway and byway was a voice of blustering conquest, bidding the weaker to stand aside or be crushed. Here no man was a human being, but each merely a portion of an inconceivably complicated mechanism . . . The smooth working of the huge machine made it only the more sinister; one had but to remember what cold tyranny, what elaborate fraud, were served by its manifold ingenuities, only to think of the cries of anguish stifled by its monotonous roar.

Gissing's anti-Establishment bias is not so much a matter of political philosophy as of temperament; the modern city offends his aesthetic sense and exacerbates his neurasthenia. The vulgarity of money-worship, the negation of culture, the unimportance of individual feelings are epitomized for Gissing, as for Dickens before him, in the horrors of modern commerce, which interests itself in 'products' rather than individuals. The passage is one of the few in Gissing's novels that a Marxist might find congenial.

The by-products of this new vulgarity are enumerated. One is the increased importance of advertising, which Gissing found so offensive. It is specifically attacked here as the epitome of commercial vulgarity. Its chief proponent in *The Crown of Life* is an Italian named Florio, who declares that advertising is 'the triumph of the century, the supreme outcome of civilisation!'

But the greatest moral outgrowth of what Gissing calls, in the long passage quoted above, the 'voice of blustering conquest', is Imperialism which is destroying both the peace and the peace of mind of the world. An advocate of Imperialism in the novel is the obnoxious Arnold Jacks, who delivers 'a dribble of commonplaces' on the subject. His nature is meant to represent those forces of the English character Gissing struggled to portray in *The Crown of Life* as responsible for Imperialist ventures. 'The prime characteristic of this nation, that personal arrogance which is the root of English freedom, which accounts for everything best, and everything worst, in the growth of English power, possessed him to the exclusion of all less essential qualities. He was the subduer amazed by improbable defiance.' Arnold's father, the more sensible John Jacks, speaks for Gissing when he says:

I'm afraid the national character is degenerating. We were always too fond of liquor . . . but worse than that is our gambling . . . We're beginning, now, to gamble for slices of the world . . . Our pride, if we don't look out, will turn to bluffing and bullying . . . hear the roaring of the Jingoes . . . Johnson defined Patriotism . . . as the last refuge of a scoundrel; it looks as if it might presently be the last refuge of a fool.

Piers Otway joins in this lament, complaining, as Yeats was to do two decades later, that 'the best hold back, keep silence', while the worst make themselves heard. Piers says: 'We ought to be rapidly outgrowing warfare . . . It seems a commonplace that everyone should look to that end, and strive for it. Yet we're going back – there's a military reaction – fighting is glorified by everyone who has a loud voice, and in no country more than England.' He adds that 'the world's only hope' is 'peace made a religion. The forms don't matter; only let the supreme end be peace.' Irene's anti-jingoism is even more forcefully expressed; she too speaks for Gissing:

what has pluck or heroism to do with bloodshed? How can anyone imagine that courage is only shown in fighting? . . . one knows very well how easy it must be for any coward or brute, excited to madness, to become what's called a hero [in battle]. Heroism is noble courage in ordinary life . . . Every day some braver deed is done by plain men and women . . . than was ever known on the battlefield . . . In the commonest everyday home life, doesn't any man or woman have endless chances of being brave or a coward? And this is civilised courage, not the fury of a bull at a red rag.

Gissing's pacifism is expressed with passion and eloquence in *The Crown of Life*. He would have been one of the few Englishmen unsurprised by the outbreak of the Great War.

Also familiar to the Gissing reader here is the contempt some of the central characters harbour for the lower classes and all schemes of philanthropy. 'How it relieves one to say flatly that one does *not* love the multitude!' declares Mrs Borisoff, one of the novel's more sympathetic characters. Piers observes that nothing is too bad to say of 'the crowd . . . At its best, a smiling simpleton; at its worst, a murderous maniac'.

Another recognizable element is the book's perspective on marriage and the relation of the sexes, a perspective not limited to the story of Piers and Irene. The Hannafords, like Gissing and Edith, 'were completely alienated; but for their child, they would long ago have parted.' Unable to get a divorce because of the unwillingness of one partner, the other partner, as Gissing puts it, remains 'a martyr to national morality' – as he felt himself to be. Piers's father makes a disastrous marriage because of his incapacity for choice and deliberation when it comes to selecting a wife: 'He was ardent and impulsive; marriage becoming a necessity, he clutched at the first chance . . . and the result was calamitous.' Mrs Borisoff, on the other hand, has the sort of idealized wedded relationship Gissing so often thought about. She and her husband are good friends but find from time to time they must get away from one another. They go off on trips by themselves when they feel so inclined. 'Love has nothing whatever to do with marriage, in the statistical – the ordinary – sense of the term', Mrs Borisoff says. 'Marriage is a practical concern of mankind at large; Love is a personal experience of the very few . . . You can no more choose to be a lover, than to be a poet.'

From beginning to end *The Crown of Life*, one of Gissing's most interesting books, is imbued with the novelist's feeling that perhaps he was destined to love and be loved after all. Love is everywhere, on every page.

III

Meredith's advice notwithstanding – 'you cannot have novels on periods so long ago. A novel can only reflect successfully the moods of men and women around us' – Gissing continued to work sporadically on 'The Vanquished Roman' in the spring of 1899. He also visited Algernon in Worcestershire, where Margaret and Walter were staying on holiday. Gabrielle had suggested that he should bring his elder son with him to France and bring him up there, but this would have involved disclosure to the family of his marital status, and he was not prepared for that. A letter to Roberts shows evidence of Gissing's moodiness in the midst of prospective happiness. 'I wish I had died ten years ago', he told his friend. 'I should have gone away with some hope for civilisation, of which I now have none. One's choice seems to be between death in the workhouse, or by some ruffian's bullet. As for those who come after one, it is too black to think about.' He told Bertz that Methuen had decided to delay publication of *The Crown of Life* because *The Town Traveller* was still selling. 'I think it a mistake, the story being so opportune; but publishers are *always* making mistakes.' This mistake was destined to be a very bad one indeed.

Meanwhile the letters to Gabrielle continued to pour out of Dorking. He reported on the visit of the doctor, who told him that his solitary life and rigorous working habits were 'suicidal' and could lead to a total breakdown in health. 'It would have killed a weaker man, he said, long ago.' But then 'Not another man in England is so lonely as I have been.' The doctor recommended more exposure to 'open air' and said that the novelist could expect to live many years, provided he changed his mode of life. 'You, and you alone, have kept me alive', he told Gabrielle. Still, as long as they were separated he could not help having 'fits of misery':

It is mental illness, resulting from a whole lifetime of wretchedness. Since I was a boy until the day you said you loved me, I had never known a tranquil mind. The reason? – Poverty, frustrate ambition, and above all vain desire of love. Combine these things with the imaginative temper, and *must* not . . . the gravest mental suffering . . . result? . . . those black moods . . . result . . . from long, long years of solitude . . . private misery [has]kept me apart from the world.

Gissing worried that his growing fame would result in his private circumstances becoming known. There was much that he did not want Edith or the British public to know. He also worried as usual about money: 'I rank (from the pecuniary point of view) with the poorest of English novelists . . . There is something in my books which English people really *dislike*.' He told Gabrielle he hoped to support their household without using any of her money, but as it turned out she did have to contribute toward their expenses.

Their reunion was now planned to take place in Rouen in May. Mid-April found the novelist packing up his library and making other last-minute preparations for his departure from England. He stored his furniture once again, and on 22 April left Dorking for Lewes, where he would pass the time before his embarkation for France. He wrote farewell notes to Wells full of complaints ('I have got into such a loathing of the present world that I *would* not write about it just now'; 'publishers will take their own course, and on the whole they seem to know less about publishing than any order of men'); and to Hick – the last for a year and a half – containing a description of his new novel ('anti-jingo, and therefore not at all likely to be popular. But I have done without popularity for twenty years and more and must go on to the end'). Two days before he was due to travel to France, he wrote to Gabrielle: 'As this is *my last letter* to you . . . I want to ask you to forgive me all the troubles . . . which I have caused you since first we met . . . I have now but one aim in life, to prove myself worthy of the great sacrifices you have made for my sake . . . For the first time in my life I shall know happiness.'

On 6 May 1899 he crossed to Dieppe and went immediately to Rouen, where Gabrielle and her mother were waiting. On the next evening, at the cathedral in Rouen, Gissing and Gabrielle were 'married', her mother being the only witness. Gissing put on Gabrielle's finger one of the two wedding rings he had bought in London. 'In the evening, our ceremony. Dear Maman's emotion, and G.'s sweet dignity.' Such is the only account Gissing gives in the diary of this, his third wedding ceremony. Nor did he write of it to any of his family or friends, even those few who knew what he was doing. The whole business 'had . . . to be carried out with absolute secrecy toward his actual wife and most of his English friends', Wells commented later. 'Those of us who knew, thought that if he could be put into such circumstances as would at last give his very fine brain a fair chance to do good work, connivance in so petty a deception was a negligible price to pay.' Mme Fleury had probably learned from her daughter the true state of things, but she nobly notified her friends and relatives of Gabrielle's new status by sending out visiting cards on which her daughter's maiden name was crossed out and 'Gissing' substituted in its place.

IV

Gissing and Gabrielle stayed in Normandy for three weeks. 'Absolute perfection of mind and character!' the novelist wrote of her to Bertz. He added: 'For the first time in my life, I am at ease.' Bertz was one of his few correspondents throughout the rest of 1899. Early in June the pair returned to Gabrielle's mother's apartment in the Rue de Siam (Passy). The novelist settled down to a number of tasks, writing three more prefaces to Dickens and several short stories.

On 29 June he began a book about his travels in Calabria in the autumn of 1897. This was to be *By the Ionian Sea*. Writing easily, he completed the first nine chapters in two weeks. He was comfortable and content. Gabrielle's friends received him with respect, and his working conditions were ideal. Most importantly, his relationship with her seemed to be flawless. 'I have perfect intellectual companionship', he told Clara Collet. In mid-July he and Gabrielle and her mother went off on a two-months holiday to the Swiss Alps, where on 9 August 1899 he finished *By the Ionian Sea*. Also while in Switzerland he corrected proofs of *The Crown of Life* ('My best book yet for style', he noted in his diary): and wrote another story, 'Humplebee'. He told Bertz that his new life was

very different from what it was in my old miserable loneliness. I still have to shake off the effects of that long wretchedness, and perhaps I shall never wholly attain to a cheerfulness like that of other men. But, after all I have endured, an extraordinary piece of good fortune has befallen me – a thing beyond all hope. Perhaps my life may end in a tranquillity unforeseen.

As always, however, his moods varied. Reflecting on the myriad demands upon his income, he wrote petulantly to Bertz: 'I . . . shall have to be working furiously all through the winter; for the scoundrel English public will not buy my books, and my need of money will compel me to ceaseless production.'

By late September he and Gabrielle were back in Paris, where he found a cheque for £254 – the balance, after deductions, of his advance for the English and American editions of *The Crown of Life*, now scheduled for October publication. On 1 October Gissing began a new novel called 'The Coming Man' (eventually *Our Friend the Charlatan*). During this month he rewrote the early chapters several times, suddenly finding it difficult to write again. He began to be homesick for England. The Boer War had broken out, and he agreed to write a brief anti-jingo piece for a London weekly – an unpopular position to adopt at the time. He received praise from Hardy and others for his stance, but political events were to have a disastrous effect on the reception of his new novel.

By the Ionian Sea was published serially the following year. In the introductory chapter Gissing attempts to explain the particular appeal 'Magna Graecia' has for him. He says:

Every man has his intellectual desire; mine is to escape life as I know it and dream myself into that old world which was the imaginative delight of my boyhood. The names of Greece and Italy draw me as no others; they make me young again, and restore the keen impressions of that time when every new page of Greek or Latin was a new perception of things beautiful. The world of the Greeks and Romans is my land of romance.

To-day seemed to him an unreality, an idle impertinence; the real was that long-buried past which gave its meaning to all about him.

The lyrical tone is typical of the book, and *By the Ionian Sea* contains some of Gissing's best writing.

It follows faithfully enough the novelist's 1897 itinerary (Paola, Taranto, Cotrone, Catanzaro, Squillace, Reggio, and so on) and is based largely on the diary entries he made at the time. The great clarity of its style and the skill with which a number of ancient sites are viewed against the background of contemporary places and their inhabitants, undoubtedly helps account for the popularity of the volume – despite the unflattering comparison of English as opposed to Italian 'provincials'. 'These people have an innate respect for things of the mind, which is totally lacking to a typical Englishman.' Another passage likely to offend English readers at the time was prompted by his coming across the grave of a young soldier in Reggio:

The very insignificance of this young life makes the fact more touching; one thinks of the unnumbered lives sacrificed upon this soil, age after age, to the wild-beast instinct of mankind, and how pathetic the attempt to preserve the memory of one boy, so soon to become a meaningless name! His own voice seems to plead with us for a regretful thought, to speak from the stone in sad arraignment of tyranny and bloodshed. A voice which has no accent of hope. In the days to come, as through all time that is past, man will lord it over his fellows, and earth will be stained red from veins of young and old. That sweet-sounding name of *patria* becomes an illusion and a curse; linked with the pretentious modernism, *civilization*, it serves as plea to the latter-day barbarian, ravening and reckless under his civil garb.

A scholar as well as a novelist, Gissing was equipped to recapture for a modern audience 'the vanished life so dear to my imagination'. After all, as he says while describing the illness he suffered at Cotrone, 'it is better to die in a hovel by the Ionian Sea than in a cellar at Shoreditch.'

One remembers all [the Italian people] have suffered, all they have achieved in spite of wrong. Brute races have flung themselves, one after another, upon this sweet and glorious land; conquest and slavery, from age to age, have been the people's lot. Tread where one will, the soil has been drenched with blood. An immemorial woe sounds even through the lilting notes of Italian gaiety. It is a country wearied and regretful, looking ever backward to the things of old; trivial in its latter life, and unable to hope sincerely for the future.

As he looked his last upon the Ionian Sea, he tells us that he wished it were his so that he could 'wander endlessly amid the silence of the ancient world, to-day and all its sounds forgotten'. On this familiar note *By the Ionian Sea*, like several of his best works almost completely unknown to modern readers, comes to an end.

v

Late in October Miss Collet visited Paris and met Gabrielle. It was the beginning of a friendship that was to survive Gissing's death. Meanwhile he agreed to write a story (4,000 words for £20) for Shorter's new weekly, the *Sphere*. He awaited word of the first reviews of *The Crown of Life* with gloomy foreboding. 'It comes either very inappropriately, or just at the right moment. We shall see', he wrote to Bertz. 'People don't like me as an author, though they speak of me with a certain respect.'

The Crown of Life did appear at the most inopportune moment. As always in the first stages of any war, patriotic feeling was running high, fanned into flame by early disasters sustained by British troops in Africa. Methuen at first tried to cash in on the book's topicality by referring to its denunciation of Imperialism but very quickly the publishers saw their mistake and deleted from their meagre advertising any mention of the subject. But it could not be helped: the novel ran counter to popular feeling of the day, and suffered accordingly. Had it been published in the spring of 1899, as Gissing had wanted, it might well have had a different fate.

In the *Review of the Week* Roberts described the book's discussion of European politics as naïve. *Literature* called the novel 'commonplace . . . the sort of story one is accustomed to expect from lady novelists of the older school'. The *Pall Mall Gazette* (no longer, as in the heyday of W. T. Stead and John Morley, a fountainhead of liberalism), the *Speaker*, the *Guardian*, and even the *Daily Chronicle* attacked *The Crown of Life* with venom. Many other periodicals – including the *Illustrated London News*, the *Sketch*, the *Daily Telegraph*, and *The Times* – simply refused to notice the book at all.

There were a few friendly reviews. The *Graphic* called the novel Gissing's best, the pacifist *New Age* praised it, and the *St. James's Gazette* described it as 'a novel of the first rank'. Abroad the volume could be reviewed with more detachment. In Australia, for example, the *Book Lover*, in a notice that found its way into Gissing's hands, called him a 'genius', a 'master hand', and declared that he would be 'read more by the next generation than he is by this . . . The historian of the future will find in *The Crown of Life* valuable materials and testimony, when he comes to write the social history of the nineteenth century.'

The Crown of Life also called forth two new assessments of Gissing in the public press. In the *Academy* Arnold Bennett pronounced *Demos* Gissing's greatest novel and generally praised the early slum-life tales at the expense of the more recent ones. Gissing, he said, was a realist, not a pessimist: 'To take the common grey things which people know and despise, and, without tampering, to disclose their epic significance, their essential grandeur – that is realism . . . it is art, precious and indisputable. Such art has Mr Gissing accomplished.' He noted Gissing's obsession with social distinctions; he was sensitive to 'the most delicate *nuances* of them'. Gissing 'has that peculiar moral significance and weight which exist apart from . . . popularity', Bennett declared. He noted that there was little in Gissing's books 'to attract, and much to repel, the general gaze'. 'His novels contain less of potential popularity than those of almost any other living novelist of rank.' In an article in the *National Review* called 'The Slum Movement in Fiction', Gissing was said to be the master of low-life; little attention was paid here either to his later work. 'As no one else has ever done . . . [and] as no one else will ever do – Gissing writes the tragedy of Want.' *The Crown of Life* was not mentioned.

In 1912 the novel still had not sold out its (very large) first edition of 4,500 copies. Rarely reprinted since, for years it was one of the most difficult of Gissing's books to obtain. The novelist himself lost interest in it soon enough. As early as 7 November 1899 he noted in a long letter to Clodd that Meredith did not greatly care for it. That was no surprise for Meredith was a fierce militarist. But Gissing admitted that he feared 'the thing had small value'. He sounded less resigned in a letter to Bertz, who was told that *The Crown of Life* had fallen flat on its face in England, was being coldly reviewed, and would 'soon cease to be spoken of at all. This is worse luck than has befallen any book of mine for several years': indeed, the last novel of his to be so badly treated was *Born in Exile* seven years earlier. He also reiterated his worries about world militarism. 'No man living more abhors the influence of Kipling than I do', he added. 'Nothing too severe can be said against the brute savagery of Kipling's latest work [*Stalky & Co.*] . . . Such a book ought to be burnt by the hangman! It is the most vulgar and bestial production of our times.' *Stalky & Co.*, a glorification of war, was selling like hot cakes during that first autumn of the Boer War while *The Crown of Life* languished on the shelves.

In November Gissing put 'The Coming Man' aside, convinced he needed to go to the English Midlands to gather material for it, and began another novel called 'Among the Prophets'. He told Bertz it was about 'the restless seeking for a *new religion*, which leads people into Theosophy, Spiritualism, and things still more foolish'. To Miss Collet he described it similarly as being about 'new religious crazes of various kinds'. The fate of 'Among the Prophets' was an unhappy one. Gissing wrote the entire novel between late November 1899 and late January 1900, grew dissatisfied with it, asked Pinker (who disliked it) to return the manuscript to him, and ultimately destroyed it. No copies survive.

Gissing was forty-two on 22 November 1899. The war, the failure of *The Crown of Life*, the impasse he had reached in writing 'The Coming Man', and (a few weeks later) the demise of the firm of Lawrence and Bullen, combined to put him in a dark mood in December. The end of the year found him bitter. 'I limit my [New Year] wishes to individuals. Nations . . . are brutally stupid, and all one can hope is that any given mass will not bring too heavy a curse on the rest of the world', he wrote to Miss Collet. 'My agent cheers me with his prophecies that no books will be read in England for long enough to come', he added. 'That *my* books will not be read is a pretty safe forecast . . . the other novelists have been making their hundred thousand copies lately.' To Walter he sent a passionate indictment of war. 'You must understand . . . that *War* is a horrible thing which ought to be left to savages . . . What we ought to be proud of is peace and kindness – not fighting and hatred.' On New Year's Eve he wrote a gloomy letter to Bertz decrying 'this war-fever which has possession of the English.' He totalled up his earnings for the year and found the amount to be £427 – one of his better years, but by no means his best.

VI

In January 1900 a brief essay by Gissing called 'The Coming of the Preacher' was published in *Literature*. It argued that no great artists were working at the moment. 'The intellect of mankind is too uneasy; life is too anarchic. There will appear no great imaginative craftsman until the soul of the world has in some degree been set at rest.' Meanwhile Gissing laboured over 'Among the Prophets' and several stories. 'Just as I was hoping to earn a little more money comes this scoundrelly war, and the ruin of the book trade', he told Ellen. 'It's a dreary outlook for the next year or two.' He was again subject to 'ceaseless torment about money . . . And so it will be to the end.' At the same time he read Jean Izoulet's *La Cité moderne*

(1894), a treatise arguing for the unity of mankind and attempting to trace all moral good from the principle of workers' associations; it was from this book that the protagonist of *Our Friend the Charlatan* would filch his 'biosociological' theories. Late in January he finished 'Among the Prophets' and the last of his prefaces to Dickens. He continued to grumble about the war, declaring to Bertz that the great enemy of peace was finance, and telling Roberts with tragic irony that he would rather never see Walter again 'than foresee him marching in ranks, butchering or [being] butchered.' At last some good news arrived. Pinker sold the serial rights for *By the Ionian Sea* to the *Fortnightly Review* for 120 guineas: it would run from May to October 1900. Gissing turned his attention again to 'The Coming Man' and to several ideas he had for short stories.

'The House of Cobwebs' and 'The Pig and Whistle' were written in March. The former, another exercise in autobiography, is about a young novelist living in lodgings on a tiny income who is forced to become an expert in domestic economy in the course of pursuing his craft. He feels he has talent, is destined to lead 'a new school of fiction', and persists; some day, he hopes, he can live in the country. Meanwhile he has his mail sent to the post office to avoid 'shocking the nerves of the postman' by having it delivered to his wretched lodgings. He won't accept invitations for fear of betraying his poverty. He finishes his great book and has to sell the copyright for £50. Gissing's early years of struggle continued to haunt him. Indeed, he was struggling still, for the income he was earning now, in 1900, was only just sufficient to meet his heavy expenses. 'The Pig and Whistle' is about a man who declasses himself by changing his profession from schoolmaster to innkeeper in order to be assured of a steady income. The two tales were placed by Pinker for nearly £64 altogether. Gissing's stories, at least, continued to command high prices.

His inability to make any progress on 'The Coming Man' was a result, Gissing thought, of his continued absence from England. He needed to spend time there gathering materials, for he had now been away from his native land for the unprecedentedly long period of ten months. Gabrielle's brother René, who had come to live with them in the Passy flat, led an unruly life which began to interfere with the novelist's serenity and comfort. Gabrielle had to spend some of her time nursing her mother, who was unwell. Gissing's 'mother-in-law' still ruled the kitchen, however, and the meals she served were apparently spare ones. The novelist began to chafe. He decided to spend the month of April in England. 'It is almost impossible to do all one's business by correspondence, and then too I find it necessary to collect some material for my next novel', he told Bertz. He added that 'One can *never* trust a publisher', and he resumed his attack on Kipling who was 'doing incalculable harm to the human race'.

Early in April Gissing left for England. He visited Clodd and Pinker in London and spent more than a week in Wakefield (his mother and sisters still knew nothing of Gabrielle). He devoted another week, in Lincoln, to gathering material he would use in *Our Friend the Charlatan*. From Lincoln he went to St. Neots (which he would make use of both in *The Ryecroft Papers* and *Will Warburton*). He then returned to Clodd's house in London ('we had a very pleasant talk on Trollope's and Jane Austen's novels', Clodd recorded in his diary; Gissing assessed 'Trollope fairly high and Jane Austen very high in her quiet mordant humour'). The novelist wrote to Gabrielle: 'I am coming back very rich in materials. My mind is full of the new pictures . . . Happily, you understand better now the conditions of my work.' It would appear that she had objected to his going. He saw Clara Collet, Bullen, and Roberts, and visited Meredith at Box Hill for the last time. He then stayed with the Wellses for several days at their new House in Sandgate, where he also saw Hick. On 1 May 1900, the day on which the first instalment of *By the Ionian Sea* appeared in the *Fortnightly*, he returned to Paris.

There he got back to work on 'The Coming Man', recasting the whole thing in outline. He finished correcting the last proofs of *By the Ionian Sea* for the *Fortnightly*, and wrote a story, 'A Daughter of the Lodge' – like 'Humplebee' a tale of the victimization of a working-class family by a wealthy one. In reply to a letter from Miss Collet referring joyfully to the British victory at Mafeking, Gissing wrote sternly: 'I entreat you . . . not to be carried away by a natural patriotism, which, just now, may lead one into sheer betrayal of one's country's better hope . . . a just and great cause has rarely declared itself in blind violence.'

For the summer a villa had been rented at St. Honoré-les-Bains in Nièvre, and late in May Gissing, Gabrielle, and her mother travelled there and settled in for a five-months' stay. The novelist immediately immersed himself in the new book: 'Better work, I think, than I have done since "New Grub Street"', he recorded in his diary. He liked the villa, which was situated in the midst of lush vegetation and picturesque scenery.

On the first day of June Gissing received some welcome news:

Chapman and Hall had paid £130 for the cloth edition of *By the Ionian Sea*. Publication of an illustrated volume, based on sketches by Gissing himself, was scheduled for the following year, 1901. The great little book thus earned him over £255 altogether.

During the summer he worked steadily on 'The Coming Man' and made substantial progress. Further news from Pinker was both good and bad: sale of the stories 'The Scrupulous Father' and 'The Pig and Whistle' on advantageous terms, and the recommendation that 'Among the Prophets', which he had been trying unsuccessfully to place since February, should be held over. Gissing readily agreed. His mood remained sunny. 'I enjoy my quiet life here', he wrote to Clodd from St. Honoré-les-Bains. 'The country delights me', he told Walter. 'It is wonderfully like England.' He added: 'I am working better than for a long time . . . I can write nearly seven hours daily.'

Early in August Gissing wrote a long and interesting letter to Bertz. On the subject of war he struck, as so often, a remarkably prophetic note:

The newspapers lately have made me ill. It is to be feared that never again in our lifetime shall we see peace and quietness . . . A period of struggle for existence beween the nations seems to have begun, and indeed it will obviously soon be a struggle for the very means of life. This may . . . well result in a period of semi-barbarism, until – perhaps by immense slaughter, perhaps by famine and epidemics – the numbers of the human race are once more reduced.

Gissing told Bertz that he had just been paid for French translation rights of *The Unclassed* (no translation ever appeared): 'The old "Unclassed"! It was written a lifetime ago.' He complained bitterly once again about the moderate sales of his books. There were no good novelists around any more, he declared; what could one think of a reading public that bought up Hall Caine and Marie Corelli in such numbers? 'It is . . . humiliating to have to live by story-telling in a time which condemns one to mediocrity.'

About this time both Miss Orme and Clodd wrote that gossip about his private life was circulating in England. 'I knew too well that sooner or later talk would begin', he told Clodd. 'To me . . .what people say is indifferent, but I am always anxious on account of the woman who is my real wife . . . I can only live quietly on, and work. My part is chosen; there is no return, nor shall I ever wish it.' The French, he said, supposed his 'marriage' to Gabrielle to be a legal one. 'I must brave it out, satisfied with the acquaintance of a few reasonable people who know the truth, and content to let others, as long as possible, be in the dark. I do them no wrong.'

'The Coming Man' was finished on 29 August 1900. Three days later Gissing began a new book called 'An Author at Grass' (eventually *The Private Papers of Henry Ryecroft*). He described it to Bertz:

I imagine an author who has led a long Grub Street life, and who, at the age of fifty, is blest with a legacy which gives him £300 a year . . . he goes down into Somerset, establishes himself in a cottage, and passes the last five years of his life in wonderful calm and contentment. During this time he keeps a diary . . . occasional jottings of his experience and thought and memories. I, at his death, am supposed to publish selections . . . it is a great rest to my mind after so much fiction of the ordinary sort . . . the thing is doing me good.

Thus the beginnings of his most popular book.

Wells wrote praising *By the Ionian Sea* and told Gissing that his neighbour Joseph Conrad borrowed each instalment of the *Fortnightly* while the serial was running. The first draft of 'An Author at Grass' (later extensively revised) was completed on 23 October, less than two months after it had been begun. 'Have great faith in this little book', Gissing recorded in his diary. He told Bertz:

it is better than anything I have yet done – of that I feel no doubt. As to its reception by the public, that is another matter. I have expressed very freely my views with regard to the present tendencies of English life; but, at the same time, I have put into relief the old English virtues – so there will be things pleasant as well as disagreeable.

He was not sanguine, after the disaster of *The Crown of Life*, about the public's view of him. To Miss Collet, after the usual warnings about current events ('Who knows what fantastic horrors lie in wait for the world. It is at least a century and a half since civilisation was in so bad a state'), he also gave an account of *An Author at Grass*. 'A strange miscellany, this book, but, as a bit of English, the best I have yet done', he concluded.

The period in St. Honoré-les-Bains had been one of the most productive of his life. The party left on 1 November, and went to visit some of Gabrielle's relatives at Nevers in the Loire Valley – who later remembered the novelist as a sad, quiet man greatly worried about the children he had left in England. Gissing, Gabrielle, and Mme Fleury arrived back in Paris three days before the novelist's forty-third birthday.

VII

The two books Gissing brought back from Nièvre with him in November 1900 were 'The Coming Man' (published in 1901 as *Our Friend the Charlatan*) and 'An Author at Grass' (published serially in 1902 to 1903 under this title and in cloth in 1903 as *The Private Papers of Henry Ryecroft*). They vary greatly in quality. As I have suggested throughout, Gissing could only successfully write about himself. *Our Friend the Charlatan*, one of his least autobiographical novels, ranks just above *The Town Traveller* and the unfinished *Veranilda* among his undistinguished performances; *The Ryecroft Papers*, which is transparent autobiography from first to last, is one of his better books, and one of the most popular. I refrain from calling *The Ryecroft Papers* a 'great novel' because it is less fiction than a thinly disguised personal memoir. *Our Friend the Charlatan*, on the other hand, is a typical product of Gissing's satirical impulse: a comedy which is not amusing and which suffers mightily from authorial detachment. It is one of the least passionate, least eloquent, least interesting of Gissing's published works.

The satirist must be detached from his subject; he must stand away from it as he detonates the charges he has laid. In the instance of *Our Friend the Charlatan* – Gissing's twentieth published novel since 1880, and his twenty-third published volume – a curiously disembodied book is the result. None of the characters is especially admirable, though several of them (Lord Dymchurch, Lady Ogram, Constance Bride) are memorable. Unfortunately the protagonist, Dyce Lashmar, is thoroughly unlikeable and utterly unconvincing. No one could be less like Gissing himself. Into dishonest, hypocritical, insincere men the novelist had very little insight: for once he was writing about someone he knew nothing about. True, there are familiar undertones: Lashmar's yearning for financial independence, his attractiveness to women, his contemplation of suicide, his hatred of 'democracy', his 'frank contempt of the average man', his lack of sympathy for the down and out combined with his Reardonesque conviction that 'as often as not . . . the true leaders of mankind . . . struggle through their lives in poverty and neglect' and 'perish . . . for want of a little money!'

But Lashmar is not a 'Gissing-*persona*'; on the contrary, he is meant to epitomize the modern era. In his lack of principles, his insincerity, his discontent, he represents for Gissing the mediocre spirit of the age. Like Dalmaine in *Thyrza*, he is a political charlatan, pretending to have popular sympathies; like Peak in *Born in Exile,* he adopts philosophical principles in order to propitiate particular people. A moral chameleon, Lashmar 'excelled in intellectual plausibility': he is the child 'of a time which subdues everything to interest, which fosters vanity and chills the heart'. He is also seen as a disciple of Nietzsche – identified here as the father of 'the jingo impulse, and all sorts of forces making for animalism'.

Lashmar's father, a clergyman, makes one of the novel's most direct comments on the modern age:

Christianity has . . . utterly, absolutely, glaringly failed. At this moment the world . . . holds more potential barbarism than did the Roman Empire under the Antonines. Wherever I look, I see a monstrous contrast between the professions and the practice, between the assumed and the actual aims, of so-called Christian peoples. Christianity has failed to conquer the human heart.

Nor does the answer lie in political action. As in *Denzil Quarrier,* politicians are perceived as frauds. The novel tells us that 'speciousness' is the prime requisite of a successful politician; that 'Most men who go in for a Parliamentary career regard it either as a business by which they and their friends are to profit, or as an easy way of gratifying their personal vanity and ambition'; and that politics is only 'a game . . . a relaxation from serious thought and work.' The member in the seat Lashmar has his eye on 'can't put together three sentences; he never in his life had an idea. The man is a mere money-sack, propped up by toadies and imbeciles.' In *Our Friend the Charlatan* there is admiration for no one, for nothing; it is unrelieved unpleasantness from beginning to end, a Waste Land without heart or soul, full of hatred and venom.

One of the few sympathetic characters is Lord Dymchurch, a man with a title but no money, and thus 'declassed'. Ultimately he decides to become a farmer, his return to the land an emblem of his disgust with the urban social life men of his caste are expected to lead. Like Gissing he is easily discomfited, always needs money, yearns to meet educated women, dislikes emancipated women ('women militant, women in the public eye, were . . . unpleasing to him'), detests 'the craze for quasi-scientific phraseology, for sonorous explanations of the inexplicable', hates metaphysics and sociology, is naturally refined, and has two sisters in the country. 'No man saw more clearly how much there was of vanity and of evil in the unrest which rules our time. He was possessed by that turbid idealism which, in the tumult of a day without conscious guidance, is the peril of gentle souls.' He worries about 'the hostile forces everywhere leagued against' the human race: 'Life was a perpetual struggle, and, let dreamers say what they might, could never be anything else.' He doesn't care 'a rap for mankind at large . . . I ask only to be left alone, and to satisfy in quiet my sense of self-respect.' The declassed, neurasthenic nobleman would have made a much more interesting and congenial protagonist than Dyce Lashmar, the scheming, amoral anti-hero who dominates so many pages of the novel and makes it so dull.

There is also, of course, a sexual theme. Man and woman, the novel declares, are 'condemned by nature to mutual hostility'; for most men, living with a woman means 'Thought and talk drowned by a scream; nerves worried into fiddle-strings.' Was Gissing still thinking of his past life? Or was he, after only a year and a half of 'marriage' with Gabrielle, already growing restive? We know that Gissing never remained content for long. In his desire 'to unite irreconcilable things', did he contemplate trying, for example, to reconcile a French wife to an English residence? His letters of this time betray some homesickness. And his fiction, as we know, often anticipates his own future actions – or perhaps gives voice to those feelings just below the surface of conscious thought. *The Ryecroft Papers* expresses, among other things, Gissing's deep love of the English countryside and the 'contemptuous impatience' he often felt in foreign places. If *Our Friend the Charlatan* suggests a subterranean unease, *The Ryecroft Papers* even more unmistakably articulates the novelist's unchanging Englishness. Indeed, it is his most 'English' production of all.

Ryecroft speaks of missing, when out of the country, England's 'Sunday quietude'; of his love of English landscape painters; the comfort, 'stability', and order of life in England; and even the virtues of the English weather ('A better climate does not exist – for healthy people'). Significantly, there is a good deal of praise for English cooking: 'English victuals are . . . the best in the world, and English cookery is the wholesomest and the most appetizing.' English meat is lauded, foreign sauces condemned. All of this undoubtedly was aimed at the two French ladies who were keeping house for him. Nothing could more clearly betray his restiveness (and indeed, the novelist's letters were soon to complain bitterly about his French diet). On the subject of 'Englishness' Ryecroft makes an unequivocal statement about himself: 'I am quite sure that many people who have known me casually would say that my fault is a lack of geniality. To show my true self, I must be in the right mood and the right circumstances – which . . . is merely as much as saying that I am decidedly English.' Gissing's growing dissatisfaction with his French life is apparent.

Lest there be any doubt that Henry Ryecroft speaks with Gissing's voice – that he *is* Gissing, hardly disguised – consider the following. Ryecroft mentions his few friends. One of them, whose initials are 'E.B.', lives in Germany, and has long been a faithful correspondent:

For many and many a year [his] letters have made a pleasant incident in my life; more than that, they have often brought me help and comfort. It must be a rare thing for friendly correspondence to go on during the greater part of a lifetime between men of different nationalities who see each other not twice in two decades. We were young men when we first met in London, poor, struggling, full of hopes and ideals; now we look back upon those far memories from the autumn of life.

Another close friend is a novelist who earns two thousand a year from his books and 'feels a certain respect for some of my work', says Ryecroft, but not much more. No pretence of fiction is made in these accounts of Bertz and Wells. But this is by no means all. Ryecroft's account of his early days as a tutor; the story he tells (also told in *The Unclassed*) of the purchase of a first edition of Gibbon which he carried back a volume at a time to his lodgings in Islington; his stated desire 'once more before I die' to read *Don Quixote* (shortly after this Gissing began to learn Spanish in order to read it in the original); the story (recounted in a Commonplace Book entry for 1892) of the working-class man observed ordering a steak in a restaurant who couldn't work out how to eat it; the tale of the unsolicited descriptive piece published by a newspaper a day after it was submitted: a re-telling of the circumstances surrounding publication of Gissing's 'On Battersea Bridge' in 1883; the story of the steamer voyage from Corfu to Brindisi during which the ship's captain was frightened by a storm into taking refuge along the coast of Albania; the account of Ryecroft's passion for foreign travel as a young man ('to think of Italy was to feel myself goaded by a longing which at times made me literally ill') . . . Then came into my hands a . . . poor little . . . sum of money . . . for a book I had written' – all of these things are taken from Gissing's life, drawn upon without any attempt at disguise.

Ryecroft tells the reader: 'I had in me the making of a scholar. With leisure and tranquillity of mind, I should have amassed learning. Within the walls of a college, I should have lived so happily, so harmlessly, my imagination ever busy with the old world . . .'. His subjects are literature and history, and the latter has taught him to recognize the violence of man's past. This section of *The Ryecroft Papers* could just as easily be part of *In the Year of Jubilee* or *The Whirlpool*, or of a letter to Roberts or Miss Collet:

If historic times had a voice, it would sound as one long moan of anguish . . . History is a nightmare of horrors . . . make real to yourself the vision of every blood-stained page – stand in the presence of the ravening conqueror, the savage tyrant – tread the stones of the dungeon and the torture-room – feel the fire of the stake – hear the cries of that multitude which no man can number, the victims of calamity, of oppression, of fierce injustice in its myriad forms, in every land, in every age – and what joy have you of your historic reading?

The knowledge of history's horrors and the fear of modern science combine into a fierce pacifism familiar to us. 'It would be far better that England should bleed under conquest than that she should be saved by eager, or careless, acceptance of conscription', Ryecroft declares. War only comes about because leaders or people see in it 'a direct or tangible profit, or they are driven to it, with heads down, by the brute that is in them . . . There has but to arise some lord of slaughter, and the nations will be tearing at each other's throats.' As for the present: 'men are fretting, raving, killing each other for matters so trivial . . . What lunatic ever dreamed of things less consonant with the calm reason . . . in every community of men called sane?'

Ryecroft's stoicism and resignation in the face of such contemporary horrors is also Gissing's. He speaks of reading Marcus Aurelius and of the solace of learning simply 'to accept one's lot, whatever it is, as inevitable . . . Why are we here? For the same reason that has brought about the existence of a horse, or of a vine, to play the part allotted to us by nature.' Thus, though there had been a time when he dreaded death, now he enjoys walking through cemeteries. 'I read the names upon the stones, and find a deep solace in thinking that for all these the fret and the fear of life are over . . . the end having come . . . what matter if it came too late or soon?' If Ryecroft regrets anything at all, it is this: 'My life has been merely tentative, a broken series of false starts and hopeless new beginnings . . . I could revolt against the ordinance which allows me no second chance.'

Ryecroft also refers to 'nervous instability from which I have suffered since boyhood'. He shrinks, he says, from 'the noisy world', rarely hearing in his rural retreat even so much as 'a clink of crockery' or 'the closing of a door or window. Oh, blessed silence!' The following is one of the most neurasthenic passages Gissing ever wrote:

I remember the London days when sleep was broken by clash and clang, by roar and shriek, and when my first sense on returning to consciousness was hatred of the life about me. Noises of wood and metal, clattering of wheels, banging of implements, jangling of bells – all such things are bad enough, but worse still is the clamorous human voice. Nothing on earth is more irritating to me than a bellow or scream of idiot mirth, nothing more hateful than a shout or yell of brutal anger. Were it possible, I would never again hear the utterance of a human tongue, save from those few who are dear to me.

I have said that the women in his life cannot be asked to assume all the blame for Gissing's unhappiness; a man who, at forty-three, can hardly bear to listen to the 'utterance of a human tongue' must be considered by any odds difficult to get along with. The novelist was dangerously close to turning his back on the entire human race. 'My pleasure in the finest music would be greatly spoiled by having to sit amid a crowd, with some audible idiot on right hand or left', Henry Ryecroft remarks.

At least there is an acknowledgement in *The Ryecroft Papers* that it takes two to bring about the domestic imbroglios that played such havoc with Gissing's own life. 'It is so difficult for human beings to live together . . . however transitorily and even under the most favourable conditions, without some . . . mutual offence', Ryecroft says. 'The average man or woman . . . could not live without oft-recurrent squabble.' In many of the preceding novels the 'bad wife' theme was dominant; here is an admission that the average man as much as the average woman can be hard to live with. In any case, this passage makes it clear, after only a year and a half with Gabrielle, that Gissing was no more sanguine than before about 'marriage' or his future domestic happiness. The 'crown of life' now seemed more gilt than gold.

Some of the difficulties of his life, Ryecroft asserts, have arisen as a result of the uncertainties of his profession. He is, of course, a novelist; this makes inevitable financial insecurity and an unstable mode of existence. 'Through the greater part of life I was homeless', Ryecroft says. 'Many places have I inhabited . . . At any moment I might have been driven forth by . . . nagging necessity . . . Some of my abodes I have utterly forgotten . . . I was always moving.' Ryecroft refers elsewhere to 'the unspeakable blessedness of having a *home*!' and there can be no home without the sense of 'permanence' – something Gissing was deprived of for much of his life.

As a result of his experiences Ryecroft learned what it meant to have and to lack money. 'The average educated man has never stood . . . utterly alone, just clad and nothing more than that, with the problem before him of wresting his next meal.' He gives us a version of Gissing's familiar caveat: 'Starvation . . . does not necessarily produce fine literature'; on the other hand one feels uneasy about those authors who make money. Even now, Ryecroft says, he is by no means a rich man; he has never earned as much as he hoped he would. 'In my twenties I used to say to myself: what a splendid thing it will be *when* I am the possessor of a thousand pounds! Well, I have never possessed that sum . . . and now never shall.' (In his Commonplace Book Gissing noted that one of his ambitions in life was to possess £1,000.) An Englishman, Ryecroft concludes, likes to live well. 'His virtues are those of the free-handed and warm-hearted . . . man; his weaknesses come of the sense of inferiority (intensely . . . humiliating) which attaches . . . to one who cannot spend and give; his vices . . . originate in loss of self-respect due to loss of secure position.'

For a long time, Ryecroft declares, he was prevented by dire necessity from worrying about posterity's judgement on him as a writer. 'For more than six years I trod the pavement . . . [struggling] against starvation' (Gissing undoubtedly refers to the period 1878 to 1885, the years preceding *Demos*). Since then 'this pen and a scrap of paper clothed and fed me and . . . held at bay all those hostile forces of the world ranged against one who has no resource save in his own right hand . . . Hateful as is the struggle for life in every form, this rough-and-tumble of the literary arena seems to me sordid and degrading beyond all others.' It pits the intelligent educated man against 'those hostile forces of the world' usually so much more powerful than he and makes him battle against them to stay alive: in that sense the struggle is 'degrading'. The narrator of *The Ryecroft Papers* has few misconceptions left about it: 'Say what one will after a lifetime of disillusion, the author who earns largely by capable and honest work is among the few enviable mortals.' He feels nothing but pity for the 'boy of twenty, fairly educated, but without means, without help, with nothing but the glow in his brain and steadfast courage in his heart, who sits in a London garret and writes for dear life.'

In the course of his discussion of the writer's life, Ryecroft takes aim at two of Gissing's favourite targets: the reading public, and publishers. 'The public which reads . . . is very, very small; the public which would feel no lack if all book-printing ceased tomorrow, is enormous.' On publishers: 'Who knows better than I', says the man forced to sell the copyright of almost every book he wrote, 'that your representative author face to face with your representative publisher was, is, and ever will be at a ludicrous disadvantage'. George Smith is not mentioned by name, but the example Ryecroft offers of the unprincipled publisher is Gissing's favourite tale of literary exploitation: 'Think of that grey, pinched life, the latter years of which would have been so brightened had Charlotte Brontë received but . . . one third of what in the same space of time the publisher gained by her books.' Gissing never forgave Smith for taking advantage of him in his early years or for boasting how much money Gissing's favourite novelist had earned for his publishing firm.

Ryecroft's anti-democratic bias is an unmistakable distillation of the novelist's:

I am no friend of the people. As a force by which the tenor of the time is conditioned, they inspire me with distrust, with fear; as a visible multitude, they make me shrink . . . move me to abhorrence . . . Every instinct of my being is anti-democratic, and I dread to think of what our England may become when *demos* rules . . . Democracy is full of menace to all the finer hopes of civilisation . . . With barely one or two exceptions, the people are nothing to me, and the less I see of them the better . . . And to think that at one time I called myself a socialist . . . not for long, to be sure, and I suspect that there was always something in me that scoffed when my lips uttered such things. Why, no man living has a more profound sense of property than I; no man ever lived, who was, in every fibre, more vehemently an individualist.

Gissing now looks back on the period of *Workers in the Dawn* as a time of political and philosophical apostasy; no wonder he never brought the book to people's attention in later years. In the same vein Ryecroft recalls those days in which he began to write novels: 'I could never feel myself at one with the native poor among whom I dwelt . . . I came to know them too well . . . What they at heart desired was to me barren; what I coveted was to them forever incomprehensible.' The political and social perspective of *The Ryecroft Papers* is hardly different from that of *Demos*, *Thyrza*, or *The Nether World*.

On education and the social aspirations of the working classes, the perspective is of a piece. Education, says Ryecroft, 'is a thing of which only the few are capable'. And he goes on, 'I had far rather see England covered with schools of cookery than with schools of the ordinary kind . . . Little girls should be taught cooking . . . more assiduously than they are taught to read . . . Think of the glorious revolution that could be wrought . . . if it could be ordered that no maid, of whatsoever rank, might become a wife unless she had proved her ability to . . . bake a perfect loaf of bread.' What little sympathy Gissing once had for the 'odd' women seems to have evaporated altogether. This is largely because the wrong people have notions of gentility. Thus the 'worst features of the rustic mind in our day is not its ignorance or grossness, but its rebellious discontent . . . The bucolic wants to "better" himself . . . he imagines that on the pavement of London he would walk with a manlier tread.' But the 'English lower ranks' are neither teachable nor adaptable.

I have quoted from *The Ryecroft Papers* at length in order to show how completely and uncomplicatedly it speaks with Gissing's voice. The pretence of fiction is dropped altogether; what we have is the 'novel' as spiritual confession, as private memoir. It is perhaps the fullest artistic expression of the close connection between Gissing's work and his life. The novelist's description of Ryecroft is another self-portrait, and one of the most interesting of them all:

He was a struggling man, beset by poverty and other circumstances very unpropitious to mental work. Many forms of literature had he tried; in none had he been conspicuously successful; yet now and then he had managed to earn a little more money than his actual needs demanded, and thus was enabled to see something of foreign countries. Naturally a man of independent and rather scornful outlook, he had suffered much from defeated ambition, from disillusions of many kinds, from subjection to grim necessity . . . and . . . under a haunting fear of the future. The thought of dependence had always been intolerable to him; perhaps the only boast . . . from his lips was that he had never incurred debt. It was a bitter thought that after so long and hard a struggle with unkindly circumstance he might end his life as one of the defeated.

Ryecroft is just beginning to enjoy his existence when he is cut off in the prime of life, at the age of fifty. By the time *The Ryecroft Papers* was published, Gissing was approaching the untimely end of his days, at the age of forty-six. At the end of the book Ryecroft says: 'May I look back on life as a long task duly completed – a piece of biography; faulty enough, but good as I could make it.' Gissing's whole life was 'a piece of biography', a story to be told over and over again in his novels. As he says of Ryecroft in the 'Preface' to *The Ryecroft Papers*, 'he spoke of himself, and told the truth as far as mortal can tell it.'

※

CHAPTER 12

LAST THINGS, 1900–1903

Such men as I live and die alone, however much in appearance
accompanied.   *The Ryecroft Papers*

We enter the gates of life with wailing, and anguish to the
womb which brings us forth; we pass again into the outer
darkness through the valley of ghastly terrors, and leave cold
misery upon the lips of those that mourn us.
                                    'The Hope of Pessimism'

He died a month ago, over there in the South of France.
                                    Will Warburton

I

THE story of Gissing's last years is a sad one. It has been said that
the final period of his life gave him the only happiness he knew.
Certainly he was happier with Gabrielle than he was with Nell or
Edith, but one can hardly go much further than this. He was
constitutionally unable to be happy for long anywhere, under any
conditions, and a careful sifting of the evidence suggests that
eighteen months after his third 'marriage' – about the same length of
time as it took him to begin finding fault with Edith – he was
unhappy with his French *ménage*. It is suggestive that the picture
Henry Ryecroft paints for us of his ideal life in Somerset does not
include a wife.

Shortly after his return to Paris in November 1900, the first
serious complaints about foreign cooking begin to be heard. In a
letter to Hick, Gissing writes: 'Oh, an honest bit of English roast
beef! Could you put a slice in a letter?? – laden with gravy?' He was
becoming convinced that Mme Fleury, who had a heart complaint
and was being nursed by Gabrielle, was aggravating his own
condition by systematic starvation. He could not, he began to tell
his friends, get enough to eat. Late in December Gissing told Clodd
that his cough was getting bad again. He was having trouble
writing, and Gabrielle's brother René was disturbing his peace.
'Marvellous that I can work at all – a sort of despair drives me', he
recorded in his diary on the last Christmas Day of the nineteenth

century. He began the historical novel anew at the end of December. 'I really think I can make an interesting book', he wrote to Bertz. 'One thing is certain – I know my period.' But the writing was 'fearfully difficult'; it was not easy to find the right idiom for a historical novel. He also reported to Bertz that 'The Coming Man' had been used as a title before and his title would have to be changed; and that he was paying 'that terrible woman', who had been quiet lately, £104 a year. Again we hear the despairing note: 'It is a disagreeable thing to feel that, at my age, I am beginning to lose even what little public I had.' He had earned only £297 in 1900.

A French acquaintance of the novelist later described him at this period of his life. He had a 'well-shaped head' and wore a 'short and bushy moustache'. His features included a 'delicate nose', a 'high forehead', and 'long hair, already greying', which was 'brushed over his head, behind his ears and off his temples, without a parting'. He had 'expressive eyes, dilated by fever, for disease had been undermining him for a long time, and he had that hectic gauntness of those about to die of consumption' (this last was the product of hindsight).

On 22 January 1901 Queen Victoria died. 'It is impossible not to be affected by this news, for [she] has been a part of all our lives, and now that she is gone the world is greatly changed', Gissing wrote to his mother. 'Strange to think that when I was born Victoria had already reigned for twenty years, and that I am already beginning to feel old at the time of her death. I am afraid there can be no doubt that the [Boer] war killed her.' 'I confess to a little gloom over the cheerless close of the Victorian reign', he wrote to Clodd. But he was heartened late in January by Pinker's disposal of *Our Friend the Charlatan* (as it would be called): Chapman and Hall paid £350 (half down) for British and Colonial rights and Henry Holt another £100 for the American rights. The £450 was his best sale to date; the novel would appear in May 1901.

Also at the end of January he wrote 'A Charming Family', a story set in a suburban lodging-house and largely concerned with matters of class. It describes yet again the victimization of the working class, represented in the heroine, by the more prosperous middle class. Ultimately the heroine is robbed of all she has by her 'respectable' friends.

Throughout February he worked on 'The Vanquished Roman' and sifted through proposed illustrations for *By the Ionian Sea*, which would be published in cloth in June 1901. It was to be illustrated with full-page colour pictures, as well as by engravings based on his own sketches. 'I am immensely gratified by all this', he told Clara Collet. He added that his Roman novel 'will be the first really honest piece of work I have offered to my readers, for it represents the preparatory labour of years, and is written without pressure.' Meanwhile, Gabrielle's translation of *New Grub Street* began to appear in the *Journal des Débats,* much to Gissing's satisfaction: the French title was *La Rue des Meurt-de-Faim.* He spent the final days of the month reading proofs of the *de luxe* edition of *By the Ionian Sea.* The end of February found him in a gloomy mood once again, worried about his worsening health. He continued to lose weight, and he was homesick for England. His growing hatred of Paris may be glimpsed in a letter to Clodd. 'Every day gives me a deeper loathing of city life. If I cannot escape from it to die amid green fields, my end will be wretched indeed.'

Early in March Wells and his wife visited Gissing and Gabrielle in Paris. 'The apartment was bleakly furnished in the polished French way', Wells said later. Gissing 'was doing no effective work, he was thin and ailing, and he complained bitterly that his pseudo mother-in-law, who was in complete control of his domestic affairs, was starving him. The sight of us stirred him to an unwonted Anglo-mania, a stomachic nostalgia.' Gissing reported to Bertz on Wells's visit, noting that Wells sat in his new house at Sandgate near Folkestone and communicated with London by telephone. 'That kind of thing' would never fall to him, he felt.

Throughout the rest of March 1901 Gissing corrected proofs of *Our Friend the Charlatan* and *By the Ionian Sea* and worked sporadically on his Roman novel. He told Pinker that 'A Vanquished Roman' would be full of colour and movement – 'war, monkery, violent ambitions, loves etc.'. He also asked Pinker to destroy both typescripts of 'Among the Prophets' for which no publisher had been found. Early in April he sold the English copyright of his critical study of Dickens to Blackie for £50.

A doctor whom the novelist now consulted told him he had emphysema, bronchitis, and a moist spot on the right lung. He was ordered to stop working, eat more, live in the mountains, and on no account return to England where the damp climate would bring on tuberculosis. The only one of these orders Gissing took seriously was that pertaining to food. He refused to stop working – during April he brought 'A Vanquished Roman' to half its projected length – or to go to the mountains; they would only remind him, he told Wells, that they were '*not* England', to which he was determined to go anyway. 'One *health* motive would be that in England I should put on flesh, which I never can here', he wrote to Wells. The doctor's caveats depressed him. 'I had . . . positively lived, on the hope of seeing an English field, and walking in an English lane . . . I had thought night and day of a boiled potato – of a slice of English meat – of tarts and puddings – of teacakes . . . I . . . looked forward to ravening on those things.' These are the words of a man starving for food as well as for England: all pretence of happiness in his French life had now been dropped. 'The food question . . . is sufficiently serious', he told Miss Collet, 'but cannot be talked about.' His weight was down to 140 pounds. 'This time, I fear, the situation is rather grave. I must make the best fight I can.' At the end of April, perhaps to help conserve his flagging energies, Gissing abandoned his diary, not to resume writing in it for a year.

II

In May 1901 Gissing found an excuse to escape from the clutches of his austere French mother-in-law and return to England. *Literature*, which had published 'The Coming of the Preacher' in January 1900, asked him to sit for a London photographer: his photograph was to appear along with an essay on him scheduled for the July number. The chance of some free publicity at the time two of his books were to be published could not be resisted. Wells, who wanted to introduce him to his neighbours, Conrad and James, offered to put him and Gabrielle up – for she was to accompany him. The trip was to last only four days because Mme Fleury could not be left alone any longer than that.

Upon his arrival at Sandgate most of his plans were cast to the winds. Wells had asked Hick to examine Gissing, and his verdict was that the novelist 'was in the condition of a starved man . . . practically no more than a skeleton'. Mrs Wells 'set to work and fed him up', as her husband puts it, and within a week Gissing had gained seven pounds. The decision to stay on at Sandgate was reached without Gabrielle's concurrence; angered, she left for Paris to resume nursing her mother. Gissing remained. According to Hick this resolution was arrived at amicably, though the letters Gabrielle was to write afterwards were not so amicable as we shall see. Hick says: 'There was . . . no question of his leaving [her] . . . there was no row, I do not think he ever had any serious disagreement with her. He had trouble with her mother, who said he was disgusting because he wanted eggs and bacon for breakfast.'

Roberts, who agrees with Hick's account, says that Gissing's third marriage had 'come to disaster over the mere matter of the dining-table . . . he had . . . been a sad fool for not insisting good-humouredly on having the food he wanted . . . There is no doubt that the feeding in his French home was not fat, or fine.' Mme Fleury thought Gissing's gastronomic tastes were gross, and he preferred not to argue with her. One is reminded of Mrs Ormonde's characterization of Egremont in *Thyrza*: 'you are passive in great trials; it is easier for you to suffer than to act'. It is reminiscent too of what Gissing wrote to Bertz in 1894: 'I yield at once . . . under almost any kind of trouble.' And Wells said that Gissing 'never turned and fought. He always hid or fled.' He was impatient with him, accusing him of turning tail when he ought to have stood his ground. Jane Wells treated him like a foolish child.

And so Gissing stayed, getting fat on his favourite foods. By mid-June he had gained nine pounds. Conrad was invited to Sandgate to meet him, but no record of their conversation survives. *Literature*'s photographer took Gissing's photograph in Wells's study. Gissing informed Miss Collet of the state of his affairs, remarking that there had been no domestic rows in France but that a good deal of suppressed irritation had exhausted him. Wells took him to spend a day and a night with Henry James at Rye. Gissing admired James's Georgian house and was amused by his reminiscences of Turgenev in Paris. The Master found Gissing 'highly sympathetic . . . but worn almost to the bone (of sadness)'. Upon leaving, Gissing presented James with an inscribed copy of *New Grub Street*.

Pye-Smith came to examine Gissing, and confirmed Hick's diagnosis: emphysema was the novelist's only real danger, but he had to gain weight and strength. Both physicians recommended rest in a sanatorium. Hick suggested one in Suffolk, and thence Gissing planned to go at the end of June (after, that is, nearly a month at Sandgate). Gabrielle's reproaches followed him there and were directed as well at several of his English friends. Her prime target was Wells, whom she blamed for separating her from her husband. Gissing's extended stay in England was an implied criticism of her ability to care for him. Since two doctors had pronounced him nearly starved, such a criticism, had it actually been made, would have been justified. On the other hand, a forty-three-year-old man should have known how to ask for food when he wanted it. Gissing wrote to Gabrielle from Sandgate throughout June seeking to reassure her of his love, but the terms he chose in which to do this were not always happy. Informing her of his weight-gain, he declared: 'It is no joke . . . life and death are at issue, and I can no longer play with my health.' He asked if regaining his health was not 'much better than *just keeping alive*?' He gave this as one reason for not returning to France immediately: 'it would be most dangerous to incur the least risk of losing weight again.' Gabrielle must have been furious – even more so when he asked her to send him all the papers and manuscripts in his desk. He told her it was better to have a short separation during which he might strengthen himself than 'to spend this summer together and perhaps never see another . . . to spend the summer in France would almost certainly be fatal to me.' In addition to the gain of weight, he reported no bronchitis, no fever, and the cessation of his cough. As June wore on his letters became more genuinely reassuring. 'Do you imagine that one moment passes without my thinking of you and longing for you?' he wrote.

'Be patient! I love you . . . I am tormented by the longing for your companionship . . . I seem to have only half a life away from you.' He told her the breakdown in his health was the result of many years of precarious living. 'What possibility was there for me of health before our marriage, when starved emotions made me a madman?' But he admitted that his nerves had suffered in the last year or two. In his last letter to her before leaving for Suffolk, he made an extraordinary declaration:

Looking back over the last two years, I see myself as a rather poor creature, living in querulous subjection, without courage to rebel and to say: 'No, this is not the life of a *man*!' I am going to be more worthy of respect in the eyes of my wife. After all, the old predominance of the *man* is thoroughly wholesome and justifiable, but he must be *manlike* and worthy of ruling. Most contemptible is the man who lets himself be dominated even by the most beloved woman.

Gabrielle saw this as the work of Wells, and she was probably right: it sounds like the sort of thing he was always saying to Gissing. But this does not excuse the incredible letters she wrote to the Wellses in June 1901, letters full of resentment, jealousy, even hatred – after all, the Wellses had probably saved her husband's life. Nor was it their fault that her mother needed her at home. Wells later described these communications sarcastically as 'long, wonderfully phrased letters – on thin paper'. The peculiar Latin capacity for complicating simple situations impressed him anew, he said. Gabrielle's letters – not always in perfect English – were blunt, at times paranoid, and certainly less sensible than those Gissing wrote to her during their separation. 'No French doctor would ever dream of taking away an invalid from his wife – provided his wife is decent enough – to put him in the care of strangers', she told the Wellses in her opening salvo: they had known Gissing longer than he had known her, and were hardly 'strangers'. She alone, she said, knew enough of Gissing's 'peculiarities' to take care of him properly. She had letters from him, she said, *proving* that his poor health antedated their marriage, that it was due largely 'to the frightful state of his nerves, after the frightful life he had lived . . . I know perfectly well that France has not been fatal to my husband.' She feared that if he stayed in England Edith would find him, 'seize him and give herself the pleasure . . . of restoring him to the brilliant state of health and nerves he enjoyed when in care of her'. She also worried that he would end by living with his sisters: 'he has [such] admiration . . . for everything they think, say or do.' That was nonsense: as we know, Gissing could never stand Wakefield for more than a few days at a time. 'I am afraid . . . that if choice had to be made, it would not be in my favour', Gabrielle lamented. After all, she reminded Wells, the Wakefield people did not even know of her existence: how could she interfere in such circumstances? 'For them, I should be an object of unspeakable contempt . . . I have . . . made great sacrifices, of half the natural joys of every married woman, but I cannot bring myself to be treated with scorn and contempt.'

Of course Gabrielle was being irrational, but in her defence it must be said that her position was indeed equivocal, and she could not be sure that Gissing's English friends, some of whom obviously disliked her, might not persuade him to stay rather than return to France, where all her friends and relations considered Gissing and herself a contented married couple.

As the separation lengthened, Gabrielle's letters grew more plaintive and strident. A letter from Wells calling on her to be strong enough to do what was best for Gissing and to put foolish fears out of her mind elicited a long tirade from her on the weaknesses of Gissing's character. She could not feel safe as long as he was out of her sight, she said, because of his 'extraordinary, terrible, perhaps morbid *unstability* in mind, views, decision, feelings . . . [and] a quite peculiar unability of being happy for a long time in unchanged circumstances and surroundings'. This, she declared, was the result of the 'sad and miserable life' he had led for many years. She thought it would disappear once they lived together as man and wife. 'Now I have come to know that it is a constitutional feature of . . . his blood . . . and unfortunately uncurable.' She went on to discuss his 'unstability of character', his 'constant changing of moods'; she realized that 'his health . . . requires a great deal of changing . . . for some time he feels better and happy, then the bad germ in him . . . reappears, he feels the want of another change and gets discontented, hating his present conditions of living – and so on.' Such a man of moods tended to build up extraordinary dependence on people, and she was afraid, she said, that he had come to depend in this way on his family! She would never forget his telling her once that he 'had to live *for his children*'. She referred hysterically to the 'extraordinary intimacy and domination of Wakefield' and went on to abuse Gissing's innocent sisters. Here she is nowhere near the truth. When she speaks of Gissing's constitutional inability to be happy anywhere for long she is of course right. But she also dreaded 'the terrorising power', that Edith had upon him and criticized him for making so generous an allowance as £2 a week to Edith and Alfred. In his illness, she said, his financial worries should be reduced as much as possible; a cut in this allowance would be one way to lighten his financial burden. This was by no means a disinterested proposition. Gissing was 'constantly gloomy and miserably brooding over his pecuniary situation, anguish troubling him all day long, preventing him of sleep'; he was 'reduced to a nervous trembling state at every bill I showed him'. She concluded by wondering if perhaps the illness in his lungs was spreading to his brain – how else explain this 'strange complaining which had suddenly begun?' The report of the physicians was not mentioned.

Still, there is much truth in the assessment of Gissing she offered: 'Discontent is in his nature . . . paradise is always for him where he is not.' She warned against encouraging him 'in his discontented moods. With regard to practical . . . everyday life, George is like a child.' As soon as he came into contact with a worry, he thought that it would go away if circumstances altered, and this was 'the constant delusion of his mind, a product of his bad health and his deep unpracticality.'

It is not a very creditable performance. Gabrielle was trying to get her husband back by making his friends – who were doing much more than she to help him in this crisis – think that his illness was more psychosomatic than physical, even that he was being driven mad by a nervous disorder. Wells's account of his response to her is succinct:

After one or two rather hasty attempts at diplomacy I brutalized the situation. I declared that the best thing for Gissing to do would be to decide never to return to France, since there was an evident incompatibility of appetite between him and [Gabrielle], or alternatively if there was any sort of living affection still between them, which I doubted, he must stipulate as a condition of his return that the catering should be taken out of the hands of the mother and put in those of the daughter under his own direction, and finally I announced that in no circumstances would I read through . . . any further letters from [her].

No wonder Gabrielle hated him. Certainly he was wrong about Gissing's feelings for her, as the novelist's letters plainly show. But Wells's proposed domestic plan was sensible, and indeed after Gissing's return to her, due largely to Wells's insistence, 'the management of the kitchen was conducted on more reasonable lines', as Roberts reports. Gissing continued to gain weight.

   In the third week of June 1901 the novelist went to the Suffolk sanatorium recommended by Hick. He wrote to Clodd that the book he would be sending shortly (*Our Friend the Charlatan*) was 'poor stuff'. He brought Bertz up to date on the state of his affairs, commenting that he had been 'starved' in France: 'it is a very delicate subject (complicated with the mother-in-law difficulty).' He referred briefly to 'laudatory' reviews of *Our Friend the Charlatan* and *By the Ionian Sea,* both just published, and declared that perhaps after all 'success is coming. It need be so, for my expenses are . . . very heavy.' He asked Bertz, should he happen to write to Gabrielle, to 'try to impress upon her the (surely obvious) fact that nothing on earth could keep me away from her but fear of utter ruin of my health. I *must get well.*'

                                    III

Our Friend the Charlatan appeared in May and *By the Ionian Sea* just two weeks later, in June. Both, to Gissing's delight, were pleasing the reviewers.

   The *Guardian* called Lady Ogram 'a masterpiece'. The *Pall Mall Gazette* declared that the new novel 'displays . . . Mr Gissing at his best . . . he has never written a book in which the psychology was truer.' This was the general opinion. The *Daily Chronicle* compared him to Turgenev, and favourably to Zola. *Literature* compared him to Meredith, commenting that the younger novelist's 'psychology is wonderfully subtle and acute', and that Lashmar is fully the equal as a character of Sir Willoughby Patterne. The *Academy* and *The Times* also made the comparison with *The Egoist*. Only *St. James's Gazette* and the *Fortnightly Review* printed uncomplimentary notices. As so often before, Gissing fared better with the reviewers than he deserved (the comparison of the mediocre *Our Friend the Charlatan* with *The Egoist* is ludicrous). The novel was reprinted several times during the decade following its publication.

By the Ionian Sea did deserve its warm reception. This was the first opportunity Gissing had had to show his knowledge both of classical antiquity and of modern Italy, and the reviewers were not slow to observe this apparently 'new' side to him. The *Academy* hit the popular note when it commented that the book 'increases one's respect for [Gissing] . . . We know now that . . . the painter of modern squalor, sadness, gloom, and heroic futility, has had eyes continually on other scenes and other ages.' Like *Charles Dickens: A Critical Study* three years earlier, *By the Ionian Sea* gave the reading public a chance to see Gissing in another light. The *Academy* went on to compare it favourably with Paul Bourget's *Sensations d'Italie*. *Literature* made the same comparison, with similar results. It declared that Gissing had never 'been so completely successful [as a writer] as in . . . *By the Ionian Sea* . . . The book is full of masterpieces of prose writing . . . it is . . . a gem.' The *Guardian* echoed much of this praise, referring to 'the finest poetic feeling, the truest sympathy, and the clearest analysis that have ever been combined by the scholarly student with the description of travel'. The *Daily Chronicle*, the *Scotsman*, the *Westminster Gazette*, and the *Globe* also printed laudatory notices. Only the benighted *Athenaeum* was lukewarm.

In *Literature*, meanwhile, the long-promised piece on Gissing, printed with the photograph taken at Sandgate, now appeared. It was written (badly) by Morley Roberts. One of its main points was that Gissing belonged to no particular school. 'His essence lies in a bent, a mood of mind, not . . . in any subject.' Zola, said Roberts, had no influence upon Gissing. The early novels expressed what Gissing wished the world to be by showing that it possessed every conceivable opposite to his desire – thus the 'unsurpassable gloom' of a novel like *Isabel Clarendon*. In *By the Ionian Sea* he had finally declared himself. He was by nature a scholar, a man of the cloister, though not conventional. Roberts pronounced *Born in Exile* Gissing's 'masterpiece', his most moving novel. In book after book, he observed, quoting directly from the letter Gissing sent him in 1895 containing ammunition for the projected counter-attack in the *Fortnightly* on the *Spectator* for its review of *In the Year of Jubilee*, the novelist dealt with 'young men who, while fairly bred and well-educated, are without money'; in *Born in Exile*, Roberts argued, he did this better than anywhere else. He concluded: 'There are [many] ways of hating modern civilization. Mr. Gissing is an inverted idealist. He looks back.'

IV

At the sanatorium in Suffolk, where Gissing spent more than a month, he continued to put on weight and improve in health. Among the patients there was Rachel Evelyn White, a thirty-year-old lecturer in classics at Newnham College, Cambridge, who became the novelist's friend and on whom he would model the heroine of 'Miss Rodney's Leisure', one of his last stories. For the most part he read, walked, ate, and slept. The attending physician did not regard his condition as serious so long as he kept his weight up. 'Cough all but gone, temperature normal, good sleep and powerful eating. Do nothing', the novelist told Hick. To Wells he wrote: 'As always in things practical, I bungled this affair from the first. Whether it means the end of all the best things I had hoped has still to be seen.' In the final days of his stay a number of invitations to visit were received, and all were declined: Gissing planned only a short stop in Wakefield before rejoining Gabrielle and her mother, who were spending the summer in Autun, in central France.

Gabrielle wrote a long letter to Jane Wells in mid-July. She was not sure of their future plans, she said, since – unlike Gissing – she was 'not willing to move every year or so'. She begged Mrs Wells not to give credence to Gissing's 'strange complaints about not being master in his household . . . George has . . . strange fancies in his head . . . He has no idea whatever about the realities of domestic life.' She complained that she had only one servant to help at home and that Gissing preferred to live 'in his own solitary way'. She assured Mrs Wells that she, not her mother, ran the kitchen – not a very flattering admission in the circumstances. Gissing, she said, did not believe her when she told him this; he was too deeply embroiled in 'complaints, disquietude, discontent'. What she called his 'tormenting unquietness of soul' prevented him from being 'unreservedly happy; it is not in his nature.' Again she complained about money, turning her fire this time away from Edith and Alfred to declare that the amounts Gissing sent to Wakefield for the maintenance of Walter were extravagant. As for their French establishment: 'he can't expect to get everything requested for his diet and to keep expenses so low!' She waxed hysterical over Gissing's plan to visit Wakefield before joining her: 'it is certain they will do their utmost to keep him with them and away from me as long as possible.' Since, she said, 'so much sacrifice has been required from me on account of his health', he ought to forego seeing his mother, his sisters, and his son (her sacrifices are not enumerated). She dreaded, she said, 'the results of this [visit] and increased intimacy between him and his people . . . knowing as I only too well know his extreme, astonishing submissiveness to them . . . And I know their love of exercising their authority over him, and their natural animosity against everyone who appears to have some influence on him!' This is sheer paranoia. She noted that the Wellses had persuaded Gissing to tell his relatives about her, and she was grateful for that – though she thought it insulting that 'poor, weak G.' felt such trepidation about making the disclosure. So ends this awful letter.

Gissing's correspondence with Gabrielle in July 1901 chiefly concerned the question of their future residence. 'The success of my new books has very much strengthened my position', he told her. 'All I have to do now is to make for myself a healthy *home*, where I can work steadily for the greater part of every year. If this is done, we shall never again have any money troubles.' He added: 'Of course I must not lose weight, and I *must* live in a sunny, airy room; also (and most important of all) I must have peace for the nerves.' He was certain, he said, that 'I did the right thing': 'now we can try to forget all about the miseries it involved. They must never begin again. Indeed, they *cannot* . . . I must never allow myself to live in a way which reduces my strength and makes me wretched.' He noted that Suffolk was the home county of his father. 'Ah, if he had lived, how he would have rejoiced in my success! It was his one hope that I might become a man of some note.' He was certain now that he was on the verge of real fame: 'If I live another five years, my position will be very different.' He approved of her plan to spend August, September and October at Autun, and hoped they could remain together during the dangerous winter months. Again and again he reassured her of his feelings. 'The differences that have been between us seem very slight and transitory when I think of the deep, strong love which unites us, and ever will.' In the last letter he wrote to her before leaving England, however, there is a querulous note: 'Dear, [my love] is very deep and tender and lasting . . . Cannot we manage so as to live without these horrid differences? It is strange your love cannot overcome such small troubles, or direct our life into a quiet channel.' Obviously the letters he was receiving from her were not so cordial.

At Autun Gissing planned to work on the second half of 'A Vanquished Roman', thinking that he might cash in on the popularity of *By the Ionian Sea*. There was also the final revision of *An Author at Grass*, for which he also had high hopes, and several short stories to write. Meanwhile (on 30 July) he finally dispatched to Wakefield the letter disclosing his relationship with Gabrielle. It was addressed to Margaret and its chief emphasis was on Gabrielle's respectability. Gissing explained that he 'could not live on in my state of hopeless misery' – that this liaison had saved his life and preserved for his two boys the health of their father. His English friends knew Gabrielle, accepted her, and respected her, he said. (He wrote because he had decided to yield to Gabrielle's entreaties not to visit Wakefield.) The Wakefield people, who by now were used to finding out the details of Gissing's personal life long after everyone else had done so, reacted sensibly, though without joy, as Coustillas puts it – choosing merely 'to shut their eyes to this latest instance of [Gissing's] unconventional behaviour'. Their mild reaction caused him to change his mind yet again. During the second week of August, on the eve of his departure for France, he paid a two-day visit to Wakefield. It was just as well on this occasion that he disregarded Gabrielle's feelings, for it was the last time he would see any of his Wakefield relations. The family thought him 'greatly improved in health and confident in his future'. At Wakefield station, Ellen recalled later, his 'wave of the hand, and cheery smile for his boy Walter and for ourselves . . . proved to be our last farewell.' Walter was now nine years old.

v

Autun, in Burgundy, was peaceful, and Gissing went back to work. He wrote only for short periods now ('Can work only two hours a day, a wretched stint', he told Algernon), but Gabrielle and her mother paid more attention to his diet, and his health seemed to improve. Throughout September 1901 he worked on *An Author at Grass* – which, he informed Bertz, he was 'considerably altering and improving': he finished the revision during the last week of the month. He said his two new books had had 'considerable *literary* success' but had not made much money: 'This will be the case to the end – much praise and little money.' Though both *Our Friend the*

Charlatan and *By the Ionian Sea* were reprinted, the publisher never recovered his costs. Gissing told Bertz he had put aside 'A Vanquished Roman'. He could only write it in his own library. Noting the appearance of a Roman novel by Hall Caine (*The Eternal City*, 1901), he said he had probably 'waited too long' with his own. He warned Bertz not to buy the Rochester Dickens. 'It is ugly in form, and all the good of the prefaces you will find in my "Charles Dickens". The publisher is horribly mean. He sends me only one copy.'

Methuen, in fact, was finding the Rochester Edition thoroughly unrewarding, and with the publication of *Barnaby Rudge* in November 1901 the series was brought to an abrupt end. After protracted negotiations Gissing was paid nearly £46 for the prefaces he wrote. He also worked on a preface to *David Copperfield* for another collected edition of Dickens's works, for which he was paid fifteen guineas. At the request of the editor of *Literature* he wrote yet another essay on Dickens, 'Dickens in Memory' (later appended to *The Immortal Dickens*). And now Chapman and Hall asked him if he would write a new life of Dickens, based on Forster's. The novelist felt he could not do the book without access to archival material in England and suggested instead an abridgement of Forster's *Life*. Chapman and Hall agreed, and paid down immediately half of the advance of £150 Gissing had requested.

In October Gissing sent off to Pinker the revised version of *An Author at Grass* – along with a story, 'The Riding-Whip', an unpleasant little tale condemning gambling. Upon the return of the household to Paris in November the novelist was examined by a physician, who declared that Gissing now had emphysema in both lungs. The south of France was recommended. This would mean another separation from Gabrielle; Mme Fleury could not leave Paris during the winter, and Gabrielle announced that she would remain with her mother rather than her 'husband'. He spent the rest of November in Nièvre, working on his abridgement of Forster. On the eve of his forty-fourth birthday Gissing wrote a bleak letter to Wells. 'I must not pretend to care very much about the future of the human race; come what may, folly and misery are sure to be the prevalent features of life', he said. He added that he had become 'estranged by [the] unintelligibility' of the universe.

In the midst of his depression some welcome news arrived. Pinker had sold, for £150, serial rights of *An Author at Grass* to the *Fortnightly*, which had had such a success with *By the Ionian Sea*. The serial would appear in four instalments: 'Spring' in May 1902,

'Summer' in August, 'Autumn' in November, and 'Winter' in February 1903. Gissing was delighted. 'It is probably the best bit of work I shall do', he told Jane Wells. But he was quickly depressed again by considerations of health and the prospect of spending much of the forthcoming winter alone. 'It is only too probable that I shall never again see your pleasant house', he wrote to Clodd at the end of November, 'for I live the life of an invalid whom any slightest imprudence may injure seriously . . . Ceaseless care for one's physical organs has a very demoralizing effect.'

On 3 December Gissing and Gabrielle travelled to Arcachon in the south of France, where he was to spend the next four months, mostly alone, taking the 'cure' at a *pension* catering for invalids. Gabrielle returned to Paris and her mother before Christmas, and from Arcachon Gissing wrote sadly to Ellen of 'the truth about my lungs. I am threatened with gradual hardening of all the surface, which, if it went on, would . . . extinguish me.' The man who used to walk twenty miles a day now 'cannot walk a mile, and [I] pant terribly if I have to go upstairs.' But he was coughing less and the doctor thought that there was still a chance his health might improve.

In his New Year letter to Bertz, Gissing described his life as 'fatally complicated', but he had high hopes for *An Author at Grass* and ended optimistically: 'Don't be gloomy about me. I feel a great deal of vitality in me yet, and am *never* downcast by fear – unless it be fear of beggary.' In a letter to Algernon he sounded less sanguine. 'It seems to me extraordinary that only two years ago I climbed mountains. I am constantly dreaming over my old walks.' The letter ends pathetically: 'Don't let the children forget me.'

Thus ended 1901. In one respect, at least, it was a good year for Gissing. He had earned during the twelve months a total of £723, by far his best year ever financially. The last two years of his life would see a dramatic decline.

VI

In January 1902 Gissing dispatched to Pinker his abridgement of Forster's *Life of Dickens*. His health improved a little in the mild weather and he was able to take longer walks. He began to think about starting another novel, but was too depressed by his growing loneliness to write anything. 'I am sad and troubled and want my wife's company', he wrote to Gabrielle. 'It is not half a life away from you.' But Gabrielle stayed in Paris. Was she punishing him for abandoning her the previous summer? Perhaps. Like his own Henry Ryecroft, Gissing reflected that he had been homeless most of his life. He wondered where they could settle: 'we *must* have a home'. He could not wait to leave Arcachon, where life was too 'depressing'.

Towards the end of January, though he was still too unhappy to write, he planned out carefully what would be his last completed novel, *Will Warburton*. 'Some day my exile may come to an end', he told Miss Collet. In a letter to Clodd he spoke glowingly of his relationship with Gabrielle, declining to discuss the current cause of his unhappiness. 'It has been justified by the event', he said of his third 'marriage'. His state of mind was not improved by news he received from England early in February. After mistreating Alfred and threatening in public to kill Miss Orme, Edith had been taken in charge, declared insane, and committed to an asylum. At first the novelist was alarmed: this might mean more expense – the costs of Edith's incarceration and a new home for Alfred. But it transpired that Edith had saved £115 out of her allowance, enough to pay for at least two years of institutionalization ('in order to do so, she lived in miserable squalor, and all but ruined the child's health', Gissing said later). A farmer's family in Cornwall was found by Miss Orme to take Alfred on moderate terms, for his aunts in Wakefield had enough on their hands with Walter; Alfred would be watched over by Miss Orme's sister, who lived nearby. Thus Gissing, like Butler's Ernest Pontifex, farmed out both his children. Alfred would cost him about 30 shillings a month, and Walter, who was to begin school near Norwich in the autumn, about £60 a year. With Edith no longer on the loose he was free to travel in England, should he wish to do so, without fear of ambush and scandal. 'The poor creature . . . must pass altogether out of our thoughts, as one dead', he wrote to Gabrielle. 'I cannot distress myself about her fate.' So much for Edith. Her end 'has surprised nobody', he complacently informed Bertz. 'On the whole, I regard this as a good thing for the poor woman herself.' He said he was 'enormously relieved', for Alfred's sake: 'I always felt myself guilty of a crime in abandoning the poor little fellow. He will now have his chance to grow up in healthy and decent circumstances.'

Gissing soon came thoroughly to hate Arcachon. 'Oh, a beautiful house in Devonshire, with our library, our quiet garden, our quiet evening, our walks in the lovely lanes and on the hills!!!' he wrote to Gabrielle. His fantasy world was that of *The Ryecroft Papers*. He continued to worry off and on about his two sons. 'They have never known a mother, and scarcely, indeed, a father.' He said he was pleased to receive a kind and gentle letter from her: 'Now *this* is the kind of letter that does me good! . . . Always write like this – like your TRUE self!' They tentatively agreed to look for a house in the *pays basque* when he left Arcachon in April. He reported that 'The Riding-Whip' had been sold for £25.

In letters to both Wells and Clodd around this time, Gissing, whose thoughts were becoming more philosophical as his illness grew more acute, discussed the principles of his lifelong agnosticism. 'I . . . cannot doubt . . . that purpose there *is*' in life, he told Wells. 'On the other hand, I do doubt whether *we* . . . shall ever be granted an understanding of that purpose.' To Clodd he wrote:

That there is *some* order, *some* purpose, seems a certainty; my mind, at all events, refuses to grasp the idea of a universe which means nothing at all. But just as unable am I to accept any of the solutions ever proposed. Above all, it is the existence of natural beauty which haunts my thought. I can, for a time, forget the world's horrors; I can never forget the flower by the wayside and the sun falling in the west. These things have a meaning – but I doubt, I doubt – whether the mind of man will ever be permitted to know it.

This is of a piece with Gissing's lifelong scientific scepticism. He told Clodd that *An Author at Grass* was 'more serious in intention than the title would suggest.' 'I have tried to put into it a good deal of what I really think and feel in these latter days', he said. With his friends, at least, there was never any pretence that *The Ryecroft Papers* was fiction. In late February and early March, not ready as yet to begin writing his new novel, Gissing completed two more stories. 'Christopherson' is about a bibliophile and his wife who become declassed through a failure in business. They are both poor in health, but the wife, it is emphasized, is always ready to sacrifice her comfort to the husband's. Ultimately they sell their books and move to the country, where they find it possible to live happily. 'Miss Rodney's Leisure' is another tale of lodging-house life. The heroine (who, as I have said, resembles Gissing's friend Rachel Evelyn White) is a teacher who reforms the slatternly landlady and turns the household right-side-up. As usual in a Gissing tale, improvement of the working classes shows no sign of coming from within. The story is also notable for conveying a claustrophobic sense of the closeness of bodies to one another when too many people live under the same roof – a sense Gissing retained from his own lodging-house days and which he was beginning to feel again at the *pension* in Arcachon.

Throughout March, 1902 Gissing wrestled with the problem of where to live. He wanted to go back to England, but knew the climate could ruin his health. Paris, or any other large city, would also be dangerous. He needed fresh air. Settling in the south of France might involve a good deal of complication and expense in moving. Furthermore: could Gabrielle and her mother get used to living, after Paris, in provincial obscurity?

Tentatively they chose St. Jean de Luz, near Biarritz and Bayonne at the foot of the French Pyrenees, for their next experiment in living *à trois*. Meanwhile Gissing complained about the lack of privacy and the coarse conversation at the Arcachon *pension*. He begged Gabrielle to come and visit him, but she did not. 'These long absences seem . . . to put a moral distance between us', he wrote to her. He complained of insomnia and indigestion – signs of nervousness. She was reading *Jude the Obscure* and asked him what he thought of it. 'The book is far from good', Gissing replied. 'It is *not* immoral . . . but simply a bitter attack upon the cruelty of the Universe. Any one of Hardy's early books is worth a dozen times more than this.' He told her to read Gibbon, and Fitzgerald's translation of *The Rubáiyát of Omar Khayyám*.

Gissing's letters of March and April reflect his continuing depression. Gabrielle stayed away; he worked very little; his lungs were not healing. 'I no more reckon on . . . the future', he wrote to Algernon. 'A wearisome life, this homeless wandering.' In mid-April he informed Miss Collet of the St. Jean de Luz experiment. He was cheered at the prospect of abandoning Paris – 'I hope, for ever.' He told her something of *An Author at Grass*, declaring that 'this little book is more to me than anything else I have written'. But the letter ends on a note of bitterness: 'If I live a few more years, I may hope to have earned in a quarter of a century the reputation which twenty authors of to-day have achieved by the publication of a couple of volumes.'

In April Gissing worked on the first proofs of *An Author at Grass*. Also at this time he took up his diary again. The initial entries, the first in a year, are about the diary itself: 'chanced to open . . . my Diary, and found it such strange and moving reading that I have gone on, hour after hour.' The earliest entries (he began to keep the diary in 1887, the year before Nell's death) were to him the most 'moving'. He went on to speak of the recent past: 'Not much work done this last year'; however, his latest two books 'were brilliantly reviewed'. He complained about his life at Arcachon: 'Never have I lived so long in the company of blackguards.' He confessed that he '*ached* with thoughts of England' and that he was very lonely: 'Receive no letters nowadays' (Gabrielle wrote mostly postcards).

Finally, on 24 April, Gissing left Arcachon. He went immediately to St. Jean de Luz, where he put up at a boarding-house and looked for suitable lodgings. His first impressions, as so often, were positive: the combination of mountains, sea, lush countryside, and comfortable villas delighted him. He wrote enthusiastically to Gabrielle: 'I think this is certainly *the* place . . . The more I see of this country, the more I like it . . . I improve in health almost hour by hour.' After a week in St. Jean de Luz he was eating, sleeping, and walking more than he had for a long time. He and Gabrielle agreed that if he found a place he liked he would rent it for a year. Meanwhile Gabrielle and her mother would begin packing up the Passy apartment.

Gissing found what he wanted in the Ciboure section of St. Jean de Luz. Here he rented the first floor of a large furnished villa overlooking the Bay of Biscay. The rent was low, and this he hoped would please Gabrielle, who was 'almost painfully economical, like most Frenchwomen', he told Margaret. Meanwhile he waited at the St. Jean de Luz boarding-house for Gabrielle and her mother to come down. While there he corrected proofs of his abridgement of Forster. On 1 May he was delighted to receive the number of the *Fortnightly* containing the first instalment of *An Author at Grass*. He noted in his Commonplace Book the death of an aeronaut at Paris (his flying machine exploded 300 metres off the ground): 'This rather pleasing to me than otherwise. Utterly useless to any good end, such inventions, and meant, first and foremost, for use in war.' By the third week of May there was still no sign of Gabrielle and no indication of when she would be coming. Gissing wrote in his diary: 'Having . . . nothing to do, passed the day in utter idleness . . . how often in my life have I spent such a day as this, – blank, wearisome, wasted! A sort of destiny of idleness and wasted time seems to oppress a great part of my life . . . circumstances are too strong for me.' Finally he could stand it no longer and jumped on a train for Paris.

VII

Reunited with Gabrielle in the Rue de Siam, Gissing spent much of his time helping the two ladies pack their belongings. He told Bertz that if he survived 'all the horrors of the removal' he had 'a novel ready to begin' as soon as he got back to Ciboure. The month in Paris was one of 'disorder and weariness', he wrote in his diary. Pinker had sold the volume rights of *An Author at Grass* to Constable, who paid £100 plus a twenty percent royalty. Constable wanted a more descriptive title, and suggested *The Private Papers of Henry Ryecroft*.

Early in July the three went down to Ciboure and moved into their new home. Gissing immediately began to write *Will Warburton*. In his spare time he taught himself Spanish and started to work his way through *Don Quixote*: 'A great thing to be . . . achieving this old ambition', he wrote in his diary. He also completed two reviews of studies of Dickens for the new *Times Literary Supplement*.

To Bertz he sent an account of his life at St. Jean de Luz. He said he wrote every morning for three hours but that this was as much as he could manage: 'a poor account, for a man who used to write his 8 or 10 hours daily, but I am not sure that it is not better from every point of view. I have more time to *meditate* my chapters, and lose less by the necessity of recommencing.' He said the Roman novel had been put aside: 'I always keep an eye on my Sixth Century, but it is plain to me that I shall not get that book written just yet' (he still missed his library). 'Long idleness has made the money question rather a grave one, and for the present I must do what I can pretty easily.' This was a reference to *Will Warburton*, in some ways a return to Gissing's old vein, which he continued to write slowly.

The climate of southern France suited Gissing but he evidently lacked occupation. 'Somehow my interest in life is not very keen', he told Wells. 'The years go by, and I still somehow tread the earth', he wrote wearily to Hick. 'Little cough, good sleep, fair appetite – on the whole a very respectable prolongation of life.' In mid-October, in typical fashion (his more methodical system of writing notwithstanding) he decided to scrap what he had written of *Will Warburton* and start again.

In October 1902 a long article, 'The Novel of Misery', appeared in the *Quarterly Review*. It had much to say about Gissing. The author begins by declaring that of all contemporary novelists, Gissing 'has shown himself the most open to the influences of continental literature'. But he had gone beyond French naturalism, and in fact his early books owed more to Dickens than to any realistic novelist – though Gissing's portraits of 'the London populace' were much more accurate (because less idealized) than

Dickens's. A long survey of the early novels follows. (Notably, *The Unclassed* is criticized for dealing with prostitution more sentimentally than seriously: how times had changed!) 'Mr Gissing's novels . . . are a history of his opinions', the essay concludes. Gissing also came before the public with his abridgement of Forster's *Life of Dickens*. The reviews were mixed, some journals welcoming a more readable format for Forster's bulky volumes, others unhappy with Gissing's tampering.

The prospect of winter began to alarm him. 'Intolerable idiots go about prophesying a winter of unprecedented severity', he told Hick. He hoped to come to England some time in 1903. In letters to Bertz written in October and November his low spirits show through plainly, but he was satisfied that *The Ryecroft Papers*, about which (in its serial form) he had received a good deal of adulatory mail, was the best literary work he could hope to turn out. And then there were the old complaints: 'My reputation in England steadily increases . . . but . . . my fame brings me no money, my books have only the smallest sale . . . [they] are read only from the libraries. And so . . . it will be to the end . . . the richest authors, to-day, are generally the least important.' Bertz wrote that he had just read *Tess of the d'Urbervilles* and *Jude the Obscure*. Gissing replied: 'Neither of them appeals to me like Hardy's earlier books, when the idyllic spirit was unaffected by fierce pessimism . . . The end of "Tess" . . . [is] an entire artistic mistake. But I greatly admire Hardy, and am very sorry he will write no more fiction. His . . . verse has but small value.'

Having finished correcting proofs of *The Private Papers of Henry Ryecroft*, Gissing took an excursion, his first such venture, into nearby Spain. The account of it written on 8 November 1902 is the final entry in the diary. Towards the end of the month, he read Conrad's *Youth*, recently published, and on the stories in it he commented in these terms to Clodd: 'No man at present writing fiction has such grip of reality, such imaginative vigour, and such wonderful command of language, as Joseph Conrad. I think him a *great* writer – there's no other word. And, when one considers his personal history, the English of his books is something like a miracle.' Clodd passed these comments along to Conrad, who poured out his gratitude to Gissing a few days before Christmas. 'No lavishness of Dickens's imagination would have contrived [such a gift] for the felicity of a poor devil in a Christmas tale', Conrad wrote.

Gissing sounded like 'a poor devil' himself when he wrote to

Clara Collet on Christmas Eve. Though the new version of *Will Warburton* was nearly half finished, his mind was weighed down with unhappy thoughts: 'In the days gone by, I used to imagine for my later life all the evils of poverty; what I never foresaw was inability to write through failure of health . . . My inability to do any serious work takes away from any kind of enjoyment . . . On the whole', he added, 'I suspect [*Ryecroft*] the best thing I have done, or am likely to do; the thing most likely to last when all my other futile work has followed my futile life.' He begged her to read Conrad. 'He is the strongest writer . . . at present publishing in English. Marvellous writing! The other men are mere scribblers in comparison. That a foreigner should write like this, is one of the miracles of literature.'

The year 1902 – having 'passed in ailing idleness', as Gissing told Clara Collet – drew to an end. He had earned only £226 during the past twelve months.

VIII

The Private Papers of Henry Ryecroft was published in January 1903 (a few days before the last instalment of *An Author at Grass* appeared in the *Fortnightly*) to some of the best notices Gissing ever received. 'Oh, golden book of spirit and of sense', sighed the *Daily Telegraph*. The *Times Literary Supplement* (formerly *Literature*) compared him on equal terms with Balzac. Like the old Dutch painters, it said, he is 'always' convincing. 'Soberness, strength, an impeccable honesty; the unswerving, almost fatalistic acceptance of the hardest facts; a deep, painful, vital sense of the brotherhood of our bewildered humanity; and the most masculine expression of pathos to be found in any contemporary novelist – that brief, inexpressive, poignant pity for the individual, which can yet accept his pain as a necessary part of life – these are all characteristics of Mr. Gissing', the *TLS* declared. The new book, it added, was Gissing's 'fullest expression of the poetry within him . . . [he] has never written anything more remarkable.' The reviewer concluded that 'It has become the fashion, within the last two or three years, to speak of Mr Gissing as of a master.' The *Athenaeum*, in a rare favourable notice, still managed to enrage the novelist by discussing *The Ryecroft Papers* as if it were an autobiography. The *Pall Mall Gazette* called the volume Gissing's 'masterpiece'. The *Academy*'s reviewer confessed himself 'overcome' by the book, which he called 'the coping-stone' of Gissing's literary career. He added a generous tribute: a reference to the novelist's 'singleness of mind in an age of literary opportunism. Unlogrolled and unboomed . . . he has fared on through periods and popularities, winning nothing more showy than the hearty respect of everyone who can recognise a true man of letters.' *The Ryecroft Papers*, said the *Week's Survey*, a new journal, 'is one of the most distinguished books that has been written in the last ten dull years.' Only the *Morning Post* and the *Publishers' Circular* among English publications printed unfriendly notices. In Boston the *Independent* pronounced *The Ryecroft Papers* one of the best books to have appeared in English in many years.

The volume brought bundles of letters to Gissing from strangers all over the world, many of whom believed that there really had been a Henry Ryecroft. Perhaps the apotheosis was reached by a clergyman who wrote to inquire if by chance the late Mr Ryecroft's housekeeper needed employment. Gissing had never been so closely in touch with his readers. The first edition of the book sold out in a month. Three new impressions were issued in 1903 alone: the book was the hit of the season. Still, because of the advance he received and his small share of royalties, Gissing was to earn less than £200 from *The Ryecroft Papers* during what little remained of his lifetime.

Bertz had a number of objections to the book, especially the attack in it on conscription and militarism, which he felt was a criticism of Germany. Gissing replied: 'I lament the lot of the "poor devil" who makes soldiering his trade; but I lament still more the lot of quiet people whose lives are . . . made miserable by the accursed spirit of war.' He gave Bertz a thumbnail sketch of the current state of his own affairs. He had 'nearly finished' a new novel, *Will Warburton*. Despite the success of *Ryecroft*, 'The troubles about me and before me are very grave, and any day I might find the world very much my enemy. My need of money grows rather serious, for though we live . . . economically . . . I earn so little, so little!'

In February Roberts came to visit for a week. 'He complained to me when we were alone about his health, and . . . protested . . . against the meals,' Roberts said later. Gissing yearned to settle in England. He said he could not complete *Veranilda*, as the Roman novel was now called, away from the British Museum. But Gabrielle thought that her mother could not stand another move, and would not entertain the idea (Mme Fleury was to outlive Gissing by some years). Roberts was astonished at Gissing's refusal to go out of doors whenever he thought he might catch cold. 'He had developed a great fear of death, and life seemed to him extraordinarily fragile.' Roberts read *Ryecroft* for the first time on his way home, and disliked it. Its 'calculated dispirited air . . . afflicted me', he said. When he got home he wrote to Gissing at length about the book. In his reply the novelist said that the volume was 'a curious blend . . . of truth and fiction'. He added, as part of his rationale for writing such a book, that his 'delight in the beauty of the visible world, and enjoyment of the great things of literature, grow stronger. My one desire now is to *utter* this passion.' In the months following his visit, Roberts received several requests from Gissing for information about Roman law and spent many hours in the British Museum gathering it for him.

Early in March Gissing told Jane Wells that he could 'walk for an hour at a time, with not more than a dozen pauses to labour agonizingly for breath'. An invitation to lecture in England (on Dickens) had to be turned down for reasons of health. In mid-March he finished *Will Warburton* and dispatched it to Pinker, hoping for another serialization. He wrote triumphantly to Ellen that '*Ryecroft* is just announced in a *third edition*! . . . the book is being universally read . . . the success of *Ryecroft* helps to keep me cheerful and hopeful.' Gissing's tendency to quick changes of mood can be observed in a letter he wrote to Margaret just four days later: 'They tell me that [*Ryecroft*] has been the subject of conversation in every London drawing-room. And see the result in cash! Of course people who know nothing of such matters think I am drawing large sums of money.'

IX

Despite the fact that Gissing habitually referred disparagingly to *Will Warburton*, it is one of his very greatest novels, another in the long line of neglected masterpieces he gave to a largely indifferent posterity. Writing more slowly – 'meditating' his chapters, as he put it – may have been partly responsible for the book's quality; or it may simply be the result of his general unhappiness, which was so often a creative factor in his literary labours. The return to a number of well-tried themes may also be partly responsible.

Will Warburton is the last of Gissing's fictional *alter-egos*. He epitomizes in himself much of the novelist's personality, and many of the fictional personalities he had been conjuring up for a quarter of a century. 'I was always a good deal of a solitary . . . and my temper hasn't been improved by ill-luck', Warburton declares. A misogynist, a recluse (he shuts himself off 'from the outer world' for weeks at a time), a great walker (like Henry Ryecroft, Warburton walks to tire himself and sleep at night), a hater of 'society' in all its forms and of the 'cunning' of the Stock Exchange, Warburton is an educated man (a classicist, no less) whose prosperity melts away in a bad investment. To support himself he secretly 'goes behind the counter' – becomes, that is, a grocer. The novelist had always worried, as we know, about stumbling into a similar fate should his powers fail him. As illness reduced his earning power, he wrote this great fear into his last novel. Warburton shares the anxiety of Godwin Peak, and suffers the same humiliation of public 'declassment' as Kingcote in *Isabel Clarendon* when he puts his name over a shop. He also personifies one of Gissing's most ubiquitous themes: the power of money to determine the social milieu one inhabits. *Will Warburton* is a brilliant examination of the psychological impact of class barriers and pressures on a sensitive nature.

Like Peak, Warburton sees himself as an 'exile' living away from his friends and having to hide the true nature of his life, unable to meet his intellectual peers on equal terms. Like Peak, he cannot in the end stomach the social 'lie to which he was committed . . . what rendered his life intolerable was its radical dishonesty . . . Grocerdom with a clear conscience would have been a totally different thing from grocerdom surreptitiously embraced. Instead of slinking into a corner for the performance of an honourable act, he should have declared it, frankly, unaffectedly . . . as things stood, he was ashamed, degraded, not by circumstances, but by himself.' Thus Gissing describes, from the inside, the pathology of class fear and the way it can govern human intercourse.

Not surprisingly, Warburton lives in lodgings, and is cheated by his landlady. He assumes that no respectable woman will interest herself in him. He feels closer to his dead father than to his living mother. A brother died while at school. Warburton's friendship with Norbert Franks in its early stages resembles that of Gissing with Bertz and Roberts during the early London years (the novel is set in 1886). The mother and sister of Warburton live in St. Neots, where Gissing spent some time gathering material several years earlier. These placid English scenes are invoked with great fondness and loving detail – down to the wonderfully sustaining qualities of the food served. As in *The Ryecroft Papers,* Gissing's love of England and his impatience with his French 'exile' are apparent. Warburton retraces Gissing's steps too by going to the French Pyrenees (after his 'grocerdom' is revealed). There are several references in the novel to St. Jean de Luz, and while there Warburton has 'a run into Spain'.

Warburton ends with a wife (Bertha Cross) whose mother lives with them and from whom control of the domestic management of their household has to be wrested for efficiency's sake. 'I give over everything into your hands. I will never interfere; I won't say a word, whatever fault I may have to find; not a word' – thus Mrs Cross to her daughter after being relieved of her domestic charge. Did Mme Fleury make a similar declaration when Gissing returned to the fold in 1901 – or is this a case of wish-fulfilment? Mrs Cross is part Mme Fleury, part Edith Gissing.

When occasions of dispute were lacking, the day would have been long and wearisome for her had she not ceaselessly plied the domestic drudge with tasks, and narrowly watched their execution . . . Underpaid and underfed, these persons . . . were of course incompetent, careless, rebellious, and Mrs Cross found the sole genuine pleasure of her life in the war she waged with them. Having no reasonable way of spending her hours, she was thus supplied with occupation; being of acrid temper, she was thus supplied with a subject upon whom she could fearlessly exercise it; being remarkably mean of disposition, she saw in the paring-down of her servant's rations to a working minimum, at once profit and sport; lastly, being fond of the most trivial gossip, she had a never failing topic of discussion with such ladies as could endure her society.

The novel takes up in detail Warburton's attitudes towards class. 'Social grades were an inseparable part of his view of life; he recognized the existence of his superiors – though resolved to have as little to do with them as possible, and took it as a matter of course that multitudes of men should stand below his level.' Gissing goes on to define, in Warburton, the brand of middle-class paranoia to which he himself was subject throughout his adult life: 'No man was less pretentious; but his liberality of thought and behaviour consisted with a personal pride which was very much at the mercy of circumstance. Even as he could not endure subjection, so did he shrink from the thought of losing dignity in the eyes of his social inferiors.' This latter clause says much: it refers to the continuously percolating guilt about his past and the fear of revelation which haunted Gissing throughout his life and explains so much of his social conservatism. The 'guilty secret' here is the secret of Warburton's 'grocerdom'.

Written during Gissing's last months, *Will Warburton* exudes a sense of physical suffering unknown in the previous novels. The very short chapters, some of them only two or three pages, betray perhaps the novelist's failing strength. 'The struggle was telling upon his health; it showed in his face, in his bearing', Gissing writes of Warburton. He enumerates some of his sick hero's anxieties:

What if some accident . . . threw him among the weaklings? He saw his
mother, in her age and ill-health, reduced to the pittance of the poorest; his
sister going forth to earn her living; himself, a helpless burden upon both. –
Nay, was there not rat poison to be purchased? How – he cried within
himself – how, in the name of sense and mercy, is mankind content to live
on in such a world as this? By what devil are they haunted, that . . . they
neglect the means of solace suggested to every humane and rational mind
. . . Overwhelmed by the hateful unreason of it all, he felt as though his
brain reeled on the verge of madness . . . life weighed upon him with a
burden such as he had never imagined. Never had he understood before
what was meant by the sickening weariness of routine.

This gives us a fearsome glimpse into the mind of the dying novelist,
detesting his invalidism and the bleak prospects he faced if he
managed to go on living. He had always worried about being
incapacitated, unable to work, dependent on others. The possibility
of suicide, that 'means of solace' he had considered and rejected so
often before, was apparently being contemplated once again. Feeling as never before 'the humiliating circumstances of human life', as
he wrote in his Commonplace Book, Gissing in *Will Warburton*
returned to the despairing mode of the early novels. He asks: How
can one live in such a world? It is the question posed by *Workers in
the Dawn*, *The Unclassed*, *Isabel Clarendon*, *Thyrza*, *The Nether
World*. 'A horror of life seized him', Gissing writes of Warburton.
'He understood, with fearful sympathy, the impulse of those who,
rather than be any longer hustled in this howling mob, dash
themselves to destruction.'

In its indictment of the commercialization of art, *Will Warburton*
returns to themes prominent in Gissing's last half-dozen novels.
But in so far as it focuses on the status of art and of artists in society
– many of them painters and many of them starving – it is a return
to an earlier vintage. Norbert Franks, the hungry painter who
succeeds by prostituting his art, could have stepped out of the pages
of any of Gissing's first ten novels. Again we hear that the artist
must starve to succeed, and that often he is spoiled by marriage.
Franks, the Jasper Milvain of *Will Warburton*, discovers these
things for himself; ultimately his only goal in life is to make enough
money to induce Rosamund Elvan to marry him. At the end of the
novel there is a scene between the complacent Franks and victorious
Rosamund (*née* Amy Reardon) which will remind any reader of the
end of *New Grub Street*. The two speak condescendingly of their
friends Will and Bertha, who have had to settle for so much less

than they themselves. 'A grocer's wife', they say of Bertha: 'That she should have no higher ambition!'

'"We can't all achieve ambitions", cried Franks . . . "Not every girl can marry a popular portrait-painter."

'"A great artist!" exclaimed his wife, with emphasis.'

She calls him 'great' only because he is rich. To make money as an artist, the book argues, one must discard standards and ideals. Success comes with selling out, with artistic vulgarity. *Will Warburton* is a very bitter book. 'Fate has a grudge against the foolishly secure', it says, and this might be its epigraph.

The importance of money as a means of providing ease and pleasure is as patently emphasized here as in any of the early slum-life novels. 'Chance to be poor, and not only must you die when you need not, but must die with the minimum of comfort, the extreme of bodily and mental distress . . . A few coins, or pieces of printed paper to signify all that . . . No matter how pure the motive, a man cannot devote his days to squeezing out pecuniary profits without some moral detriment.' Here is the Gissing of *The Nether World*, the Gissing of the eighties, reborn as a result of the terrible struggles of his last years.

Will Warburton reminds us that a respectable woman will only marry a man with money. No truly respectable woman, for example, could love a grocer – unless she knew him to be, socially speaking, better than his profession (as Bertha knows Will to be). Rosamund's reaction to the disclosure of Will's adopted profession is interesting for its excessiveness: she sobs hysterically – and then runs off to marry the prosperous but uninteresting Norbert Franks.

There is, finally, the familiar city/country theme. It is better to go to work every day 'through lanes overhung with fruit-tree blossoms' than through 'the filth and stench and gloom and uproar' of London, the novel argues. The streets of London are called a 'vast slaughter-strewn field of battle'. The sounds of the city are 'cries of pain or of misery, shouts savage or bestial; over and through all, that low, far-off rumble or roar, which never for a moment ceases, the groan . . . of suffering multitudes'. London and Paris no longer beckoned to Gissing. He yearned only for Henry Ryecroft's country cottage.

x

In April 1903 Gissing wrote to Bertz that *The Ryecroft Papers* was 'more of a success than anything I have yet published' and told him about the third edition. Bertz, alarmed by the tone of recent letters from his friend, had inquired about Gissing's state of mind. The novelist replied: '*my* reconcilement with the state of things is rather literary than actual; as a matter of fact, I am sadly ill at ease in the world. But I fear that I am losing combative force.' He told Bertz of Roberts's visit. 'We talked of you, and the old days – ah, the old days!' A week later he wrote to Ellen, complaining of the heat and quoting a newspaper which said it was hotter in 1879. 'I was then toiling in London, and often starving – aye but I was well and young and strong, and nothing mattered.' Another letter written at this time shows the depth of his depression. 'I fall more and more into the habits of an invalid, very seldom writing any letters save those absolutely necessary', he told Justin MacCarthy. 'I can't walk much, and my work is reduced to a minimum. So things will go on, I suppose, for a few years yet. The less said of it the better.'

Gissing, Gabrielle, and Mme Fleury now moved to the neighbouring town of St. Jean Pied de Port, near Roncesvalles and farther from the sea, which the local physician felt was injurious to the novelist's health. Gissing continued to work desultorily on *Veranilda* throughout May. He pressed Pinker to sell *Will Warburton* and continued to worry about money. The funds being used to pay Edith's bills at the asylum were running out, and Walter's expenses at school were on the rise. Would there never be an end to these troubles over cash? He told Hick early in June that he had hoped *The Ryecroft Papers* would make him rich, 'but 3,000 copies in England seem to be about the extent of my public – and if you like to calculate what 3,000 shillings amount to, you will see what a literary "success" [means].'

In June they all moved again, seeking an even healthier climate for the ailing novelist – first to Cambo-les-Bains and then to Ispoure, at the foot of the Pyrenees. Here Gissing seemed to feel better; his breathing improved. Still, he could not shake off his general discomfiture. 'It is just a year now since I came to the Basque country, and I cannot remember in all my life a year so unprofitable', he told Clodd. The letter concluded: 'Don't, don't speak of my coming there! I fear I shall not live to do so, and the mere thought of eating an English potato at your table makes me frantic with homesickness.' He described himself to Bertz at the end of June as 'weak and pain-ridden . . . to a dangerous degree'.

In July Gissing's affairs brightened. Pinker sold *Will Warburton* to Constable for an advance of £300 against a royalty of twenty per cent up to 2,500 copies and twenty-five per cent thereafter. Gissing told Bertz he was feeling better and making some progress on *Veranilda* – 'But I live in fear of breaking down . . . oh, the torments of the last half-year!' He complained of insomnia. Early in August his health was better. He even began to contemplate his next book: it would be another historical novel, set in Greece during the Golden Age and he would need to work in the British Museum. He told Meredith he hoped to see him in England in 1904. In a long letter written at the end of August Gissing brought Wells up to date on his affairs. He said he had completed a third of the Roman novel 'which has haunted my mind for the last ten years'. There was more praise for Conrad, whose volume *Typhoon* he had managed to get hold of. He said he had seen in an English newspaper a notice of the death of W. E. Henley: the obituary had put the deceased man's worth at more than £800. 'Amazing! How on earth did he amass that wealth?' Such an amount now seemed incredibly large to Gissing, who had earned over £700 just two years earlier, in 1901.

Around the same time he told Roberts he faced 'sheer pauperdom' if he did not finish his new novel by the end of the year: 'In short I have not often . . . been nearer to an appalling crisis.' During the last two years of his life, 1902 and 1903, he earned only £442 altogether. He was delighted, however, when Pinker managed to sell the Roman novel, sight unseen, to Constable; the terms were identical with those given for *Will Warburton*, including the advance of £300. (In the case of both novels half the advance was paid down, the rest to await publication.) Gissing stipulated that *Veranilda* was to appear before *Will Warburton* . But it was proving increasingly difficult to write. 'I am often troubled with doubts', he told Bertz, 'thinking the whole thing a mere worthless effort of the imagination. Yet . . . I sometimes feel that I have got hold of the spirit of the 6th. Century.' St. Jean de Luz, he said, had been a mistake, but St. Jean Pied de Port suited him well – though he complained about the lack of library resources: 'The need of books is becoming a very serious matter for me.' He ended: 'All good be with you.' It was his last letter to Bertz.

He wrote a long letter to Wells in mid-October, largely in response to Wells's recently published *Mankind in the Making*. Among the many issues he debated with Wells here three are of special interest. As so often before, he came down against schemes of universal education. 'Genius', he wrote, 'is stifled a thousand times for once that it comes to fruit; but one cannot forget the law of humanity which says that all good shall be won "not without dust and heat". I fear the over-much encouraging of the young by making things easy for them.' Wells had declared that the average London working-girl possessed a tenth part of the English language. Gissing said he should have substituted 'thousandth' for 'tenth': 'I have known some whose vocabulary was, I swear, barely 200 words.' And he condemned Wells's tolerant view of literary censorship and his suggestion that books be marked for 'children' or 'adults': 'I fear humanity must go on in the old way, getting good here and evil there, each reader finding pasture or poison as his nature may be. The label 'adult' would merely introduce into the world a new prurience', Gissing said, accurately anticipating the chief result in our time of film censorship and systems of audience-rating.

At the same time the novelist wrote what turned out to be his last letter to Clodd. He said he felt 'drawn every day, in spirit', to south-eastern Europe, by which he meant Italy and Greece. 'Here [in France] I cannot feel myself at home; the country has no true charm for me; I want to feel the Mediterranean somewhere near.' In another vein: 'The one thing I greatly envy any man is the possession of a home. I have never had one since I was a boy, and now, I fear, never shall' (Henry Ryecroft, of course, says exactly the same thing). *Veranilda*, he told Clodd, would not 'be bad . . . but it is harder work than any I ever did – not a line that does not ask sweat of the brain.' The letter ends as the last letter to Bertz ended: 'All good be with you.'

As November set in Gissing again began to worry about the winter. Should he go somewhere else? He decided that a journey would be the greater danger. He dispatched to Pinker the first twenty-two chapters of *Veranilda* just before his forty-sixth birthday. By the end of the month he estimated that he had written three-quarters of the novel, and that he would finish it in January. In the last letter he wrote to Wakefield he told Ellen of the book's progress, and added a short sermon on 'the disastrous effect of too much wealth. I have great fears that England is being ruined by this – this, and excessive poverty.' At the end of November Gissing wrote to Wells – also for the last time. 'I want very badly to see England, and my friends there', he said, but his health would not permit the trip. He referred to the slow growth of *Veranilda*, 'which has hovered before me so long', and remarked longingly at the end of the letter: 'How full your life must be of work and pleasure.'

XI

During the first week of December 1903 Gissing wrote his last story, 'Topham's Chance'. It is a pathetic tale of a wealthy grocer whose children marry and leave home to avoid living in the same town as their tradesman father; the grocer decides to study for the Church so that the family will no longer be 'ashamed' of him. Topham himself is a highly educated man toiling in a correspondence school because of a guilty secret in his past. The subjects of Gissing's last works are the same as those of his first.

On 8 December, after taking a walk on a cold day, Gissing caught a chill. Several days later pneumonia developed in his already ravaged lungs. During the following week either myocarditis or pericarditis set in – an infection of the heart muscle or surrounding membrane, caused by an extension of pleuritis. On the 21st a local doctor told Gabrielle that the novelist was past hope and might not live another day. As it turned out, he lingered on through a week of terrible pain – 'of cruel suffering, of veritable torture, of delirium and of terrible attacks of nerves', Gabrielle was to say later.

'Pain I cannot endure, and I . . . think with apprehension of being subjected to the trial of long death-bed torments', says Henry Ryecroft. 'Most solemnly do I hope that in the latter days no long illness awaits me. May I pass quickly from this life of quiet enjoyment to final peace.' 'It had always been his wish to die suddenly', Gissing says of Ryecroft in the 'Preface' to the book. 'He dreaded the thought of illness, chiefly because of the trouble it gave to others.' These hopes, transparently the novelist's own, were not to be fulfilled. Gissing had also worried, in *The Ryecroft Papers*, about dying away from his native land. Yet here he was – dying, like Godwin Peak, 'in exile'.

On 23 December Gabrielle sent a telegram to Wells, and what followed next might have been the dénouement of a comic opera. 'Come and see me', she cabled cryptically. 'What for?' he replied. The next day Gabrielle telegraphed that Gissing was dying. Wells, who had a bad cold, wired Roberts and asked him to go to the Pyrenees in his place. Roberts was seriously ill at the time. He told Wells he should not travel, but that he would go if Wells was absolutely unable to. On Christmas Eve Wells started for the *pays basque*. Gabrielle, meanwhile, had asked the English chaplain at St. Jean de Luz, Theodore Cooper, to come over – not for religious solace but because, she believed, Gissing would like another Englishman to speak to. Cooper, described by Wells as 'a tremulous, obstinate little being', left an account of his visit. Gissing told him he was dying and asked the clergyman to send him back to England so that he could be treated by an English doctor. Cooper told Gissing of a Dr Malpas, an English physician living at Biarritz; Gissing begged that he be sent for, and he was. The next morning, Christmas morning, Cooper came again. The novelist was in great pain. Cooper says he leaned over the bed and declared, 'My friend, you are going home.' Distinctly and clearly, he says, came the reply: 'God's will be done.' It is highly unlikely that Gissing said any such thing; Cooper's version is distorted by the delusion that the novelist had become a Christian on his deathbed. More characteristic are some of Gissing's last reflections as reported by Gabrielle. He had 'no thought of horror, but of mere bewilderment'. He spoke of having 'done . . . nothing . . . How I wasted the golden days! How strong I was!' He told her: 'Life is meaningless.' He pictured himself 'on the deck of a steamer, approaching the English coast!'

On the afternoon of Christmas Day both Wells and Dr Malpas arrived. The latter saw immediately that Gissing was beyond help. Wells took over the sick-room, saying later that Gabrielle was 'extremely incompetent' and that Mme Fleury remained in her room. Some relatives of Gabrielle's were on the scene, but Wells managed to get rid of them. A nurse was found. Wells then girded himself for the battle against his old enemy. He argued in the very death-chamber with Gabrielle about the respective merits of English and French theories of nursing – whether or not to give the patient liquids, what to feed him (a light diet had been prescribed), whether to keep him warm or cool. At one point Wells apparently threw open all the windows in the house. He maintained later that Gabrielle did nothing but wander around wringing her hands and crying, 'Oh, poor George, poor George', and telling everyone how much it pained her to see her husband dying. He also charged that she was reluctant to provide handkerchiefs and towels for wiping the patient's face and body because of the cost of cleaning them. She in turn would contend that Wells himself 'killed' Gissing by feeding him broth, wine, and coffee in quick succession. Wells declared that she had starved him again, this time beyond repair. He and Hick agreed later that 'French starvation caused Gissing to go to pieces . . . His life was probably sacrificed . . . to silly incompetence, want of nursing, etc.' Wells says that Gissing was delirious most of the time he was there. 'There was no ice available and his chest had to be kept cool by continually dipping handkerchiefs in methylated spirits and putting them on him' – these were the famous handker-chiefs he and Gabrielle supposedly quarrelled about. The nurse, says Wells, had dirty finger nails and spent most of the time sleeping by the fire.

The brilliantly written account of the death of George Ponderevo in Wells's *Tono-Bungay* (1908) is a highly personalized picture of Gissing's last days. Ponderevo dies in a little village in the *pays basque*,

strangely changed under the shadow of oncoming death, with his skin lax and yellow and glistening with sweat, his eyes large and glassy, his countenance unfamiliar through the growth of a beard, his nose pinched and thin. Never had he looked so small as now . . . from those slimy tormented lips . . . came nothing but dreams and disconnected fancies . . . It seemed such nonsense that he should have to suffer so.

In his autobiography Wells says that Gissing was lucid only once while he was at his bedside, and in that moment 'entreated me to take him back to England'.

For the rest of the time this gaunt, dishevelled, unshaven, flushed, bright-eyed being who sat up in bed and gestured weakly with his lean hand, was exalted. He had passed altogether into that fantastic pseudo-Roman world of which Wakefield Grammar School had laid the foundations . . . 'Who are these magnificent beings advancing upon us?' [he asked]. Or again, 'What is all this splendour? What does it portend?' He babbled in Latin; he chanted fragments of Gregorian music. All the accumulation of material that he had made for *Veranilda* . . . was hurrying faster and brighter across the mirrors of his brain before the lights went out for ever.

Throughout the 26th Wells sat by Gissing's bedside, wiping his mouth and lips and watching him struggle for breath as the fluid-level rose in his diseased lungs. It was on this night that he took advantage of Gabrielle's brief absence from the sick-room to conduct his *blitzkrieg* feeding of the 'starving' patient. He also wrote to Gosse, requesting him to apply for a Royal pension for Gissing's sons, and cabled Roberts, asking him to come if he possibly could (Roberts left for the Pyrenees the next day). On the 27th Wells and Cooper both departed, the former ill himself and seeing plainly that nothing more could be done. Upon his departure he told Gabrielle once again that she had starved her husband to death. She retorted that Gissing might have recovered had not he, Wells, overfed him, thus driving the patient's temperature up and putting an extra strain on his heart (modern medicine seems to be on Gabrielle's side). 'I treated her harshly', Wells admitted later, but he said in his own defence: 'Her sense of proportion was inadequate and her need for sympathy untimely.' He did not take up the question of the possible injury he did Gissing by overfeeding him (in all likelihood it made little difference by that time). Gissing continued to suffer great pain while his wife and his friend said their unpleasant farewells. Gabrielle wrote to Clara Collet and Bertz on the 27th to inform them that Gissing was dying. She told Bertz that the novelist kept muttering 'about his *Veranilda* which he leaves unachieved, with just 5 – the 5 last chapters missing!'

Due to a series of mishaps, Roberts was delayed on his journey and Gabrielle was alone with her husband at the end. She sat up with him on this, his last night alive. 'Your brother had a devoted wife: she was unsparing of herself', the clergyman Cooper wrote later to Ellen Gissing. This picture of Gabrielle (stoutly defended by Roberts) must after all be balanced against Wells's prejudiced account.

'Death inspires me with no fear . . . There is no such dignity as that of death', Gissing had written in *The Ryecroft Papers*. He had none the less added: 'I have had no time; I have only been preparing myself – a mere apprentice to life . . . And is this all? A man's life can be so brief and vain?' Ryecroft also declares that 'the last thought of my brain as I lie dying will be that of sunshine upon an English meadow.' But Gissing was delirious during most of the night of 27 December, and according to Gabrielle he spent much of it reciting the *Te Deum,* crying out 'that he saw the other world, hell and all the devils', and babbling about popes and cardinals. On the morning of the 28th, after an injection of morphia, he briefly 'regained consciousness, recognised me and showed great feeling', Gabrielle told Bertz.

Gissing had written to her in 1898: 'My beloved, how I hope that a word of tenderness, spoken as you can speak it, will be the last thing I hear on earth.' In this, at least, it would appear that he got his wish. 'His eyes did not leave me until he breathed his last, and he gave me the most moving, the most heartbreaking mute farewell', Gabrielle told Bertz. 'He had lost all power of speech, and from 8 o'clock in the morning until 1:15 p.m. when he died, he made violent but vain efforts to speak to me . . . One could live for centuries and still have in the "mind's eye" this tragic and agonising scene, this cruel ending of a life filled with misery of every kind.' She added that the 'inarticulate sounds' Gissing made towards the end left her supremely frustrated: 'I should so have wished to gather his last words, his last thoughts, and not even this consolation was afforded me!' By a strange coincidence he died on the same day of the year as his father – 28 December.

'Such men as I live and die alone, however much in appearance accompanied', the novelist had declared in *The Ryecroft Papers*. In *Thyrza* Gissing had written of Gilbert Grail: 'Only when he lay in his last sleep would it truly be said of him that he rested.' About suffering he was never wrong.

※

CHAPTER 13

AFTERWARDS

The end of a novel, like the end of a children's dinner-party,
must be made up of sweetmeats and sugar-plums.
Trollope, *Barchester Towers*

Here lie I, Ross Mallard; who can say no good of myself, yet
have as little right to say ill; who had no faith whereby to direct
my steps, yet often felt that some such was needful; who spent
all my strength on a task which I knew to be vain; who suffered
much and joyed rarely; whose happiest day was his last.
The Emancipated

There is no such dignity as that of death.
The Ryecroft Papers

I

ROBERTS arrived at St. Jean Pied de Port on the day after
Gissing's death. He described Gabrielle, 'the only woman who had
given [Gissing] any happiness', as 'completely broken down'. She
told Roberts that at the last, 'in his agony', the novelist had 'cried
aloud for death'. Roberts viewed his dead friend:

He looked strangely and peculiarly intellectual, as so often happens after
death . . . Curiously . . . he had grown a little beard in his last illness . . .
As I stood by the dead-bed knowing . . . that he had died at last in the
strange anguish which . . . he had feared, it seemed to me that here was a
man who had been born to inherit grief. He had never known pure peace or
utter joy . . . I looked back across the toilsome path by which he had come
hither to the end, and it seemed to me that from the very first he had been
doomed . . . I put my hand upon his forehead and said farewell.

The body was buried (after an Anglican ceremony, which would
have appalled Gissing) in the English cemetery at St. Jean de Luz
overlooking the Bay of Biscay, a view the novelist had enjoyed. A
large number of the English residents there turned out for the
ceremony.

A long obituary appeared immediately in *The Times*. It described
Gissing's career; the 'guilty secret' of his past was still unknown.
The usual mistake about *The Unclassed* being his first novel was

repeated. The notice said in part: 'Mr. Gissing . . . [had] a determination to tell what he believed to be the truth and nothing else . . . A good classical scholar and a man of the highest literary ideals, he cared little or nothing for what the average reading public thought of his work.' The obituary went on to compare Gissing to Balzac in his desire 'to picture the truth of life' through accumulation of detail. 'The result', said *The Times*, 'was a series of books which, if they cannot justly be called great work, were at least the work of a very able and conscientious literary artist, whose purity and solidity may win him a better chance of being read a hundred years hence than many writers of greater grace and more deliberately sought charm.'

Most of the other major newspapers and journals printed highly flattering notices (even the *Athenaeum*, come round at last). The *Pall Mall Gazette*, in whose pages the novelist's periodical career had begun, remarked that Gissing was 'a writer excelled by none of his contemporaries in justness of observation and . . . tenacious fidelity in the description of what he observed'. The *Speaker* declared that Gissing's novels 'are never likely to be read less than they are read at present, and that can be said of very few novelists'. This was the sort of thing that undoubtedly aroused the jealousy of Wells, whose books were so patently aimed at the popular market.

Ellen Gissing wrote her own memorial essay, published years later in the volume of *Family Letters* she and Algernon edited. It is a tender, mellow, affectionate remembrance. In the course of it Ellen says that 'a note of depression was the most strongly marked of all of [Gissing's] characteristics. One always felt that his enjoyment . . . would be followed . . . by a sinking of spirit.'

Hearing of Gissing's death, Clodd wrote in his diary: 'Storm-tossed, sincere and brave fellow: for him welcome rest: I loved him.'

Just a week after Gissing's death, Wells began the campaign of vilification in which he was to persevere for the next four decades. Asked by Gosse to supply some information about Gissing for the application being filed for the boys' Civil List pension, Wells wrote: 'Gissing was a most amiable decent man but an absolute fool, outside the covers of a book . . . there is nothing lurid and bad but much that is pitiful in his life.' He told Gosse as much as he knew about Gissing. Gabrielle he described as 'pathetic . . . devoted and exasperatingly incompetent.' He asked Gosse to get some money for the education of the boys, which he felt Gissing would have cared deeply about. He ended on a note of grudging admiration: 'in money matters he was a most scrupulous man. That's not so common as it might be in our profession. He was one of the most clean minded and decent of men.' Walter and Alfred were ultimately granted yearly pensions of £37 each.

Frederic Harrison was astonished to receive a mourning card written in French. Knowing nothing of Gabrielle, he asked Wells for an explanation and Wells supplied it. In the course of his reply Harrison said he was amused by the public impression that Gissing had emerged from the slum-life he wrote about – the 'myth' of the novelist's 'grinding poverty, solitude, neglect' – when in fact up to the age of eighteen 'he had a perfectly comfortable, easy, successful and even brilliant life, with every prospect of a fine career. That he threw away . . . [and] passed through a year or two of acute pressure and dreadful suffering – for which he alone was responsible.' He had a penchant, Harrison said, 'for trying what misery was like. He was a sort of amateur Fakir of modern slum life.' His first two marriages, Harrison thought, were the result of 'an incurable turn for a solitary life and the study of misery and the sordid'. He said he loved Gissing but thought him, despite his fascination with misery, 'the most hardened egotist and the most refined sybarite I knew'. He commented that no one seemed to have heard of Gissing's 'earliest and in many ways his best book – savage and foul as it is'.

Meanwhile a genuine controversy had swirled up. Two weeks after the novelist's demise a report of his deathbed conversion, attributed to Theodore Cooper, was published in the *Church Times*. Undoubtedly Cooper had been confused by Gissing's mutterings about popes and cardinals and the *Te Deum* and did not realize that it was *Veranilda* he had on his mind. Roberts wrote immediately to the *Church Times* and the *Westminster Gazette*, which also picked the conversion story up, to deny it absolutely. Gissing, he declared, had never had 'the slightest sympathy with any creed whatsoever . . . During the whole of our long intimacy I never knew him to waver from that point of view . . . he could barely understand how any one in the full possession of his faculties could subscribe to any formulated doctrines.' To Clodd, equally incensed at this gratuitous muddling of their friend's beliefs, Roberts wrote: 'I . . . let the damned clergy bury him [at St. Jean de Luz] because I didn't want to make a row. Now I wish I had done it.'

Dozens of articles on Gissing and his work appeared in the popular press. In February 1904, to take just two examples, both the *Independent Review* in England and the *Atlantic Monthly* in America published long appreciations. The former commented that Gissing's great subjects are 'the vital importance of culture, and the degrading effects of poverty'. It added: 'we realise what culture and its absence mean . . . far more vividly from Gissing's pictures, alive as they are with the very breath of reality, than from any essays of the moralist.' He loved the past and hated the present precisely because of the culture of the one and the vulgarity of the other. For Gissing, the writer noted, culture is 'incompatible with poverty'. Thus we seek wealth, with tragic consequences. It is a highly intelligent essay. The *Atlantic* concluded: 'He did enough to make his fame secure.'

II

Gissing's will, written in 1897, left his estate to Edith and his sons, with Algernon and Miss Collet named as executors. Though he had nearly five years in which to do it, he made no codicil in Gabrielle's favour. This made her position somewhat awkward. When she proposed coming to England in the spring of 1904 to see the Gissing family and some of his English friends, Wells, for one, argued against the trip. The chances of a Civil List pension for the boys might be compromised, he said, by a woman going around the country calling herself Gabrielle Gissing when everyone knew that Gissing's wife was in an asylum. But Gabrielle had the good sense to ignore him and the pension, as I have said, was granted (Wells and Miss Collet were appointed its administrators; but Wells soon found he could not get on with Miss Collet, who was a staunch friend of Gabrielle, and resigned his office). Gabrielle had been shattered by the novelist's death. The letters she wrote in the first half of 1904 demonstrate a deep, almost hysterical, grief. She told Miss Collet in one of them that she would '*never* . . . drop George's name': he would not want her to, she was certain. Nor would she be governed by anything her arch-enemy Wells thought or said. Miss Collet agreed that attempts at concealment were ridiculous and likely to be counter-productive. Nor did she have any use for Wells, whom she quite properly considered no longer a friend of the family. So Gabrielle made her visit as arranged and most of Gissing's friends greeted her warmly. It was while she was in England that the Civil List pensions were granted to Gissing's sons – 'in recognition of the literary services of their father and of his straitened circumstances'.

And now the story of *Veranilda* must be told. In January 1904

Algernon asked Wells to write a preface to the novel, which Constable would bring out in its unfinished form that autumn. Wells wrote a preface – a preposterous, patronizing preface. It began reasonably enough, correcting some of the public notions about Gissing then current and emphasizing the late novelist's 'consuming passion for learning' from the time he was a schoolboy. But, Wells said, his scholarship put him 'out of touch with life' from his adolescence onwards. The essay went on to emphasize Gissing's 'practical incapacity, that curious inability to do the sane, secure thing . . . he had some sort of blindness toward his fellow men, so that he never entirely grasped the spirit of everyday life . . . [and] misunderstood, blundered, was nervously diffident, and wilful and spasmodic in common affairs.' His decision to become a novelist Wells coolly called 'ill-advised'. He added: 'it was surely the most unhappy and presumptuous of undertakings' to write 'that misconceived series of novels'. Gissing's fiction, Wells went on, is largely 'about people he did not understand . . . and . . . ways of life into which he had never entered'; much of it is therefore 'incurably unconvincing'. This, however, did not deter Gissing, who drove himself to produce an 'unending, inky succession of words'. There are a few paragraphs about *Veranilda* at the end.

Thus the second-rate novelist wrote of the first-rate one, recently dead and supposedly a friend. Wells portrayed himself as astonished when the family rejected the arrogant, tactless preface and asked Frederic Harrison, now seventy-three, to write one instead. Clara Collet, to whom Wells showed the spurned essay, remarked huffily but with insight that 'Literary criticism . . . generally tells more about the critic than about his subject.' Out of pique Wells published his piece in the *Monthly Review* four weeks before *Veranilda* appeared and again in the *Eclectic Review* two months after it appeared, doing his best to sabotage its reception. This, predictably, started an argument in the press about Gissing's merits as a novelist, and for the most part Wells received the drubbing he deserved. The *British Weekly* declared that he 'neither understands how great a writer Gissing was, nor . . . the secret of his greatness'; the *Globe* said Wells was utterly 'lacking in insight'; the *Outlook* and the *New York Tribune* condemned Wells's ruthlessness. Stung by these attacks, Wells fought back by declaring that Gissing had not thought much of his books, so why should anyone else? He deliberately exploited his friend's modesty and self-deprecation to defend himself, which was perhaps even more unforgivable than the original attack.

When *Veranilda* was finally published, on 28 September 1904, interest in it understandably was running high, and all the journals rushed to review it. Harrison's senile preface did the novel's reception no good. Rightly citing Gissing's 'really fine scholarship and classical learning', he went overboard altogether in calling *Veranilda* 'the most important book which . . . Gissing ever produced: that one of his writings which will have the most continuing life . . . his best and most original work'. It was a better novel, Harrison said, than any of 'the studies of contemporary life which first made [Gissing's] fame' – some of which, he admitted, he had not read. Of course such a silly statement cried out to be contradicted. Most of the reviewers were not slow to point out that *Veranilda*, while a fine piece of scholarship, as a novel was little more than an interesting failure. The sixth-century Roman scene is evoked with great skill, certainly, but also unselectively, the plot is mere melodrama, and the characters are uninteresting (though the 'lassitude and impotence' of the hero, Basil, give him some resemblance to Gissing's moody English protagonists, as Korg points out). Gissing made the same mistake here that George Eliot made in *Romola*: he substituted scholarship for story-telling, and the result is something virtually unreadable as fiction. It is sad that he devoted so many of his last months to so hopeless an undertaking; but it is characteristic of the man that in the end his hatred of modern life drove him back not merely to the past, but to the most remote corner of the past – a corner even Gibbon knew practically nothing about.

The *Daily Chronicle* called 'this mutilated and unfinished book' pathetic. The *Manchester Guardian*'s notice shrewdly rated the novel 'the cold performance of a writer who was capable of passion and penetration' and violently contradicted the judgement of Harrison's preface, asserting that Gissing would be remembered for *New Grub Street* and *In the Year of Jubilee*. The *TLS* kindly commented that the book was 'the work of a scholar – mellow and serene': indeed, it said, 'Gissing seems to know [the sixth century] as well as if he had lived in it in a previous incarnation.' The *Outlook* fired upon the distortions of the preface ('the sort of thing that makes us despair of serious English criticism') and declared that Gissing was 'a master' when it came to illuminating 'contemporary life' but that *Veranilda* was little more than 'a monument of archaeological research'. The *Illustrated London News*, the *Speaker*, the *Week's Survey*, the *Academy*, the *Bookman*, and of course the *Athenaeum* printed unfavourable notices. A few enthusiastic reviews did appear (the *Scotsman*, the *World*, the *Spectator*, the *Morning Post*, the *New York Times*, the *New York Tribune*).

Veranilda was not a popular success, but the widespread attention it received, both before and after publication, stimulated further interest in Gissing and his work. In the months following September 1904 a number of longer articles on Gissing appeared in the journals. In November the *National Review* published a piece called 'The Spokesman of Despair'. 'Never writer wrote with deeper conviction than George Gissing', said the author, 'and this fact alone . . . separates [his work] at once from the common ruck of novel-writing.' *New Grub Street*, *The Odd Women*, and *The Nether World* ('that nightmare book') are given special praise. Six months later the *Manchester Quarterly* published a long discussion of Gissing focused mainly on *The Nether World* ('its tragic squalor is magnificent') and *In the Year of Jubilee*. Already, in 1905, *New Grub Street* was cited as Gissing's 'most famous novel'. His work, the writer declared, 'will be our enduring possession'.

III

On the first anniversary of Gissing's death – 28 December 1904 – Gabrielle and Clara Collet, like Sidney and Jane in *The Nether World*, met in a graveyard. It was, of course, at St. Jean de Luz, and the discussion centred on the novelist's posthumous reputation.

Nothing did more for that reputation than *Will Warburton*, which was a popular success and received generally favourable notices. Again, contemporary reviewers did Gissing justice. The novel was serialized, as he had wished, in the *New Age*, January to June 1905; it was published by Constable in June 1905. The *Morning Leader* rated it 'more mature, more generous, more human than anything else Gissing wrote'. The four major characters, it declared, 'are masterpieces'. The *TLS* commented shrewdly that Gissing's 'best books were those which he wrote "in exile" . . . One remembers such books as one remembers some hideous nightmare.' The hero of Gissing's last novel, Edward Garnett commented in the *Speaker*, is transparently like Gissing himself: 'modest, but timidly self-conscious, high-principled, generously self-sacrificing, but morbidly reserved and full of self-distrust'. Enthusiastic notices appeared almost everywhere. Only the *Outlook* and the *Illustrated London News* printed unfavourable reviews. It was a complete turn-around from *Veranilda* (which the *TLS* had called, among other things, 'dead as a doornail') – as indeed it should have been. Roberts placed *Will Warburton* below only *The Ryecroft Papers* among Gissing's later books.

Will Warburton went through three editions from 1905 to 1915; in the ten years about 8,000 copies of the novel were sold. It has been virtually unobtainable since the 1920s. Three-quarters of a century ago the book was received with the enthusiasm it merited; its obscurity since then has been a fate more cruel and unjust than that met by any of Gissing's other novels.

The last of the immediate posthumous publications was *The House of Cobwebs*, a selection (by Algernon) of fifteen stories by Gissing written between 1893 and 1903. The new collection, designed as a companion-volume to *Human Odds and Ends*, was published in May 1906 by Constable, and sold well: it went through three editions in seven months. The stories were preceded by a foolish preface, full of mistakes, commissioned by Constable and written by one Thomas Seccombe, who declared that Gissing would always be read by recluses and night-school students, and that while the novelist 'understood the theory of composition . . . he was unable to exhibit it in action'. Yet again Gissing was unfortunate in his 'introducer'. The reviews, however, were more appreciative than the preface. The *Daily News* pronounced the stories 'profound, searching, movingly realistic'. In the *Speaker* Edward Garnett compared Gissing to Balzac, and Arthur Waugh, in the *Daily Chronicle*, also gave *The House of Cobwebs* high marks. The reviewer in the *Glasgow Herald* thought that Gissing 'raised English fiction higher into the region of pure literature than any writer since Thackeray'. Only the *Gentleman's Magazine* and the reliable *Athenaeum* printed unfavourable notices. As I have said, Gissing was never at his best in his short fiction; the reviewers dealt with this volume generously.

IV

Through the influence of Wells, Algernon was granted a pension of £100 from the Royal Literary Fund. This, added to his brother's posthumous royalties and the boys' Civil List pension, allowed him to give the novelist's sons a good education and to pay Edith's bills at the asylum. Still, impractical as ever, he ended by selling most of the valuable manuscripts he owned for small sums. In his last years he took to his old practice of borrowing money from anyone who would lend it. He died in 1937. Partly as a result of his improvidence, old Mrs Gissing spent her last years in Wakefield in comparative poverty: she died in 1913. Clara Collet helped pay Edith's bills, and also made presents of money to Walter and Alfred from time to time. Edith died, still institutionalized, in 1917. Miss Collet lived on until 1948. Gabrielle was kept at arm's length by the women in Wakefield. Her correspondence with Gissing's English connections diminished over the years, and finally ceased altogether. Her mother died in 1910. Shortly before his death in 1931, Bertz, out of respect for Gabrielle and regard for his friend's memory, destroyed all the letters he had received from Gissing before Nell's death (letters written, that is, from 1879 to 1888: a sad loss to us). Gabrielle, who lived until 1954, shortly after the novelist's death destroyed the letters she had written to Gissing; while she tampered with many of them, at least she left to posterity most of the letters he wrote to her. Alfred Gissing lived until 1975. Margaret died in 1930, Ellen in 1938; neither of the novelist's sisters ever married. Wells lived until 1945, Hick until 1932, Clodd until 1930. Roberts died in 1942. His condescending, inaccurate 'biography' of Gissing, *The Private Life of Henry Maitland*, appeared in 1912. In this same year an unsympathetic critical study of Gissing (the first) was published by Frank Swinnerton. Another storm of controversy around Gissing's name and posthumous reputation ensued, with Wells, of course, defending Swinnerton. Gabrielle, Miss Collet, Clodd, W. H. Hudson, and other members of the Gissing 'circle' cut Roberts cold from the moment his book came out. It depicted Gissing as a sensual weakling, and also gave the public its first peek into the guilty secrets of the novelist's early years.

Between 1908 and 1913 Constable sold 20,000 copies of *The Ryecroft Papers* in a sixpenny edition; in his old age Alfred Gissing was still receiving royalties on it. But most of Gissing's other books were out of print by the time World War II began. Two decades later, in the 1960s, Gissing again came into vogue; there is a discussion of the 'revival' in the Appendix to this volume.

v

'It is not every day that you will get a gentleman and a scholar, with the gift for . . . fiction, knowing the . . . "nether world" of London – the lower middle class, the artisan class, the latter-day medley of "half-baked" humanity which is gradually creating the "labour movement," men and girls – as Gissing knew them, from the inside.' Thus the *TLS* in 1906. In almost every way that counts,

Dickens is a better novelist than Gissing. But one of Gissing's greatest accomplishments is that he portrayed this 'nether world' more realistically and objectively than Dickens, always so tangled in his various sentimentalities. Rarely indeed does knowledge of the lower depths coexist with the ability to articulate what one has seen and felt there. In another piece on Gissing, published a year after his death, the *TLS* sought to define the type of characters he wrote about. Gissing, said the writer, was interested in

those who dwell on the edge of the abyss, in continual danger of falling into it, deteriorating mentally and morally in the endeavour to keep out of it, cut off from the saving grace of culture by carking material cares: a world in which the battle is to the strong, and the delicately and sensitively organized go under in the struggle with those of coarser fibre . . . the tragedy of Gissing's heroes and heroines is that their circumstances are unfavourable to the life of refinement and leisure and culture for which their gifts qualify them, and for which they long.

'Book after book', the *TLS* writer added, 'reads like the protest and the bitter cry of the weak man who is hurt by the hustling in spite of his contempt for it.' All of which is to say, very eloquently, what we now know: that Gissing's books are about aspects of himself and of his own experience, that we cannot study them without studying *him*; and that, as the *TLS* also said, the gloomier the ironies of his life made him the better his writing was likely to be. Gissing himself paired 'art' and 'misery'.

So the personality of Gissing is dramatized in his fiction. 'But for my Greek and Latin poets, I should perhaps have been brutalized in the long years of poverty', he had written to Gabrielle in 1898. 'How many a time I have read Homer when I was living in a wretched garret, and had scarcely enough to eat!' Few Englishmen of letters could have written such a statement; few Englishmen of letters found themselves in such anomalous circumstances. It is perhaps worth recalling once more what Gissing told Roberts about his fiction: 'The most characteristic, the most important, part of my work is that which deals with a class of young men distinctive of our time – well-educated, fairly bred, *but without money*.' Roberts commented on this: 'The sort of poverty which crushed the aspiring is the keynote to the best work he did . . . He played all these parts himself.' This may help explain why Gissing's work is so personal. It is difficult to imagine him writing anything that does not reflect his own personality and experience, his own fears and concerns and hopes. Even *Veranilda* is an extension of his character – in its focus upon a most inaccessible period of his beloved classical past.

Gissing's bad luck, his masochism, his restlessness, his guilt, his insecurity, prevented him from feeling at home in *any* class – indeed made him feel, as Walter Allen has said, 'permanently estranged, at odds with society', the ultimate outsider. From his Owens College period onwards he never relaxed, felt comfortable, or had any measure of mental ease. Always he felt the need to prove, or disprove, something: and so he worked himself to death, producing 27 volumes in 26 years. 'Out of his first great disaster sprang all the rest', Roberts said of him. 'His ill luck began early . . . [and] lasted even beyond the grave.' The result was a large portion of unhappiness for Gissing, but for us a fascinating series of books. At his best Gissing is as good as any novelist; at his worst, he is still interesting. The man who wrote *The Nether World*, *New Grub Street*, and *The Whirlpool* is not just another minor Victorian novelist. Roberts said of Gissing after his death: 'He was always in exile.' Surely his reputation has served its appointed time in the shades of obscurity and his 'exile' may be ended.

APPENDIX

۞

SOME NOTES ON THE GISSING REVIVAL

SERIOUS interest in Gissing revived around 1961. I shall take that year as my starting-point in this brief survey of what the Gissing revival has produced.

First, new editions of Gissing's work. Several paperback editions of Gissing's novels appeared in 1961 – *The Private Papers of Henry Ryecroft*, edited by V. S. Pritchett (New York: New American Library, Signet paperback); the same novel was brought out unedited in this year by Doubleday (New York: Anchor Dolphin paperback); and Doubleday also published a new edition of *New Grub Street* in the same format. In 1962 came a paperback edition of *New Grub Street*, edited by Irving Howe (Boston: Houghton Mifflin; Riverside paperback). *By the Ionian Sea* was re-published in 1963 with a Foreword by Frank Swinnerton (London: Richards Press). *Les Carnets d'Henry Ryecroft (The Private Papers of Henry Ryecroft)*, edited by Pierre Coustillas – a bilingual edition – was published in 1966 (Paris: Aubier Montaigne). In the next year another edition of *New Grub Street* appeared, this one edited in cloth by John Gross (London: The Bodley Head, 1967). In 1968 came still another edition of *New Grub Street*, edited by Bernard Bergonzi (Harmondsworth, England: Penguin; Magnolia, Mass.: Peter Smith; Penguin paperback – reprinted in 1976 and 1978). In the same year (1968) appeared a new edition of *The Odd Women*, edited by Swinnerton (London: Anthony Blond; New York: Stein and Day), and three essays by Gissing were reprinted together under the title *Notes on Social Democracy*, edited by Jacob Korg (London: Enitharmon Press). In 1969 the Harvester Press (then in Hassocks, Sussex; now in Brighton) initiated its critical edition of Gissing's works by bringing out a two-volume edition of *Isabel Clarendon*, edited by Coustillas. *Gissing's Writings on Dickens: A Bio-Bibliographical Survey*, edited by Coustillas (Enitharmon), also appeared in 1969. Two essays not previously identified as being by Gissing were reprinted here, both from the *TLS* – 'Mr. Swinburne on Dickens' (25 July 1902) and 'Mr. Kitton's Life of Dickens' (15 August 1902) – and the editor added a helpful essay of his own which recapitulates the extent of Gissing's interest in and work on his great predecessor. Three more Gissing volumes appeared in 1970. Two of Gissing's previously unpublished tales were brought out as '*My First Rehearsal*' and '*My Clerical Rival*', edited by Coustillas (Enitharmon). Coustillas also edited a collection of manuscripts published for the first time as *George Gissing: Essays and Fiction* (Baltimore: Johns Hopkins Press), which includes two essays (the important 'Hope of Pessimism', and

'Along Shore'), a *novella* ('All for Love'), and six short stories written between 1879 and 1884 ('The Last Half-Crown', 'Cain and Abel', 'The Quarry on the Heath', 'The Lady of the Dedication', 'Mutimer's Choice', and 'Their Pretty Ways'). The editor's long introduction to this volume is especially helpful. Also in 1970 *Born in Exile*, edited by Walter Allen, was republished in cloth (London: Gollancz). *The Odd Women* (New York: Norton; Norton paperback) was published in 1971; having become a minor document of the women's movement of the seventies, it has been reprinted several times since. The lesser-known *A Victim of Circumstances* (New York: Books for Libraries Press), a collection of late stories, also reappeared in 1971. Harvester published *Demos*, edited by Coustillas, in 1972. *The Nether World*, edited by Walter Allen (London: J. M. Dent; New York: E. P. Dutton; Everyman's Library paperback) was published in 1973 (and reprinted in 1975). In 1974 came another edition of *The Nether World*, this one edited by John Goode (Harvester, and Madison, N.J.: Fairleigh Dickinson University Press); *Thyrza*, edited by Jacob Korg (Harvester and Fairleigh Dickinson); *Sleeping Fires*, edited by Coustillas (Harvester); and Coustillas's edition of *Demos* in paperback (Harvester). In 1976 Harvester and Fairleigh Dickinson brought out *The Unclassed*, edited by Korg; *In the Year of Jubilee*, edited by P. F. Kropholler, with an Introduction by Gillian Tindall; and *Our Friend the Charlatan*, edited by Coustillas. Also in 1976 *Workers in the Dawn* was republished by Garland (New York and London; three volumes in one). *The Emancipated*, edited by Coustillas, and *The Whirlpool*, edited by Patrick Parrinder, were published by Harvester and Fairleigh Dickinson in 1977. In 1978 the same two brought out *Born in Exile*, edited by Coustillas, in both cloth and paper. In this year too *George Gissing on Fiction*, edited by Jacob and Cynthia Korg, was published by Enitharmon; this volume reproduces sections of Gissing's letters (many of them to Algernon) which deal with the writing of novels, and two essays – 'The Coming of the Preacher' and 'The English Novel of the Eighteenth Century'. In 1979 Harvester and the Humanities Press brought out new editions of *The Crown of Life*, edited by Michel Ballard, and *Denzil Quarrier*, edited by John Halperin.

The sum total: 32 editions in 18 years (including seven in paperback), 27 of which appeared between 1968 and 1979. With the exception of Hardy, no other Victorian novelist has been reprinted so prodigiously since 1968. (I do not include in these figures novels by Gissing which apparently also exist in unreliable reprint–facsimile editions published by Abrahams' Magazine Services [New York], 1968–71. I have not reviewed these, but they are said to include *Workers in the Dawn*, *The Unclassed*, *Demos*, *Thyrza*, *A Life's Morning*, *The Emancipated*, *Denzil Quarrier*, *Born in Exile*, *The Odd Women*, *In the Year of Jubilee*, *Eve's Ransom*, *The Paying Guest*, *The Whirlpool*, *The Town Traveller*, *The Crown of Life*, *Our Friend the Charlatan*, *Veranilda*, and *Will Warburton* – eighteen in all.)

Next, editions of Gissing's letters and private papers. In 1961 two collections of the novelist's letters were published – the first such volumes to appear since the *Letters of George Gissing to Members of His Family*, edited by Algernon and Ellen Gissing (London: Constable) came out in 1927. These were *The Letters of George Gissing to Eduard Bertz, 1887–1903*, edited by Arthur C. Young (New Brunswick, N.J.: Rutgers University Press; London: Constable), and *George Gissing and H. G. Wells: Their Friendship and Correspondence*, edited by Royal A. Gettmann (Urbana: University of Illinois Press). *The Letters of George Gissing to Gabrielle Fleury*, edited by Pierre Coustillas (New York: New York Public Library), was published in 1964. These, plus the volume of family letters, remain the major collections in print. Other smaller collections of letters published recently include *Henry Hick's Recollections of George Gissing, Together with Gissing's Letters to Henry Hick* and *The Letters of George Gissing to Edward Clodd*, both edited by Coustillas and brought out by Enitharmon in 1973. Another important volume containing personal writings of the novelist is *George Gissing's Commonplace Book*, edited by Jacob Korg (New York: New York Public Library, 1962). Gissing's diary, covering the years 1887 to 1902, has been published under the unwieldy title *London and the Life of Literature in Late Victorian England: The Diary of George Gissing, Novelist*, edited by Coustillas (Harvester; and Lewisburg, Pa.: Bucknell University Press, 1978).

Finally, bibliographical, biographical, and critical volumes on Gissing published since 1961 (I omit articles, and previously published book-length studies). After Morley Roberts's untrustworthy *The Private Life of Henry Maitland* (1912), Wells's acidulous and highly inaccurate 'reminiscences' in *Experiment in Autobiography* (1934), S. V. Gapp's brilliant *George Gissing, Classicist* (1936), Mabel Collins Donnelly's unsatisfactory critical biography *George Gissing: Grave Comedian* (1954), A. C. Ward's unsympathetic *Gissing* (1959), and Orwell's incisive and influential essay 'George Gissing' (written in 1948 but not published until 1960), the most important study to appear was Jacob Korg's splendid *George Gissing: A Critical Biography* (Seattle: University of Washington Press, 1963; London: Methuen, 1965). This book gave impetus to Gissing studies nearly two decades ago, superseding previous biocriticism and opening Gissing studies to others who had the desire to work on Gissing but not the tools. Indeed, few if any sustained discussions of the novelist and his work published after Korg's book have been as informative or incisive. In 1965 Korg helped found, and became the first editor of, *The Gissing Newsletter* – in its seventeenth year now, edited by Pierre Coustillas, and published in Dorking, Surrey, by C. C. Kohler (12, Horsham Road). Oswald H. Davis, in *George Gissing: A Study in Literary Leanings* (London: Johnson Publications, 1966; reprinted in 1974 by Kohler and Coombes, with a Foreword by Coustillas), pays little attention either to chronology or any standards of critical objectivity in his survey of the novels and stories. Also in 1966 the third edition of Frank Swinnerton's *George Gissing* was issued by the Kennikat Press (Port Washington, N.Y.) with a new Introduction by the author. The book is unsympathetic to Gissing; its interest today, since its only noteworthiness is the damage it did to Gissing's reputation in 1912, is historical. In 1968 Coustillas edited *Collected Articles on George Gissing* (London: Frank Cass: New York: Barnes and Noble), which reprints sixteen essays culled from various sources. Also in 1968 appeared P. J. Keating's *George Gissing: 'New Grub Street'* (London: Edward Arnold), which contributes little to our understanding of the novel. Next to come out was Coustillas's *George Gissing at Alderley Edge* (London: Enitharmon, 1969), a brief but interesting account of the two years (1871 to 1872) Gissing spent at the boarding school in Cheshire. In *Gissing East and West: Four Aspects* (London: Enitharmon, 1970), Coustillas discusses problems and opportunities for the would-be Gissing scholar in search of materials and information. *The Rediscovery of George Gissing* (London: National Book League, 1971) is a pamphlet designed by Coustillas and John Spiers as a companion-guide to the Gissing Exhibition of that year at the National Book League (Albemarle Street, London). The two authors put together here an informative and original combination of bibliography and biography – this is perhaps the best of the shorter studies of Gissing published recently. Also in 1971 appeared Coustillas's *Gissing's Writings on Dickens* (Enitharmon). The Critical Heritage people got around to Gissing in 1972; *Gissing: The Critical Heritage,* edited by Coustillas and Colin Partridge (London and Boston: Routledge and Kegan Paul), is a comprehensive and useful compilation of contemporary reactions to Gissing's novels. In 1974 appeared *George Gissing: An Annotated Bibliography of Writings about Him,* edited and annotated by Joseph J. Wolff (Dekalb, Ill.: Northern Illinois University Press), which lists secondary material published between 1880 and 1970 and summarizes briefly the content of each item listed. This volume is efficiently organized and arranged, the annotations lucid and helpful; it is not complete, however, and its index is useless. Also in 1974 came Gillian Tindall's *The Born Exile: George Gissing* (London: Temple Smith; New York: Barnes and Noble), which is long on fascinating psychoanalysis but short on sensible literary criticism. Still, any student of Gissing will find this book illuminating and provocative. Adrian Poole's *Gissing in Context* (London: Macmillan; Totowa, N.J.: Rowman and Littlefield), which purports to discuss the intellectual and literary climate in which Gissing's books were written but in fact fails to do so, appeared in 1975. In the same year Michael Collie's *George Gissing: A Bibliography* was published (Toronto: University of Toronto Press). This volume, as well as two others by Collie – *George Gissing: A Biography* (Folkestone: Dawson, 1977) and *The Alien Art: A Critical Study of George Gissing's Novels* (Dawson; and Hamden, Conn.: Archon Books, 1979) – must be read with extreme caution; all have inaccuracies, and the 'biography' is especially capricious with the facts of Gissing's life. John Goode's *George Gissing: Ideology and Fiction* (London: Vision Press, 1978; New York: Barnes and Noble, 1979) is little more than an 'introduction' to Gissing, notable chiefly for its impenetrable prose. In 1981 J. P. Michaux published *George Gissing: Critical Essays* (London: Vision Press; New York: Barnes and Noble), an excellent collection of twenty one reprinted pieces.

Again figures are relevant here. Between 1961 and 1978 there have appeared seven volumes of Gissing's private writings and sixteen biocritical or bibliographical volumes. Fifteen of these latter have come out since 1968. In the last twelve years alone, 44 Gissing-related volumes have been published – 30 editions and 13 secondary works – which averages out to 3.7 per year. This is a genuine revival. Certainly less has been published on Gissing in recent years than on Hardy or Trollope or the Brontës, and there is still much less in print on Gissing than there is on Dickens or George Eliot. But just as certainly Gissing has been keeping pace with such other acknowledged 'major' Victorian novelists as Thackeray, Mrs Gaskell, and Meredith, and for whatever it is worth, he is leagues ahead of Disraeli, Collins, Butler, and George Moore. It is a pace that suits him, and that may yet quicken even more.

NOTE

In the recently discovered preface to the Rochester Edition of *David Copperfield*, Gissing writes that that novel was Dickens's own favourite among his books because it was his most autobiographical work – a sentiment with which Gissing readily sympathizes. Of *Copperfield*, Gissing adds: 'The book is fortunate in its autobiographical form, which burdens us as little as may be with exigencies of "plot". For the contrivance of a plot Dickens had no aptitude . . . [He] lacked almost entirely the novelist's power of inventing plausible circumstances.'

Dickens's essential conservatism is also noted in the preface. 'Dickens, with his intensely practical commonsense . . . never desired a social revolution; he believed firmly in the subordination of ranks, and shows throughout his writings that he regarded "humility" as a natural and laudable attribute of the lowly class'. Clearly Gissing approves of what he calls 'the conservatism which lay deep in [Dickens's] mind'; the younger novelist characterizes it as 'the root of so much in him that was good and great'.

A NOTE ON REFERENCES

SINCE among other things I wish to tell a story, I have chosen not to interrupt the text with notes. Research for the present study has not been lacking, however, and those who wish to look up my sources will find them in the Chapter Notes at the end of this book.

Wherever possible, references to Gissing's novels are to the critical edition being published a volume at a time by the Harvester Press (about a dozen volumes in print as of this writing); but since so much of Gissing's work is hard to obtain in *any* edition, some of my citations may be difficult for others to look up. I cannot help this. References to Gissing's letters and other private writings and to work by other scholars are also given in notes.

Throughout notes I have used the following abbreviations for frequently cited works (dates of composition and of publication of primary materials may be found in the Chronological Listing of Works Discussed at the end of this volume; individual shorter works are listed there):

I. WORKS BY GISSING

AHC	*An Heiress on Condition* (Philadelphia, 1923); story
ALM	*A Life's Morning*
B	*Brownie*, Introduction by G. E. Hastings, V. Starrett, and T. O. Mabbott (New York, 1931); stories
BE	*Born in Exile*
BIS	*By the Ionian Sea*; travel
CD	*Charles Dickens: A Critical Study*; criticism
CL	*The Crown of Life*
D	*Demos*
DQ	*Denzil Quarrier*
ER	*Eve's Ransom*
GGEF	*George Gissing: Essays and Fiction*, ed. Pierre Coustillas (Baltimore, 1970)
HC	*The House of Cobwebs*, Introduction by Thomas Seccombe (London, 1906); stories
HOE	*Human Odds and Ends: Stories and Sketches* (London, 1897); stories
IC	*Isabel Clarendon* (2 vols.)

ID	*The Immortal Dickens* (London, 1925); essays
IYJ	*In the Year of Jubilee*
MFR	'My First Rehearsal' and 'My Clerical Rival', ed. Pierre Coustillas (London, 1970); stories
NGS	*New Grub Street*
NSD	'Notes on Social Democracy', ed. Jacob Korg (London, 1968); essays
NW	*The Nether World*
OFC	*Our Friend the Charlatan*
OW	*The Odd Women*
PG	*The Paying Guest*
PPHR	*The Private Papers of Henry Ryecroft*
SF	*Sleeping Fires*
SFOT	*The Sins of the Fathers and Other Tales,* Introduction by Vincent Starrett (Chicago, 1924); stories
T	*Thyrza*
TE	*The Emancipated*
TT	*The Town Traveller*
TW	*The Whirlpool*
U	*The Unclassed*
V	*Veranilda*
WD	*Workers in the Dawn*
WW	*Will Warburton*

II. LETTERS AND PRIVATE PAPERS

Bertz	*The Letters of George Gissing to Eduard Bertz, 1887–1903,* ed. Arthur C. Young (New Brunswick, N.J., 1961)
CB	*George Gissing's Commonplace Book,* ed. Jacob Korg (New York, 1962)
Clodd	*George Gissing's Letters to Edward Clodd,* ed. Pierre Coustillas (London, 1973)
Diary	*London and the Life of Literature in Late Victorian England: The Diary of George Gissing, Novelist,* ed. Pierre Coustillas (Hassocks, Sussex, 1978)
Family Letters	*Letters of George Gissing to Members of His Family,* ed. Algernon and Ellen Gissing (London, 1927)
Fiction	*George Gissing on Fiction,* ed. Jacob and Cynthia Korg (London, 1978)

Gabrielle	*The Letters of George Gissing to Gabrielle Fleury,* ed. Pierre Coustillas (New York, 1964)
Hick	*Henry Hick's Recollections of George Gissing, Together with Gissing's Letters to Henry Hick,* ed. Pierre Coustillas (London, 1973)
MB	*George Gissing's Memorandum Book* (unpublished; MS in Huntington Library, San Marino, Ca.)
Wells	*George Gissing and H. G. Wells: Their Friendship and Correspondence,* ed. Royal A. Gettmann (Urbana, Ill., 1961)

III. CRITICAL AND BIOGRAPHICAL STUDIES

Autobiography	H. G. Wells, *Experiment in Autobiography* (London, 1934)
'Bibliography'	Pierre Coustillas, 'Gissing's Short Stories: A Bibliography', *English Literature in Transition,* 7, No. 2 (June 1964)
Biography	Norman and Jeanne Mackenzie, *H. G. Wells: A Biography* (New York, 1971)
CAGG	*Collected Articles on George Gissing,* ed. Pierre Coustillas (New York, 1968)
Coustillas	Pierre Coustillas, *George Gissing: The Dynamics of Frustration* (unpublished; since page-references to the typescript would help no one, I cite chapters only)
Critical Heritage	*George Gissing: The Critical Heritage,* ed. Pierre Coustillas and Colin Partridge (London and Boston, 1972)
Goode	John Goode, *George Gissing: Ideology and Fiction* (London, 1978; New York, 1979)
'Humanist'	Jacob Korg, 'George Gissing: Humanist in Exile', in *The Victorian Experience: The Novelists,* ed. Richard A. Levine (Athens, Ohio, 1976), pp. 239–73
Korg	Jacob Korg, *George Gissing: A Critical Biography* (Seattle, 1963)
'Political Responses'	Pierre Coustillas, 'Political Responses to *Demos*', in *Politics in Literature in the Nineteenth Century* (Lille, 1974), pp. 155–84
Poole	Adrian Poole, *Gissing in Context* (London, 1975)

Roberts   Morley Roberts, *The Private Life of Henry Mait-
                   land* (London, 1912)

'Short Stories'   Pierre Coustillas and Robert Selig, 'Gissing's
                   American Short Stories', *The Book Collector*, 29,
                   No. 3 (Autumn 1980), Note 430

Spiers   John Spiers and Pierre Coustillas, *The Rediscovery
                   of George Gissing* (London, 1971)

Tindall   Gillian Tindall, *The Born Exile: George Gissing*
                   (London, 1974)

NOTES

CHAPTER 1

I

THE critic quoted in the opening paragraph is Pierre Coustillas – from his Introduction to the Diary, p. 10. The quotation from the *TLS* is taken from 'Gissing's Heroines', unsigned (28 Dec. 1956), p. 780; reprinted in *CAGG*, pp. 58–63. Gissing on novel-writing is quoted by Coustillas in his Introduction to the Diary, p. 1.

The Orwell quotation comes from 'George Gissing', written in 1948 but not published until 1960 in the June number of *London Magazine*, pp. 36–43. It is reprinted in *CAGG*, pp. 50–7.

II

Gissing's comment on *Adam Bede* may be found in *CB*, p. 35. The passages on Gissing's 'Victorianism' quoted in the text are taken from Orwell, *CAGG*, pp. 50 and 56, and 'Gissing's Heroines', *CAGG*, p. 63. The quotation from Masterman's *In Peril of Change* is taken from the *Critical Heritage*, p. 489. Surely it is going much too far to say, as Irving Howe has done, that 'the techniques of modern novelists . . . do not figure in Gissing's books' and to cite lack of 'burrowing psychological analysis' as proof of this. See Howe's 'George Gissing: Poet of Fatigue', originally published as part of an Introduction to the Riverside edition of *NGS* in 1962 and reprinted in *CAGG*, pp. 119–25. The opinion of Greenough White, whose essay 'A Novelist of the Hour' (actually a review of *TW; Sewanee Review*, July 1898) – is also reprinted in *CAGG* (pp. 142–51) – is more to the point: 'Mr. Gissing is at his best in describing a psychological crisis, a moment of supreme nervous tension.'

Comments on Gissing by V. S. Pritchett cited in this chapter are taken from his Introduction to *PPHR* (New York: New American Library, 1961).

For Biffen's comments on the literary uses of the 'ignobly decent' and the rest of his theories of fiction (with few of which Gissing agrees), see *NGS*, Chs. 10 and 16.

III

Wells's characterization of Gissing's novels as the '*genre* of nervous exhaustion' was made, before the two men ever met (their first meeting was on 20 Nov. 1896), in an essay called 'The Depressed School', published in the *Saturday Review* for 27 Apr. 1895. In this essay Wells deals at some length with the just-published *Eve's Ransom*; his celebrated comment is made in connection with that novel. The portion of 'The Depressed School' given over to *Eve's Ransom* is reprinted in *Wells*, pp. 234–7.

James on Gissing is quoted without attribution by Tindall, p. 238; it is also quoted without attribution in 'The Permanent Stranger,' *TLS* for 14 Feb. 1948, p. 92 (reprinted in *CAGG*, pp. 43–9). The original source of the quotation apparently is a letter from James to Sidney Colvin dated 28 Dec. 1903 (the day on which Gissing died) and published in E. V. Lucas, *The Colvins and Their Friends* (New York, 1928), p. 279.

The quotation from Roberts appears on p. 109.

The *TLS* is quoted from *Critical Heritage*, p. 480. The passage from *U* is quoted from p. 165. The quotation from Snow is taken from *Homecomings* (London: Macmillan, 1956), pp. 40–1. Conrad on autobiography in fiction is taken from 'A Familiar Preface' to *A Personal Record*.

IV

The letter to Algernon Gissing may be found in *Family Letters*, p. 169. The quotation from *PPHR* is in fact the novel's last sentence (Winter, 26).

Ellen Gissing's comment on her brother appears in the volume of *Family Letters*. For the context of Gissing's comment (written in 1900) on the 'suffering poor', see *CB*, p. 54.

The critic quoted in the final paragraph is Russell Kirk, in 'Who Knows George Gissing?', originally published in the *Western Humanities Review* for Summer 1950, reprinted in *CAGG*, pp. 3–13.

CHAPTER 2

I

MY account of the cloakroom incident at Owens College is indebted to Coustillas, Ch. II; Roberts, pp. 16 and 28; Korg, pp. 4 and 13; and Tindall, p. 10.

II

The description of Wakefield is Russell Kirk's in *CAGG*, p. 3. The details of Gissing's birthplace are taken largely from Coustillas, Ch. I. The quotation from Hick appears on p. 6. Gissing's remark about his father was made to Roberts (quoted on p. 16); his comment on dreams of his father may be found in *CB*, p. 26. My discussion of Thomas Gissing is indebted to Coustillas, Ch. I, and Tindall, p. 50. The quotation from Coustillas appears in Ch. I. The critic quoted on 'class' is Walter Allen, writing in 'The Permanent Stranger' (unsigned), *TLS* for 14 Feb. 1948, p. 92; the essay is reprinted in *CAGG*, pp. 43–9.

The characterization of Gissing's mother as 'unknown' is made by Tindall and discussed by her on pp. 56–69, *passim*. Much of the rest of my discussion of Mrs Gissing is indebted to Coustillas, Ch. I. Gissing's description of his mother as 'a stranger' occurs in an unpublished letter (Yale University Library) to his brother Algernon (26 Oct. 1884). Gissing's remark about never having received a caress from his mother is made in a letter to Gabrielle Fleury (4 Feb. 1899), quoted from *Gabrielle*, p. 104. The quotation from *Hick* appears on p. 7.

The discussion of Gissing's brothers and sisters is indebted to Coustillas, Ch. I. The quotation fron *CB* may be found on p. 23.

The quotations from *Hick* appear on p. 8. The details of Gissing's early schooling are taken from Coustillas, Ch. II, and Korg, Ch. I.

The quotations from Ellen Gissing are taken from Appendix C of *Family Letters*, pp. 403–4.

The quotations from Roberts appear on pp. 23 and 16.

The two quotations from Roberts (on Nell) occur on pp. 24 and 26, respectively. On Gissing's early attitudes toward Nell see Coustillas, Ch. II, and Korg, Ch. I, esp. p. 12.

Gissing mentions *The Ordeal of Richard Feverel* as one of his favourite novels in a piece he wrote for *Pearson's Weekly* for 30 June 1894.

On the 'guilty secret' motif see Tindall, Ch. 3. The quotation from Tindall appears on p. 130.

My account of Gissing's life between his arrest and his departure for America is indebted to Coustillas, Ch. II. Gissing's possible clerkship is mentioned by Korg, p. 15.

CHAPTER 3

I

MY account of Gissing in America is taken largely from Korg, Ch. I; Coustillas, Ch. III; and *Family Letters*, Section I.

The description of Gissing at Waltham High School is quoted from George A. Stearns, 'George Gissing in America', published in *Bookman* (New York) for Aug. 1926, pp. 683–4.

The story of Martha Barnes and the quotation from Coustillas are taken from Coustillas, Ch. III.

II

Whelpdale's account of his experiences in Chicago may be found in *NGS*, Ch. 28. Gissing's own feelings about this time in his life were not so sanguine in after years, as I suggest in the text. See, for example, Noel Ainslie, 'Some Recollections of George Gissing', published in *Gentleman's Magazine* for Feb. 1906. See also Coustillas, Ch. III.

'The Sins of the Fathers' was published in the *Chicago Tribune* for 10 Mar. 1877. 'R.I.P.' appeared in the *Tribune* on 31 Mar. 1877. 'Too Dearly Bought', signed 'G.R.G.', was published in the *Tribune* on 4 Apr. 1877. The passage quoted from this story may be found in *SFOT*, pp. 88–9. 'The Warden's Daughter' was published in the *Chicago Journal* on 28 Apr. 1877. 'Gretchen', signed 'G.R.G.', appeared in the *Tribune* on 12 May. 'Twenty Pounds' was published in the *Journal* on 9 May 1877 but was probably written after 'Gretchen'. The passage quoted from 'Twenty Pounds' may be found in *B*, p. 48. 'Joseph Yates' appeared in the *Evening Post* on 2 June 1877. 'Brownie' was published in the *Tribune* on 29 July 1877 (in all likelihood after Gissing had left Chicago). I am indebted for some of this information to 'Short Stories', p. 428.

III

Much of my information about Gissing in Troy, as well as the quoted phrase, is taken from Korg, p. 19. See also Roberts, p. 35, and *NGS*, Ch. 28. The quotation from Roberts on starvation appears on p. 38.

The quotation from Coustillas on Gissing's departure from Wakefield is taken from Ch. III.

IV

The quotation from Gissing on his early years in London appears in *CB*, p. 16. For his account in *PPHR* of this period of his life, see Spring, 4–12. The passage quoted from *PPHR* is taken from Spring, 7 and 10, *passim*.

My account of Gissing's early period in London is indebted to Coustillas, Ch. IV; Korg, Ch. I; and Roberts, Ch. II (the quotations from Roberts appear on p. 43).

For Roberts on Nell, see pp. 40–1. Coustillas's account of Gissing's first years with Nell and of the fund left by his father from which he benefited is given in Ch. IV. On Gissing's clerkship, see Korg, p. 25.

My account of Bertz is indebted to Korg, p. 23; Arthur C. Young's Introduction to *Bertz*, esp. p. xxviii, but also xxii and xxiv; and Coustillas, Ch. IV. See also Arthur C. Young, 'George Gissing's Friendship with Eduard Bertz', in *Nineteenth Century Fiction* (Dec. 1958), 227–37.

The quotation from *U* appears on pp. 41–2.

My information on Gissing's lecturing plans and his tutorials is taken largely from Coustillas, Ch. IV. The quotation from the letter to Algernon about popular education appears in *Family Letters*, pp. 42–3.

The quotation from Gissing on *WD* is taken from *Family Letters*, pp. 49–50.

V

What I say in the text about Gissing's first marriage and its relationship to *WD* is indebted partly to Tindall, p. 81, who makes a point similar to mine. I am also indebted to the discussions by Korg, p. 26, and Coustillas, Ch. IV. The quotation from Roberts appears on p. 112.

Gissing's characterization of *WD* appears in *Family Letters*, p. 74. The quotation from *TW* may be found in III, i.

The quotations in this part of the text from *WD* are taken, respectively, from I, 197; I, 247; I, 237 and 255–6, *passim*; and I, 106. The quotation from Roberts appears on p. 306.

Gissing on *WD* is quoted from *Family Letters*, p. 56.

On the 'emancipation' of Helen, see Vol. I, Chs. xiii–xiv.

The quotation about 'doubt' appears in II, 42.

On Bertz's influence on the German chapters of *WD*, see Korg, p. 20; Young's Introduction to *Bertz*, p. xxiii; and Coustillas, Ch. IV.

Passages from *WD* quoted in this part of the text are as follows: III, 190–2; III, 10; III, 257; III, 321; III, 63–4; III, 69; III, 384; III, 353; III, 17; III, 77; III, 270; III, 38; III, 261 and 35; III, 209; III, 323; III, 324; III, 374; II, 297; and I, 241.

VI

The letter to Algernon, written on 7 Feb. 1880, may be found in *Family Letters*, p. 57. My information on Gissing's agreement with Remington and Co. is taken from Coustillas, Ch. IV.

VII

For Gissing's letters to Algernon on the new novel see *Family Letters*, pp. 64–5.

The letter to William may be found in *Family Letters*, p. 69.

My account of Gissing's reaction to William's death is taken from Coustillas, Ch. IV.

On the financial results of the publication of *WD* see Korg, p. 43, and Coustillas, Ch. V. For reviews of *WD* see *Critical Heritage*, pp. 51–64. For Gissing's comment on the gloominess of *WD* and his statement of aims as a novelist see *Family Letters*, pp. 72 and 83. For his complaints about the reviews see *Family Letters*, p. 81.

For Harrison's opinion of *WD*, see *Critical Heritage*, pp. 53–5, and *Family Letters*, pp. 77–9. My account of the help Harrison gave Gissing during 1880 is indebted to Korg, pp. 45–6, and Coustillas, Ch. V..On Gissing's 'double life', see Korg, p. 45.

VIII

My account of Gissing's activities during the winter of 1881 is indebted largely to Korg, pp. 46–7. For Roberts on Gissing during this period see Roberts, pp. 31–2 and 41–2, *passim*. The letters to Algernon quoted in the text appear in *Family Letters*, pp. 85–7, *passim.*, and pp. 93–4.

My account of Gissing's activities during the early part of 1881, especially his association with the Harrisons, is taken from Coustillas, Ch. V. Austin Harrison's reminiscences of Gissing may be found in 'George Gissing', in the *Nineteenth Century* for Sept. 1906, pp. 453–63; 'Memories of Gissing – London Rambles with my Unconventional Tutor', in *T.P.'s and Cassell's Weekly* for 24 Apr. 1926, p. 23; and in his memoir of his father, *Frederic Harrison, Thoughts and Memories* (London, 1926), pp. 80–4 and 110–12.

Gissing's 1881 letters to Algernon and Ellen may be found in *Family Letters*, pp. 106, 97–8, and 101, respectively, and Korg, p. 48.

The letter to Algernon (*Family Letters*, p. 97) describing Gissing's nervousness was actually written in May 1881, but it may be considered an accurate description of the novelist's state of mind throughout much of the rest of this year. The account of Gissing's troubles with Nell during the winter of 1882 is indebted to Coustillas, Ch. V, and Korg, pp. 49–50.

The story of the purchase of Gibbon is recounted in *Family Letters*, p. 113, and by Coustillas, Ch. V.

The letter to Ellen quoted in the text appears in *Family Letters*, p. 107.

IX

The quotations from 'The Lady of the Dedication' are taken from *GGEF*, pp. 232–3.

The quotation from Korg appears on p. 51. Gissing's reasons for not publishing the 'pessimistic article' are outlined in a letter to Algernon dated 6 Oct. 1882; see *Family Letters*, p. 120. The quotations in the text from 'The Hope of Pessimism' are taken from *GGEF*, pp. 88, 91–2, 95, and 97, respectively.

CHAPTER 4

I

MY account of the fate of 'Mrs. Grundy's Enemies' is indebted to Coustillas, Ch. V, and Korg, pp. 53–4.

My account of Gissing's relations with Nell during 1883 is based on the discussions by Coustillas, Ch. V, and Korg, pp. 58–9.

The quotation from Gissing's letter to Algernon is taken from *Family Letters*, p. 126. The summary of the letters about writing fiction is indebted to Korg, p. 60.

My account of the publishing agreement between Gissing and Chapman and Hall for *U* is taken from Coustillas, Ch. V.

II

Quotations from the letters to Algernon appear in *Family Letters*, pp. 138–9, 140, and 142.

Quotations in the text from *U* are taken from the following pages: on Waymark on life, art, and radicalism, pp. 117, 211–12, and 54; on Hogarth and Waymark's first book, pp. 123 and 290; on Schopenhauer, p. 225; the description of Waymark appears on p. 40; on Waymark and poverty, pp. 61 and 53. Gissing's comment on the 'class' question appears in an 1895 preface to *U*; see *Critical Heritage*, p. 75. For Waymark on women and love, see *U*, p. 82; on Harriet and Casti, pp. 202 and 163–5; on the importance of money, p. 53.

Gissing's suggestion of a pseudonym for publication of *ALM* is recounted by Coustillas, Ch. VI.

III

Gissing's reaction to the poor notices is quoted from an unpublished letter (dated 19 Nov. 1884) at the University of Pennsylvania. The exchange between Gissing and Harrison is recounted by Coustillas, Ch. VI.

For reviews of *U* see *Critical Heritage*, pp. 66–73 and 75–8.

The letters to Algernon are quoted from *Family Letters*, pp. 150–1, and *Fiction*, pp. 34–6, *passim*.

Gissing's account of the projected theme of *D* appears in an unpublished letter to Algernon (dated 29 June 1884) in the Berg Collection of the New York Public Library.

The quotation from Korg appears on p. 70; my account of Gissing's feelings about his new social life is indebted to Korg, pp. 70–1.

The letter to Algernon about landladies may be found in *Family Letters*, pp. 150–1. Roberts's account of the flat is given on pp. 66, 107, and 109, *passim*.

My description of Gissing's activities during the first half of 1885 is indebted to Coustillas, Ch. VI.

The letters to Algernon on the ending of *IC* are quoted from *Family Letters*, pp. 163–4 and 166. Cf. James's critical prefaces, esp. that to *The Portrait of A Lady* (the novel appeared before Gissing made these statements, the preface afterwards). In his notice of *IC*, the *Pall Mall Gazette*'s anonymous reviewer said that Gissing's method of ending the novel reminded him of James's usual practice of 'leaving nearly all the threads of his story hanging loose at the end'. See the *Pall Mall Gazette* for 30 Apr. 1886, p. 6. James himself, though confessing to a 'persistent taste for Gissing', felt that often in Gissing's novels 'the whole business of distribution and composition' was 'cast to the winds'. See James's *Notes on Novelists* (London: J. M. Dent, 1914), p. 346; and Ch. 10, Section I of the present study.

Quotations from *Family Letters* showing Gissing's state of mind during 1885 (especially during the summer months) appear on pp. 158, 167, and 169, respectively.

The letters to Algernon are quoted from *Fiction*, p. 38, and *Family Letters*, pp. 169–71, *passim*.

IV

For Gissing's comments on Morris and on the conservative nature of *D* see *Family Letters*, pp. 169 and 172–4, *passim*.

My account of Gissing's growing conservatism is indebted to Korg, pp. 89–90, and Tindall, pp. 101–15, *passim*. The quotation from *DQ* appears on p. 32. The quotation from Roberts is taken from the Introduction he wrote to an American edition of *D* (New York: E. P. Dutton, n.d.), pp. vii and ix. The *Spectator* review of *D* appeared on 10 Apr. 1886. The quotation from S. V. Gapp is taken from *George Gissing, Classicist* (Philadelphia: University of Pennsylvania Press, 1936), the relevant section of which is reprinted in *CAGG* as 'Influence of the Classics on Gissing's Novels of Modern Life', pp. 83–98 (the passage quoted in the text may be found on p. 94). For Roberts's comment see pp. 79 and 292. The quotation from More is taken from *Selected Shelburne Essays* (London: Oxford University Press, 1935), p. 35. The quotation from Coustillas appears in his Introduction to the Diary, p. 12. Korg is quoted from 'Humanist', p. 260. Garnett is quoted from *Critical Heritage*, p. 486.

My account of the contractual arrangements for *IC* and of the events surrounding the writing of *D* in late 1885 are taken from Coustillas, Ch. VI.

v

Quotations in the text on Kingcote's resemblances to Gissing are as follows: *IC*, II, 222; II, 212; I, 128; I, 8; II, 188; II, 275; Coustillas's Introduction to *IC* (Brighton: Harvester Press, 1969), 2 vols., vol. i, pp. xxxv–xxxvi; *IC*, II, 108; II, 111; II, 279; I, 177; I, 212; II, 81; Roberts, p. 306; and *IC*, I, 6.

On Mrs Kingcote, see II, 206.

Passages in which Isabel is treated as the ideal woman abound; see, for example, I, 49.

On marriage see II, 178 and 126.

On the money theme see I, 8, and I, 183.

On education and 'progress', see I, 240, 178–9, and 185.

On children see II, 101; on the need for companionship see II, 168 and I, 52.

On the country and the city see I, 174 and II, 91 and 95–6.

On the writing of fiction see II, 141; on Meredith see II, 36.

On the autobiographical element in Wilfrid in *ALM* see p. 15.

On autobiographical elements of Emily see pp. 240 and 112; *Hick*, p. 6; and *ALM*, pp. 68, 76–7, and 211, respectively.

On exogamous marriage and Dagworthy see pp. 202, 117, and 119.

On industry and the country see pp. 64, 73, 195, and 133.

On marriage and housekeeping see pp. 114, 200–1, and 213–14.

On pessimism see pp. 65, 211, 212, and 210.

The 'impenetrable' passages may be found on pp. 69–70 and 92.

On money see pp. 40–1, 95, 135–6, 209, 239, and 84.

On education and politics see pp. 14, 75, 32, and 281.

On art see p. 293.

CHAPTER 5

I

MY account of the events surrounding the composition of the last volume of *D* is indebted to 'Political Responses', p. 156, and the Introduction by Morley Roberts to *D* cited earlier (New York: E. P. Dutton, n.d.), pp. vi–vii. Gissing's feelings about *D* are given in an unpublished holograph letter, dated 6 Mar. 1886, in the Berg Collection of the New York Public Library.

Extracts from contemporary reviews of *D* are reprinted in *Critical Heritage*, pp. 79–93. My quotations from the reviews are taken from this volume; from 'Political Responses', pp. 165 and *passim*; and from an Introduction by Pierre Coustillas to *D* (Brighton: Harvester Press, 1972), p. xxi. See also *Family Letters*, pp. 177 and 185. A partial history of the reputation of *D*, and of criticism of it, may be found in 'Political Responses', pp. 168–77, *passim*.

II

The quotation from Roberts is taken from his Introduction to *D* (see above), pp. v–vi.

On class distinctions in *D*, see pp. 137, 282, 334, 444–5, and 350–1.

The meaning of 'demos' is discussed by S. V. Gapp in the essay on the influence of the classics on Gissing; see *CAGG*, p. 84.

On Gissing's condemnation of the working class, see pp. 136, 238, 149, 245, 376, 237, 367, and 301.

On the anti-socialist theme, see pp. 416, 387, 453–4, 238, and 450; Roberts's Introduction to *D* (see above), p. viii; and *D*, pp. 386 and 381–2.

On education and humanitarianism, see pp. 382, 470, 384–5, and 405. The quotation from Roberts is taken from his Introduction, p. viii.

The description of the East End graveyard may be found on p. 221.

On money see pp. 278, 27, 195, 383, and 96.

On politicians, industry, and the countryside, see pp. 244, 1, 26, 201, 67–8, 281, 338–9, and 77.

On anti-modernism, see pp. 385, 339, 225–6, and 349.

On pessimism see pp. 397 and 24.

On puritanism and asceticism see pp. 156, 258, 475, and 384. The letters to Gabrielle (3 Oct. and 10 Aug. 1898) are quoted from *Gabrielle*, pp. 71 and 40, respectively.

On autobiographical elements of Mutimer see pp. 411 and 302. On autobiographical elements of Eldon, see pp. 75–6 and 69.

On Emma's storytelling, see pp. 394–5.

III

Gissing's comments on *IC* are taken from *Family Letters*, p. 180. Contemporary reviews of *IC* may be found in *Critical Heritage*, pp. 94–101.

My information on sales and editions of *D* is taken from Coustillas, Ch. VII.

The letter to Ellen may be found in *Family Letters*, p. 176.

On Gissing's trip to Paris, see Korg, p. 98, and Coustillas, Ch. VI.

On Gissing's state of mind in the spring of 1886 see *Family Letters*, pp. 182 and 189.

IV

On Gissing and Hardy, see Coustillas, Ch. VII, and 'Some Unpublished Letters from Gissing to Hardy', in *English Literature in Transition*, Vol. ix, No. 4 (Fall, 1966).

On Smith, Elder's response to and offer for *T*, see Coustillas, Ch. VII, and Korg, p. 101.

The quotations from Gissing's letters are taken from *Fiction*, p. 40; *Bertz*, p. 4; and *Family Letters*, pp. 181, 184, and 188–9. The quotation from *CB* (entry for 1887) appears on p. 29.

On social and literary questions discussed by Gissing in connection with *T*, see *Family Letters*, pp. 43, 183, and 185.

An account of Gladstone's reading of *T* is given by Coustillas in 'Political Responses', p. 168.

On reform, see *T*, pp. 82, 136, 139–40, 127–8, 296–7, 422 (on Cornelius Vanderbilt), 426, 14–15, 87, 93, and 92.

On Gissing's hatred of the working classes see pp. 37, 87, 38, 343; and *CB*, p. 52 (entry for early 1891). On his mistrust of social theory see p. 176.

On Egremont see pp. 83, 420–1, 455, 56, 428, 10, 252, 6, and 342.

On Grail see pp. 69–70, and 144; on Newthorpe see p. 477.

On asceticism see pp. 119 and 158. On marriage see pp. 413 and 386.

On neurasthenia and London see pp. 108, 98, 319, 73, and 111–12. On poverty and art, see pp. 478 and 486. The references to Virginia Woolf are to *A Room of One's Own* (London, 1929), and a short essay called 'George Gissing', published in *The Common Reader* (second series; New York and London, 1932), pp. 198–203.

On money see pp. 134, 138, and 81. On pessimism see pp. 348, 422, 468, and 474.

V

For contemporary reviews of *T* see *Critical Heritage*, pp. 102–9. Other reactions to the novel mentioned here are taken from Coustillas, Ch. VII. The essays on Gissing by Stead and Edith Sichel from which excerpts are taken are reprinted in *Critical Heritage*, pp. 110–26. The quotation from Roberts appears on p. 129. Gissing's reaction to Miss Sichel's essay is noted in the Diary (entry for 9 June 1889), p. 153.

VI

My account of Gissing's activities during the winter of 1887 is indebted to Coustillas, Ch. VII. The quotations from Gissing's letters are taken from *Family Letters*, pp. 193 and 190, respectively.

My information on Gissing's activities during the spring of 1887 is taken from Korg, pp. 107–8, and Coustillas, Ch. VII. On the fate of 'Clement Dorricott' see the Diary, p. 31 (entry for 7 June 1888). The quotations from Gissing's letters are taken from *Family Letters*, pp. 192 and 191, respectively.

Gissing on his own work is quoted from *Family Letters*, p. 193. On Charlotte Brontë see Korg, pp. 108–9; *Family Letters*, p. 191; *Bertz*, pp. 5–6; *CB*, p. 29; *Family Letters*, p. 222; and *Fiction*, p. 45. See also Korg, p. 109; A. C. Young's note in *Bertz*, p. 6n.; Goode, p. 18; and Roberts, p. 90.

On Gissing's activities during the summer of 1887 see Korg, p. 109, and Coustillas, Ch. VII. Clodd's account of Gissing is quoted by Coustillas from Clodd's *Memories*, p. 165.

The letter to Margaret about Clerkenwell may be found in *Family Letters*, p. 199.

The letter (unpublished) to Ellen on the Jubilee, dated 21 June 1887, is in the Berg Collection of the New York Public Library. The letter to Algernon may be found in *Family Letters*, pp. 195–6.

On Mudie and *Thyrza*, see Coustillas, Ch. VII. The letter to Ellen appears in *Family Letters*, p. 196 (the part about Haggard is unpublished; the letter, dated 8 July 1887, is in the Yale Library). The comment about Mrs Harrison is made in an unpublished letter to Ellen (11 Sept. 1887 – also in the Yale Library). Roberts's comment on Gissing's misanthropy may be found in Roberts, p. 70. On the coal business, see Roberts, p. 75. The 'optimistic' letter to Ellen is given in *Family Letters*, p. 201. See Roberts, p. 77, on the matter of Gissing's exclamation.

For a full account of the story of the publication of *ALM* see Coustillas, Ch. VII. The quotations from the letters to Ellen may be found in *Family Letters*, pp. 202 and 209.

Gissing's state of mind early in 1888 is recounted by Coustillas, Ch. VII. Gissing's comments on his own mood (extracts from his Diary) are given in *Family Letters*, pp. 207 and 208.

My account of Gissing's stay in Eastbourne is based on that given by Coustillas, Ch. VII.

On the death of Nell see Roberts, pp. 58–62; Coustillas, Ch. VII; Korg, pp. 110–11; and the Diary, p. 23.

The Diary entries on Nell are dated 1 and 2 March 1888.

The (unpublished) letter to Algernon, quoted by Korg (p. 111), is in the Berg Collection of the New York Public Library. The account of Nell's funeral is taken from Coustillas, Ch. VII.

CHAPTER 6

I

THE letter to Ellen is given in *Family Letters*, p. 210. The quotations from Roberts appear on pp. 61–2, 133, 105, and 131, respectively. The letters to Gabrielle (26 Mar. 1899 and 6 Aug. 1898) are quoted from *Gabrielle*, pp. 122 and 34, respectively. The subsequent quotation from the letter to Ellen appears on p. 211 of *Family Letters*. The longer passage quoted from Roberts is taken from pp. 58–9. The quotation from Coustillas is taken from his Introduction to the Diary, p. 10.

Gissing's letter to Ellen on his 'companionlessness' may be found in *Family Letters*, p. 211. The quotation from the Diary on loneliness appears on p. 28. The library visit is recounted in the Diary, p. 24 (15 Mar. 1888).

The letter to Margaret is quoted from *Family Letters*, p. 213. The Diary entries on early death appear on p. 30 (3 June 1888).

The letter to Ellen on solitude appears in *Family Letters*, p. 216. The Diary entry appears on p. 32 (17 June 1888). The last series of quotations in this paragraph is taken from *Family Letters*, pp. 217–20, *passim*.

Gissing on his own moods is quoted from the Diary, p. 31 (11 June 1888). The 'suicidal mood' is reported in the Diary, p. 36 (9 July 1888).

For Gissing on his new 'cheerfulness' see *Family Letters*, p. 222. My account of Gissing's activities during Aug. and Sept. 1888 is indebted to Coustillas, Ch. VII. Gissing's reference to his mother's unintellectualism is contained in an unpublished letter to Ellen dated 13 Sept. 1888 (in the Boston Public Library).

II

On money – its effects and importance – poverty, the poor, and the rich see *NW*, pp. 370, 296, 52, 185, 392, 6, 4, and 41; the Diary entry for 2 Apr. 1888 (pp. 25–6); *NW*, pp. 109–10; *Family Letters*, p. 116; *NW*, p. 175; Roberts, p. 84; and *NW*, p. 377.

On specifically autobiographical elements in *NW*, including those in Kirkwood, Scawthorne, and other people and events, see *NW*, pp. 374–5, 373, 143, 194, and 76.

On philanthropy, idealism, radicalism, and education see *NW*, pp. 253, 232, 236, 79, and 82.

On general pessimism (the Church, fate, death, the waste land motif, etc.) and Dickens see *NW*, pp. 319, 50, 55, 314, 356, 129–30; 'Humanist', p. 255; *NW*, pp. 2, 344, 203, 248, 74; and *CB*, p. 33.

III

The letter to Ellen about Rome (dated 4 Nov. 1885) may be found in *Family Letters*, pp. 172–3. The Diary entries appear on pp. 45–6 (3 and 7 Oct. 1888). Quotations from the letter to Bertz are taken from *Bertz*, pp. 9–10.

My account of Gissing's stay and activities in Paris is indebted to Korg's, pp. 121–2.

The Diary entry on art and working-people appears on p. 54 (19 Oct. 1888). The commentary by Korg appears on p. 122.

The account of the journey southward is given by Coustillas, Ch. VIII (to which I am chiefly indebted here), and Korg, pp. 122–3. The letter to Ellen is quoted from *Family Letters*, p. 229.

The letter to Bertz appears on p. 12, that to Ellen in *Family Letters*, pp. 236 and 238–9. The Diary entry may be found on p. 63 (4 Nov. 1888).

The Diary entry on *ALM* may be found on p. 71 (15 Nov. 1888). The letter to Bertz is quoted from pp. 19–20.

The *Vanity Fair* notice of *ALM* was published on 15 June 1889, p. 454. For the *Spectator* review, see *Critical Heritage*, pp. 132–3. The *Whitehall Review* notice was published on 13 Dec. 1888, p. 20. All other references to and quotations from contemporary reviews (published mostly in Dec. 1888 and Jan. 1889) of *ALM* are taken from *Critical Heritage*, pp. 127–33. Gissing's attitude toward *ALM* is discussed by Coustillas in Ch. VIII and accompanying notes.

IV

On the meeting with Shortridge and the Germans and the departure for Rome see Coustillas, Ch. VIII, and Korg, pp. 125–6.

Quotations from letters to Bertz are taken from pp. 30 and 51. The letter to Ellen is given in *Family Letters*, p. 269. Quotations from the letter to Margaret may be found in *Family Letters*, pp. 261 and 260.

The Diary entry on Gissing's 'happiness of mind' appears on p. 98 (14 Dec. 1888). The Diary entry on New Year's Eve 1888 appears on p. 114.

V

Quotations from the letter to Bertz about homesickness for Rome and hatred of tourists are taken from *Bertz*, pp. 32–3.

The letter to Bertz declining the German visit may be found on p. 38. The letter to Ellen is quoted from *Family Letters*, p. 269. The letters to Bertz are quoted from pp. 49, 38–42, and 46 respectively.

The Diary notes the discovery and dispatch of the epigraph for *NW* – see p. 140 (24 Feb. 1889); the English translation is by Elaine P. Halperin. On Gissing's ramble through Brussels see Korg, p. 128.

VI

The quotation from the letter to Bertz appears on p. 53. The description of the awful London day (7 Mar. 1889) appears in the Diary, p. 142.

On the West End (15 Mar. 1889), see the Diary, p. 143. The (unpublished) letter to Ellen (11 Mar. 1889) is in the Yale University Library. Korg on *TE* is quoted from p. 130; see also p. 132.

Gissing's comments on his social life (3 and 6 Apr. 1889) are quoted from the Diary, p. 146. On Gissing's new friends, see Coustillas, Ch. IX.

The letter to Bertz appears on p. 56. Bertz's description of *NW* as 'classical' is recounted by Gissing to Algernon in a letter given in *Fiction*, p. 54.

For Gissing to Algernon on the short story and other matters see *Fiction*, pp. 49–54, *passim*.

On Plitt's mistress see the Diary, p. 148.

For contemporary reviews of *NW* (including Bertz's essay) see *Critical Heritage*, pp. 134–56, and Coustillas, Ch. IX. Gissing's comment on Farrar's essay is quoted from *Bertz*, p. 75.

On the new cheap edition of *NW* see Coustillas, Ch. IX.

VII

The quotations in the opening paragraph appear in letters to Bertz (2 June and 4 Aug. 1889), pp. 61 and 68.

The Diary entries quoted in this paragraph are, respectively, for 30 May 1889, p. 152; 13 Aug. 1889, p. 159; 1 Sept. 1889, p. 163; and 10 Sept. 1889, p. 165.

The account of Gissing's negotiation with Bentley and his financial situation at the time are given in the Diary, 23–4 and 27 Sept. 1889, p. 167.

VIII

For Korg on *TE* see pp. 133–40, *passim*. See also pp. 141–2. On Margaret see *Bertz*, p. 71, and the Diary, p. 161. The quotation from the letter to Bertz about *TE* is taken from p. 79.

On puritanism in *TE* see pp. 320, 375, 199, 103, 101, and 100, respectively.

The quotation from Roberts appears on p. 116. The quotation from *CB* appears on p. 47.

On art and the artist in *TE* see pp. 28, 80, and 268.

On the marriage theme see pp. 50, 301, and 269.

On autobiographical elements and characters other than Mallard see pp. 22, 248, 134, 268, 266, and 297.

Quotations linking Gissing and Mallard are taken, respectively, from pp. 7, 433, 333, 446, 78, 325, 439, 456, 330, 96, 101, 194–5, and 169.

IX

The letter to Bertz is quoted from p. 77. For the letter to Algernon see *Family Letters*, pp. 287–8. The letters to Ellen appear in *Family Letters*, pp. 289–91, *passim*.

On 'Women Literature' see the Diary, p. 169 (15 Oct. 1889).

The letter to Bertz appears on pp. 78–9. The letter to Ellen mentioning the new novel is quoted from *Family Letters*, p. 291.

The (unpublished) letter to Margaret, dated 29 Sept. 1889, is in the Berg Collection, New York Public Library.

CHAPTER 7

I

GISSING's letter to his mother is quoted from *Family Letters,* pp. 294 and 293. The Diary entry (24 Nov. 1889) is quoted from pp. 179–80.

Gissing's dislike of Athens, the Greeks, and Greek life is recorded in the Diary (entries for 19, 21, and 26 Nov. and 2 and 4 Dec. 1889), pp. 175–6, 184, 181, and 185, respectively.

The 'last' letter to Bertz appears on p. 91. The long quoted passage is taken from the Diary (10 Dec. 1889), p. 189.

II

The Diary entry for 25 Dec. 1889 is quoted from p. 195.

The Diary entry for 7 Jan. 1890 is quoted from p. 201. Gissing's illness in Naples is recounted by Korg, p. 148.

The letters written to Bertz on board ship are dated 22, 25, and 26 Feb. 1890 and are quoted from pp. 99–102, *passim.* The Diary entry (25 Feb. 1890) is quoted from pp. 209–10. The importance for Gissing of the incident on board ship is discussed by Coustillas, Ch. IX.

III

The letter to Ellen is quoted from *Family Letters,* p. 307. My account of Gissing's activities during Mar. 1890 is based mainly on Diary entries, pp. 210–11. The reference to the 'new story' is dated 13 Mar. 1890, p. 211. The reference to not having enough to eat is quoted from the Diary, p. 211 (entry for 14 Mar. 1890). Roberts's comment on *TE* is reported in a Diary entry for 27 Mar. 1890, p. 212.

Ellen's attitude toward *TE* is noted in a Diary entry for 1 Apr. 1890, p. 212. Gissing's reply, dated the same day, is reprinted in *More Books,* Nov. 1947, pp. 335–6 (Boston Public Library).

For reviews of *TE* see *Critical Heritage,* pp. 157–68, *passim,* and Coustillas, Ch. X. For the exchange between Gissing and Bertz on *TE* see *Bertz,* pp. 106–7.

IV

The story of the dress suit is recounted by Korg, p. 150. The Diary entry for 12 June 1890 appears on p. 219, those for 29–30 June 1890 on p. 220. The Diary entry on the new story (15 July 1890) is quoted from p. 221; those for 28–9 July 1890 appear on p. 222. The Diary entries for 2–4 Aug. 1890 appear on p. 223.

The long letter to Bertz, dated 22 June 1890, is quoted from pp. 107–9.

For the story of Gissing's fleeting acquaintance with Connie Ash, see Young's discussion in *Bertz,* p. 110n, and Coustillas, Ch. X. Coustillas also gives an account of the unpublished letters (dated 9 and 12 Aug. 1890) which Gissing wrote to his sisters and which are quoted in my text (see notes 20 and 22 of Coustillas's Ch. X). The letter to Bertz of 15 Aug. 1890 is quoted from p. 110.

The Diary entries for 15, 16, 18, and 19 Sept. 1890 are quoted from p. 226.

The long letter to Bertz on marriage, etc., is dated 6 Sept. 1890 and quoted from pp. 111–12.

On Edith Underwood, see Coustillas, Ch. X; Korg, p. 151; Roberts, pp. 134–51, *passim*; and *Autobiography*, pp. 483 and 489.

My discussion of the relationship between Edith and Gissing in the autumn of 1890 is indebted to Coustillas's in Ch. X (the speculations on the nature of the relationship are wholly my own).

The letter to Bertz (25 Oct. 1890) is quoted from p. 113. The letter to Algernon (undated, but written in Oct.) is quoted from *Family Letters*, p. 311.

The (unpublished) letter to Ellen, dated 7 Oct. 1890, is in the Berg Collection, New York Public Library.

The Diary entry (22 Nov. 1890) is quoted from p. 230.

For an account of Gissing's activities during Dec. 1890, see Coustillas, Ch. X.

The Diary entry (31 Dec. 1890) is quoted from p. 234.

V

On Gissing's decision to marry Edith see Roberts, pp. 155–6.

Korg on Gissing's second marriage is quoted from p. 153.

My discussion of Gissing's second marriage is based in part on Coustillas's account (Ch. X), and also on Korg's (p. 153).

The letter to Bertz (23 Jan. 1891) is quoted from pp. 115–16. That to Ellen (20 Jan. 1891) is quoted from *Family Letters*, pp. 312–13.

The quotation from the Diary (entry for 25 Feb. 1891) is taken from p. 240.

Gissing's letter to Mrs Harrison is discussed by Korg, p. 153; it is mentioned in the Diary (entry for 21 Apr. 1891), p. 244. The leter to Ellen (20 Jan. 1891) is quoted from *Family Letters*, pp. 312–13. Coustillas is quoted from the end of his Ch. X.

VI

Quotations from *NGS* in this section are cited by chapter number only due to the unusually large number of texts available.

On Reardon see Chs. 5, 15, 6, 27, 5, 6, 31, 37, and 27, respectively.

On Biffen see Ch. 10. On naturalism see *ID*, p. 216, and *Gabrielle*, p. 37 (letter of 8 Aug. 1898).

On Milvain see Chs. 30, 24, and 36.

On Whelpdale and Yule see Chs. 28, 20, 10, 30, and 7.x

On literature as a business see Chs. 3, 1, 18, 4, and 15.

On marriage without money see Chs. 22, 27, 24, 17, and 19.

On money and the horrors of poverty see Chs. 3, 4, 18, 21, 7, 15, and 3. The quotation from Roberts is taken from p. 178. The passages quoted from Tindall appear on p. 185.

Gissing's reference to his 2nd marriage is quoted from a letter written to Gabrielle Fleury in 1898, the text of which will be quoted and discussed in greater detail in Ch. 10.

The final quotation from *NGS* is taken from Ch. 27.

VII

Roberts's description of Gissing may be found on pp. 158–80, *passim*.

The quotations from *CB* are taken from pp. 44 and 25.

The letter to Algernon about *NGS* is quoted from *Family Letters*, p. 315. The passages quoted from the letter to Bertz (5 Mar. 1891) appear on pp. 118–19.

On the early days of Gissing's life with Edith see Coustillas, Ch. XI. The (unpublished) letter to Ellen (7 Mar. 1891) is in the Yale University Library. The *CB* entry on *Pilgrim's Progress* appears on p. 52.

On the *Pall Mall Gazette*'s attempt to interview Gissing see the Diary, p. 243 (entry for 2 Apr. 1891). The letter to Bertz is quoted from p. 120.

For reviews of *NGS*, see the *Critical Heritage*, pp. 169–87, and Coustillas, Ch. XI.

Bertz's reaction to *NGS* is reported by Gissing in a letter to Ellen (29 Apr. 1891); see *Family Letters*, pp. 318–19, for this, and also for Gissing's response to his mother's and Ellen's reaction to *NGS*. Gissing's letter to Bertz on *NGS* (26 Apr. 1891) may be found on pp. 121–3.

The Diary entry quoted (27 May 1891) appears on p. 247.

For Gissing's activities at this time, see the Diary entries for 29 May, 2 June, 15 June, and 21 June (pp. 247–9). The Diary entries on *BE* (17 and 20 July 1891) appear on p. 251. The letter to Algernon (23 July 1891) is quoted from *Family Letters*, p. 322

The Oxford/Cambridge letter to Bertz (26 Apr. 1891) appears on p. 121. My account of Gissing's activities during July 1891 is indebted largely to Coustillas, Ch. XI.

VIII

For Smith, Elder's correspondence on *BE* and Gissing's response, see the Diary (entries for 7 and 9 Aug. 1891), p. 253. The quotations from the letters to Bertz (27 Aug. and 21 Sept. 1891) appear on pp. 130 and 135.

On the 'large canvas' see the Diary (3 Sept. 1891), p. 255. The letter to Bertz on *DQ* (dated 18 October 1891) is quoted from pp. 137–8.

On 'A Victim of Circumstances' see Coustillas, Ch. XI. The Diary entry on *DQ*'s change of title (20 Nov. 1891) appears on p. 261. Lawrence and Bullen on *DQ* is quoted from the Diary, p. 262 (entry for 25 Nov. 1891), and from an unpublished letter (in the Berg Collection, New York Public Library) written by Gissing in Nov. 1891 (undated). My account of Lawrence and Bullen's handling of *DQ* is indebted to Coustillas, Ch. XI. The discussion of Lawrence and Bullen's relationship with Gissing is indebted to Korg, p. 179.

On the birth of Gissing's son see the Diary entry for 10 Dec. 1891, p. 263, and Korg, p. 183.

Gissing to Bertz on *BE* (16 Dec. 1891) is quoted from pp. 140–1.

The Diary entries quoted at the end of this section are for 22, 25, and 30 Dec. 1891; all appear on p. 265.

IX

Roberts is quoted from p. 307. The letter to Bertz (20 May 1892) may be found on p. 153.

Poole's excellent discussion of *BE* makes a point similar to mine about 'the psychology of exile' – see p. 173. The letter to Ellen (20 Jan. 1891) is quoted from *Family Letters*, pp. 312–13.

Quotations from *BE*, available in a variety of editions, are by book and chapter number only (thus, for example, II, iii would indicate Part II, Ch. 3, and so on).

On the general resemblances between Peak and Gissing, see I, ii; I, i; III, v; II, iv; I, v; II, ii; II, iii; V, ii; Korg, p. 170; V, iii; VII, i; and V, i.

On class see I, iii; II, ii; III, v; III, i; II, iii; and II, iii.

On 'exile' see I, iii; I, v; VII, i; VII, iii; VI, iii; II, ii; III, iv; VII, i; and *CB*, p. 53.

On women and marriage see II, i; III, iv; VII, iii; II, ii; II, iv; III, ii; VI, iii; VII, i; III, ii; VI, iii; V, iv; IV, iii; III, iii; III, ii; I, ii; and Roberts, p. 259.

On religion see IV, iii; III, iii; V, iv; and *CB*, p. 48.

The last passage quoted from *BE* (on pessimism) appears in III, i.

References to *DQ* are to chapter numbers only.

On towns see Ch. XVII. On convention see Chs. XIV and IX.

On the marriage and education themes see Chs. VII and IX.

On feminism see Chs. XV, III, XIII, XV, and IX, respectively.

On politics, see Chs. XIX, III, XI, XVII, III, VI, and III, respectively.

CHAPTER 8

I

THE quotations in the opening paragraph are from the Diary (3, 4, and 30 Jan. and 16 Feb. 1892), pp. 266, 268, and 270. The letters to Bertz are quoted from pp. 143–4, 140, and 144, respectively; those to Algernon are quoted from *Fiction*, pp. 67–8, and *Family Letters*, p. 325.

For contemporary reviews of *DQ*, see *Critical Heritage*, pp. 188–95, and Coustillas, Ch. XI.

II

The quotation from Roberts's article, reprinted in its entirety in *Critical Heritage* (pp. 208–14), appears on pp. 210–11 of that volume.

The letter to Ellen is quoted from *Family Letters*, pp. 326–7.

The quotation from *CB* appears on p. 50, those from Roberts on pp. 186–8 and 192. The Diary entries for 30 Apr. and 6 and 13 May 1892 may be found on pp. 277–8.

For contemporary reviews of *BE* see *Critical Heritage*, pp. 196–207. On sales of *BE*, see Coustillas, Ch. XI.

The letters to Bertz (1 and 20 May 1892) are quoted from pp. 151–5, *passim*.

III

The letters to Bertz (19 June and 30 Aug. 1892) are quoted from pp. 156 and 158–60. The Diary entries for 1, 10, and 30 July and 4 Oct. 1892 may be found on pp. 280–2 and 286.

My account of the terms offered and accepted for *OW* is indebted to Coustillas, Ch. XI.

The Diary entries for 5 and 9 Dec. 1892 are quoted from p. 291.

The letter to Bertz (2 Dec. 1892) is quoted from pp. 163–5, *passim*.

The letter to Ellen is quoted from *Family Letters*, p. 330.

IV

The letters to Bertz (15 Jan., 11 Mar., and 16 Apr. 1893) are quoted from pp. 166 and 169–70. The letter to Algernon is quoted from *Family Letters*, p. 332.

The Diary entry for 24 Jan. 1893 appears on p. 295; that for 7 Feb. 1893 appears on pp. 296–7.

On the visit of Gissing's mother to Exeter and the final abandonment of 'The Iron Gods' see the Diary entries for late Apr. – p. 302, *passim*.

v

Quotations from *OW* are taken from the Norton paperback edition, the most readily available modern text.

On the 'odd' women see pp. 37 and 52. On love and the novel see pp. 68 and 58.

On women's education see *OW*, p. 56; the letter to Bertz (2 June 1893), p. 171; the (unpublished) letter to Blackwood (6 Dec. 1892, National Library of Scotland, Edinburgh); and *OW*, pp. 61, 99, 102, 107, and 135–6, respectively.

On women and marriage see *OW*, pp. 59, 239, 80, 305, and 268, respectively.

On Gissing and Everard see pp. 85, 145, 176, 254, 265, and 282, respectively.

On Monica and Widdowson see pp. 201, 246, 152–3, 162, 196–7, 236, 200, 224, and 237–9, respectively.

The quotations from Tindall appear on pp. 162, 161, and 203.

vi

The letter to Bertz (2 June 1893) is quoted from p. 172.

For contemporary reviews of *OW*, see *Critical Heritage*, pp. 215–24, and Coustillas, Ch. XI. The *Echo* essay is reprinted in its entirety in *Critical Heritage*, pp. 225–8.

My account of Clara Collet is indebted largely to Coustillas, Ch. XII.

The letter to Algernon is quoted from *Family Letters*, p. 334.

The account given of Gissing's negotiations with regard to his short stories is indebted to Korg, pp. 193–4, and Coustillas, Ch. XII.

The letter to Bertz (29 Sept. 1893) is quoted from pp. 176–8.

Quotations from ' A Lodger in Maze Pond' are taken from *HC*, pp. 249 and 257–61, *passim*.

Quotations from 'A Capitalist' are taken from *HC*, pp. 29 and 37.

The quotation from *CB* appears on p. 53.

vii

On the Baker Street flat suicide see the Diary (entry for 2 Sept. 1893), p. 314.

The reference to Shorter may be found in the Diary (entry for 19 Sept. 1893), p. 316. On 'Miss Lord' and money see the Diary (entry for 16 Oct. 1893), pp. 318–19.

The letter to Bertz (19 Nov. 1893) is quoted from p. 180. The Diary entries for 21 and 22 Nov. 1893 may be found on pp. 321–2.

The two stories discussed here are reprinted in *HOE*.

The letter to Bertz (19 Jan. 1894) is quoted from pp. 181–3, *passim*.

The letter to Paisley is quoted from Coustillas, Ch. XII. It is dated 13 Jan. 1894; reprinted in the *Gissing Newsletter* for June 1965; and may be found in the Colgate University Library.

The letter to Bertz (19 Jan. 1894) is quoted from pp. 181–3. My account of the genesis of *ER* is indebted to Coustillas, Ch. XII. The comment on domestic troubles is quoted from the Diary (entry for 4 Jan. 1894), p. 326; that on finishing the first volume of 'Miss Lord' (26 Jan. 1894) is quoted from p. 328.

My account of Gissing's financial situation in Jan. 1894 is indebted to Korg, p. 194.

The Diary entry (15 Mar. 1894) is quoted from p. 332.

The letter to Bertz (25 Mar. 1894) appears on p. 184.

On finishing 'Miss Lord', see the Diary (12 and 13 Apr. 1894), p. 335. The (unpublished) note to Bullen (dated 14 Apr. 1894) is in the Berg Collection of the New York Public Library. The details of Bullen's terms for *IYJ* are taken from Coustillas, Ch. XII.

The Diary entry on the new serial (29 Mar. 1894) is quoted from p. 333. The reference to *ER* is quoted from the Diary (entry for 19 Apr. 1894), p. 335.

On Gissing's trip to Halesworth see Korg, p. 198, and the Diary (26 May 1894), p. 338. Two decades later Halesworth's most famous inhabitants would be Duncan Grant and Vanessa Bell and her children, who lived out the war there.

Stead's letter is quoted in the Diary (19 June 1894), p. 340. The Diary entries on *ER* (4, 22, and 29 June 1894) are quoted from pp. 339–40.

The letter to Bertz (24 June 1894) is quoted from pp. 185–7.

The letter to Clara Collet – quoted by Coustillas, Ch. XII – is dated 26 Aug. 1894.

VIII

Quotations from *IYJ* are as follows:

On Barmby, Lord, and women see pp. 319 and 229.

On the Peacheys see *CB*, p. 38; and *IYJ*, pp. 401, 53, 253, 7, 168, 245, 168, 242, and 241; Roberts, p. 197; and *IYJ*, pp. 244, 243, 241, 385, 242, and 379, respectively.

On Tarrant and marriage see pp. 144, 355, 198, 335, 436, 413, 430, 410, 412, 149, 193, 199, 411, 205, 411, 201, 375, 413, 178, and 410, respectively.

On Nancy and class see pp. 15 and 80.

On Jessica Morgan, Barmby, and education see pp. 147–8, 214, and 405.

On women, the home, and the anti-feminist theme see pp. 44, 95, 297, 429, and 414.

On the suburbs, Crewe, and advertising see pp. 218, 60, 114, 424, 74, 309; and *CB*, p. 45.

Quotations from *ER* are by chapter number only.

On Hilliard, women, and marriage see Chs. I, IV, XX, and XXII.

On money, see Chs. XXIV, XX, and XXI.

On Birmingham, see Ch. III. The quotation about Hilliard at the end of the novel is taken from Ch. XXVII.

CHAPTER 9

I

THE letter to Bertz (2 Oct. 1894) appears on pp. 188–9. My account of Gissing's activities during the latter half of Sept. 1894 is based largely upon the Diary, pp. 347–9.

The Diary entry on 'Their Pretty Ways' (4 Oct. 1894) may be found on p. 349; quotations from the story are taken from *GGEF*, pp. 256–7.

The Diary entry for 10 Oct. 1894 may be found on p. 350. Korg says this entry 'marks the point at which Gissing began to realize that his marriage might become too great a hardship to bear' (p. 199), but as my discussion of *IYJ* shows, the novelist must have reached this conclusion long before 10 Oct. 1894. Indeed, Korg himself says that Gissing 'had given up hope of winning affectionate companionship from Edith within two years after their marriage' (that is, early in 1893).

Comments on the company at the Society of Authors may be found in a letter to Bertz (24 Nov. 1894), p. 190, and in the Diary (entry for 19 Nov. 1894), p. 354.

My information on Gissing's income is taken from Coustillas, Ch. XIII. The letter to Bertz (24 Nov. 1894) is quoted from p. 191.

II

Contemporary reviews of *IYJ*, along with the full text of Gissing's letter to Roberts, may be found in *Critical Heritage,* pp. 229–47. Additional information about contemporary reviews and sales of *IYJ* and about Gissing's agreement with Lawrence and Bullen for *ER* is taken from Coustillas, Ch. XIII.

The quotation from the letter to Bertz (30 Dec. 1894) appears on p. 192. The comment on *Esther Waters* is quoted from the Diary (entry for 9 Dec. 1894), p. 356. On the agreement with Jerome, see Coustillas, Ch. XIII. For the Diary entry on earnings (31 Dec. 1894), see p. 358.

The letter to Algernon (9 Jan. 1895) is quoted from *Fiction,* p. 80. The Diary entries (16 Jan. and 13 Feb. 1895) are quoted from pp. 360 and 363.

On Martha Barnes, see the Diary (entry for 21 Feb. 1895), p. 364. For the entries on *SF* see the Diary (1 and 4 Mar. 1895), p. 365. The letter to Bertz (26 Mar. 1895) is quoted from p. 197. The (unpublished) letter to Roberts (5 Mar. 1895) is in the Berg Collection of the New York Public Library.

The (unpublished) letter to Colles (dated 19 Jan. 1895) is in the Carl H. Pforzheimer Library.

My information on sales of *ER* is taken from Coustillas, Ch. XIII.

For contemporary reviews of *ER* see *Critical Heritage,* pp. 248–54, and Coustillas, Ch. XIII. Quotations from 'The Depressed School' are taken from *Wells,* pp. 236–7.

III

On Greece in *SF* see pp. 11, 75–6, and 229.

On having an adolescent son see p. 54.

Passages on marriage are quoted from *SF,* pp. 141, 52, 39, 150, 140, 195, 219, and 194, respectively.

On the 'guilty secret' see p. 37.

On 'sleeping fires' and love see pp. 184–5, 191, and 218.

Passages on asceticism and related issues are quoted from pp. 149, 216, 197, 153, 215, and 221–2, respectively.

IV

The Diary entry (16 Apr. 1895) is quoted from p. 371. Gissing's reply to Clodd is quoted from *Clodd,* pp. 34–5. The Diary entry on the Derby (29 May 1895) appears on p. 374. For the description of Gissing by W. Robertson Nicoll see Korg, pp. 200 and 291n. The quotation from Hick appears in *Hick,* p. 9.

The comment made to Colles appears in an unpublished letter (5 Aug. 1895) in the Carl H. Pforzheimer Library. On the arrival of Bertz's cheque, see the Diary (9 May 1895), p. 373. Gissing's letter to Bertz of 9 May 1895 is quoted from pp. 198–99.

Quotations from 'The Place of Realism in Fiction' are taken from *Fiction*, pp. 84–6, *passim*.

Quotations from the letter to Bertz (23 June 1895) appear on p. 200.

On the reprinting of Gissing's novels, see Korg, p. 202.

                                         V

See the appropriate sections of *HOE*, *passim*, for the following quoted passages cited.

The quotation from 'The Medicine Man' appears on p. 182; that from 'An Old Maid's Triumph' appears on p. 200.

The passage from 'A Profitable Weakness' is quoted from p. 231. The quotation from 'A Free Woman' appears on p. 292. For the relevant section of *WD* alluded to in the text in connection with 'A Son of the Soil', see *WD*, III, 136.

The passages quoted from 'Out of the Fashion' appear on pp. 306 and 308.

                                        VI

The quotations are from the Diary (25 July and 20 Aug. 1895), pp. 381 and 384. The letter to Hardy (3 Sept. 1895) is in the Dorset County Museum. Gissing's desire to get back to writing novels is expressed in an unpublished letter to Colles (12 Aug. 1895), in the Carl H. Pforzheimer Library. The letter to Bertz (27 Aug. 1895) is quoted from pp. 202–4.

The visit to Meredith is recounted in the Diary (3 Sept. 1895), pp. 385–6.

Gissing's account of the dinner at Box Hill is given in the Diary (12 Sept. 1895), p. 387. On the visit to Hardy see the Diary (entries for 14–16 Sept. 1895), pp. 387–8.

The letter to Bertz about Hardy (22 Sept. 1895) is quoted from pp. 205–6.

On the familiarity of Gissing's name to readers of the popular press see Coustillas, Ch. XIII.

On Gissing's will see the Diary (26 and 28 Sept. 1895), p. 389, and Coustillas, Ch. XIII.

My account of the new edition of *U* is indebted to that provided by Coustillas, Ch. XIII.

The letters to Bertz (12 Nov. and 18 Dec. 1895 and 15 Jan. 1896) are quoted from pp. 207–8 and 210–12.

On *Jude the Obscure* see *Hick*, pp. 23–4.

                                       VII

Cassell's advertisement for *PG* is given in a note by Pierre Coustillas (the editor) in *Hick*, pp. 23–4. Gissing's reaction is quoted from *Hick*, p. 24.

The letters to Hick (14 and 29 Nov. 1895 and 6 Jan. 1896) are quoted from pp. 21–4.

Reviews of *SF* are quoted from *Critical Heritage*, pp. 260–3, and Coustillas, Ch. XIII. Coustillas's notion (Ch. XIII) that reviewers showed 'flagrant incompetence' in preferring *SF* to *ER* is nonsense.

Reviews of *PG* are quoted from *Critical Heritage,* pp. 264–8, and Coustillas, Ch. XIII.

The essay by Frederic is reprinted in *Critical Heritage,* pp. 255–9; that by Mrs Michaelis appears in the same volume, pp. 269–75.

VIII

The first quotation in this section is from the Diary (18 Jan. 1896), p. 400.

Gissing on Alfred's birth is quoted from an unpublished letter to Algernon (20 Jan. 1896), in the Yale Library, and *Hick,* p. 26. The Diary entry on Edith (23 Jan. 1896) appears on p. 401.

On the trip to Mudie's see the Diary (12 Feb. 1896), p. 402. Gissing's (unpublished) letter to Bullen on *IC,* dated 12 Feb. 1896, is in the Berg Collection of the New York Public Library. Coustillas, in Ch. XIII, gives a detailed account of the circumstances surrounding Gissing's decision not to reprint *IC.*

The Diary entries quoted are for 13, 14, and 16 Feb. 1896, pp. 402–3. The letter to Bertz (23 Feb. 1896) is quoted from p. 213.

The letter to Algernon (3 Mar. 1896) is quoted from *Family Letters,* p. 345.

My account of Gissing's removal of Walter from Epsom is indebted to Coustillas, Ch. XIII. The letter to Bertz (16 Apr. 1896) is quoted from p. 217.

The (unpublished) letters to Algernon (22 Apr. 1896) and Miss Collet (23 Apr. 1896) are quoted by Coustillas, Ch. XIII. The Diary entry (23 Apr. 1896) on the scene with Edith appears on p. 408. The quotation from Tindall appears on p. 218.

IX

The letters to Bertz (9, 20, and 28 May 1896) are quoted from pp. 219–21, *passim.* These letters show that *TW* and 'Benedict's Household' were by no means entirely different stories, as some critics have supposed. The (unpublished) letter to Roberts (27 May 1896), which is in the Berg Collection of the New York Public Library, is quoted both in Roberts, p. 195, and *Fiction,* p. 81. On Gissing's difficulties with 'Benedict' (Rolfe) see the Diary (26 May 1896), p. 411.

The Diary entry on Meredith (12 May 1896) appears on p. 410. Coustillas's 'Bibliography' mistakenly lists 'A Yorkshire Lass' as having been written in June 1895. The letter to Bertz (3 Aug. 1896) is quoted from p. 222.

The letters to Hick (10 and 14 June 1896) are quoted from pp. 27–8; that to Algernon (19 June 1896) appears in *Family Letters,* p. 348.

On the Omar Khayyám dinner and Frederic Harrison see the Diary (20 June 1896), p. 413. Zangwill's reminiscence may be found in 'Without Prejudice: George Gissing', *To-Day,* 3 Feb. 1904, pp. 433–4.

The Diary entry on Walter (9 Aug. 1896) appears on p. 418. The letter to Bertz (3 Aug. 1896) appears on pp. 222–3.

Hick's account of the Sept. 1896 visit to Epsom is given on p. 10.

The letters to Bertz (27 Sept. and 9 Oct. 1896) are quoted from pp. 224 and 225.

My account of Gissing's first meeting with Wells and of Wells's background is indebted chiefly to Korg, pp. 206–7; see also Coustillas, Ch. XIV.

The Diary entries on Wells (20 and 26 Nov. 1896) are quoted from pp. 427

and 428. Wells's comments on Gissing in this paragraph are taken from *Autobiography*, pp. 481, 486, and 483. Gissing is quoted from a letter to Wells (8 Dec. 1896); see *Wells*, p. 38.

The letters to Bertz (27 Sept. and 6 Dec. 1896) are quoted from pp. 224–6.

The description of the visit to Wells is taken from the Diary (16 Dec. 1896), p. 429.

On *TW* see the Diary (18 Dec. 1896), p. 429. The details of Bullen's terms for *TW* are taken from Coustillas, Ch. XIV, and the Diary (21 Dec. 1896), p. 430. The (unpublished) letter to Algernon (17 Dec. 1896) is in the Yale Library.

x

Quotations from *TW* are by Book and chapter number (thus II,iii would refer to Part the Second, third chapter).

The first quotations are taken from III,v and II,xii.

On housekeeping and servants see I,xii; II,v; and III,i.

On women see III, iii; I,iv; and II,xi.

On Alma see II,i.

On Rolfe and his similarities to Gissing see I,i; I,iii; I,i; I,xi; III,i; I,ix; II,i; III,vi; Roberts, p. 192, and *TW*, II,ii; II,iii; II,x; III,vi; III,i; II,ix; II,xiv; III,i; III,vi; III,ii; III,i; III,iii; III,ii; and III,ix.

On the city, the country, and the environment see III,ii; II,ix; III,vii; III,xiii (on Henrietta Winter); III,i; and II,ii.

On war and Imperialism, see I,ii; III,xiii; and Tindall, p. 251.

Miscellaneous autobiographical passages are quoted from *TW*, II,iv; II,vii; III,vii; III,viii; and III,v.

xi

On the Dickens monograph, see the Diary (27 Dec. 1896), p. 430.

The letter to Clara Collet (30 Nov. 1896) is quoted by Coustillas, Ch. XIV.

For Shorter's request and Gissing's response, see the Diary (8 and 9 Jan. 1897), p. 432. The Diary entry for 5 Feb. 1897 appears on p. 434; that for 2 June 1897 appears on p. 435.

CHAPTER 10

I

On the events of 10 Feb. 1897, see Roberts, pp. 198–9.

On the visits to Hick and Pye-Smith see *Hick*, pp. 10–11. On the 'miserable peace' see Roberts, p. 199.

The letters to Algernon, both unpublished and both in the Yale Library, are dated 17 Feb. and 21 March. 1897. The letters to Hick (27 Feb. and 16 Mar. 1897) are quoted from pp. 34–5. The letter to Miss Collet, dated 18 Feb. 1897, is quoted by Coustillas, Ch. XIV.

The quotations from Wells are taken from 'George Gissing : An Impression', *Monthly Review*, Aug. 1904, pp. 160–72, reprinted in *Wells*, pp. 260–77: this was the preface to *V* commissioned and later suppressed by the Gissing family (see Ch. 12); and *Biography*, p. 134.

Reviews of *TW* are quoted from *Critical Heritage*, pp. 277–305, and Coustillas, Ch. XIV.

Wells's essay, 'The Novels of Mr George Gissing', is reprinted in *Wells*, pp. 242–59, Gissing's letter to Wells (7 Aug. 1897) is quoted from *Wells*, pp. 47–8.

The *Sewanee Review* essay is reprinted in *CAGG*, pp. 142–51. James's piece is reprinted in his *Notes on Novelists* (New York, 1914), pp. 436–45.

My information on sales and editions of *TW*, as well as my account of Gissing's rejection of the 16-guineas offer, is indebted to Coustillas, Ch. XIV.

II

The letter to Hick (13 Apr. 1897) is quoted from pp. 37–8. The quotation from Bertz's letter to Gissing (? Apr. 1897) is quoted from p. 229.

The letter to Hick (16 May 1897) is quoted from pp. 38–9.

The visit to Pye-Smith is chronicled in the Diary (1 June 1897), p. 435, and *Hick*, p. 40.

The letter to Hick (2 June 1897) is quoted from p. 40. Rothenstein is quoted from his *Men and Memories*, Vol. I (London, 1931), pp. 302–4. The account of the luncheon with Beerbohm (the descriptive phrase is Gissing's) and Rothenstein is given in the Diary (7 June 1897), p. 436.

The letters to Bertz (13 and 15 June 1897) are quoted from pp. 231–3.

Details regarding terms of publication of *HOE* are taken from Coustillas, Ch. XIV.

On Castle Bolton and its literary uses see Coustillas, Ch. XIV. The letter to Hick (28 July 1897) is quoted from p. 41. The Diary entries (11, 12, 16, 17, 21, and 24 Aug. 1897) are quoted from pp. 441–2.

The quotations from Roberts appears on pp. 201 and 202–3.

The Diary entry (25 Aug. 1897) is quoted from p. 443. The letters to Hick (30 Aug. and 10 Sept. 1897) are quoted from pp. 42–4. On Miss Orme see the Diary (10 Sept. 1897), p. 445. The passage quoted from the letter to Bertz (13 Sept. 1897) appears on p. 236. See the Diary for 6, 7, and 17 Sept. 1897, pp. 444–5, on Gissing's final days with Edith. The letter to Wells (21 Sept. 1897) is quoted from p. 56.

III

On Gissing's amendment of his will, see Coustillas, Ch. XV. On his new capacity for work, see Gissing's Diary (29 Oct. 1897), p. 452. Quotations from the letter to Bertz (29 Oct. 1897) appear on p. 239. The letter to Mrs Wells (3 Oct. 1897) is quoted from pp. 60–1.

'George Gissing's Novels' (*National Review*, Oct. 1897) is reprinted in *Critical Heritage*, pp. 306–15.

The letter to Wells (13 Nov. 1897) is quoted from p. 65. The Diary entry (15 Nov. 1897) is quoted from p. 455.

Reviews of *HOE* are quoted from *Critical Heritage*, pp. 316–19, and Coustillas, Ch. XV.

IV

Quotations from *CD* are based on the pagination of the first edition (reprinted by Haskell House, New York, 1974).

On Dickens's genius see pp. 166, 171, 184, 193, and 192; on his limitations see pp. 85, 95, 45, 52, 96, 197, 27, 101, and 201.

The summing-up is quoted from p. 50. On *Little Dorrit* see p. 86.

On general aspects of autobiography in *CD* see pp. 227 and 217.

Quotations from *CD* relating to specific areas of resemblance between Gissing and Dickens are as follows:

On travel see p. 240; on Dickens's ability to write amid distractions, see pp. 234–5; on his inability to withstand popular neglect, see p. 72; on the hatred of modern life, see pp. 13–14, 18, 208, 59, 38, and 129.

On conservatism see pp. 77, 110, 196, 198, 202, 209, and 215.

On religion, puritanism, and social tyranny see pp. 121–2 and 205.

On women see pp. 155, 161, 162–3, 133–5, 137–8, 141, and 153.

For the matter discussed in the final paragraph of this section, see Roberts, pp. 207–8, and Korg, p. 219. The quotations from Roberts appear on pp. 210, 212, and 218.

v

The Diary entry for 22 Nov. 1897 appears on p. 459; that for 1 Dec. 1897 is quoted from p. 464. The letter to Colles (26 Dec. 1897; in the Carl H. Pforzheimer Library) is quoted by Coustillas, Ch. XV.

vi

The Diary entries on Edith (27 and 30 Dec. 1897) appear on pp. 477–8.

The letter to Wells (6 Jan. 1898) is quoted from pp. 73–5.

The letter to Bertz (13 Jan. 1898) is quoted from pp. 242–5. The quoted passage from the letter to Ellen (23 Jan. 1898) appears in *Family Letters*, p. 364. The letter to Wells (27 Jan. 1898) is quoted from pp. 82–3.

The quoted passage in the letter to Wells (18 Feb. 1898) appears on p. 91. The letter to Bertz (10 Feb. 1898) is quoted from p. 245.

Details of the terms offered for *TT* are given by Coustillas, Ch. XV.

On the Dreyfus affair see the Diary (entry for 24 Feb. 1898), p. 484. On Edith's behaviour see the Diary (entry for 3 Mar. 1898), p. 485.

On the proposed Thackeray volume see the Diary (entry for 8 Mar. 1898), p. 485. The letter to Bertz (8 Mar. 1898) is quoted from p. 247.

Reviews of *CD* are quoted from *Critical Heritage*, pp. 320–37, and Coustillas, Ch. XV.

vii

The quotations from Wells are taken from *Autobiography*, pp. 487–8. Hornung on Gissing is quoted from 'George Gissing' in *Author* for 1 Feb. 1904, pp. 131–2. Dunne is quoted in *Wells*, p. 38n.

The account of Edith's behaviour in London is indebted to Coustillas, Ch. XV.

The Diary entries on Bertz and the German visit (14 and 15 Apr. 1898) are quoted from p. 490. The letter to Bertz (10 Feb. 1898) is quoted from p. 245. On Gissing's return to London, see the Diary (entry for 20 Apr. 1898), p. 490.

For Gissing's pleas for secrecy about his new address see Roberts, p. 219 (7 May 1898); Hick, p. 50 (22 May 1898); and *Bertz*, p. 249 (17 May 1898).

On Gissing's financial worries, see the Diary (entry for 21 May 1898), p. 493. On *TT* and the loan to Algernon see the Diary (entry for 10 May 1898), p. 492.

Quotations from 'Fate and the Apothecary' are taken from *HC*, pp. 217–18 and 223.

The Diary entry on Edith (17 June 1898) is quoted from p. 495. Quoted passages from the letter to Hick (17 June 1898) appear on pp. 51–2.

Details of the terms for the Rochester Edition are given by Coustillas, Ch. XV. Gissing's characterization of the work as 'easy' is made in a letter to Bertz (1 July 1898), p. 250.

The letter to Wells (26 June 1898) is quoted from pp. 102–3; that to Bertz (1 July 1898) is quoted from pp. 250–1.

The letter to Clara Collet (dated 3 Jan. 1898) is given by Coustillas, Ch. XV. My account of Mrs Williams is taken from Coustillas, Ch. XV.

Wells on Gabrielle Fleury is quoted from *Autobiography*, p. 489. Roberts on Gabrielle is quoted from p. 259. Gissing on Gabrielle is quoted in *Biography*, p. 135.

My account of Gabrielle's background is taken from Coustillas, Ch. XVI.

VIII

The Diary entry (10 July 1898) appears on p. 497. The letter to Wells (19 July 1898) is quoted from p. 107.

The Diary entry on Gabrielle (26 July 1898) is quoted from p. 498. The letters to Gabrielle (late July 1898) are quoted from *Gabrielle,* pp. 27–8.

On Edith's terms for a separation and her behaviour in Aug. 1898 see Korg. p. 226, and Coustillas, Ch. XVI. The letter to Roberts is given by him on p. 220. Gissing's letter to Wells about Mrs Williams is given on p. 109; see also p. 110n (for Wells's opinion of Gabrielle).

The letters to Gabrielle (early Aug. 1898 and 5–10 Aug. 1898) are quoted from pp. 29, 31–8, and 40, *passim.*

Roberts on Gabrielle is quoted from pp. 229 and 231; Wells, from p. 110n. Quotations from the letters to Wells (20, 26, and 27 Aug. 1898) appear on pp. 116, 118, and 119.

The letters to Gabrielle (14, 16, 18, 25, 29, and 30 Aug. 1898) are quoted from pp. 41–6, 48, and 51–3, *passim.*

IX

Reviews of *TT* are quoted from *Critical Heritage,* pp. 338–51, and Coustillas, Ch. XVI; sales figures are taken from Coustillas, Ch. XVI.

The letter to Clodd (1 Sept. 1898) is quoted from pp. 51–2. The letter to Bertz (4 Sept. 1898) is quoted from pp. 251–2.

The Diary entry for 7 Sept. 1898 appears on p. 501.

Quotations from the letters to Gabrielle (7, 9, 11, and 12 Sept. 1898) are taken from pp. 55, 58–60, and 62.

The letter to Gabrielle of 1 Oct. 1898 is quoted from pp. 69–70.

The letter about Edith and divorce (16 Aug. 1898) appears in *Gabrielle,* p. 44. The Diary entry for 15 Oct. 1898 may be found on p. 503.

The letters to Gabrielle (3 and 23 Oct. and 6 and 13 Nov. 1898) are quoted from pp. 71–3 and 75–9, *passim.*

The letter to Roberts is quoted from pp. 236–7; on the possibility of an American divorce see Roberts, p. 238. The quotations from *OW* are taken from p. 285.

The letter to Bertz (1 Nov. 1898) is quoted from pp. 252–4.

The letters to Gabrielle (29 Aug., 15 Sept., and 23 Oct. 1898) are quoted from pp. 51, 63–4, and 73.

CHAPTER 11

I

The letters to Gabrielle (20, 22, and 27 Nov. 1898; 11, 18, 24, and late Dec. 1898; and 1 Jan. 1899) are quoted from pp. 82, 84–6, and 88–94.

Passages quoted from the letters to Gabrielle (15 and 25 Jan. 1899) may be found on pp. 95 and 97.

Miss Collet's comment is quoted by Gissing in a letter to Gabrielle (29 Jan. 1899), p. 98. The (unpublished) letter to Roberts (3 Feb. 1899) is in the Berg Collection of the New York Public Library. Gissing further quotes Miss Collet in a letter to Gabrielle (16 Feb. 1899), p. 109.

Information about the financial arrangements for *CL* is taken from Coustillas, Ch. XVI. The letter to Wells (28 Mar. 1899) is quoted from p. 135.

The letters to Gabrielle (25, 29, and 31 Jan. 1899; 4, 15, and 25 Feb. 1899; and 1, 5, 8, 12, and 16 Mar. 1899) are quoted from pp. 96, 98–104, 108–9, 112–13, 115, 117, and 119.

II

Quotations from the prefaces to Dickens's novels are taken from the English edition of *ID*.

Passages quoted from the prefaces to *Oliver Twist* and *Dombey and Son* appear on pp. 93, 110, 81–2, 125, 100, 122, and 139.

On *The Old Curiosity Shop* see pp. 201 and 208–9.

On *Bleak House* see pp. 234–5 and 241.

Quotations from 'A Poor Gentleman' are taken from *HC*, pp. 113 and 115.

The letter to Bertz (17 Jan. 1899) is quoted from pp. 254–6. The quotation on love is taken from *CL*, p. 131. The quotation from the letter to Gabrielle (3 Oct. 1898) appears on p. 71.

On Piers Otway as an autobiographical creation see *CL*, pp. 15, 55, 69, 108, 184, 164, 165, 167, 168, 170, 268, 172–3, 249–50, 267, 286–7, 193–5, 272, and 273.

On the modern age see pp. 79, 156, 290, and 163–4.

On advertising see p. 261.

On Arnold Jacks, Imperialism, peace, and heroism see pp. 119, 238, 180, 289, and 309.

On the poor see pp. 281 and 290–1.

On marriage and the relations of the sexes see pp. 16, 96, 67, and 195–6.

III

The quotation from Meredith is taken from Coustillas (who quotes Clodd), Ch. XVI. The letter to Roberts is quoted from *Roberts*, pp. 241–2. The letter to Bertz (31 Mar. 1899) is quoted from p. 259.

Quoted passages from the letters to Gabrielle (27 Mar. and 1 and 4 Apr. 1899) may be found on pp. 121–3 and 125–7.

The letter to Wells (21 Apr. 1899) is quoted from p. 137; that to Hick (27 Apr. 1899) is quoted from p. 56; that to Gabrielle (4 May 1899) is quoted from p. 130.

The Diary entry (7 May 1899) appears on p. 513. The passage quoted from Wells is taken from *Autobiography*, p. 489.

IV

The letter to Bertz (12 May 1899) is quoted from p. 260.

The letter to Miss Collet (22 July 1899) is quoted by Coustillas, Ch. XVII. The Diary entry (16 Aug. 1899) may be found on p. 517. Quoted passages from the letters to Bertz (23 July and Aug. 1899) appear on pp. 263 and 265.

Passages quoted from *BIS* may be found on pp. 13, 105, 151, 197–8, 115, 116–17, and 203, respectively.

V

The letter to Bertz (22 Oct. 1899) is quoted from pp. 265 and 267.

Quotations from contemporary reviews of *CL* are taken from *Critical Heritage*, pp. 352–68, and Coustillas, Ch. XVII.

The commercial failure of *CL* is recounted by Coustillas, Ch. XVII. Gissing's letter to Clodd (7 Nov. 1899) is quoted from p. 57.

The letter to Bertz (11 Dec. 1899) is quoted from pp. 268–9.

The letter to Miss Collet (29 Dec. 1899) is quoted from *Family Letters*, p. 366. My account of the fate of 'Among the Prophets' is indebted to Coustillas, Ch. XVII.

Quoted passages from the letters to Miss Collet and Walter (both 29 Dec. 1899) may be found in *Family Letters*, pp. 366–7. The letter to Bertz (31 Dec. 1899) is quoted from pp. 271–2.

VI

'The Coming of the Preacher' appeared in *Literature*, 13 (Jan. 1900), pp. 15–16, and is quoted from *Fiction*, pp. 94–6.

The quoted passage from the letter to Ellen (2 Jan. 1900) is taken from *Family Letters*, p. 368. The (unpublished) letter to Roberts (10 Feb. 1900) is in the Berg Collection of the New York Public Library.

My account of Gissing during March 1900 is indebted to Coustillas, Ch. XVII. The letters to Bertz (11 and 28 Mar. 1900) are quoted from pp. 276–8.

The quotation from Clodd's diary is taken from *Clodd*, p. 60. The letter to Gabrielle (20 Apr. 1900) is quoted from p. 131.

For the letter to Clara Collet (23 May 1900), see *Family Letters*, p. 369. The Diary entry (30 May 1900) appears on p. 524.

The letter to Clodd (7 June 1900) is quoted from p. 67. The letter to Walter (17 June 1900) appears in *Family Letters*, pp. 370–1.

The letter to Bertz (5 Aug. 1900) is quoted from pp. 284–5.

The letter to Clodd (28 Aug. 1900) is quoted from p. 69. The letter to Bertz (30 Sept. 1900) is quoted from pp. 287–8.

Wells on Conrad may be found in a letter to Gissing dated 19 Oct. 1900 – in *Wells*, p. 146. The Diary entries on *PPHR* (23 Oct. 1900) appear on p. 533. The letter to Bertz (24 Oct. 1900) is quoted from p. 289. The letters to Miss Collet (24 Oct. and 2 Nov. 1900) appear in *Family Letters*, pp. 372–3.

The characterization of Gissing by Gabrielle's Nevers relatives was reported to the present writer by their daughter, the late Denise Le Mallier.

VII

Quotations from *OFC* are as follows:

On Lashmar and Gissing see pp. 235, 397, and 387.

On Lashmar as the spirit of the age see pp. 165, 285, and 235.

Lashmar's father is quoted from pp. 263–4.

On politics see pp. 69, 375, 121, 78, and 188.

On 'vintage Gissing themes' in *OFC* see pp. 298, 235–6, 299, 219, 309, 213–14, 404–5, 240, 138, and 135, respectively.

Due to the number of texts available, quotations from *PPHR* are cited by section and chapter only.

On Gissing's 'Englishness' see Spring, 2; Summer, 2; Summer, 4; Summer, 25; Winter, 13; Summer, 14; Winter, 7; Winter, 8; and Summer, 18.

On miscellaneous autobiography see Autumn, 7; Summer, 23; Winter, 17; Autumn, 19; Summer, 26; Winter, 1; Summer, 25; Autumn, 5; Winter, 6; Spring, 8; Spring, 12; Autumn, 9–10; Spring, 7; Spring, 12; Spring, 17; Winter, 17; Spring, 19; Summer, 7; Spring, 19; Autumn, 24; Autumn, 13; Autumn, 12; Winter, 16; and Autumn, 23.

On the Ryecroft/Gissing 'personality' and neurasthenia see Spring, 7; Spring, 17; Spring 19; Autumn, 15; Autumn, 2; Winter, 25; Spring, 23; and Summer, 6.

On the writer's home and homelessness see Spring, 2; Spring, 10; Summer, 12; and Winter, 15.

On poverty see Spring, 1; Spring, 4; Autumn, 15; Spring, 10; Winter, 9; Autumn, 6; Autumn, 15; Autumn, 21; Spring, 5; Spring, 11; Winter, 24; Summer, 23; Winter, 3; and Summer, 21. The *CB* entry (1903) appears on p. 67.

On writing as a profession see Spring, 1; Spring, 9; Spring, 18; Autumn, 16; Summer, 23; Autumn, 21; Spring, 22; and Autumn, 22.

On the conservatism of Ryecroft/Gissing, including views on education, see Spring, 16; Summer, 20; Summer, 22; Spring, 19; Summer, 12; Autumn, 15; Spring, 22; Winter, 11; Autumn, 17; and Summer, 17.

The quotations in the final two paragraphs are taken from the 'Preface' to *PPHR*, and Winter, 26.

CHAPTER 12

I

THE letter to Hick (17 Dec. 1900) is quoted from p. 58. The Diary entry (25 Dec. 1900) appears on p. 534. The letter to Bertz (26 Dec. 1900) is quoted from pp. 291–2.

The description of Gissing is by Henry-D. Davray and is quoted by Coustillas, Ch. XVII.

Gissing's letter to his mother (23 Jan. 1901) appears in *Family Letters*, pp. 374–5. The letter to Clodd (24 Jan. 1901) is quoted from p. 72.

The letter to Miss Collet on *BIS* (17 Feb. 1901) appears in *Family Letters*, p. 375. The letter to Clodd (28 Feb. 1901) is quoted from p. 72.

Wells is quoted from *Autobiography*, p. 490. The letter to Bertz (17 Mar. 1901) is quoted from pp. 293–4.

Gissing's letters to Pinker, both in the Berg Collection of the New York Public Library and both unpublished, are dated 6 Apr. and 13 Mar. 1901. On Gissing's illness in March–April 1901, see Korg, p. 246, and the Diary (entry for 26 Apr. 1901), p. 539. Gissing also wrote a detailed letter to Hick (8 Apr. 1901, pp. 58–60) on his illness and the French physician's diagnosis and advice.

The letters to Wells (12 and 26 Apr. 1901) are quoted from pp. 153 and 156. Roberts is quoted from pp. 251–2. The letters to Miss Collet (12 Apr. and 2 May 1901) are quoted by Coustillas, Ch. XVII, and in *Family Letters*, p. 376.

II

Hick on Gissing's condition is quoted from Roberts, p. 253, and *Hick*, p. 12. Wells is quoted from *Autobiography*, p. 490. The longer passage quoted from *Hick* also appears on p. 12. The quotation from Roberts may be found on p. 254.

The letter to Miss Collet and the comments of Henry James are quoted by Coustillas, Ch. XVIII.

Gissing's letters to Gabrielle (6, 7, 10, 11, and 13 June 1901) are quoted from pp. 134–8, *passim*.

Wells on Gabrielle is quoted in *Autobiography*, p. 490. For Gabrielle's letters to the Wellses (10 and 24 June 1901), see *Wells*, pp. 162–77, *passim*. Wells's final response to Gabrielle is paraphrased by him in *Autobiography*, p. 490. The quotation from Roberts is taken from p. 257.

The letter to Clodd (17 June 1901) appears on pp. 73–4. The letters to Bertz (20 and 22 June 1901) are quoted from pp. 295–7.

III

Reviews of *OFC* and *BIS* are quoted from *Critical Heritage*, pp. 369–89, and Coustillas, Ch. XVIII.

Roberts's essay, 'George Gissing', is reprinted in *Critical Heritage*, pp. 389–92.

IV

The letter to Hick (2 July 1901) appears on p. 61. The letter to Wells (25 June 1901) is quoted from p. 181.

For Gabrielle's letter to Jane Wells (12 July 1901), see *Wells*, pp. 182–5 and 187–8.

Gissing's letters to Gabrielle (1, 3, 4, and 5 July 1901) may be found on pp. 139–42.

Gissing's (unpublished) letter to Margaret about Gabrielle is in the Berg Collection of the New York Public Library. Coustillas is quoted from Ch. XVIII. Ellen Gissing is quoted from Appendix C to *Family Letters*, p. 406.

V

The letter to Algernon (Aug. 1901) appears in *Family Letters*, p. 377. The letters to Bertz (8 and 25 Sept. 1901) are quoted from pp. 299 and 302.

The story of Gissing's negotiations with Methuen over payments for his prefaces to Dickens is told by Coustillas, Ch. XVIII. Gissing's other activities in connection with Dickens are discussed by Coustillas, Ch. XVIII.

The letter to Wells (21 Nov. 1901) is quoted from pp. 196–7.

The letter to Mrs Wells (30 Nov. 1901) is quoted from p. 201. The letter to Clodd (29 Nov. 1901) is quoted from p. 76.

The letter to Ellen (8 Dec. 1901) appears in *Family Letters*, p. 378.

The letter to Bertz (27 Dec. 1901) is quoted from pp. 303–4. The letter to Algernon (28 Dec. 1901) appears in *Family Letters*, pp. 379–80.

VI

The letters to Gabrielle (16, 19, and 23 Jan. 1902) are quoted from pp. 147–9.

The letter to Clara Collet (31 Jan. 1902) is quoted from *Family Letters*, p. 381. The passage from the letter to Clodd (8 Jan. 1902) is taken from p. 79. On Edith's incarceration and the placement of Alfred, see Korg, pp. 248–9; Coustillas, Ch. XVIII; and a letter from Gissing to Gabrielle (20 Feb. 1902), p. 153. The next quotation from a letter to Gabrielle (4 Feb. 1902) appears on p. 150. The letter to Bertz (24 Feb. 1902) may be found on pp. 305–6.

The letters to Gabrielle (4 and 13 Feb. 1902) quoted in the text may be found on pp. 151–2.

The letter to Wells (19 Feb. 1902) is quoted from pp. 203–4. The passages from the letter to Clodd (1 Mar. 1902) appear on p. 82.

The letters to Gabrielle (6, 14, and 20 Mar. 1902) are quoted from pp. 156–8.

Passages from the letters to Algernon (14 Mar. and 5 Apr. 1902) are taken from *Family Letters*, p. 382. The letter to Clara Collet (16 Apr. 1902) appears in *Family Letters*, pp. 383–4. The comment on Paris may be found in a Diary entry for 14 Apr. 1902, p. 541.

The Diary entries (7, 8, 10, and 12 Apr. 1902) are quoted from pp. 540–1.

Passages quoted from the letters to Gabrielle (25 and 29 Apr. 1902) may be found on pp. 160 and 162–3. The (unpublished) letter to Margaret (2 May 1902) is in the Berg Collection of the New York Public Library. The entry in *CB* (14 May 1902) is quoted from p. 27. The Diary entry (21 May 1902) appears on p. 545.

VII

The letter to Bertz (3 June 1902) is quoted from pp. 308–9. The Diary entries quoted (1 and 15 July 1902) appear on pp. 546 and 547.

The letter to Bertz (27 July 1902) is quoted from pp. 310–11.

The letter to Wells (10 Aug. 1902) is quoted from p. 209. The letter to Hick (24 Aug. 1902) appears on p. 63.

'The Novel of Misery' is reprinted in *Critical Heritage*, pp. 396–402. Reviews of Gissing's abridgement of Forster's *Life of Dickens* may be found in *Critical Heritage*, pp. 403–8.

The letter to Hick (26 Oct. 1902) is quoted from p. 65. Passages quoted from the letters to Bertz (26 Oct. and 16 Nov. 1902) may be found on pp. 311–15.

The letter to Clodd about Conrad (30 Nov. 1902) is quoted from pp. 88–9. Conrad's letter to Gissing is quoted in Coustillas's headnote to Letter xxxi in *Clodd*, p. 86.

The letter to Clara Collet (24 Dec. 1902) appears in *Family Letters*, pp. 390–1.

VIII

Reviews of *PPHR* are quoted from *Critical Heritage*, pp. 409–29, and Coustillas, Ch. XIX. Information about sales of *PPHR* is taken from Coustillas, Ch. XIX.

The letter to Bertz (15 Feb. 1903) is quoted from pp. 315–16.

Roberts's account of his visit to Gissing and of their correspondence during the winter of 1903 may be found on pp. 259–67, *passim*. In *The Private Life of*

Henry Maitland the visit to the south of France is erroneously described as having taken place in 1902.

The letter to Mrs Wells (8 Mar. 1903) is given in *Wells*, p. 212. The letter to Ellen (21 Mar. 1903) appears in *Family Letters*, p. 392. The letter to Margaret (25 Mar. 1903) is quoted from *Family Letters*, p. 393.

IX

Page-references to *WW* are to the 1st edition (1905).

Quotations in the opening paragraphs on autobiography in *WW* are taken from pp. 181, 187–8, 29, 151, 252, 295, 285, 68, 26, 207, 109; *CB*, p. 54; *WW*, pp. 154 and 162–3; *CB*, p. 27; and *WW*, p. 114.

On other themes in *WW* see pp. 332–3, 160, 15, 124, 164–5, 151, 216, 145, 22, and 160–1, respectively.

X

The letter to Bertz (5 Apr. 1903) is quoted from pp. 318–19. The letter to Ellen (12 Apr. 1903) may be found in *Family Letters*, pp. 393–4. The letter to Justin MacCarthy is quoted by Coustillas, Ch. XIX.

On the move to St. Jean Pied de Port, see Korg, p. 250. The letter to Hick (3 June 1903) appears on pp. 66–7.

The letter to Clodd (16 June 1903) is quoted from pp. 90–2. The letter to Bertz (27 June 1903) appears on p. 320.

The details of Pinker's sale of *WW* are given by Coustillas, Ch. XIX. The letter to Bertz (10 July 1903) is quoted from p. 321. On Gissing's future literary plans, see Coustillas, Ch. XIX.

The letter to Wells (31 Aug. 1903) appears on pp. 213–16. The letter to Roberts is quoted from p. 273.

My discussion of publishing arrangements for *V* is indebted to Coustillas, Ch. XIX.

The letter to Bertz (4 Oct. 1903) appears on pp. 322–3.

The letter to Wells (12 Oct. 1903) may be found on pp. 217–23. I quote it from pp. 220–2, *passim*.

The letter to Clodd (17 Oct. 1903) appears on pp. 93–5.

The letter to Ellen (11 Nov. 1903) is quoted from *Family Letters*, p. 395. The letter to Wells (27 Nov. 1903) appears on pp. 223–5.

XI

I quote Gabrielle on Gissing's suffering from a letter she wrote to Bertz (17 Jan. 1904; unpublished, in the Yale Library), translated and quoted by Coustillas, Ch. XIX.

Quotations from *PPHR* are taken from Autumn, 12 and 5, and the book's 'Preface'.

My account of the various telegrams is indebted to Coustillas, Ch. XIX.

Theodore Cooper's account of Gissing may be found in Appendix A to *Family Letters*, pp. 397–9. Gabrielle is quoted from the passage she wrote in *CB*, p. 67, and from a letter to Clodd (27 Feb. 1904); the latter may be found in *Clodd*, p. 100.

Wells's account of the trip he made to the Pyrénées and of what happened at Gissing's bedside may be found in *Autobiography*, pp. 491–3. On the dispute between Wells and Gabrielle, see Tindall, p. 248, and *Biography*, p. 181. On the 'starvation' and alleged incompetent treatment of Gissing, see the letter Hick wrote to Wells (23 Feb. 1904), quoted in *Wells*, p. 153n; see also *Hick*, p. 12.

The passage quoted from *Tono-Bungay* may be found in IV, 1, vii.

The letter Gabrielle wrote to Bertz (27 Dec. 1903) is quoted from *Bertz*, p. 324.

Cooper is quoted from *Family Letters*, Appendix A, p. 399.

Gabrielle's account of Gissing's last hours is contained in the (unpublished) letter to Bertz of 17 Jan. 1904, cited above. It is quoted at length by Coustillas, Ch. XIX. The letter from Gissing to Gabrielle quoted in the text (9 Sept. 1898) appears in *Gabrielle*, p. 7.

The final two quotations are from *PPHR*, Autumn, 5, and *T*, p. 72.

CHAPTER 13

I

ROBERTS is quoted from pp. 279–82.

The Times obituary (29 Dec. 1903) is reprinted in *Family Letters*, pp. 400–2. Quotations from the *Pall Mall Gazette* and the *Speaker* are taken from Coustillas, Ch. XX.

Ellen's impressions are quoted from Appendix C of *Family Letters*, p. 404.

Clodd is quoted from p. 95.

Wells is quoted from pp. 225–6 and 228–9. The letter to Gosse is dated 4 Jan. 1904.

Harrison on Gissing (letter to Wells of 4 Feb. 1904) is quoted from *Wells*, pp. 231–3.

Roberts's letter to the *Westminster Gazette* (11 Jan. 1904, p. 12) is quoted by Coustillas, Ch. XX. The letter to the *Church Times* is quoted from Roberts, pp. 286–7. Roberts's letter to Clodd (11 Jan. 1904) is quoted from *Clodd*, p. 97.

The two essays quoted in the text may be found in *Critical Heritage*, pp. 430–4.

II

Gabrielle's letter to Miss Collet (11 Apr. 1904) is quoted by Coustillas, Ch. XX. The Civil List pension documents are quoted by Coustillas, Ch. XX.

Wells's preface to *V* was published in the *Monthly Review* for Aug. 1904 (and again in the *Eclectic Review* for Nov. 1904) under the title 'George Gissing: An Impression'. It is reprinted in *Wells*, pp. 260–77.

The letter Miss Collet wrote to Wells about *V* (unpublished; dated 21 May 1904) is in the University of Illinois Library. The comments on Wells's essay are quoted from Coustillas, Ch. XX.

For Korg on *V* see pp. 255–6.

Contemporary reviews of *V* are quoted from *Critical Heritage*, pp. 437–55, and Coustillas, Ch. XX.

The essays by Jane H. Findlater and Allan Monkhouse may be found in *Critical Heritage*, pp. 456–78.

III

An account of Gabrielle's meeting with Miss Collet on 28 Dec. 1904 is given by Coustillas, Ch. XX.

Contemporary reviews of *WW* are cited from *Critical Heritage,* pp. 479–87, and Coustillas, Ch. XXI.

My information on sales of *WW* is taken from Coustillas, Ch. XXI.

For informaion about the publication and success of *HC*, see Coustillas, Ch. XXI. Reviews of *HC* are quoted from *Critical Heritage,* pp. 493–508, and Coustillas, Ch. XXI.

IV

The last years of the rest of the Gissings and of the Gissing 'circle', and the continuing popularity of *PPHR*, is discussed by Coustillas, Ch. XXI.

V

The *TLS* is quoted, first, from a review of *HC* published on 8 June 1906, 208–9, reprinted in *Critical Heritage,* pp. 504–7 (the passage I quote appears on p. 507); and second, from an article published on 7 Oct. 1904, 303.

The letter to Gabrielle (26 Aug. 1898) is quoted from p. 49. Gissing's letter to Roberts and Roberts's reaction to it may be found in Roberts, pp. 311–13.

Walter Allen is quoted from 'The Permanent Stranger', *TLS,* 14 Feb. 1948, 92. The last two quotations from Roberts are taken from pp. 300–1 and 305.

APPENDIX

THE Abrahams list is taken from Tindall, p. 278. It may also be worth pointing out that an increasing number of translations of Gissing's novels has been appearing in recent years – most notably in Japan and Italy, but also in France, Sweden, China, and even Korea.

Coustillas's *Collected Articles on George Gissing* contains the following items: Russell Kirk, 'Who Knows George Gissing?'; Stanley Alden, 'George Gissing, Humanist'; Ruth Capers McKay, 'George Gissing as a Portrayer of Society'; 'The Permanent Stranger' (published anonymously, written by Walter Allen), reprinted from *TLS*; George Orwell, 'George Gissing'; 'Gissing's Heroes' (anonymous), reprinted from *TLS;* Jacob Korg, 'Division of Purpose in George Gissing'; Samuel Vogt Gapp, 'Influence of the Classics on Gissing's Novels of Modern Life'; Gilbert Phelps, 'Gissing, Turgenev and Dostoyevsky'; C. J. Francis, 'Gissing and Schopenhauer'; Irving Howe, 'George Gissing: Poet of Fatigue'; V. S. Pritchett, ' "Grub Street" '; Jacob Korg, 'The Spiritual Theme of "Born in Exile" '; Greenough White, 'A Novelist of the Hour'; Jackson I. Cope, 'Definition as Structure in "The Ryecroft Papers" '; Jacob Korg, 'The Main Source of "The Ryecroft Papers" '.

CHRONOLOGICAL LISTING OF
WORKS DISCUSSED

MUCH of the information given here about the stories is available in Pierre Coustillas's bibliographical article published in *English Literature in Transition* and cited in the Note on References towards the end of this volume. Abbreviated references in parentheses are to volumes in which stories and essays subsequently appeared – either for the first time, or as reprints (see the Note on References for full citations).

No attempt is made here to give a complete bibliography of Gissing's work. This is readily available elsewhere. I list here for the reader's convenience those items mentioned in the course of the present study. Dates of publication of letters and other private writings of Gissing are given in the Note on References.

1877

March – 'The Sins of the Fathers' (*SFOT*)
March – 'R.I.P.' (*SFOT*)
April – 'Too Dearly Bought' (*SFOT*)
April – 'The Warden's Daughter' (*B*)
May – 'Gretchen' (*SFOT*)
May – 'Twenty Pounds' (*B*)
May – 'Joseph Yates' (*B*)
May – 'A Terrible Mistake'
May – 'A Mother's Hope'
June – 'The Artist's Child'
July – 'An English Coast–Picture'
July – 'Brownie' (*B*)

1880

Workers in the Dawn (written 1879)
January – 'The Last Half-Crown' (*GGEF*)
January – 'Cain and Abel' (*GGEF*)
February – 'All for Love' (*GGEF*)
September – 'Notes on Social Democracy' (written Aug. 1880)
'My First Rehearsal' (written during 1880)
'My Clerical Rival' (written during 1880)

1881

Autumn – 'The Quarry on the Heath' (*GGEF*)

1882

October – 'The Hope of Pessimism' (*GGEF*)
Autumn – 'The Lady of the Dedication' (*GGEF*)

1884

The Unclassed (written 1882–3)
June and July – 'Mutimer's Choice' (*GGEF*)

1886

Demos (written 1885–6)
Isabel Clarendon (written 1884–5)

1887

Thyrza (written 1886–7)

1888

A Life's Morning (written 1885)

1889

The Nether World (written 1888)

1890

The Emancipated (written 1889)

1891

New Grub Street (written 1890)

1892

Denzil Quarrier (written 1891)
Born in Exile (written 1891)
(Note: *Born in Exile* was written Mar.–July 1891 and *Denzil Quarrier* in Oct.–Nov. 1891, but *Denzil Quarrier* appeared first – in February 1892; *Born in Exile* was published Apr. 1892.)

1893

The Odd Women (written 1892)
December–'The Day of Silence' (*HOE*; written Aug. 1893)

1894

In the Year of Jubilee (written 1894)
March – 'Our Mr. Jupp' (*HOE*; written Aug. 1893)
April – 'A Capitalist' (*HC*; written Aug. 1893)
September – 'Comrades in Arms' (*HOE*; written Dec. 1893)

1895

Eve's Ransom (written 1894)
Sleeping Fires (written 1895)
January – 'The Salt of the Earth' (*HC*; written Oct. 1894)
February – 'A Lodger in Maze Pond' (*HC*; written Aug. 1893)
February – 'The Poet's Portmanteau' (*HOE*; written Dec. 1893)
April – 'In Honour Bound' (*HOE*; written Dec. 1893)
September – 'Their Pretty Ways' (*GGEF*; written Oct. 1894)
October – 'The Medicine Man' (*HOE*; written Aug. 1895)

October – 'Raw Material' (*HOE*; written Aug. 1895)
October – 'Two Collectors' (*HOE*; written Sept. 1895)
October – 'An Old Maid's Triumph' (*HOE*; written Aug. 1895)
November – 'The Invincible Curate' (*HOE*; written Aug. 1895)
November – 'The Tout of Yarmouth Bridge' (*HOE*; written Aug. 1895)
November – 'A Well-Meaning Man' (*HOE*; written Sept. 1895)
November – 'A Song of Sixpence' (*HOE*; written Sept. 1895)
December – 'A Profitable Weakness' (*HOE*; written Sept. 1895)
December – 'The Beggar's Nurse' (*HOE*; written Sept. 1895)
December – 'An Inspiration' (*HOE*; written Nov. 1894)
December – 'Transplanted' (*HOE*; written Dec. 1895)

1896

The Paying Guest (written 1895)
January – 'A Parent's Feelings' (*HOE*; written Sept. 1895)
January – 'Lord Dunfield' (*HOE*; written Sept. 1895)
January – 'The Foolish Virgin' (written Oct.–Nov. 1895)
January – 'The Little Woman from Lancashire' (*HOE*; written Sept. 1895)
February – 'In No-Man's Land' (*HOE*; written Sept. 1895)
February – 'At High Pressure' (*HOE*; written Sept. 1895)
February – 'A Conversion' (*HOE*; written Sept. 1895)
March – 'A Free Woman' (*HOE*; written Sept. 1895)
March – 'A Son of the Soil' (*HOE*; written Sept. 1895)
March – 'Out of the Fashion' (*HOE*; written Sept. 1895)
June – 'The Justice and the Vagabond' (*HOE*; written June 1895)
July – 'The Firebrand' (*HOE*; written June 1895)
August – 'A Yorkshire Lass' (written June 1896)
August – 'The Prize Lodger' (*HOE*; written Oct. 1895)

1897

The Whirlpool (written 1896)
Human Odds and Ends (stories; written 1893–6)

1898

Charles Dickens: A Critical Study (written 1897)
The Town Traveller (written 1897)
(Note: *The Town Traveller* was written June–July 1897 and *Charles Dickens: A Critical Study* Sept.–Nov. 1897, but *Charles Dickens* appeared first, in Feb. 1898; *The Town Traveller* was published Aug. 1898.)

1899

The Crown of Life (written 1898–9)
May – 'Fate and the Apothecary' (*HC*; written June 1898)
October – 'A Poor Gentleman' (*HC*; written Jan.–Feb. 1899)

1900

By the Ionian Sea (travel; written 1899)
March – 'Humplebee' (*HC*; written Aug. 1899)
August – 'The House of Cobwebs' (*HC*; written Mar. 1900)

1901

Our Friend the Charlatan (written 1899–1900)
February – 'The Scrupulous Father' (*HC*; written June 1899)
May – 'A Charming Family' (*HC*; written Jan. 1901)
August – 'A Daughter of the Lodge' (*HC*; written May 1900)

1902

The Private Papers of Henry Ryecroft (published 1902–3; written 1900–1)
March – 'The Riding-Whip' (*HC*; written summer–autumn 1901)
September – 'Christopherson' (*HC*; written Feb.–Mar. 1902)

1903

December – 'Topham's Chance' (*HC*; written in 1903)
December – 'Miss Rodney's Leisure' (*HC*; written Feb.–Mar. 1902)

1904

Veranilda (unfinished; written 1900–1 and 1903)
December – 'The Pig and Whistle' (*HC*; written Mar. 1900)

1905

Will Warburton (written 1902–3)

1906

The House of Cobwebs (stories; written 1893–1903)

1923

An Heiress on Condition (story; written Feb. 1880)

1924

The Sins of the Fathers and Other Tales (stories)

1925

The Immortal Dickens (essays; written 1898–1900)

1928

A Yorkshire Lass (story; written June 1896)

1931

Brownie (stories)

1938

George Gissing: Stories and Sketches (fiction)

1970

George Gissing: Essays and Fiction (stories and non-fiction)
My First Rehearsal and My Clerical Rival (stories; written 1880)

1981

Introduction to Rochester Edition of Dickens's *David Copperfield* (in *The Dickensian*, Spring)

INDEX

OXFORD

MORE OXFORD PAPERBACKS

Details of a selection of other books follow. A complete list of Oxford Paperbacks, including The World's Classics, Twentieth-Century Classics, OPUS, Past Masters, Oxford Authors, Oxford Shakespeare, and Oxford Paperback Reference, is available in the UK from the General Publicity Department, Oxford University Press (JH), Walton Street, Oxford OX2 6DP.

In the USA, complete lists are available from the Paperbacks Marketing Manager, Oxford University Press, 200 Madison Avenue, New York, NY 10016.

Oxford Paperbacks are available from all good bookshops. In case of difficulty, customers in the UK can order direct from Oxford University Press Bookshop, 116 High Street, Oxford, Freepost, OX1 4BR, enclosing full payment. Please add 10 per cent of published price for postage and packing.

WAR IN EUROPEAN HISTORY

Michael Howard

This book offers a fascinating study of warfare as it has developed in Western Europe from the warring knights of the Dark Ages to the nuclear weapons of the present day, illustrating how war has changed society and how society in its turn has shaped the pattern of warfare.

'Wars have often determined the character of society. Society in exchange has determined the character of wars. This is the theme of Michael Howard's stimulating book. It is written with all his usual skill and in its small compass is perhaps the most original book he has written. Though he surveys a thousand years of history, he does so without sinking in a slough of facts and draws a broad outline of developments which will delight the general reader.' A. J. P. Taylor, *Observer*

'It is, at one and the same time, the plain man's guide to the subject, an essential introduction for serious students, and in its later stages a thought-provoking contribution.' Michael Mallet, *Sunday Times*

WAR AND THE LIBERAL CONSCIENCE

Michael Howard

Is war rooted in the vested interests of the ruling classes? Can political disputes be settled by civilized negotiation? Ought states to steer clear of other states' internal conflicts? Such questions reflect the confusion that still besets liberal-minded men in the face of war, despite centuries during which they have tried to discover its causes and secure its abolition. Michael Howard traces the pattern in their attitudes from Erasmus to the Americans after Vietnam, and concludes that peacemaking 'is a task which has to be tackled afresh every day of our lives'.

'This book is so well written that it could be read as a novel—except few novels are so interesting . . . To take one strand of history and unravel it in this way is not only a service to historians but to the ordinary bus-riding liberal anxious to clarify his own thoughts.' *Books and Bookmen*

An Opus book

THE ECONOMY OF ENGLAND, 1450–1750

D. C. Coleman

Two centuries ago the Industrial Revolution began transforming the economy of England into the form in which we know it today. But what sort of economy did England have in preceding centuries? Professor Coleman gives us an account of three centuries of English economic life, stretching from the Wars of the Roses almost to the accession of George III. He never allows us to forget that the economic world in which the men and women of the day lived and died was only one aspect of their historical context. And just as he puts the economy of England into its social and political setting, so he also presents it in its changing relationship with the economy of Europe and the wider world. In this last connection the period from 1650 to 1750, rarely treated as a whole, receives particular emphasis as marking the economic divergence of England from the Continent.

'Professor Coleman brings a welcome freshness of learning and originality of style to the subject-matter which makes this work an excellent statement of the more temperate position which lies between 'old' and 'new' economic historians.' Barry Supple, *Times Literary Supplement*

An Opus book

THE AGE OF SCANDAL

T. H. White

Towards the end of the eighteenth century the literary sway of Johnson, Pope, and Swift gave way to a more aristocratic set of literati of whom Horace Walpole is the best known. T. H. White christened this period between the Classical and Romantic movements 'the age of scandal', and wrote this witty portrait in celebration of the flamboyant and gossip-ridden society that suggested its name.

EARLY MODERN FRANCE
1560–1715
Robin Briggs

This book provides an overall interpretation of a decisive period in French history, from the chaos of the Wars of Religion to the death of Louis XIV. A clear but economical narrative of the major political events is combined with an analysis of the long-term factors which decisively moulded the evolution of both state and society.

'A very fine, thorough and conscientious study of a formative period of French History . . . his account of the French provinces in the age of Richelieu and Louis XIV . . . is one of the best things of its kind in English.' *Sunday Telegraph*

'this vigorously-written book deserves wide use as an introduction to absolutist France' *History*

An OPUS book

THE AGE OF AUSTERITY, 1945–1951
Edited by Michael Sissons and Philip French

Fifteen leading writers examine the key personalities, fashions, and occasions of the period. Contributors include: Anthony Howard, David Hughes, David Marquand, John Gross, and Michael Frayn. One of the best books on this watershed in modern British history.

'intensely readable' *Guardian*

'A highly talented team.' *Daily Mail*

ENGLAND IN THE REIGN OF CHARLES II

David Ogg

The subject of this book is the England and the Empire over which Charles II ruled. It presents an analysis of institutions together with a narrative of the events in which these institutions were strained and tested—the last two Anglo-Dutch Wars, the Popish Plot, the early struggles of party politics, the organized attacks on the corporations, and the continual contest between a wily monarch and a parliament increasingly conscious of its strength.

PASSAGES IN THE LIFE OF A RADICAL

Samuel Bamford

Samuel Bamford was a radical Manchester weaver, a dedicated reformer, and a man of lively and independent spirit. This book is his account of political and industrial opposition to the landed interests of British government in the early nineteenth century. It covers the years between 1816 and 1821—a time of catastrophic recession for Lancashire weavers. The central chapters contain his eyewitness account of the Peterloo Massacre and the events leading up to it. He was later arrested and imprisoned for High Treason, which put an end to his active participation in the reform movement. His picture of contemporary working-class social and political life is not only one of the most important documents of early radicalism, but also a fascinating record of the times.

'*Passages* is an important and impressive book, of interest to all concerned with early radicalism.' *British Book News*

'A great text of English Radicalism.' *Sunday Times*

THE IMPACT OF ENGLISH TOWNS,
1700–1800

P. J. Corfield

English towns in the eighteenth century displayed great vitality and diversity. While elegant social life was in its heyday in Bath, Hogarth was painting the horrors of London's Gin Lane, and the first Liverpool Docks were opened in an atmosphere of confidence. The book examines both the impact on English towns and their collective influence on the wider economy and society. The towns were a powerful force for change, but urban growth is not presented as the 'first cause' of industrialization. Drawing upon much new material, what Dr Corfield's synthesis reveals is the complexity of the transformation that eighteenth-century towns were themselves undergoing.

'Penelope Corfield looks back on eighteenth-century England from a refreshingly new vantage point . . . All in all, the work succeeds admirably in fulfilling its primary objective of providing an account for the 'general reader as well as for students'. Among professional historians it is certain to stimulate a new appreciation of that hitherto neglected urban terrain that lies between the early modern town and the Victorian city.'
Journal of Economic History

An Opus book

A THEORY OF ECONOMIC HISTORY

John Hicks

Economists are inclined to think of the market economy as always existing, just developing or 'growing'; historians (and anthropologists) know very well that that is not the case. An attempt is made in this book to build a bridge between their opposing views. Its subject is the evolution of the market economy, its forms and institutions; an evolution which has great things to its credit, but has many darker sides. Some of the dark sides—slavery and usury and the darker aspects of colonization—are given considerable attention. The discussion culminates in an analysis of the Industrial Revolution. Examples drawn from four thousand years of history illustrate this celebrated study.